Multicultural Education

Multicultural Education
Issues and Perspectives

THIRD EDITION

Edited by

JAMES A. BANKS
University of Washington, Seattle

CHERRY A. McGEE BANKS
University of Washington, Bothell

ALLYN AND BACON

Boston   London   Toronto   Sydney   Tokyo   Singapore

Series Editor: Frances Helland
Editorial Assistant: Nihad Farooq
Marketing Manager: Kathy Hunter
Editorial Production Service: Grace Sheldrick, Wordsworth Associates
Manufacturing Buyer: Megan Cochran
Cover Administrator: Linda Knowles
Interior Designer: Greta D. Sibley

Library of Congress Cataloging-in-Publication Data
Multicultural education : issues and perspectives / edited by James A.
    Banks, Cherry A. McGee Banks. — 3rd ed.
        p.   cm.
    Includes bibliographical references and index.
    ISBN 0-205-18896-6
        1. Multicultural education—United States. 2. Minorities-
    -Education—United States. 3. Educational anthropology—United
    States. 4. Educational equalization—United States. I. Banks,
    James A. II. Banks, Cherry A. McGee.
    LC1099.3.M85 1997
    370.19'314—dc20   96—16038
                                                              CIP

Printed in the United States of America
10 9 8 7 6 5 4 3 2 1   01 00 99 98 97 96

Photo Credits:
Will Faller: pp. xvi (top & bottom), 84 (center & bottom), 192 (top & center), 298 (top),
    384 (center);
Stephen Marks: pp. xiv (center), 128 (center);
Jim Pickerell: pp. 84 (top), 192 (bottom), 298 (center), 384 (bottom);
Brian Smith: pp. 128 (top & bottom), 298 (bottom).

Brief Contents

v

Contents

Preface

As we enter the twenty-first century, it is essential that the nation's schools help future citizens acquire the knowledge, values, and skills needed to participate in the forging of a democratic and just society that fosters the common good. A democratic and just society must enable groups on the margins to participate fully in the making and perpetuation of a moral and civic community that promotes the nation's democratic ideals. These ideals are set forth in the nation's founding documents, such as the Declaration of Independence, the Constitution, and the Bill of Rights. An important aim of multicultural education is to actualize for all people in the United States the democratic ideals that the founding fathers intended for an elite few.

The United States is sharply divided along racial, gender, and social-class lines. These divisions are caused by political, social, and economic factors that prevent large segments of society from fully participating in the commonwealth. The quest by most marginalized groups for inclusion has been an elusive one. Multicultural education, which involves transforming the schools in ways that promote educational equality and justice for all groups, can play an important role in helping the nation's schools—and the larger society—to promote national unity. This goal can be greatly facilitated by constructing institutions that promote inclusion and a national culture that reflects the experiences, struggles, and visions of all groups, thus fostering the common good.

Several developments within the United States and the rest of the world make multicultural education essential as we enter a new century. They include the workforce demands of the twenty-first century, the demographic changes in the nation's population, the widening gap between the rich and the poor, and the global challenges the nation faces. As we enter the twenty-first century, students must be able to compete in a global economy that is primarily service- and knowledge-oriented. However, if significant educational reforms are not successfully implemented, there will be a mismatch between the knowledge and skills demands of the work force and the knowledge and skills of a large proportion of U.S. workers. Many of these workers will be women, people of color, and immigrants. Between now and the turn of the century, about 83 percent of the new entrants to the U.S. work force will be members of these groups.

Approaches to school reform that do not include important aspects of multicultural education will not be successful because the learning and motivational characteristics of students from diverse cultural groups often differ in significant ways from those institutionalized within the school. Demographers predict that students of color will make up about 46 percent of the nation's school-age population by the year 2020. These students are already large majorities in the nation's forty-seven urban school districts that are members of the Council of the Great City Schools. In 1992, students of color made up 76.5 percent of the student population in those districts. Students of color also make up a majority of the students who attend the public schools in California, our most populous state.

Not only will tomorrow's students become increasingly diverse, but they will also become increasingly poor. The gap between the relatively affluent 85 percent of U.S. society and the desperately poor 15 percent of the population continues to widen. Women and children are highly concentrated among the low-income population. In 1995, about 20.6 percent of children in the United States lived in poverty; 25.3 percent lived in families headed by a single parent.

As important as it is for multicultural education to help students from diverse cultural groups attain the academic skills needed to function in a knowledge society, a pluralistic education is an imperative for all students. A multicultural education is an education for life in a free and democratic society. It helps students transcend their cultural boundaries and acquire the knowledge, attitudes, and skills needed to engage in public discourse with people who differ from themselves and to participate in the creation of a civic culture that works for the common good. Multicultural education also helps students acquire the skills needed to participate in civic action, which is an integral part of a democratic nation.

A major goal of multicultural education is to "Americanize" the United States by helping the nation realize in practice ideals that are part of its founding documents. Education that promotes our common heritage by empowering groups on the margins of society to participate in a common, shared civic culture is essential for the survival of a democratic, pluralistic nation in the next century.

Multicultural Education: Issues and Perspectives, Third Edition, is designed to help present and future educators acquire the concepts, paradigms, and explanations needed to become effective practitioners in a culturally and racially diverse society. This third edition has been revised to reflect current and emerging research, concepts, and debates about the education of students from both genders and from different cultural, racial, and ethnic groups. Exceptionality is a part of our concept of diversity because there are exceptional students in each group discussed in this book.

Five chapters are new to this edition. These include chapter 2 by Frederick D. Erickson on culture; chapter 11 by Janet Ward Schofield on the colorblind perspective; chapter 14 on school inclusion and multicultural issues by Luanna H. Meyer, Beth Harry, and Mara Sapon-Shevin; chapter 15 on gifted students by Rena F. Subotnik; and chapter 16 on school reform and academic achievement by Sonia Nieto. Each chapter in *Multicultural Education*, Third Edition, contains new data, interpretations, and developments. The Multicultural Resources in the Appendix have been substantially revised and updated. The Glossary has been revised to incorporate new census data.

This book consists of six parts. The chapters in Part One discuss how race, gender, class, and exceptionality interact to influence student behavior. Social class and religion and their effects on education are discussed in Part Two. Part Three describes how educational opportunity differs for female and male students and how schools can foster gender equity. The issues, problems, and opportunities for educating students of color and students with language differences are discussed in Part Four. The addition of chapter 11 on the colorblind perspective highlights the importance of race when teaching about differences. Part Five focuses on exceptionality, describing the issues involved in creating equal educational opportunity for students who have disabilities and who are gifted. The final part of *Multicultural Education*, Part Six, discusses multicultural education as a process of school reform and ways to increase student academic achievement.

The Appendix consists of a list of books for further reading. The Glossary defines many of the key concepts and terms used in the book.

Acknowledgments

We are grateful to the authors who revised their chapters for this third edition of *Multicultural Education* and to the new authors for writing their chapters and then revising them in response to our comments and suggestions. We want to thank Academic Press and Professor Janet Ward Schofield for permitting us to reprint her chapter on the colorblind perspective from another source.

Grace Sheldrick, Wordsworth Associates, has provided the editorial and production service for our books for more than a decade. We are deeply grateful to her for her professionalism and wisdom. We also want to thank Angela M. Banks for help with several computer and technical tasks in the preparation of the manuscript. Our daughters, Angela and Patricia, continue to be a source of encouragement and inspiration for our work.

J. A. B.
C. A. M. B.

Multicultural education helps students from diverse cultural, racial, and ethnic groups to attain the knowledge, attitudes, and skills needed to function effectively in a diverse nation and world.

PART

ONE

Issues and Concepts

The chapters in this first part of the book define the major concepts and issues in multicultural education, describe the diverse meanings of culture, and describe the ways in which variables such as race, class, gender, and exceptionality influence student behavior. Various aspects and definitions of culture are discussed. Culture is conceptualized as a dynamic and complex process of construction; its invisible and implicit characteristics are emphasized. The problems that result when culture is essentialized are described.

Multicultural education is an idea, an educational reform movement, and a process whose major goal is to change the structure of educational institutions so that male and female students, exceptional students, and students who are members of diverse racial, ethnic, and cultural groups will have an equal chance to achieve academically in school. It is necessary to conceptualize the school as a social system in order to implement multicultural education successfully. Each major variable in the school, such as its culture, power relationships, the curriculum and materials, and the attitudes and beliefs of the staff, must be changed in ways that will allow the school to promote educational equality for students from diverse groups.

To transform the schools, educators must be knowledgeable about the influence of particular groups on student behavior. The chapters in this part of the book describe the nature of culture and groups in the United States as well as the ways in which they interact to influence student behavior.

Chapter 1

Multicultural Education: Characteristics and Goals

James A. Banks

THE NATURE OF MULTICULTURAL EDUCATION

Multicultural education is at least three things: an idea or concept, an educational reform movement, and a process. Multicultural education incorporates the idea that all students—regardless of their gender and social class and their ethnic, racial, or cultural characteristics—should have an equal opportunity to learn in school. Another important idea in multicultural education is that some students, because of these characteristics, have a better chance to learn in schools as they are currently structured than do students who belong to other groups or who have different cultural characteristics.

Some institutional characteristics of schools systematically deny some groups of students equal educational opportunities. For example, in the early grades, girls and boys achieve equally in mathematics and science. However, the achievement test scores of girls fall considerably behind those of boys as children progress through the grades (Grossman & Grossman, 1994; Sadker & Sadker, 1994). Girls are less likely than boys to participate in class discussions and to be encouraged by teachers to participate. Girls are more likely than boys to be silent in the classroom. However, not all school practices favor males. As Sadker, Sadker, and Long point out in chapter 6, boys are more likely to be disciplined than are girls, even when their behavior does not differ from the girls'. They are also more likely than girls to be classified as learning disabled. Males of color, especially African American males, experience a highly disproportionate rate of disciplinary actions and suspensions in school. Some writers have described the situation of African American males as a "crisis" and have called them "endangered" in U.S. society (Gibbs, 1988).

In the early grades, the academic achievement of students of color such as African Americans, Hispanics, and American Indians is close to parity with the achievement of White mainstream students. However, the longer these students of color remain in school, the more their achievement lags behind that of White mainstream students. Social-class status is also strongly related to academic achievement. Persell, in chapter 4, describes how students from the middle and upper classes are treated more positively in schools than are lower-class students and are given a better chance to learn. Exceptional students, whether they are physically or mentally disabled or gifted and talented, often find that they do not experience equal educational opportunities in the schools. The chapters in Part V of this book describe the problems that such exceptional students experience in schools and suggest ways that teachers and other educators can increase their chances for educational success.

Multicultural education is also a reform movement that is trying to change the schools and other educational institutions so that students from all social class, gender, racial, and cultural groups will have an equal opportunity to learn. Multicultural education involves changes in the total school or educational environment; it is not limited to curricular changes. The variables in the school environment that multicultural education tries to transform are identified and discussed later in this chapter (see Figure 1.5).

Multicultural education is also a process whose goals will never be fully realized. Educational equality, like liberty and justice, are ideals toward which human beings work but never fully attain. Racism, sexism, and discrimination against people with disabilities will exist to some extent no matter how hard we work to eliminate these problems. When prejudice and discrimination are reduced toward one group, they are usually directed toward another group or they take new forms. Because the goals of multicultural education can never be fully attained, we should work continually to increase educational equality for all students.

Multicultural education must be viewed as an ongoing process, and not as something that we "do" and thereby solve the problems that are the targets of multicultural educational reform. When I asked one school administrator what efforts were being taken to implement multicultural education in his school district, he told me that the district had "done" multicultural education last year and that it was now initiating other reforms, such as improving the students' reading scores. This administrator not only misunderstood the nature and scope of multicultural education, but he also did not understand that it could help raise the students' reading scores. A major goal of multicultural education is to improve academic achievement (Banks & Banks, 1995).

MULTICULTURAL EDUCATION: AN INTERNATIONAL REFORM MOVEMENT

Since World War II, many immigrants and groups have settled in the United Kingdom and in nations on the European continent, including France, the Netherlands, Germany, Sweden, and Switzerland (Figueroa, 1995; Hoff, 1995). Some of these immigrants, such as the Asians and West Indians in England and the North Africans and Indochinese in France, have come from former colonies. Many Southern and Eastern European immigrants have settled in Western and Northern European nations in search of upward social mobility and other opportunities. Groups such as Italians,

Greeks, and Turks have migrated to Northern and Western European nations in large numbers. Ethnic and immigrant populations have also increased significantly in Australia and Canada since World War II (Allan & Hill, 1995; Moodley, 1995).

Most of the immigrant and ethnic groups in Europe, Australia, and Canada face problems similar to those experienced by ethnic groups in the United States. Groups such as the Jamaicans in England, the Algerians in France, and the Aborigines in Australia experience achievement problems in the schools and prejudice and discrimination in both the schools and society at large. The problems that Greeks and Italians experience in Australia indicate that race is not always a factor when ethnic conflict and tension develop.

The United Kingdom, various nations on the European continent, and Australia and Canada have implemented a variety of programs to increase the achievement of ethnic and immigrant students and to help students and teachers develop more positive attitudes toward racial, cultural, ethnic, and language diversity (Banks & Lynch, 1986; Figueroa, 1995).

THE HISTORICAL DEVELOPMENT OF MULTICULTURAL EDUCATION

Multicultural education grew out of the ferment of the civil rights movement of the 1960s. During this decade, African Americans embarked on a quest for their rights that was unprecedented in the United States. A major goal of the civil rights movement of the 1960s was to eliminate discrimination in public accommodations, housing, employment, and education. The consequences of the civil rights movement had a significant influence on educational institutions as ethnic groups—first African Americans and then other groups—demanded that the schools and other educational institutions reform their curricula so that they would reflect their experiences, histories, cultures, and perspectives. Ethnic groups also demanded that the schools hire more Black and Brown teachers and administrators so that their children would have more successful role models. Ethnic groups pushed for community control of schools in their neighborhoods and for the revision of textbooks to make them reflect the diversity of peoples in the United States.

The first responses of schools and educators to the ethnic movements of the 1960s were hurried. Courses and programs were developed without the thought and careful planning needed to make them educationally sound or to institutionalize them within the educational system. Holidays and other special days, ethnic celebrations, and courses that focused on one ethnic group were the dominant characteristics of school reforms related to ethnic and cultural diversity during the 1960s and early 1970s. Grant and Sleeter, in chapter 3, call this approach *single group* studies. The ethnic studies courses developed and implemented during this period were usually electives and were taken primarily by students who were members of the group that was the subject of the course.

The apparent success of the civil rights movement, plus growing rage and a liberal national atmosphere, stimulated other victimized groups to take actions to eliminate discrimination against them and to demand that the educational system respond to their needs, aspirations, cultures, and histories. The women's rights movement emerged as one of the most significant social reform movements of the late twentieth century (Schmitz, Butler, Rosenfelt, & Guy-Sheftal, 1995). During the 1960s and 1970s, discrimination against women in employment, income, and education was widespread and often blatant. The women's rights movement articulated and publicized how discrimination and institutionalized sexism limited the opportunities of women and adversely affected the nation. The leaders of this movement, such as Betty Friedan and Gloria Steinem, demanded that political, social, economic, and educational institutions act to eliminate sex discrimination and to provide opportunities for women to actualize their talents and realize their ambitions (Steinem, 1995). Major goals of the women's rights movement included equal pay for equal work, the elimination of laws that discriminated against women and made them second-class citizens, the hiring of more women in leadership positions, and greater participation of men in household work and child rearing.

When *feminists* (people who work for the political, social, and economic equality of the *sexes*) looked at educational institutions, they noted problems similar to those identified by ethnic groups of color. Textbooks and curricula were dominated by men; women were largely invisible. Feminists pointed out that history textbooks were dominated by political and military history—areas in which men had been the main participants (Trecker, 1973). Social and family history and the history of labor and of ordinary people were largely ignored. Feminists pushed for the revision of textbooks to include more history about the important roles of women in the development of the nation and the world. They also demanded that more women be hired for administrative positions in the schools. Although most teachers in the elementary schools were women, most administrators were men.

Other marginalized groups, stimulated by the social ferment and the quest for human rights during the 1970s, articulated their grievances and demanded that institutions be reformed so they would face less discrimination and acquire more human rights. People with disabilities, senior citizens, and gay rights advocates were among the groups that organized politically during this period and made significant inroads in changing institutions and laws. Advocates for citizens with disabilities attained significant legal victories during the 1970s. The Education for All Handicapped Children Act of 1975 (P.L. 94-142), which required that students with disabilities be educated in the least restricted environment and institutionalized the word *mainstreaming* in education, was perhaps the most significant legal victory of the movement for the rights of students with disabilities in education (see chapters 13 and 14).

HOW MULTICULTURAL EDUCATION DEVELOPED

Multicultural education emerged from the diverse courses, programs, and practices that educational institutions devised to respond to the demands, needs, and aspirations of the various groups. Consequently, as Grant and Sleeter point out in chapter 3, multicultural education is not in actual practice one identifiable course or educational program. Rather, practicing educators use the term *multicultural education* to describe a wide variety of programs and practices related to educational equity, women, ethnic groups, language minorities, low-income groups, and people with disabilities. In one school district, multicultural education may mean a curriculum that incorporates the experiences of ethnic groups of color; in another, a program may include the experiences of both ethnic groups and women. In a third school district, this term may be used the way it is by me and by other authors, such as Grant and Sleeter (1986a) and Baptiste (1986), that is, to mean a *total school reform effort designed to increase educational equity for a range of cultural, ethnic, and economic groups.* This broader and more comprehensive notion of multicultural education is discussed in the last part of this chapter. It differs from the limited concept of multicultural education, in which it is viewed as curriculum reform.

MULTICULTURAL EDUCATION AND TENSION AMONG DIVERSE GROUPS

The challenge to multicultural educators, in both theory and practice, is how to increase equity for a particular victimized group without further limiting the opportunities of another. Even though the various groups that are targeted for empowerment and equity in multicultural education share many needs and goals, sometimes they perceive their needs as divergent, conflicting, and inconsistent, as some feminist and ethnic group advocates have in the past (Albrecht & Brewer, 1990). Butler describes this phenomenon in chapter 8. A major cause of the tension among various marginalized groups may be institutionalized practices within society that promote tension, conflict, and divisiveness among them. If this is the case, as some radical scholars suggest (Barton & Walker, 1983), perhaps an important goal of multicultural education should be to help students who are members of particular victimized groups better understand how their fates are tied to those of other powerless groups and the significant benefits that can result from multicultural political coalitions. These coalitions could be cogent vehicles for social change and reform. Jesse Jackson's attempt to form what he called a Rainbow Coalition at the national level in the 1980s had as one of its major goals the formulation of an effective political coalition made up of people from both gender groups and from different racial, ethnic, cultural, and social-class groups.

THE NATURE OF CULTURE IN THE UNITED STATES

The United States, like other Western nation-states such as the United Kingdom, Australia, and Canada, is a multicultural society. The United States consists of a shared core culture as well as many subcultures. In this book, we call the larger shared core culture the *macroculture;* the smaller cultures, which are a part of the core culture, are called *microcultures.* It is important to distinguish the macroculture from the various microcultures because the values, norms, and characteristics of the mainstream (macroculture) are frequently mediated by, as well as interpreted and expressed differently within, various microcultures. These differences often lead to cultural mis-understandings, conflicts, and institutionalized discrimination.

Students who are members of certain cultural, religious, and ethnic groups are sometimes socialized to act and think in certain ways at home but differently at school. One example of this behavior is children who are taught the creation story in the book of Genesis at home but are expected to accept in school the evolutionary explanation of the development and emergence of human beings. A challenge that multi-cultural education faces is how to help students from diverse groups mediate between their home and community cultures and the school culture. Students should acquire the knowledge, attitudes, and skills needed to function effectively in each cultural setting. They should also be competent to function within and across other microcultures in their society, within the national macroculture, and within the world community.

The Meaning of Culture

Bullivant (1993) defines *culture* as a group's program for survival in and adaptation to its environment. The cultural program consists of knowledge, concepts, and values shared by group members through systems of communication. Culture also consists of the shared beliefs, symbols, and interpretations within a human group. Most social scientists today view culture as consisting primarily of the symbolic, ideational, and intangible aspects of human societies. The essence of a culture is not its artifacts, tools, or other tangible cultural elements but how the members of the group interpret, use, and perceive them. It is the values, symbols, interpretations, and perspectives that distinguish one people from another in modernized societies; it is not material objects and other tangible aspects of human societies (Banks, 1994a; 1994b). People within a culture usually interpret the meanings of symbols, artifacts, and behaviors in the same or in similar ways.

Identifying and Describing the U.S. Core Culture

The United States, like other nation-states, has a shared set of values, ideations, and symbols that constitute the core or overarching culture. This culture is shared to some extent by all the diverse cultural and ethnic groups that make up the nation-state. It is difficult to identify and describe the overarching culture in the United States because it is such a diverse and complex nation. It is easier to identify the core culture within an isolated premodern society, such as the Maoris before the Europeans came to New Zealand, than within highly pluralistic, modernized societies such as the United States, Canada, and Australia (Lisitzky, 1956).

When trying to identify the distinguishing characteristics of U.S. culture, one should realize that the political institutions within the United States, which reflect some of the nation's core values, were heavily influenced by the British. U.S. political ideals and institutions were also influenced by Native American political institutions and practices, especially those related to making group decisions, such as in the League of the Iroquois (Weatherford, 1988).

Equality

A key component in the U.S. core culture is the idea, expressed in the Declaration of Independence in 1776, that "all men are created equal, that they are endowed by their Creator with certain unalienable rights, that among these are life, liberty, and the pursuit of happiness" (Declaration of Independence, 1968, pp. 447–449). When this idea was expressed by the nation's founding fathers in 1776, it was considered radical. A common belief in the eighteenth century was that human beings were not born with equal rights; that some people had few rights and others, such as kings, had divine rights given by God. When considering the idea that "all men are created equal" is a key component of U.S. culture, one should remember to distinguish between a nation's ideals and its actual practices, as well as between the meaning of the idea when it was expressed in 1776 and its meaning today. When the nation's founding fathers expressed this idea in 1776, their conception of men was limited to White males who owned property (Franklin & McNeil, 1995). White men without property, White women, and all African Americans and Indians were not included in their notion of people who were equal or who had "certain unalienable rights."

Although the idea of equality expressed by the founding fathers in 1776 had a very limited meaning at that time, it has proven to be a powerful and important idea in the quest for human rights in the United States. Throughout the nation's history since 1776, victimized and excluded groups such as women, African Americans, Indians, and other cultural and ethnic groups have used this cogent idea to justify and defend the extension of human rights to them and to end institutional discrimination, such as sexism, racism, and discrimination against people with disabilities. As a result, human rights have gradually been extended to various groups throughout U.S. history. The extension of these rights has been neither constant nor linear. Rather, periods of extension of rights have often been followed by periods of retrenchment and conservatism. Schlesinger (1986) calls these patterns "cycles of American history." The United States is still a long way from realizing the ideals expressed in the Declaration of Independence in 1776. However, these ideals remain an important part of U.S. culture and are still used by victimized groups to justify their struggles for human rights and equality.

Individualism and Individual Opportunity

Two other important ideas in the common overarching U.S. culture are individualism and individual social mobility (Garretson, 1976). Individualism as an ideal is extreme in the U.S. core culture. Individual success is more important than commitment to family, community, and nation-state. An individual is expected to experience success by his or her sole efforts. Many Americans believe that a person can go from rags to riches within a generation and that every American boy can, but not necessarily will, become president.

Individuals are expected to experience success by hard work and to pull themselves up by their bootstraps. This idea was epitomized by fictional characters such as Ragged

Dick, one of the heroes created by the popular writer Horatio Alger. Ragged Dick attained success by valiantly overcoming poverty and adversity. A related belief is that if you do not succeed, it is because of your own shortcomings, such as being lazy or unambitious; failure is consequently your own fault. These beliefs are taught in the schools with success stories and myths about such U.S. heroes as George Washington, Thomas Jefferson, and Abraham Lincoln. The beliefs about individualism in American culture are related to the Protestant work ethic. This is the belief that hard work by the individual is morally good and that laziness is sinful. This belief is a legacy of the British Puritan settlers in colonial New England. It has had a powerful and significant influence on U.S. culture.

Groups and Individual Opportunity

The belief in individual opportunity has proven tenacious in U.S. society. It remains strong in American culture despite the fact that individuals' chances for upward social, economic, and educational mobility in the United States are highly related to the social-class, ethnic, gender, and other ascribed groups to which they belong (Knapp & Woolverton, 1995). Social scientists have amply documented the extent of social class stratification in the United States and the ways in which people's chances in life are affected by the groups to which they belong (Green, 1981; Domhoff, 1983). Jencks and his associates (1972) have documented thoroughly the extent to which educational opportunity and life chances are related to social class. The chapters in this book on social class, gender, and ethnicity belie the notion that individual opportunity is a dominant characteristic of U.S. society. Yet the belief in individual opportunity remains strong in the United States.

Individualism and Groupism

Although the groups to which people belong have a cogent influence on their life chances in the United States, Americans—particularly those in the mainstream—are highly individualistic in their value orientations and behaviors. The strength of the nuclear family reinforces individualism in U.S. culture. One result of the strong individualism is that married children usually expect their older parents to live independently or in homes for senior citizens rather than with them.

The strong individualism in U.S. culture contrasts sharply with the groupism and group commitment found in Asian nations, such as China and Japan (Butterfield, 1982; Reischauer, 1981). Individualism is viewed rather negatively in these societies. One is expected to be committed first to the family and group and then to oneself. Some U.S. social scientists, such as Lash (1978) and Bellah and associates (1985), lament the extent of individualism in U.S. society. They believe it is harmful to the common national culture. Some observers believe that groupism is too strong in China and Japan and that individualism should be more valued in those nations. Perhaps modernized, pluralistic nation-states can best benefit from a balance between individualism and groupism, with neither characteristic dominating.

Expansionism and Manifest Destiny

Other overarching U.S. values that social scientists have identified include the desire to conquer or exploit the natural environment, materialism and consumption, and the belief in the nation's inherent superiority. These beliefs justified Manifest Destiny and U.S. expansion to the West and into other nations and the annexation of one-third of Mexico's territory in 1848. These observations, which reveal the less positive side of U.S. national values, have been developed by social scientists interested in understanding the complex nature of American society (DeMontilla, 1975; Greenbaum, 1974).

Greenbaum (1974) believes that distance is also a key value in U.S. society. He uses this word to describe the formal nature of bureaucratic institutions, as well as unfriendliness and detachment in social relationships. Greenbaum argues that the Anglo-Saxon Protestants, the dominant cultural group in U.S. society, have often used distance in their relationships with other ethnic and cultural groups to keep them confined to their social-class status and group.

In his discussion of the nature of values in U.S. society, Myrdal (1962) contends that a major ethical inconsistency exists in U.S. society. He calls this inconsistency "the American dilemma. " He states that American Creed values, such as equality and human dignity, exist in U.S. society as ideals. However, they exist alongside the institutionalized discriminatory treatment of African Americans and other ethnic and cultural groups in U.S. society. This variance creates a dilemma in the American mind because Americans try to reconcile their democratic ideals with their treatment of victimized groups. Myrdal states that this dilemma has been an important factor that has enabled ethnic groups to fight discrimination effectively. In their efforts to resolve their dilemma when the inconsistencies between their ideals and actions are pointed out to them by human-rights advocates, Americans, according to Myrdal, often support the elimination of practices that are inconsistent with their democratic ideals or the American Creed. Some writers have refuted Myrdal's hypothesis and contend that most Americans do not experience such a dilemma (Ellison, 1973).

Microcultures in the United States

A nation as culturally diverse as the United States consists of a common overarching culture, as well as of a series of microcultures (see Figure 1.1). These microcultures share most of the core values of the nation-state, but these values are often mediated by the various microcultures and are interpreted differently within them. Microcultures sometimes have values that are somewhat alien to the national core culture. Also, some of the core national values and behaviors may seem somewhat alien in certain microcultures or may take on different forms.

The strong belief in individuality and individualism that exists within the national macroculture is often much less endorsed by some ethnic communities and is somewhat alien within them. African Americans and Hispanic Americans who have not experienced high levels of cultural assimilation into the mainstream culture are much more group oriented than are mainstream Americans. Schools in the United States are

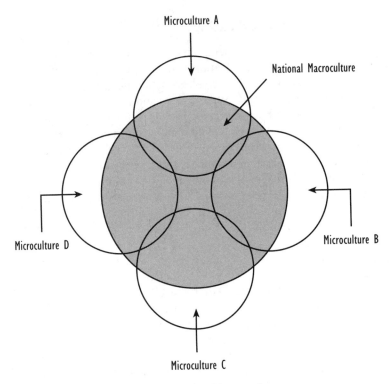

Figure 1.1 Microcultures and the National Macroculture

The shaded area represents the national macroculture. A, B, C, and D represent microcultures that consist of unique institutions, values, and cultural elements that are nonuniversalized and are shared primarily by members of specific cultural groups. A major goal of the school should be to help students acquire the knowledge, skills, and attitudes needed to function effectively within the national macroculture, their own microcultures, and within and across other microcultures.

highly individualistic in their learning and teaching styles, evaluation procedures, and norms. Many students, particularly African Americans, Hispanics, and American Indians, are group oriented (Hale, 1994; Irvine & York, 1995). These students experience problems in the highly individualistic learning environment of the school. Teachers can enhance the learning opportunities of these students, who are also called *field dependent* or *field sensitive*, by using cooperative teaching strategies that have been developed and field-tested by researchers such as Slavin (1995) and Cohen (1994).

Some emerging theories indicate that female students may have preferred ways of knowing, thinking, and learning that differ to some extent from those most often preferred by males (Belenky, Clinchy, Goldberger, & Tarule, 1986; Halpern, 1986; Taylor, Gilligan, & Sullivan, 1995). Maher (1987) describes the dominant inquiry model used in social science as male constructed and dominated. She contends that it strives for objectivity: "Personal feelings, biases, and prejudices are considered inevitable limitations" (p. 186). Feminist pedagogy is based on different assumptions about the nature of knowledge and results in a different teaching method. According to Maher, feminist pedagogy enhances the learning of females and deepens the insight of males. In chapter 7, Tetreault describes feminist pedagogy techniques she uses to motivate students and to enhance their understandings.

After completing a major research study on women's ways of knowing, Belenky and her colleagues (1986) concluded that conceptions of knowledge and truth in the core culture and in educational institutions "have been shaped throughout history by the male-dominated majority culture. Drawing on their own perspectives and visions, men have constructed the prevailing theories, written history, and set values that have become the guiding principles for men and women alike" (p. 5).

These researchers also found an inconsistency between the kind of knowledge most appealing to women and the kind that was emphasized in most educational institutions. Most of the women interviewed in their study considered personalized knowledge and knowledge that resulted from first-hand observation most appealing. However, most educational institutions emphasize abstract, "out-of-context" knowledge (Belenky et al., 1986, p. 200). Ramírez and Castañeda (1974) found that Mexican American students who were socialized within traditional cultures also considered personalized and humanized knowledge more appealing than abstract knowledge. They also responded positively to knowledge that was presented in a humanized or story format.

Research by Gilligan (1982) provides some clues that help us better understand the findings by Belenky and her colleagues about the kind of knowledge women find most appealing. Gilligan describes caring, interconnection, and sensitivity to the needs of other people as dominant values among women and the female microculture in the United States. By contrast, she found that the values of men were more characterized by separation and individualism.

A major goal of multicultural education is to change teaching and learning approaches so that students of both genders and from diverse cultural and ethnic groups will have equal opportunities to learn in educational institutions. This goal suggests that major changes ought to be made in the ways that educational programs are conceptualized, organized, and taught. Educational approaches need to be transformed.

In her research on identifying and labeling students with mental retardation, Mercer (1973) found that a disproportionate number of African American and Hispanic students were labeled *mentally retarded* because the testing procedures used in intelligence tests "reflect the abilities and skills valued by the American core culture," (p. 32) which Mercer describes as predominantly White, Anglo-Saxon, and middle and upper class. She also points out that measures of general intelligence consist primarily of items related to verbal skills and knowledge. Most African American and Hispanic students are socialized within microcultures that differ in significant ways from the U.S. core culture. These students often have not had an equal opportunity to learn the knowledge and skills that are measured in mental ability tests. Consequently, a disproportionate percentage of African American and Hispanic students are labeled *mentally retarded* and are placed in classes for slow learners. Mental retardation, as Mercer points out, is a *socially determined* status. When students are placed in classes for the mentally retarded, the self-fulfilling prophecy develops. Students begin to act and think as though they are mentally retarded.

Groups and Group Identification

Thus far, this chapter has discussed the various microcultures that make up U.S. society. Individuals learn the values, symbols, and other components of their culture from their social group. The group is the social system that carries a culture. People belong to and live in social groups (Bullivant, 1993). A group is a collectivity of persons who share an identity, a feeling of unity. A group is also a social system that has a social structure of interrelated roles (Theodorson & Theodorson, 1969). The group's program for survival, values, ideations, and shared symbols constitutes its culture.

The study of groups is the major focus in sociology. Sociologists believe that the group has a strong influence on the behavior of individuals, that behavior is shaped by group norms, and that the group equips individuals with the behavior patterns they need to adapt to their physical, social, and metaphysical environments. Sociologists also assume that groups have independent characteristics; they are more than aggregates of individuals. Groups possess a continuity that transcends the lives of individuals.

Sociologists also assume that knowledge about groups to which an individual belongs provides important clues to and explanations for the individual's behavior. Goodman and Marx (1982) write, "Such factors as shared religion, nationality, age, sex, marital status, and education have proved to be important determinants of what people believe, feel, and do" (p. 7). Although membership in a gender, racial, ethnic, social-class, or religious group can provide us with important clues about individuals' behavior, it cannot enable us to predict behavior. Knowing one's group affiliation can enable us to state that a certain type of behavior is probable. Membership in a particular *group* does not determine behavior but makes certain types of behavior more probable.

There are several important reasons that knowledge of group characteristics and modalities can enable us to predict the probability of an individual's behavior but not the precise behavior. This is, in part, because each individual belongs to several groups at the same time (see Figure 1.2). An individual may be White, Catholic, female, and middle class, all at the same time. She might have a strong identification with one of these groups and a very weak or almost nonexistent identification with another. A person can be a member of a particular group, such as the Catholic church, and have a weak identification with the group and a weak commitment to the tenets of the Catholic faith. Religious identification might be another individual's strongest group identification. Identification with and attachments to different groups may also conflict. A woman who has a strong Catholic identification but is also a feminist might find it difficult to reconcile her beliefs about equality for women with some positions of the Catholic church, such as its prohibiting women from becoming ordained priests.

The more we know about a student's level of identification with a particular group and the extent to which socialization has taken place within that group, the more accurately we can predict, explain, and understand the student's behavior in the classroom. A knowledge of the importance of a group to a student at a particular time of life and within a particular social context will also help us understand the student's behavior. Ethnic identity may become more important to a person who becomes a part of an ethnic minority when he or she previously belonged to the majority. Many Whites

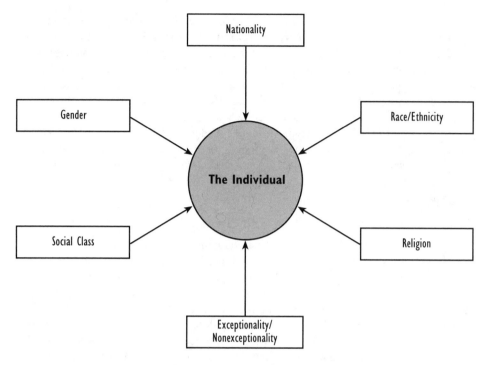

Figure 1.2 Multiple Group Memberships

An individual belongs to several different groups at the same time. This figure shows the major groups discussed in this book.

who have moved from the U.S. mainland to Hawaii have commented on how their sense of ethnic identity increased and they began to feel marginalized. Group identity may also increase when the group feels threatened, when a social movement arises to promote its rights, or when the group attempts to revitalize its culture.

The Teaching Implications of Group Identification

What are the implications of group membership and group identity for teaching? As you read the chapters in this book that describe the characteristics of the two gender groups and of social-class, racial, ethnic, religious, and exceptional groups, bear in mind that individuals within these groups manifest these behaviors to various degrees. *Also remember that individual students are members of several of these groups at the same time.* Above I describe the core U.S. culture as having highly individualistic values and beliefs. However, research by Gilligan (1982) indicates that the values of women, as compared with those of men, are more often characterized by caring, interconnection, and sensitivity to the needs of others. This observation indicates how core values within the macroculture are often mediated by microcultures within various gender, ethnic, and cultural groups.

As stated above, researchers have found that some students of color such as African

Americans and Mexican Americans often have field-sensitive learning styles and therefore prefer more personalized learning approaches (Ramírez & Castañeda, 1974). Think about what this means. This research describes a group characteristic of these students and not the behavior of a particular African American or Mexican American student. It suggests that there is a higher probability that these students will have field-sensitive learning styles than will middle-class Anglo-American students. However, students within all ethnic, racial, and social-class groups have different learning styles (Irvine & York, 1995). Those groups influence students' behavior, such as their learning style, interactively, because they are members of several groups at the same time. *Knowledge of the characteristics of groups to which students belong, about the importance of each of these groups to them, and of the extent to which individuals have been socialized within each group will give the teacher important clues to students' behavior.*

The Interaction of Race, Class, and Gender

When using our knowledge of groups to understand student behavior, we should also consider the ways that such variables as class, race, and gender interact and intersect to influence student behavior. Middle-class and more highly assimilated Mexican American students tend to be more field independent than do lower-class and less assimilated Mexican American students. African American students tend to be more field dependent (group oriented) than are White students; females tend to be more field dependent than are male students. Therefore, it can be hypothesized that African American females would be the most field dependent when compared to African American and White males and White females. This finding was made by Perney (1976).

Unfortunately, the researcher did not include a social-class measure in the study. After doing a comprehensive review of research on the ways that race, class, and gender influence student behavior in education, Grant and Sleeter (1986b) concluded that we must look at the ways these variables interact in order to fully understand student behavior.

Figure 1.3 illustrates how the major groups discussed in this book—*gender, race* or *ethnicity, social class, religion,* and *exceptionality*—influence student behavior, both singly and interactively. The figure also shows that other variables, such as geographic region and age, also influence an individual's behavior. The ways these variables influence selected student behaviors are described in Table 1.1.

THE SOCIAL CONSTRUCTION OF CATEGORIES

The major variables and categories discussed in this book, such as gender, race, ethnicity, class, and exceptionality, are social categories (Berger & Luckman, 1967; Mannheim, 1936). The criteria for whether an individual belongs to one of these categories are determined by human beings and consequently are socially constructed. Religion is also a social category. Religious institutions, symbols, and artifacts are created by human beings to satisfy their metaphysical needs.

These categories are usually related to the physical characteristics of individuals. In some cases, as when they have severe or obvious physical disabilities, the relationship between the labels given to individuals and their physical characteristics is direct and

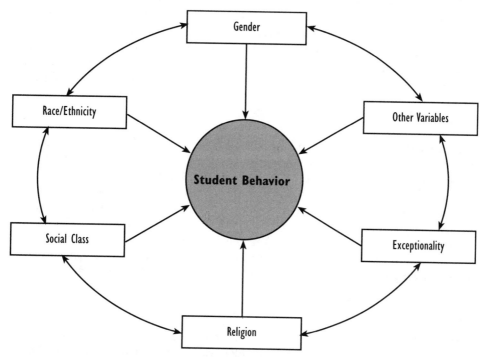

Figure 1.3 The Intersection of Variables

The major variables of gender, race or ethnicity, social class, religion, and exceptionality influence student behavior, both singly and interactively. Other variables, such as region and age, also influence student behavior.

Table 1.1 Singular and Combined Effects of Variables

Student Behavior	Gender Effects	Race/ Ethnicity Effects	Social-Class Effects	Religious Effects	Combined Effects
Learning Styles (Field Independent/Field Dependent)	X[a]	X			X
Internality/Externality			X		
Fear of Success	X	X			?
Self-Esteem	X	X			?
Individual vs. Group Orientation	X	X	X		?

[a] An X indicates that the variable influences the student behavior described in the far-left column. An X in the far-right column means that research indicates that two or more variables combine to influence the described behavior. A question mark indicates that the research is unclear about the combined effects of the variables.

would be made in almost any culture or social system. The relationship between categories that are used to classify individuals and their physical characteristics, however, is usually indirect and complex. Even though one's sex is determined primarily by physical characteristics (such as genitalia, chromosome patterns, etc.,), gender is a social construction created and shaped by the society in which individuals and groups function.

Gender

Gender consists of the socially and psychologically appropriate behavior for males and females sanctioned by and expected within a society. Gender role expectations vary across cultures and at different times in a society and within microcultures in the same society. Traditionally, normative behavior for males and females has varied among mainstream Americans, African Americans, Native Americans, and Hispanic Americans. Gender role expectations also vary somewhat across social classes within the same society. In the White mainstream society in the 1940s and 1950s, upper-middle-class women often received negative sanctions when they worked outside the home, whereas women in working-class families were frequently expected to become wage earners.

Race

Race is a socially determined category that is related to physical characteristics in a complex way. Two individuals with nearly identical physical characteristics, or phenotypes, can be classified as members of different races in two different societies. In the United States, where racial categories are well defined and highly inflexible, an individual with any acknowledged or publicly known African ancestry is considered Black. One who looks completely Caucasian but who acknowledges some African ancestry is classified as Black. Such an individual would be considered White in Puerto Rico. In Puerto Rico, hair texture, social status, and degree of eminence in the community are often as important as—if not more important than—physical characteristics in determining an individual's racial group or category. There is a saying in Puerto Rico that "money lightens," which means that upward social mobility considerably enhances an individual's opportunity to be classified as White. There is a strong relationship between race and social class in Puerto Rico and in most other Caribbean and Latin American nations.

Our discussion of race as a social category indicates that the criteria for determining the characteristics of a particular race vary across cultures, that an individual considered Black in one society may be considered White in another, and that racial categories reflect the social, economic, and political characteristics of a society.

Social Class

Social scientists find it difficult to agree on criteria for determining social class. The problem is complicated by the fact that societies are constantly in the throes of change. During the 1950s, social scientists often attributed characteristics to the lower class that are found in the middle class today, such as single-parent and female-headed households, high divorce rates, and substance abuse. Today, these characteristics are no longer rare among the middle class, even though their frequency is still higher among lower-class families. Variables such as income, education, occupation, life-style, and values are among the most frequently used indices to determine social-class status in the United States (Warner, with Meeker & Eells, 1960). However, there is considerable disagreement among social scientists about which variables are the most important in determining the social-class status of an individual or family.

Social-class criteria also vary somewhat among various ethnic and racial groups in the United States. Teachers, preachers, and other service professionals were upper class in many rural African American communities in the South in the 1950s and 1960s but were considered middle class by mainstream White society. The systems of social stratification that exist in the mainstream society and in various microcultures are not necessarily identical.

Exceptionality

Exceptionality is also a social category. Whether a person is considered disabled or gifted is determined by criteria developed by society. As Shaver and Curtis (1981) point out, disabilities are not necessarily handicaps, and the two should be distinguished. They write, "A disability or combination of disabilities becomes a handicap only when the condition limits or impedes the person's ability to function normally" (p. 1). A person with a particular disability, such as having one arm, might have a successful college career, experience no barriers to his achievements in college, and graduate with honors. However, he may find that when he tries to enter the job market, his opportunities are severely limited because potential employers view him as unable to perform well in some situations in which, in fact, he could perform effectively (Shaver & Curtis, 1981). This individual has a disability but was viewed as handicapped in one situation—the job market—but not in another—his university.

Mercer (1973) has extensively studied the social process by which individuals become labeled as persons with mental retardation. She points out that even though their physical characteristics may increase their chance of being labeled persons with mental retardation, the two are not perfectly correlated. Two people with the same biological characteristics may be considered persons with mental retardation in one social system and not in another social system. An individual may be considered a person with mental retardation at school but not at home. She writes, "Mental retardation is not a characteristic of the individual, nor a meaning inherent in behavior, but a socially determined status, which [people] may occupy in some social systems and not in others" (p. 31). She states that people can change their role by changing their social group.

The highly disproportionate number of African Americans, Hispanics, and particularly males classified as *learning disabled* by the school indicates the extent to which exceptionality is a social category. Mercer (1973) found that the school labeled more people *mentally retarded* than did any other institution (p. 96). Many African American and Hispanic students who are labeled *mentally retarded* function normally and are considered normal in their homes and communities. Boys are more often classified as mentally retarded than are girls. The school, as Mercer and other researchers have pointed out, uses criteria to determine the mental ability of students of color that conflict with their home and community cultures. Some students in all ethnic and cultural groups are mentally retarded and deserve special instruction, programs, and services, as the authors in Part Five of this book suggest. However, the percentage of students of color in these programs is too high. The percentage of students in each ethnic group labeled mentally retarded should be about the same as the total percentage of that group in school.

Giftedness is also a social category (Sapon-Shevin, 1994). Important results of the socially constructed nature of giftedness are the considerable disagreement among experts about how the concept should be defined and the often inconsistent views about how to identify gifted students (Sisk, 1987). The highly disproportionate percentage of middle- and upper-middle-class mainstream students categorized as gifted compared to lower-class students and students of color such as African Americans, Hispanics, and American Indians is also evidence of the social origin of the category. Many students who are classified as gifted do have special talents and abilities, and they do need special instruction.

In chapter 15, Subotnik describes the characteristics of these students and ways in which their needs can be met. However, some students who are classified as gifted by school districts merely have parents with the knowledge, political skills, and power to force the school to classify their children as gifted, which will provide them with special instruction and educational enrichment. In some racially mixed school districts, the gifted programs are made up primarily of middle-class and upper-middle-class mainstream students.

Schools should try to satisfy the needs of students with special gifts and talents; however, they should also make sure that students from all social-class, cultural, and ethnic groups have an equal opportunity to participate in programs for academically and creatively talented students. If schools or districts do not have a population in their gifted programs that represents their various cultural, racial, and ethnic groups, steps should be taken to examine the criteria used to identify gifted students and to develop procedures to correct the disproportion. Both excellence and equality should be major goals of education in a pluralistic society.

THE DIMENSIONS OF MULTICULTURAL EDUCATION

When many teachers think of multicultural education, they think only or primarily of content related to ethnic, racial, and cultural groups. Conceptualizing multicultural education exclusively as content related to various ethnic and cultural groups is problematic for several reasons. Teachers who cannot easily see how their content is related to cultural and normative issues will easily dismiss multicultural education with the argument that it is not relevant to their disciplines. This is done frequently by secondary math and science teachers.

The "irrelevant of content argument" can become a legitimized form of resistance to multicultural education when it is conceptualized primarily or exclusively as content. Math and science teachers often state, "Multicultural education is fine for social studies and literature teachers, but it has nothing to do with me. Math and science are the same, regardless of the culture or the kids." Multicultural education needs to be more broadly defined and understood so that teachers from a wide range of disciplines can respond to it in appropriate ways and resistance to it can be minimized.

Multicultural education is a broad concept with several different and important dimensions (Banks, 1995a). Practicing educators can use the dimensions as a guide to school reform when trying to implement multicultural education. The dimensions are (1) content integration, (2) the knowledge construction process, (3) prejudice reduction, (4) an equity pedagogy; and (5) an empowering school culture and social structure. Each of the dimensions is defined and illustrated below.

Content Integration

Content integration deals with the extent to which teachers use examples and content from a variety of cultures and groups to illustrate key concepts, principles, generalizations, and theories in their subject area or discipline. The infusion of ethnic and cultural content into the subject area should be logical and not contrived.

More opportunities exist for the integration of ethnic and cultural content in some subject areas than in others. In the social studies, the language arts, and music, frequent and ample opportunities exist for teachers to use ethnic and cultural content to illustrate concepts, themes, and principles. There are also opportunities to integrate multicultural content into math and science. However, the opportunities are not as ample as they are in social studies, the language arts, and music.

The Knowledge Construction Process

The knowledge construction process relates to the extent to which teachers help students to understand, investigate, and determine how the implicit cultural assumptions, frames of references, perspectives, and biases within a discipline influence the ways in which knowledge is constructed within it (Banks, 1996).

Students can analyze the knowledge construction process in science by studying how racism has been perpetuated in science by genetic theories of intelligence, Darwinism, and eugenics. In his important book *The Mismeasure of Man*, Gould (1981) describes how scientific racism developed and was influential in the nineteenth and twentieth centuries. Scientific racism has had and continues to have a significant influence on the interpretations of mental ability tests in the United States.

The publication of *The Bell Curve* (Herrnstein & Murray, 1994), its widespread and enthusiastic public reception, and the social context out of which it emerged provide an excellent case study for discussion and analysis by students who are studying knowledge construction. Herrnstein and Murray contend that low-income groups and African Americans have less cognitive abilities than other groups and that these differences are inherited. Students can examine the arguments made by the authors, their major assumptions, and how their conclusions relate to the social and political context.

Gould (1994) contends that the arguments made by Herrnstein and Murray reflect the social context of the times, "a historical moment of unprecedented ungenerosity, when a mood for slashing social programs can be powerfully abetted by an argument that beneficiaries cannot be helped, owing to inborn cognitive limits expressed as low I. Q. scores" (p. 139). Students should also study counter-arguments to *The Bell Curve* made by respected scientists. A good source is *The Bell Curve: History, Documents, Opinions*, edited by Jacoby and Glauberman (1995).

Students can examine the knowledge construction process in the social studies when they study such units and topics as the European discovery of America and the westward movement. The teacher can ask the students the latent meanings of concepts such as the *European discovery of America* and the *New World*. The students can discuss what these concepts imply or suggest about the Native American cultures that had existed in the Americas for about 40,000 years before the Europeans arrived. When studying the westward movement, the teacher can ask the students, "Whose point of view or perspective does this concept reflect, that of the European Americans or the Lakota Sioux?" "Who was moving west?" "How might a Lakota Sioux historian describe this period in United States history?" "What are other ways of thinking about and describing the westward movement?"

Prejudice Reduction

Prejudice reduction describes lessons and activities teachers use to help students develop positive attitudes toward different racial, ethnic, and cultural groups. Research indicates that children come to school with many negative attitudes toward and misconceptions about different racial and ethnic groups (Phinney & Rotheram, 1987). Research also indicates that lessons, units, and teaching materials that include content about different racial and ethnic groups can help students to develop more positive intergroup attitudes if certain conditions exist in the teaching situation (Banks, 1995b). These conditions include positive images of the ethnic groups in the materials and the use of multiethnic materials in a consistent and sequential way.

Allport's (1954) contact hypothesis provides several useful guidelines for helping students to develop more positive interracial attitudes and actions in contact situations. He states that contact between groups will improve intergroup relations when the contact is characterized by these conditions: (1) equal status; (2) cooperation rather than competition; (3) sanction by authorities such as teachers and administrators; and (4) characterized by interpersonal interactions in which students become acquainted as individuals. Stephan and Stephan (1996) in their book, *Intergroup Relations*, provide a comprehensive and helpful discussion of the contact hypothesis.

An Equity Pedagogy

Teachers in each discipline can analyze their teaching procedures and styles to determine the extent to which they reflect multicultural issues and concerns. An equity pedagogy exists when teachers modify their teaching in ways that will facilitate the academic achievement of students from diverse racial, cultural, gender, and social-class groups (Banks, C. A. M., & Banks, J. A., 1995). This includes using a variety of teaching styles and approaches that are consistent with the wide range of learning styles within various cultural and ethnic groups, being demanding but highly personalized when working with groups such as Native American and Alaskan students, and using cooperative learning techniques in math and science instruction in order to enhance the academic achievement of students of color (Davidson, 1990).

Several of the chapters in this book discuss ways in which teachers can modify their instruction in order to increase the academic achievement of students from different cultural groups and from both gender groups, including the chapters that constitute Parts Three and Four.

An Empowering School Culture

Another important dimension of multicultural education is a school culture and organization that promotes gender, racial, and social-class equity. The culture and organization of the school must be examined by all members of the school staff. They all must also participate in restructuring it. Grouping and labeling practices, sports participation, disproportionality in achievement, disproportionality in enrollment in gifted and special education programs, and the interaction of the staff and the students across ethnic and racial lines are important variables that need to be examined in order to create a school culture that empowers students from diverse racial and ethnic groups and from both gender groups.

Figure 1.4 summarizes the dimensions of multicultural education described above. The next section of this chapter identifies the major variables of the school that must be changed in order to institutionalize a school culture that empowers students from diverse cultural, racial, ethnic, and social-class groups.

The School as a Social System

To implement multicultural education successfully, we must think of the school as a social system in which all of its major variables are closely interrelated. Thinking of the school as a social system suggests that we must formulate and initiate a change strategy that reforms the total school environment to implement multicultural education. The major school variables that must be reformed are presented in Figure 1.5.

Reforming any one of the variables in Figure 1.5, such as the formalized curriculum or curricular materials, is necessary but not sufficient. Multicultural and sensitive teaching materials are ineffective in the hands of teachers who have negative attitudes toward different racial, ethnic, and cultural groups. Such teachers are rarely likely to use multicultural materials or to use them detrimentally. Thus, helping teachers and other members of the school staff to gain knowledge about diverse groups and democratic attitudes and values is essential when implementing multicultural programs.

To implement multicultural education in a school, we must reform its power relationships, the verbal interaction between teachers and students, the culture of the school, the curriculum, extracurricular activities, attitudes toward minority languages, the testing program, and grouping practices. The institutional norms, social structures, cause-belief statements, values, and goals of the school must be transformed and reconstructed.

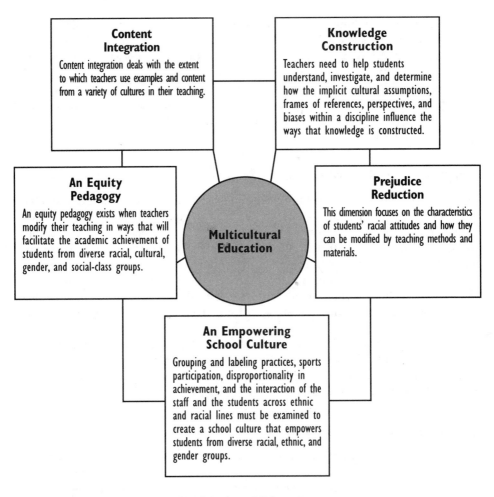

Figure 1.4 The Dimensions of Multicultural Education

Major attention should be focused on the school's hidden curriculum and its implicit norms and values. A school has both a manifest and a hidden curriculum. The manifest curriculum consists of such factors as guides, textbooks, bulletin boards, and lesson plans. These aspects of the school environment are important and must be reformed to create a school culture that promotes positive attitudes toward diverse cultural groups and helps students from these groups experience academic success. However, the school's hidden or latent curriculum is often more cogent than its manifest or overt curriculum. The latent curriculum has been defined as the one that no teacher explicitly teaches but that all students learn. It is that powerful part of the school culture that communicates to students the school's attitudes toward a range of issues and problems, including how the school views them as human beings and its attitudes toward males, females, exceptional students, and students from various religious,

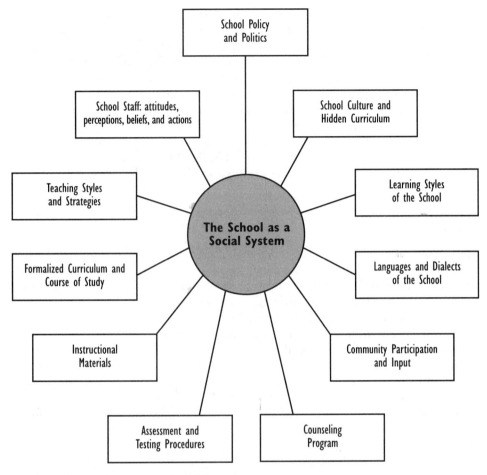

Figure 1.5 The School as a Social System

The total school environment is a system consisting of a number of major identifiable variables and factors, such as a school culture, school policy and politics, and the formalized curriculum and course of study. Any of these factors may be the focus of initial school reform, but changes must take place in each of them to create and sustain an effective multicultural school environment.

Adapted with permission from James A. Banks (Ed.), *Education in the 80s: Multiethnic Education* (Washington, DC: National Education Association, 1981), Figure 2, p. 22.

cultural, racial, and ethnic groups. Jackson (1992) calls the latent curriculum the "untaught lessons."

When formulating plans for multicultural education, educators should conceptualize the school as a microculture that has norms, values, statuses, and goals like other social systems. The school has a dominant culture and a variety of microcultures. Almost all classrooms in the United States are multicultural because White students, as well as Black and Brown students, are socialized within diverse cultures. Teachers also come from many different groups. Many teachers were socialized in cultures other than the Anglo mainstream, although these may be forgotten and repressed. Teachers can get in touch with their own cultures and use the perspectives and insights they acquired as vehicles for helping them relate to and understand the cultures of their students.

The school should be a cultural environment in which acculturation takes place; teachers and students should assimilate some of the views, perspectives, and ethos of each other as they interact. Teachers and students will be enriched by this process, and the academic achievement of students from diverse groups will be enhanced because their perspectives will be legitimized in the school. Both teachers and students will be enriched by this process of cultural sharing and interaction.

SUMMARY

Multicultural education is an idea stating that all students, regardless of the groups to which they belong, such as those related to gender, ethnicity, race, culture, social class, religion, or exceptionality, should experience educational equality in the schools. Some students, because of their particular characteristics, have a better chance to succeed in school as it is currently structured than have students from other groups. Multicultural education is also a reform movement designed to bring about a transformation of the school so that students from both genders and from diverse cultural and ethnic groups will have an equal chance to experience school success. Multicultural education views the school as a social system that consists of highly interrelated parts and variables. Therefore, in order to transform the school to bring about educational equality, all the major components of the school must be substantially changed. A focus on any one variable in the school, such as the formalized curriculum, will not implement multicultural education.

Multicultural education is a continuing process because the idealized goals it tries to actualize—such as educational equality and the eradication of all forms of discrimination—can never be fully achieved in a human society. Multicultural education, which was born during the social protest of the 1960s and 1970s, is an international movement that exists in various nations on the European continent and in Australia, the United Kingdom, and Canada. A major goal of multicultural education is to help students to develop the knowledge, attitudes, and skills needed to function within their own microcultures, the U.S. macroculture, other microcultures, and within the global community.

Questions and Activities

1. What are the three components or elements of multicultural education?
2. How does Banks define *multicultural education?*
3. Find other definitions of multicultural education in several books listed under the category "Issues and Concepts" in the Appendix. How are the definitions of multicultural education in these books alike and different from the one presented in this chapter?

4. In what ways did the civil rights and women's rights movements of the 1960s and 1970s influence the development of multicultural education?

5. Ask several teachers and other practicing educators to give you their views and definitions of multicultural education. What generalizations can you make about their responses?

6. Visit a local school and, by observing several classes as well as by interviewing several teachers and the principal, describe what curricular and other practices related to multicultural education have been implemented in the school. Share your report with your classmates or workshop colleagues.

7. What major tensions exist among groups such as various racial and ethnic groups and between feminists and ethnic minorities? Can multicultural education help reduce such tensions? If so, how?

8. What is a macroculture? A microculture?

9. How is *culture* defined? What are the most important components of culture in a modernized society?

10. List and define several core or overarching values and characteristics that make up the macroculture in the United States. To what extent are these values and characteristics consistent with practices in U.S. society? To what extent are they ideals that are inconsistent with realities in U.S. society?

11. What problems result when ideals in U.S. society are taught to students as if they were realities? Give examples of this.

12. How is individualism viewed differently in the United States and in nations such as China and Japan? Why? What are the behavioral consequences of these varying notions of individualism?

13. What is the American dilemma defined by Myrdal? To what extent is this concept an accurate description of values in U.S. society? Explain.

14. How do the preferred ways of learning and knowing among women and students of color often influence their experiences in the schools as they are currently structured? In what ways can school reform help make the school environment more consistent with the learning and cognitive styles of women and students of color?

15. In what ways does the process of identifying and labeling students with mental retardation discriminate against groups such as African Americans and Hispanics?

16. In what ways can the characteristics of a group help us understand an individual's behavior? In what ways are group characteristics limited in explaining an individual's behavior?

17. How do such variables as race, class, and gender interact to influence the behavior of students? Give examples to support your response.

18. What is meant by the "social construction of categories"? In what ways are concepts such as gender, race, social class, and exceptionality social categories?

19. List and define the five dimensions of multicultural education. How can these dimensions be used to facilitate school reform?

References

Albrecht, L. and Brewer, R. M. (Eds.). (1990). *Bridges of Power: Women's Multicultural Alliances.* Philadelphia: New Society Publishers.

Allan, R. and Hill, B. (1995). Multicultural Education in Australia: Historical Development and Current Status. In J. A. Banks and C. A. M. Banks (Eds.). *Handbook of Research on Multicultural Education* (pp. 763–777). New York: Macmillan.

Allport, G. W. (1954). *The Nature of Prejudice.* Reading, MA: Addison-Wesley.

Banks, C. A. M. and Banks, J. A. (1995). Equity Pedagogy: An Essential Component of Multicultural Education. *Theory into Practice, 34*(3), 152–158.

Banks, J. A. (1994a). *Multiethnic Education: Theory and Practice* (3rd ed.). Boston: Allyn and Bacon.

Banks, J. A. (1994b). *An Introduction to Multicultural Education.* Boston: Allyn and Bacon.

Banks, J. A. (1995a). Multicultural Education: Historical Development, Dimensions, and Practice. In J. A. Banks and C. A. M. Banks (Eds.). *Handbook of Research on Multicultural Education* (pp. 3–24). New York: Macmillan.

Banks, J. A. (1995b). Multicultural Education: Its Effects on Students' Racial and Gender Role Attitudes. In J. A. Banks and C. A. M. Banks (Eds.). *Handbook of Research on Multicultural Education* (pp. 617–627). New York: Macmillan.

Banks, J. A. (Ed.) (1996). *Multicultural Education, Transformative Knowledge, and Action.* New York: Teachers College Press.

Banks, J. A. & Banks, C. A. M. (Eds.). (1995) *Handbook of Research on Multicultural Education.* New York: Macmillan.

Banks, J. A. and Lynch, J. (Eds.). (1986). *Multicultural Education in Western Societies.* London: Cassell.

Baptiste, H. P. Jr. (1986, Winter). Multicultural Education and Urban Schools from a Sociohistorical Perspective: Internalizing Multiculturalism. *Journal of Educational Equity and Leadership* 6, 295–312.

Barton, L. and Walker, S. (Eds.). (1983). *Race, Class and Education.* London: Croom Helm.

Belenky, M. F. , Clinchy, B. M., Goldberger, N. R., and Tarule, J. M. (1986). *Women's Ways of Knowing: The Development of Self, Voice and Mind.* New York: Basic Books.

Bellah, R. N., Madsen, R., Sullivan, W. M., Swidler, A., and Tipton, S. M. (1985). *Habits of the Heart: Individualism and Commitment in American Life.* New York: Harper and Row.

Berger, P. L. and Luckman, T. (1967). *The Social Construction of Reality: A Treatise in the Sociology of Knowledge.* New York: Doubleday and Co.

Bullivant, B. (1993). Culture: Its Nature and Meaning for Educators. In J. A. Banks and C. A. M. Banks (Eds.). *Multicultural Education: Issues and Perspectives* (2nd ed., pp. 29–47). Boston: Allyn and Bacon.

Butterfield, F. (1982). *China: Alive in the Bitter Sea.* New York: Bantam Books.

Cohen, E. G. (1994). *Designing Groupwork: Strategies for Heterogeneous Classrooms* (2nd ed.) New York: Teachers College Press.

Davidson, N. (Ed.). (1990). *Cooperative Learning in Mathematics: A Handbook for Teachers.* Menlo Park, CA: Addison-Wesley.

Declaration of Independence. In *The Annals of America*, Vol. 2 (pp. 447–449). Chicago: Encyclopaedia Britannica.

DeMontilla, A. N. (1975). *Americanization in Puerto Rico and the Public-School System, 1900–1930*. San Juan: University of Puerto Rico, Editorial Universitaria.

Domhoff, G. W. (1983). *Who Rules America Now?* New York: Simon & Schuster.

Ellison, R. (1973). An American Dilemma: A Review. In J. A. Ladner (Ed.). *The Death of White Sociology* (pp. 81–95). New York: Vintage Books.

Figueroa, P. (1995). Multicultural Education in the United Kingdom: Historical Development and Current Status. In J. A. Banks and C. A. M. Banks (Eds.). *Handbook of Research on Multicultural Education* (pp. 778–800). New York: Macmillan.

Franklin, J. H. and McNeil, G. R. (Eds.). (1995). *African Americans and the Living Constitution*. Washington, DC: Smithsonian Institution Press.

Garretson, L. R. (1976). *American Culture: An Anthropological Perspective*. Dubuque: Wm. C. Brown Co.

Gibbs, J. T. (Ed.). (1988). *Young, Black, and Male in America: An Endangered Species*. Dover, MA: Auburn House Publishing.

Gilligan, C. (1982). *In a Different Voice: Psychological Theory and Women's Development*. Cambridge: Harvard University Press.

Goodman, N. and Marx, G. T. (1982). *Society Today* (4th ed.). New York: Random House.

Gould, S. J. (1981). *The Mismeasure of Man*. New York: Norton.

Gould, S. J. (1994). Curveball. *The New Yorker, 70*(38), 139–149.

Grant, C. A. and Sleeter, C. E. (1986a). *After the School Bell Rings*. Philadelphia: The Falmer Press.

Grant, C. A. and Sleeter, C. E. (1986b). Race, Class, and Gender in Education Research: An Argument for Integrative Analysis. *Review of Educational Research, 56*, 195–211.

Green, P. (1981). *The Pursuit of Inequality*. New York: Pantheon Books.

Greenbaum, W. (1974, August). America in Search of a New Ideal: An Essay on the Rise of Pluralism. *Harvard Educational Review, 44*, 411–440.

Grossman, H. and Grossman, S. H. (1994). *Gender Issues in Education*. Boston: Allyn and Bacon.

Hale, J. E. (1994). *Unbank the Fire: Visions for the Education of African American Children*. Baltimore: The Johns Hopkins University Press.

Halpern, D. F. (1986). *Sex Differences in Cognitive Abilities*. Hillsdale, NJ: Lawrence Erlbaum Associates, Inc.

Herrnstein, R. J. & Murray, C. (1994). *The Bell Curve: Intelligence and Class Structure in American Life*. New York: The Free Press.

Hoff, G. (1995). Multicultural Education in Germany: Historical Developments and Current Status. In J. A. Banks and C. A. M. Banks (Eds.). *Handbook of Research on Multicultural Education* (pp, 821–838). New York: Macmillan.

Irvine, J. J. & York, E. D. (1995). Learning Styles and Culturally Diverse Students: A Literature Review. In J. A. Banks and C. A. M. Banks (Eds.). *Handbook of Research on Multicultural Education* (pp. 484–497). New York: Macmillan.

Jackson, P. W. (1992). *Untaught Lessons*. New York: Teachers College Press.

Jacoby, R. and Glauberman, N. (Eds.) (1995). *The Bell Curve Debate: History, Documents, Opinions*. New York: Times Books/Random House.

Jencks, C., Smith, M., Acland, H., Bane, M. J., Cohen, D., Gintis, H., Heyns, B., and Michelson, S.. (1972). *Inequality: A Reassessment of the Effect of Family and Schooling in America*. New York: Basic Books.

Knapp, M. S. and Woolverton, S. (1995). Social Class and Schooling. In J. A. Banks and C. A. M. Banks (Eds.). *Handbook of Research on Multicultural Education* (pp. 548–569). New York: Macmillan.

Lasch, C. (1978). *The Culture of Narcissism*. New York: Norton.

Lisitzky, G. (1956). *Four Ways of Being Human: An Introduction to Anthropology*. New York: Viking Press.

Maher, F. A. (1987, March). Inquiry Teaching and Feminist Pedagogy. *Social Education, 51*(3), 186–192.

Mannheim, K. (1936). *Ideology and Utopia: An Introduction to the Sociology of Knowledge*. New York: Harcourt Brace.

Mercer, J. R. (1973). *Labeling the Mentally Retarded: Clinical and Social System Perspectives on Mental Retardation*. Berkeley: University of California Press.

Moodley, K. A. (1995). Multicultural Education in Canada: Historical Development and Current Status. In J. A. Banks & C. A. M. Banks (Eds.). *Handbook of Research on Multicultural Education* (pp. 801–820). New York: Macmillan.

Myrdal, G. with the assistance of Sterner, R. and Rose, A. (1962). *An American Dilemma: The Negro Problem and Modern Democracy* (anniv. ed.). New York: Harper and Row.

Perney, V. H. (1976). Effects of Race and Sex on Field Dependence–Independence in Children. *Perceptual and Motor Skills, 42*, 975–980.

Phinney, J. S. and Rotheram, M. J. (Eds.). (1987). *Children's Ethnic Socialization: Pluralism and Development*. Beverly Hills, CA: Sage.

Ramírez, M. and Castañeda, A. (1974). *Cultural Democracy, Bicognitive Development and Education*. New York: Academic Press.

Reischauer, E. O. (1981). *The Japanese*. Cambridge: Harvard University Press.

Sadker, M.P. and Sadker, D.M. (1994). *Failing at Fairness: How America's Schools Cheat Girls*. New York: Charles Scribner's Sons.

Sapon-Shevin, M. (1994). *Playing Favorites: Gifted Education and the Disruption of Community*. Albany: State University of New York Press.

Schlesinger, A. M. Jr. (1986). *The Cycles of American History*. Boston: Houghton Mifflin.

Schmitz, B., Butler, J., Rosenfelt, D., and Guy-Sheftal, B. (1995). Women's Studies and Curriculum Transformation. In J. A. Banks & C. A. M. Banks (Eds.). *Handbook of Research on Multicultural Education* (pp. 708–728). New York: Macmillan.

Shaver, J. P. and Curtis, C. K. (1981). *Handicapism and Equal Opportunity: Teaching about the Disabled in Social Studies*. Reston, VA: The Foundation for Exceptional Children.

Sisk, D. (1987). *Creative Teaching of the Gifted*. New York: McGraw-Hill Book Co.

Slavin, R. E. (1995). Cooperative Learning and Intergroup Relations. In J. A. Banks and C. A. M. Banks (Eds.). *Handbook of Research on Multicultural Education* (pp. 628–634). New York: Macmillan.

Steinem, G. (1995). *Outrageous Acts and Everyday Rebellions*. New York: Holt.

Stephan, W. G. and Stephan, C. W. (1996). *Intergroup Relations*. Madison, WI: Brown & Benchmark Publishers.

Taylor, J. M., Gilligan, C., and Sullivan, A. M. (1995). *Between Voice and Silence: Women and Girls, Race and Relationships*. Cambridge: Harvard University Press.

Theodorson, G. A. and Theodorson, A. G. (1969). *A Modern Dictionary of Sociology*. New York: Barnes and Noble.

Trecker, J. L. (1973). Teaching the Role of Women in American History. In J. A. Banks (Ed.). *Teaching Ethnic Studies: Concepts and Strategies* (pp. 279–297). Washington, DC: National Council for the Social Studies. (NCSS 43rd Yearbook)

Warner, W. L. with Meeker, M. and Eells, K. (1960). *Social Class in America* (reissued ed.). New York: Harper Torchbooks.

Weatherford, J. (1988). *Indian Givers: How the Indians of the Americas Transformed the World*. New York: Fawcett Columbine.

Chapter 2

Culture in Society and in Educational Practices

Frederick Erickson

A group of first graders and their teacher are in the midst of a reading lesson in a classroom in Berkeley, California. The children read aloud in chorus from their reading book:

1   T: All right, class, read that and remember your endings.

2   CC: What did Little Duck see? (final *t* of "what" deleted)

3   T: Wha_t_. (emphasizing final *t*)

4   CC: What (final *t* deleted as in turn 2)

5   T: I still don't hear this sad little "t."

6   CC: What did—what did—what—(final *t*'s deleted)

7   T: Wha_t_.

8   T&CC: What did Little Duck see? (final *t* spoken)

9   T: OK, very good

(From Piestrup, 1973)

What's cultural in this picture? How are those aspects of culture, and other aspects as well, related to issues of multicultural education? This chapter tries to answer these questions by considering various ways in which culture has been thought of and how those varying definitions of culture have relevance for education in general and for multicultural education in particular. The chapter first surveys a number of issues broadly in an overview. Later in the chapter, as the issues are revisited more closely, pertinent citations are included.

CULTURE: AN OVERVIEW

In a sense, everything in education relates to culture—to its acquisition, its transmission, and its invention. Culture is in us and all around us, just as is the air we breathe. It is personal, familial, communal, institutional, and societal in its scope and distribution.

Yet culture is a notion that is often difficult to grasp. As we learn and use culture in daily life, it becomes habitual. Our habits become for the most part invisible to us. Thus, culture shifts in and outside our reflective awareness. We don't think much about the structure and characteristics of culture as we use it, just as we don't think reflectively about any familiar tool in the midst of its use. If we hammer things a lot, we don't think about the precise weight or chemical composition of the steel of the hammer, especially as we are actually hammering; and when we speak to someone we know well we are unlikely to think reflectively about the sound system, grammar, vocabulary, and rhetorical conventions of our language, especially as we are doing things in the midst of our speaking.

Just as hammers and languages are tools by which we get things done, so is culture; indeed, culture can be thought of as the primary human toolkit. Culture is a product of human creativity in action, which, once we have it, enables us to extend our activity still further. In the sense that culture is entirely the product of human activity, an artifact, it is not like the air we breathe. By analogy to computers, which are information tools, culture can be considered as the software—the coding systems for doing meaning and executing sequences of work—by which our human physiological and cognitive hardware is able to operate so that we can make sense and take action with others in daily life. Culture structures the "default" conditions of the everyday practices of being human.

Another way to think of culture is as a sedimentation of the historical experience of persons and of social groupings of various kinds, such as nuclear family and kin, gender, ethnicity, race, and social class, all with differing access to power in society. We have become increasingly aware that the invention and sharing of culture (in other words, its production and reproduction) happen through processes that are profoundly political in nature, having to do with access to and distribution of social power. In these processes of cultural production and reproduction, the intimate politics of immediate social relations face-to-face are combined with a more public politics in the social forces and processes of economy and society writ large. How does the sedimentation of historical experience as culture take place? What are the micro and macro political circumstances in which culture is learned and invented? How does culture get distributed, similarly and differently within and across human groups and within and between human generations?

These are questions not only for social scientists or for social philosophers to address; they also are questions that raise issues that are essential for consideration by educators. Culture, as it is more and less visible and invisible to its users, is profoundly involved in the processes and contents of education. Culture shapes and is shaped by the learning and teaching that happen during the practical conduct of daily life within all the educational settings we encounter as learning environments throughout the human life span, in families, in school classrooms, in community settings, and in the workplace. There is some evidence that we begin to learn culture in the womb, and we continue to learn new culture until we die. Yet people learn differing sets and subsets of culture, and they can unlearn culture—shedding it as well as adopting it. At the individual and at the group level, some aspects of culture undergo change and other aspects stay the same, within a single human life and across generations.

Educators address these issues every time they teach and every time they design curriculum. They may be addressed by educators explicitly and within conscious awareness, or they may be addressed implicitly and outside conscious awareness. But at every moment in the conduct of educational practice, cultural issues and choices are at stake. This chapter makes some of those issues and choices more explicit.

Two final orienting assumptions are implicit in the previous discussion. First, everybody is cultural even though not all culture is equal. Every person and social group possesses and uses culture as a tool for the conduct of human activity. This means that culture is not the possession or characteristic of an exotic other, but of all of us, the dominant and the dominated alike. In other words, and to put it more bluntly, within U.S. society White people are just as cultural as are people of color (indeed the terms *White* and *people of color* represent cultural categories that are socially constructed). Moreover, White Anglo-Saxon Protestants (WASPs) are just as cultural as are Jews or Catholics; men are just as cultural as women; adults are just as cultural as teenagers; northerners are just as cultural as southerners; English speakers are just as cultural as the speakers of other languages; and native-born Americans are just as cultural as immigrants or citizens who reside in other countries. This is to say, Americans of African or European or Asian descent are just as cultural as people who live in Africa, Europe, or Asia. To reiterate, everybody in the world is cultural, even though not all culture is equal.

The second orienting assumption is that everybody is multicultural. Every person and every human group possesses both culture and cultural diversity. For example, Americans of Mexican descent are not culturally identical to Puerto Ricans who live on the mainland, but not all Mexican Americans or Puerto Ricans (or White Episcopalians, for that matter) are culturally identical even if they live in the same neighborhood and attend the same school or church. Members of the same family also are culturally diverse. In fact, we often encounter cultural difference as individual difference, as well as encountering culture in its more institutionalized manifestations, such as school literacy, the legal system, or the broadcast media. An important way we meet culture is in the particular people with whom we interact daily.

It is not possible for individuals to grow up in a complex modern society without acquiring differing subsets of culture—differing software packages that are tools that can be used in differing kinds of human activity; tools that in part enable and frame the activities in which they are used. From the nuclear family, through early and later schooling, through peer networks, and through life at work, we encounter, learn, and to some extent help create differing microcultures and subcultures. Just as everyone learns differing variants and styles of the various languages we speak so that everybody is multilingual (even those of us who only speak English), so everybody is multicultural. No matter how culturally isolated some person's lives may appear, in large-scale modern societies (and even in small-scale traditional societies) each member carries a considerable amount of that society's cultural diversity inside. This insight appears in an article by Goodenough—"Multiculturalism as the Normal Human Experience" (Goodenough, 1976).

If it is true that every person and human group is both cultural and multicultural, then a multicultural perspective on the aims and conduct of education is of primary importance. That assumption guides this chapter. First it considers a variety of definitions of culture. Then it discusses issues of how culture is organized and distributed in society that have special relevance for education. The discussion comments on teaching and learning in multicultural classrooms, in the light of the conceptions of culture previously discussed. The chapter concludes with a discussion of the diversity of culture not only within society but also within the person and the implications of that diversity for multicultural education.

ALTERNATIVE DEFINITIONS AND CONCEPTIONS OF CULTURE

Attempts at formal definitions of culture have not been fruitful; even the experts have not been able to agree on what culture "really" is. Yet some ways of thinking about culture seem increasingly to be inadequate and misleading and others are more useful. Presented here is a range of definitions, emphasizing the differing conceptions of culture that underly the various definitions.

Culture as Cultivation

All conceptions of culture imply a distinction between the cultural and the natural. "Cultivation" transforms the natural, in a social sense, just as agriculture transforms nature in a biological and chemical sense. Cultivating the soil makes for fewer weeds than in nature (indeed, the distinction between what is considered weed and what is considered plant is a cultural one). Cultivation requires effort and method—it evokes images of straight furrows, of working, and of planning for the future harvest.

The agricultural metaphor for culture bears a family resemblance to an artistic one. In the fine arts, cultivation also involves disciplining the natural—the fingers learn to find keys on the piano; the painter's eye and hand and the ballerina's feet are schooled by artistic convention. Thus, in ordinary use, culture has come to mean "high culture"—what we find in the museum, the symphony hall, the theater, the library. In those institutions we find cultural products whose value is defined by elite tastes, which are defined and framed reflexively by those cultural products.

In contrast to prestigious high culture there is also "low culture"—popular culture—which is another sense in which the term *culture* is used. Some artifacts of U.S. popular culture, such as blue jeans and popular music, have been adopted throughout the world. In the realm of popular culture, fashions change across time and across various social groups and social sectors, just as they do in the realm of high culture. We have diverse artifacts and practices of popular culture with differential appeal, such as classic rock 'n roll, rap, country, and Cajun music. We have Western cowboy boots, motorcycle boots, hiking boots, upland game hunting boots, and Nike basketball sneakers, each with a different resonance among subgroups within U.S. society, and each potentially able to serve as badges of personal and group identity.

In the social sciences, the term *culture* refers to phenomena that are less mystifying than those of so-called high culture and less sensational than those of popular culture. In the social scientific sense, culture is seen as something everyone has and makes use of routinely, regardless of social position. It refers to the patterns for sense-making that are part of the organization of the conduct of everyday life.

This egalitarian notion of culture arose among Western Europeans in the Enlightenment (Vico, 1725/1968) and it developed further in the early Romantic period, foreshadowed by Rousseau and continued by the brothers Grimm and by von Humboldt. The Grimms collected folktales from German peasants whose language and folk knowledge had been made fun of by aristocrats in earlier times. This shift toward greater respect for the lifeways of ordinary people happened between the mid-eighteenth and the early nineteenth centuries.*

Culture as Tradition

By the early nineteenth century culture was beginning to be seen as *tradition*—that which is handed down across generations. Within anthropology during the nineteenth century, culture was seen as a sum total of social inheritance. In 1871, anthropologist Sir Edward Burnett Tylor presented this broad definition: "Culture or Civilization…is that complex whole which includes knowledge, belief, art, morals, law, custom, and any other capabilities and habits acquired by man as a member of society" (Tylor, 1871/1970, p. l).

As genetic theory was developing, culture came to be seen as a kind of gene pool existing at the level of social symbolism and meaning rather than biology. By 1917, an American anthropologist called culture the "superorganic," meaning that it had an ideational rather than material existence (Kroeber, 1917). Following Tylor and others, Kroeber assumed that culture was a whole system consisting of interrelated parts, not literally a living organism but metaphorically similar to one.

Yet the notion of culture remained fuzzy among social scientists. Near the end of his career Kroeber collaborated with Kluckhohn in a review of the uses of the term *culture*. Their review of anthropology and sociology publications turned up hundreds of citations and differing shadings of meaning for the word (Kroeber & Kluckhohn, 1952). Since then no scholar has tried to claim a single, authoritative meaning of the term.

---

*This change in popular opinion is reflected even in productions of musical high culture. Composing for German courtiers in the late Baroque era, J. S. Bach wrote the "Peasant Cantata" in which he mocked the musical and speech style of German farm workers, portraying them in parody as dishonest and igno-rant, albeit amiable. By the 1780s, however, the French playwright Beaumarchais in "The Marriage of Figaro" presented the lower-class character of a barber in a sympathetic light. The play was censored as revolutionary by the royal French court and was similarly regarded as suspect by the imperial court of Vienna before Mozart took the risk of adapting the play for his opera of the same name.

Culture as Information Bits

Currently, one conception of culture considers it by analogy to information bits in a computer as well as to genetic information in a breeding population. According to this view, culture can be thought of as consisting of many small chunks of knowledge that are stored as a large pool of information within a bounded social group (see Goodenough, 1981). No single member of the group has learned all knowledge that is possessed within the group as a whole. The amounts and kinds of information known are seen as varying widely across individuals and subgroups within the total population.

This variation can be understood by analogy to language. What we call a *language* has a sound system (pronunciation), a syntax (grammar), and a lexicon (vocabulary). Those who understand the literal meaning of a sound system, a syntax, and a lexicon are termed members of the same *language community*. Subsets of the language are called *dialects*—they are spoken by members of subgroups within the overall language community. Dialects may vary in some aspects of pronunciation of vowels or consonants, or in some aspects of grammar, or in vocabulary, but any dialect is still intelligible overall to speakers of other dialects within the language. Each person within a language community speaks a unique form of that language, called an *idiolect* (i.e., no one individual actually speaks "English"; all individuals pronounce the language sounds in slightly differing ways and use grammar and vocabulary in individually distinct ways, in a kind of personal dialect). By this analogy, an overall general culture = language, while dialect = subculture, and idiolect = microculture, which can be thought of as a personal or immediately local variation on a subculture or general culture.

Culture as Symbol System

Another conception considers culture as a more limited set of large chunks of knowledge—conceptual structures that frame or constitute what is taken as "reality" by members of a social group (Geertz, 1973). These central organizing constructs—core symbols—are seen as being shared widely throughout the group. The routine ways of acting and making sense that are used by members of the group tend to repeat the major framing patterns again and again, just as within a musical composition many variations can be written on a few underlying thematic elements. This conception of culture emphasizes relatively tight organization of patterns, coherence in the overall meaning system, and identical (or at least closely shared) understanding of symbols and shared sentiments regarding those symbols among the members of the social group.

Culture as Social Process

A third conception treats social structure and culture as intertwined (Bourdieu, 1977; Bourdieu & Passeron, 1977; Williams, 1983). Some work within this stream of approaches emphasizes the diversity of cultural knowledge within a given social unit (Barth, 1969; 1989). Cultural difference is seen as tracing lines of status, power, and political interest within and across the subgroups and institutions found in the total social unit. This variation in cultural difference within a social unit can be seen as analogous to the ways in which differences in air pressure or temperature are displayed on a weather map. There is variation in temperature in the earth's atmosphere, and it is nonrandomly distributed. There is variation in culture within a human society or social unit, and it, too, is nonrandomly distributed, closely related to the differential allocation of power and prestige within the society.

One school of thought within this third mode sees culture not so much as a cognitive template for the routine conduct of everyday life, but as residing in the conduct of everyday life itself (Bourdieu, 1977; Ortner, 1984). This conduct is seen as *practice*, as routine activity that is habitual and goal-directed (Connell, 1982). Practices are daily and customary, but they also tend toward a projected outcome, although the aims in such "projects" may not be entirely conscious ones. Thus, the person engaged in the practical conduct of everyday life can be seen as not simply following cultural "rules" (as in the first conception of culture) or as responding to cultural symbols always in the same ways (as is implied in the second conception of culture) but as being strategic—an active agent who uses culture as tools adaptively, employing novel means when necessary to achieve desired ends.

The first and second conceptions of culture can be criticized as presuming that human actors are the passive recipients of shaping by their social circumstances and that once having acquired culture passively (through learning) they are on "automatic pilot," capable only of following general cultural rules or scripts and incapable of acting adaptively in unique local circumstances. These views consider the cultural actor as a robot or as a "social dope" (Garfinkel & Sacks, 1970); they leave no room for human agency. Practice theory, on the other hand, takes realistic account of how habitual and conservative our daily conduct is, but it leaves room for the assumption that individuals can make sense adaptively within their practices, rather than simply following cultural rules.

The school of thought which sees culture as inherently related to issues of social structure and power also tends to see culture as arising through social conflict, with the possibility of differing interest groups becoming progressively more culturally different across time even though the groups may be in continual contact. From this perspective the emphasis is not on culture as a general integrated system but on the content of cultural knowledge and practice within the specific life situations of the persons and groups by whom such knowledge is held and such practices are undertaken. Key questions in this perspective are, "Given certain kinds of daily experience, what kinds of sense do people make of it, and how does this sense-making influence their customary actions?" This position assumes that new culture—whether conceived as small information bits or as larger structures of concept and activity—is being transformed continually within the contradictions experienced in daily life. These new cultural forms are accepted, learned, and remembered, or rejected, ignored, and forgotten, depending on where one sits in the social order, and depending on the particular circumstances in the situation in which the new culture is invented.

Overall, the third conception of culture emphasizes three related points: (1) the systematic variation of culture in relation to the allocation of power in society; (2) social conflict as a fundamental process by which cultural variation is organized, through which traditional culture is being simultaneously forced on people and contested, and through which new culture is continually being invented; and (3) human agency in the use of cultural tools, both tools inherited through tradition and tools invented through their use in practice within changing circumstances (Giddens, 1984).

Culture as Motive and Emotion

Another contemporary approach considers both the cognitive and the emotional/motivational force of culture (Lutz, 1990). We learn customs, but why do we become emotionally attached to them? How do we come to desire and work for ends and to use means for reaching those ends that are culturally enjoined? We do not act on culturally defined goals simply because we are forced to do so, although in situations of unequal power subordinates may "fake it"—they may feign more allegiance to cultural norms such as politeness or diligence than they in fact are feeling. Still, culturally defined love objects are genuinely yearned for, culturally defined careers do become the objects of genuine aspiration and striving, and customs that are culturally defined as repulsive, such as eating sea slugs, evoke strong emotional reactions of disgust in some social groups, even though those same food practices are seen as normal or even highly desirable in other social groups.

Contemporary neuroscience shows that when we engage in routine activities not only are the neural networks activated that involve prior cognitive learning (i.e., neural connections to the cerebral cortex), but that neural connections to our emotional states at the time of initial learning are also activated (i.e., neural connections to the limbic system). Thus, our repetition of certain customary activities evokes and reinforces emotional feelings as well as thoughts and skills (D'Andrade & Strauss, 1992). Through continued participation in daily life we thus acquire *cultural models* for its conduct that involve feeling in our knowing. In an important sense that went unrecognized in earlier cognitive psychology, all our cognitions are "hot cognitions" and learning is a profoundly emotional activity as well as a cognitive one.

Now, more than forty years since Kroeber and Kluckhohn's review of social scientists' use of the term *culture*, formal definitions, while overlapping, still do not agree exactly. Yet culture is generally seen as a product of human activity that is used as a tool. It is seen as learned and transmitted from our elders and also as invented within current situations. How much and in what ways culture is shared within and between identifiable human groups is an issue on which there is much debate currently. Power and politics seem to be involved in the processes by which culture is learned, shared, and changed. Culture, in other words, takes shape in the weight of human history. Some aspects of culture are explicit, and others are implicit, learned, and shared outside conscious awareness. Our moods and desires as well as our thoughts are culturally constructed.

Culture can be thought of as a construction—it constructs us and we construct it. That is, all thoughts, feelings, and human activity are not simply natural, but are the result of historical and personal experiences that become sedimented as culture in habit. Culture varies, somehow, from one person or group to another. Since our subjective world—what we see, know, and want—is culturally constructed, and since culture varies, that is, persons really do not inhabit the same subjective worlds even though they may seem to do so. Even though some of us show up in what seems to be the same event, how we experience it is never quite the same across the various individuals who have joined together in interaction. Thus, there is no single or determinative human world as a fixed point of reference. Individually and collectively, we make cultural worlds and they are multiple. This point has profound implications for educators, as is discussed in the following sections.

As human beings not only do we live in webs of meaning, caring, and desire that we ourselves create and that create us, but those webs hang in social gravity (Geertz, 1973, p. 5). Within the webs all our activity is vested in the weight of history, that is, in a social world of inequality all movement is up or down. Earlier conceptions of culture described it and human actions guided or framed by it as existing in a universe without gravity. Movement was thus unconstrained; it had no effort, no force. There was no domination or subordination, no resistance or compliance in such a cultural world. In more recent conceptions of culture we are coming to see that living in a gravity-ridden social and cultural universe we always have weight. We are culturally constructed and constructing beings, and in that construction we are never standing still.

CULTURAL ISSUES IN EDUCATION AND SOCIETY

The previous discussion provides a framework for the four main issues that have special relevance for educators: (1) the notion of culture as invisible as well as visible; (2) the politics of cultural difference in school and society; (3) the inherent diversity of cultures and subcultures within human social groups; and (4) the diversity of cultures within the individual—a perspective on the self as multiculturally constructed.

Invisible Culture

The distinction between visible and invisible culture has also been called explicit/implicit or overt/covert. (Hall, 1959; 1976; Philips, 1983). Much of culture is not only held outside conscious awareness but is also learned and taught outside awareness—hence neither the cultural insiders nor the newcomers are aware that certain aspects of their culture exist. In multicultural education and in discussions of cultural diversity more generally the focus has been on visible, explicit aspects of culture, such as language, dress, food habits, religion, and aesthetic conventions. While important, these visible aspects of culture, which are taught deliberately and learned (at least to some extent) consciously, are only the tip of the iceberg of culture.

Implicit and invisible aspects of culture are also important. How long in clock time one can be late before being impolite, how one conceives or experiences emotional or physical pain, how one displays such pain behaviorally, what topics should be avoided at the beginning of a conversation, how one shows interest or attention through listening behavior, how loud is too loud or not loud enough in speaking, how one shows that one would like the speaker to move on to the next point—these are all aspects of culture that we learn and use without realizing it. When we meet other people whose invisible cultural assumptions and patterns for action differ from those we have learned and expect implicitly, we usually don't recognize what they are doing as cultural in origin. Rather, we see them as rude or uncooperative. We may apply clinical labels to the other people—passive aggressive, low self-esteem.

Differences in invisible culture can be troublesome in circumstances of intergroup conflict. The difficulty lies in our inability to recognize others' differences in ways of acting as cultural rather than personal. We tend to naturalize other people's behavior and blame them—attributing intentions, judging competence—without realizing that we are experiencing culture rather than nature.

Modern society exacerbates the difficulties that can result from differences in invisible culture. Formal organizations and institutions, such as hospitals, workplaces, the legal system, and schools, become collection sites for invisible cultural difference. If the differences were more visible, we might see less misattribution, in the absence of intergroup conflict. For example, if we were to meet a woman in a hospital emergency room who was wearing exotic dress, speaking a language other than English, and carrying food that looked and smelled strange, we would not assume that we understood her thoughts and feelings or that she necessarily understood ours. Yet when such a person is dressed similarly to us, speaks English, and does not differ from us in other obvious ways, we may fail to recognize the invisible cultural orientations that differ between us, and a cycle of mutual misattribution can start.

Aspects of invisible culture have been identified by anthropologists with linguistic and cognitive orientations (Gumperz, 1982; Hymes, 1974). They make a helpful distinction between language community and speech community or network. Those people in the same language community share knowledge of the sound system, grammar, and vocabulary of a language. But within the same language community there are diverse speech communities or networks—sets of persons who share assumptions about the purposes of speaking, modes of politeness, topics of interest, ways of responding to others. Those cultural assumptions concerning ways of speaking differ considerably, even though at a general level all are uttering the same language. That is, language community differences are visible, but speech community differences are often invisible.

Yet cultural difference, visible and invisible, doesn't always lead to trouble between people. These differences become more troublesome in some circumstances than in others. That leads to a consideration of the circumstances of intercultural contact.

The Politics of Cultural Difference: Boundaries and Borders

The introductory discussion states that cultural difference demarcates lines of political difference, and often of domination. By analogy to a weather map, boundaries of cultural difference can be seen as isobars of power, rank, and prestige in society. One can trace boundaries of networks of members who share cultural knowledge of various sorts, of language, social ideology and values, religious beliefs, technical knowledge, preferences is aesthetic tastes—in recreation and sport, in personal dress and popular music tastes, and in cultivated tastes in the fine arts, cuisine, and literature. Because these preferences have differing prestige value they have been called *cultural capital* (Bourdieu, 1977; Bourdieu & Passeron, 1977). Such preferences also become symbols, or badges of group identity—markers of ethnicity, religion, gender, or social class.

The presence of cultural difference in society does not necessarily lead to conflict, however, nor need it lead to difficulty in education. The presence of conflict depends on whether cultural difference is being treated as a *boundary* or as a *border* (Barth, 1969; Giroux, 1991; McDermott & Gospodinoff, 1979/1981). A cultural *boundary* refers to the presence of some kind of cultural difference. As noted earlier, cultural boundaries are characteristic of all human societies, traditional as well as modern. A *border* is a social construct that is political in origin. Across a border power is exercised, as in the political border between two nations.

When a cultural boundary is treated as a cultural border, differences in rights and obligations are powerfully attached to the presence or absence of certain kinds of cultural knowledge. Consider, for example, the political/cultural border between the United States and Mexico. On either side of the border are people who speak English and people who speak Spanish; that is, the boundaries of language community cross over the lines demarcating national citizenship. Yet on either side of the border, fluency in Spanish—which is an aspect of cultural knowledge—is differentially rewarded or punished. On the Mexican side of the border, fluency in Spanish is an advantage legally, educationally, and in the conduct of much daily life, while on the United States side, the same cultural knowledge is disadvantaged, indeed in parts of South Texas speaking Spanish is still stigmatized.

When one arrives at a cultural border, one's cultural knowledge may be held up for scrutiny—stopped and frisked. An ancient example comes from the Book of Judges. At approximately 800 B.C., the Hebrews were not yet fully unified politically under a monarch and they had not yet completely occupied the territory of Canaan. They were a loose federation of kinship groups or clans that periodically came together in an unstable and tense alliance against common enemies. A dispute broke out between soldiers of two of the clans, the men of Ephraim and the men of Gilead. After defeat in a battle with the Ammonites, the common enemy, the men of Ephraim were trying to escape across fords in the Jordan River. The fords were guarded on the Hebrew-occupied side of the river by Gileadites. The men of Gilead checked the clan identity of the retreating soldiers by testing their cultural knowledge: "When any of the fugitives of Ephraim said, 'Let me go over,' the men of Gilead said to him, 'Are you an Ephraimite?' When he said, 'No,' they said to him, 'Then say Shibboleth.' He said 'Sibboleth,' for he could not pronounce it correctly. Then they seized him and slew him at the fords of the Jordan" (Judges 12: 5b-6a, RSV). The two clans of Hebrews differed in their pronunciation of the initial sibilant in the word *Shibboleth*. The Gileadites used the /sh/ phoneme for that consonant, while the Ephraimites used the /s/ phoneme. The Gileadite soldiers were aware of this cultural difference and made use of it to construct a sociolinguistic test at a geographic and political border, which, because of the test imposed, became a cultural border as well.

In modern societies the same thing can happen when one enters the emergency room of a hospital and speaks to an admitting clerk, or when one speaks to the maitre d' at a restaurant. It also can happen in school classrooms. Yet cultural boundaries (the objective presence of cultural difference) need not necessarily be treated as cultural borders. This is a matter of socially constructed *framing*. The framing of cultural difference as boundary or as border can change over time. Sometimes that change is very rapid, as in the following example (Fanon, 1963). In Algeria shortly before France gave up colonial rule, the pronunciation of the announcers on the state radio was made a cultural border issue by the independence movement. Complaints were voiced that Radio Algiers was not employing native Algerians. This practice was seen as another symbol of colonial oppression by France. Radio Algiers sent out a statement that its announcers were in fact Algerians. The independence movement then asked why the radio announcers spoke cosmopolitan French rather than the Algerian dialect. The complaints about the announcers became increasingly strident in the independence-oriented press, right up to Independence Day. After that day the announcers on Radio Algiers continued to speak cosmopolitan French but public complaint ended instantly. The reason for the complaint was gone, and so a small feature of cultural difference, which had been framed for a time as a cultural border, was reframed as a cultural boundary.

These two examples suggest that cultural difference, rather than being considered a cause of conflict in society (and in education), is more appropriately seen as a *resource* for conflict. If people have a reason to look for trouble, cultural difference—especially one that becomes a badge of social identity—can be used to start a fight. But the causes of the fight go beyond the cultural difference itself.

Cultural Differentiation as a Political Process

What happens over time when certain aspects of cultural difference get treated as border issues? Examples from language suggest that the differences become more extreme on either side. This suggests that political conflict, explicit and implicit, is a major engine of culture change. Such conflict generates cultural resistance. Labov (1963) found that on Martha's Vineyard, a small island off the coast of Massachusetts, certain sound features in the islanders' dialect became increasingly divergent from the more "standard" English spoken by summer tourists as the number of tourists staying on the island in the summer increased over time, although the islanders were not aware consciously that this was happening. Firsthand contacts with a standard model of American English had been increasing for the islanders, but across a generation their speech was becoming more different from that of the mainlanders.

A similar process of divergence was reported as taking place across the time span of half hour interviews in experimental situations (Giles & Powesland, 1975). Speakers of differing British regional dialects were paired for two-person discussions. In some discussions, mild discomfort and conflict was experimentally introduced, while in other discussions conflict was not introduced. In the discussions with conflict and discomfort, by the end of a half-hour each person was speaking a broader form of his or her regional dialect than before the discussion began. In other words, if a Yorkshireman were talking to a person from Dorsetshire, he would become more distinctly Yorkshire in his pronunciation and the Dorset man would become more Dorsetshire in his pronunciation as the conversation between the two progressed. Conversely, when conflict was not introduced and the two parties spoke comfortably, pronunciation features that differed between their two dialects became less distinct—they were converging in speech style rather than diverging.

This example suggests that cultural divergence is a result rather than a cause of social conflict. Bateson (1972) called the tendency of subsystems to evolve in increasingly differentiated ways *complementary schismogenesis* which seems to be the process by which cultural resistance over time results in culture change. It should be emphasized, however, that such change can occur entirely outside the conscious awareness of those involved in it as well as in situations of more explicit, conscious awareness in which people are deliberate regarding the change they are struggling to produce.

The classic view of culture in social science was as a total system, with integrated parts, the operation of which tended toward maintaining a steady state. As we have seen, culture now seems to be more labile than that—variable in the moment. This raises the question of how we conceive of culture change—as loss, as gain, as a mixture of both, or less evaluatively as change. We must also consider how culture is shared within human groups. We usually think of ethnic and racial groups (and perhaps gender categories as well) as necessarily identifying cultural boundaries. Such groups, we may assume, are defined by shared culture among their members. Barth (1969) contends, however, that culture sharing is not the crucial defining attribute of ethnic group membership. Rather, the ethnic or racial group is more appropriately considered as an economic and political interest group. Features of culture may be considered as identity badges, indicating group membership. But culture sharing is not essential for this, according to Barth. There may be much cultural diversity within the same named social category. He used as an example the Pathans, who live as a numerical minority on one side of the border between Pakistan and Afghanistan and as a majority on the other side. Some Pathans are herders—more so on the Afghan side of the border. Other Pathans are farmers—more on the Pakistani side. Yet both herders and farmers will identify as Pathan and are so regarded by ethnic others on either side of the border.

Culture Change as Culture Loss—or Not

When we think of ethnic/racial groups and cultural groups as having the same boundaries—the traditional view—we are sometimes to think of culture change as culture loss. Members of an ethnic group can blame themselves for losing a language, a religion, a household practice. Native Americans, for example, have mourned the passing of old culture and gone beyond mourning to self-blame, considering themselves less Indian than their forebears. Yet if a Koyukon Athabaskan now uses a snowmobile rather than a dog team and sled, does that mean he or she is any less Koyukon than before? Not necessarily, if we follow Barth's analysis. What is essential for the maintenance of ethnic groups and ethnic identity are not the specifics of culture traits practiced by the members, rather, being ethnic counts economically and politically in the larger society. Even the specific ways in which it counts to be ethnic can change, yet if there continue to be economic and political consequences of being identified as ethnic, especially if that is to the advantage of the members, then the ethnic group continues.

The classic view makes culture the defining attribute of ethnic identity. It becomes easy then to see culture change as culture loss. This can be thought of as the leaky bucket perspective on culture change: as if culture were held in a human group as water is contained in a bucket. Change then becomes the holes in the bucket. As one carries such a bucket over time and space, the water gradually drains out. Alternatively, we can conceive of the bucket of culture as always full. Air may replace the water, but the bucket is never empty. The contemporary Koyukon society, with its snowmobile practices, can be considered just as full culturally as the Koyukon society in the days of sled and dog team. What's in the bucket is different now, but the bucket is still not empty. During the summer people in an Odawa community in Northern Ontario wear tee shirts as they fish from aluminum boats powered by outboard motors. They no longer wear buckskin and use birchbark canoes. Yet they continue to fish, and they do so with differing fishing rights from those of White Canadians. Moreover, they still consider themselves Odawa, as distinct from White Canadians in neighboring villages who also fish from aluminum boats while wearing tee shirts.

Culture and Collective Identity Formation

To call something *cultural* has in itself political implications. Because so many aspects of culture are transparent to its users in their use, ordinarily we do not think about or notice them. Yet in complex and diverse modern societies, as ethnic, racial, religious and gender identification becomes self-aware among identification group members, they begin to notice their customary practices and to identify them as cultural. As with ethnic identification, cultural identification is always relational and comparative— with reference to an other. In the early nineteenth century, for example, German *Kultur* began to be invoked by German intellectuals in contrast and opposition to the French and Italians, whose tastes in literature and music, architecture, and clothing had previously set the standard of what was desirable in upper-class polite society. Without the presence of French and Italian models to compete with, Germans may not have become so aware of their own Germanness. This awareness progressed beyond rediscovery to invention, with German intellectuals such as Wagner helping to *create* a Germanic heritage with the support of the ruling interests in German society. With this rise in in-group awareness and solidarity came a heightened awareness of boundaries with non-Teutonic others. To the extent that this perception of out-groups was invidious the boundaries became borders.

We see a similar phenomenon today with the rise of religious nationalism and of ethnic and racial nationalism. With in-group identification there is always the possibility for treating boundaries as borders. Especially when heightening of cultural awareness and identification is used as a political strategy for changing power relations in society, or for legitimating territorial or colonial expansion, in-group solidarity and identification can become demonic. As Said notes (1978) in commenting on the colonial relationship between Europe and a perceived Orient that was a cultural creation of Europeans themselves, when more powerful nations or interest groups identify some Other as exotic and different there can be a tendency for the more powerful to project their own flaws, contradictions, and hostilities on the constructed Other. Such projections are reciprocated by those who have been "Othered" in a process of mutual border framing. Through this process of projective "Othering," negative cultural stereotypes result, making the fostering of intercultural and multicultural awareness a tricky business indeed.

Ethnic identification need not necessarily lead to Othering in the negative sense, however—the comparisons with those who differ from "Us" need not be invidious. Cultural differences can be framed as boundaries rather than as borders even though such framing takes effort to maintain. It should be noted, however, that an increase in the deliberateness and intensity of cultural awareness necessarily involves a comparative awareness. The construction of in-group identity is a relational process through which a definition of Other as well as of Self, of Them as well as of Us—and in the case of subordinated groups a specific identification of aspects of oppression—becomes more focal in conscious awareness.

TEACHING AND LEARNING MULTICULTURALLY
Emphasizing Invisible as well as Visible Culture

Schools can support or hinder the development of healthy identity and of intergroup awareness. The discussion now turns to teaching and learning in classrooms (see Mehan et al., 1995). This chapter emphasizes the importance of culture and criticizes our tendencies to essentialize it. When we essentialize culture, assuming that all persons in a given social category are culturally similar and focusing on the unitary cultures of various Others without reflecting on our own cultures and their diversity, we open a Pandora's box of opportunity for negative attribution. Sometimes social scientific notions of culture, especially of culture as a unified system and of group membership as culturally defined, have provided a justification for intergroup stereotypes. When these stereotypes come with social scientific warrant, we call them *neo-stereotypes*.

Teaching about the cultural practices of other people without stereotyping or misinterpreting them and teaching about one's own cultural practices without invidiously characterizing the practices of other people should be the aims of multicultural education. In situations of intergroup conflict these aims can be ideals that are difficult to attain. Educators should face such difficulty realistically.

One problem in multicultural curriculum and pedagogy is the overemphasis on visible (explicit) culture at the expense of the invisible and implicit. Focusing mainly on explicit culture can be misleading. Even when we do this respectfully of the lifeways of others, focus on visible culture easily slides into too comfortable a stance for considering other people—a stance of cultural romance or cultural tourism.

Particular traits of visible culture, often treated in isolation, have become the basis for much of what we teach about cultural diversity in schools. Some educators speak critically of "*piñata* curriculum," "snowshoe curriculum," and "holidays and heroes" in characterizing this approach.

By treating cultural practices as sets of static facts we trivialize them in superficiality and we make it seem as if culture were necessarily unchanging. What if Mexican Americans were to have a party and *not* break a *piñata*? Would they be any less Mexican? In Alaskan Athabascan villages, snowmobiles rather than sled dogs and snowshoes are the preferred mode of winter transportation. Are the villagers any less Indian? They are, only if we adopt an essentialist view of culture, with its accompanying "leaky bucket" image of culture change.

A way to teach about explicit culture without overgeneralizing about the lifeways of other people is to emphasize the variability of culture within social groups and the continual presence of cultural change as well as cultural continuity across time. Unfortunately, published multicultural materials that have an essentialist emphasis may not lend themselves well to this method. Yet in every classroom there is a resource for the study of within-group cultural diversity as well as between-group diversity. That resource is the everyday experience and cultural practices of the students and teachers themselves. (This is most easily done in a self-contained classroom, and so this discussion may seem most relevant for elementary school teaching, but many of the issues and approaches mentioned can be undertaken by high school and college teachers as well.)

Critical Autobiography as Curriculum and as Action Research

Critically reflective autobiography by students and oral history of their families—a form of community action research—can become important parts of a multicultural curriculum. Even in a classroom with a student population highly segregated by race or by social class, reflective investigation of their own lives and of family and local community histories by students will reveal diversity as well as similarity (hooks, 1993; Torres-Guzman, 1992; Skilton Sylvester, 1994; Wiggington, 1986; Witherell & Noddings, 1991). Not all the Italian Americans in a classroom have had the same family experience of immigration. Not all the African American students whose forebears moved from the rural South to a large city have had the same experience of urbanization. As a result of differing life experiences there are differences in cultural funds of knowledge between families who on the surface appear to be demographically similar—differences in family microcultures (see Moll, 1990).

Some of these differences across families also reveal similarity—as in variations on a common theme of life experience, such as that of the experience of racism by African Americans. But not all the experiences, even of racism within a given racial group, are identical. Thus, diversity and similarity always accompany one another in the real stories of people in human groups. Those stories have involved struggles to change, to resist. Contemporary community issues, as students address them through local community study, also provide opportunities for students to take action to improve the circumstances of their lives and, in the process, come to see themselves and their families not simply as passive recipients of social and cultural influences, but as active agents who are making sense and making their lives.

Direct connections between the daily lives of students outside the classroom and the content of instruction in history, social studies, and literature can make the stated curriculum come alive. These connections also afford the teacher an opportunity to learn the cultural backgrounds and cultural diversity that he or she confronts with each set of students. As stated earlier, formal organizations in modern societies become collection sites for cultural diversity. This is true for every school classroom. Each new set of students represents a unique sampling from the universe of local cultural diversity present in the school area. Simply knowing that one has three Haitian students and four Cambodian students—or seventeen girls and eleven boys—in a certain classroom, for example, does not tell that teacher anything (necessarily) about the specific cultural backgrounds of those students and their families and their assumptions about ethnicity, race, or gender, given the cultural diversity that is possible within any social category. The teacher's tasks are to know not only about Haitians or Cambodians in general, or about girls and boys in general, but also about *these students in particular*. By making particular student culture and family history a deliberate object of study by all the students in the classroom, the teacher can learn much about what he or she needs to know in order to teach the particular students in ways that are sensitive and powerfully engaging, intellectually and emotionally.

As our standards for what students need to learn change from the lower-order mastery of facts and simple skills to higher-order reasoning and the construction of knowledge that is personally distinctive and meaningful (in other words, as we move from an essentialist understanding of curriculum teaching and learning to a more constructivist one), our conceptions of culture in muliticultural education also need to become more constructivist and less essentialist. Teaching about culture as socially constructed and continually changing is thus consistent with contemporary definitions of good pedagogy as well as being consistent with recent developments in culture theory and social theory.

Reframing Borders as Boundaries in the Classroom

This approach frames the cultural diversity to be found in the classroom group in terms of cultural boundaries rather than cultural borders. Even when cultural difference and group identity are highly politicized in the wider society, by approaching the culture of students forthrightly in the classroom they can be depoliticized to a remarkable extent (or perhaps we might think of it as being repoliticized in a positive rather than negative frame).

A problem comes with teaching second-culture skills and knowledge as morality rather than as pragmatic skills for survival and success. Delpit (1995) observes that for students of color in the United States the school's "second-culture" often appears alien and dominating. Culturally mainstream ways of speaking and writing represent a "language and culture of power" that minority students need to master for success in the wider society. But this culture of power can be taught unsuccessfully in two ways. In the first, the teacher attempts to teach the second-culture skills in a moralizing way—the right way to act and to be. That is likely to stimulate student resistance and thus is a teaching strategy that risks student refusal to learn. (Consider the word *ain't*. Teachers for generations have been teaching working-class students not to say *ain't* as a moral lesson. Yet inside and outside the classroom the students still say *ain't*.)

Another unsuccessful way to teach a second-culture skill is implicitly, according to Delpit. She observes that among well-meaning middle-class White teachers, some aspects of the language of power are part of the teacher's own invisible culture. Taking it for granted herself, she does not teach it explicitly to working-class African American students.

Delpit (1995) recommends an alternative approach—to teach second-culture skills explicitly and carefully but without moralizing. The school's language and culture of power can be presented as a situational dialect, to be used pragmatically for special situations, such as job interviews, formal writing, and college admissions interviews. When combined with reflective self-study of the student's own language use in the family, among peers, and in the neighborhood—study by which the student explores his or her own repertoire of differing speech styles used in differing situations—explicit teaching and learning of the language of power can be framed not as a matter of cultural borders but of cultural boundaries. This approach takes a critical and strategic view of mulitculturalism, for survival reasons.

Multicultural Pedagogy as Emancipatory

Other multicultural educators recommend a critical approach to cultures of domination and to the phenomenon of domination. Ladson-Billings (1994) describes African American and White teachers who are effective with African American students. They taught in a variety of styles, but one common approach was to deal directly and explicitly with issues of injustice and oppression and the privileging of mainstream knowledge and perspectives as they came up in the curriculum and in the reported daily experiences of their students. Trueba (1994), Nieto (1995), McCarthy (1993), Perry and Fraser (1993), Sleeter and Grant (1993), Apple (1993), and Giroux (1991) recommend a similar approach, sometimes called critical pedagogy, counter-hegemonic pedagogy, or emancipatory pedagogy.

Cultural hegemony refers to the established view of things—a commonsense view of what is and why things happen that serves the interests of those people already privileged in a society. When the school presents a comfortable established view of the nature of U.S. society and of the goodness and inherent rightness of school knowledge and school literacy, that is hegemonic. Students whose lives are not affirmed by the establishment seem intuitively not to accept hegemonic content and methods of instruction. They often resist, consciously or unconsciously, covertly as well as overtly.

Multicultural education has an opportunity and a challenge to be counter-hegemonic. When such issues as racism, class privilege, and sexism are left silent in the classroom, the implicit message for students of color appears to be that the teacher and the school do not acknowledge that experiences of oppression exist. If only the standard language, the standard American history, and the voices and lives of White men appear in the curriculum, the further implicit message (by what is left in and what is left out of the knowledge presented as legitimate by the school) seems to be that real America and real school is only about the cultural mainstream and its establishment ideology. This approach especially marginalizes the students of color who come to school already marginalized by life experience and by the historical experience of oppression in their ethnic or racial communities. Such a hegemonic approach also marginalizes female students (Sadker & Sadker, 1994). Marginalization is alienating, and one response to alienation is resistance—the very thing that makes teaching and learning more difficult for students and their teachers.

Ironically, for teachers to name and acknowledge tough social issues, rather than turning students against school and the teacher, makes it more possible for students who have experienced oppression to affiliate with the teacher and with school learning.

By taking the moralizing that characterizes culturally hegemonic teaching out of the picture, reframing second-culture acquisition as strategically instrumental rather than inherently right, a teacher facilitates second-culture learning by students from nonmainstream backgrounds. Through such teaching, cultural borders are reframed as boundaries, and the politics of the dominant culture and cultures are, to some extent at least, depoliticized in the classroom. The cycles of resistance and schismogenesis that are stimulated by hegemonic curriculum and teaching do not get set off.

The role of resistance to cultures of domination in student disaffiliation from school learning is a fundamental issue in public education in the United States, Canada, Australia, and also in Britain and the rest of Europe (Apple, 1993; Willis, 1977; Giroux, 1983). Ogbu (1987/1992) has argued that for students of "caste-like" minority background in the United States (from groups with historic experiences of stigma and limitation of economic opportunity, such as African Americans, Mexican Americans, Puerto Ricans, and Native Americans), resistance to school is almost inevitable because of the effects of group history. Fordham (1993) has shown that African American high school students in Washington, DC, defined achieving in school as "acting White." Other scholars, (Erickson, 1987/92; Foley, 1991; Trueba, 1994) have acknowledged Ogbu's insight while observing that student resistance can come not only as a result of group history of oppression, but also of oppressive and alienating circumstances of teaching and learning within the school itself. Another difficulty with Ogbu's position is that it leaves no room for the possibility of school change.

A major theme here is that when business is done as usual in school, student resistance results from that, as well as from influences from the wider society on students. In the short run, we cannot change the wider society. But we can make school learning environments less alienating. Multicultural education, especially critical or antiracist multicultural education, is a way to change the business as usual of schools. When that happens, as Ladson-Billings (1994) and others have shown, minority students of the backgrounds categorized as "caste-like" rise to the occasion. When treated with dignity and taught skillfully, such students affiliate with the school and achieve. Group history of oppression no doubt makes students and parents wary of school and its claims that the standard ways of teaching are good for you. This is to say that trust of a school's good intentions, especially by students and parents of color, is not automatic. But relationships of mutual trust and respect can be established between teachers and students in the classroom. Sensitive multicultural pedagogy is one foundation for such trust.

Conventional Teaching as Cultural Border Wars

Conversely, for teachers to treat the dominant culture in the curriculum as a matter of cultural borders rather than of boundaries can make the classroom an unsafe place for students. It makes the classroom learning environment untrustable and can invite student resistance. A vivid example of such culture conflict is seen in the first-grade reading lesson at the beginning of this chapter:

1   T: All right, class, read that and remember your endings.

2   CC: What did Little Duck see? (final *t* of "what" deleted)

3   T: Wha<u>t</u>. (emphasizing final *t*)

4   CC: What (final *t* deleted as in turn 2)

5   T: I still don't hear this sad little "t."

6   CC: What did—what did—what—(final *t*'s deleted)

7   T: Wha<u>t</u>.

8   T&CC: What did Little Duck see? (final *t* spoken)

9   T: OK, very good

The example comes from first-grade classrooms in Berkeley, California, attended by both predominantly working-class African American children and predominantly middle-class White children (Piestrap, 1973). In some classrooms the teachers were African American, and in others the teachers were White.

Piestrup found the phenomenon of language style divergence that increases over time in situations of conflict, also reported by Labov (1963) and Giles and Powesland (1975). At the beginning of the school year many of the African American children spoke Black dialect (sometimes termed *Black Nonstandard Vernacular*). In the classrooms in which the teachers—whether African American or White—negatively sanctioned the children's use of Black dialect, by the end of the year those children spoke a broader form of the dialect in the classroom than they had done at the beginning of the year. The converse was also true in Piestrup's findings. Regardless of whether the teacher was African American or White, if the teacher did not publicly rebuke children for speaking Black dialect, by the end of the year those children's classroom speech more closely approached standard English.

The transcribed example shows one scene of rebuke for language style that Piestrup found in a number of the classrooms. Here, the teacher was correcting African American children's nonstandard pronunciation. An alternative focus of instruction could have been comprehension—understanding what was in the story. The teacher chose to focus on final consonant deletion (the final /t/ in the word *what*). In so doing the teacher was making that cultural feature of language style a cultural border issue— just as the Ephraimites treated the pronunciation of the final sound in the word Shibboleth so long ago. But the children's not articulating the final /t/ in *what* could have been treated as a cultural boundary issue.

Framed in that way, the speech style difference (which probably did not interfere with the teachers' ability to hear the child's speech as intelligible in terms of literal, referential meaning) need not have gotten in the way of the discussion. Rather, the teacher, the child, and the other children in the group could have gone on to consider what Little Duck saw. There is now considerable evidence that pronouncing words in a nonstandard way does not interfere with children's ability either to decode written standard English (that is, to read letter combinations as identifiable words) or to understand the sense of a written passage at the level of a sentence or paragraph.

Why did the teacher insist on the final /t/? One explanation could be class bias or some other source of ethnocentrism, since final consonant deletion is not correct in terms of the dominant cultural style of official school literacy. Another, related explanation is possible. Deletion of a final /t/ also violates a key cultural assumption in one of the professional subcultures of educators—the assumption from behaviorist learning theory that mastery of subskills (such as pronouncing the final consonant) must necessarily precede mastery of more complex skills (such as comprehension at the word or sentence level). This ladder-of-skills cultural belief of educators is increasingly being challenged by advocates of whole language approaches to literacy as well as by sociolinguists and cognitive psychologists who study processes of learning to read.

Both sets of beliefs can be seen as hegemonic, reinforcing one another's commonsense validity. The general cultural value of correctness of standard English seems to be confirmed by the professional cultural belief in a ladder-of-skills approach to pedagogy. Of course, the teacher should correct mistakes, the reasoning goes; that's the teacher's job. Thus, we see how what may have begun as an ethnic and social class marker in speech style (standard English) gets used as a sociolinguistic test at a cultural border in what seem to be a professionally responsible pedagogy. The justification of that pedagogy results in ways of teaching that are culturally biased and needlessly alienating for those students who come to school speaking a dialect other than the culturally dominant one.*

Between teachers and students the discomfort of such interchanges as shown in the example, repeating day after day across the school year, according to Piestrup, led to dialect divergence on the part of the students. Considering that these were first graders, not adolescents, we can see the dialect divergence as a nondeliberate form of student resistance on the part of the students, outside their conscious awareness. These regressive social relationships between teachers and students, which become more negative, can happen for many reasons, not only because of cultural difference; when cultural difference is treated as a border issue in the classroom it becomes a rich resource for ongoing conflictual relationships between teachers and students (McDermott & Gospodinoff, 1979/81).

In the previous example, the cultural assumptions behind the standard pedagogy are so much a part of professional common sense that we might consider them an aspect

---

*To underscore the point discussed earlier in reference to Delpit (1995), my argument is not that standard forms of speech and writing should never be taught, but rather that this is not the way to teach them, for the unintended negative consequences of treating language difference as a cultural border outweigh the positive consequences that such instruction is intended to achieve. Framing the speech style as a cultural boundary issue and conducting this lesson not as a reading lesson but as a practice session in talking standard English would change the micropolitics and the affect of the learning environment in subtle but profound ways for those students who do not come to school already speaking in a culturally dominant manner. Do we want all students to master standard English as part of their multicultural competence? If so, this analysis suggests that the last thing we should do is to treat students as we can see them having been treated in the example.

of invisible culture. The teacher might say, "I wasn't doing anything *cultural*; I was just teaching the children to read correctly." The children's lack of cooperation might not be seen as cultural resistance. Rather, the cultural issue might be clinicalized. The uncooperative children might be seen as passive-aggressive or as suffering from low self-esteem. If they shifted in their seats a lot they might be considered hyperactive.

Aspects of invisible culture often get used as diagnostic indicators with clinical significance, especially in the early grades. For example, if a child comes from a home in which adults do not routinely ask them teacher-like known-information questions (questions to which the adults already know the answer), such questions by a teacher can seem confusing or intimidating initially (Heath, 1983). "What color is this?" the kindergarten teacher says on the first day of school, holding up a red piece of construction paper in front of an African American child whose mother is on welfare. "Aonh-oh" (I don't know) the child replies, thinking there must be some trick, because anybody can see that the paper is red. "Lacking in reading readiness," the teacher thinks to herself, writes this in the child's permanent record, and assigns the child to the bottom reading group.

Once again we find ourselves with the Ephraimites on the banks of the Jordan River, witnessing the consequences of a cultural border test. Yet because we don't recognize knowing about teacher-like questions as a distinct cultural skill, we may not see the teacher's informal readiness test as cultural, or as culturally biased. Such framing of cultural difference as a border can be done inadvertently by teachers who are members of the cultural minority student's own ethnic group and speech community as well as by teachers who are of majority background. Recall that Piestrup found the African American students' speech style diverging from the standard style in classrooms where such speech style was rebuked, regardless of whether the teacher were White or African American. What mattered was not the race of the teacher but the teacher's cultural practices in pedagogy—responsive or unresponsive?

The cultural responsiveness or relevance of a classroom learning environment can differ in contradictory ways between the visible and the invisible aspects of culture. For example, in the same multiracial kindergarten or first-grade classroom in which a teacher uses informal tests of reading readiness that treat invisible cultural knowledge and skill as a cultural border (such as recognition of teacher-questions and how to answer them) the teacher may have put a picture of Frederick Douglass on the wall, read a book about his life, presented information on West Africa in a positive light, and taught basic vocabulary in Yoruba or Swahili. Yet hanging a picture of Douglass, the African American abolitionist, on the wall next to a picture of George Washington, the White slave holder, or introducing students to an African language doesn't make that classroom fully multicultural, if invisible aspects of the communicative cultural practices of African American students are still being treated in invidious ways. Such contradictions between formal and informal culture must be confusing and alienating for students, even though that alienation may be experienced by them outside conscious awareness. This is why attention to issues of invisible informal culture as well as those of visible formal culture seems so important for the success of attempts at multicultural education.

CONCLUSION: ON DIVERSITY OF TONGUES AND THEIR EDUCATIONAL POTENTIAL

The Russian literary critic Bakhtin (1981) provides us with a final way to consider culture in its continuity and in its diversity, as transmitted across generations and as invented in the present moment. He studied the novel as it emerged in the sixteenth and eighteenth centuries in Spain and France and in England respectively and as it developed in England, France, and Russia in the nineteenth centuries. Bakhtin noted that the classic novelists depicted a variety of ways of speaking across their various characters, who differed in social class, gender, and region. That diversity he called *heteroglossia*, from the Greek meaning "differing tongues." He believed that a fine novel encapsulated key aspects of the total diversity in speech styles found in the society at the historical moment in which that novel was written. To produce such a text convincingly the author must have incorporated the diversity of tongues present in the society.

Bakhtin (1981) also observed a personal heteroglossia within the characters of the novel akin to that in its author. For example, in Cervante's *Don Quixote* Bakhtin noticed that usually the good Don, of bourgeois background, spoke in an imitation of the literary romance. Thus, his speech style sounded like the Spanish of the nobility. Sancho Panza, the peasant, usually spoke in the speech style of the lower classes. Yet once in a while, when engaged with the Don, or when reflecting to himself on what he had been experiencing, Sancho's speech drifted slightly toward the more prestigious style of Spanish. This tendency, apparent from the beginning of the modern novel, was more pronounced in nineteenth-century French and Russian novels. Russian serfs, for example, were depicted as speaking in a variety of speech styles—what Bakhtin called "social languages"—some more elevated and agentive, some more subordinated and passive. World view, personal status, and agency seemed to shift, as did the character's language style.

Bakhtin's insights suggest ways of understanding how cultural diversity is organized and distributed within a society and within persons. There is heteroglossia within a society. Members of distinct social categories and social networks speak more often than not in differing ways (reminiscent of the "speech community" notion discussed earlier). Men do tend to speak differently from women, African Americans from Whites, working-class people from upper-middle-class people, gay from straight, fundamentalist Christians from Unitarians, physicians from lawyers (and physicians from nurses). These ways of speaking are relatively continuously distributed within the various social groupings; they become badges of identity of such groupings; and for the most major social categories such as class, gender, race and ethnicity, and religion these social languages tend to persist across generations. In other words, social divisions and cultural and linguistic diversity appear to be consistently reproduced in society across time.

Moreover, the differing ways of speaking carry with them differing points of view that are the result of differing life experience of the speakers and, as the feminist slogan puts it, "the personal is political." Thus, the historical experience of a group and its particular political interests in assuming that things are really one way rather than some other—its ideology—come with the social language of the group, as uttered by a particular member of that group. Ways of speaking, then, are discourses—whole sets of assumptions about the world and roles for being in the world that are entailed in certain ways of creating oral and written texts (Foucault, 1979; Gee, 1990). Much more is involved than language style alone. To the extent that various group interests and their discourses are involved with the distribution of power in society, there can be conflict and contradiction between ways of speaking and thinking as well as between social groupings. A discourse is in a sense a social institution or a subculture.

Yet the consistency of cultural reproduction is not unitary or absolute. There is also heteroglossia within persons. Each person's life experience differs somewhat from others, and every person lives in a variety of social situations each day. Differing social situations provide differing ecologies of relationship with other people. They evoke differing aspects of the individual's overall repertoire of ways of speaking. One speaks differently to one's mother than to one's siblings, to one's teacher than to one's mother. Sometimes in complex relationships, such as that between an employer or supervisor who is also a friend or between spouses who are simultaneously lovers, parents, and administrators of household resources, a variety of interrelated voices are evoked from moment to moment in what appears to be the same social situation. The utterances of persons in dialogue lean on one another in mutual influence, Bakhtin claimed. Thus, the phenomenon of ways of speaking (and of discourses) is inherently labile as well as stable. Culture at the group level varies in part because individuals differ among one another and within themselves as they find themselves in differing social circumstances.

As diverse persons show up in the scenes of daily life they bring their heteroglossia with them. There can be affiliation as well as conflict across those cultural differences. And discourses can be contested; they can be interrupted or interrogated. When that happens the assumptions of the discourse become visible and available for criticism. If a person or a group were to change discourses in a conflict that would be to take a different stance in the world. One may feel as if that is not permitted or as if that is one's right.

Since the discourses vary within persons as well as between groups, whatever conflict or affiliation there may be between the discourses in society is experienced within the personality. This means that the diversity of tongues and of voices within the person has profound emotional content and profound significance for personal identity and wholeness.

Schools are collection sites for diversity of voice and identity. Schools ask of students that they try on new discourses, new ways of speaking and thinking, new ways of being a self, and to appropriate them as their own. At their best, schools ask this of teachers as well, in order that they may come into closer awareness of and engagement with the voices of their students and also develop intellectually within their careers, appropriating within themselves more of the various discourses and literacies of their society. That is personally risky business, both for students and teachers. When discourses, or cultures, are in conflict in society then conflict can be experienced within the self over which discourses are being tried on.

Students and teachers come to school already having appropriated multiple voices and cultures. One task of education can be reflection on the voices one already has.

Multicultural education, especially that which considers invisible as well as visible culture, can assist in that process of personal and group reflection. Teachers and students, by looking within themselves, can come to see that everybody is cultural and multicultural, including themselves. By listening to the discourses around them and also within them and testing how those discourses feel—more like self, more like other, owned or alienated—students and their teachers can accept that not all cultures are equal. If school is a secure place to try on new cultures and voices, if cultural diversity is treated as boundaries rather than as borders, then students and their teachers can establish safe spaces in which to explore growing relationships with new cultures and old ones.

Ultimately, for persons in complex multicultural societies, growth into maturity involves coming to terms with the diversity of voices and cultures within. This is especially the case when the cultures and voices have been in conflict in the wider society and when the person is a member of a dominated group. Then, coming to terms with one's own diversity means making some kind of just peace with the voices within. For example, in every man there are the voices of women, and in every woman there are the voices of men. Are these voices alien and in conflict within the person, or have they been appropriated within the self? Can a woman come to terms with the male voices within without acquiescing to male hegemony and adopting an alienated self? In every White person in the United States, because of our historical experience, there are not only White voices but also Black ones. What do those voices sound more like, Amos and Andy or Frederick Douglass? Aunt Jemima or Alice Walker? How have those voices been appropriated within the person, and what role has the school played in facilitating that process? In every African American in the United States there are not only Black voices but also White ones. How can the African American come to terms with the White voices within, forgiving and making peace with them, coming to own them while at the same time affirming and owning the Black voices, holding a continuing sense of the injustice of continuing racism? Doing all of that is necessary to mature into full adulthood as an African American (Cross, 1991; Helms, 1990).

To come to terms with the diversity of voices within is an educative task for society, for the individual, and for the school. It is what growing up means in a multicultural society and in a multicultural world. When the voices of the school curriculum and of its teaching and learning are fully multicultural, then the appropriation of multiple voices—in dignity and without coercion, keeping a critical stance without despair—becomes possible for all students. This is a noble aim for multicultural education. How hard it is to achieve, yet how necessary. This becomes more apparent to educators as we become able to think more deeply about culture, its nuances, and its diversity in school and in society.

AFTERWORD

What we are talking about is creating a new tradition, telling "new stories" that are fundamentally different by virtue of the role that the lives of the historically oppressed have assumed in their construction. This is a matter of redefining American culture, not once and for all, but in the negotiated meanings that are always emerging out of a curricular process. ... It is in the day-to-day interactions of teachers and students, dealing with a transformed curriculum and attempting to create a transformed, democratic classroom, that the new common culture will be created and continually recreated.

(Perry & Fraser, 1993, pp. 19–20)

Questions and Activities

1. The author describes six conceptions of culture: (1) culture as cultivation; (2) culture as tradition; (3) culture as information bits; (4) culture as a symbol system; (5) culture as social process; and (6) culture as motive and emotion. Form groups in your class or workshop that consist of five people each to explore the diverse meanings of culture. Ask one student or workshop participant in each group to become an expert on one conception of culture given by the author. Discuss how the different conceptions of culture are both alike and different. Explain each definition by giving examples.

2. What does the author mean by implicit and invisible aspects of culture? In what ways are these aspects of culture important? Give some examples of invisible aspects of culture. What are some non-examples of the concept?

3. In what ways might differences in invisible culture cause conflict? Give specific examples.

4. According to the author, what problems result when teachers focus on visible (explicit) culture at the expense of invisible and implicit culture? What kinds of educational practices result when teachers focus on visible and tangible aspects of culture?

5. How does the author distinguish between a cultural boundary and a cultural border? Why is this distinction important? Is a cultural boundary always a cultural border? Explain.

6. According to the author, does cultural change necessarily mean cultural loss? Explain why or why not.

7. The author states that we sometime "essentialize" culture. What does he mean? What problems result, in his view, when culture is essentialized?

8. The author states that "our conceptions of culture in multicultural education need to become more constructivist and less essentialist." Explain what he means by this statement and its implications for educational practice.

9. The author states that "Multicultural education has an opportunity and a challenge to be counter-hegemonic." Explain the meaning of this statement and give examples of how this might be done by classroom teachers.

References

Apple, M. W. (1993). *Official Knowledge: Democratic Education in a Conservative Age.* New York: Routledge.

Bakhtin, M. M. (1981). *The Dialogic Imagination.* M. Holquist (Ed.). Trans. by C. Emerson and M. Holquist. Austin: University of Texas Press.

Barth, F. (1969). *Ethnic Groups and Boundaries: The Social Organization of Culture Difference.* Boston: Little, Brown.

Barth, F. (1989). The Analysis of Culture in Complex Societies. *Ethnos 54,* 120–142.

Bateson, G., Jackson, D., Haley, J., and J. Weakland. (1972). Toward a Theory of Schizophrenia. In G. Bateson (Ed.). *Steps Toward an Ecology of Mind* (pp. 201–227). New York: Ballantine Books.

Bourdieu, P. (1977). *Outline of a Theory of Practice.* Cambridge Studies in Social Anthropology 16. Cambridge: Cambridge University Press.

Bourdieu, P. and Passeron, J. C. (1977). *Reproduction: In Education, Society and Culture.* Beverly Hills, CA: Sage Books.

Bourdieu, P. and Passeron, J. C. (1984). *Distinction: A Social Critique of the Judgement of Taste.* Trans. by R. Nice. Cambridge: Harvard University Press.

Connell, R. (1982). *Making the Difference: Schools, Families, and Social Division.* Sydney: Allen and Unwin.

Cross, W. E. (1991). *Shades of Black: Diversity in African American Identity.* Philadelphia: University of Pennyslvania.

D'Andrade, R. G. and Strauss, C. (Eds.). (1992). *Human Motives and Cultural Models.* New York: Cambridge University Press.

Delpit, L. (1995). *Other People's Children: Cultural Conflict in the Classroom.* New York: New Press.

Erickson, F. (1987/1992). Transformation and School Success: The Politics and Culture of Educational Achievement. *Anthropology and Education Quarterly, 18* (4), 335–356.

Fanon, F. (1963). *The Wretched of the Earth.* Trans. by C. Farrington. New York: Grove Press.

Foley, D. E. (1991). Reconsidering Anthropological Explanations of Ethnic School Failure. *Anthropology and Education Quarterly, 22*(1), 60–86.

Fordham, S. (1993). "Those Loud Black Girls": (Black) Women, Silence, and Gender "Passing" in the Academy. *Anthropology and Education Quarterly, 24*(1), 3–33.

Foucault, M. (1979). *Discipline and Punish: The Birth of the Prison.* New York: Random House/Vintage Books.

Garfinkel, H. and Sacks, H. (1970). The Formal Properties of Practical Actions. In J. C. McKinney and E. A. Tiryakian (Eds.). *Theoretical Sociology* (pp. 331–336). New York: Appleton-Century-Crofts.

Gee, J. (1990). *Social Linguistics and Literacies: Ideology in Discourses.* Philadelphia: The Falmer Press.

Geertz, C. (1973). *The Interpretation of Cultures.* New York: Basic Books.

Giddens, A. (1984). *The Constitution of Society: Outline of the Theory of Structuration.* Berkeley: University of California Press.

Giles, H. and Powesland, P. F. (1975). *Speech Style and Social Evaluation.* London: Academic Press.

Giroux, H. A. (1983). Theories of Reproduction and Resistance: A Critical Analysis. *Harvard Educational Review, 53,* 257–293.

Giroux, H. (1991). *Border Crossings: Cultural Workers and the Politics of Education.* New York: Routledge.

Goodenough, W. (1976). Multiculturalism as the Normal Human Experience. *Anthropology and Education Quarterly,* 7(4), 4–7.

Goodenough, W. (1981). *Culture, Language and Society.* Menlo Park, CA: Benjamin/Cummins Publishing.

Gumperz, J. J. (1982). *Discourse Strategies.* Cambridge: Cambridge University Press.

Hall, E. T. (1959). *The Silent Language.* New York: Doubleday.

Hall, E. T. (1976). *Beyond Culture.* New York: Doubleday.

Heath, S. B. (1983). *Ways with Words: Language, Life, and Work in Communities and Classrooms.* Cambridge: Cambridge University Press.

Helms, J. (1990). *Black and White Racial Identity.* New York: Greenwood Press.

hooks, b. (1993). Transformative Pedagogy and Multiculturalism. In T. Perry and J. W. Fraser (Eds.). *Freedom's Plow: Teaching in the Multicultural Classroom* (pp. 91–98). New York: Routledge.

Hymes, D. H. (1974). *Foundations in Sociolinguistics: An Ethnographic Approach.* Philadelphia: University of Pennsylvania Press.

Kroeber, A. L. (1917). The Superorganic. *American Anthropologist, 19,* 163–213.

Kroeber, A. L. and Kluckhohn, C. (1952). *Culture: A Critical Review of Concepts and Definitions,* Vol. 47(1). Cambridge: Peabody Museum of American Archaeology and Ethnology, Harvard University.

Labov, W. (1963). The Social Motivation of a Sound Change. *Word, 19,* 273–309.

Ladson-Billings, G. (1994). *The Dreamkeepers: Successful Teachers of African-American Children.* San Francisco: Jossey-Bass Publishers.

Lutz, C. A. (1990). *Language and the Politics of Emotion.* New York: Cambridge University Press.

McCarthy, C. (1993). After the Canon: Knowledge and Ideological Representation in the Multicultural Discourse on Curriculum Reform. In C. McCarthy and W. Crichlow (Eds.). *Race, Identity, and Representation in Education* (pp. 289–305). New York: Routledge.

McDermott, R. P. and Gospodinoff, K. (1979/1981). Social Contexts for Ethnic Borders and School Failure. In A. Wolfgang (Ed.). *Nonverbal Behavior: Applications and Cultural Implications* (pp. 175–195). New York: Academic Press.

Mehan, H., Wills, J. S., Okamoto, D., and Lintz, A. (1995). Ethnographic Studies of Multicultural Education in Classrooms and Schools. In J. A. Banks and C. A. M. Banks (Eds.). *Handbook of Research on Multicultural Education* (pp. 129–44). New York: Macmillan.

Moll, L. C. (Ed.). (1990). *Vygotsky and Education: Instructional Implications and Applications of Sociohistorical Psychology.* New York: Cambridge University Press.

Nieto, S. (Ed.). (1995). *Affirming Diversity: The Sociopolitical Context of Multicultural Education* (2nd ed.). New York: Longman Press.

Ogbu, J. U. (1987/1992). Variability in Minority School Performance: A Problem in Search of an Explanation. *Anthropology and Education Quarterly, 18*(4), 312–334.

Ortner, S. B. (1984). Theory in Anthropology since the Sixties. *Comparative Studies in Society and History, 26*(1), 126–166.

Perry, T. and Fraser, J.W. (Eds.). (1993). *Freedom's Plow: Teaching in the Multicultural Classroom.* New York: Routledge.

Philips, S. U. (1983). *The Invisible Culture: Communication in School and Community on the Warm Springs Indian Reservation.* New York: Longman.

Piestrup, A. M. (1973). *Black Dialect Interferences and Accomodations of Reading Instruction in First Grade.* Washington, DC: National Institute of Mental Health. (ERIC Document Reproduction Service No. ED 119 113.)

Sadker, M. and Sadker, D. (1994). *Failing at Fairness: How America's Schools Cheat Girls.* New York: Scribner's.

Said, E. W. (1978). *Orientalism.* New York: Pantheon Books.

Skilton Sylvester, P. (1994). Elementary School Curricula and Urban Transformation. *Harvard Educational Review 64,* 309–331.

Sleeter, C. E. and Grant, C. A. (1993). *Making Choices for Multicultural Education.* New York: Merrill/Macmillan.

Torres-Guzman, M. (1992). Stories of Hope in the Midst of Despair: Culturally Responsive Education for Latino Students in an Alternative High School in New York City. In M. Saravia-Shore and S. F. Arvizu (Eds.). *Cross-Cultural Literacy: Ethnographies of Communication in Multiethnic Classrooms* (pp. 477–490). New York: Garland Publishing, Inc.

Trueba, H. T. (1994). Reflections on Alternative Visions of Schooling. In *Anthropology and Education Quarterly.* Theme Issue: Alternative Visions of Schooling: Success Stories in Minority Settings. G. Ernst, E. Stratzner, and H. Trueba (Eds.). *25* (3), 376–393.

Tylor, E. B. (1871/1970). *Primitive Culture: Researches into the Development of Mythology, Philosophy, Religion, Language, Art, and Custom.* London: Murray.

Wiggington, S. (1986). *Sometimes a Shining Moment: The Foxfire Experience.* Garden City, NY: Anchor Books.

Williams, R. (1983). *Culture and Society.* New York: Columbia University Press.

Willis, P. E. (1977). *Learning to Labor: How Working Class Kids Get Working Class Jobs.* New York: Columbia University Press.

Witherell, C. and Noddings, N. (1991). *Stories Lives Tell: Narrative and Dialogue in Education.* New York: Teachers College Press.

Chapter 3

Race, Class, Gender, and Disability in the Classroom

Carl A. Grant and Christine E. Sleeter

Schools have always been a focal point of debate. What should be taught? How should students be organized for instruction? How should teachers be prepared? What constitute acceptable standards? As we move closer to the year 2000, several developments and tensions in society have fueled renewed debate about schooling.

First, since the 1980s, the United States has had to come to terms with its loss of firm economic standing in the global arena. For example, "In the last decade, American savings have plummeted and American investment has been increasingly financed by foreign capital" (Rivlin, 1992, p. 6). While a variety of interpretations can be given for the U.S. decline in world economic status, business leaders have directed considerable attention to schools. Beginning with *A Nation at Risk* in 1983, a spate of reform reports elaborated on the "rising tide of mediocrity" presumed to be spreading from the schools to the rest of society (National Commission on Excellence in Education, 1983). These reports have led to the current federal education strategy, America 2000, which advocates the systematic restructuring of schools by focusing on results rather than procedures; developing new world class standards and voluntary achievement tests; requiring more math, science, and computer literacy; allowing parental choice of schools; and creating more rigorous programs of instruction. Students at risk of failure are to be identified and remediated (U.S. Department of Education, 1991).

Second, as transnational corporations exported jobs to third world nations in order to cut wages, many middle-class and working-class people in the United States experienced an erosion of their life-styles, and the poverty level rose, especially among women and children. Compared to the postwar economic boom, the 1970s, 1980s, and 1990s were decades in which Americans had to learn to settle for less: fewer jobs were available, prices rose, real income of a large proportion of the population fell, and White middle-class families experienced some of the hard times poor families had always lived with (Newman, 1993; Rivlin, 1992; Shor, 1986). Many people grew skeptical of their ability to achieve the American dream. Katherine Newman (1993) listened to people describing their concerns and fears:

> I'll never have what my parents had. I can't even dream
> of that. I'm living a lifestyle that's way lower than it was
> when I was growing up and it's depressing. . . . Even if you
> are a hard worker and you never skipped a beat, you fol-
> lowed all the rules, did everything they told you you were
> supposed to do, it's still horrendous. (p. 3)

Furthermore, domestic social problems such as drug use and teen pregnancy seemed to be concentrated in a growing underclass dependent on welfare. Middle-class people in the United States, increasingly concerned about their ability to maintain their own standard of living, have become less tolerant of those who are poor. As schooling has become increasingly a prerequisite for employment, its payoff has seemed less certain, and competition for the good jobs has seemed keener.

Third, the United States has experienced tremendous growth in ethnic and racial diversity, especially through immigration, and public debate about what that diversity should mean has become prolific. For example, a special issue of *Time* magazine placed actor Edward James Olmos's picture on the cover, under the caption "Magnifico! Hispanic culture breaks out of the barrio" (*Time Magazine*, 1988). Readers of *Time* were told about problems confronting the United States as it moves "Beyond the melting pot"; the main problem would be learning to "maintain a distinct national identity" that builds on commonalities while embracing ethnic diversity (Henry III, 1990). Most talk in popular literature centered on trying to identify what we have in common in order to promote national unity. While some people argued that new commonalities could be forged from diverse cultural input, others insisted that all immigrants must be turned into "Americans" who embrace traditional definitions of American culture. Discussions of immigration often publicized Asians as the model minority, attributing their presumed success to their embracing of traditional U.S. culture and values. Educators agreed that schools would need to respond to growing racial and ethnic diversity, but disagreed about whether schools should promote cultural assimilation or pluralism.

Fourth, racial minority groups experienced tension between achieving steady gains in education, as reflected in years of schooling obtained, SAT scores, and other standardized test scores; and simultaneous lack of economic progress and even erosion of gains in life-style, economic status, and rights. For example, between 1970 and 1987 the White–African American education gap closed from 2.3 years to 3 months (U.S. Bureau of the Census, 1989, p. 69) and has since remained at 3 to 4 months (National Center for Education Statistics, 1993). At the same time, however, poverty and unemployment hit communities of color harder than White communities (U.S. Bureau of the Census, 1992a), President Bush vetoed the Civil Rights Act of 1990, and the legality of scholarships for minority students was seriously questioned. These occurrences led to growing frustration. For example, Terkel (1988) reported the following comment:

> I think Reagan made it very accepted to be a white
> bigot. It's the most fashionable thing. Now they say: America
> is white. America isn't single women on welfare. Why should
> us taxpayers support these people who ride on our backs and
> bring this country down? I'm afraid of what's gonna happen
> to blacks in this country. There are a fortunate few who will
> get over. But for the many, no way.... The dividing line is
> becoming clear and the bitterness is growing. You can't help
> but wonder why. (pp. 67–68)

Even Asian Americans, held up as the model group who had made it, were not nearly as successful uniformly as the media suggested. It is revealing that some of the most outspoken critics of this stereotype have been Japanese Americans, the group often touted as most successful (Jiobu, 1988; Omatsu, 1994; Suzuki, 1989; Takaki, 1989). But many people in the United States, seeing White women and people of color in professional and administrative positions, believed racism and sexism were no longer problems. Ironically, despite gains in years of schooling and test scores, following the reform reports of the early 1980s, racial and ethnic minority children were described as "at risk of failure" rather than as "promising achievers" (Swadener, 1990).

People in the United States with disabilities also experienced both gains and losses. Although special education had expanded services to students with disabilities in schools, they, too, were disproportionately hit by economic losses and threatened by the raising of standards in schools. A triumph was passage of the Americans with Disabilities Act, designed to protect people with disabilities from discrimination, but some observers adopted a wait-and-see attitude because of many loopholes in the act (The Americans with Disabilities Act: Where We Are Now?, 1991).

Fifth, universities became actively engaged in promoting diversity. Since the 1960s, there have been growing bodies of scholarship by scholars of color, women, and critical theorists who created new ethnic studies and women's studies courses, programs, and curricular requirements. You may have taken such a course yourself. The amount of research and curriculum that was multicultural mushroomed, advancing perspectives that differed in some cases sharply from those of most political and economic leaders.

All of this may seem removed from you and your classroom. But students whose parents have been experiencing the tensions discussed here are in your classroom, and local community and business leaders as well as spokespeople for oppressed groups are probably recommending what they believe schools should do to address these issues. And probably you have come across reports of tensions surrounding these issues in the media. For example, as the states of California and New York have wrestled with what a multicultural curriculum should look like, and as universities have begun requiring multicultural coursework, critics have charged minority groups with attempting to tear the United States apart (Schlesinger, 1992). Yet, advocates of multicultural education argue that most curricula are no more than cosmetically multicultural (Sleeter & Grant, 1993), and that weak treatments of historic injustices mask very real concerns.

A major thread running through the debates about schooling is the relative importance of preparing students for jobs versus preparing them as citizens. Schools have always done both, but recently much of the talk about what schools should do has emphasized job preparation and maintained silence about citizenship. What kind of a nation do we want for ourselves and our children, given the challenges and problems we have been facing? How should limited resources be distributed, given our diversity and virtually everyone's desire for a good life? How should we address the fact that there are not enough good jobs to go around?

Most students we teach usually give one of three reasons for wanting to become teachers: (1) they love kids, (2) they want to help students, (3) they want to make school more exciting than when they were students. If one of these is the reason you chose to enter the teaching profession, then we hope you will see the demographic and social trends described above as being challenging and will realize that your love and help are needed, not just for some students, but for *all* students.

This chapter discusses the importance of race, class, gender, and disability in classroom life and provides alternative approaches to dealing with these issues in the classroom.

RACE, CLASS, GENDER, DISABILITY, AND CLASSROOM LIFE

Ask yourself what you know about race, class, gender, and disability as they apply to classroom life. Could you write one or two good paragraphs about what these words mean? How similar or different would your meanings be from those of your classmates? How much do these ascribed characteristics influence the way you think about teaching? If you and your classmates organize into small discussion groups (try it) and listen closely to each other, you will probably notice some distinct differences in the ways you see the importance of these factors. The point of such an exercise is not to show that you have different ideas and interpretations, but to challenge you to think clearly about what your ideas and interpretations mean for working with your students: How will you bring excellence and equity to your teaching?

Race, social class, and gender are used to construct categories of people in society. On your college application form, you were probably asked to indicate your race, gender, disability, and parents' place of employment. Most institutions want to know such information. It provides the institution with the ability to analyze and report data related to any or all of your ascribed characteristics. Social scientists studying school practices often report results according to race, class, or gender. As a teacher, it is essential for you to understand how the dymanics of race, class, gender, and disability can influence your knowledge and understanding of your students. It is also important for you to consider these dyanamics collectively and not separately. Each of your students is a member of multiple status groups, and these simultaneous memberships, in interaction with dynamics in the broader society, influence the students' perceptions and actions.

For example, a child in the classroom is not just Asian American but also male, middle class, native-English speaking, and not disabled. Thus, he is a member of an oppressed racial group, but also of a gender group and a social class that historically have oppressed others. Therefore, his view of reality and his actions based on that view will differ from those of a middle-class Asian American girl whose first language is Korean, or a lower-class Asian American boy whose first language is Hmong and who has spina bifida. A teacher's failure to consider the integration of race, social class, and gender could lead at times to an oversimplified or inaccurate understanding of what occurs in schools, and therefore to an inappropriate or simplistic prescription for educational equity and excellence. You may have noticed, for example, teachers assuming (often mistakenly) that middle- and lower-class Mexican American students identify strongly with each other and that they view issues in much the same way, or that African American male students have the same goals and views as African American female students.

We often begin working with teacher education students by having them take a self-inventory of the sociocultural groups they have been exposed to in their own schooling, religious, or work situations. The more honest you are in thinking about your familiarity with the backgrounds of different children, the more readily you can begin to learn about people you have had little exposure to. It will be a much greater limitation on your ability to teach well if you assume you know more about different students than you actually know, than if you recognize whose lives are unfamiliar to you, so that you can learn.

APPROACHES TO MULTICULTURAL EDUCATION

Educators often work with students of color, students from low income backgrounds, and White female students according to one of five approaches to multicultural education. As we briefly explain these approaches, ask yourself which one you are most comfortable using in your teaching. Before we begin this discussion, you should understand two important points. First, space does not allow for a complete discussion of each approach; for a thorough discussion, please refer to *Making Choices for Multicultural Education: Five Approaches to Race, Class and Gender* (Sleeter & Grant, 1993). Second, if you discover that you are a true eclectic or that none of the approaches satisfies your teaching style, that is fine, as long as you are not straddling the fence. Indecision, dissatisfaction, and frustration in teaching style and technique may confuse your students. Also, to be the dynamic teacher you want to be, you need a teaching philosophy that is well thought out and makes learning exciting for your students. Good teaching requires that you have a comprehensive understanding of what you are doing in the classroom, why, and how you are doing it.

Teaching the Exceptional and Culturally Different

If you believe that a teacher's chief responsibility is to prepare all students to fit into and achieve within the existing school and society, this approach may be particularly appealing to you. It may be especially appealing if students of color, special-education students, White female students, or low-income students are behind in the main subject areas of the traditional curriculum. The goals of this approach are to equip students with the cognitive skills, concepts, information, language, and values traditionally required by U.S. society, and eventually to enable them to hold a job and function within society's institutions and culture. Teachers using this approach often begin by determining the achievement levels of students, comparing their achievement to grade-level norms, and then working diligently to help those who are behind to catch up.

A good deal of research documents learning strengths of students of different sociocultural groups, suggesting that if a teacher learns to identify and build on their strengths, students will learn much more effectively than if a teacher assumes the child cannot learn very well. For example, Shade (1989) synthesized research on the learning style of African Americans and concluded that, "from all indications their knowledge is gained most effectively through kinetic and tactile senses, through the keen observation of the human scene, and through verbal description. This difference in perception manifests itself, not only in worldview but also in modality preference, cue selection, and pictorial perception" (p. 110). Teachers who understand this will read the classroom behavior of such children accurately and adjust their instructional processes accordingly without lowering their expectations for learning.

As another example, gender differences in math achievement may be due partly to instructional styles that favor males. Fennema and Peterson (1987) suggest that girls learn math better when taught through cooperative rather than competitive procedures. More recently, Pearson (1992) discovered that, at the college level, the majority of the female students studied preferred a more collaborative and intimate learning environment. The success of adapting instruction to students' strengths was demonstrated dramatically by teacher Jaime Escalante in an East Los Angeles high school. He attributed his success mainly to high expectations, developing students' teamwork, and offering them challenging and interesting instruction (Escalante & Dirmann, 1990).

Starting where the students are and using instructional techniques and content familiar to them are important. For example, one teacher who used this approach helped two African American students who had moved from a large urban area to a much smaller college town to catch up on their writing skills by having them write letters to the friends they left in the city. A second teacher grouped the girls in her ninth-grade class who were having problems in algebra, allowing them to work together, support one another, and not be intimidated by the boys in the class who had received the kind of socialization that produces good math students. A third teacher provided two students with learning disabilities with materials written at their reading level that covered concepts comparable to those the rest of the class was reading. A fourth teacher placed two Latino students with limited English-speaking abilities into a transitional bilingual program. A teacher may believe that only one or two students in the classroom need this approach, or that all of them do, especially if the school is located in an inner-city community or barrio.

In sum, the heart of this approach is building bridges for students to help them acquire the cognitive skills and knowledge expected of the so-called average White middle-class student. This approach accepts that there is a body of knowledge all students should learn, but that teachers should teach that knowledge in whatever way works so students understand and learn it.

Human Relations Approach

If you believe that a major purpose of the school is to help students learn to live together harmoniously in a world that is becoming smaller and smaller, and if you believe that greater social equality will result if students learn to respect one another regardless of race, class, gender, or disability, then this approach may be of special interest to you. Its goal is to promote a feeling of unity, tolerance, and acceptance among people: "I am okay and you are okay."

The human relations approach teaches positive feelings among all students, promotes group identity and pride for students of color, reduces stereotypes, and works to eliminate prejudice and biases. For example, a teacher of a fourth-grade multiracial, mainstreamed classroom spends considerable time during the first two weeks of each semester, and some time thereafter, doing activities to promote good human relations in the class. Early in the semester he uses a sociogram to learn student friendship patterns and to make certain that every child has a buddy. He also uses this activity to discover how negative or positive the boy-girl relationships are. He uses sentence-completion activities to discover how students are feeling about themselves and their family members. Based on these data, he integrates into his curriculum concepts of social acceptance and humanness for all people, the reduction and elimination of stereotypes, and information to help students feel good about themselves and their people. Also he regularly brings to his classroom speakers who represent the diversity in society to show all students that they too can be successful.

The curriculum for the human relations approach addresses individual differences and similarities. It includes contributions of the groups of which the students are members and provides accurate information about various ethnic, racial, disability, gender, or social-class groups about whom the students hold stereotypes. Instructional procedures include a good deal of cooperative learning, role playing, and vicarious or real experiences to help the students develop appreciation of others. Advocates of this approach suggest that it should be comprehensive, integrated into several subject areas, and schoolwide. For example, a school attempting to promote gender equality is working at cross-purposes if lessons in language arts teach students to recognize sex stereotypes, while in the science class girls are not expected to perform as well as boys and thus are not pushed to do so. These contradictory attitudes simply reaffirm sex stereotypes.

While the "teaching the exceptional and culturally different" approach emphasizes helping students acquire cognitive skills and knowledge in the traditional curriculum, the human relations approach focuses on attitudes and feelings students have about themselves and each other.

Single-Group Studies

We use the phrase *single-group studies* to refer to the study of a particular group of people, for example, Asian American studies or Native American studies. The single-group studies approach seeks to raise the social status of the target group by helping young people examine how the group has been oppressed historically and what its capabilities and achievements have been. Unlike the two previous approaches, this one (as well as the next two) views school knowledge as political rather than neutral and presents alternatives to the existing Eurocentric, male-dominant curriculum. It focuses on one specific group at a time so the history, perspectives, and worldview of that group can be developed coherently, rather than piecemeal. It also examines the current social status of the group and actions taken historically as well as contemporarily to further the interests of the group. Its advocates hope that students will develop more respect for the group and also the knowledge and commitment to work to improve the group's status in society.

Single-group studies are oriented toward political action and liberation. For example, in his discussion of the development of Asian American studies, Omatsu (1994) explains that

> The redefinition [of the Asian American experience]
> began with an analysis of power and domination in American
> society. It provided a way for understanding the historical
> forces surrounding us. And most importantly, it presented a
> strategy and challenge for changing our future. (p. 33)

Women's studies, according to Westkott (1983), is intended "to change the sexist world." Women's studies corrects history that has been written almost solely by White men about White men. It teaches students about the oppression women face and provides female students with accurate knowledge, purpose, and understanding of themselves. For students of color, ethnic studies provides the intellectual offensive for the social and political struggle for liberation and cultural integrity (Cortada, 1974). The student works to develop what Freire (1970) calls a "critical consciousness."

Since the late 1960s and early 1970s, scholars have generated an enormous amount of research about various oppressed groups and have begun to map out new conceptual frameworks within various disciplines. For example, Afrocentric scholars redefined the starting point of African American history from slavery to ancient Africa, and in the process rewrote story lines for African American history. Beginning history with a group other than European males enables one to view historic events very differently. A group's story may begin in Asia and move east, or South or Central America and move north, or Europe and move west, or right here on the North American continent thousands of years ago. Further, the story is different if one views the group as having started from a position of strength (for example, African civilizations), then having been subjugated and now attempting to rebuild that strength, rather than starting in a position of weakness (such as slavery) and now attempting to rise.

A single-group studies curriculum includes units or courses about the history and culture of a group (for example, African American history, Chicano literature). It teaches how the group has been victimized and has struggled to gain respect, as well as about current social issues facing the group. It is essential that such curricula be based on scholarship by people who have studied the group in depth, rather than on your own ideas about what you think might be important.

Beginning in the late 1980s, Afrocentric curricula and schools received considerable publicity and discussion. As reported in *Education Week,*

> School districts in Atlanta, Indianapolis, Milwaukee,
> Pittsburgh, Washington, and other cities are in various
> stages of adopting Afrocentric programs inspired, in part, by
> a curriculum pioneered in the predominantly white
> Portland, Ore. school system. (Viadero, 1990, p. 1)

The *African American Baseline Essays* (Portland Public Schools, 1989), developed under the leadership of Asa Hilliard III, provide teachers with content in six subject areas on achievements of people of African descent from the time of ancient Egypt to the present. Afrocentric schools represent a serious attempt to implement the single-group studies approach because of the failure of schools to successfully educate African American children. Afrocentric public schools have received considerable recent publicity, but Ratteray (1990) notes that more than 400 independent African American schools exist, a few being more than 100 years old. The main rationale for such schools is that "Current practice, even in desegregated settings, effectively excludes African American males [and females, to a lesser degree] from the mainstream culture" (Leake & Leake, 1992, p. 25). Desegregated schools still operate on a Eurocentric model, and many African American students experience serious alienation. Rather than continuing to accept poor academic achievement and cultural marginality, the African American communities in several large school districts decided to try Afrocentric schools with Afrocentric curricula.

These developments sparked much controversy. While educators such as Hilliard maintain that they are an antidote to the "colonial Western approach to history and academic work" and that they develop strong self-concepts in African American students, opponents maintain that such curricula are too politicized and stretch truth (Leo, 1990). From our perspective, all curricula and school programs are political and try to teach someone's version of the truth; at least Afrocentric curricula are more direct about this than traditional Eurocentric, male-dominant curricula.

Although single-group studies focuses mainly on the curriculum, they also give some attention to instructional processes that benefit the target group. Women's studies programs, for example, have developed what is known as "feminist pedagogy." This is a teaching approach that attempts to empower students. The main idea is that in the traditional classroom, women are socialized to accept other people's ideas. By reading text materials that were written mainly by men, providing a male interpretation of the world, women learn not to interpret the world for themselves. In the feminist classroom, women learn to trust and develop their own insights. The feminist teacher may assign material to read and encourage students to generate discussion and reflections about the material. The discussion and personal reflection are important parts of the process, during which "control shifts from me, the teacher, the arbiter of knowing, to the interactions of students and myself with the subject matter" (Tetreault, 1989, p. 137).

In summary, the single-group studies approach is aimed toward social change. It challenges the knowledge normally taught in schools, arguing that knowledge reinforces control by White wealthy men over everyone else. It offers an in-depth study of oppressed groups for the purpose of empowering group members, developing in them a sense of pride and group consciousness, and helping members of dominant groups understand where others are coming from.

Multicultural Education Approach

Multicultural education has become the most popular term used by educators to describe education for pluralism. We apply the term to a particular approach that most advocates of multicultural education prefer. As you will notice, this approach synthesizes many ideas from the previous three approaches.

The societal goals of this approach are to reduce prejudice and discrimination against oppressed groups, to work toward equal opportunity and social justice for all groups, and to effect an equitable distribution of power among members of the different cultural groups. The multicultural education approach attempts to reform the total schooling process for all children, regardless of whether the school is an all-White suburban school or a multiracial urban school. Schools that are reformed around principles of pluralism and equality would then contribute to broader social reform.

Various practices and processes in the school are reconstructed so the school models equality and pluralism. For example, the curriculum is organized around concepts basic to each discipline, but content elaborating on those concepts is drawn from the experiences and perspectives of several different U.S. groups. If you are teaching literature, you select literature written by members of different groups. This not only teaches students that groups other than Whites have produced literature; it also enriches the concept of literature because it enables students to experience different literature forms that are common to all writing. For example, the universal struggle for self-discovery and cultural connection within a White-dominant society can be examined by reading about a Puerto Rican girl in *Felita* (Mohr, 1990), a Chinese girl in *Dragonwings* (Yep, 1975), an African American boy in *Scorpions* (Myers, 1990), and a European American girl in *The Great Gilly Hopkins* (Paterson, 1987).

It is also important that the contributions and perspectives you select depict each group as the group would depict itself and show the group as active and dynamic. This requires that you learn about various groups and become aware of what is important and meaningful to them. For example, teachers wishing to teach about famous Native Americans should ask members of different Native American tribes whom they would like to see celebrated, instead of holding up to their students Pocahontas, Kateri Tekakwitha, or Sacajawea. These Native Americans are often thought among their people to have served White interests more than Native American interests. Additionally, African Americans are becoming increasingly concerned because the African American athlete or entertainer is often held up as the hero and heroine for the group, instead of African Americans who have done well in other areas of life, such as science or literature.

In this approach, instruction starts by assuming that students are capable of learning complex material and performing at a high level of skill. Each student has a personal, unique learning style that teachers discover and build on when teaching. The teacher draws on and uses the conceptual schemes (ways of thinking, knowledge about the world) students bring to school. Cooperative learning is fostered, and both boys and girls are treated equally, in a nonsexist manner. A staff as diverse as possible is hired and assigned responsibilities nonstereotypically. More than one language is taught; all students become at least bilingual. The multicultural education approach, more than the previous three, advocates total school reform to make the school reflect diversity. It also advocates giving equal attention to a variety of cultural groups regardless of whether specific groups are represented in the school's student population.

Education That Is Multicultural and Social Reconstructionist

Reflect back on the various forms of social inequality mentioned at the opening of this chapter. Education that is multicultural and social reconstructionist deals more directly than the other approaches have with oppression and social structural inequality based on race, social class, gender, and disability. Its purpose is to prepare future citizens to reconstruct society so that it better serves the interests of all groups of people, especially those who are of color, poor, female, and/or disabled. The phrase *education that is multicultural*, Grant (1978) explains, means that the entire education program is redesigned to reflect the concerns of diverse (race, class, gender, and disability) groups. Its orientation and focus are on the whole education process. Social reconstructionism seeks to reform society toward greater equity in race, class, gender, and disability. It draws on the penetrating vision of George Bernard Shaw (1980), who exclaimed, "You see things, and you say, 'Why?' But I dream things that never were, and I say, 'Why not?'" (p. 681).

As noted above, this approach extends the multicultural education approach, in that the curriculum and instruction of these two approaches are very similar. However, there are four practices unique to education that is multicultural and social reconstructionist.

First, democracy is actively practiced in the schools. Having students read the Constitution and hear lectures on the three branches of government is a passive way to learn about democracy. For students to understand democracy they must *live* it. They must practice politics, debate, social action, and the use of power. In the classroom this means that students will be given the opportunity to direct a good deal of their learning and to learn how to be responsible for that direction. This does not mean that teachers abdicate the running of their classroom to the students, but rather that they guide and direct students so they learn how to learn and develop skills for wise decision-making. Shor (1980) describes this as helping students become subjects rather than objects in the classroom, and Freire (1985) says it will produce women and men "who organize themselves reflectively for action rather than men [and women] who are organized for passivity" (p. 82).

Second, students learn how to analyze institutional inequality within their own life circumstances. Anyon (1981) tells us that we have a practical consciousness that coexists with a theoretical consciousness. Practical consciousness refers to one's common-sense understanding of one's own life, how "the system" works and "everyday attempts to resolve the class, race, gender and other contradictions one faces" (p. 126). Theoretical consciousness refers to dominant social ideologies—explanations one learns about how the world works, that assume conditions to be fair and just for everyone. As you know, these two sets of consciousness do not always mesh; most of us learn to live within the boundaries of both of them. For example, students of color are taught that education is the doorway to success and that if they obey the teacher and do their work they will succeed. However, studies indicate that many students of color who comply with school rules and teachers' requests still do not receive the career guidance and school work necessary for becoming successful (Grant & Sleeter, 1986). Furthermore, education pays off better for Whites than for people of color; for example in 1991, the average full-time working White person with four years of high school earned $17,520, whereas the average Black and Hispanic full-time worker with the same amount of education earned $13,878 and $14,644 respectively (U.S. Bureau of the Census, 1992b). This approach teaches students to question what they hear about how society works from other sources and to analyze the experiences of people like themselves to understand more fully what the problems actually are in order to prepare themselves to change unfair social processes.

Third, students learn to use social action skills. Bennett (1990) describes social action skills as "the knowledge, attitudes and skills that are necessary for active citizen participation" (p. 307). In this approach the school is seen as a laboratory or training ground for preparing students to be more socially active. Banks (1994) says that oppressed ethnic groups

> must also develop a sense of political efficacy, and be given
> practice in social action strategies which teaches them how to
> get power without violence and further exclusion.... A curricu-
> lum designed to help liberate marginalized ethnic groups
> should emphasize opportunities for social action, in which stu-
> dents have experience obtaining and exercising power. (p. 216)

For example, some stories that elementary school children read could deal with issues involving discrimination and oppression and could suggest ways to deal with such problems. Students of all ages can be taught to identify sexist advertising of products sold in their community and how to take action to encourage advertisers to stop these types of practices. Advocates of this approach do not expect children to reconstruct the world, but they do expect the schools to teach students how to do their part in helping the nation achieve excellence and equity in all areas of life.

Fourth is building bridges across various oppressed groups (e.g., people who are poor, people of color, and White women) so they can work together to advance their common interests. This is important because it can energize and strengthen struggles against oppression. However, getting groups to work together is difficult because members often believe that they would have to place some of their goals second to those of other groups. Further, racial groups find themselves divided along gender and class lines to the extent that middle-class males of all colors fail to take seriously the concerns of women and of lower-class members of their own groups. Childs (1994) describes "transcommunal" organizations, such as the African-American/Korean alliance in Los Angeles, which bring different groups together to identify and work on common concerns. Albrecht and Brewer's book (1990), *Bridges of Power: Women's Multicultural Alliances*, addresses concerns and issues women face in attempting to coalesce across racial and social-class lines.

You now have an idea of the approaches used to teach multicultural education. Which one best suits your teaching philosophy and style? An equally important question is, Which approach will best help to bring excellence and equity to education? We next provide an example of how one teacher brings both excellence and equity to her classroom.

Ms. Julie Wilson and Her Approach to Teaching

The following example describes a few days in the teaching life of Ms. Julie Wilson, a first-year teacher in a medium-large city. Which approach to multicultural education do you think Ms. Wilson is using? Which of her teaching actions do you agree or disagree with? What would you do if assigned to her class?

May 23

Julie Wilson was happy, but also sad that she had just completed her last exam at State U. As she walked back to her apartment, she wondered where she would be this time next year. She had applied for ten teaching positions and had been interviewed three times. As Julie entered her apartment building, she stopped to check the mail. A large, fat, white envelope addressed to her was stuffed into the small mailbox. She hurriedly tore it open and quickly read the first sentence. "We are pleased to offer you a teaching position...." "Julie leaped up the stairs three at a time. She burst into the apartment, waving the letter at her two roommates. "I've got a job! I got the job at Hoover Elementary. My first teaching job, a fifth-grade class!"

Hoover Elementary had been a part of a desegregation plan that brought together students from several different neighborhoods in the city. Hoover was situated in an urban-renewal area to which city officials were giving a lot of time and attention and on which they were spending a considerable amount of money. The city officials wanted to bring the Whites back into the city from suburbs and to encourage the middle-class people of color to remain in the city. They also wanted to improve the life chances for the poor. Julie had been hired because the principal was looking for teachers who had some record of success in working with diverse students. Julie had a 3.5 grade point average and had worked with a diverse student population in her practicum and student teaching experience. She had strong letters of recommendation from her cooperating teacher and university supervisor. Julie also had spent her last two summers working as a counselor in a camp that enrolled a wide diversity of students.

August 25

Julie was very pleased with the way her classroom looked. She had spent the last three days getting it ready for the first day of school. Plants, posters, goldfish, and an old rocking chair added to the warmth of an attractive classroom. There was also a big sign across the room saying "Welcome Fifth Graders." Tomorrow was the big day.

August 26

Twenty-eight students entered Julie's classroom: fifteen girls and thirteen boys. There were ten White students, three Hmong students, six Latino students, and nine African

American students. Three of the students were learning disabled, and two were in wheelchairs. Eleven of the students were from middle-class homes, nine were from working-class homes, and the remaining eight were from very poor homes. Julie greeted each student with a big smile and a friendly hello as they entered the room. She asked their names and told them hers. She then asked them to take the seat with their name on the desk.

After the school bell rang, Julie introduced herself to the whole class. She told them that she had spent most of her summer in England, and that while she was there she had often thought about this day—her first day as a teacher. She talked briefly about some of the places she had visited in England as she pointed to the places on a map. She concluded her introduction by telling them a few things about her family. Her mother and father owned a dairy farm in Wisconsin, and she had one older brother, Wayne, and two younger sisters, Mary and Patricia. Julie asked if there were any students new to the school. Lester, an African American male, raised his hand, along with a female Hmong student, Mai-ka. She asked Mai-ka if she would like to tell the class her complete name, how she had spent her summer, and one favorite thing she liked to do. Then she asked the same of Michael. After Mai-ka and Michael finished introducing themselves, Julie invited the other students to do the same. Julie then asked Marie to tell Mai-ka and Michael about Hoover Elementary.

Once the opening greetings were completed, Julie began a discussion about the importance of the fifth grade and how special this grade was. She explained that this is a grade and class where a lot of learning would take place, along with a lot of fun. As Julie spoke, the students were listening intently. Julie radiated warmth and authority. Some of the students glanced at each other unsmilingly as she spoke of the hard work; however, when she mentioned "a lot of fun," the entire class perked up and looked at each other with big grins on their faces.

Julie had begun working on her educational philosophy in the Introduction to Education course at State U. Although she was continually modifying the way she thought about teaching, her basic philosophical beliefs had remained much the same. One of her major beliefs was that the students should actively participate in planning and shaping their own educational experiences. This, she believed, was as important for fifth graders as twelfth graders.

Julie asked the class if they were ready to take care of their classroom governance—deciding on rules, helpers, a discipline code, and time for classroom meetings. The class responded enthusiastically. The first thing the students wanted to do was to decide on the class rules. Several began to volunteer rules:

> "No stealing."
>
> "No rock throwing on the playground."
>
> "No sharpening pencils after the bell rings."
>
> "No fighting."

As the students offered suggestions, Julie wrote them on the chalkboard. After giving about sixteen suggestions, the class concluded. Julie commented, "All the rules seem very important"; she then asked the class what they should do with the rules.

One student, Richard, suggested that they be written on poster board and placed in the upper corner of the room for all to see. Other class members said, "Yes, this is what we did last year in fourth grade." William, however, said, "Yes, we did do this, but we rarely followed the rules after the first day we made them." Julie assured the class this would not be the case this year, and that they would have a weekly classroom meeting, run by an elected official of the class. She then asked if they thought it would be helpful if they wrote their rules using positive statements, instead of "no" or negative statements. The class said yes and began to change statements such as "no stealing" to "always ask before borrowing," and "no rock throwing" to "rock throwing can severely hurt a friend." Once the rules were completed, the class elected their officers.

After the classroom governance was taken care of, Julie asked the students if they would like her to read them a story. An enthusiastic yes followed her question. Julie glanced at the clock as she picked up *To Break the Silence* (Barrett, 1986) from the desk. The book is a varied collection of short stories, especially for young readers, written by authors of different racial backgrounds. It was 11:35. She could hardly believe the morning had gone by so quickly. She read for twenty minutes. All the students seemed to be enjoying the story, except Lester and Ben, two African American male students. Lester and Ben were drawing pictures, communicating nonverbally between themselves, and ignoring the rest of the class members. Julie decided that because they were quiet and not creating a disturbance she would leave them alone.

After lunch, Julie had the class do two activities designed to help her learn about each student both socially and academically. She had the students do a self-concept activity, in which they did sentence completions that asked them to express how they felt about themselves. Then she had them play math and reading games to assess informally their math and reading skills. These activities took the entire afternoon, and Julie was as pleased as the students when the school day came to an end.

When Julie arrived at her apartment, she felt exhausted. She had a quick dinner and shower and then crawled into bed. She set the alarm for 7 P.M., and fell quickly asleep.

By 10:30 that night she had examined the students' self-concept activity and compared the information she had collected from the informal math and reading assessment with the official information from the students' cumulative record cards. She thought about each student's achievement record, social background, race, gender, and exceptionality. She said aloud, "I need to make plans soon to meet every parent. I need to find out about the students' lives at home, the parents' expectations, and if I can get some of them to volunteer."

Julie turned off her desk lamp at 11:45 to retire for the evening. She read a few pages from Richard Wright's *Native Son* and then turned out the light. Tonight she was going to sleep with less tension and nervousness than she had the night before. She felt good about the way things had gone today and was looking forward to tomorrow. As Julie slept, she dreamed of her class. Their faces and most of their names and backgrounds floated through her mind.

Eight of the ten White students were from Briar Creek, a solid middle-class single-unit housing community; these students were performing at grade level or above in all scholastic areas, and each of them was at least a year ahead in some core area subject. Charles, who had used a wheelchair since he was in an automobile accident three years ago, was three years ahead in both reading and math. However, Elaine and Bob had chosen a mixture of positive and negative adjectives when doing the self-concept activity, and this concerned Julie. She would keep her eye on them to try to determine the cause of their problems.

Estelle and Todd, the other two White students, were between six months and a year behind in most academic areas. Estelle had been diagnosed as learning disabled, but the information in her personal cumulative file folder seemed ambiguous about the cause of her problem. Julie wondered if Estelle was classified as L.D. based on uncertain reasons. She recalled an article that discussed the learning-disability label as being a social construction rather than a medical condition.

All three of the Hmong students were at grade level or very close in their subjects. However, two of them, Mai-ka and Chee, were having some difficulty speaking English. The Kaying family owned a restaurant in the neighborhood. The rumor mill reported that they were doing very well financially, so well that they had recently opened a restaurant in the downtown area of the city. All of the six Hispanic students were Mexican American, born in the United States. Marie, José, and Lourdes were bilingual, and the other three were monolingual, with English being their primary language. Marie, José, and Lourdes were from working-class homes, and Richard, Jesus, and Carmen were from very poor homes. Lourdes, Carmen, and Richard's achievement scores were at least two years ahead of their grade level. José was working at grade level, and Marie and Jesus were one to two years behind.

Five of the African American students—Lester, Ben, Gloria, Sharon, and Susan—were all performing two years behind grade level in all core area subjects. All five lived in the Wendell Phillips low-rent projects. Two African American students—Shelly and Ernestine—lived in Briar Creek and were performing above grade level in all academic areas. Dolores and Gerard lived in Chatham, a working-class predominantly African American neighborhood; both were performing above grade level in all subjects, except Gerard, who was behind in math. Gerard also had chosen several negative words when doing the self-concept activity.

All students in Julie's class were obedient and came from families that encouraged getting a good education.

May 25, 7:30 A.M.

Julie liked arriving early at school. The engineer, Mike, usually had a pot of coffee perking when she arrived. This was her time to get everything ready for the day. She had been teaching for almost one school year and was proud and pleased with how everything was going. The school principal, Mr. Griffin, had been in her class three times for formal visits and had told others, "Julie is an excellent teacher." He usually offered her one or two minor suggestions, such as "Don't call the roll every day; learn to take your attendance silently," and "The museum has an excellent exhibit on food and the human body your class may enjoy."

Julie had also been surprised by several things. She was surprised at how quickly most of the teachers left school at the end of the day. Out of a staff of twenty classroom teachers, only about five or six came early or stayed late. Even more surprising to her was how she and the other teachers who either came early or stayed late were chided about this behavior. She was surprised at the large number of worksheets and ditto sheets used and at how closely many teachers followed the outline in the books regardless of the needs of students. Also, she noticed, there was a common belief among the staff that her instructional style would not work.

Julie had made several changes in the curriculum. She had adopted a tradebook approach to reading and integrated that with her language arts. She made available to the students a wide assortment of books that featured different races, exceptionalities, and socioeconomic classes. In some stories, both males and females were featured doing traditional as well as nontraditional things. Stories were set in urban and rural settings, and some featured children with disabilities. It had taken Julie several months to get such a diverse collection of books for her students, and she had even spent some of her own money for the books, but the excitement the students had shown about the materials made the expense worthwhile.

She also had several computers in her class. There was a computer lab down the hall, but Julie wanted her students to use the computer on a regular basis. When she discovered that Richard's father owned a computer store, she convinced him to lend the class two computer systems, and she convinced Mr. Griffin to purchase six more at cost. Several of the students from Briar Creek had computers at home. Charles and Elaine, Julie discovered, were wizards at the computer. Julie encouraged them to help the other students (and herself—since she had taken only one computer course at State U). The two students enjoyed this assignment and often had a small group of students remain after school to receive their help. Julie was pleased at how well Charles and Elaine handled this responsibility. Lester and Ben were Charles's favorite students, they liked the computer; but Julie believed they liked Charles and his electric wheelchair even more. Julie had heard them say on several occasions that Charles was "cool." Lester's and Ben's work was showing a steady improvement, and Charles enjoyed having two good friends. This friendship, Julie believed, had excellent mutual benefits for all concerned, including herself.

Julie's mathematics pedagogy was built on two principles. First, she built on the thinking and life experiences of the students. Second, she sought to provide students with insights into the role of mathematics within the various contexts of society. These two principles of mathematics pedagogy guided her daily teaching. Julie often took her class to the supermarket, to the bank, and to engineering firms. She made certain that she selected firms that employed men and women of color and White women in positions of leadership. She often requested that a representative from these groups spend a few minutes with the students, explaining their roles and duties. On one occasion, Julie's students questioned a federal government official about the purpose and intent of the U.S. Census. One biracial student asked, "How are racial categories constructed?"

Julie took the students on field trips to supermarkets in different areas of town so the students could compare prices and quality of products (e.g., fruit, meat, and vegetables) between the suburban area and the inner-city area. On two occasions this led to a letter-writing campaign to the owner of the food chain to explain their findings. The students also wondered why the cost of gas was cheaper in the suburban areas than in the inner-city area. This became a math, social studies, and language arts lesson. Letters were written and interviews conducted to ascertain the cost of delivering the gas to the inner city as compared to the suburban area of the city, and to ascertain the rental fee for service station property in the inner city in comparison to the suburban areas. Math skills were used to determine if there needed to be a difference in gas prices between the areas after rental fees and delivery charges were taken into consideration.

Julie used advertisements and editorials from newspapers and magazines to help students see the real-life use of such concepts as sexism, justice, and equity. Julie supplemented her social studies curriculum on a regular basis. She found the text biased in several areas. She would integrate into the assigned curriculum information from the history and culture of different racial and ethnic groups. For example, when teaching about the settling of the local community years ago, she invited a Native American female historian and a White historian to give views on how the settling took place and on problems and issues associated with it. She invited an African American historian and a Latino historian to discuss what was presently happening in the area.

Students were usually encouraged to undertake different projects to provide a comprehensive perspective on the social studies unit under study. Choices were up to the student, but Julie maintained high expectations and insisted that excellence in every phase of the work was always necessary for each student. She made certain that during the semester each student was a project leader. She also made certain that boys and girls worked together. For example, Julie knew that Ben, Lester, and Charles usually stayed close together and did not have a girl as a member of their project team. She also knew that Carmen was assertive and had useful knowledge about the project on which they were working. She put Carmen on the project team.

Julie did have two problems with her class that she could not figure out. Shelly and Ernestine did not get along well with any of the African American students, especially Ben and Lester. George and Hank, two White boys from Briar Creek, had considerable difficulty getting along with José and went out of their way to be mean to Lourdes and Marie. Julie was puzzled by George's and Hank's behavior; she did not think it was racially motivated because both of the boys got along pretty well with Shelly. She labored over this problem and discussed it with the school counselor. She wondered if she didn't have a problem related to a combination of race, class, and gender in George's and Hank's relationship with José, Lourdes, and Marie. She also concluded that she might have a social-class problem among the African American students. Julie decided to discuss her concerns with the students individually. After some discussion, she discovered that Shelly's and Ernestine's problem with Ben and Lester was related to social class and color. Both Shelly and Ernestine had very fair skin color. They had grown up in a predominantly White middle-class community and had spent very little time around other African American students. Ben and Lester were dark-skinned male students who lived in a very poor neighborhood. Julie felt that if her assumptions were true, she would need help with this problem. She was successful in getting an African American child psychiatrist to talk to her class. She did this in relationship to an art unit that examined "color, attitude, and feelings." His discussion enabled Julie to continue her discussion with Shelly and Ernestine and get them to examine their prejudice.

George and Hank admitted to Julie, after several discussions, that they did not care too much for any girls. But Hispanic girls who wore funny clothes and ate non-

American foods were a big bore. It took Julie several months of talking with George and Hank, using different reading materials and having them all work on a group project under her direction, to get George and Hank to reduce some of their prejudices. At the end of the semester, Julie still believed this problem had not been completely resolved. Thus, she shared it with the sixth grade teacher.

At the end of the school year, Julie felt very good about her first year. She knew she had grown as a teacher. She believed her professors at State U, her cooperating teacher, and her university supervisor would give her very high marks. They had encouraged her to become a reflective teacher—committed, responsible, and wholehearted in her teaching effort. Julie believed she was well on her way to becoming a reflective teacher, and she looked forward to her second year with enthusiasm.

She also realized that her sensitivity to things she did not know had grown, and she planned to engage in some learning over the summer. As she had become aware of resentments that students from low-income families felt toward students from upper-income families, she began to wonder what the city was doing to address poverty. She heard that the NAACP (National Association for the Advancement of Colored People), some Latino community leaders, and heads of homeless shelters were trying to work with the city council, and she wanted to find out more about how these groups viewed poverty in the city. She decided to join the NAACP so she could become more familiar with its activities. She also wanted to spend time with some Latino families, because before her teaching experience she had never talked directly with Latino adults; her principal suggested she should meet Luis Reyes, who directed a local community center and could help her do this. In addition, Julie felt somewhat overwhelmed by the amount of background information she had never learned about different groups in the United States and decided to start reading; because she enjoyed novels, she would start with some by Toni Morrison, Louise Erdrich, James Baldwin, and Maxine Hong Kingston. She would also read the novel by Sylvia Plath, *The Bell Jar*.

From what you know of Julie, what is her approach to multicultural education? Would you be comfortable doing as Julie did? Discuss Julie's teaching with your classmates. How would you change it?

CONCLUSION

In Julie's classroom, as in yours, race, class, gender, and disability are ascribed characteristics students bring to school that cannot be ignored. To teach with excellence, Julie had to affirm her students' diversity. Why do we say this?

For one thing, Julie needed to pay attention to her students' identities to help them achieve. She needed to acknowledge the importance of African American males to American life to hold the interest of Lester and Ben; she needed to acknowledge Mai-ka's and Chee's prior learning to help them learn English and school material; she needed to become familiar with her students' learning styles so her teaching would be most effective.

For another thing, Julie needed to pay attention to her students' personal and social needs to help them perceive school as a positive experience. Some of her students disliked other students because of prejudices and stereotypes. Some of her students did not know how to relate to people in wheelchairs or to people who looked or talked differently. Some of her students felt negative about their own abilities. These attitudes interfere not only with achievement, but also with one's quality of life, both as students today and later as adults in a pluralistic society.

Julie realized over the year the extent to which schools are connected with their social context. She remembered having to take a course called School and Society and had not understood why it was required. She remembered reading about societal pressures on schools; over the year she had come to see how societal pressures translated into funding, programs, and local debates that directly affected resources and guidelines in her classroom. Further, she realized the extent to which students are connected with their own cultural context. The African American students, for example, emphasized their African American identity and did not want to be regarded as White; teachers who tried to be color blind regarded this as a problem, but teachers who found the community's diversity to be interesting saw it as a strength. On the other hand, immigrant students tried hard to fit in; Julie would not have understood why without considering why their families had immigrated and the pressures the children experienced.

Julie also knew that the future of the United States depends on its diverse children. Her students will all be U.S. adults one day, regardless of the quality of their education. But what kind of adults will they become? Julie wanted them all to be skilled in a variety of areas, to be clear and critical thinkers, and to have a sense of social justice and caring for others. Julie had some personal selfish motives for this: She knew her own well-being in old age would depend directly on the ability of today's children to care for older people when they become adults. She also knew her students of today would be shaping the society in which her own children would one day grow up. She wanted to make sure they were as well prepared as possible to be productive citizens who had a vision of a better society. She drew from all of the approaches, at one time or another, to address specific problems and needs she saw in the classroom. But the approach she emphasized, and the one that guided her planning, was education that is multicultural and social reconstructionist.

How will you approach excellence and equity in your own classroom? We can guarantee that all your students will have their identities shaped partly by their race, social class, and gender; all of them will notice and respond in one way or another to people who differ from themselves; and all of them will grow up in a society that is still in many ways racist, sexist, and classist. You are the only one who can guarantee what you will do about that.

Questions and Activities

1. Why is it important for teachers to strive to attain both excellence and equity for their students? What can you do to try to achieve both goals in your teaching?

2. What does each of these terms mean to you in relationship to classroom life: *race, class, gender, and disability?* How are your notions of these concepts similar to and different from those of your classmates?

3. Give an example of how such variables as race, language, class, and gender interact to influence the behavior of a particular student.

4. Name the five approaches to multicultural education identified by Grant and Sleeter. What are the assumptions and instructional goals of each approach?

5. In what significant ways does the "education that is multicultural and social reconstructionist" approach differ from the other four approaches? What problems might a teacher experience when trying to implement this approach in the classroom? How might these problems be reduced or solved?

6. Visit a school in your community and interview several teachers and the principal about activities and programs the school has implemented in multicultural education. Using the typology of multicultural education described by the authors, determine what approach or combination of approaches to multicultural education are being used within the school. Share your findings with your classmates or fellow workshop participants.

7. Which approach to multicultural education is Ms. Wilson using? Which aspects of her teaching do you especially like? Which aspects would you change?

8. Which approach to multicultural education described by the authors would you be the most comfortable using? Why?

References

Albrecht, L. and Brewer, R. (1990). *Bridges of Power: Women's Multicultural Alliances.* Philadelphia: New Society Publishers.

Anyon, J. (1981). Elementary Schooling and Distinctions of Social Class. *Interchange, 12,*118–132.

Banks, J. A. (1994). *Multiethnic Education: Theory and Practice* (3rd ed.). Boston: Allyn and Bacon.

Barrett, P. A. (Ed.). (1986). *To Break the Silence.* New York: Dell Publishing Company.

Bennett, C. E. (1990). *Comprehensive Multicultural Education* (2nd ed.). Boston: Allyn and Bacon.

Childs, J. B. (1994). The Value of Transcommunal Identity Politics. *Z Magazine 7 (7/8),* 48–51.

Cortada, R. E. (1974). *Black Studies: An Urban and Comparative Curriculum.* Greenwich: Xerox Publishing Group.

Escalante, J. and Dirmann, J. (1990). The Jaime Escalante Math Program. *Journal of Negro Education, 59,* 407–423.

Fennema, E. and Peterson, P. L. (1987). Effective Teaching for Girls and Boys: The Same or Different? In D. C. Berliner and B. V. Rosenshine (Eds.). *Talks to Teachers* (pp. 111–125). New York: Random House.

Freire, P. (1970). *Pedagogy of the Oppressed.* New York: The Seaburg Press.

Freire, P. (1985). *The Politics of Education: Culture, Power, and Liberation*. Trans. by D. Macedo. Boston: Bergin and Garvey.

Grant, C. (1978). Education That Is Multicultural—Isn't That What We Mean? *Journal of Teacher Education, 29*, 45–49.

Grant, C. A. and Sleeter, C. E. (1986). *After the School Bell Rings*. Philadelphia: Falmer Press.

Henry III, W. A. (1990, July 16). Beyond the Melting Pot. *Time*, 28–31.

Jiobu, R. (1988). *Ethnicity and Assimilation*. Albany, NY: SUNY Press.

Leake, D. O. & Leake, B. L. (1992). Islands of Hope: Milwaukee's African American Immersion Schools. *The Journal of Negro Education 61*(1), 24–29.

Leo, J. (1990, Nov. 12). A Fringe History of the World. *U.S. News and World Report*, 25–26.

Mohr, N. (1990). *Felita*. New York: Bantam.

Myers, W. D. (1990). *Scorpions*. New York: Harper Trophy.

National Center for Education Statistics. (1993). *Digest of Education Statistics: 1993*. U.S. Department of Education. Washington, DC: U.S. Government Printing Office.

National Commission on Excellence in Education. (1983). *A Nation at Risk*. Washington, DC: U.S. Government Printing Office.

Newman, K. S. (1993). *Declining Fortunes: The Withering of the American Dream*. New York: Basic Books.

Omatsu, G. (1994). The "Four Prisons" and the Movements of Liberation: Asian American Activism from the 1960s to the 1990s. In K. Aguilar-San Juan (Ed.). *The State of Asian America* (pp. 19–70). Boston: South End Press.

Paterson, K. (1987). *The Great Gilly Hopkins*. New York: Harper Trophy.

Pearson, C. S. (1992). Women as Learners: Diversity and Educational Quality. *Journal of Developmental Education, 16*(2), 2–4, 6, 8, 10, 38–39.

Portland Public Schools. (1989). *African American Baseline Essays*. Portland, OR: Portland Public Schools.

Ratteray, J. D. (1990). African-American Achievement: A Research Agenda Emphasizing Independent Schools. In K. Lomotey (Ed.). *Going to School: The African-American Experience* (pp. 197–208). Albany, NY: SUNY Press.

Rivlin, A. M. (1992). *Reviving the American Dream: The Economy, the States, and the Federal Government*. Washington, DC: The Brookings Institution.

Schlesinger, A. M. (1992). *The Disuniting of America*. New York: Norton.

Shade, B. J. (1989). Afro-American Cognitive Patterns: A Review of the Research. In B. J. Shade (Ed.). *Culture, Style and the Educative Process* (pp. 94–115). Springfield, IL: Charles C. Thomas Publisher.

Shaw, G. B. (1980). Back to Methuselah. In J. Bartlett (Ed.). *Familiar Quotations*. Boston: Little, Brown.

Shor, I. (1980). *Critical Teaching and Everyday Life*. Boston: South End Press.

Shor, I. (1986). *Culture Wars*. Boston: Routledge and Kegan Paul.

Sleeter, C. E. and Grant, C. A. (1991). Textbooks and Race, Class, Gender, and Disability. In M. W. Apple and L. K. Christian-Smith (Eds.). *Politics of the Textbook* (pp. 78–110). New York: Routledge, Chapman and Hall.

Sleeter, C. E. and Grant, C. A. (1993). *Making Choices for Multicultural Education: Five Approaches to Race, Class and Gender* (2nd ed.). New York: Merrill.

Suzuki, B. (1989, November/December). Asian Americans as the 'Model Minority.' *Change*, 13–19.

Swadener, E. B. (1990, Fall). Children and Families 'At Risk.' *Educational Foundations*, 17–39.

Takaki, R. (1989). *The Fourth Iron Cage: Race and Political Economy in the 1990's.* Paper presented at the Green Bay Colloquium on Ethnicity and Public Policy, Green Bay, WI.

Terkel, S. (1988). *The Great Divide: Second Thoughts on the American Dream.* New York: Pantheon Books.

Tetreault, M. K. T. (1989). Integrating Content about Women and Gender into the Curriculum. In J. A. Banks & C. A. M. Banks (Eds.). *Multicultural Education: Issues and Perspectives* (1st ed.), (pp. 124–144). Boston: Allyn and Bacon.

The Americans with Disabilities Act: Where Are We Now? (1991). *The Disability Rag 12,*(1), 11–19.

Time Magazine (1988, July 11). *Hispanic Americans* (Special Issue), *132*(2).

U.S. Bureau of the Census. (1989). *Statistical Abstracts of the United States 1989.* Washington, DC: U.S. Government Printing Office.

U.S. Bureau of the Census. (1992a). *Statistical Abstracts of the United States, 1992.* Washington, DC: U.S. Government Printing Office.

U.S. Bureau of the Census. (1992b). *Educational Attainment in the United States: March 1991 and 1990.* Current Population Report. Series P-20, No. 462. Washington, DC: U.S. Government Printing Office.

U.S. Department of Education. (1991). *America 2000: An Education Strategy.* Washington, DC: U.S. Government Printing Office.

Viadero, D. (1990, November 28). Battle over Multicultural Education Rises in Intensity. *Education Week*, 10, 11.

Westkott, M. (1983). Women's Studies as a Strategy for Change: Between Criticism and Vision. In G. Bowles and R. D. Klein (Eds.). *Theories of Women's Studies* (pp. 210–218). London: Routledge and Kegan Paul.

Yep, L. (1975). *Dragonwings.* New York: Harper and Row.

Students from different social-class and religious groups cooperatively pursue common goals in the effective multicultural school.

Social Class and Religion

The two chapters in Part Two of this book discuss the effects of two powerful variables on student behavior, beliefs, and achievement: social class and religion. Social class is a powerful variable in U.S. society despite entrenched beliefs about individual opportunity in the United States. As Persell points out in chapter 4, three children born at the same time but into different social classes have very unequal educational opportunities. Students from the lower, middle, and upper classes usually attend different kinds of schools and have teachers who have different beliefs and expectations about their academic achievement. The structure of educational institutions also favors middle- and upper-class students. Structures such as tracking, IQ tests, and programs for gifted and mentally retarded students are highly biased in favor of middle- and upper-class students. Persell suggests ways in which teachers and other educators can create equal educational opportunities for students from different social classes.

Students who are socialized within religious families and communities often have beliefs and behaviors that conflict with those of the school. Religious fundamentalists often challenge the scientific theories taught by schools about the origin of human beings. They also attack textbooks and fictional books assigned by teachers that they believe violate or contradict their doctrines. Conflicts about the right to pray in the school sometimes divide communities. The school should help students mediate between their home culture and the school culture. Uphoff, in chapter 5, describes some promising ways in which this can be done.

Chapter 4

Social Class and Educational Equality

Caroline Hodges Persell

Picture three babies born at the same time, but to parents of different social-class backgrounds. The first baby is born into a wealthy, well-educated, business or professional family. The second is born into a middle-class family in which both parents attended college and have middle-level managerial jobs. The third is born into a poor family in which neither parent finished high school or has a steady job. Will these children receive the same education? Although the United States is based on the promise of equal opportunity for all people, the educational experiences of these three children are likely to be quite different.

Education in the United States is not a single, uniform system that is available to every child in the same way. Children of different social classes are likely to attend different types of schools, to receive different types of instruction, to study different curricula, and to leave school at different rates and times. As a result, when children end their schooling, they differ more than when they entered, and these differences may be used by society in an effort to legitimate adult inequalities. If we understand better how schools may help construct inequalities, we may be in a better position to try to change them.

The nature and meaning of social class are issues often debated by social scientists. Researchers often measure social class by asking survey questions about a person's or a family's educational level, occupation, rank in an organization, and earnings (Persell, 1990). Several features of social class in the United States are worth special mention. Social-class inequality is greater in the United States than in any other industrial or postindustrial society in the world. Germany, Japan, Italy, France, Switzerland, England, Sweden, and the Netherlands, all have considerably less social-class inequality than the United States. Moreover, income inequality has increased in the United States during the last twenty years, which has increased inequality among children as well (Lichter & Eggebeen, 1993). At the same time, the United States has an historical belief in opportunity for all, regardless of their social origins.

This paradox of great and growing inequality and the belief in opportunity for all creates a special problem for the United States, namely, the "management of ambition" (Brint & Karabel, 1989, p. 7). Many more people aspire to high-paying careers than can actually enter them. One result has been the growth of educational credentialism (Collins, 1979), which means that more and more education is required for all jobs, especially professional and managerial occupations. This means that education is playing an ever-increasing role in the process of sorting people into their highly unequal adult positions. This sorting does not happen randomly, however.

Social class has been consistently related to educational success through time (Coleman, Campbell, Hobson, McPartland, Mood, Weinfeld & York, 1986; Goldstein, 1967; Grissmer, Kirby, Berends, & Williamson, 1994; Hanson, 1994; Mare, 1981; Mayeske & Wisler, 1972). Although there are a number of exceptions, students from higher social-class backgrounds tend to get better grades and to stay in school longer than do students from lower-class backgrounds. The question is, why does this happen? Does the educational system contribute to the widening of educational results over time? I argue that three features of U.S. education increase educational inequalities:

1. The structure of schooling in the United States
2. The beliefs held by many members of U.S. society and hence by many educators
3. Certain curricular and teaching practices in U.S. schools

The *structure of schooling* refers to such features as differences among urban, rural, and suburban schools, and differences between public and private schools. *Educational beliefs* includes beliefs about IQ (intelligence quotient) and cultural deprivation, two sets of ideas that have been offered to explain why lower-class children often do less well in school. *Curricular and teaching practices* include tracking of students into certain curricula, teachers' expectations about what different children can learn, and differences in the quantity and quality of what is taught.

This chapter reviews research showing differences in educational structures, beliefs, and practices; examines how these differences are related to the social-class backgrounds of students; considers the consequences they have for student achievement; and analyzes how they affect individuals' adult lives. Lest this be too depressing an account, at the end of the chapter I suggest some ways that teachers and other educators might work to improve education.

EDUCATIONAL STRUCTURES

The three babies described above are not likely to attend the same school, even if they live in the same area. Most students in the United States attend schools that are relatively alike with respect to the social-class backgrounds of the other students. One reason this happens is that people in the United States tend to live in areas that are fairly similar with respect to class and race. If they attend their neighborhood school, they are with students from similar backgrounds. If children grow up in a fairly diverse area such as a large city, mixed suburb, or rural area, they are less likely to attend the same schools. The states with the most private schools, for example, are the states with the largest concentrations of urban areas (Coleman, Hoffer, & Kilgore, 1982). If, by chance, students of different backgrounds do attend the same school, they are very likely to experience different programs of study because of tracking and ability grouping.

In older suburbs or cities, children of higher-class families are more likely to attend homogeneous neighborhood schools, selective public schools, or private schools, and to be in higher tracks; lower-class children are also likely to attend school together. Middle-class families try to send their children to special public schools, parochial schools, or private schools if they can afford them.

Private day and boarding schools are also relatively similar with respect to social class, despite the fact that some scholarships are awarded. Researchers who studied elite boarding schools, for example, found that 46 percent of the families had incomes of more than $100,000 per year in the early 1980s (Cookson & Persell, 1985; Persell & Cookson, 1985).

Let's look more closely at elite private schools and exclusive suburban schools, which are overwhelmingly attended by upper- and upper-middle-class students; at parochial schools, attended by middle-class and working-class students; and at large urban public schools, heavily attended by lower-class pupils. Although these descriptions gloss over many distinctions within each major type of school, they do convey some of the range of differences that exist under the overly broad umbrella we call U.S. education.

Schools of the Upper and Upper-Middle Classes

At most upper- and upper-middle-class high schools, the grounds are spacious and well kept; the computer, laboratory, language, and athletic facilities are extensive; the teachers are well educated and responsive to students and parents; classes are small; nearly every student studies a college preparatory curriculum; and considerable homework is assigned.

At the private schools, these tendencies are often intensified. The schools are quite small, with few having more than 1,200 students. Teachers do not have tenure or belong to unions, so they can be fired by the headmaster or headmistress if they are considered unresponsive to students or parents. Classes are small, often having no more than fifteen students, and sometimes fewer. Numerous advanced placement courses offer the possibility of college credit. Students remark that it is not "cool to be dumb around here" (Cookson & Persell, 1985, p. 95). Most students watch very little television during the school week and do a great deal of homework (Cookson & Persell, 1985). They have many opportunities for extracurricular activities, such as debate and drama clubs, publications, and music, and the chance to learn sports that colleges value, such as crew, ice hockey, squash, and lacrosse. Students have both academic and personal advisors who monitor their progress, help them solve problems, and try to help them have a successful school experience.

Affluent suburban communities have a robust tax base to support annual costs that in the 1990s often exceeded $10,000 per pupil. School board members are elected by members of the community who may know them. Private schools are run by self-perpetuating boards of trustees, many of whom are graduates of the school. The school head is chosen by the board of trustees and may be replaced by them if they are not satisfied.

Private Parochial Schools

Many differences exist among parochial schools, but in general these schools are also relatively small. More of the high school students in them study an academic program and do more homework than do their public-school peers. They also are subjected to somewhat stricter discipline (Coleman, Hoffer, & Kilgore, 1982). The classes, however, are often larger than elite private, suburban, or urban school classes, with sometimes as many as forty or fifty pupils per class. Some non-Catholic middle- and working-class parents, especially those in urban areas, send their children to parochial schools (Coleman, Hoffer, & Kilgore, 1982).

The costs at parochial schools are relatively low, especially compared to private schools, because these schools are subsidized by religious groups. These schools have relatively low teacher salaries and usually have no teachers' unions. Currently, there are more lay teachers and fewer nuns, sisters, priests, and brothers as teachers. The schools are governed by the religious authority that runs them.

Urban Schools

Urban schools are usually quite large, and they are part of an even larger school system that is invariably highly bureaucratic. They usually offer varied courses of study, including academic, vocational, and general curricular tracks. The school systems of large cities and older, larger suburbs tend to lack both political and economic resources. These systems are generally highly centralized, with school board members generally elected on a citywide basis. School board members are often concerned members of the community who may send their own children to private schools, and they may have little knowledge about or power over the daily operations of the public system. The authority of professional educators is often buttressed by bureaucratic procedures and by unionization of teachers and administrators. At least one observer (Rogers, 1968) has described the system as one of organizational paralysis, rather than governance.

Economically, the large city school systems are also relatively powerless. Their shrinking tax bases make them dependent on nonlocal sources (state and federal monies) to balance their budgets. Moreover, the property tax base of public education in the United States results in vastly unequal resources for urban, suburban, and rural schools, and for major regional variations in educational expenditures. Unequal educational expenditures have been challenged in the courts in several states, including New Jersey and Texas (Berne & Picus, 1994).

In general, then, a child's social-class background is related to the school attended, the size of the school, the political and economic resources available to the school, the curricula offered, and the ensuing educational opportunities (Persell, Cookson, & Catsambis, 1992).

EDUCATIONAL BELIEFS

Two educational concepts have been particularly important in influencing educational practices in the twentieth century. These are *IQ* and *cultural deprivation*, or what in the 1990s have been called *at risk* students. (For a critique of the currently popular "at-risk" construct, see Swadener and Lubeck, 1995, who develop the contrasting idea of children and families "at promise," in classrooms that offer children a place where they find acceptance and possibility). These concepts have dominated explanations of differences in school achievement among students of different social classes. Considerable attention has been devoted to determining which concept provides the more correct explanation. However, even though they seem to be competing explanations, they actually have many common assumptions and share many significant consequences.

A great deal of educational thought and research have been devoted to the study of intelligence quotient, or IQ. The concept of IQ has been used to explain why some children learn more slowly than others, why African American children do less well in school than White children, and why lower-class children do less well than middle- and upper-middle-class children. The latest example of this argument is the highly controversial book, *The Bell Curve*, by Richard Herrnstein and Charles Murray (1994). IQ tests are often used to justify variations in education, achievement, and rewards. The justification usually is that because some people are more intelligent than others, they are entitled to more opportunities and rewards, including curricular track placement and exposure to special educational programs and resources.

IQ tests, however, were designed to differentiate people. This was done by dropping from the final intelligence test those items that everyone answered correctly (about 60 percent of the initial items) and including only those questions that some portion (about 40 to 60 percent) of the respondents answered incorrectly. This was done even when the rejected items might represent the best possible measure of achievement or aptitude.

Critics of IQ tests have raised a number of good points about the accuracy of the tests. For example, IQ tests do not measure such important features of intelligence as creative or divergent thinking, logic, and critical reasoning. The idea of multiple intelligences is well developed by Howard Gardner in his book *Frames of Mind* (Gardner, 1983). Stephen Jay Gould's *The Mismeasure of Man* (1981) may still be the single best critical analysis of IQ tests.

IQ tests have good predictive validity for grades in school, which was what Binet designed them for originally. One important question is, how valid are IQ tests or grades for predicting success in life? Many studies show little relationship between educational achievement and performance on the job, in a variety of occupations (Berg, 1970; Collins, 1979; Hoyt, 1965; McClelland, 1974; Taylor, Smith, & Ghiselin, 1963).

IQ testing, especially at an early age, may be inefficient because it may rule out the late bloomer, the early rebel, or the child whose family does not stress test-taking skills. Yet, those people may have a great deal to contribute to society.

IQ tests are criticized for being culturally biased. To do well on an IQ test, an individual needs to have learned White middle-class, U.S. English. One section of the WPPSI (Wechsler Preschool-Primary Scale of Intelligence) requires children to repeat sentences verbatim to the examiner. Children who know a different dialect may provide a simultaneous translation of the sentence read and say it in their own dialect, but they are penalized for not repeating the sentence exactly. They have shown a much more advanced skill than rote memory, but in the test scoring it is a handicap. Even non-verbal tasks such as stacking blocks can be culturally loaded, because more middle-class homes have blocks than do lower-class homes. The ideological significance of IQ tests becomes most apparent in the explanations that have been offered for different educational results.

There is a big controversy in the behavioral and social sciences over whether differences in IQ test scores among students of different classes are the result of genetic deficits (nature) or of cultural deprivation (nurture). Advocates of each position take for granted the importance of IQ test scores.

Arthur Jensen rekindled the genetic controversy when he asserted in 1969 that 80 percent of the variation in intelligence is determined by heredity (Jensen, 1969). Even though it is clear that some portion of IQ is transmitted genetically from parent to child, no one knows exactly how much. A continuing study of more than 100 identical and fraternal twins, separated in infancy and reared apart, found that about 70 percent of the variation in IQ was associated with genetic variation (Bouchard, Lykken, McGue, Segal, & Tellegen, 1990). The authors of the study note that genetic differences may influence the environments that children and adolescents find congenial. Thus, even though heredity may play an important role, the environment in which an individual is raised is also very important. Their results do not detract from the value or importance of parenting, education, and other shaping influences. We know that traits such as height, which are highly heritable, can vary dramatically in different environments.

Economic and social environments facilitate the development of genetic potential. This fact has led to another explanation for differential school achievement, namely, cultural deprivation. The cultural deprivation (or children "at risk") explanation sees low-income or minority children as failing to achieve in school because of their deficient home environments, disorganized family structure, inadequate child-rearing patterns, undeveloped language and values, and low self-esteem.

Consider the issue of self-esteem, which is related to a person's social status. If cultural deprivation and family deficiencies were the factors that produced low self-esteem in children, we would expect very young children to show the same low self-esteem that older ones do. But the reverse is the case. The older the children and the more time they spend in school, the more their self-esteem plummets (Bridgeman & Shipman, 1975). This result suggests that something happens to the initially high self-esteem of lower-class youngsters as they encounter predominantly middle-class institutions. Hence, it is not the so-called pathology of their homes that seems to affect their self-esteem, but something else.

Much of the social science literature has been filled with debates between the IQ and cultural deprivation positions, in what might be today's version of a nature-nurture controversy. But this controversy directs attention away from the common premises and consequences shared by both explanations of differences in test performance and school achievement. These premises include the following:

1. Both genetic and cultural-deficit theorists assume that IQ is important for success in life and appear to agree with the necessity of early testing and selection in schools. They do not question the widespread use of tests designed to differentiate children.

2. Supporters of both theories place the blame for academic failure on children and their families. Thus, they divert attention from the entire educational system and how it produces certain outcomes, including failure among certain types of children. (Not every upper-class child has a high IQ, but do you think that those with lower IQs are allowed to fail at the same rate as lower-class and minority children?)

3. Accepting these theories removes responsibility from educators, because failure presumably lies with the children.

4. These concepts have self-fulfilling potency; that is, if teachers believe that children cannot learn because of their genetic or cultural deficits or because they are "at risk," they will expect less of them and teach them less, and, indeed, it is likely that the children will learn less. Their lower grades tend to confirm the predictions. Hence, the self-fulfilling nature of the prophecy.

5. These theories divert attention from questions about how children learn and what kinds of cognitive skills they have. Such theories make it less likely that effective forms of teaching and learning will happen.

6. Finally, and perhaps most important, the genetic and cultural-deficit theories of differences in school achievement offer compensatory education as the sole solution to poverty, thus diverting attention from structured inequalities of power and wealth in society. Thus, both views leave existing structures of inequalities unchallenged.

I am not suggesting that no intellectual or cultural differences exist between individuals. Differences in intelligence or culture may affect the speed at which students can learn certain things and may influence the effectiveness of different pedagogical approaches. What is important, however, is how intellectual differences are labeled, regarded, and treated by schools, because those beliefs contribute to the maintenance of educational and social inequalities.

In China, for example, where different concepts of individual intellectual abilities have prevailed, teachers work with slow learners until they learn. As the leaders of a school in Peking said, "Of course people differ in ability. But a student who is weak in one field may be strong in another. And these abilities are not something innate and unchanging. Abilities grow when they are made use of, through practice. ...As abilities grow by being used they are not constant, and it does not make any sense to say that a given individual has so and so much ability" (Feinberg, 1975, p. 204).

The widespread use of IQ testing and the explanations offered for differences in

IQ and school achievement are critically important for the curricular and teaching practices in U.S. schools. European schools are much less likely to use IQ tests than are American schools.

CURRICULAR AND TEACHING PRACTICES

As noted earlier, schools attended by children of different social classes vary in terms of what proportion of their students study an academic curriculum. They also vary in terms of how much work they expect and demand of their students. Two curricular and teaching practices in particular highlight how school experiences vary by the students' social class, namely, tracking and teachers' expectations.

Tracking

The first recorded instance of tracking was the Harris plan in St. Louis, begun in 1867. Since then, tracking has followed a curious pattern in the United States of alternate popularity and disuse. In the 1920s and 1930s, when many foreign immigrants settled in the United States, tracking increased greatly. Thereafter, it fell into decline until the late 1950s, when it was revived, apparently in response to the USSR's launching of Sputnik and the competitive concern in the United States with identifying and educating the gifted (Conant, 1961; Oakes, 1985). That period was also marked by large migrations of rural southern African Americans to northern cities and by an influx of Puerto Rican and Mexican American migrants into the United States. Tracking today is widespread, particularly in large, diverse school systems and in schools serving primarily lower-class students (Finley, 1984). It is less prevalent, and less rigid when it occurs, in upper-middle-class suburban and private schools and in parochial schools (Jones, Vanfossen, & Spade, 1985). As we discuss below, there is also a movement toward detracking in some communities and schools.

What exactly is tracking? To address this question, we need to examine the distinction between ability grouping and curriculum differentiation. Proponents of ability grouping stress flexible subject-area assignment. By this they mean that students are assigned to learning groups on the basis of their background and achievement in a subject area at any given moment, and that skills and knowledge are evaluated at relatively frequent intervals. Students showing gains can be shifted readily into another group. They might also be in different ability groups in different subjects, according to their own rate of growth in each subject. This practice suggests a common curriculum shared by all students, with only the mix of student abilities being varied. It also assumes that, within that curriculum, all groups are taught the same material.

In fact, it seems that group placement becomes self-perpetuating, that students are often grouped at the same level in all subjects, and that even a shared curriculum may be taught differently to different groups. This is especially likely to happen in large, bureaucratic, urban public schools. Quite often, different ability groups are assigned to different courses of study, resulting in simultaneous grouping by curriculum and ability. Rosenbaum (1976) notes that although ability grouping and curriculum grouping may appear different to educators, in fact they share several social similarities: (1) Students are placed with those defined as similar to themselves and are segregated from those deemed different; (2) group placement is done on the basis of criteria such as ability or postgraduate plans that are unequally esteemed. Thus, group membership immediately ranks students in a status hierarchy, formally stating that some students are better than others (Rosenbaum, 1976). Following Rosenbaum, the general term of tracking is applied here to both types of grouping.

On what basis are students assigned to tracks? Three major criteria have been noted in the literature: (1) standardized test scores; (2) teacher grades, recommendations, or opinions about pupils; and (3) pupil race and socioeconomic class. Test scores are usually based on large group-administered aptitude tests, a method considered least valid by test-givers. Teacher opinions about students may be influenced by test scores, pupil social class, or ethnicity, as discussed below. Social class and ethnicity have been found in some research studies to be directly related to track assignments as well, even when ability and teacher recommendations were similar (Brookover, Leu, & Kariger, 1965; Rist, 1970). Thus, the social-class background of students is related to the prevalence of tracking in the schools and to the ways track assignments are made. Furthermore, while there is some relationship between tested ability and track placement, it is highly imperfect (Dreeben & Barr, 1988; Pallas, Entwisle, Alexander, & Stluka, 1994).

Once students are assigned to different tracks, what happens to them? Researchers suggest that tracking has effects through at least three mechanisms. These are instructional, social, and institutional in nature, and all three may operate together. The major *instructional processes* that have been observed to vary according to track placement include the unequal allocation of educational resources, the instruction offered, student teacher interactions, and student-student interactions. Dreeben & Barr (1988) found variations in the content, pacing, and quantity of instruction in different tracks. Higher ranked reading groups were taught more (and learned more) words than lower ranked reading groups, according to Gamoran (1984, 1986). Hallinan studied within-class ability grouping in thirty-four elementary school classes. She found that ability grouping affects the learning of students in higher and lower groups because it influences their opportunities for learning, the instructional climate, and the student aptitudes clustered in the different groups. "High-ability" groups spend "more time on tasks" during class; that is, more class time is devoted to actual teaching activities. Also, teachers use more interesting teaching methods and materials. Finally, teachers hold higher expectations, and the other students support learning more in the higher-ability groups. As a result, the aptitude of students in the higher groups tends to develop more than does the aptitude of students in the lower group (Hallinan, 1987).

In secondary schools, college-track students consistently receive better teachers, class materials, laboratory facilities, field trips, and visitors than their lower-track counterparts (Findley & Bryan, 1975; Goodlad, 1984; Oakes, 1985; Rosenbaum, 1976; Schafer, Olexa, & Polk, 1973). Oakes observed that teachers of high-track students set aside more time for student learning and devoted more class time to learning activities. Fewer students in these classes engaged in " off-task" activities (Oakes, 1985, p. 111). Oakes also found that "students are being exposed to knowledge and taught behaviors that differ not only educationally but also in socially important ways. Students at the top are exposed to the knowledge that is highly valued in our culture, knowledge that identifies its possessors as 'educated'" (Oakes, 1985, pp. 91–92). Similarly, those students are taught critical thinking, creativity, and independence. Students at the bottom are denied access to these educationally and socially important experiences (Oakes, 1985, p. 92).

Freiberg (1970) found that higher-track students received more empathy, praise, and use of their ideas, as well as less direction and criticism, than did lower-track students. Oakes (1985) observed that teachers spent more time in low-track classes on discipline and that students in those classes perceived their teachers as more punitive than did students in high-track classes.

Socially, tracks may create settings that shape students' self-esteem and expectations about academic performance. For example, Rosenbaum (1976) reported that more than one-third of lower-track (noncollege) students mentioned "blatant insults directed at them by teachers and administrators. 'Teachers are always telling us how dumb we are.'" One articulate general track student in that study reported that he sought academic help from a teacher but was told that he was not smart enough to learn the material. Several students reported that a lower-track student who asks a guidance counselor for a change of classes is not only prevented from changing but is also insulted for being so presumptuous as to make the request. Rosenbaum (1976) was told by one teacher, "You're wasting your time asking these kids for their opinions. There's not an idea in any of their heads." As the researcher notes, "This comment was not expressed in the privacy of the teacher's room; it was said at a normal volume in a quiet classroom full of students!" (pp. 179–180).

Students have been observed to pick up on the negative evaluations associated with lower-track placement. They may make fun of lower-track students, call them unflattering names, or stop associating with them (Rosenbaum, 1976). Hence, a major result of tracking is differential respect from peers and teachers, with implications for both instruction and esteem.

Institutionally, tracking creates groups of students who are understood by teachers and parents as having certain qualities and capacities, above and beyond the actual skills they possess. The symbolic value of track placement thus creates expectations in teachers and parents, independent of student performance. These expectations affect placement in subsequent levels of the educational system (Gamoran, 1984). Ability groups limit teachers' perceptions of what grades are appropriate for students in different tracks (Reuman, 1989). Both parents and teachers rated children in higher reading groups as more competent and likely to do better in the future than children in low reading groups, even when children's initial performance levels and parents' prior beliefs about their children's abilities were held constant (Pallas et al., 1994, p. 41).

Further consequences of tracking include segregation of students by social class and ethnicity (Esposito, 1973; *Hobson v. Hansen*, 1967; Oakes, 1985; *Racial and Social Isolation in the Schools*, 1969), unequal learning by students in different tracks (Findley & Bryan, 1970a, 1970b; Oakes, 1985; Rosenbaum, 1976; Shafer, Olexa, & Polk, 1973), and unequal chances to attend college (Alexander, Cook, & McDill, 1978; Alexander & Eckland, 1975; Jaffe & Adams, 1970; Jones, Spade, & Vanfossen, 1987; Rosenbaum,

1976, 1980). The percentage of students in an academic curriculum may be the single most significant structural difference between different types of schools. Noncollege preparatory programs may foreclose future opportunities for young persons by failing to provide them with the courses or training necessary for admission to institutions of higher education, or for pursuing particular college majors (Hallinan, 1987a, 1987b).

In recent years tracking has come under considerable attack, and a movement toward "detracking" has gained support (Braddock & McPartland, 1990; Oakes, 1985, 1992; Wheelock, 1992). Research is currently being conducted by Jeannie Oakes, Amy Wells, and others at UCLA on the consequences of efforts to detrack; interested educators can watch for the results of their research when it is published. Because of the great inequality in U.S. society, it is possible that there may be some resistance to genuine detracking.

Teachers' Expectations

Educational structures such as schools that are socioeconomically homogeneous, concepts such as IQ or "at risk," and practices such as tracking go a long way toward shaping the expectations teachers hold about students. Teacher training and textbooks have tended to attribute educational failures to deficiencies in the children. Often, such deficiencies are assumed to reside in the social characteristics of the pupils, such as their social-class background, ethnicity, language, or behavior, rather than in social structure. In a review of relevant research, Persell found that student social class was related to teacher expectations when other factors such as race were not more salient, when expectations were engendered by real children, or when teachers had a chance to draw inferences about a student's social class rather than simply being told his or her background (Persell, 1977). Sometimes social class was related to teacher expectations even when the child's current IQ and achievement were comparable. That is, teachers held lower expectations for lower-class children than for middle-class children even when those children had similar IQ scores and achievement.

Teachers' expectations may also be influenced by the behavior and physical appearance of the children (Ritts, Patterson, & Tubbs, 1992). Social class may influence teacher expectations directly or indirectly through test scores, appearance, language style, speed of task performance, and behavior. All of these traits are themselves culturally defined and are related to class position. Moreover, teacher expectations are influenced more by negative information about pupil characteristics than by positive data. It is important to know this because much of the information teachers gain about low income children seems to be negative.

Another factor that may influence teacher expectations and pupil performance is the operation of the cultural capital possessed by families of higher social classes. As used here, the term *cultural capital* refers to the cultural resources and assets that families bring to their interactions with school personnel. By virtue of their own educational credentials and knowledge of educational institutions, parents, especially mothers, are able to help their children get the right teachers and courses and do extra work at home if necessary (Baker & Stevenson, 1986; Grissmer et al., 1994; Lareau, 1989; Useem, 1990).

If teacher expectations are often influenced by the social class of students, do those expectations have significant consequences for students? Research on this question has produced seemingly contradictory results. The controversy began with the publication of *Pygmalion in the Classroom* (Rosenthal & Jacobson, 1968). That book suggested that the expectations of classroom teachers might powerfully influence the achievement of students. Hundreds of studies on the possibility of "expectancy effects" have been conducted since then (Cooper & Good, 1983). One thing is clear: only expectations that teachers truly believe are likely to affect their behaviors.

When teachers hold higher expectations for pupils, how does this affect their behavior? Their expectations seem to affect the frequency of interaction they have with their pupils and the kinds of behaviors they show toward different children. Teachers spend more time interacting with pupils for whom they have higher expectations (Persell, 1977). For example, Brophy and Good (1970) found that students for whom teachers held high expectations were praised more frequently when correct and were criticized less frequently when wrong or unresponsive than were pupils for whom teachers had low expectations.

Rosenthal (1974) believes that teachers convey their expectations in at least four related ways. He bases this judgment on his review of 285 studies of interpersonal influence, including at least 80 in classrooms or other settings. First, he sees a general climate factor, consisting of the overall warmth a teacher shows to children, with more shown to high-expectancy students. Second, he sees students for whom high expectations are held as receiving more praise for doing something right than do students for whom low expectations are held. Third, Rosenthal notes that high-expectancy students are taught more than are low expectancy students. This is consistent with research by others and summarized by Persell (1977). Fourth, Rosenthal indicates that expectancy may be affected by a response opportunity factor. That is, students for whom the teacher has higher expectations are called on more often and are given more chances to reply, as well as more frequent and more difficult questions.

A fifth way teachers convey their expectations, which Rosenthal does not mention but which has been observed by others, is the different type of curricula teachers may present to children for whom they have different expectations. One study found that teachers report that they present completely different types of economics to students of differently perceived abilities (Keddie, 1971). Another study reported that teachers use more reading texts and more difficult ones with the top reading group (Alpert, 1975).

Clearly, there is evidence that at least some teachers behave differently toward students for whom they hold different expectations. The critical question remains: Do these expectations and behaviors actually affect students? That is, do the students think differently about themselves or learn more as a result of the expectations teachers hold? Therein lies the heart of the "Pygmalion effect" controversy.

When teachers hold definite expectations and when those expectations are reflected in their behavior toward children, these expectations are related to student cognitive changes, even when pupil IQ and achievement are controlled. Moreover, negative expectations, which can be observed only in natural settings because it is unethical to induce negative expectations experimentally, appear to have even more powerful consequences than do positive expectation. Moreover, socially vulnerable children (i.e., younger, lower-class, and minority children) seem to be more suscepti-ble to lower teacher expectations (Rosenthal & Jacobson, 1968).

CONSEQUENCES OF SOCIAL CLASS AND EDUCATIONAL INEQUALITY

This profile of social-class differences in education in the United States is oversimpli-fied, but considerable evidence suggests that the general patterns described here do exist. Social-class backgrounds affect where students go to school and what happens to them once they are there. As a result, lower-class students are less likely to be exposed to valued curricula, are taught less of whatever curricula they do study, and are expected to do less work in the classroom and outside of it. Hence, they learn less and are less well prepared for the next level of education.

Although students have many reasons for dropping out of school or for failing to continue, their experiences in school may contribute to their desire to continue or to quit. Coleman, Hoffer, and Kilgore found that 24 percent of public high school stu-dents dropped out, compared to 12 percent of Catholic and 13 percent of other private school students (Coleman, Hoffer, & Kilgore, 1982). Social class is a more important cause of lost talent among U.S. youth in the late high school and post-high school years than gender or race, according to Hanson (1994).

Similarly, college attendance depends on a number of factors, including access to the necessary financial resources. Nevertheless, it is striking how differently students at different schools fare. Graduation from a private rather than a public high school is related to attending a four-year (rather than a two-year) college (Falsey & Heyns, 1984), attending a highly selective college (Persell, Cookson, & Catsambis, 1992), and earning higher income in adult life (Lewis & Wanner, 1979). Even within the same school, track placement is related to college attendance (Alexander, Cook, & McDill, 1978; Alexander & McDill, 1976; Jaffe & Adams, 1970; Rosenbaum, 1976, 1980). College attendance, in turn, is related to the adult positions and earnings one attains (Kamens, 1974; Tinto, 1980; Useem, 1984; Useem & Karabel, 1986). In 1987, women college graduates aged thirty to thirty-four earned 83 percent more than did women with a high school education, and the comparable premium for men was 57 percent more (U.S. Department of Education, 1990). Thus, educational inequalities help cre-ate and legitimate economic and social inequalities.

However, most educators do not want to enhance and legitimate social inequalities. Therefore, it seems reasonable to ask, What can they do to try to change these patterns?

RECOMMENDATIONS FOR ACTION

Teachers, educators, and concerned citizens might consider the following actions:

1. Working politically to increase the educational resources available to all children, not just those in wealthy school districts, and not just the gifted

and talented. Those concerned might do this by joining a political party that works to advance the interests of the less advantaged members of society, by attending political meetings, and by holding candidates accountable for their positions on education. We can join other people interested in scrutinizing candidates' records of support for education, and contribute time, money, or both to the campaigns of candidates seeking to defeat incumbents who have not supported quality education for all children.

2. Working to reduce economic inequalities in society. This can be done by supporting income-tax reforms at the national level that benefit hard-working low- and middle-income families, by opposing tax cuts for the rich, by supporting job programs at reasonable wages and health care for those who can work, and by providing aid for poor parents who are unable to work.

3. Working to build economically and racially integrated communities. This can be done by choosing to live in such a community, by supporting federal subsidies for low-income housing in mixed-income areas, and by opposing efforts to restrict access to certain communities by members of particular ethnic or income groups. Such restrictions might take the form of zoning that prohibits the construction of high-rise housing for low-income groups or limits housing lots to a large size, such as two acres.

4. Working to support prenatal care for all pregnant women. Currently, about one-quarter of them receive no prenatal care. Helping all pregnant women could reduce or eliminate perhaps one-third of all learning disorders (Hodgkinson, 1989).

5. Working to support Head Start programs for all eligible children. Only 16 percent of low-income children eligible for the preschool program for four-year-olds are now enrolled in it, yet Head Start has a proven track record. Every dollar invested in quality preschool education yields $4.75 because of lower costs later on for special education and public assistance and for the incarceration of people convicted of committing crimes *(Children's Defense Fund: A Call for Action, 1988;* Weikart & Schweinhart, 1984).

6. Using tests for diagnosing rather than dismissing students. For example, instead of taking a low IQ test score as evidence that a child cannot learn, we can examine what parts of a particular test were difficult for that child. If necessary, we can obtain further, individual testing to identify and analyze what skills the child needs to develop and devise strategies for teaching those specific skills. We can try alternative teaching strategies with each child until we find one that works. If a child has difficulty learning to read phonetically, for example, we might try teaching that child a different way, perhaps visually. We can help children with various kinds of learning disabilities learn ways to compensate for their difficulties. For example, planning their work in advance, organizing it so that they have enough time to complete the necessary steps, and allowing time for someone else to check their spelling are all compensatory strategies that can be adopted to good effect by children trying to overcome various learning disabilities.

7. Working on finding what abilities students do have, rather than on deciding that they haven't any. For example, if a student has strong artistic, musical, athletic, or auditory talents, but is weaker in the verbal or mathematical areas, we can help that child find ways into the academic subjects through these strengths.

8. Supporting efforts at detracking.

9. Committing to the use of a variety of pedagogical techniques, curricular assignments, and projects that address the learning needs of individual children.

10. Expecting and demanding a lot from students in the way of effort, thought, and work. We can help students take pride in themselves and their work by teaching them what first-rate work should look like. The written materials students get from teachers and schools and the appearance of the classrooms, hallways, and school should all convey a sense of care, quality, and value. We can carefully check the work students do, suggest constructive ways they might improve it, and expect them to do better the next time.

11. Teaching students content and subject matter. We can show students that we value them and their learning by devoting class time to pedagogically useful tasks, by refusing to waste class time on frivolous activities, and by trying to stick to an annual schedule of curricular coverage.

12. Helping students see how education is relevant and useful for their lives, perhaps by bringing back graduates who have used school as a springboard to better themselves and their worlds. Schools might keep a roster of successful graduates and post pictures and stories about them for current students to see. We can bring in examples that link learning with life accomplishments so students can begin to see connections between school and life. For example, we might invite people who run their own business to talk about how they use math, or bring in people who work in social service organizations to show how they use writing in their daily work.

SUMMARY

This chapter explores how educational structures, beliefs, and practices contribute to unequal educational outcomes. To achieve greater educational equality, educators must understand what social-class differences presently exist in those structures, beliefs, and practices. If these differences are understood, then the educational experiences of children of all social classes might be made more similar.

The higher one's social-class background, the more likely one is to attend a smaller school with more resources, smaller classes, and an academic curriculum. Achieving greater educational equality means making such school experiences available to all students, regardless of their social-class backgrounds.

Two different educational beliefs exist about why some children learn better than others, namely, beliefs about IQ and beliefs about cultural deprivation or being "at risk." Rather than sinking into the controversy over which one provides a better explanation for educational failure, this chapter considers what these beliefs have in common and examines how they both blame the victims for their failure and divert attention from how the social organization of schools may help to create failures. These beliefs also influence the curricular and teaching practices of schools attended by children of different social classes.

The educational process of tracking refers to the segregation of students into different learning or curriculum groups that are unequally ranked in a prestige hierarchy. Whether based on ability grouping or curricular grouping, such tracking tends to reduce learning opportunities for students in the lower groups, while increasing such opportunities for students in higher groups. As a result, this educational practice contributes to educational inequalities. The detracking movement represents an important effort toward achieving greater educational equality.

Teachers may unconsciously form different learning expectations about students of different social-class backgrounds. When teachers hold higher expectations for students, they tend to spend more time interacting with those students, praise them more, teach them more, call on them more often, and offer them a more socially valued curriculum. When teachers hold higher expectations, and when those expectations are evident in their behavior, they increase student learning. Thus, achieving greater educational equality means that teachers' expectations for lower-class students need to be raised.

Because the educational structures, beliefs, and practices examined here are related to unequal educational attainment, and because educational success is related to lifetime occupations and earnings, it is important that educational inequalities be reduced. This chapter recommends a number of steps that concerned educators and citizens can take to promote educational and social equality.

Questions and Activities

1. According to Persell, in what ways do schools contribute to inequality? What evidence does the author give to support her position?

2. Give examples of how each of the following factors contributes to educational inequality: (a) educational structures; (b) beliefs of teachers and administrators; and (c) educational practices.

3. What are the major characteristics of each of the following types of schools: (a) elite private schools and exclusive suburban schools; (b) parochial schools; and (c) large urban public school systems?

4. Why do students from different social-class backgrounds often attend different schools or get assigned to different tracks when they attend the same schools? How does the social-class background of students influence the kind of education they often receive?

5. Visit and observe in (a) a local elite private school; (b) a school in an upper-middle-class suburb; and (c) an inner-city school. How are these schools alike? How are they different? Based on your visits and observations, what tentative generalizations can you make about education, social class, and inequality? To what extent are your generalizations similar to and different from those of Persell?

6. What are some of the major limitations of IQ tests? What cautions should teachers bear in mind when interpreting IQ tests, particularly the scores of lower-class and ethnic minority students?

7. How are the genetic and cultural-deprivation explanations of the low achievement of low-income students alike and different?

8. What is the self-fulfilling prophecy? How does it affect teacher expectations?

9. What is tracking? Why do you think tracking is more widespread in large, diverse school systems and in schools serving primarily lower-class students than in upper-middle-class suburban, private, and parochial schools?

10. How do the school experiences of students in lower and higher tracks differ? How does tracking contribute to educational inequality? What is detracking?

11. How do factors related to social class influence teacher expectations of students?

12. How do teacher expectations influence how teachers and pupils interact, what students are taught, and what students achieve?

References

Alexander, K. L., Cook, M., and McDill, E. L. (1978). Curriculum Tracking and Educational Stratification: Some Further Evidence. *American Sociological Review, 43*, pp. 47–66.

Alexander, K. L. and Eckland, B. K. (1975, June). Contextual Effects in the High School Attainment Process. *American Sociological Review, 40*, (3), pp. 402–416.

Alexander, K. L. and McDill, E. L. (1976, December). Selection and Allocation within Schools: Some Causes and Consequences of Curriculum Placement. *American Sociological Review, 41*(6), pp. 963–980.

Alpert, J. L. (1975, May). Do Teachers Adapt Methods and Materials to Ability Groups in Reading? *California Journal of Education Research, 26*(3), pp. 120–123.

Baker, D. P. and Stevenson, D. L. (1986, July). Mothers' Strategies for Children's School Achievement: Managing the Transition to High School. *Sociology of Education, 59*, pp. 156–166.

Berg, I. E. (1970). *Education and Jobs: The Great Training Robbery.* New York: Praeger.

Berne, R. and Picus, L. O. (Eds.). (1994). *Outcome Equity in Education.* Thousand Oaks, CA: Corwin Press.

Bouchard, T. J. Jr., Lykken, D. T., McGue, M., Segal, N. L., & Tellegen, A. (1990, October 12). Sources of Human Psychological Differences: The Minnesota Study of Twins Reared Apart. *Science, 250,* pp. 223–228.

Braddock, J. H. II and McPartland, J. M. (1990). *Alternatives to Tracking. Educational Leadership, 47*(7), pp. 76–79.

Bridgeman, B. and Shipman, V. (1975). *Predictive Value of Measures of Self-Esteem and Achievement Motivation in Four-to-Nine-Year Old-Low-Income Children* (ETS-Head Start Longitudinal Study). Princeton, NJ: Educational Testing Service.

Brint, S. and Karabel, J. (1989). *The Diverted Dream: Community Colleges and the Promise of Educational Opportunity in America, 1900–1985.* New York: Oxford University Press.

Brookover, W. B., Leu, D. J., and Kariger, R. H. (1965). *Tracking.* Unpublished manuscript (mimeo). Kalamazoo: Western Michigan University.

Brophy, J. E. and Good, T. L. (1970). Teachers' Communication of Differential Expectations for Children's Classroom Performance: Some Behavioral Data. *Journal of Educational Psychology, 61*(5), pp. 365–374.

Children's Defense Fund: A Call for Action. (1988). Washington, DC: Children's Defense Fund.

Coleman, J. S., Campbell, E. Q., Hobson, C. J. , McPartland, J., Mood, A. M., Weinfeld, F. D., and York, R. L. (1966). *Equality of Educational Opportunity.* Washington, DC: U.S. Government Printing Office.

Coleman, J. S., Hoffer, T., and Kilgore, S. (1982). *High School Achievement.* New York: Basic Books.

Collins, R. (1979). *The Credential Society.* New York: Academic Press.

Conant, J. B. (1961). *Slums and Suburbs.* New York: McGraw Hill.

Cookson, P. W. Jr., and Persell, C. H. (1985). *Preparing for Power: America's Elite Boarding Schools.* New York: Basic Books.

Cooper, H. M. and Good, T. L. (1983). *Pygmalion Grows Up.* New York: Longman.

Dreeben, R. and Barr, R. (1988). Classroom Composition and the Design of Instruction. *Sociology of Education, 61*, pp. 129–142.

Esposito, D. (1973, Spring). Homogeneous and Heterogeneous Ability Grouping: Principal Findings and Implications for Evaluating and Designing More Effective Educational Environments. *Review of Educational Research, 43*(2), pp. 163–179;

Falsey, B. and Heyns, B. (1984). The College Channel: Private and Public Schools Reconsidered. *Sociology of Education, 57*(2), pp. 111–122.

Feinberg, W. (1975, Summer). Educational Equality under Two Conflicting Models of Educational Development. *Theory and Society, 2*, pp. 183–210.

Findley, W. G. and Bryan, M. M. (1970a). *Ability Grouping: 1970–1, Common Practices in the Use of Tests for Grouping Students in Public Schools.* Athens: University of Georgia Center for Educational Improvement. ED 048381.

Findley, W. G. and Bryan, M. M. (1970b). *Ability Grouping: 1970–1 The Impact of Ability Grouping on School Achievement, Affective Development, Ethnic Separation and Socioeconomic Separation.* Athens: University of Georgia Center for Educational Improvement. ED 048382.

Findley, W. G. and Bryan, M. M. (1975). *The Pros and Cons of Ability Grouping.* Bloomington, IN: Phi Delta Kappa.

Finley, M. K. (1984, October). Teachers and Tracking in a Comprehensive High School. *Sociology of Education, 57*(4), 233–243.

Freiberg, H. J. (1970). *The Effects of Ability Grouping on Interactions in the Classroom.* (ERIC Document Reproduction Service No. ED 053194.

Gamoran, A. (1984). Teaching, Grouping, and Learning: A Study of the Consequences of Educational Stratification. Unpublished doctoral dissertation, Department of Education, University of Chicago.

Gamoran, A. (1986). Instructional and Institutional Effects of Ability Grouping. *Sociology of Education*, pp. 185–198.

Gardner, H. (1983). *Frames of Mind.* New York: Basic Books.

Goldstein, B. (1967). *Low Income Youth in Urban Areas: A Critical Review of the Literature.* New York: Holt, Rinehart, and Winston.

Goodlad, J. I. (1984). *A Place Called School.* New York: McGraw-Hill.

Gould, S. J. (1981). *The Mismeasure of Man.* New York: Norton.

Grissmer, D. W., Kirby, S. N., Berends, M., and Williamson, S. (1994) *Student Achievement and the Changing American Family.* Santa Monica, CA: Rand.

Hallinan, M. T. (1987a). Ability Grouping and Student Learning. In M. T. Hallinan (Ed.). *The Social Organization of Schools: New Conceptualizations of the Learning Process* (pp. 41–69). New York: Plenum.

Hallinan, M. T. (1987b). The Social Organization of Schools: An Overview. In M. T. Hallinan (Ed.). *The Social Organization of the Schools: New Conceptualizations of the Learning Process* (pp. 1–12). New York: Plenum.

Hanson, S. L. (1994). Lost Talent: Unrealized Educational Aspirations and Expectations among U.S. Youths. *Sociology of Education, 3*(3), pp. 159–183.

Herrnstein, R. J. and C. Murray (1994). *The Bell Curve.* New York: Free Press.

Hobson v. *Hansen.* Congressional Record. (1967, June 21). pp. 6721–16766.

Hodgkinson, H. L. (1989). *The Same Client: The Demographics of Education and Service Delivery Systems.* Washington, DC: I.E.L.

Hoyt, D. P. (1965). *The Relationship between College Grades and Adult Achievement: A Review of the Literature.* Res. Rep. No. 7. Iowa City: American College Testing Program.

Jaffe, A. and Adams, W. (1970). *Academic and Socio-Economic Factors Related to Entrance and Retention at Two- and Four-Year Colleges in the Late 1960's.* New York: Columbia University Bureau of Applied Social Research.

Jensen, A. R. (1969, Winter). How Much Can We Boost I.Q. and Scholastic Achievement? *Harvard Educational Review, 39*(1), pp. 1–123.

Jones, J. D., Spade, J. Z., and Vanfossen, B. E. (1987, April). Curriculum Tracking and Status Maintenance. *Sociology of Education, 60*(2), pp. 104–122.

Jones, J. D., Vanfossen, B. E., and Spade, J. Z. (1985). Curriculum Placement: Individual and School Effects Using the High School and Beyond Data. Paper presented at the American Sociological Association Annual Meeting, Washington, DC.

Kamens, D. (1974, Summer). Colleges and Elite Formation: The Case of Prestigious American Colleges. *Sociology of Education, 47*(3), pp. 354–378.

Keddie, N. (Ed.). (1971). Classroom Knowledge. In M. F. D. Young (Ed.). *Knowledge and Control* (pp. 133–160). London: Collier, Macmillan.

Lareau, A. (1989). *Home Advantage.* Philadelphia: The Falmer Press.

Lewis, L. S. and Wanner, R. A. (1979). Private Schooling and the Status Attainment Process. *Sociology of Education, 52*(2), 99–112.

Lichter, D.T. and Eggebeen, D.J. (1993, March.) Rich Kids, Poor Kids: Changing Income Inequality among American Children. *Social Forces, 71*(3), pp. 761–780.

Mare, R. (1981, February). Change and Stability in Educational Stratification. *American Sociological Review 46,* pp. 72–87.

Mayeske, G. W. and Wisler, C. E. (1972). *A Study of Our Nation's Schools.* Washington, DC: U.S. Government Printing Office.

McClelland, D. C. (1974). Testing for Competence Rather Than for "Intelligence." In A. Gartner, C. Greer, and F. Riessman (Eds.). *The New Assault on Equality* (pp. 163–197). New York: Social Policy.

Oakes, J. (1985). *Keeping Track: How Schools Structure Inequality.* New Haven: Yale University Press.

Oakes, J. and Lipton, M. (1992). Detracking Schools: Early Lessons from the Field. *Phi Delta Kappan, 73*(6) pp. 448–454.

Pallas, A. M., Entwisle, D. R., Alexander, K. L., and Stluka, M. F. (1994, January). Ability-Group Effects: Instructional, Social, or Institutional? *Sociology of Education 67,* pp. 27–46.

Persell, C. H. (1977). *Education and inequality: A theoretical and empirical synthesis.* New York: Free Press.

Persell, C. H. (1990). *Understanding Society* (3rd ed). New York: Harper & Row.

Persell, C. H. and Cookson, P. W. Jr. (1985, December). Chartering and Bartering: Elite Education and Social Reproduction. *Social Problems, 33*(2), pp. 114–129.

Persell, C. H., Cookson, P.W. Jr. and Catsambis, S. (1992). Family Background, High School Type, and College Attendance: A Conjoint System of Cultural Capital Transmission. *Journal of Research on Adolescence 2*(1), pp. 1–23.

Racial and Social Isolation in the Schools. (1969). Albany: New York State Education Department.

Reuman, D. A. (1989). How Social Comparison Mediates the Relation between Ability-Grouping Practices and Students' Achievement Expectancies in Mathematics. *Journal of Educational Psychology, 81,* pp. 178–189.

Rist, R. C. (1970). Student Social Class and Teacher Expectations. *Harvard Educational Review, 40*(3). pp. 411–451.

Ritts, V., Patterson, M. L., and Tubbs, M. E. (1992). Expectations, Impressions, and Judgments of Physically Attractive Students: A Review. *Review of Educational Research, 62*(4), pp. 413–426.

Rogers, D. (1968). *110 Livingston Street: Politics and Bureaucracy in the New York City School System.* New York: Random House.

Rogers, D. and Chung, N. H. (1983). *110 Livingston Street Revisited: Decentralization in Action.* New York: New York University Press.

Rosenbaum, J. E. (1976). *Making Inequality.* New York: Wiley-Interscience.

Rosenbaum, J. E. (1980, April). Track Misperceptions and Frustrated College Plans: An Analysis of the Effects of Tracks and Track Perceptions in the National Longitudinal Survey. *Sociology of Education, 53*(2), pp. 74–88.

Rosenthal, R. (1974). The Pygmalion Effect: What You Expect Is What You Get. *Psychology Today Library Cassette, 12.* New York: Ziff-Davis.

Rosenthal, R. and Jacobson, L. (1968). *Pygmalion in the Classroom*. New York: Holt, Rinehart, and Winston.

Schafer, W. E., Olexa, C., and Polk, K. (1973). Programmed for Social Class: Tracking in American High Schools. In N. K. Denzin (Ed.). *Children and Their Caretakers* (pp. 220–226). New Brunswick, NJ: Transaction Books.

Swadener, B.B. and Lubeck, S. (Eds.). (1995). *Children and Families "at Promise."* Albany, NY: SUNY Press.

Taylor, C., Smith, W. R., and Ghiselin, B. (1963). The Creative and Other Contributions of One Sample of Research Scientists. In C. W. Taylor and F. Barron (Eds.). *Scientific Creativity: Its Recognition and Development* (pp. 53–76). New York: Wiley.

Tinto, V. (1980). College Origin and Patterns of Status Attainment. *Sociology of Work and Occupations, 7*(4), pp. 457–486.

U.S. Department of Education. (1990). *The Condition of Education 1990*, Vol. 2, *Postsecondary Education*. Washington, DC: U.S. Government Printing Office.

Useem, E. L. (1990, April). *Social Class and Ability Group Placement in Mathematics in the Transition to Seventh Grade: The Role of Parental Involvement*. Paper presented at the American Educational Research Association Annual Meeting, Boston.

Useem, M. (1984). *The Inner Circle: Large Corporations and the Rise of Business Political Activity in the U.S. and U.K.* New York: Oxford University Press.

Useem, M. and Karabel, J. (1986, April). Educational Pathways to Top Corporate Management. *American Sociological Review, 51*(2), pp. 184–200.

Weikart, D. and Schweinhart, L. J. (1984). *Changed Lives: The Effects of the Perry Preschool Program on Youths through Age 19*. Ypsilanti, MI: High Scope.

Wheelock, A. (1992). *Crossing the Tracks: How "Untracking" Can Save America's Schools*. New York: New Press.

Chapter 5

Religious Diversity and Education

James K. Uphoff

A beautiful new mosque stands with its center dome and twin minarets vivid against the blue sky. Where in the United States is this religious center located? In Washington, D.C., where many nations of the world send their diplomats? In New York City, the home of the United Nations? In Los Angeles? The answer to each of these questions is no.

The mosque is located on the flat, fertile farmland of northwest Ohio, just south of Toledo, deep in the heart of the midwestern United States. Another attractive mosque is being built near I-75 just north of Cincinnati, Ohio. Unusual? Yes, but a vivid sign of the changing times as religions in the United States become more diverse.

Watching local law enforcement officers chain and padlock a church door on the television news a few years ago was unsettling to many people. Yet this scenario did happen in rural Nebraska, when a small independent Protestant church decided to defy a state law requiring all teachers in the state to be certified. This church had recently created its own small school, which met in the church. However, the teaching staff did not meet the qualifications set by the law. The minister made national news as he, on behalf of the congregation, defied the law and all attempts of the authorities to reach a compromise.

In California's San Ramone School District, some parents raised objections to an education curriculum because it called for teachers and students to use decision-making techniques and because it was alleged to be teaching "secular humanism," considered by some people to be a type of religion ("Alleged 'Secular Humanism' Courses Attacked," 1986). This example is only the tip of a large iceberg of formal objections that have been made in school districts throughout the nation. More than ever before, school materials and teaching methods, standards, and requirements are being challenged on religious grounds as groups and individuals fight back against what they perceive as the antireligious nature of the public schools.

A January 14, 1995, headline in the *Dayton (Oh.) Daily News* read, "Prayerful

Return? For some the abandoned activity never left the halls of learning" (Hundley, 1995). The issues of whether prayer or silence can be permitted in a public school and, if so, under what conditions remain very current in this final decade of the century. Secretary of Education and former Governor of South Carolina, Richard Riley, has supported voluntary school prayer so long as "it's not coercive or intrusive on other children" (Winik, 1995, p. 6). He does not, however, support a constitutional amendment on school prayer.

A mid-decade cover story in *Newsweek* (Alter & Wingert, 1995) indicates that elements of religion are on the "front burner" of public interest and concern. Entitled "Shame. How do we bring back a sense of right and wrong?" the feature raises more questions about the role of religion in our diverse culture and our schools. Who determines what is right and wrong and by what criteria are such shame-inducing decisions to be made?

This chapter helps you better understand the religious element of cultural diversity. If the United States is to function as a cohesive unit, it must be able to accommodate the diversity within it. Teachers have a key role to play, but they can perform it only if they fully understand the play and the audiences who will attend.

To help teachers prepare for this theater, this chapter provides definitions of religion, a glimpse at the importance of religion, a brief review of relevant U.S. history, an examination of constitutional issues involved, facts and figures about the religious diversity within the United States, and a focus on the educational implications of all of these factors.

DEFINITIONS OF RELIGION

Before we can discuss religion, we must come to some common agreement about what religion is. The word is a common one that seems easy to define but in fact is difficult to explain. Nearly everyone uses the term, but few have a well-developed idea of what we mean. Wilson (1982) contends, "Often, one's definition of 'religion' reveals much more about the point of view or prejudices of the definer than it does about religion itself" (p. 18). He feels that the definition can be either negative or positive, depending on the emotions it calls forth in the speaker.

Albanese (1981) states, "Everyone knows what religion is—that is, until one tries to define it. It is in the act of defining that religion seems to slip away" (p. 2). She believes that the difficulty exists because religion crosses many boundaries, even though the purpose of most definitions is to establish boundaries.

We provide a definition by describing examples, thus providing each of us with a more common picture on which to build our look at the educational implications of religious diversity. As we focus our camera on this concept, we need to use both a close-up and a wide-angle lens. These views give us first the narrow definition most commonly used and then the much broader definition used by the U.S. Supreme Court in several landmark cases regarding church and state.

If we were to play a word-association game using the term *religion*, the responses would probably include at least some of the following: buildings of worship; traditions and festivals; names of organized groups; special objects, symbols, or literature; sets of beliefs; and specific types of persons or roles. Thus, such words as *church, temple, pagoda, shrine, confirmation, bar/bat mitzvah, Hindu, Shinto, Buddhist, Society of Mary, cross, Star of David, clerical collar, Upanishad, Koran, baptism, creed, priest, monk, nun, minister, rabbi, mullah,* and *evangelist* would be commonly stated by people using this narrowly focused view of religion.

The wide-angle view was described by the leaders of the Public Education Religion Studies Center (PERSC) in their 1974 book, *Questions and Answers* (Bracher, Panoch, Piediscalzi, & Uphoff, 1974):

> The broad definition envisions religion as any faith or set of values to which an individual or group gives ultimate loyalty. . . . Buddhism, Taoism, Ethical Culture, secularism, humanists, scientism, nationalism, money, and power illustrate this concept of religion. (p. 5)

The U.S. Supreme Court has for several decades been using this broader definition as it has made decisions. Thus, Madeline Murray O'Hare, an avowed atheist, has been considered by some to be a very religious person by this broad definition.

Several of the most recent church-state cases currently on appeal in the federal courts involve this broader definition. One federal judge found that secular humanism is a religion, that many textbooks discuss its beliefs, and that other religions such as Christianity do not have their own beliefs included in those same textbooks; thus, more than forty textbooks must be withdrawn from the public schools. Judge William Brevard Hand's ruling in *Smith et al.* v. *Board of School Commissioners of Mobile County et al.* of March 4, 1987, represented a direct use of the broader definition even though it was overturned on appeal to higher courts.

One important aspect of this dual definition is that many individuals use and live by both. Often referred to as *crypto* (hidden) religion, these people use a sectarian (narrow definition) mask to hide an ultimate concern. They often use the same symbols as those whose prime belief is a more traditional form of religion. For instance, such groups as the Ku Klux Klan use the Christian *cross* as a symbol of their "WASP-supremacy ultimate concern religion." Other people believe in the acquisition of power or wealth, doing everything they can to obtain them, even though they outwardly profess belief in the giving, sharing, and serving creeds of a particular church.

Thus, the broad definition, because it so clearly includes values and the valuing process, must also be used as we proceed through this chapter. We can understand the many educational implications of religious diversity in the United States and in the world at large only if we use both views. These views include the traditional notion of religion (being Jewish or Christian, for example) and the idea of religion as any strong faith.

Importance of Religion

For what idea, principle, cause, belief, or value would you be willing to give your life? As each of us answers this question of ultimate commitment, we state the importance of our religion. In the history of humanity, millions of people have answered this question through action. Countless lives have been given in defense of religious beliefs. There has been no shortage of examples, from the earliest hunter who believed in the security of family and died while protecting that family, to those who blow themselves up as they conduct holy war.

It is our own system of values and beliefs that makes each example positive or negative. Such emotion-laden terms as *religious fanatic, heroic,* and *martyr* provide clues as to how we perceive a particular event.

If human beings are willing to die for a belief, then they are even more willing to suffer lesser penalties such as ridicule, separation, torture, imprisonment, fines, or restrictions, on behalf of their beliefs. British and American women of the early twentieth century who fought for women's rights certainly suffered as a result of their beliefs. Today, parents who decide to school their children at home have often found themselves in court facing state charges for disobeying school-attendance laws. The Holocaust Museum in Washington, D.C., highlights the number of non-Jews who literally risked and gave their own lives to save Jews from Hitler's forces.

Religion is an important element in the lives of many people; to some, it is the most important element. It has been the source of strength in times of trouble. Certainly this has been the case for African Americans in their history in the United States. African American historian Barbara Green (1984) writes of the relationship between the survival skills and the folklore of Blacks. The spirituals they sang provided them with comfort, hope, and strength. Green states, "The performance of work songs and spirituals was just as important as the songs themselves. Singing them sharpened memory skills; taught language skills, religious values, and survival strategy; and cultivated group identity" (p. 94).

Much of the civil rights movement of the last half of this century had a strong foundation within the churches and synagogues of the United States. People opposed to integration were often placed in the position of being opposed to their own church bodies or to religion in general. Churches became divided, and crypto religions developed.

The public schools often became the battleground for these contrasting belief systems. Governors who stood at the schoolhouse door to prevent integration were endorsed by some ministers and condemned by others. The schools were in the middle. Today, the schools are still in the middle. One example is when laws are passed requiring schools to teach sex education while many individuals and churches object with such vigor that they withdraw their children from school and establish new, private schools.

It should be no wonder, then, that public education as an arm of the state should have found itself frequently at odds with first one religious group and then another, as the United States has become ever more diverse and religiously pluralistic. Goodrich (1994) addressed this diversity in his article "Religion is Alive and Diverse in US." Also, *Newsweek's* November 28, 1994, cover story was entitled "The search for the sacred: America's quest for spiritual meaning." Both publications strongly make the point that religion is very much a significant part of the lives of millions of Americans and thus worthy of being studied by their children.

We Are What We Were

Historically the United States has always had a number of different religions. The similar, yet very different, religions of the Native Americans were well in place when the Europeans arrived. These newcomers brought with them a collection of similar, yet very different, forms of Christianity. Several colonies adopted nearly exclusively a single form of this religion (for example, the Puritans and Congregationalists in Massachusetts, and the Anglicans and Episcopalians in Virginia), while others were settled by a variety of groups. Pennsylvania, for instance, became home to Quakers, Lutherans, Baptists, and many others.

Three different types of school systems developed, in part as a result of these patterns of religious settlement. The New England colonies developed public school laws (Massachusetts Laws of 1642 and 1647) that required an elementary school for every 50 families and a grammar school for every 100 families. However, since the government was essentially a theocracy, in which the church and state were essentially one, the name of those laws was "Ye Old Deluder Satan Act," and their purpose was to teach the children to read and write so they would be able to read the scriptures on their own and thus "ward off ye old deluder Satan." This *public* parochial *school* became the model for much of American education.

Because of the geographic size of the Southern colonies and the dominance by the Anglican Church of England, most schooling was done by traveling teachers who would stay for several months, visiting first one plantation and then another. Most children did not attend school; usually only boys from the wealthier families were so privileged. Apprenticeships were widely used for the less well-to-do. Formal education was much more a system of private schooling.

The middle colonies tended to have very diverse settlement patterns. No single religion dominated, but because religion was felt by many people to be a major reason for having formal education, little agreement among the various religious groups was possible. Therefore, a system of parochial schools resulted, with each group establishing its own schools.

Even amid this diversity, however, there was oneness of religion, a religious unity among Americans. Albanese (1981) says that religious unity refers to the "dominant and public cluster of organizations, ideas, and moral values which, historically and geographically, have characterized this country" (p. 10). Today, this is often referred to as the Judeo-Christian tradition. For some people, this ethic has become a civil religion, in which patriotism and nationalism become an ultimate concern, a cryptoreligion.

As each new wave of immigrants came into the United States, the oneness expanded to accommodate the new arrivals even as the established religions changed and adapted to the new setting. Some geographic areas became closely associated with a particular group, such as the Amish in Pennsylvania. Add to the problems associated with religious differences the difficulties of language, dress, and food and we can understand the assimilation problems experienced by immigrating groups. Most recently the new immigrants have come from non-Christian lands and are of a different race, thus making for a more difficult assimilation.

The process of assimilation did not always work smoothly. The religious oneness described above was nearly always patterned after the Massachusetts public school model—public parochial schools. Cincinnati's Bible War in 1869–1870 is one example of the assimilation process not working well. The public schools required the reading of the King James version of the Bible, which was objectionable to the large Catholic population, to Jews, and to others. Those in charge argued that the "common schools" were an appropriate place for the "common religion" to be taught. This religion was, however, a generalized Protestant version of Christianity and thus was not acceptable to all students (Michaelsen, 1970).

From the inception of the United States, the most fundamental question asked about religion and education has been, "To what extent should the public schools be an extension of the oneness of religion, an extension of the separateness of the many religions, or no extension of any kind of religion?" The many court cases in this century have been part of the process of trying to answer this question. The line separating church and state has always been unclear. Two centuries ago, the framers of the constitution addressed this question; legislative bodies and the courts have tried to clarify it; but it remains an issue very important to many people.

Constitutional Issues

The First Amendment to the U.S. Constitution says clearly: "Congress shall make no law respecting an establishment of religion, or prohibiting the free exercise thereof." The key word here is *Congress*, because not until the Fourteenth Amendment was adopted (1868) and gave to the citizens of the states all of the rights they had as citizens of the nation did the federal separation of church and state have any influence on the schools. In fact, not until the 1830s did the Commonwealth of Massachusetts repeal such laws as mandatory church membership as a requirement for holding a public office.

The constitutional separation of church and state has two key elements: no state support to create or maintain a religion (establishment), and no state laws against the practice of a religion (prohibition). Most constitutional cases regarding religion and the schools have dealt with the "establishment clause"; that is, the state (public school) cannot help to establish a religion by requiring prayer, Bible reading, or devotional moments of silent meditation or by permitting the use of school buildings or funds for religious instruction. Busing children to parochial schools for safety reasons and using public funds to purchase nonreligious textbooks are legal.

The Supreme Court gave strong support to the need for and appropriateness of teaching about religion in the public schools. On June 17, 1963, the Court gave its opinion on the cases of *Abington* v. *Schempp and Murray* (son of Madeline Murray O'Hare) v. *Curlett*, which dealt with required prayer and Bible reading in school. Associate Justice Tom Clark wrote the majority opinion, which included the following statement (author's emphasis):

> It might well be said that one's education is not complete without a *study* of comparative religion or the history of religion and its relationship to the advancement of civilization. It certainly may be said that the Bible is worthy of *study* for its

literary and historic qualities. Nothing we have said here
indicates that such *study* of the Bible or of religion, when presented objectively as part of a secular program of education,
may not be effected consistent with the First Amendment.

Because the headlines following this decision were inaccurate and misleading
("Prayer Banned—Bible Banned"), many educators as well as parents and other citizens were angry, perplexed, and concerned. Almost immediately the school curriculum
guides and materials were subjected to self-censoring, first by educators and then by
publishers. So much censorship occurred so rapidly that the American Association of
School Administrators published a book in 1964 entitled *Religion in the Public Schools.*
The association took a strong and clear position in support of the valid academic
study of religion in the public schools when it stated:

> A curriculum which ignored religion would itself have
> serious implications. It would seem to proclaim that religion
> has not been as real in men's lives as health, or politics, or
> economics. By omission it would appear to deny that reli-
> gion has been and is important in man's history—a denial of
> the obvious. In day by day practice, the topic cannot be
> avoided. As an integral part of man's culture, it must be
> included.

Even though the need for and appropriateness of teaching about religion has
been strongly shown since 1963, not everyone in the nation concurs. Problems occur
when the public feels that schools are teaching about the religions of other lands but
are giving little attention to religions of this land. The emotions schools had hoped to
avoid by focusing only on remote and thus less controversial peoples are now in the
headlines and in the courts.

Other constitutional issues have addressed how much power the state actually
has to regulate religious schools, to require attendance at an approved school (religious
or public), and to provide aid (what kind, how much, etc.). A 1980s case, for example,
that began in Dayton, Ohio, involved the issue of whether the state civil rights commission had the power to investigate a teacher's charge that she had been dismissed
from a private Christian school because she exercised her civil right to question an
administrative decision. The school contends that because the school is a religious
institution, civil rights laws do not apply to how it treats its own personnel. This is
one of a new type of church-state cases focusing on prohibiting the free exercise
thereof clause of the First Amendment.

The founders of the United States had either experienced firsthand or knew about
the unwelcome combination of church and state in Europe. Wars, inquisitions, and the
absence of freedom were fresh in their minds as they developed the Constitution.
The quality of their work is seen today in the fact that in the more than 200 years that
have passed, the United States has become even more religiously diverse but has
avoided the major problems of lasting and often violent interreligious conflicts too
often found elsewhere in the world.

RELIGIOUS DIVERSITY IN THE UNITED STATES

Lessons from history tell us that religious, ethnic, and language diversity within a nation or other area often lead to many problems. Such examples as Ireland, India, Pakistan, Sri Lanka, and Belgium come to mind. Diversity, however, also exists within particular religions and even within particular denominations of a religion. Conflicts during the 1980s within the Southern Baptist Convention and a split in the Lutheran Church Missouri Synod—both separate Christian denominations—illustrate the point.

If we are to learn from history, we must be more knowledgeable about our own religious diversity and learn how to respond to it more appropriately. This section examines the extent of religious diversity within the United States and within Christianity, the major religious groups.

As a nation, the United States began with a diversity of peoples and their beliefs. The dominant common Western European heritage, although not one of peace and goodwill among themselves, was clearly Christian in a general way. While some early settlers were deeply religious and came to this land in order to practice their religion, others came for different reasons, including economic gain, adventure, and escape from legal or other problems. It must be noted that some of those who sought religious freedom were, in turn, unwilling to grant it to others; Rhode Island was founded by people whose religious beliefs were not welcome in neighboring Massachusetts.

Specific data on religious diversity in the United States are difficult to find. One must turn to a variety of sources and sometimes use information from different studies to gain even a fuzzy picture of how many religions are practiced today in the United States. There is always a danger that comparisons of religions are being made between apples and oranges.

A massive 1980 survey of Judeo-Christian denominations (*The New Book of American Rankings*, 1984) found more than 228 different church groups. A few, 17 out of 111 who returned surveys, reported having more than one million adherents and another 25 church bodies claimed between 100,000 and one million members. After Roman Catholics, who accounted for 42 percent of the total, the figures dropped dramatically to 14.5 percent for Southern Baptists and 10.3 percent for Methodists. A total of 108 'denominations' were listed for the other 33.2 percent, with no one group claiming more than 2.6 percent of the total.

Add to these data the fact that there are thousands of local churches not affiliated with any larger body, synod, or organization. Many of these independent churches grew in number of adherents during the 1970s and 1980s. Television evangelists, at least until their scandals of the late 1980s, experienced large and growing video congregations, which were also outside of the enumerations of the survey cited above.

Still other groups that stand partially or totally outside the Judeo-Christian realm (Unification Church of the Rev. Sun Myung Moon, the Scientologists, and the Hare Krishna movement, for example) experienced growth during the 1970s. Precise numbers for such groups are not available.

Gaustad's (1976) data indicate that as the United States has grown over the years, the percentage of the population claiming a religious affiliation has also grown.

Another way to say this is that as the United States has become more diverse in the social and religious aspects of its peoples, a larger percentage of people have become affiliated with a religious body. Gaustad reports that in 1865, 26 percent claimed a religious affiliation. This percentage rose over the years to 44 percent in 1930 and 62 percent in 1970, the final year for these data.

Table 5.1, from *Statistical Abstract of the United States* (U.S. Bureau of the Census, 1994), summarizes data on religious preference, church membership, and attendance from 1957 to 1991 for the noninstitutional population of the United States eighteen years old and over. The table indicates that this population showed the following religious preferences in 1991: Protestant, 56 percent; Catholic, 25 percent; Jewish, 2 percent, and other, 6 percent. Although 89 percent of this population expressed a religious preference (11 percent expressed no preference), only 68 percent were church or synagogue members and only 42 percent actually attended churches or synagogues.

The 1991 Yearbook of American and Canadian Churches (Jacquet & Jones, 1991), reporting data from the Gallup organization, found that worship attendance by adults has remained remarkably steady over a fifty-year period, moving from 41 percent in 1939 to only 43 percent in 1989 after a nearly twenty-year decline. However, the worship attendance of U.S. teens has grown significantly from 50 percent in 1980 to 57 percent in 1989. Such figures are, however, called into question by a study by C. Kirk Hadaway (Keeler, 1994). The study suggests that the "real attendance rate is only half the reported rate" (6C), a difference some are calling "The God Gap."

The December 17, 1990, issue of *Newsweek* included a seven-page story entitled "A Time to Seek—with babes in arms and doubts in mind, a generation looks to religion." Noting the clear trend of former baby boomers to return to religion, the article reports the following:

- At one time or another, roughly two-thirds of baby boomers dropped out of organized religion. But in recent years, more than one-third of the dropouts have returned.
- About 57 percent—43 million people—now attend church or synagogue.
- More than 80 percent of the boomers consider themselves religious and believe in life after death.
- The biggest group of returnees (about 60 percent) are married with children.
- The least likely to have returned are married couples without kids. (p. 51)

According to *The New Book of American Rankings*, the percentage of Christian-Judaic adherents varies greatly by state. Rhode Island leads the list, with 75.5 percent, Utah follows closely, with 75.2 percent; Alaska, with 30.8 percent, and Nevada, with 29.3 percent, are at the bottom of the rankings. In general, the New England area and the Upper Midwest and Plains states have the highest percentages of adherents, and the West has the lowest.

Data for Christians and Jews are much easier to obtain than is accurate and reliable information for other religions. Only the former tend to maintain records and statistics (many of which are less than complete and current). Most information for other

Table 5.1 Religious Preference, Church Membership, and Attendance: 1957 to 1991

(**In percent.** Covers civilian noninstitutional population, 18 years old and over. Data represent averages of the combined results of several surveys during year. Data are subject to sampling variability; see sources)

Year	Religious Preference					Church/ Synagogue Members	Persons Attending Church/ Synagogue[1]	Age and Religion	Church/ Synagogue Members, 1991
	Protestant	Catholic	Jewish	Other	None				
1957	66	26	3	1	3	[2]73	47	18–29 years old	60
1967	67	25	3	3	2	[3]73	43	30–49 years old	67
1975	62	27	2	4	6	71	41	50 years and over	76
1980	61	28	2	2	7	69	40	East[4]	69
1985	57	28	2	4	9	71	42	Midwest[5]	66
1990	56	25	2	6	11	65	40	South[6]	76
1991	56	25	2	6	11	68	42	West[7]	54

[1] Persons who attended a church or synagogue in the last seven days.

[2] 1952 data.

[3] 1965 data.

[4] ME, NH, RI, NY, CT, VT, MA, NJ, PA, WV, DE, MD, and DC.

[5] OH, IN, IL, MI, MN, WI, IA, ND, SD, KS, NE, and MO.

[6] KY, TN, VA, NC, SC, GA, FL, AL, MS, TX, AR, OK, and LA.

[7] AZ, NM, CO, NV, MT, ID, WY, UT, CA, WA, OR, AK, and HI.

Sources: Princeton Religion Research Center, Princeton, NJ, "Emerging Trends," periodical. Based on surveys conducted by The Gallup Organization, Inc.; U.S. Bureau of the Census, *Statistical Abstract of the United States*, (114th ed.). Washington, DC: U.S. Government Printing Office, 1994.

religions is based on informed estimates. What follows, then, should be viewed as general patterns rather than as hard data.

Immigration reports provide a basis for enlightened conjecture as to how many adherents there are for each religion. *The World Almanac and Book of Facts: 1995* (1995) indicates that the total percentage of European immigrants to the United States went down from 33.8 percent in 1961 to only 17.8 percent for the following decade and down further to 10.4 percent for the 1981–1990 period. In sharp contrast is the number of immigrants from Asia. Figures for these immigrants went up dramatically, from 12.9 percent of total immigrants in the 1960s to 35.3 percent in the 1970s and 37.3 percent in the 1980s. The figures for African immigrants rose from 0.9 percent to 1.8 percent and to 2.4 percent in the 1980s. Those for immigrants from South and Central America and from Australia both declined a little. The continued emigration of the many refugees from Southeast Asia during the 1980s maintained this pattern and probably increased the influx of persons from non–Christian-Judaic backgrounds, thus further increasing the religious diversity of the United States.

Other data that support these conclusions indicate that in 1957 there were only 10,000 Buddhists in the United States, but in 1970, 100,000 were here. (*Historical Statistics of the United States: Colonial Times to 1970*, Part 1, 1989). However, the *Handbook of Denominations in the U.S.* (Hill, 1990), published in 1990, shows 250,000 Buddhists in the United States.

Jacquet and Jones's (1991) *Yearbook of American and Canadian Churches* indicates that practicing Jews in the United States numbered 3,750,000, with a more inclusive count totaling 5,981,000 Jewish ''adherents.'' This larger group made up about 2 percent of the total U.S. population according to *Statistical Abstracts of the United States: 1994*. The U.S. Jewish population in 1960 numbered 5,367,000, thus giving a growth rate over thirty years of only about 11.4 percent (*Historical Statistics of the United States: Colonial Times to 1970*, Part 1, 1989).

In contrast, U.S. believers of the Muslim faith were estimated to number 3,000,000 in the 1990 *Handbook of Denominations in the U.S.* (Hill, 1990) The 1995 *World Almanac* gives a figure of 6,000,000 Muslim adherents within the United States. Even though these figures are not as precise as those for Christianity and Judaism, they do clearly indicate a significant growth rate for followers of Islam.

Christianity remains the largest religion in the United States, and Judaism may have already been surpassed for its number-two ranking by Muslim followers. This increase in the numbers of Muslims has resulted from immigration from such areas as Lebanon, Iran, Egypt, India, and Pakistan, as well as from the growth of the Black Muslims.

Given the fact that U.S. schools and textbooks have paid little attention to the teachings of the Islamic faith, this growth will represent a challenge. According to Uphoff (1974), "William J. Griswold, a key investigator in a thorough study of U.S. textbooks and their treatment of Islam in history, reports that twenty-seven of forty-five texts examined either have nothing on the Muslim world, are biased, simplistic, and error-filled, or are scanty and not always dependable in their treatment of Islam" (p. 201).

Such lack of knowledge about the Islamic faith and those who follow it led to major problems following the outbreak of the Persian Gulf War in January 1991. The January 27, 1991, issue of the *Dayton Daily News* ran a front-page story with the following headlines: "Ignorance Turns to Violence: Arab-Americans the Target of Misplaced Anger in Cleveland." The February 4, 1991, issue of *Time* addressed similar violence and then informed its readers that

> the attacks are one measure of widespread ignorance about the Arab-American community. Few are aware, for example, of the degree to which Arab-Americans have flourished in this country, rising to the ranks of White House chief of staff and Senate majority leader. ...Arab-Americans are better educated than the U.S. population as a whole, more likely to hold management or professional positions, and wealthier: an average household income of $22,973 is above the U.S. average of $20,973. (pp. 18–19)

The ABC-TV news program "Nightline" focused its February 8, 1991, show on the backlash against Arab Americans. It reported the frequent use of such derogatory terms as *camel jockey* and said that slogans such as "Arabs Go Home!" were being used much more often along with more violent actions. The show also reported that hate crimes against Arab Americans numbered forty-one in all of 1990, but that a total of thirty-six had been documented in January 1991.

It is obvious that such actions clearly demonstrate ignorance about the religion of Islam and the people who practice it. The problem becomes even more serious when we realize that this religion has the same roots as Christianity and Judaism (all three trace their heritage back to Abraham) and that Islam's adherents make up a sizable proportion of the U.S. population.

A report on languages other than English spoken in the United States is another source of data for our conjecturing about the nation's religious diversity. According to the report, in 1980 the primary languages spoken at home by persons between the ages of five and seventeen were as follows:

- Vietnamese, spoken by 64,000
- Korean, 60,000
- Japanese, 34,000
- Filipino, 63,000
- Chinese, 114,000
- Other non-European, 544,000

Spanish was the largest, with 2,952,000 speakers, but most of these children are within the Christian tradition, given their cultural heritage. Hundreds of thousands of children speaking languages other than English at home and coming from nations where religions other than Christianity and Judaism are practiced are now common in the United States and its schools.

The New Book of World Rankings (Kurian, 1991) has developed what it calls a homogeneity index to use when comparing nations on a scale of internal diversity. The book's introduction states:

> Political stability is often associated with linguistic and ethnic homogeneity. While developed societies in the West are moving toward pluralism and multi-culturalism, traditional societies in Asia and Africa are moving toward mono-cultures. Many governments are striving to create nations from heterogeneous populations and finding the task difficult. Because the primary loyalty of an individual in traditional societies is to his race, language, and religion, ethnicity becomes the basis for factional and separatist tendencies. (p. 43–44)

The index includes 135 countries, with the highest ranking indicating the most homogeneity. North and South Korea are tied for first and second place, with a homogeneity percentage of 100. Others in the top ten include South Yemen, Portugal, Japan, Haiti, Puerto Rico, Hong Kong, and Germany. The United States ranks 82:135, with a homogeneity percentage of only 50. These data indicate that the United States is among the most diverse nations in the world in terms of ethnicity, race, language, and religion.

Changes have also taken place within the dominant Christian community of the United States. Membership in many mainline denominations has declined during the past ten to twenty years, while fundamentalist religions have experienced growth. The figures below illustrate these patterns of growth and decline (Jacquet & Jones, 1991):

Denominations with Their Highest Membership Figures between 1960 and 1970

Christian Church (Disciples of Christ) (1965)

Church of the Brethren (1960)

Episcopal Church (1965)

Evangelical Lutheran Church in America (1965)

Lutheran Church—Missouri Synod (1970)

Presbyterian Church (USA) (1965)

Reformed Church in America (1965)

United Church of Christ (1960)

United Methodist Church (1965)

Denominations with Their Highest Membership Figures in 1989

Assemblies of God

Christian and Missionary Alliance

Church of Jesus Christ of Latter-Day Saints

Church of the Nazarene

Jehovah's Witnesses

Roman Catholic Church

Salvation Army

Seventh-Day Adventists

Southern Baptist Convention

Within many mainstream churches, movement also occurred during the 1970s and 1980s. Hill (1990) describes it as "the infusion of unfamiliar styles of Christian practice and expression into existing denominations" (pp. 262–263). He talks about many people who remain happily Lutheran or Episcopalian or Roman Catholic "while embracing new forms of spirituality that are more often 'Spirit-filled' than 'pentecostal.' " Hill contends that this movement was away from authority within a church and toward greater individuality. He sees a "moving from tradition to immediacy; from church as authoritative institution to free-form congregations and each individual; from prescribed worship to informal gatherings" (pp. 262–263). Combined with the other growing diversities of religious groups within the United States, schools now face a different public.

This change gave public school leaders many more headaches because they had to deal more frequently with individuals and with individual congregations than with only the local ministerial association. There was more scrutiny of more aspects of public education by more people than ever before in the nation's history.

EDUCATIONAL IMPLICATIONS

The high level of religious diversity in the United States is a fact. The public schools, which at one time were a public extension of a generalized Protestant belief system, can no longer fill that role. On the other hand, these same schools must be sure that they do not move in the opposite direction, to a position of open hostility to religion.

The mission of the public schools is a broad one and may go beyond what some religious groups deem acceptable. For example, people who object to the teaching of critical-thinking skills (and there are some) will most likely have to find an alternative to public education. Although the public schools cannot be all things to all people— they must be sure to be fair to all, respect all, and be open to all.

Specific implications of this state of diversity are focused on the following eight aspects of education:

1. Curriculum resources such as textbooks, library books, films, and speakers

2. Subject matter to be included in the curriculum, whether elective or required, such as values clarification, sex and health education, and religion

3. School rules of all types, such as teacher qualifications, school attendance, discipline, and dress codes, whether from the federal, state, or local level

4. Student services, such as psychological counseling, testing, and health care

5. School calendar decisions, historically tied to Christmas and Easter

6. Scheduling of student activities that interfere with the religious obser-
   vances of some students (e.g., athletic events on Friday nights)

7. Teaching methods that require student behaviors objectionable to some
   people, such as value clarification, decision-making, and thinking and
   debating skills

8. School financing, especially where local voters must approve new monies
   for the school budget, but even at the state level, where legislators are subject to intense political pressure

The factors described here have too often caused significant controversies within
a community, a state, or the entire nation. Headlines, television cameras, angry pro-
testers, emotional meetings, and court cases have been too common. To avoid such negative situations, every educator must first become better informed about religion in
general, and especially about its influence on human beings now and throughout history. The academic study of religion is vital for both teachers and students. Within the
public schools, the best place for this type of study to occur is wherever it logically falls
in the regular curriculum. In a home economics unit on food preparation, for example,
it would be logical to include how some religions have given their adherents rules to follow regarding the handling and consumption of foods in their daily lives. During a
unit on the Colonial period of American history, students could study the roles of the
various churches and how each affected the geographic area in which it was dominant.
The effects of beliefs on the decisions of individual leaders could be examined.

Curriculum resources need to be examined carefully. Earlier in this chapter the
lack of appropriate treatment of Islamic peoples and beliefs in U.S. history textbooks
was cited. An Associated Press story on May 28, 1986, carried the headline "Most High
School Texts Neglect Religion, Group Says." The article quotes People for the
American Way as follows: "Students aren't learning about America's rich and diverse
religious heritage because textbook publishers are still afraid of offending anyone, from
moral majoritarians to civil libertarians" (*The Journal Herald*, 1986, p. 16).

Another report, by the well-respected Association for Supervision and Curriculum
Development, refers to the "benign neglect" of religion by textbooks at all levels. It
states that "an elementary student can come away from a textbook account of the
Crusades, for example, with the notion that these wars to win the Holy Land for
Christendom were little more than exotic shopping expeditions" ("Panel of Educators
Ask End to 'Neglect' about Religions," 1987, p. 1+).

It is interesting that liberal and conservative political action groups, as well as educational groups, have arrived at the same conclusions regarding the inappropriate
treatment of religion in school textbooks. This was exactly the basis used by Judge
William Brevard Hand in his decision to ban dozens of books from use in schools.

In addition to becoming better educated about religion, educators must use appropriate teaching methods. The continuing controversy over the teaching of evolution
and the call for the balancing inclusion of "creation science" illustrate the need to use
effective and sensitive teaching methods. People who accept the story of creation in
Genesis and teach it to their children are highly offended when their children are told
by teachers that the parents are wrong. The anger of the parents is understandable.

How a teacher handles the teaching of evolution is crucial. Two possible exam questions illustrate how easy it is to avoid a direct confrontation with these children and their parents, and at the same time continue to teach the prescribed curriculum:

Poor   It took millions of years for the earth to evolve to its present state. (True/False)

Better   Evolutionists believe that it took millions of years for the earth to evolve to its present state. (True/False)

The first question requires the child to agree with a statement of "fact." The second question allows the child to answer that one group of people has a different set of beliefs than the child has, while at the same time protecting his or her own integrity. The difference is subtle, but powerful. The second question respects diversity of beliefs while teaching scientific information—that is, information about evolutionary theory. No child is forced to go against personal or family beliefs.

Such a change in teaching approaches will help reduce conflict between home and school. However, we need to be aware from the beginning that not everyone will be satisfied. Some people have such a narrow belief system that the public school system will never be able to satisfy them.

Teachers of all subject areas can benefit from the work done on teaching about religion by the National Council for the Social Studies (NCSS). The January 1981 issue of *Social Education* has as its theme "Teaching about Religion: Vistas Unlimited" and includes an article entitled "Instructional Issues in Teaching about Religion." This article calls for teachers to use a wide range of methodologies, including the use of music, skits, art, and role playing (Uphoff, 1981). It is next to impossible to teach students to think critically if they are limited to a single source of information, the textbook. A teacher's academic knowledge about religion as distinguished from personal, experiential knowledge is vital. The importance of the teacher's objectivity is also stressed, and specific teacher behaviors to bring this about are presented.

The NCSS (1984) published its official position, in an article entitled "Including the Study about Religions in the Social Studies Curriculum: A Position Statement and Guidelines." The fourteen guidelines it recommends are specific and helpful. Two guidelines are:

- Study about religions should stress the influence of religions on history, culture, the arts, and contemporary issues.

- Study about religions should be descriptive, nonconfessional, and conducted in an environment free of advocacy.

Sources of further help on teaching about religion within the public schools of the nation are available as follows:

- *Religion and Education*, a professional journal published at Webster University is available by contacting Cathy Heidemann at Webster University, 470 Lockwood, St. Louis, MO 63119-3194.

- The *Religion and Public Education Resource Center* contains all kinds of materials and curriculum guides. It is located at the Butte County Office of Education IRC in Oroville, CA 95395, tel. (916) 538-7847. It is jointly operated by California State University: Chico and Professor Bruce Grelle.

- The Association for Supervision and Curriculum Development has one of its Network groups devoted to this general topic, *The Religion and Public Education Network*. Nominal dues of $10 can be sent to Dr. Austin Creel, Dept. of Religion, Univ. of Florida, Box 117410, Gainesville, FL 32611-7410.

- *The Freedom Forum First Amendment Center* has published a guide entitled, *Finding Common Ground: A First Amendment Guide to Religion and Public Education.* Call (615) 321–9588 for details.

SUMMARY

The United States is a religiously diverse nation and is becoming more so every day. If the United States is to avoid the fractionalization and inner turmoil that have destroyed other diverse nations, the public schools must lead the nation in being sensitive to the diversity itself, and by helping students to learn about each other as well as about people in other parts of the world.

The old etiquette guide about not discussing religion or politics in mixed company has done more harm than good. It is not an appropriate policy for the schools of the United States as they prepare students for life in the twenty-first century.

Questions and Activities

1. What is the broad definition of religion developed by the Public Education Religious Studies Center? How is this definition of religion similar to and different from other definitions of religion with which you are familiar? With your own personal definition of religion?

2. What are the educational consequences of broad and narrow definitions of religion?

3. Prepare a report indicating the role religion has played in the history and culture of an ethnic group, such as Jewish Americans or African Americans. Helpful references are Irving Howe's *World of Our Fathers: The Journey of the East European Jews to America and the Life They Found and Made* (New York: Simon & Schuster, 1976); E. Franklin Frazier's *The Negro Church in America* (New York: Schocken Books, 1964); and *The Black Church in the African American Experience* (Durham, NC: Duke University Press, 1990) by C. Eric Lincoln and Lawrence H. Mamiya.

4. Uphoff points out that an increasing number of children now in U.S. schools have come from nations where religions other than Christianity and Judaism are common. This means that religious diversity is increasing in U.S. schools. What are the educational implications of the increasing religious diversity in U.S. schools?

5. Controversies have developed in many communities about the way Christmas is celebrated in the schools. In some communities, the school boards have established policies that prevent teachers from using religious songs or symbols in holiday celebrations during the Christmas season. What is your opinion of such school board policies? Give reasons to support your position.

6. According to the author, why is it important for students to study religion in the public schools?

7. Why do textbooks tend to ignore religion? How can teachers supplement the textbook treatment of religion? What guidelines should teachers keep in mind when teaching about religion in public schools? What knowledge and sensitivities should they have?

8. To develop a better understanding of religious and cultural diversity in U.S. society, attend services at several religious institutions within your community or region, such as a synagogue, a Catholic church, an African American Baptist church, a Buddhist temple, and a mosque. How are the services and rituals at these institutions alike and different?

References

Albanese, C. L. (1981). *America: Religions and Religion.* Belmont, CA: Wadsworth Publishing Co.

"Alleged 'Secular Humanism' Courses Attacked." (1986, October 15). *Education Week, 5*, p. 12.

Alter, J. and Wingert, P. (1995, February 6) Shame. How Do We Bring Back a Sense of Right and Wrong? *Newsweek*, pp. 20–25.

A Time to Seek. (1990, December 17). *Newsweek*, p. 51.

Bracher, P., Panoch, J. V., Piediscalzi, N., and Uphoff, J. K. (1974). *Public Education Religion Studies: Questions and Answers.* Dayton, OH: Public Education Religion Studies Center, Wright State University.

Gaustad, E. S. (1976). *Historical Atlas of Religion in America* (Rev. Ed.). New York: Harper & Row.

Goodrich, L. J. (1994, January 10). Religion is Alive and Diverse in US. *The Christian Science Monitor*, pp. 11–13.

Green, B. L. (1984). Solace, Self-Esteem, and Solidarity: The Role of Afro-American Folklore in the Education and Acculturation of Black Americans. *Texas Tech Journal of Education, 2*(1), p. 94.

Hill, S. S. (Ed.). (1990). *Handbook of Denominations in the U.S.* (9th Ed.). Nashville: Abington Press.

Historical Statistics of the United States: Colonial Times to 1970, Part 1. (1989). Washington, DC: U.S. Department of Commerce, Bureau of the Census.

Hundley, W. (1995, January 14). Prayerful Return? For Some the Abandoned Activity Never Left the Halls of Learning. *Dayton Daily News*, 6C.

Jacquet, C. H., Jr., and Jones, A. M. (Eds.). (1991). *Yearbook of American and Canadian Churches.* Nashville: Abington Press.

Keeler, B. (1994, January 20). Study Says We Lie about How Often We Go to Church. *Dayton Daily News,* 6C.

Kurian, G. T. (1991). *The New Book of World Rankings.* New York: Facts on File Publications.

Michaelsen, R. (1970). *Piety in the Public School.* New York: Macmillan.

Most High School Texts Neglect Religion, Group Says (1986, May 28). *The Journal Herald* (Dayton, OH), 16.

National Council for the Social Studies. (1985). Including the Study about Religion in the Social Studies Curriculum: A Position Statement and Guidelines. *Social Education, 49*(5), pp. 413–414.

Panel of Educators Ask End to 'Neglect' about Religions. (1987, July 2). *New York Times, 1*(9), 28.

The New Book of American Rankings. (1984). New York: Facts on File Publications.

The Search for the Sacred. (1994, November 28). *Newsweek,* 52+.

The World Almanac and Book of Facts: 1995. (1995). New York: World Almanac.

Time (1991, February 4), 18–19.

Uphoff, J. K. (1974). Religious Minorities: In or Out of the Culturally Pluralistic Curriculum? *Educational Leadership, 32*(3), 199–202.

Uphoff, J. K. (1981). Instructional Issues in Teaching about Religion. *Social Education, 45*(1), 22–27.

U.S. Bureau of the Census (1994). *Statistical Abstract of the United States: 1994,* 114th ed. Washington, DC: U.S. Government Printing Office.

Wilson, J. F. (1982). *Religion: A Preface.* Englewood Cliffs, NJ: Prentice-Hall.

Winik, L. W. (1995, March 19). Who Is Responsible? *Parade,* 6.

In classrooms and schools where gender equity exists, both male and female students are able to successfully pursue their interests and to actualize their talents, gifts, and academic promise.

PART

THREE

Gender

Social, economic, and political conditions for women have improved substantially since the women's rights movement emerged as part of the civil rights movement of the 1960s and 1970s. However, gender discrimination and inequality still exist in schools and in society at large. In 1992, the median earnings for women who were full-time workers were 71 percent of those for men, up from 70.2 percent in 1988. The status of women in the United States within the last two decades has changed substantially. More women are now working outside the home than ever before, and more women are heads of households. In 1993, 57.9 percent of women worked outside the home, making up 46 percent of the total work force. In 1990, 17 percent of households in the United States were headed by women. A growing percentage of women and their dependents constitute the nation's poor. Some writers use the term *the feminization of poverty* to describe this development. In 1989, almost half of poor families in the United States were headed by women.

The chapters in this part of the book describe the status of women in the United States, the ways in which schools perpetuate gender discrimination, and strategies that educators can use to create equal educational opportunities for female and male students. As Sadker, Sadker, and Long point out in chapter 6, both males and females are harmed by sexual stereotypes and gender discrimination. Tetreault describes how school knowledge is dominated by male perspectives and how teachers can infuse their curricula with perspectives from both genders and thereby expand their students' thinking and insights. Butler discusses how women of color have often been ignored by the women's movement, which is predominately a White, middle-class phenomenon. She describes perspectives and content that will enable teachers to integrate their curricula with the experiences and cultures of women of color.

Chapter 6

Gender and Educational Equality

Myra Sadker, David Sadker, and Lynette Long

"Boys are doctors. Girls are nurses," insisted the kindergarten class. Amazed that young children could be so firm in their stereotype, the teacher took the twenty-two youngsters on a field trip to a nearby hospital. She introduced them to a female doctor and a male nurse who talked with them about their jobs and gave them a tour of the hospital.

Upon returning to the classroom, the teacher emphasized her point, "Now you can see that boys can be nurses. Girls can be doctors."

"No they can't," the students insisted.

"What do you mean?" The teacher was stunned. "We visited the hospital and met a man who is a nurse and a woman who is a doctor. You saw them. They talked with you."

"Yes," chorused the children triumphantly, "but they lied" (Sadker, Sadker, & Klein, 1986).

As this real-life anecdote shows, sometimes it is easier to split an atom than to change an attitude. The past two decades have seen tremendous strides in abolishing sexism, but entrenched resistance remains. From the books they read, to the role models they see, to the way they are treated in classrooms, girls and boys continue to learn subtle yet powerful messages about separate and unequal opportunities based on gender.

This chapter provides an overview of how sexism operates in school, from curriculum and instruction to administration. Through a report card, it also shows the cost of sex bias: its influence on our nation's children. After highlighting current issues, the chapter concludes with strategies educators can use to make sure their classrooms are fair to all students regardless of gender.

CURRICULAR MATERIALS

Central to academic progress are the textbooks, workbooks, tests, encyclopedias, paperbacks, computer software, and a variety of other instructional materials teachers use every day. Administrators and teachers select educational materials based on a variety of criteria, including how well they match the needs of a particular school or group of students, how clearly they present the desired material, and how practical the materials are in terms of affordability and availability. These experts must also consider whether curricular materials reflect equity in their presentation of males and females.

Six Forms of Bias

Below is a description of six forms of sex bias educators can use to evaluate materials for gender equity (Sadker & Sadker, 1982a, 1982b). The description of each form reviews research and presents historical perspectives on how the form has been manifested in instructional material. Following these six forms of bias, the state of gender equity in curriculum today is assessed.

Linguistic Bias

Referring to the use of masculine terms and pronouns in curriculum materials, linguistic bias is one of the easiest forms of sex bias to detect and eliminate. In history texts, terms such as *caveman, forefathers,* and *mankind* inherently deny the contributions of women. Similarly, masculine occupational titles such as *mailman, policeman,* and *businessman* are labels that deny the participation of women in our society. So does use of the pronoun *he* to refer to all people.

Another form of linguistic bias occurs when women are identified in terms of being someone's wife or possession, as in this sentence: "Winston Williams and his wife and children moved to New York." When this is reworded to read, "The Williams family moved to New York," all members of the family are considered equally.

Stereotyping

Many studies indicate that children and adults have been stereotyped in textbooks. Boys typically are portrayed as exhibiting one set of values, behaviors, and roles, whereas girls are drawn with a different set of characteristics. In reading books, boys routinely have been shown as ingenious, creative, brave, athletic, achieving, and curious. Girls have been portrayed as dependent, passive, fearful, and docile victims. Adults have also been stereotyped in roles and careers. In a study of seventy-seven basal readers published between 1980 and 1982, Britton and Lumpkin found a total of 5,501 careers depicted; 64 percent were attributed to Anglo males, 14 percent to Anglo females, 17 percent to males of color, and 5 percent to females of color. The most common careers shown for Anglo males were soldier, farmer, doctor, and police officer. The most frequently shown role models for males of color were worker, farmer, warrior, Indian chief, and hunter. The most common careers for White women were mother, teacher, author, and princess. For females of color, mother and teacher also headed the list, followed by slave, worker, porter, and artist (Britton & Lumpkin, 1983).

Invisibility

Women have made significant contributions to the growth and development of the United States, yet few have appeared in the history books children are assigned to read. This form of sex bias (invisibility, or omission) has characterized not only history books, but also texts in reading, language arts, mathematics, science, spelling, and vocational education. For example, a 1972 study of science, math, reading, spelling, and social studies textbooks found that only 31 percent of all illustrations included females and that the percentage of females decreased as the grade level increased (Weitzman & Rizzo, 1974).

In another study, researchers analyzed 134 elementary readers and found males pictured twice as often as females and portrayed in three times as many occupations (Women on Words and Images, 1975). A 1970 study of history texts found that students had to read more than 500 pages before they found one page of information about women (Trecker, 1977). New history texts, published in the 1990s, still devote only 2 or 3 percent of book space to discussing the experiences or contributions of women (Sadker & Sadker, 1994). When girls and women are systematically excluded from curricular material, students are deprived of information about half the nation's people. When asked to name twenty famous women from American history, most students cannot do it. Typically, they list fewer than five (Sadker & Sadker, 1994).

Imbalance

Textbooks perpetuate bias by presenting only one interpretation of an issue, situation, or group of people. Often this one-sided view is presented because the author has limited space or decides that it is not feasible to present all sides of an issue in elementary textbooks. History textbooks contain many examples of imbalance, mostly minimizing the role of women. For example, Janice Trecker studied the most widely used history textbooks and found more information on women's skirt lengths than on the suffragist movement (Trecker, 1977). As a result of such imbalanced presentation, millions of students have been given limited perspectives concerning the contributions, struggles, and participation of women in U.S. society. Although more recent textbook studies show improvement, problems remain.

Unreality

Many textbooks have presented an unrealistic portrayal of U.S. history and contemporary life experience by glossing over controversial topics and avoiding discussion of discrimination and prejudice. For example, almost 50 percent of all marriages end in divorce, and one-third of all children will live with a single parent during part of their lives. Yet many textbooks portray the typical U.S. family as one having two adults, two children, a dog, and a house in suburbia. When controversial issues are not presented, students are denied the information they need to confront contemporary problems.

Fragmentation

Textbooks fragment the contributions of women by treating these contributions as unique occurrences rather than integrating them into the main body of the text. In fragmented textbooks, the contributions of important women are often highlighted in separate boxes or are contained in a separate chapter. Fragmentation communicates to readers that women are an interesting diversion but that their contributions do not constitute the mainstream of history and literature. Fragmentation and isolation also occur when women are depicted as interacting only among themselves and as having little or no influence on society as a whole. For example, textbook discussions of feminism often talk about how women are affected by this contemporary movement, but there is little analysis of the effect of the women's movement on other groups and on social issues.

Recent Progress

In 1972, Scott, Foresman, the first company to publish nonsexist guidelines, suggested that the achievements of women be recognized; that women and girls be given the same respect as men and boys; that abilities, traits, interests, and activities should not be assigned on the basis of male or female stereotypes; and that sexist language be avoided. Today most textbook publishers edit books for sexist language and produce guidelines for authors to improve the image of women. By following these guidelines and avoiding the six forms of sex bias presented here, authors can develop nonsexist texts and other curricular materials.

Although bias in educational materials still exists, some gains were made in the 1980s. For example, a study of the story problems in mathematics textbooks from the mid-1930s to the late 1980s found a greater proportion of story problems about women in textbooks used in the 1980s than in the 1970s or before (Nibbelink, Stockdale, & Mangru, 1986). A study of the Newbery Medal Award books from 1977 through 1984 also found the portrayal of women and girls less stereotypic. Also, compared to a 1971 study, the number of books with girls and women as the main character has increased substantially (Kinman & Henderson, 1985). Basal science texts are also more sensitive to the issue of sexism. A study of the illustrations of seven elementary science textbook series found that female children are represented with greater frequency than male children (Powell & Garcia, 1985). Unfortunately, gains in history have not been as impressive, and reviews of history textbooks have found that the contributions of women are still minimized (Davis, Ponder, Burlbaw, Garza-Lubeck, & Moss, 1986; Sadker & Sadker, 1994). To represent an accurate view of history, textbooks need to portray the role of the average, as well as the exceptional, woman in our nation's history.

The influence of sex bias in curriculum materials is significant. Misrepresentations and omissions can negatively affect the self-image, goals, and philosophy of girls. Children need strong, positive role models for the development of self-esteem. When females are omitted from books, a hidden curriculum is created, one that teaches children that females are less important and less significant in our society than males.

In contrast, studies show that bias-free materials can have a positive influence and can encourage students at various grade levels to change attitudes and behaviors as a result of their reading materials. One researcher found that children in grades 1 through 5 developed less stereotyped attitudes about jobs and activities after reading about people who successfully fought sex discrimination in nontraditional jobs (Scott, 1977). In a similar study, children who read instructional materials about girls in non-traditional roles were more likely to think that girls could perform the nontraditional activity of the narrative than children who read the same materials with boys as the main characters (Scott, 1986).

Educators who select gender-fair materials can encourage significant changes in their students. Bias-free materials in literature expand students' knowledge of changing sex roles and encourage greater flexibility in attitudes regarding appropriate behavior for females and males. In science and math, gender-fair materials provide females with encouragement to enter careers in these areas. In history, bias-free materials provide role models and demonstrate contributions of women in the history of this nation. But gender-fair curricular materials by themselves are not sufficient to create a nonsexist educational environment. Attention must also be paid to the process of instruction.

Instruction

The following scene, a general music class in action, reflects the subtle ways sex bias can permeate the instructional process (Carter, 1987).

As the bell rings, students take their seats. The girls are clustered in the front and on the right-hand side of the room, while the boys are predominantly on the other side of the room and in the back. This seating arrangement doesn't bother the students, they choose their own seats, and it doesn't seem to bother their teacher, Mrs. Howe, who makes no comment about the segregated arrangement.

Mrs. Howe starts the lesson by playing part of Mozart's *Symphony Concertante* on the casette player. After about five minutes, she turns to the class with questions.

Mrs. Howe: Who can tell me the name of this composer?

(A few hands are raised when John shouts out "Bruce Springsteen." After the laughter dies down, Mrs. Howe calls on Mitch.)

Mitch: Haydn.

Mrs. Howe: Why do you think so?

Mitch: Because yesterday you played Haydn.

Mrs. Howe: Close. Eric what do you think?

Eric: I don't know.

Mrs. Howe: Come on, Eric. During the last two weeks we have been listening to various Classical period composers. Out of those we've listened to, who wrote this piece?

(Silence)

MRS. HOWE: John, can you help Eric out?

JOHN: Beethoven.

MRS. HOWE: No, it's not Beethoven. Beethoven was more a Romantic period composer. Think.

(Mrs. Howe finally calls on Pam, who has had her hand half-raised during this discussion.)

PAM: I'm not sure, but is it Mozart?

MRS. HOWE: Uh-huh. Anyone else agree with Pam?

MITCH (CALLS OUT): It's Mozart. It's similar to the Mozart concerto you played yesterday.

MRS. HOWE: Very good. Can you tell us if this is another concerto he wrote?

MITCH: Yes, it's a violin concerto.

MRS. HOWE: That's almost right. It's a special concerto written for two instruments. To help you figure out the other instrument, let's listen to more of the piece.

(Mrs. Howe plays more of the piece and calls on Mitch.)

MITCH: Another violin.

MRS. HOWE: Peter?

PETER: A cello.

MRS. HOWE: You're all close. It's another string instrument, but it's not another violin or a cello.

RUTH (CALLS OUT): What about a viola?

MRS. HOWE: Ruth, you know I don't allow shouting out. Raise your hand next time. Peter?

PETER: A viola.

MRS. HOWE: Very good. This is a special kind of concerto Mozart wrote for both the violin and viola called *Symphony Concertante*. One reason why I want you to listen to it is to notice the difference between the violin and the viola. Let's listen to the melody as played first by the violin then the viola. Listen for the similarities and differences between the two.

This scenario demonstrates several important interaction patterns; in this sex-segregated classroom, Mrs. Howe called on the boys more often than the girls and asked them more higher-order and lower-order questions. She gave male students more specific feedback, including praise, constructive criticism, and remediation. Research shows that from grade school to graduate school, most classrooms demonstrate similar instructional patterns.

One large study conducted in the fourth, sixth, and eighth grades in more than 100 classrooms in four states and the District of Columbia found that teachers gave boys more academic attention than girls. They asked them more questions and gave them more precise and clear feedback concerning the quality of their responses. In contrast, girls were more likely to be ignored or given diffuse evaluation of the academic quality of their work (Sadker, M., & Sadker, D., 1985). Other research shows that these same patterns are prevalent at the secondary and postsecondary levels (Sadker, Sadker, & Klein, 1991).

One reason boys get more teacher attention is that they demand it. More likely to shout out questions and answers, they dominate the classroom airwaves. However, when boys call out, teachers accept their comments. In contrast, when girls call out teachers are more likely to reprimand them by saying things like, "In this class, we raise our hands before talking."

Another factor allowing boys to dominate classroom interaction is the widespread sex segregation that characterizes classrooms. Occasionally teachers divide their classrooms into sex-segregated lines, teams, work and play areas, and seating arrangements. More frequently, students sex-segregate themselves. Drawn to the sections of the classroom where the more assertive boys are clustered, the teacher is positioned to keep interacting with male students.

The conclusion of most interaction studies is that teachers give more attention (positive, negative, and neutral) to male students. However, some researchers emphasize that low-achieving males get most of the negative attention, while high-achieving boys get more positive and constructive academic contacts. But no matter whether they are high or low achievers, female students are more likely to be invisible and ignored (Brophy & Good, 1974; Sadker & Sadker, 1994).

The gender difference in classroom communications is more than a mere counting game of who gets the teacher's attention and who doesn't. Teacher attention is a vote of high expectations and commitment to a student. Decades of research show that students who are actively involved in classroom discussion are more likely to achieve and to express positive attitudes toward schools and learning (Flanders, 1970).

Most teachers do not want to be biased in their treatment of students and are completely unaware of inequitable interaction. On the positive side, studies show that with resources, awareness, and training, teachers can eliminate these patterns and achieve equity in how they teach female and male students. Given the crucial nature of this pervasive problem, it is unfortunate that most schools of education still do not include the issue in their teaching-preparation programs.

School Administration

Effective research on schools has highlighted the crucial role of the principal in encouraging student achievement. When principals become instructional leaders, student performance is enhanced. Student achievement scores rise when the principal is visible throughout the school, especially in classrooms; encourages staff to work as a team in meeting school goals; holds high expectations; and is actively involved in observing and analyzing the instructional process. To accomplish these goals, an effective administrator must have extensive teaching experience, a thorough understanding of the teaching-learning process, and positive human relations skills. Although women excel in these areas, the world of school administration still belongs to men.

Almost 70 percent of teachers in the United States are women, yet women account for less than 30 percent of the administrators. Research shows that women who attain positions in administration are as competent as or more competent than their male counterparts (Gross & Trask, 1965). Female administrators excel at the human relations skills essential to effective leadership. More aware of the problems facing teachers and more supportive of their staffs, female administrators create democratic school climates and are rated high in the areas of productivity and morale.

Women as administrators also have a positive influence on students. They focus more energy on the teaching-learning process and monitor student learning more carefully than their male colleagues do. One study showed that students of all socioeconomic levels achieved more in schools with female principals (Gross & Trask, 1965). Given this research-based demonstration of competence, the question remains, Why are so few women managing schools?

Historical Perspective

During the 1920s, women were well represented as leaders in educational administration. Two-thirds of the nation's superintendents in the West and Midwest were women. In 1928, 55 percent of all elementary school principals were women. But many of these early small schools served grades 1 through 8, and typically the eighth-grade teacher was also designated as the principal. As schools grew and full-time administrators became the norm, the number of women in administrative positions dropped precipitously. By the mid-1970s only 13 percent of the nation's principalships were filled by women. In terms of school level, only 18 percent of elementary school principals, 3 percent of junior high school principals, and less than 2 percent of senior high principals were female. By the early 1980s, some gains had been achieved, with women comprising 23 percent of elementary principals and 10 percent of secondary principals (Sadker, 1985).

Today women have higher career aspirations and have attained higher levels of education and training than ever before. By 1980, women had earned one-third of all doctorates and one-half of all masters degrees in educational administration. More than 50 percent of female teachers now express interest in educational administration.

Prejudice

Although the 1980s saw more female principals than the previous decades, problems remain. Women still are not selected as frequently as men: the higher the rung on the ladder, the fewer the women in administration. Study after study has demonstrated that when an equally qualified man and woman apply for the same administrative position, the man is more likely to get the job (Smith, Kalvelage, & Schmuck, 1982). Women must be more qualified, more experienced, and more skilled than their male colleagues to secure the administrative appointment. Male superintendents often view women through stereotypic lenses. They see them as too emotional and indecisive for administration, unable to manage budgets and finance, and plagued with problems related to menstruation and pregnancy.

Besides these blatant discriminatory attitudes, other informal barriers inhibit the entrance and promotion of women in educational administration. Job descriptions are often written in sex-stereotyped language that discourages women from applying. Women who decide to apply may find application forms that request personal information, such as marital status or number of children, questions implying that women are too busy with family responsibilities to do an adequate job. Female candidates for administrative positions find themselves facing screening committees comprised primarily of male personnel. Often these committees have a pro-male bias and favor applicants with so-called preadministrative experience, such as coaching.

Another barrier to administrative advancement is that most women enter teaching not as a stepping-stone to management but rather to work closely with children. Administrative duties away from the classroom are less attractive to these women who view their role primarily as working with children. Some women are also concerned about time commitments that may impinge on home and family responsibilities.

The result of prejudice as well as personal constraint is a dearth of women in administrative roles. Students are denied appropriate role models as well as the opportunity to be led by some of the best talent available to U.S. schools. When politics and prejudice control the selection process, schools and children lose access to the best leadership available.

REPORT CARD: THE COST OF SEXISM IN SCHOOL

Below is a report card you will not find in any elementary or secondary school (Sadker & Sadker, 1982a, 1982b; Sadker & Sadker, 1994). Nevertheless, it is an important evaluation. It reflects the loss that both girls and boys suffer because of sex bias in society and in education. Years after the passage of Title IX of the Education Amendments of 1972, the law that prohibits sex discrimination in schools receiving federal financial assistance, gender inequities continue to permeate schools.

Academic

Girls

- In the early grades, girls score ahead of boys in verbal skills; their academic performance is equal to that of boys in math and almost equal to boys in science. However, as they progress through school, their achievement test scores show significant decline. The scores of boys, on the other hand, continue to rise and eventually reach and surpass those of their female counterparts, particularly in the areas of math and science. Girls are the only group in our society that begins school ahead and ends up behind.

- Sex differences in mathematics become apparent at the middle school level. Male superiority increases as the level of mathematics becomes more difficult.

- Males outperform females on both the verbal and mathematics subsections of the Scholastic Assessment Test (SAT), and females do less well on the American College Testing Program Examination (ACT).

- The College Board Achievement Tests are required for admission to more selective colleges and universities. There are a total of fourteen achievement tests ranging from physics to U.S. history to foreign languages. Males outperform females on eleven of these tests by an average of twenty-five to thirty points. Females score only three or four points higher on only three achievements tests.

- Girls attain far fewer National Merit Scholarships awarded each year. These awards are based on the higher Preliminary Scholastic Aptitude Tests (PSAT) scores attained by boys.

- On tests for admission to graduate and professional schools, males outperform females on the Graduate Record Exam (GRE), the Medical College Admissions Test (MCAT), the Graduate Management Admissions Test (GMAT), and admissions tests for law, dental, and optometry schools.

- In spite of performance decline on standardized achievement tests, girls frequently receive better grades in school. This may be one of the rewards they get for being more quiet and docile in the classroom. However, their silence may be at the cost of achievement, independence, and self-reliance.

- Girls are more likely to be invisible members of classrooms. They receive fewer academic contacts, less praise and constructive feedback, fewer complex and abstract questions, and less instruction on how to do things for themselves.

- Girls who are gifted, especially in math and science, are less likely to participate in special or accelerated programs to develop their talent. Girls who suffer from learning disabilities are also less likely to be identified or to participate in special-education programs than are learning-disabled boys.

Boys

- Boys are more likely to be scolded and reprimanded in classrooms. Also, boys are more likely to be referred to school authorities for disciplinary action than are girls.

- Boys are far more likely to be identified as exhibiting learning disabilities, reading problems, and mental retardation.

- Not only are boys more likely to be identified as having greater learning and reading disabilities, but they also receive lower grades, and are more likely to be grade repeaters.

- The National Assessment of Educational Progress indicates that males perform significantly below females in writing achievement.

Psychological and Physical

Girls

- Although women achieve better grades than men, they are less likely to believe they can do college work. Females exhibit lower self-esteem than do males during secondary and higher education.

- Girls have less confidence than boys in their mathematical ability. The sex typing of mathematics as a masculine discipline may also be related to low female confidence and performance.

- Girls have a less positive attitude toward science than do boys. High school students view science, especially physical science, as a masculine subject.

- Despite extraordinary strides made by females in high school athletics, boys' participation and sports budgets are almost twice that of girls.

- One in ten teenage girls becomes pregnant every year. More than 40 percent of all adolescent girls who drop out of school do so because of pregnancy. Teenage pregnancy is related to a constellation of factors, including poverty, low self-esteem, academic failure, and the perception of few life options.

Boys

- Society socializes boys into an active, independent, and aggressive role. But such behavior is incongruent with school norms and rituals that stress quiet behavior and docility. This results in a pattern of role conflict for boys, particularly during the elementary years.

- Hyperactivity is estimated to be nine times more prevalent in boys than in girls. Boys are more likely to be identified as having emotional problems, and statistics indicate a higher suicide rate among males.

- Boys are taught stereotyped behaviors earlier and more harshly than girls; there is a greater probability that such stereotyped behavior will stay with them for life.

- Conforming to the male sex-role stereotype takes a psychological toll. Boys who score high on sex-appropriate behavior tests also score highest on anxiety tests.

- Males are less likely than females to be close friends with one another. When asked, most men identify women as their closest friends.

- Until recently, programs focusing on adolescent sexuality and teen pregnancy were directed almost exclusively at females. Males were ignored, and this permissive "boys will be boys" attitude translated into sexual irresponsibility.

- Males are more likely to succumb to serious disease and be victims of accidents or violence. The average life expectancy of men is approximately eight years shorter than that of women.

Career and Family Relationships

Girls

- When elementary school girls are asked to describe what they want to do when they grow up, they identify fewer career options than boys do.

- Starting at the middle school level, girls say that mathematics and science are less important and useful to career goals. The majority of girls enter college without completing four years of high school mathematics. This lack of preparation serves as a "critical filter" inhibiting or preventing girls from entering many careers in science, math, and technology.

- Girls from lower socioeconomic backgrounds are less likely to have plans for college than are those from more affluent families. Family finances are less likely to affect the college options of males.

- Teenagers who become mothers earn only about half the income of females who delay childbearing. When families are headed by young mothers, they are far more likely to be in poverty.

- In urban areas, many young males who drop out of school are likely to return to school. For young females who drop out, the return rate is very low.

- The preparation and counseling girls receive in school contribute to the economic penalties that they encounter in the workplace. Although over 90 percent of the girls in U.S. classrooms will work in the paid labor force for all or part of their lives, the following statistics reveal the cost of the bias they encounter.

- More than one-half of families headed by women live below the poverty level.

- A woman with a college degree typically earns little more than a male who is a high school dropout.

- A woman with a masters will earn approximately the same as a man with a bachelor's degree.

- While the typical working woman earns approximately 75 percent of a male worker's income, minority women earn even less.

- A majority of women work not for "extra" cash, but because of economic necessity. They are single, widowed, divorced, or separated, or married to spouses barely earning subsistence wages.

Boys

- Teachers and counselors often advise boys to enter sex-stereotyped careers and limit their potential in occupations such as kindergarten teacher, nurse, or secretary.

- Many boys build career expectations that are higher than their abilities. This results in later compromise, disappointment, and frustration.

- Both at school and at home, boys are taught to hide or suppress their emotions; as adults, they may find it difficult or impossible to show feelings toward their family and friends.

- Boys are actively discouraged from playing with dolls (except those that play sports or wage war). Few schools provide programs that encourage boys to learn about the skills of parenting. Many men, through absence and apathy, become not so much parents as "transparents." In fact, the typical father spends only twelve minutes a day interacting with his children.

- Men and women vary in their beliefs of the important aspects of a father's role. Men emphasize the need for the father to earn a good income and to provide solutions to family problems. Women, on the other hand, stress the need for fathers to assist in caring for children and in responding to the emotional needs of the family. These differing perceptions of fatherhood lead to family strain and anxiety.

- Scientific advances involving the analysis of blood and other body fluids now make possible genetic testing for paternity. Such testing, along with the passage of stricter laws and enforcement procedures for child support, have major implications for the role of males in parenting.

Even as this report card calls attention to remaining sex disparities in academic achievement, research in this area is undergoing a great deal of activity and change. Meta-analyses conducted at the end of the 1980s and in the early 1990s hold hope that these disparities are shrinking (Sadker, Sadker, & Klein, 1991). The gender gap is disappearing in verbal abilities and has decreased significantly in mathematics and spatial skills. This decrease is occurring extremely quickly and at a time when equal treatment of males and females has been encouraged. Such rapid change suggests that the academic gender gap has been caused more by socialization than by biological factors (Hyde, Fenneman, & Lamon, 1990; Hyde & Lynn, 1988). You will need to keep up with current research for the most up-to-date information on differences in how boys and girls achieve in school.

ONGOING PROBLEMS AND NEW ISSUES

The cost of sexism is obvious. As educators and other professionals fight the traditional barriers to female achievement, new issues are emerging for the 1990s. Many topics have attracted current attention, including nonsexist parenting and the role of fathers, and the potential conflict between cultural background and gender equity. In this chapter, two issues are explored in greater detail. It is important to note current developments related to single-sex schools, since research in the late 1980s demonstrated how viable these are for girls' achievement. Even as the evidence mounts in favor of these schools, they face extinction during the decade of the nineties. Also, since legal decisions in the 1980s threatened the power and coverage of Title IX (which prohibits sex discrimination in education), developments surrounding this law are discussed.

Single-Sex Schools

The past decades have witnessed a precipitous decline in U.S. single-sex secondary and postsecondary schools. The number of women's colleges has dwindled from almost 300 to fewer than 100. The widespread belief that single-sex education is an anachronism has caused many schools to become coeducational institutions or to close their doors. Single-sex high schools, typically private and parochial, are also vanishing. Further, Title IX, with good intention, has encouraged coeducation in all but the most limited public school situations, such as contact sports and sex education.

The trend toward coeducation continues on a national scale despite research suggesting the benefits of single-sex schools for female students. These benefits include increased academic achievement, self-esteem, and career salience, as well as a decrease in sex-role stereotyping. One study found that students in girls' schools in the United States expressed greater interest in both mathematics and English, took more mathematics courses, did more homework, and had more positive attitudes toward academic achievement (Lee & Bryk, 1986). Finally, research shows that girls in single-sex schools show more interest in the feminist movement and are less sex-role stereotyped than are their peers in coeducational schools (Sadker & Sadker, 1994). Recently, concern over gender bias in coeducation has prompted a resurgence of interest in girls' schools and women's colleges.

Title IX

By the mid-1970s, Title IX of the 1972 Educational Amendments was being implemented, with varying degrees of success, in the nation's 16,000 school districts. The Title IX legislation prohibits sex discrimination in all educational programs receiving federal assistance. Widely known for its application to sports, Title IX also prohibits sex discrimination in counseling, discipline, testing, admissions, medical facilities, the treatment of students, financial aid, and a host of educational activities. Although theoretically the vast majority of programs should have eliminated sex bias in the past decade, the reality has been less positive. Too often, sexist practices continue because of the unwillingness of parents and students to lodge complaints, or because of the slow pace of federal enforcement practices.

In the 1980s, the Grove City College case dealt Title IX a serious blow. The Supreme Court ruled that federal funds must be traced directly to the discriminatory activity before Title IX can be enforced. This decision meant that elementary and secondary schools as well as colleges and vocational programs could practice sex discrimination in all their programs except those directly receiving federal support. If a library was built with federal funds, for example, Title IX would prohibit sex discrimination in the library only. On the same campus or school, however, financial aid could be given legally only to male students without violating federal law. The Grove City College case jeopardized not only Title IX, but also much of the civil rights legislation currently on the books. At the end of the 1980s, Congress passed the Civil Rights Restoration Act, which nullified the Grove City College case. This new legislation should revitalize Title IX and protect all students and educators from sex discrimination if any school program receives federal assistance.

Creating Gender-Fair Education

Although the struggle against a sexist educational system is long and difficult, change is already taking place. Consider the following:

- Although both girls and boys typically picture sex-stereotyped occupations, girls are beginning to view more prestigious and lucrative professional careers as both attainable and desirable (Lenerz, 1987).

- In 1960 women comprised 35 percent of students in higher education. Today they are the majority.

- In 1958 the labor force participation rate of women stood at 33 percent; by 1990 it had reached 45 percent. Although most women are still overrepresented in low-paying jobs, barriers are falling as some women are entering higher-level positions previously held only by men (National Commission on Working Women, 1986; National Commission on Working Women, 1990).

- More than 600,000 students participated in a *Weekly Reader* national survey on the future. From ten statements describing the future, the largest number of students strongly agreed with the item predicting equal treatment of the sexes. Overwhelmingly, our nation's young people express egalitarian attitudes about roles for women and men (Johnson, 1987).

While change is possible, it takes time, effort, and commitment to break down barriers that have been in place for centuries. Following are ten key steps you can take to build nonsexist classrooms today (Sadker & Sadker, 1986).

1. If the textbooks you are given to use with students are biased, you may wish to confront this bias rather than ignore it. Discuss the issue directly with your students. It's entirely appropriate to acknowledge that texts are not always perfect. By engaging your students in a discussion about textbook omission and stereotyping, you can introduce them to important social issues and develop critical reading skills as well.

2. Supplementary materials can offset the influence of unrepresentative textbooks. School, university, and local libraries often have information on the lives and contributions of women and minority-group members.

3. Have your students help you assemble bulletin boards and other instructional displays. Teach them about the forms of bias and make sure that the displays they assemble are bias free.

4. Analyze your seating chart to determine whether there are pockets of race or gender segregation in your classroom. When your students work in groups, check to see if they are representative of the different populations in the class.

5. When students themselves form segregated groups, you may need to intervene. Establish ground rules to ensure that work and play groups and teams are representative. Explain to students why segregation on any basis (race, religion, national origin, or gender) is harmful to learning and the principles of a democratic society.

6. Reinforcement can be effective for increasing the amount of time boys and girls work and play in coeducational arrangements. In one study, teachers made a consistent effort to praise girls and boys who were working and playing cooperatively together. When teachers praised in this way, the amount of time girls and boys spent working and playing cooperatively increased.

7. Peer tutoring and cooperative learning can encourage gender integration. Moreover, these techniques increase achievement not only for the students being helped, but for those doing the helping as well. Even though the research shows that peer tutoring and cooperative learning are effective techniques, they should be used as supplements to (not replacements for) teacher-led instruction. Also, both peer tutoring and cooperative learning are much more powerful when students receive training in how to tutor and work constructively with others. Where such training is not given, boys tend to dominate cooperative learning groups.

8. Most teachers find it difficult to track their own questioning patterns while they are teaching. Try to have someone do this for you. Make arrangements to have a professional whose feedback you value (a supervisor, your principal, another teacher) come into your classroom and observe. Your observer can tally how many questions you ask boys and how many you ask girls, how many questions you ask majority and how many you ask minority students. Then you can consider the race and sex of your involved and silent students and determine whether one sex or race is receiving more than its fair share of your time and attention.

9. Because teachers may find it difficult to have professional observers come into their classrooms on a regular basis, many have found it helpful to have students keep a tally of questioning patterns. Before you do this, you may want to explain to the class how important it is for all students to get involved in classroom discussion.

10. Because research on sex equity in education is occurring at a rapid pace, it is important to continue your reading and professional development in this area. Be alert for articles and other publications on the topic, and be careful that your own rights are not denied because of sex discrimination.

When teachers become aware of the nature and cost of sex bias in schools, they can make an important difference in the lives of their students. Teachers can reduce sexism in schools or even make it obsolete. They can make sex equity a reality for children in our schools. Then tomorrow's children, boys and girls, need not suffer from the limiting effects of sexism in school.

Questions and Activities

1. The authors of this chapter list six forms of gender bias that you can use when evaluating instructional materials: (a) linguistic bias, (b) stereotyping, (c) invisibility, (d) imbalance, (e) unreality, and (f) fragmentation. Define each form of bias. Examine a sample of social studies, language arts, reading, science, or mathematics textbooks (or a combination of two kinds of textbooks) to determine whether they contain any of these forms of gender bias. Share your findings with your classmates or workshop participants.

2. Give some examples of how teachers can supplement textbooks to help to eliminate the six forms of gender bias identified in activity 1 above.

3. What are some of the behavioral and attitudinal consequences for students of gender bias in curriculum materials? Of gender-fair curriculum materials?

4. In what ways do Mrs. Howe's interactions with the boys and girls during the music lesson indicate gender bias? How can Mrs. Howe be helped to change her behavior and to make it more gender fair?

5. Observe lessons being taught in several classrooms that include boys and girls and students from different racial and ethnic groups. Did the ways the teachers interacted with males and female students differ? If so, in what ways? Did the teachers interact with students from different ethnic groups differently? If so, in what ways? Did you notice any ways that gender and ethnicity combined to influence the ways the teachers interacted with particular students? If so, explain.

6. What are the major reasons there are fewer women than men who are educational administrators? Are more women likely to become educational administrators in the future? Why or why not?

7. Girls start out in school ahead of boys in speaking, reading, and counting. Boys surpass girls in math performance by junior high school. Why do you think this happens? Recent research indicates that the disparities in the academic achievement of boys and girls are declining. Why do you think they are?

8. In what ways, according to the authors, are single-sex schools beneficial for females? Why do you think all-girls schools are vanishing? Do you think this trend should be halted? Why or why not?

9. After reading this chapter, do you think there are some ways you can change your behavior to make it more gender fair? If yes, in what ways? If no, why not?

References

Britton, G., and Lumpkin, M. (1983). Females and Minorities in Basal Readers. *Interracial Books for Children Bulletin, 14*(6), 47.

Brophy, J., and Good, T. (1974). *Teacher Student Relationships: Causes and Consequences.* New York: Holt, Rinehart and Winston.

Carter, R. (1987). Unpublished class paper. American University, Washington, DC. Used with permission.

Davis, O. L. Jr., Ponder, G., Burlbaw, L., Garza-Lubeck, M., and Moss, A. (1986). *Looking at History: A Review of Major U.S. History Textbooks.* Washington, DC: People for the American Way.

Flanders, N. (1970). *Analyzing Teaching Behaviors.* Reading, MA: Addison-Wesley.

Gross, N. and Trask, A. (1965). *Men and Women as Elementary School Principals.* Cambridge: Harvard University Press.

Hyde, J., Fenneman, E., and Lamon, S. (1990). Gender Differences in Mathematical Performance: A Meta-Analysis. *Psychological Bulletin, 107,* 139–155.

Hyde, J., and Lynn, M. (1988). Gender Differences in Verbal Activity: A Meta-Analysis. *Psychological Bulletin, 104,* 53–69.

Johnson, L. (1987, May-June). Children's Visions of the Future. *The Futurist, 21*(3), 36–40.

Kinman, J. and Henderson, D. (1985, May). An Analysis of Sexism in Newbery Medal Award Books from 1977 to 1984. *The Reading Teacher, 38,* 885–889.

Lee, V. and Bryk, A. (1986, October). Effects of Single-Sex Secondary Schools on Student Achievement and Attitudes. *Journal of Educational Psychology, 78*(5), 381–395.

Lenerz, K. (1987). *Factors Related to Educational and Occupational Orientations in Early Adolescence.* Paper presented at the American Educational Research Association, Washington, DC.

National Commission on Working Women. (1986). *An Overview of Women in the Workforce.* Washington, DC.

National Commission on Working Women. (1990). *Wider Opportunities for Women.* Washington, DC: Women and Work.

Nibbelink, W., Stockdale, S., and Mangru, M. (1986, October). Sex Role Assignments in Elementary School Mathematics Textbooks. *The Arithmetic Teacher, 34,* 19–21.

Powell, R. and Garcia, J. (1985). The Portrayal of Minorities and Women in Selected Elementary Science Series. *Journal of Research in Science Teaching 22*(6) 519–533.

Sadker, D. and Sadker, M. (1985, January). Is the O.K. Classroom O.K.? *Phi Delta Kappan, 66,* 358–361.

Sadker, M. (1985). Women in Educational Administration. Washington, DC: The Mid-Atlantic Center for Sex Equity.

Sadker, M. and Sadker, D. (1982a). *Sex Equity Handbook for Schools.* New York: Longman.

Sadker, M. and Sadker, D. (1982b, reprinted and updated, 1990). The Report Card. *Sex Equity Handbook for Schools.* New York: Longman. Reprinted, Carnegie Foundation.

Sadker, M. and Sadker, D. (1994, updated for this chapter). *Failing at Fairness: How America's Schools Cheat Girls.* New York: Scribners. The Report Card copyright of David and Myra Sadker. All rights reserved; no part may be reproduced or transmitted without permission from the authors.

Sadker, M. and Sadker, D. (1985). *Effectiveness and Equity in College Teaching: Final Report.* Washington, DC: Fund for the Improvement of Education.

Sadker, M. and Sadker, D. (1986). *PEPA (Principal Effectiveness, Pupil Achievement): A Training Program for Principals and Other Educational Leaders.* Washington, DC: American University. Ten steps copyright of David and Myra Sadker. All rights reserved.

Sadker, M. and Sadker, D. (1994). *Failing at Fairness: How America's Schools Cheat Girls.* New York: Scribners.

Sadker, M., Sadker, D., and Klein, S. (1986, Autumn). Abolishing Misperceptions about Sex Equity in Education. *Theory into Practice, 25,* 220–226.

Sadker, M., Sadker, D., and Klein, S. (1991). The Issue of Gender in Elementary and Secondary Education. *Review of Research in Education.* Washington, DC: American Educational Research Association.

Scott, K. (1977). Elementary Pupils' Perceptions of Reading and Social Studies Materials: Does the Sex of the Main Character Make a Difference? (Dissertation, University of Washington). *Dissertation Abstracts,* 780973.

Scott, K. (1986, Spring). Effects of Sex-Fair Reading Materials on Pupils' Attitudes, Comprehension, and Interest. *American Educational Research Journal, 23,* 105–116.

Smith, M., Kalvelage, J., and Schmuck, P. (1982). *Women Getting Together and Getting Ahead.* Washington, DC: Women's Educational Equity Act Program.

Trecker, J. L. (1977). Women in U.S. History High-School Textbooks. In J. Pottker and A. Fishel (Eds.). *Sex Bias in the Schools: The Research Evidence* (pp. 146–161). Cranbury, CT: Associated University Presses.

Weitzman, L. and Rizzo, D. (1974). *Biased Textbooks.* Washington, DC: The Resource Center on Sex Roles in Education.

Women on Words and Images. (1975). *Dick and Jane as Victims: Sex Stereotyping in Children's Readers.* Princeton, NJ: Women on Words and Images.

Chapter 7

Classrooms for Diversity: Rethinking Curriculum and Pedagogy

Mary Kay Thompson Tetreault

> It's time to start learning about things they told you you
> didn't need to know—learning about me, instead of learning
> about them, starting to learn about her instead of learning
> about him. It's a connection that makes education education.
> (A student of European and African American ancestry)

This student's reflection on her education signals a twin transformation that is pushing us to rethink our traditional ways of teaching. The first is that students in our classrooms are increasingly more diverse and the second is that traditional course content has been enriched by the new scholarship on women, cultural studies, and multiculturalism. It is in the classroom that these transformations intersect, and it rests on the teacher to make education "education" for this student and the majority who feel their education was not made for them—women of all backgrounds, people of color, and men who lack privilege because of their social class—by bringing the two together. The current challenges to classroom teachers are not only to incorporate multiple perspectives into the curriculum but also to engage in pedagogical practices that bring in the voices of students as a source for learning rather than managing or controlling them.

FEMINIST PHASE THEORY

One of the most effective ways I have found to set a frame for envisioning a gender-balanced, multicultural curriculum, while at the same time capturing the reforms that have occurred over the past twenty-five years, is feminist phase theory. Conceptually rooted in the scholarship on women, feminist phase theory is a classification system of the evolution in thought about the incorporation of women's traditions, history, and experiences into selected disciplines. The model I have developed identifies five common phases of thinking about women: *male-defined curriculum, contribution curriculum, bifocal curriculum, women's curriculum,* and *gender-balanced curriculum.* A gender-balanced perspective, one that is rooted in feminist scholarship, takes into account the experiences, perspectives, and voices of women as well as men. It examines the similarities and differences between women and men but also considers how gender interacts with such factors as ethnicity and class.

The language of this system or schema, particularly the word *phase*, and the description of one phase and then another suggest a sequential hierarchy in which one phase supplants another. Before reviewing the schema, please refrain from thinking of these phases in a linear fashion; envision them as a series of intersecting circles, or patches on a quilt, or threads in a tapestry, which interact and undergo changes in response to one another. It is more accurate to view the phases as different emphases that coexist in feminist research. The important thing is that teachers, scholars, and curriculum developers ask and answer certain questions at each phase.

In the section that follows, I identify key concepts and questions articulated initially at each phase, using examples from history, literature, and science, and then I discuss how the phases interact and undergo changes in response to one another. The final part of this chapter shows teachers grappling with the intersection of changes in the disciplines and changes in the student population and presents four themes of analysis: mastery, voice, authority and positionality. The chapter concludes with specific objectives, practices, and teaching suggestions for incorporating content about women into the K–12 curriculum in social studies, language arts, and science.

Male-Defined Curriculum

Male-defined curricula rest on the assumption that the male experience is universal, that it is representative of humanity, and that it constitutes a basis for generalizing about all human beings. The knowledge that is researched and taught, the substance of learning, is knowledge articulated by and about men. There is little or no consciousness in it that the existence of women as a group is an anomaly calling for a broader definition of knowledge. The female experience is subsumed under the male experience. For example, feminist scientists have cited methodological problems in some research about sex differences that draws conclusions about females based on experiments done only on males or that uses limited (usually White, middle class) experimental populations from which scientists draw conclusions about all males and females.

The incorporation of women into the curriculum has not only taught us about women's lives but has also led to questions about our lopsided rendition of men's lives, wherein we pay attention primarily to men in the public world and conceal their lives in the private world. Historians, for example, are posing a series of interesting questions about men's history: What do we need to unlearn about men's history? What are the taken-for-granted truths about men's history that we need to rethink? How do we get at the significant masculine truths? Is man's primary sense of self defined in relation to the public sphere only? How does it relate to boyhood, adolescence, family, life, recreation, and love? What does this imply about the teaching of history?

Feminist scholarship, like African American, Native American, Latino, and Asian scholarship, reveals the systematic and contestable exclusions in the male-defined curriculum. When we examine it through the lens of this scholarship, we are forced to reconsider our understanding of the most fundamental conceptualization of knowledge and social relations within our society. We understand in a new way that knowledge is a social construction, written by individual human beings who live and think at a particular time and within a particular social framework. All works in literature, science, and history, for example, have an author—male or female, White, or ethnic or racial minority, elite or middle-class or occasionally poor—with motivations and beliefs. The scientist's questions and activities, for instance, are shaped, often unconsciously, by the great social issues of the day (see Table 7.1). Different perspectives on the same subject will change the patterns discerned.

Table 7.1 Male-Defined Curriculum

Characteristics of Phase	Questions Commonly Asked about Women in History*	Questions Commonly Asked about Women in Literature*	Questions Commonly Asked about Women in Science*
The absence of women is not noted. There is no consciousness that the male experience is a "particular knowledge" selected from a wider universe of possible knowledge and experience. It is valued, emphasized, and viewed as the knowledge most worth having.	Who is the author of a particular history? What is her or his race, ethnicity, religion, ideological orientation, social class, place of origin and historical period? How does incorporating women's experiences lead to new understandings of the most fundamental ordering of social relations, institutions, and power arrangements? How can we define the content and methodology of history, so it will be a history of us all?	How is traditional humanism, with an integrated self at its center and an authentic view of life, in effect part of patriarchal ideology? How can the objectivist illusion be dismantled? How can the idea of a literary canon of "great literature" be challenged? How are writing and reading political acts? How do race, class, and gender relate to the conflict, sufferings, and passions that attend these realities? How can we study language as specific *discourse*, that is specific linguistic strategies in specific situations, rather than as universal language?	How do scientific studies reveal cultural values? What cultural, historical, and gender values are projected onto the physical and natural world? How might gender be a bias that influences choice of questions, hypotheses, subjects, experimented design, or theory formation in science? What is the underlying philosophy of an andocentric science that values objectivity, rationality, and dominance? How can the distance between the subject and the scientific observer be shortened so that the scientist has some feeling for or empathy with the organism? How can gender play a crucial role in transforming science?

*New questions generated by feminist scholars.

Contribution Curriculum

Early efforts to reclaim women's rightful place in the curriculum were a search for missing women within a male framework. Although there was the recognition that women were missing, men continued to serve as the norm, the representative, the universal human being. Outstanding women emerged who fit this male norm of excellence or greatness or conformed to implicit assumptions about appropriate roles for women outside the home. In literature, female authors were added who performed well within the masculine tradition, internalizing its standards of art and its views on social roles. Great women of science, who have made it in the male scientific world, most frequently Marie Curie, for example, were added.

Examples of contribution history can be seen in U.S. history textbooks. They now include the contributions of notable American women who were outstanding in the public sphere as rulers or as contributors to wars or reform movements to a remarkable degree. Queen Liliuokalani, Hawaii's first reigning queen and a nationalist, is included in the story of the kingdom's annexation. Molly Pitcher and Deborah Sampson are depicted as contributors to the Revolutionary War, as is Clara Barton to the Civil War effort. Some authors have also included women who conform to the assumption that it is acceptable for women to engage in activities outside the home if they are an extension of women's nurturing role within the family. Examples of this are Dorothea Dix, Jane Addams, Eleanor Roosevelt, and Mary McLeod Bethune (Tetreault, 1986).

The lesson to be learned from understanding these limitations of early contribution history is not to disregard the study of notable women, but to include those who worked to reshape the world according to a feminist reordering of values. This includes efforts to increase women's self determination through a feminist transformation of the home, increased education, women's rights to control their bodies, to increase their political rights, and to improve their economic status. A history with women at the center moves beyond paying attention to caring for the unfortunate in the public sphere to how exceptional women influenced the lives of women in general (see Table 7.2). Just as Mary McLeod Bethune's role in the New Deal is worth teaching to our students, so is her aggressive work to project a positive image of Black women to the nation through her work in Black women's clubs and the launching of the *Afro-American Woman's Journal.*

Bifocal Curriculum

In bifocal curricula, feminist scholars have made an important shift, from a perspective that views men as the norm to one that opens up the possibility of seeing the world through women's eyes. This dual vision, or bifocal perspective, generated global questions about women and about the differences between women and men. Historians investigated the separation between the public and the private sphere and asked, for example, how the division between them explains women's lives. Some elaborated on the construct by identifying arenas of female power in the domestic sphere. Literary critics aimed to provide a new understanding of a distinctively female literary tradi-

Table 7.2 Contribution Curriculum

Characteristics of Phase	Questions Commonly Asked about Women in History	Questions Commonly Asked about Women in Literature	Questions Commonly Asked about Women in Science
The absence of women is not noted. There is a search for missing women according to a male norm of greatness, excellence, or humanness. Women are considered exceptional, deviant, or other. Women are added into history, but the content and notions of historical significance are not challenged.	Who are the notable women missing from history and what did they and ordinary women contribute in areas or movements traditionally dominated by men, for example during major wars or during reform movements like abolitionism or the labor movement? What did notable and ordinary women contribute in areas that are an extension of women's traditional roles, for example, caring for the poor and the sick? How have major economic and political changes like industrialization or extension of the franchise affected women in the public sphere? How did notable and ordinary women respond to their oppression, particularly through women's rights organizations? *Who were outstanding women who advocated a feminist transformation of the home, who contributed to women's greater self-determination through increased education, the right to control their bodies, to increase their political rights, and to improve their economic status? *What did women contribute through the settlement house and labor movements?	Who are the missing female authors whose subject matter and use of language and form meet the male norm of "masterpiece?" What primary biological facts and interpretations are missing about major female authors?	Who are the notable women scientists who have made contributions to mainstream science? How is women's different (and inferior) nature related to hormones, brain lateralization, and sociobiology? Where are the missing females in scientific experiments? What is the current status of women within the scientific profession? *How does adding minority women into the history of science reveal patterns of exclusion and recast definitions of what it means to practice science and to be a scientist? *How is the exclusion of women from science related to the way science is done and thought? *What is the usual pattern of women working in science? How is it the same as or different from the pattern of notable women? *How do our definitions of science need to be broadened to evaluate women's contributions to science? Do institutions of science need to be reshaped to accommodate women? If so, how?

*New questions generated by feminist scholars.

tion and a theory of women's literary creativity. They sought to provide models for understanding the dynamics of female literary response to male literary assertion and coercion. Scientists grapple with definitions of woman's and man's nature by asking how the public and private, biology and culture, and personal and impersonal inform each other and affect men and women, science, and nature.

Scholars have pointed out some of the problems with bifocal knowledge. Thinking about women and men is dualistic and dichotomized. Women and men are thought of as having different spheres, different notions of what is of value in life, different ways of imagining the human condition, and different associations with nature and culture. But both views are valued. In short, women are thought of as a group that is complementary but equal to men; there are some truths for men and there are some truths for women. General analyses of men's and women's experiences often come dangerously close to reiterating the sexual stereotypes scholars are trying to overcome. Because many believe that the public sphere is more valuable than the private sphere, there is a tendency to slip back into thinking of women as inferior and subordinate.

The generalized view of women and men that predominates in the bifocal curriculum often does not allow for distinctions within groups as large and as complex as women and men. Important factors like historical period, geographic location, structural barriers, race, paternity, sexual orientation, and social class, to name a few, clearly make a difference.

Other common emphases in the bifocal curriculum are the oppression of women and exploration of that oppression. Exposés of woman-hating in history and literature are common. The emphasis is on the misogyny (the hatred of women) of the human experience, particularly the means men have used to advance their authority and to assert or imply female inferiority. The paradoxes of women's existence are sometimes overlooked with this emphasis on oppression. For example, although women have been excluded from positions of power, a few of them as wives and daughters in powerful families were often closer to actual power than were men. If some women were dissatisfied with their status and role, most women adjusted and resisted efforts to improve women's lot. Too much emphasis on women's oppression perpetuates a patriarchal framework presenting women as primarily passive, reacting only to the pressures of a sexist society. In the main, it emphasizes men thinking and women being thought about.

Women's scholarship during the 1970s and 1980s has helped us see that understanding women's oppression is more complex than we initially thought. We do not yet have adequate concepts to explain gender systems, founded on a division of labor and sexual asymmetry. To understand gender systems, it is necessary to take a structural and experiential perspective that asks from a woman's point of view where we are agents and where we are not; where our relations with men are egalitarian and where they are not. This questioning may lead to explanations of why women's experiences and interpretations of their world can differ significantly from men's.

Further, the concepts with which we approach our analysis need to be questioned. Anthropologists have pointed out that our way of seeing the world—for instance, the idea of complementary spheres for women (the private sphere) and men (the public sphere)—is a product of our experience in a Western, modern, industrial, capitalistic state with a specific history. We distort our understanding of other social systems by imposing our world view on them. Feminist critics are calling for rethinking, not only of categories like the domestic versus the public sphere, and production and reproduction but even of categories like gender itself.

Feminist scholars have helped us see the urgency of probing and analyzing the interactive nature of the oppressions of race, ethnicity, class, and gender. We are reminded that we can no longer take a liberal reformist approach that does not probe the needs of the system that are being satisfied by oppression. We have to take seriously the model of feminist scholarship that analyzes women's status within the social, cultural, historical, political, and economic contexts. Only then will issues of gender be understood in relation to the economic needs of both male dominance and capitalism that undergird such oppressions.

One of the most important things we have learned about a bifocal perspective is the danger of generalizing too much, of longing for women's history, instead of writing histories about women. We must guard against establishing a feminist version of great literature and then resisting any modifications or additions to it. We have also learned that the traditional disciplines are limited in their ability to shed light on gender complexities, and it becomes apparent that there is a need for an interdisciplinary perspective (see Table 7.3).

Women's Curriculum

The most important idea to emerge in women's scholarship is that women's activities, not men's, are the measure of significance. What was formerly devalued, the content of women's everyday lives, assumes new value as scholars investigate female rituals, housework, childbearing, child rearing, female sexuality, female friendship, and studies of the life cycle. For instance, scientists investigate how research on areas of primary interest to women—menstruation, childbirth, and menopause—challenge existing scientific theories. Historians document women's efforts to break out of their traditional sphere of the home in a way that uses women's activities, not men's, as the measure of historical significance. These activities include women's education, women's paid work and volunteer work outside the home, particularly in women's clubs and associations. Of equal importance is the development of a collective feminist consciousness, that is, of women's consciousness of their own distinct role in society. Analyses begun in the bifocal phase continue to explore what sex and gender have meant for the majority of women.

Bifocal Curriculum

As scholars look more closely at the complex patterns of women's lives, they see the need for a pluralistic conceptualization of women. Although thinking of women as a monolithic group provides valuable information about patterns of continuity and change in those areas most central to women's lives, generalizing about a group as vast and diverse as women leads to inaccuracies. The subtle interactions among gender and other variables are investigated. Historians ask how the particulars of race, ethnicity, social class, marital status, and sexual orientation challenge the homogeneity of women's experiences.

Table 7.3 Bifocal Curriculum

Characteristics of Phase	Questions Commonly Asked about Women in History	Questions Commonly Asked about Women in Literature	Questions Commonly Asked about Women in Science
Human experience is conceptualized primarily in dualist categories: male and female, private and public, agency and communion. Emphasis is on a complementary but equal conceptualization of men's and women's spheres and personal qualities. There is a focus on women's oppression and on misogyny. Women's efforts to overcome the oppression are presented. Efforts to include women lead to the insight that the traditional content, structure, and methodology of the disciplines are more appropriate to the male experience.	How does the vision between the public and the private sphere explain women's lives? Who oppressed women, and how were they oppressed? *What are forms of power and value in women's worlds? *How have women been excluded from and deprived of power and value in men's spheres? *How do gender systems create divisions between the sexes such that experience and interpretations of their world can differ significantly from men's? *How can we rethink categories like public and private, productive and reproductive, sex and gender?	Who are the missing minor female authors whose books are unobtainable, whose lives have never been written, and whose works have been studied casually, if at all? How is literature a record of the collective consciouness of patriarchy? What myths and stereotypes about women are present in male literature? How can we critique the meritocratic pretensions of traditional literary history? How can we pair opposite-sex texts in literature as a way of understanding the differences between women's and men's experiences? How is literature one of the expressive modes of a female subculture that developed with the distinction of separate spheres for women and men? *How can feminist literary critics resist establishing their own great canon of literature and any additions to it?	How have the sciences defined (and misdefined) the nature of women? Why are there so few women scientists? What social and psychological forces have kept women in the lower ranks or out of science entirely? How do women fit into the study of history of science and health care? How do scientific findings, originally carried out on males of a species, change when carried out on the females of the same species? How do the theories and interpretations of sociobiology require constant testing and change to fit the theory for males and females with regard to competition, sexual selection, and infanticide? How does the science/gender system—the network of associations and disjunctions between public and private, personal and impersonal, and masculine and feminine—inform each other and affect men and women, science and nature? *What are the structural barriers to women in science?

*New questions generated by feminist scholars.

Questions about sex and gender are set within historical, ideological, and cultural contexts, including the culture's definition of the facts of biological development and what they mean for individuals. Researchers ask, for example, Why are these attitudes toward sexuality prevalent at this time in history? What are the ways in which sexual words, categories, and ideology mirror the organization of society as a whole? What are the socioeconomic factors contributing to them? How do current conceptions of the body reflect social experiences and professional needs?

Life histories and autobiographies shed light on societies' perceptions of women and women's perceptions of themselves. Women's individual experiences are revealed through these stories and contribute to the fashioning of the human experience from the perspective of women.

Scholars find it necessary to draw on other disciplines for a clearer vision of the social structure and culture of societies as individuals encounter them in their daily life. Likewise, there are calls for new unifying frameworks and different ways to think of periods in history and literature to identify concepts that accommodate women's history and traditions. There is also a more complex conceptualization of historical time. The emphases in much history are on events, a unit of time too brief to afford a sense of structural change, changes in the way people think about their own reality, and the possibilities for other realities. *L'Ecole des Annales* in France (a group of historians who pioneered the use of public records such as birth, marriage, and death certificates in historical analysis) has distinguished between events and what they call the *longue durée* (Letters to the Editors, 1982). By the *longue durée* they mean the slow, glacial changes, requiring hundreds of years to complete, that represent significant shifts in the way people think.

Examples of areas of women's history that lend themselves to the concept are the structural change from a male-dominated to an egalitarian perspective, and the transformation of women's traditional role in the family to their present roles as wives, mothers, and paid workers outside the home. Also important is the demographic change in the average number of children per woman of childbearing age from seven to fewer than two children between 1800 and 1990 (see Table 7.4).

Gender-Balanced Curriculum

This phase continues many of the inquiries begun in the women's curriculum phase but articulates questions about how women and men relate to and complement one another. Conscious of the limitations of seeing women in isolation and aware of the relational character of gender, researchers search for the nodal points at which women's and men's experiences intersect. Historians and literary critics ask if the private, as well as the public, aspects of life are presented as a continuum in women's and men's experience.

Women's Curriculum

The pluralistic and multifocal conception of women that emerged in the women's curriculum phase is extended to human beings. A central idea in this phase is *positionality* (Alcoff, 1988; Haraway, 1988; Harding, 1991). Positionality means that important

Table 7.4 Women's Curriculum

Characteristics of Phase	Questions Commonly Asked about Women in History	Questions Commonly Asked about Women in Literature	Questions Commonly Asked about Women in Science
Scholarly inquiry pursues new questions, new categories, and new notions of significance that illuminate women's traditions, history, culture, values, visions, and perspectives. A pluralistic conception of women emerges that acknowledges diversity and recognizes that variables besides gender shape women's lives—for example, race, ethnicity, and social class. Women's experience is allowed to speak for itself. Feminist history is rooted in the personal and the specific; it builds from that to the general. The public and the private are seen as a continuum in women's experiences. Women's experience is analyzed within the social, cultural, historical, political, and economic contexts. Efforts are made to reconceptualize knowledge to encompass the female experience. The conceptualization of knowledge is not characterized by disciplinary thinking but becomes multidisciplinary.	What were the majority of women doing at a particular time in history? What was the significance of these activities? How can female friendship between kin, mothers, daughters, and friends be analyzed as one aspect of women's overall relations with others? What kind of productive work, paid and unpaid, did women do and under what conditions? What were the reproductive activities of women? How did they reproduce the American family? How did the variables of race, ethnicity, social class, marital status, and sexual preference affect women's experience? What new categories need to be added to the study of history, for instance, housework, childbearing, and child rearing? How have women of different races and classes interacted throughout history? What are appropriate ways of organizing or periodizing women's history? For example, how will examining women's experiences at each stage of the life span help us to understand women's experiences on their own terms?	What does women's sphere —for example, domesticity and family, education, marriage, sexuality, and love— reveal about our culture? How can we contrast the fictional image of women in literature with the complexity and variety of the roles of individual women in real life as workers, housewives, revolutionaries, mothers, lovers, and so on? How do the particulars of race, ethnicity, social class, marital status, and sexual orientation, as revealed in literature, challenge the thematic homogeneity of women's experiences? How does literature portray what binds women together and what separates them because of race, ethnicity, social class, marital status, and sexual orientation? How does the social and historical context of a work of literature shed light on it?	How do the cultural dualisms associated with masculinity and femininity permeate scientific thought and discourse? How does women's actual experiences, as compared to the physician's analysis or scientific theory, challenge the traditional paradigms of science and of the health care systems? How does research on areas of primary interest to women, for instance, menopause, childbirth and menstruation/ estrus, challenge existing scientific theories? How do variables other than sex and gender, such as age, species, and individual variation, challenge current theories? How do the experience of female primates and the variation among species of primates, for example, competition among women, female agency in sexuality, and infanticide, test the traditional paradigms?

aspects of our identity (for example, our gender, our race, our class, our age, and so on) are markers of relational positions rather than essential qualities. Their effects and implications change according to context. Recently, feminist thinkers have seen knowledge as valid when it comes from an acknowledgment of the knower's specific position in any context, one always defined by gender, race, class, and other variables.

Scientists ask explicit questions about male-female relations in animals and inquire about how such variables as age, species, and individual variation challenge current theories. Accompanying this particularistic perspective is attention to the larger context, for example, the interplay among situation, meaning, economic systems, family organization, and political systems. Thus, historians ask how gender inequities are linked to economics, family organization, marriage, ritual, and politics. Research scientists probe how differences between the male and female body have been used to justify a social agenda that privileges men economically, socially, and politically. In this phase, a revolutionary relationship comes to exist between things traditionally treated as serious, primarily the activities of men in the public sphere, and those things formerly perceived as trivial, namely the activities of women in the private sphere.

This new relationship leads to a recentering of knowledge in the disciplines, a shift from a male-centered perspective to one that includes both females and males. This reconceptualization of knowledge works toward a more holistic view of human experience. As in the previous stage, the conceptualization of knowledge is characterized by multidisciplinary thinking.

Feminist scholars have cautioned against moving too quickly from women's curricula to gender-balanced curricula. As the historian Gerda Lerner (1982) once observed, our decade-and-a-half-old investigation of women's history is only a speck on the horizon compared to the centuries-old tradition of male-defined history. By turning too quickly to studies of gender, we risk short-circuiting important directions in women's studies and again having women's history and experiences subsumed under those of men. It remains politically important for feminists to defend women as women in order to counteract the male domination that continues to exist. French philosopher Julia Kristeva (cited in Moi, 1985), however, pushes us to new considerations when she urges women (and men) to recognize the falsifying nature of masculinity and femininity, to explore how the fact of being born male or female determines one's position in relation to power, and to envision more fluid gender identities that have the potential to liberate both women and men to a fuller personhood (see Table 7.5).

CHANGING TRADITIONAL WAYS OF TEACHING

Feminist scholarship has helped us understand that all knowledge, and therefore all classroom knowledge, is a *social construction*. The male-dominated disciplines have given us a discourse that silences or marginalizes other ways of knowing. One book, *Women's Ways of Knowing* (Belenky, Clinchy, Goldberger, & Tarule, 1986), evoked a deep and widespread response, in part because the authors pointed out that education rewards certain kinds of learners and particular perspectives on knowledge. To educate students for a complex, multicultural, multiracial world, we need to include the perspec-

Table 7.5 Gender-Balanced Curriculum

Characteristics of Phase	Questions Commonly Asked about Women in History	Questions Commonly Asked about Women in Literature	Questions Commonly Asked about Women in Science
A multifocal, gender-balanced perspective is sought that weaves together women's and men's experiences into multi-layered composites of human experience. At this stage, scholars are conscious of positionality. Positionality represents the insight that all women and men must be located in historical contexts, contexts defined in terms of race, class, culture, and age, as well as gender, and that they gain their knowledge and their power from the specifics of their situations. Scholars must begin to define what binds together and what separates the various segments of humanity. Scholars have a deepened understanding of how the private as well as the public form a continuum in individual experience. They search for the nodal points at which comparative treatment of men's and women's experience is possible. Efforts are made to reconceptualize knowledge to reflect this multilayered composite of women's and men's experience. The conceptualization of knowledge is not characterized by disciplinary thinking but becomes multidisciplinary.	What is the knower's specific position in this historical context? How is gender asymmetry linked to economic systems, family organizations, marriage, ritual, and political systems? How can we compare women and men in all aspects of their lives to reveal gender as a crucial historical determinant? Are the private, as well as the public, aspects of history presented as a continuum in women's and men's experiences? How is gender a social construction? What does the particular construction of gender in a society tell us about the society that so constructed gender? What is the intricate relation between the construction of gender and the structure of power? How can we expand our conceptualization of historical time to a pluralistic one that conceives of three levels of history: structures, trends, and events? How can we unify approaches and types of knowledge of all social sciences and history as a means of investigating specific problems in relational history?	How does the author's specific position, as defined by gender, race, and class, affect this literary work? How can we validate the full range of human expression by selecting literature according to its insight into any aspect of human experience rather than according to how it measures up to a predetermined canon? Is the private as well as the public sphere presented as a continuum in women's and men's experiences? How can we pair opposite-sex texts in literature as a way of understanding how female and male characters experience "maleness" and "femaleness" as a continuum of "humanness"? How do the variables of race, ethnicity, social class, marital status, and sexual orientation affect the experience of female and male literary characters? How can we rethink the concept of periodicity to accentuate the continuity of life and to contain the multitude of previously ignored literary works, for example, instead of Puritanism, the contexts for and consequences of sexuality? How can we deconstruct the opposition between masculinity and femininity?	What explicit questions need to be raised about male-female relations in animals? How do variables such as age, species, and individual variation challenge current theories? What are the limits to generalizing beyond the data collected on limited samples to other genders, species, and conditions not sampled in the experimental protocol? How have sex differences been used to assign men and women to particular roles in the social heirarchy? How have differences between the male and female body been used to justify a social agenda that privileges men economically, socially, and politically?

tives and voices of those who have not been traditionally included— women of all backgrounds, people of color, and females and males who perceive their education as not made for them.

Feminist teachers are demonstrating how they transform courses through their attention to cultural, ethnic and gender diversity and give concrete form to the complexity of the struggles over knowledge, access, and power (hooks, 1994; Maher & Tetreault, 1994; Weiler, 1988). In a study, *The Feminist Classroom*, Frances Maher and I (Maher & Tetreault, 1994) show how all students may benefit from, and how some are even inspired by, college courses transformed by their professor's attention to cultural, ethnic, and gender diversity. We have found that the themes we used to analyze teaching and learning in seventeen classrooms on six campuses across the country apply to elementary and secondary classrooms as well. The four themes, *mastery, voice, authority* and *positionality*, all relate to issues present in today's classroom. Although all four deal with reconstituted relationships between new students and new disciplinary frameworks, the themes of mastery and authority focus on knowledge and its sources; voice and positionality on the students themselves.

Mastery has traditionally meant the goal of an individual student's rational comprehension of the material on the teacher's and expert's terms. Women (and other marginalized groups) must often give up their voices when they seek mastery on the terms of the dominant culture. We found classrooms undergoing a shift away from unidimensional sources of expertise to a multiplicity of new information and insights. Students were no longer mastering a specific body of material nor were they emphasizing subjective experiences that risk excluding students from a wealth of knowledge. Rather, they were struggling through or integrating often widely various interpretations of texts, scientific research, and social problems. These teachers redefined mastery as *interpretation*, as increasingly sophisticated handling of the topics at hand, informed by but not limited to the students' links to the material from their own experience. For example, a Japanese American student reread an Emily Dickinson poem about silences and invisibilities to comment on her gender and ethnic marginality.

> I couldn't help thinking of the idea of a mute culture within a dominant culture. A "nobody" knowing she's different from the dominant culture keeps silent.... But to be somebody! How dreary! How public! So when you become a somebody and buy into the dominant culture, you have to live in their roles.
>
> A silly example: It's like watching a Walt Disney movie as a child where Hayley Mills and these other girls dance and primp before a party singing "Femininity," how being a woman is all about looking pretty and smiling pretty and acting stupid to attract men. As a child I ate it up, at least it seemed benign. But once your eye gets put out and you realize how this vision has warped you, it would split your heart to try and believe that again, it would strike you dead.

Students were stretched by such broadenings of interpretative frameworks and indeed became authorities for one another. A male student in the same class said:

> I could read Dickinson a thousand times and probably never try to relate to that because it just would never make an impression on me, but having the girls in that class interested in that particular topic,—"How does that relate to me as a woman?"—then I sit back and I think that's a really good question. Although I'm male I can learn how women react to women's text as opposed to maybe the way I react to it or the teacher reacts to it.

The teachers in our study consciously used their *authority* to give students responsibility for their own learning (Finke, 1993). Students and professors became authorities for one another to the extent that they were explicit about themselves as social and political actors with respect to a text or an issue (Tetreault, 1991). The teachers also struggled with reconceptualizing the grounds for their own authority, both over the subject matter and with students, because their traditional positions as the sole representatives of expertise were called into question by these multiple new sources of knowledge. These professors shared a sense of their authority as grounded in their own experiences and in their intellectual engagement with feminist scholarship and other relevant fields.

As important as the rethinking of the disciplines is the power of expression that these new forms of knowledge, coming from the students' questions as well as from new topics, give to women and other previously silenced groups. We explored the effects on students through our theme of voice. *Voice* is frequently defined as the awakening of the students' own responses. However, we came to think of these classrooms as arenas where teachers and students fashion their voices rather than "find" them, as they produce relevant experiences to shape a narrative of an emerging self.

Our fourth theme is *positionality*, which was defined in the section on gender-balanced curriculum. Positionality helps us to see the multiple ways in which the complex dynamics of difference and inequality, which come from outside society, also operate powerfully inside the classroom itself. Much of our emphasis in the past twenty-five years has been on the consequences of sexism and racism on females and students of color. We have learned much about how universalizing the position of maleness leads to intellectual domination. Some educators and theorists are arguing that we need to become conscious in similar ways about the effects of universalizing the position of Whiteness (Frankenberg, 1993; McIntosh, 1988; Tatum, 1992). For example, how do assumptions of Whiteness or maleness shape the construction of knowledge in classrooms? How do those assumptions contribute to the intellectual domination of groups'? Why is it that when we think of the development of racial identity in our students, we think primarily of students of color rather than White students? What happens in classrooms where Whiteness is marked, revealed as a position? In our culture, the presumptions of Whiteness or maleness act to constrict voice by universalizing the dominant positions, by letting them float free of "position."

We are beginning to understand that the process of reconstructing knowledge depends on those in the dominant group acknowledging their own positions and the privilege that accompanies them. We need to understand more about how the dominant culture shapes assumptions and therefore shapes knowledge, even when the topic is ostensibly about the "other." Understanding all the ways in which positionality shapes learning is a long, interactive process.

In the lessons that follow, I attempt to model teaching that is constructed to reveal the particular and the common denominators of human experience. These sample lessons are organized by the subject areas of language arts, science, and social studies, but they can be adapted to other subject areas as well.

Language Arts

Analyzing Children's Literature

Suggested Activities

Ask students to locate five of their favorite children's books, to read or reread them, and to keep a written record of their reactions to the books. Either on the chalkboard or on a sheet of newsprint, keep a record of the students' (and your) book choices. Divide the class into small groups according to the same or similar favorite books, and have students share their written reactions to the books. Ask the groups to keep a record of the most noteworthy ideas that emerge from their small-group discussions. When you bring the small groups together, ask each group to present its noteworthy ideas. Ideas that emerge may be as follows:

How differently they read the book now than at the time of their first reading

The differences and similarities in so-called girls books and boys books

The importance of multicultural or international perspectives

What the stories reveal about the culture in which the stories are set.

A follow-up activity could be to interview grandparents, parents, teachers, and other adults about characters and stories they remember from childhood. Questions to ask include, How do they recall feeling about those stories? Have images of female and male behavior or expectations in children's stories changed? Is race or ethnicity treated similarly or differently?

Pairing Female and Male Autobiographies

Suggested Activities

Pairings of autobiographies by male and female authors can contribute greatly to students' multifocal, relational understanding of the human experience. Two pairings I have found to be particularly illuminating are *Black Boy* by Richard Wright (1945) and *Woman Warrior* by Maxine Hong Kingston (1976). Another interesting pairing is Maya Angelou's *I Know Why the Caged Bird Sings* (Angelou, 1969) and Mark Twain's *Huckleberry Finn* (Clemens, 1912).

One professor we observed at Lewis and Clark College, Dorothy Berkson, uses teaching logs to demystify the process of interpretation by linking the students' emotional connections to texts with their intellectual analysis. She asks her students to select a passage that puzzles or engages them or triggers a strong emotional reaction. Believing that some of the best criticism starts with such reactions, she asks the students next to paraphrase the passage they have chosen, to understand what it means, or, in a sense, to master it. They are then asked to look at it again, to become conscious of what cannot be captured by paraphrase as well as any concerns or questions that escaped them before. They finally place the passage in the context of the entire text, using the following questions: "Where does it happen? Are there other passages that relate to it? that contradict it? that confirm it? that raise more questions about it?" Concluding with a summary of where this procedure has taken them, they turn in these logs at the end of each class. Returned to the students with Berkson's comments, the logs then become the basis for the students' formal paper. This process forces students to reengage with the text over and over again, to engage in continuous reinterpretation of the text rather than to think they have arrived at some final mastery.

Science

Fear of Science: Fact or Fantasy?

Suggested Activities

Fear of science and math contributes to the limited participation of some students, most often female, in math and science classes. Their inadequate participation limits their choice of most undergraduate majors that depend on a minimum of three years of high school mathematics. The following exercise was designed by the Math and Science Education for Women Project at the Lawrence Hall of Science (Fraser, 1982). The purpose of the exercise is to decrease female and male students' fear of science by enabling them to function as researchers who define the problem and generate solutions to it.

Ask students to complete the following sentence by writing for about fifteen minutes:

When I think about science, I . . .

When they are finished, divide students into groups of five or six to discuss their responses to the cue. Ask each group to state the most important things it has learned. Discuss fear of science with the class and whether there is a difference in how girls and boys feel about science. What could be some reasons for these differences or similarities? When the findings from this exercise are clear, suggest to students that they broaden their research to include other students and teachers in the school. Have each group brainstorm questions that might appear on a science attitude questionnaire. Put the questions on the chalkboard. Analyze the questions and decide on the ten best questions.

Decide with the class what group of students and teachers you will research and how you will do it; for example, other science classes, all ninth-grade science classes, or the entire school during second period. Obtain permission to conduct the survey from the administration and other teachers or classes involved in your research project. Have the class do the survey or questionnaire as a pilot activity. Analyze the questions for sex differences and make minor revisions before giving the survey and questionnaire to your research group. Distribute the survey or conduct interviews. Have the students decide how to analyze the information. Let each group decide how it will display findings and information. Have each group give (1) a report to the class on what it found, using graph displays to convey the information; and (2) recommendations for decreasing science anxiety in the school. Place the entire student research project in the school library, main office, or gymnasium, where the rest of the school population can see the results. Have a student summarize and write an article for the school paper.

Doing Science

Suggested Activities

Evelyn Fox Keller's (1983) biography of Barbara McClintoch, *A Feeling for the Organism*, allows students to explore the conditions under which dissent in science arises, the function it serves, and the plurality of values and goals it reflects. Questions her story prompts are, What role do interests, individual and collective, play in the evolution of scientific knowledge? Do all scientists seek the same kinds of explanations? Are the kinds of questions they ask the same? Do differences in methodology between different subdisciplines ever permit the same kinds of answers? Do female and male scientists approach their research differently? This book is difficult reading for high school or college students, but it is manageable if they read carefully and thoroughly. The best way I have found to help them manage is to ask them to read a chapter or section and to come to class with their questions about the reading and to propose some answers.

Social Studies

My Family's Work History

Suggested Activities

Women and men of different social classes, ethnic groups, and geographic locations have done various kinds of work inside and outside their homes in agricultural, industrial, and postindustrial economies. Before introducing students to the history of work, I pique their interest by asking them to complete a Family Work Chart (see Table 7.6). When their charts are complete, the students and I build a work chronology from 1890 to the present. Our work chronology contains information gleaned from the textbook and library sources about important inventions, laws, demographics, and labor history.

I then reproduce the work chronology on a chart so they can compare their family's history. By seeing their families' histories alongside major events in our collective work history, students can see how their family was related to society. A sample of items from our chart looks like this (Chapman, 1979):

Table 7.6 Family Work Chart

| | | | Work Experience | |
| | | | After Marriage | |
	Year of Birth	Before Marriage	While Children Were Young?	When Children Were Grown?
Your Maternal Side				
Mother				
Grandmother				
Grandfather				
Great-grandmother				
Great-grandfather				
Great-grandmother				
Great-grandfather				
Your Paternal Side				
Father				
Grandmother				
Grandfather				
Great-grandmother				
Great-grandfather				
Great-grandmother				
Great-grandfather				

This activity was developed by Carol Frenier. Reprinted with permission from the Education Development Center from Adeline Naiman, Project Director, *Sally Garcia Family Resource Guide,* Unit 3 of *The Role of Women in American Society* (Newton, Mass.: Education Development Center, Inc., 1978), p. 62.

Historical Events	*Your Family History*
1890 Women are 17 percent of labor force	
1915 Telephone connects New York and San Francisco	
1924 Restriction of immigration	

Students conclude this unit by writing about a major theme in their family's work history. They might focus on how the lives of the women in the family differed from the lives of the men. They might focus on how their family's race or ethnicity shaped their work history.

Integrating the Public and Private Spheres

Suggested Activities

Human life is lived in both the public and the private spheres in wartime as well as in peacetime. By asking students consciously to examine individuals' lives as citizens, workers, family members, friends, members of social groups, and individuals, they learn more about the interaction of these roles in both spheres. War is an extraordinary time when the nation's underlying assumptions about these roles are often put to the test. By having students examine the interaction of these roles in wartime, they can see some of our underlying assumptions about the roles and how they are manipulated for the purposes of war. Through researching the histories of their families, and by reading primary source accounts, viewing films, and reading their textbook, they will see the complexity and variety of human experiences in the United States during World War II.

Students research their family's history during World War II by gathering family documents and artifacts and by interviewing at least one relative who was an adult during World War II. Students draw up questions beforehand to find out how the individual's social roles were affected by the war. During the two weeks they are researching their family's history, two class periods are spent on this project. During the first period, students give oral reports to a small group of fellow students in read-around groups.

Appropriate readings and films on World War II are widely available. Studs Terkel's (1984) book *The Good War* is particularly useful because of the variety of people the author interviewed. For instance, students can read about the internment of Japanese Americans and can role play an account read. Their textbook may provide good background information. My students answer two questions in this unit: World War II has been described as a 'good war.' From the materials you have examined, was it a good war for individuals' lives as citizens, workers, family members, friends, and members of social groups? How were their experiences similar to or different from those of your relatives?

SUMMARY

This chapter has illustrated how women's studies is challenging male domination over curricular content. The evolution of that challenge is illuminated by understanding the different emphases that coexist in male-defined, contribution, bifocal, women's and gender-balanced curricula. We now have a conceptual framework for a curriculum that interweaves issues of gender with ethnicity, culture, and class. This framework acknowledges and celebrates a multifocal, relational view of the human experience.

The idea of the phases of feminist scholarship as a series of intersecting circles, or patches on a quilt, or threads on a tapestry suggests parallel ways to think about a class of students. Each student brings to your classroom a particular positionality that shapes his or her way of knowing. Your challenge as a teacher is to interweave the individual truths with course content into complex understandings that legitimize students' voices.

This relational knowledge, with the authority of the school behind it, has the potential to help students analyze their own social, cultural, historical, political, and economic contexts. The goal of relational knowledge is to build a world in which the oppressions of race, gender, and class, on which capitalism and patriarchy depend, are challenged by critical citizens in a democratic society.

Questions and Activities

1. What is a gender-balanced, multicultural curriculum?

2. What is feminist phase theory?

3. Define and give an example of each of the following phases of the feminist phase theory developed and described by the author: (a) male-defined curriculum; (b) contribution curriculum; (c) bifocal curriculum; (d) women's curriculum; (e) gender-balanced curriculum.

4. What problems do the contribution and bifocal phases have? How do the women's curriculum and gender-balanced curriculum phases help solve these problems?

5. The author states that "knowledge is a social construction." What does this mean? In what ways is the new scholarship on women and ethnic groups alike? In what ways does the new scholarship on women and ethnic groups challenge the dominant knowledge established in the society and presented in textbooks? Give examples.

6. Examine the treatment of women in a sample of social studies, language arts, mathematics, or science textbooks (or a combination of two types of textbooks). Which phase or phases of the feminist phase theory presented by the author best describe the treatment of women in the textbooks you examined ?

7. What is the *longue durée?* Why is it important in the study of social history, particularly women's history?

8. Research your family history, paying particular attention to the roles, careers, and influence of women in your family's saga. Also describe your ethnic heritage and the influence of ethnicity on your family's past and present. Share your family history with a group of your classmates or workshop participants.

References

Alcoff, L. (1988, Spring). Cultural Feminism versus Post-Structuralism: The Identity Crisis in Feminist Theory. *Signs, 13,* 405–436.

Angelou, M. (1969). *I Know Why the Caged Bird Sings.* New York: Bantam Books.

Belenky, M., Clinchy, B., Goldberger, N., and Tarule, J. (1986). *Women's Ways of Knowing: The Development of Self, Body and Mind.* New York: Basic Books.

Chapman, A. (Ed.). (1979). *Approaches to Women's History.* Washington, DC: American Historical Association.

Clemens, S. (1912). *The Adventures of Huckleberry Finn.* New York: Collier.

Finke, L. (1993). Knowledge as Bait: Feminism Voice, and the Pedagogical Unconscious. *College English,* *55*(1), 7–27.

Frankenberg, R. (1993). *White Women Race Matters: The Social Construction of Whiteness.* Minneapolis: University of Minnesota Press.

Fraser, S. (1982). *Spaces: Solving Problems of Access to Careers in Engineering and Science.* Berkeley: University of California, Lawrence Hall of Science.

Haraway, D. (1988). Situated Knowledges: The Science Question in Feminism and the Privilege of Partial Perspective. *Feminist Studies, 14*(3), 575–599.

Harding, S . (1991) *Whose Science? Whose Knowledge? Thinking from Women's Lives.* Ithaca, NY: Cornell University Press.

hooks, b. (1994). *Teaching to Transgress: Education as the Practice of Freedom.* New York: Routledge.

Keller, E. F. (1983). *A Feeling for the Organism: The Life and Work of Barbara McClintoch.* San Francisco: W. H. Freeman.

Kingston, M. H. (1976). *The Woman Warrior.* New York: Alfred Knopf.

Lerner, G. (1982). Reputed to have said this at a conference on women's history.

Letters to the Editor. (1982). *Social Education, 46*(6), 378–380.

Maher, F. and Tetreault, M. K. (1994). *The Feminist Classroom.* New York: Basic Books.

McIntosh, P. (1988). *Understanding Correspondences between White Privilege and Male Privilege through Women's Studies Work.* Wellesley, MA: Wellesley Center for Research on Women.

Moi, T. (1985). *Sexual/Textual Politics.* New York: Methuen.

Tatum, B . (l992). Talking about Race, Learning about Racism: The Application of Racial Identity Development Theory in the Classroom. *Harvard Educational Review, 62*(1), l–24.

Terkel, S. (1984). *The Good War: An Oral History of World War II.* New York: Pantheon Books.

Tetreault, C. (l99l) *Metacommunication in a Women's Studies Classroom.* Unpublished senior honors thesis, Vassar College. Chapel Hill: University of North Carolina.

Tetreault, M. K. T. (1986). Integrating Women's History: The Case of United States History Textbooks. *The History Teacher, 19*(2) 211–262.

Weiler, K. (1988). *Women Teaching for Change: Gender, Class, and Power.* South Hadley, MA: Bergin and Garvey.

Wright, R. (1945). *Black Boy.* New York: Harper and Brothers.

Chapter 8

Transforming the Curriculum: Teaching about Women of Color

Johnnella E. Butler

Many efforts to include women and issues of gender into what is called the mainstream curriculum focus on White, middle-class women from the United States and on women from other nations and cultures. Generally, we have taken the White, middle-class woman's experience as the norm when examining and talking about women's lives. When we want to know about women's lives that differ from that norm, we generally have explored the global experience (Gross, 1987). Curiously, when we deal with cultures of other nations, we seem to grasp that before we can have a proper understanding of the women in these cultures, we must adopt a multicultural perspective. It seems less apparent to us that to understand the lives of women in the United States, a cross-ethnic, multiethnic perspective that takes into account the structures and representations of racism and their effects is necessary.

This chapter focuses on teaching about women of color in the United States and also describes an approach useful for studying and teaching about all women in U.S. society. The discussion is rooted in the method of critical pedagogy developing in this country that is influenced by Brazilian educator and activist Paulo Friere. I see feminist pedagogy as an evolution of this critical pedagogy, as well as the pedagogy implicit in ethnic studies. The context of this chapter is the dialectical, dialogic, and critical relationship between modernism and postmodernism that Henry Giroux calls for and demonstrates (Giroux, 1994). Giroux examines especially the central issues of the postmodern debate and the "challenges and provocations they provide to modernity's conception of history, agency, representation, culture, and the responsibility of individuals" (p. 347). Rather than criticize and dismiss modernity's conceptions, Giroux calls for the engagement of the relationships between modernism and postmodernism, describing today's youth—our students—as bordering the two. Transformation, as described in this chapter, is offered as the philosophical perspective for such dialogues. The content, context of, and pedagogy for teaching about women of color in the United States is part of that dialogue.

Examples are provided throughout to keep the theory from seeming only abstract and unrelated to those involved in the teaching process—the student and the teacher. Although I do not provide suggested activities for kindergarten and grades 1 through 12, I do provide information and a conceptual framework, the appropriate starting points for such activities. The appendix of this book includes bibliographic resources for content about the lives of women of color. They also provide a starting point. Much work has yet to be done to make this information available to most teachers.

WHY WOMEN OF COLOR?

The phrase *women of color* came into use gradually during the 1970s. It immediately brings to mind differences of race and culture. It also makes clear that African American women are not the only women of color. In a democratically structured society with a great power imbalance signified by race and class privilege, labels representative of reality for those outside the realm of power are difficult to determine. The form of that power is both cultural and political and consequently further complicates labeling. Selecting the phrase *women of color* by many women of U.S. ethnic groups of color is part of their struggle to be recognized with dignity for their humanity, racial heritage, and cultural heritage as they work within the women's movement of the United States. The effort of women of color to name themselves is similar to attempts by African Americans and other ethnic groups to define with dignity their race and ethnicity and to counter the many stereotypical names bestowed on them. Because we tend to use the word *women* to be all-inclusive and general, we usually obscure both the differences and the similarities among women.

With the decline of the civil rights movement of the 1960s, the women's movement in the second half of the twentieth century got under way. Not long after, African American women began to articulate the differences they experienced as African American women, not only because of the racism within the women's movement or the sexism within the African American community, but also because of their vastly differing historical reality. One major question posed by Toni Cade's pioneering anthology, *The Black Woman*, remains applicable: "How relevant are the truths, the experiences, the findings of White women to Black women? Are women after all, simply women?" Cade answers the question then as it might still be answered today: "I don't know that our priorities are the same, that our concerns and methods are the same, or even similar enough so that we can afford to depend on this new field of experts (White, female). It is rather obvious that we do not. It is obvious that we are turning to each other" (Cade, 1970, p. 9).

This anthology served as a turning point in the experience of the African American woman. Previously, White males, for the most part, had interpreted her realities, her activities, and her contributions. The Moynihan Report of 1965, the most notable example of this scholarship, received the widest publicity and acceptance by U.S. society at large. Blaming African American social and economic problems on the Black family, Daniel Moynihan argues that Black families, dominated by women, are generally pathological and pathogenic. His scholarship directly opposes the scholarship of Billingsley and others, which demonstrates the organizational differences between Black and White family units, the existence of a vital African American culture on which to base solutions to the problems, and the effects of racism, sexism, classism, and ethnocentrism in shaping the Black reality and government policy and societal attitudes towards that reality (Billingsley, 1968; Ladner, 1973; McAdoo, 1981; Moynihan, 1965). Bambara's anthology responded directly to such attacks and resulting policy, calling for Black women's direct involvement in both defining the problems and fashioning the solutions.

Although we are beyond the point of the complete invisibility and complete distortion of women of color in the academic branch of the women's movement (women's studies), African American women must still demand to be heard, must insist on being dealt with from the perspective of the experiences of women of color, just as they did in 1970, as the blurb in the paperback *The Black Woman* implies: "Black Women Speak Out. A Brilliant and Challenging Assembly of Voices That Demand to Be Heard." By the latter part of the 1970s, the logic of a dialogue among women of color became a matter of course. We find, as in Cade's *The Black Woman* Black women speaking to one another in publications such as *Conditions: Five, The Black Women's Issue*, and women of color speaking in the pioneering *This Bridge Called My Back: Writings by Radical Women of Color* (Conditions: Five, 1979; Moraga & Anzaldua, 1981). The academic community began to recognize U.S. women of color who identify with the Third World, both for ancestral heritage and for related conditions of colonization; in 1980 we see, for example, the publication of Dexter Fisher's anthology *The Third Woman: Minority Women Writers of the United States* (Fisher, 1980), another milestone giving voice to U.S. women of color.

The most familiar ethnic groups of color are the Asian Americans, African Americans, Hispanic Americans, and Native Americans. Yet within each group there are cultural, class, and racial distinctions. These ethnic groups can be further delineated: Asian Americans consist of Chinese Americans, Japanese Americans, Filipino Americans, Korean Americans, in addition to the more recent immigrants from Southeast Asia. African Americans consist of the U.S. African American and the West Indian or African Caribbean immigrants. The number of African immigrants is most likely too small and diverse to consider as a group; however, their presence should be acknowledged. Hispanic Americans, or Latino Americans as some prefer, are largely Puerto Rican, Chicano, and Cuban. The Native American is made up of many tribal groups such as Sioux, Apache, Navajo, and Creek.

The phrase *women of color* helps women of all these groups acknowledge both their individual ethnicity and their racial solidarity as members of groups that are racial minorities in the United States, as well as a majority as people of color in the world. The concept also acknowledges similarity in historical experiences and position in relation to the White American. In addition, the use of the phrase and the concept *women of color* implies the existence of the race and ethnicity of White women, for whom the word *women* wrongly indicates a norm for all women or wrongly excludes other women.

WHAT WE LEARN FROM STUDYING WOMEN OF COLOR

When we study women of color, we raise our awareness and understanding of the experiences of all women either implicitly or directly. Quite significantly, because of the imbalanced power relationship between White women and women of color, information about one group tends to make more apparent the experiences of the other group. It is well known, for example, that ideals of beauty in the United States are based on the blond, blue-eyed model. Dialogue about the reactions to that model in the experience of women of color, both within their ethnic groups and as they relate to White women, ultimately reveals that White women often judge themselves by that model of beauty. White women also serve simultaneously as reminders or representatives of that ideal to women of color and, most frequently, to themselves as failures to meet the ideal.

Another way of stating this is that a way of understanding an oppressor is to study the oppressed. Thus, we come to another level of awareness and understanding when we study women of color. We see clearly that White women function both as women who share certain similar experiences with women of color and as oppressors of women of color. This is one of the most difficult realities to cope with while maintaining productive, generative dialogue among women while teaching and conducting scholarship. White women who justifiably see themselves as oppressed by White men find it difficult to separate themselves from the effects of and power shared with White men. White women share with White men an ethnicity, an ancestral heritage, racial dominance, and certain powers and privileges by virtue of class, race, and ethnicity, by race and ethnicity if not class, and always by virtue of White skin privilege (Frye, 1983; McIntosh, 1987).

The growing scholarship on women of color gives us much to teach about women's lives, their joys and celebrations, and their oppressions. I cannot begin to relate the content you must deal with in order to know women's lives. However, the books in the appendix can provide a beginning guide for you to become familiar with the history and culture of women of color. When we study women of color, we raise our awareness and understanding of the experiences of all women either explicit or implicitly.

Once we realize that all women are not White, and once we understand the implications of this realization, we see immediately the importance of race, ethnicity, and class when considering gender. Interestingly, much scholarship that intends to illustrate and analyze class dynamics is blind to racial and ethnic dynamics. In similar fashion, much scholarship that illustrates and analyzes racial dynamics and class dynamics fails to see ethnic dynamics. Other scholarship gives short shrift to, or even ignores, class. We have begun to grapple with the connectedness of the four big -isms—racism, sexism, classism, and ethnocentrism.

Much scholarship in women's studies, however, fails to work within the context of race, class, ethnicity, and gender and their related -isms, which modulate each other to a greater or lesser extent. Elizabeth V. Spelman illustrates how the racist equating of Blackness with lustfulness in Western culture modulates sexism toward African American women (Spelman, 1982). One resulting stereotype is that the African

American woman has a bestial sexuality and, as such, deserves or expects to be raped. This racism is also modulated by an ethnocentrism that further devalues the African American woman, thereby justifying the sexism. Classism may also modulate this sexism if the perpetrator is of a higher class status than are most African American women. However, if this cannot be claimed, racism, ethnocentrism, or both will suffice. Nonetheless, each is operative to some degree. Lower-class Whites or Whites of the same economic class as African Americans can invoke skin privilege to differentiate within the class common denominator. The categories of race, class, ethnicity, and gender are connected and interrelated; likewise their related -isms and their correctives.

Attention to race makes us aware of the differing perspectives that women have about race and skin color—perceptions of what is beautiful, ugly, attractive, repulsive, what is ordinary or exotic, pure or evil, based on racist stereotypes; the role that color plays in women's lives; and the norms by which women judge themselves physically. Attention to race also brings us to a realization that White women, too, are members of a race with stereotypes about looks and behavior. Attention to race in women's lives, with the particular understanding that race has a function for White women as well, reveals the oppression of racism, both from the point of view of one oppressed and of one who oppresses or participates in oppression by virtue of privilege.

Attention to class reveals, among other things, that because of different historical experiences, class means different things to different groups. Not necessarily measured by financial status, neighborhood, and level of education, class status frequently is measured by various ways in which one approximates variations on the Anglo-American norm of middle to upper class. Simultaneously, our society insists on formally measuring class status by economic means. The market/consumer representation of the U.S. citizen drives goals and concepts of self-worth and continues in various representations of the Dynasty, Yuppie, and Buppie that gained currency during the 1980s. Yet for the woman of color, as for the man of color, the dynamic of social class becoming a measure for success is particularly insidious, threatening to destroy the affirmation of ethnic strengths that may be closely related to a generative, self-identity. For example, Chinese Americans who have reached a high education level may move from Chinatown in a conflicting effort to succeed and participate in U.S. society. Adherence to the Anglo-American norm dictates certain dress, foods, and life-style, as well as a sense of superiority of the Anglo values. Ties to family and friends may be questioned, and the very traditions and understandings that provided the source of strength for coping in the White world may be devalued and discarded rather than transformed and adapted to the U.S. context.

Ethnicity, as a category of analysis, reveals the cultural traditions, perspectives, values, and choices that shape women's lives and their position in society, ranging from hairstyles and jewelry adornment to modes of worship and ways of perceiving a divine force, from values to the perception of women's roles and the roles of men. Ethnicity, our cultural and historical heritage, shapes our perception of race and racism, sex and sexism, class and classism.

The element of power or lack of power has a great deal to do with the benefits or deficits of race and ethnicity. Similar to the example regarding classism, ethnic traditions, kinships, and values that are sustaining in the context of an ethnic group that is a minority, and thus, powerless, may become deficits when interacting with the majority or dominant society. On the other hand, when one becomes secure in one's ethnic identity, deficits of powerlessness and the moves to various levels of success (access to limited power) can be negotiated through variations on those strengths. Kinship networks, for example, are of primary importance to people of color for cultural reasons and for survival. Women's friendships often have particular significance, specifically friendships of younger women with older women. The structure of the larger U.S. society does not make allowances for such friendships. Most of us do not live in extended families or in neighborhoods near relatives. Women of color frequently insist that they maintain such relationships over great distances. Time spent with family, especially extended family, must have priority at various times during the year, not just for tradition's sake, but for maintaining a sense of rootedness, for a dose of shared wisdom, a balanced perspective of who you are, and often, simply for that affirmation that Momma or Aunt Elizabeth loves you. Ethnic identity provides a basis on which women of color celebrate who they are and where they come from in the awareness that they are not simply victims of ethnocentrism and other -isms.

Ethnicity is important in women's lives. Most important, ethnicity reveals that besides the usually acknowledged European American ethnic groups, White Anglo-Saxon Protestants are an ethnic group. Even though it is an ethnicity that boasts a defining dominance that makes it unnecessary to name itself, it is an ethnicity. That it is an ethnicity to which many Whites have subscribed, rather than one to which they belong by lineage, frequently is cause for confusion. However, it is no less an ethnicity for this reason.

The presence of Anglo-American ethnicity within the ethnicity of ethnic groups of color is often cause for confusion. Nonetheless, U.S. ethnic groups of color manifest ethnicities that constantly balance, integrate, and synthesize the Western European Anglo-American, with what has become, with syncretism over the years, Chinese American, Japanese American, African American, Chicano, Native American, and Puerto Rican American. In a similar fashion, the English who came here syncretized with the values that emanated from being on this continent and became English Americans. They maintained a position of power so that other Europeans syncretized to their English or Colonial American culture eventually resulted in their being called Americans. The assumption that people living in the United States are called Americans and that those living in other nations in the hemisphere are Latin Americans, Caribbean Americans, or Canadians attests to this assumed and enforced position of power.

Religion is closely related to ethnicity. Its values are sometimes indistinguishable from ethnic values, and it defines women's experiences in similar ways. Ethnicity as a category of analysis reveals sources of identity, sources of sustenance and celebration, as well as the cultural dynamics that shape women's experience. It makes apparent the necessity of viewing women pluralistically.

Once we view women pluralistically, gender roles begin to assume differing degrees of importance. By virtue of the modulation of the other categories, women may see gender, sexual identity, sexism, and homophobia to be of lesser or greater importance. Gender roles for women of color are more apparently designated, determined, or modulated by ethnicity, race, and sexism. Therefore, racism may assume primary importance as an oppressive force with which to reckon. The African American woman harassed in the workplace because she wears her hair in intricate braids and wears clothes associated with her African heritage receives harsh treatment because of racism, not sexism. Racism also caused African American women to be denied the right to vote after White women gained suffrage rights. Gender, sexual identity, and race become related targets for discrimination as a result of ethnic and/or religious values; an individual's conceptualization of gender roles may be in conflict with that of her racial/ethnic group. Thus, while key aspects of women's identities are connected and interrelated, they can be so in conflict as well as in harmony.

WOMEN OF COLOR: THE AGENT OF TRANSFORMATION

In dealing with the commonalities and differences among women, a necessity in teaching about women of color, I am reminded that the title of Paula Giddings's work on African American women is taken from Anna J. Cooper's observation: "When and where I enter, then and there the whole…race enters with me" (Giddings, 1984, p. 82). Repeated in many forms by women of color from the nineteenth-century struggle for the vote to the present-day women's movement, this truth ultimately contains the goal of transformation of the curriculum: a curriculum that reflects all of us, egalitarian, communal, nonhierarchical, and pluralistic. Women of color are inextricably related to men of color by virtue of ethnicity and traditions as well as by common conditions of oppression. Therefore, at minimum, their struggle against sexism and racism is waged simultaneously. The experiences and destinies of women and men of color are linked. This reality poses a special problem in the relationship between White women and women of color. Moreover, in emphasizing the commonalities of privilege between White men and women, the oppressive relationship between men of color and White men, women of color and White men, and men of color and White women—all implied in Anna J. Cooper's observation—the teaching about women of color provides the naturally pluralistic, multidimensional catalyst for transformation. As such, women of color are agents of transformation.

This section defines transformation and provides the theoretical framework for the pedagogy and methodology of transformation. The final section discusses aspects of the process of teaching about women of color, which, though closely related to the theoretical framework, manifest themselves in very concrete ways.

A review of feminist pedagogy over the past twenty years or so reveals a call for teaching from multifocal, multidimensional, multicultural, pluralistic, interdisciplinary perspectives. This call, largely consistent with the pedagogy and methodology implied thus far in this chapter, can be accomplished only through transformation. Although many theorists and teachers now see this point, the terminology has still to be corrected to illustrate the process. In fact, we often use the words *mainstreaming, balancing, integration,* and *transformation* interchangeably. Mainstreaming, balancing, and integration imply adding women to an established, accepted, and unchangeable body of knowledge. The experience of White, middle-class women has provided a norm in a way that White

Anglo-American male ethnicity provides a norm. All other women's experience is added to and measured by those racial, class, ethnic, and gender roles and experiences.

Transformation, which does away with the dominance of norms, allows us to see the many aspects of women's lives. Understanding the significance of naming the action of treating women's lives through a pluralistic process—transformation—leads naturally to a convergence between women's studies and ethnic studies. This convergence is necessary to give us the information that illuminates the function and content of race, class, and ethnicity in women's lives and in relation to gender. In similar fashion, treating the lives of people of color through a pluralistic process leads to the same convergence, illuminating the functions and content of race, class, and gender in relation to lives of ethnic Americans and in relation to ethnicity.

We still need to come to grips with exactly what is meant by this pluralistic, multidimensional, interdisciplinary scholarship and pedagogy; much of the scholarship on, about, and even frequently by women of color renders them systematically invisible, erasing their experience or part of it. White, middle-class, male, and Anglo-American are the imposed norms corresponding to race, class, gender, and ethnicity. In contrasting and comparing experiences of pioneers, White males and females when dealing with Native Americans, for example, often speak of "the male," "the female," and "the Indian." Somehow, those of a different ethnicity and race are assumed to be male. Therefore, both the female and the male Indian experience is observed and distorted. They must be viewed both separately and together to get a more complete view, just as to have a more complete view of the pioneer experience, the White male and White female experiences must be studied both separately and together. Thus, even in our attempts to correct misinformation resulting from measurement by one norm, we can reinforce measurement by others if we do not see the interaction of the categories, the interaction of the -isms, as explained in the previous section. This pluralistic process and eye are demanded in order to understand the particulars and the generalities of people's lives.

Why is it so easy to impose these norms, effectively to erase the experience of others? I do not think erasing these experiences is always intentional. I do, however, think that it results from the dominance of the Western cultural norms of individuality, singularity, rationality, masculinity, and Whiteness at the expense of the communal, the plural, the intuitive, the feminine, and people of color. A brief look at Elizabeth Spelman's seminal work, "Theories of Race and Gender: The Erasure of Black Women," explains the important aspects of how this erasure comes about (Spelman, 1982, pp. 57–59). Then, a consideration of the philosophical makeup of transformation both tells us how our thinking makes it happen and how we can think to prevent it from happening.

Spelman gives examples of erasure of the Black woman, similar to the examples I have provided. She analyzes concepts that assume primacy of sexism over racism. Furthermore, she rejects the additive approach to analyzing sexism, an approach that assumes a sameness of women modeled on the White, middle-class, Anglo-oriented woman. Spelman shows that it is premature to argue that sexism and racism are either mutually exclusive, totally dependent on one another, or in a causal relationship with one another. She discusses how women differ by race, class, and culture or ethnicity.

Most important, she demonstrates that Black does not simply indicate victim. Black indicates a culture; in the United States the African American culture. She suggests, then, that we present women's studies in a way that makes it a given that women are diverse, that their diversity is apparent in their experiences with oppression and in their participation in U.S. culture. To teach about women in this manner, our goal must not be additive, that is, integrating, mainstreaming, or balancing the curriculum. Rather, *transformation* must be our goal.

Essentially, transformation is the process of revealing unity among human beings and the world, as well as revealing important differences. Transformation implies acknowledging and benefiting from the interaction among sameness and diversity, groups and individuals. The maxim on which transformation rests may be stated as an essential affirmation of the West African proverb, "I am because we are. We are because I am." The communality, the human unity implicit in the proverb operate in African traditional (philosophical) thought in regard to human beings, other categories of life, categories of knowledge, ways of thinking and being (Davidson, 1969; Mbiti, 1975). It is in opposition to the European, Western pivotal axiom, on which integration, balancing, and mainstreaming rest (as expressed through the White, middle-class, Anglo norm in the United States), "I think; therefore, I am," as expressed by Descartes.

The former is in tune with a pluralistic, multidimensional process; the latter with a monolithic, one-dimensional process. Stated succinctly as "I am we," the West African proverb provides the rationale for the interaction and modulation of the categories of race, class, gender, and ethnicity, for the interaction and modulation of their respective -isms, for the interaction and modulation of the objective and subjective, the rational and the intuitive, the feminine and the masculine, all those things that we, as Westerners, see as either opposite or standing rigidly alone. This is the breakdown of what is variously called critical pedagogy, feminist pedagogy, or multifocal teaching, when the ends are the comprehension of and involvement with cultural, class, racial, and gender diversity toward the end not of tolerance, but rather of an egalitarian world based on communal relationships within humanity. Elsa Barkley Brown gives us an insightful and useful discussion of teaching African American women's history in a way consistent with transformation as I have described it that creates "a polyrhythmic, 'nonsymmetrical,' nonlinear structure in which individual and community are not competing entities (Brown, 1989, p. 926)."

To realize this transformation, we must redefine categories and displace criteria that have served as norms in order to bring about the life context (norms and values) as follows:

1. Nonhierarchical terms and contexts for human institutions, rituals, and action

2. A respect for the interaction and existence of both diversity and sameness (a removal of measurement by norms perpetuating otherness, silence, and erasure)

3. A balancing and interaction between the individual and the group

4. A concept of humanity emanating from interdependence of human beings on one another and on the world environment, both natural and human created

5. A concept of humanity emanating from a sense of self that is not totally abstract and totally individually defined (I think; therefore, I am), but that is both abstract *and* concrete, individually *and* communally defined (I am we; I am because we are; we are because I am).

Such a context applies to pedagogy and scholarship, the dissemination and ordering of knowledge in all disciplines and fields. Within this context (the context in which the world does operate and against which the Western individualistic, singular concept of humanity militates), it becomes possible for us to understand the popular music form rap as an Americanized, Westernized version of African praise singing, functioning, obviously, for decidedly different cultural and social reasons. It becomes possible to understand the syncretization of cultures that produced Haitian voudon, Cuban santeria, and Brazilian candomble from Catholicism and the religion of the Yoruba. It becomes possible to understand what is happening when a Japanese American student is finding it difficult to reconcile traditional Buddhist values with her American life. It becomes possible to understand that Maxine Hong Kingston's *Woman Warrior* is essentially about the struggle to syncretize Chinese ways within the United States, whose dominant culture devalues and coerces against syncretization, seeking to impose White, middle-class conformity.

Thinking in this manner is foreign to the mainstream of thought in the United States, although it is alive and well in Native American traditional philosophy, in Taoist philosophy, in African traditional philosophy, and in African American folklore. It is so foreign, in fact, that I realized that in order to bring about this context, we must commit certain so-called sins. Philosopher Elizabeth Minnich suggested to me that these sins might be more aptly characterized as heresies, because they are strongly at variance with established modes of thought and values.

The following heresies challenge and ultimately displace the ways in which the Western mind orders the world (Education for Critical Consciousness, 1973; Friere, 1969). They emanate from the experiences of people of color, the nature of their oppression, and the way the world operates. Adopting them is a necessity for teaching about women of color. Using the heresies to teach women's studies, to teach about the lives of all women, becomes natural when we study women of color and leads naturally to the transformation of the curriculum to a pluralistic, egalitarian, multidimensional curriculum.

Heresy #1 The goal of interaction among human beings, action, and ideas must be seen not only as synthesis, but also as the identification of opposites and differences. These opposites and differences may or may not be resolved; they may function together by virtue of the similarities identified and the tensions they generate as they move ultimately toward resolution.

Heresy #2 We *can* address a multiplicity of concerns, approaches, and subjects, without a neutral or dominant center. Reality reflects opposites as well as overlaps in what are perceived as opposites. There exist no pure, distinct opposites. Human experience has multiple, interconnected centerings.

Heresy #3 It is not reductive to look at gender, race, class, and culture as parts of a complex whole. The more different voices we have, the closer we are to the whole.

Heresy #4 Transformation demands an understanding of ethnicity that takes into account the differing cultural continua (in the United States, Western European, Anglo-American, African, Asian, Native American) and their similarities.

Heresy # 5 Transformation demands a relinquishing of the primary definitiveness of gender, race, class or culture, and ethnicity as they interact with theory, methodology, pedagogy, institutionalization, and action, both in synthesis and in a dynamic that functions as opposite and same simultaneously. A variation on this heresy is that although all -isms are not the same, they are connected and operate as such; likewise, their correctives.

Heresy #6 The Anglo-American, and ultimately the Western, norm must be seen as only one of many norms, and also as one that enjoys privilege and power that has colonized, and may continue to colonize, other norms.

Heresy #7 Feelings are direct lines to better thinking. The intuitive as well as the rational is part of the process of moving from the familiar to the unfamiliar in acquiring knowledge.

Heresy #8 Knowledge is identity and identity is knowledge. All knowledge is explicitly and implicitly related to who we are, both as individuals and as groups.

Engaging transformation through these eight heresies means addressing the connections among human beings, among human beings and the environment, and among experiences, categories of identity; using the intuitive *and* the congitive; displacing dominating norms; exploring the comparative and relational aspects of various norms as well as the conflictual aspects; and acknowledging the power of knowledge to define self , others, and experience. Transformation, then, provides the basis of a pedagogy that stems from teaching about the experience of women of color in a way that engages both how women of color are constructed as subject, with an implicit understanding of how the student is constructed as subject.

Such an approach may prove helpful in teaching other content to today's postmodern youth who Giroux describes as "border youth," that is, youth for whom "plurality and contingency—whether mediated through the media or through the dislocations spurned by the economic system, the rise of new social movements or the crisis of representation—have resulted in a world with few secure psychological, economic, or intelectual markers. ... [they] increasingly inhabit shifting cultural and social spheres marked by a plurality of languages and cultures" (Giroux, 1994, p. 355). As stated at the beginning of this chapter, the content, context of, and pedagogy for teaching about women of color in the United States is part of the needed dialogue between modernism and postmodernism. The fragmentation and dislocation of women of color in relation to what and how we teach frequently reflects and refracts the objectification of the student when we teach as if we are filling empty repositories, fulfilling Freire's banking concept (1969).

As the agent of transformation, women of color as subject content in the humanities and social sciences provide an excellent point for engaging our modern/postmodern conflict. It provides also a philosophical perspective, transformation, for a generative pedagogy that fosters students as subjects, generates knowledge and understanding through building on the interconnections among student, teacher, and content, and engages the conflictive from the strength of the multiply-centered, relational context.

TEACHING ABOUT WOMEN OF COLOR

The first six heresies essentially address content and methodology for gathering and interpreting content. They inform decisions such as the following:

1. Not teaching Linda Brent's *Narrative* as the single example of the slave experience of African American women in the nineteenth century, but rather presenting it as a representative example of the slave experience of African American women that occurs within a contradictory, paradoxical world that had free Black women such as Charlotte Forten Grimke and African American abolitionist women such as Sojourner Truth. The picture of Black women that emerges then becomes one that illuminates their complexity of experiences and their differing interactions with White people rather than an aberrant experience.

2. Not simply teaching about pioneer women in the West, but teaching about Native American women, perhaps through their stories, which they have passed on to their children and their children's children using the word to advance those concepts crucial to cultural survival. The picture of settling the West becomes more balanced, suggesting clearly to students the different perspectives and power relationships. The Native American becomes a subject—one who acts and interacts, rather than an object of Whites, portrayed as the only subjects.

3. Not choosing biographies for children of a White woman, an Asian American woman, and an African American woman, but rather finding ways through biography, poetry, and storytelling to introduce children to different women's experiences, different according to race, class, ethnicity, and gender roles. The emphases are on the connectedness of experiences and on the differences among experiences, the communality among human beings, and the interrelatedness among experiences and ways of learning.

The last two heresies directly address process. After accurate content, process is the most important part of teaching. Students who learn in an environment that is sensitive to their feelings and that supports and encourages the pursuit of knowledge will consistently meet new knowledge and new situations with the necessary openness and understanding for human development and progress. If this sounds moralistic, we must remember that the stated and implied goal of critical pedagogy and feminist pedagogy, as well as of efforts to transform the curriculum with content about women and ethnicity, is to provide an education that more accurately reflects the history and composition of the world, that demonstrates the relationship of what we learn to how we live, and that implicitly and explicitly reveals the relationship between knowledge and social action. Process is most important, then, in helping students develop ways throughout their education to reach the closest approximation of truth toward the end of a better, more democratic human condition.

The key to understanding the teaching process in any classroom in which teaching about women of color from the perspective of transformation is a goal is recognizing that the content alters all students' perceptions of themselves. First, they begin to realize that we can never say women to mean all women, that we must particularize the term as appropriate to context and understanding (for example, White, middle-class women; Chinese American, lower-class women; middle-class, Mexican American women). Next, students begin to understand that using White, middle-class women as the norm will seem distortingly reductive. White women's ethnic, regional, class, and gender commonalities and differences soon become apparent, and the role in oppression of the imposed Anglo-American ethnic conformity stands out. Student reactions may range from surprise, to excitement about learning more, to hostility and anger. In the volume *Gendered Subjects*, Margo Culley details much of what happens. Her opening paragraph summarizes her main thesis:

> Teaching about gender and race can create classrooms that are charged arenas. Students enter these classrooms imbued with the values of the dominant culture: they believe that success in conventional terms is largely a matter of will and that those who do not have it all have experienced a failure of will. Closer and closer ties between corporate America and higher education, as well as the "upscaling" of the student body, make it even harder to hear the voices from the margin within the academy. Bringing those voices to the center of the classroom means disorganizing ideology and disorienting individuals. Sometimes, as suddenly as the fragments in a kaleidoscope rearrange to totally change the picture, our work alters the ground of being for our students (and perhaps even for ourselves). When this happens, classrooms can become explosive, but potentially transformative arenas of dialogue. (Culley, 1985, p. 209)

While Culley's observation is eleven years old at this writing, reports from faculty in various workshops I have conducted nationwide suggest that it still holds.

"Altering the ground of being" happens to some extent on all levels. The White girl kindergarten pupil's sense of the world is frequently challenged when she discovers that heroines do not necessarily look like her. Awareness of the ways in which the world around children is ordered occurs earlier than most of us may imagine. My niece, barely four years old, told my father in a definitive tone as we entered a church farther from her home than the church to which she belongs, "Gramps, this is the Black church." We had not referred to the church as such, yet clearly that Catholic congregation was predominantly Black and the girl's home congregation predominantly White. Her younger sister, at age three, told her mother that the kids in the day school she attended were "not like me." She then pointed to the brown, back side of her hand. Young children notice difference. We direct what they do with and think of that difference.

Teaching young children about women of color gives male and female children of all backgrounds a sense of the diversity of people, of the various roles in which women function in U.S. culture, of the various joys and sorrows, triumphs and struggles they encounter. Seeds of awareness of the power relationships between male and female, among racial, ethnic, and class groups are sown and nurtured.

Teaching about women of color early in students' academic experience allows the voices of the margin to be heard and to become a part of the matrix of reality. Teaching about women of color reveals race, ethnicity, gender, and class as essential components of human identity and also questions ideology and ways of being. It encourages an openness to understanding, difference and similarity, and the foreign and the commonplace necessary to the mind-set of curiosity and fascination for knowledge that we all want to inspire in our students no matter what the subject. Moreover, it highlights connections among human beings and human experiences and reveals relationships among actions one to another.

Culley also observes that "anger is the energy mediating the transformation from damage to wholeness," the damage being the values and perspectives of the dominant culture that have shaped opinions based on a seriously flawed and skewed American history and interpretation of the present (Culley, 1985, p. 212). Certain reactions occur and are part of the process of teaching about women of color. Because they can occur at all levels to a greater or lesser extent, it is useful to look for variations on their themes.

It is important to recognize that these reactions occur within the context of student and teacher expectations. Students are concerned about grading, teachers about evaluations by superiors and students. Frequently, fear of, disdain for, or hesitancy about feminist perspectives by some students may create a tense, hostile atmosphere. Similarly, fear of, disdain for, or hesitancy about studying people different from you (particularly by the White student) or people similar to you (particularly by the student of color or of a culture related to people of color) also may create a tense, hostile atmosphere. Student expectations of teachers, expectations modulated by the ethnicity, race, class, and gender of the teacher, may encourage students to presume that a teacher will take a certain position. The teacher's need to inspire students to perform with excellence may become a teacher's priority at the expense of presenting material that may at first confuse the students or challenge their opinions. It is important to treat these reactions as though they are as much a part of the process of teaching as the form of presentation, the exams, and the content, for, indeed, they are. Moreover, they can affect the success of the teaching of the material about women of color.

Specifically, these reactions are part of the overall process of moving from the familiar to the unfamiliar. As heresy #7 guides us, "Feelings are direct lines to better thinking." Affective reactions to content, such as anger, guilt, and feelings of displacement, when recognized for what they are, lead to the desired cognitive reaction, the conceptualization of the facts so that knowledge becomes useful as the closest approximation to the truth. As Japanese American female students first read accounts by Issei (first-generation) women about their picture bride experiences, their reactions might at first be mixed. Raising the issue of Japanese immigration to the United States during the late nineteenth century may not only challenge the exotic stereotype of the Japanese woman, but it may also engender anger toward Japanese males, because of students' incomplete access to history. White students may respond with guilt or indifference because of the policy of a government whose composition is essentially White, Anglo-oriented, and with which they identify. Japanese American male students may become defensive, desirous of hearing Japanese American men's stories about picture bride marriages. African American male and female students may draw analogies between the Japanese American experience and the African American experience. Such analogies may be welcomed or resented by other students. Of course, students from varied backgrounds may respond to learning about Issei women with a reinforced or instilled pride in Japanese ancestry or with a newfound interest in immigration history.

Teacher presentation of Issei women's experience as picture brides should include, of course, lectures, readings, films, and videos about the experience of male Issei immigrants to the United States during the first quarter of the twentieth century, the cheap labor they provided, the impossibility of return to Japan due to low wages, the male-female ratio of Japanese Americans at the turn of the century, and the tradition of arranged marriage in Japan. Presentations should also anticipate, however, student reaction based on their generally ill-informed or limited knowledge about the subject. Discussion and analysis of the students' initial perspectives on Issei women, of how those perspectives have changed given the historical, cultural, and sociological information, allow for learning about and reading Issei women's accounts to become an occasion, then, for expressing feelings of guilt, shame, anger, pride, interest, and curiosity, and for getting at the reasons for those feelings.

Understanding those feelings and working with them to move the student from a familiar that may be comprised of damaging misinformation and even bigotry, to a balanced understanding, sometimes become major portions of the content, especially when anger or guilt is directed toward a specific group—other students, the teacher, or perhaps even the self. Then it becomes necessary for the teacher to use what I call pressure release sessions. The need for such sessions may manifest itself in many ways. For example,

> the fear of being regarded by peers or by the professor as racist, sexist or "politically incorrect" can polarize a classroom. If the [teacher] participates unconsciously in this fear and emotional self-protection, the classroom experience will degenerate to hopeless polarization, and even overt hostility. He or she must constantly stand outside the classroom experience and anticipate such dynamics. ..."Pressure release" discussions work best when the teacher directly acknowledges and calls attention to the tension in the classroom. The teacher may initiate the discussion or allow it to come about in whatever way he or she feels most comfortable. (Butler, 1985, p. 236)

The hostility, fear, and hesitancy "can be converted to fertile ground for profound academic experiences…'profound' because the students' knowledge is challenged, expanded, or reinforced" (Butler, 1985, p. 236) by a subject matter that is simultaneously affective and cognitive, resonant with the humanness of life in both form and content. Students learn from these pressure release sessions, as they must learn in life, to achieve balance and harmony in whatever pursuits, that paradoxes and contradictions are sometimes resolved and sometimes stand separately yet function together (recall heresy #1).

Teaching about women of color can often spark resistance to the teacher or cause students to question subject veracity. For example, students usually are taught that the latter part of the nineteenth century and the turn of the century was a time of expansion for the United States—the Progressive Era. Learning of the experiences of Native American and Mexican women who were subjected to particular horrors as the United States pushed westward, or reading about restrictions on Chinese immigrant women who were not allowed to enter the United States with the Chinese men who provided what was tantamount to slave labor for the building of the railroads, students begin to realize that this time was anything but progressive or expansive.

Teaching about Ida Wells-Barnett, the African American woman who waged the antilynching campaigns at the end of the nineteenth century and well into the twentieth century, also belies the progress of that time. Ida Wells-Barnett brings to the fore the horror of lynchings of African American men, women, and children, the inhuman practice of castration that was part of the lynching of Black males, the stereotyped ideas of African American men and women, ideas that were, as Giddings reminds us, "older than the Republic itself—for they were rooted in the European minds that shaped America" (Giddings, 1984, p. 31). Furthermore, Wells-Barnett's life work reveals the racism of White women in the suffragist movement of the early twentieth century, a reflection of the racism in that movement's nineteenth-century manifestation.

The ever-present interaction of racism and sexism, the stereotyping of African American men and women as bestial, the unfounded labeling of African American men as rapists in search of White women, and the horrid participation in all of this by White men and women in all stations of life, make for difficult history for any teacher to teach and for any student to study. The threat to the perfect founding fathers and Miss Liberty versions are apparent. Such content is often resisted by African American and White students alike, perhaps for different reasons, including rage, anger, or shame that such atrocities were endured by people like them; indifference in the face of reality because "nothing like that will happen again"; and anger, guilt, or shame that people of their race were responsible for such hideous atrocities. Furthermore, all students may resent the upsetting of their neatly packaged understandings of U.S. history and of their world.

The teacher must know the content and be willing to facilitate the pressure release sessions that undoubtedly will be needed. Pressure release sessions must help students sort out facts from feelings and, most of all, must clarify the relevance of the material to understanding the world in which we live and to preventing such atrocities from recurring. Also, in teaching about the Issei women and about the life of Ida Wells-Barnett, teachers must never let the class lose sight of the vision these women had, how they dealt with joy and sorrow, the triumphs and struggles of their lives, the contributions to both their own people and to U.S. life at large.

In addition to variations on anger, guilt, and challenges to credibility in learning about women of color, students become more aware of the positive aspects of race and ethnicity and frequently begin to take pride in their identities. As heresy #8 states, "Knowledge is identity and identity is knowledge. All knowledge is explicitly and implicitly related to who we are, both as individuals and as groups." The teacher, however, must watch for overzealous pride as well as unadmitted uneasiness with one's ethnic or racial identity. White students, in particular, may react in a generally unexpected manner. Some may predictably claim their Irish ancestry; others may be confused as to their ethnicity, for they may come from German and Scottish ancestry, which early on assumed Anglo-American identity. Students of Anglo-American ancestry, however, may hesitate to embrace that terminology, for it might suggest to them, in the context of the experiences of women and men of color, an abuse of power and "all things horrible in this country," as one upset student once complained to me. Here teachers must be adept not only at conveying facts, but also at explaining the effects of culture, race, gender, and ethnicity in recording and interpreting historical facts. They also must be able to convey to students both the beautiful and the ugly in all of us. Thus, the African American teacher may find himself or herself explaining the cultural value of Anglo-American or Yankee humor, of Yankee precision in gardening, of Yankee thriftiness, of the conflicting values of the founding fathers, and how we all share, in some way, that heritage. At whatever age this occurs, students must be helped to understand the dichotomous, hierarchical past of that identity and to move toward expressing their awareness in a pluralistic context.

Now that we have explored the why of the phrase *women of color*, identified the essence of what we learn when we study women of color, discussed the theory of transformation and its heresies, and identified and discussed the most frequent reactions of students to the subject matter, we focus on the teacher.

CONCLUSION

Teaching about women of color should result in conveying information about a group of people largely invisible in our curricula in a way that encourages students to seek further knowledge and ultimately begin to correct and reorder the flawed perception of the world based on racism, sexism, classism, and ethnocentrism. To do so is no mean feat. Redefining one's world involves not only the inclusion of previously ignored content, but also the revision, deletion, and correction of accepted content in light of missing and ignored content. As such, it might require a redesignation of historical periods, a renaming of literary periods, and a complete reworking of sociological methodology to reflect the ethnic and cultural standards at work. This chapter, then, is essentially an introduction to the journey that teachers must embark on to begin providing for students a curriculum that reflects the reality of the past, prepares students to deal with and understand the present, and creates the basis for a more humane, productive, caring future.

The implications of teaching about women of color are far-reaching, involving many people in many different capacities. New texts need to be written for college-level students. Teacher education must be restructured to include not only the transformed content but also the pedagogy that reflects how our nation and the world are multicultural, multiethnic, multiracial, multifocal, and multidimensional. College texts, children's books, and other materials need to be devised to help teach this curriculum. School administrators, school boards, parents, and teachers need to participate in and contribute to this transformation in all ways that influence what our children learn.

For teachers and those studying to be teachers, the immediate implications of a transformed curriculum can seem overwhelming, for transformation is a process that will take longer than our lifetimes. Presently, we are in the formative stages of understanding what must be done to correct the damage in order to lead to wholeness. I suggest that we begin small. That is, decide to include women of color in your classes this year. Begin adding some aspect of that topic to every unit. Pay close attention to how that addition relates to what you already teach. Does it expand the topic? Does it present material you already cover within that expansion? Can you delete some accepted, repetitive material and still meet your objectives? Does the new material conflict with the old? How? Is that conflict a valuable learning resource for your students? Answering such questions will move you quickly from simply adding to re-visioning and transforming. Continue to do this each year. Gradually, other central topics will emerge about men of color, White men, White women, class, race, ethnicity, and gender. By beginning with studying women of color, the curriculum then will have evolved to be truly pluralistic.

This chapter pays the most attention to the student. The teacher, who embarks on this long journey, must be determined to succeed. Why? Because all the conflicting emotions, the sometimes painful movement from the familiar to the unfamiliar, are experienced by the teacher as well. We have been shaped by the same damaging, ill-informed view of the world as our students. Often, as we try to resolve their conflicts, we are simultaneously working through our own. Above all, we must demand honesty of ourselves before we can succeed.

Another important task of the teacher is changing how, in our attempts to change the construction of the student as object, a receptacle of information, we have constructed the student as a distant, theoretical, abstract subject. John Shilb cogently describes what it means to change how we construct the student as subject:

> Changing how the student is constructed as subject
> entails a number of related teaching practices. It means considering how social differences can affect the interests, backgrounds, learning styles, and degrees of confidence that students bring to the classroom. It means examining how authority operates there as well as in the larger society, analyzing how traditional power relations might be rethought or merely reinforced when teachers and students meet. It means taking students' accounts of their own experiences as

at least potentially legitimate avenues to knowledge. It means recognizing that learning can involve intuition and emotion, not just cold, hard logic. Overall, it means taking as a central classroom aim the empowerment of students as conscious, active subjects in the learning process, thereby enhancing their capacity to develop a more democratic world. (Shilb, 1992, p. 65)

The difficulty of the process of transformation is one factor contributing to the maintenance of the status quo. Often we look for the easiest way out. It is easier to work with students who are not puzzled, concerned, or bothered by what they are studying. We, as teachers, must be willing to admit that we do not know everything, but that we do know how to go about learning in a way that reaches the closest approximation of the truth. Our reach must always exceed our grasp, and, in doing so, we will encourage the excellence, the passion, the curiosity, the respect, and the love needed to create superb scholarship and encourage thinking, open-minded, caring, knowledgeable students.

Questions and Activities

1. When Butler uses the phrase *women of color,* to what specific ethnic groups is she referring? Why did this phrase emerge, and what purpose does it serve?

2. How can a study of women of color help broaden our understanding of White women? Of women in general?

3. In what ways, according to Butler, is ethnicity an important variable in women's lives? Give specific examples from this chapter to support your response.

4. How does racism, combined with sexism, influence the ways in which people view and respond to women of color?

5. What does the author mean by transformation and a *transformed curriculum?* How does a transformed curriculum differ from a mainstream or balanced curriculum?

6. How can content about women of color serve as a vehicle for transforming the school curriculum?

7. The author lists eight heresies, or assumptions, about reality that differ fundamentally from dominant modes of thought and values. Why does she believe these heresies are essential when teaching about women of color?

8. The author states that teaching about women of color may spark resistance to the teacher, the subject, or both. What examples of content does she describe that may evoke student resistance? Why, according to Butler, might students resist this content? What tips does she give teachers for handling student resistance?

9. Develop a teaching unit in which you incorporate content about women of color, using the transformation approach described in this chapter. Useful references on women of color are found in the appendix ("Gender" section).

References

Billinglsey, A. (1968). *Black Families in White America*. Englewood Cliffs, NJ: Prentice-Hall.

Brown, E. B. (1989). African American Women's Quilting: A Framework for Conceptualizing and Teaching African American Women's History. *Signs: Journal of Women in Culture and Society, 14*(4), 921–929.

Cade, T. (1970). *The Black Woman: An Anthology*. New York: New American Library.

Conditions, Five (1979, Autumn). *The Black Woman's Issue 2*,(3).

Culley, M. (1985). Anger and Authority in the Introductory Women's Studies Classroom. In M. Culley and C. Portuges (Eds.). *Gendered Subjects: The Dynamics of Feminist Teaching*. Boston: Routledge and Kegan Paul.

Davidson, B. (1969). *The African Genius*. Boston: Little, Brown.

Fisher, D. (1980). (Ed.). *The Third Woman: Minority Women Writers of the United States*. Boston: Houghton Mifflin.

Friere, P. (1969). *Pedagogy of the Oppressed*. New York: Seabury.

Friere, P. (1973). *Education for Critical Consciousness*. New York: Seabury.

Frye, M. (1983). On Being White: Toward a Feminist Understanding of Race and Race Supremacy. In M. Frye (Ed.). *The Politics of Reality: Essays in Feminist Theory*. (pp. 110–127). Trumansburg, NY: The Crossing Press.

Giddings, P. (1984). *When and Where I Enter: The Impact of Black Women on Race and Sex in America*. New York: William Morrow.

Giroux, H. (1994). Slacking Off: Border Youth and Postmodern Education. *Journal of Advanced Composition, 14*(2), 347–366.

Gross, S. H. (1987, March). Women's History for Global Learning. *Social Education, 51*(3), 194–198.

Ladner, J. (Ed.). (1973). *The Death of White Sociology*. New York: Vintage.

Mbiti, J. (1975). *Introduction to African Religion*. London: Heinemann.

McAdoo, H. (Ed.). (1981). *Black Families*. Beverly Hills, CA: Sage Publications.

McIntosh, P. (1987). *Understanding Correspondence between White Privilege and Male Privilege through Women's Studies Work*. Unpublished paper presented at the National Women's Studies Association Annual Meeting, Atlanta, GA.

Moraga, C. and Anzaldua, G. (Eds.). (1981). *This Bridge Called My Back: Writings by Radical Women of Color*. Watertown, MA: Persephone Press.

Moynihan, D. (1965). *The Negro Family*. Washington, DC: U.S. Department of Labor.

Shilb, J. (1992). Poststructuralism, Politics, and the Subject of Pedagogy. In M. Kecht (Ed.). *Pedagogy Is Politics: Literary Theory and Critical Teaching* (pp. 62–85). Urbana: University of Illinois Press.

Spelman, E. V. (1982). Theories of Gender and Race: The Erasure of Black Women. *Quest: A Feminist Quarterly, 5*(4), 36–62.

Ethnic, cultural, and language diversity in today's classrooms present rich opportunities and possibilities as well as challenges to classroom teachers.

Race, Ethnicity, and Language

The drastic increase in the percentage of students of color and of language minority students in the nation's schools is one of the most significant developments in education in the last several decades. The growth in the percentage of students of color and of language minority students in the nation's schools results from several factors, including the new wave of immigration that began after 1968 and the aging of the White population. The nation's classrooms are experiencing the largest influx of immigrant students since the turn of the century. The United States received nearly one million immigrants in 1980, more than in any year up to that time since 1914. Today, more than 600,000 people make the United States their home each year, most of whom come from nations in Asia and Latin America.

Demographers predict that if current trends continue, about 46 percent of the nation's school-age youths will be of color by the year 2020. In 1992, students of color made up 76.5 percent of the student population in the forty-seven districts that make up the Council of the Great City Schools. They were a majority of the students in the state of California. Another important characteristic of today's students is the large percentage who are poor and who live in female-headed households. Today, about one out of every five students lives in a poor family.

While the percentage of students of color in the nation's schools is increasing rapidly, the percentage of teachers of color is decreasing sharply. In 1980, teachers of color made up 12.5 percent of the nation's teachers. If current declining trends continue, they will make up about 5 percent of the nation's teachers by the turn of the century. In the year 2000, most students in the nation's cities and a significant percentage of those in suburban school districts will be students of color, and more of the teachers than today will be White and mainstream. This development underscores the need for all teachers to develop the knowledge, attitudes, and skills needed to work effectively with students from diverse racial, ethnic, social-class, and language groups.

Chapter 9

Educational Equality
for Students of Color

Geneva Gay

Despite its desirability, to date the goal of achieving educational equality for students of color has been elusive and unattainable. Reasons for this are complicated. Some are associated with how educational equality is typically conceived. Others may be located in the indicators that are most often used to determine the educational attainment of students from different ethnic groups, and whether these indicators are culturally sensitive enough to be valid measures of the academic performance of students of color. Still other reasons may have to do with the quality of the opportunities and experiences students from different ethnic groups receive in educational processes as they matriculate through school. This chapter explores these issues as a basis for establishing some foundations for proposals about how education can be reformed to move closer toward achieving the goal of equality, in both the processes and outcomes of learning, for students of color.

CONCEPTION OF EDUCATIONAL EQUALITY

Educational equality in the United States is popularly understood to mean the *physical access* of African Americans, Latino, Asian Americans, and American Indians to the same schools and instructional programs as middle-class European American students. The prevailing assumption is that when these groups become students in majority schools, equal educational opportunity is achieved. Until recently little attention was given to the quality of the curriculum content and instructional processes as key factors in formulas for educational equity.

For those who accept a strictly de jure or legal conception of desegregation, the issue of educational inequality is largely resolved. After all, they argue, federal and state laws now exist prohibiting educational discrimination on the basis of race, color, creed, gender, nationality, and social class. For these people, the persisting discrepancies between the academic achievement, quality of school life, and other indicators of school success of students of color and European Americans are not a result of differences in educational opportunities at all. Rather, these problems are matters of personal abilities, aspirations, and responsibiities. Students of color and poverty do not do as well in school as their middle-class White counterparts because of individual deficiencies, not because of discrepancies in opportunities perpetuated by schools that serve systematically to their detriment.

These notions of educational inequality, and attributions of responsibility for it, are overly simplistic, naive, and culturally insensitive. They assume that the education European American students are receiving is universally desirable, and that the only way for youths of color to get a comparable education is to imitate Whites. Given the great diversity in quality of the teachers, facilities, resources, and instruction that exists in U.S. schools, including predominantly European American ones, these conceptions are inadequate. Any viable definitions of and approaches to educational equality must take into consideration the *quality of instructional opportunities*, not merely the place where students attend school. Legal mandates guaranteeing the accessibility of schooling to all students do not ensure quality unless the opportunities themselves are of equal status (Astin, 1985). And, under no circumstances can identical educational opportunities for very diverse groups and individuals (whether that diversity stems from class, gender, race, ethnicity, nationality, or personal traits) constitute equality.

Equating sameness of opportunity with educational equality ignores the more fundamental issue of quality of learning opportunity, and how this has to be understood and acted on within the contexts of ethnic and cultural diversity. It also fails to acknowledge the fact that treating different individuals identically is inherently discriminatory. Their differentness demands variability in treatment so that each can have the best chances to perform at maximum capabilities. Thus, equality of educational opportunities should be understood to mean *equity, parity,* and *comparability* of treatment based on diagnosed needs of diverse individuals and groups. How can this be accomplished? Should the *processes of schooling* be given much more attention in efforts to achieve educational equality for students of color? Or, as Grant and Sleeter might ask, what should happen "after the school bell rings" (Grant & Sleeter, 1986) for students of color if they are to receive educational equality? Answers to these questions are contingent on a clear understanding of the various inequalities that now exist. These issues and inequities and some possible solutions to them are discussed in the subsequent sections of this chapter.

EDUCATIONAL ATTAINMENT OF STUDENTS OF COLOR

Despite legal mandates prohibiting them, educational inequalities continue to prevail at crisis levels today. A report on the educational status of African Americans by the College Entrance Examination Board (*Equality and Excellence*, 1985, p. vii) concluded that "although many of the legal barriers to educational opportunity have been removed, education—to a large extent—remains separate and unequal in the United

States." This inequality becomes clearer when the current educational status of students of color, especially African Americans, Mexican Americans, Puerto Ricans, and American Indians, and the pervasiveness of the problems these groups encounter in schools, are analyzed. The situation is not quite as serious for Asian Americans, at least on some standardized test measures of school achievements, school attendance, and graduation rates.

Unquestionably, some significant progress has been made in the last thirty years in the social conditions of schooling for and academic achievement of students of color. This is evident in increasing rates of high school graduation; some steady but small improvements in proficiency levels in the academic core subjects (math, science, reading, writing, social studies); and the enactment of federal legislation (such as the Indian Education Act, Chapter 1, and the Bilingual Education Act), which pays for supplementary instructional services for educationally and economically disadvantaged children in kindergarten through grade twelve to assure them equal access to high quality academic achievement. Of these federal initiatives, Chapter 1 is the most notable for its duration and magnitude of funding. The beneficiaries of Chapter 1 services include approximately 5 percent Native and Asian Americans, 28 percent African Americans, 27 percent Latinos, and 41 percent European Americans (U.S. Department of Education, 1994a).

During the late 1980s and early 1990s, many federal and state efforts toward equalizing access to educational resources experienced serious cutbacks. For instance:

- 750,000 children were disqualified from receiving services from Chapter 1 programs.

- Requirements for schools receiving federal funds to comply with anti-discrimination laws were relaxed.

- New funding arrangements that benefit rural and private schools at the expense of urban and inner-city schools were instituted.

- Drastic cuts were made in the funding of bilingual, migrant, Indian, and gender equity educational initiatives. (*Teachers' View on Equity and Excellence*, 1983, pp. 4–5)

These changes were due to less money available, unsympathetic national administrations, and a general overall climate of conservatism toward social service programs.

Other serious problems exist that negatively affect the educational opportunities of students of color and testify to the persistence of educational inequality. Most elementary and secondary schools in the United States continue to be racially segregated. Students of color now constitute the majority population in at least 41 of the nation's 100 largest school districts, and this distribution is increasing yearly. This number is probably an underestimate since 15 of the largest districts located in cities with large numbers of people of color populations (such as Atlanta, New Orleans, and St. Louis) did not report their student enrollments by ethnicity. In the 41 school systems, the percentages of students of color range from a low of 53.3 percent in Pittsburgh, Pennsylvania, to 96.6 percent in Washington, DC. In 22 of these districts, the percentage is 75 or higher (U.S. Department of Education, 1991). African Americans comprise 16.7 percent of U.S. public school students, Latinos 11.9, American Indians/Alaskan Natives

1.1, and Asian/Pacific Islanders 2.9. Together, they accounted for a total of 32.6 percent of all public school students in 1992. This percentage is expected to continue to increase well into the twenty-first century (*Education That Works*, 1990; Olivas, 1986, pp. 1–25; Orum, 1986; U.S. Bureau of the Census, 1990; U.S. Department of Education, 1990). According to Celis (1993), in the 1991–92 school year 66 percent of African Americans and 74.3 percent of Latinos attended schools where the majority student population was African American, Latino, or a combination of these two. High percentages of these groups are located in central cities. For example in 1992, 32.5 percent of African American and 20.8 percent of Latino students attended schools in central cities. Approximately 8 percent of Native Americans attend Bureau of Indian Affairs (BIA) tribal schools, 36 percent attend public schools with Indian enrollment of 25 percent of more, and the other 56 percent attend schools with low Indian and Native Alaskan (less than 25 percent) populations. The number of students who have difficulty speaking English increased by 27 percent between 1980 and 1990 (U.S. Department of Education, 1994d, 1995). The populations of students of color also are distributed unequally throughout the United States: African Americans are clustered in the Southeast and the Great Lakes areas; Latinos in the Southwest; Asian Americans along the Pacific Coast; and American Indians and Native Alaskans in the Great Plains states and Alaska.

Yet, the ethnicity of teachers, administrators, and policymakers in these districts is the reverse. European Americans far outnumber educators of color in all school leadership and instructional positions. In fact, the numbers of school teachers and administrators of color declined steadily for about fifteen years before an increase occurred in 1991. The percentage of African American teachers declined from 12.0 in 1970 to an all-time low of 6.9 percent in 1987. By 1991 this percentage had increased to 8.3. In 1987 Latinos comprised 1.9 percent of all elementary and secondary teachers in the United States; this had increased to 3.4 by 1991. The number of American Indian/Alaskan Native and Asian/Pacific Islander teachers in the same year was 0.8 and 1.0 percent, respectively. The ratios of students-to-teachers by ethnic groups are African Americans 2:1 (approximately 16.7 percent students and 8 percent teachers); Latinos more than 3:1 (11.9 percent students, 3.4 percent teachers); Asian/Pacific Islanders, 2:1; and American Indian/Native Alaskan, 1:1 (*USA Today*, 1986; Orum, 1986; U.S. Department of Education, 1993). Traditionally, urban schools have had less money, fewer resources and poorer facilities, larger numbers of inexperienced teachers, greater management problems, and higher turnover rates among teachers, administrators, and students (see Chapter 4 for a more detailed discussion). Moreover, too few systematic and sustained high-quality teacher education and leadership development programs exist to prepare educators to work effectively with urban students of color.

These situations lead to some obvious conclusions. One is that the ethnic, class, and racial disparities that currently exist between teachers and students will continue unabated in the future. Another is that teachers will inevitably encounter children of color. Their instructional effectiveness and the extent to which educational equality exist for the greater number of students will depend largely on teachers "understanding a broad array of histories, personal experiences, cultural practices, languages, and needs" (Miller-Lachmann & Taylor, 1995, p. 62).

Although the levels of educational attainment of students of color, as measured by such factors as high school graduation, daily attendance records, persistence rates, and levels of acdemic proficiency, are increasing for successive generations, the dropout rates continue to be a major problem. According to Bureau of Census statistics the high school completion rates in 1993 for European Americans twenty-five years or older was 81.5 percent compared to 70.4 percent for African Americans, and 53.1 percent for Latinos. No data were reported for the high school graduation rates of American Indian/Native Alaskans (Kominski & Adams, 1994).

The dropout rate for African Americans declined between 1970 and 1993 from 30 to 12.5 percent, compared to 15.2 and 7.3 percent for European Americans. Yet this rate continues to be higher than the national average (10. 6 percent). The situation is even worse for Latinos. Their national average dropout rate (30.7) in 1993 was almost two and a half times that of African Americans and and more than four times that of European Americans (U.S. Department of Education, 1994a, 1994d). In some school districts the dropout rates far excede the national averages. A 1986 California State University System Advisory Council on Educational Equity reported that Latinos had the highest dropout rate of all ethnic groups in California. Some school districts indicated that as many as 40 percent of Latino students left school before grade 10. However, approximately 50 percent of Mexican Americans and Puerto Ricans drop out of high school before graduation. In some urban school districts, such as Chicago, Boston, New York, and Philadelphia, the dropout rate for Puerto Ricans has been as high as 70 percent (Nielsen, 1986; Nieto, 1995; Orum, 1986; Santiago, 1986). Unfortunately, given other achievement patterns, there is no reason to be hopeful that this rate has changed significantly in the last eight years.

For most ethnic groups the school dropout rates of males excede those of females. This pattern also prevails across time periods. The exception is African Americans. Female dropouts were greater than males by 1.7 percent in 1990 (13.4 compared to 15.1), and 1.5 percent in 1992 (12.3 compared to 13.8). By 1993 the difference had dropped to 0.8 percent, when the dropout rate for African American females was 12.9 percent compared to 12.1 percent for males (U.S. Department of Education, 1994a).

Dropout rates for American Indians, Native Alaskans, and Asian Americans/ Pacific Islanders are not reported as systematically as for African Americans, Latinos, and European Americans. But, given the general educational status of American Indians on other measures of school success that indicate that their situation is comparable to that of African Americans and Latinos, their dropout rates may likewise be as high or higher. Given that the high school completion rates of many Asian American groups excede the national averages, their dropout rates also may be far lower, but the gender pattern is similar. Yu, Doi, and Chang (1986) found that more Asian males leave school prior to graduation than females.

Another school attendance factor that contributes to the educational inequality of students of color is *school delay*. Defined by Nielsen (1986, p. 79) as "the discrepancy between the educational level reached by students and the normal level corresponding to their age," school delay rates are substantially greater for African Americans, Latinos, and American Indians than for European and Asian Americans. These groups repeat grades more often and generally take longer to complete school.

Since 1980 the percentage of students of color below modal grade (the grade in which most children of a certain age are enrolled) has increased substantially. African American males have the highest below modal grade averages. In 1985 (the latest data available) their representation in this category was 32.4 percent for eight-year-olds and 44.2 percent for thirteen-year-olds, compared to 24 and 29.1 percent for White eight- and thirteen-year old males, and 19.9 and 35 percent for eight- and thirteen-year-old African American females (U.S. Department of Education, 1990). Thus, by age thirteen almost one-half of African American males and one-third Latinos have repeated a grade at least once (Miller-Lachmann & Taylor, 1995).

School delays are more serious than they might first appear. They may initiate a cumulative process that ultimately results in the child's leaving school completely. Delayed students are likely to be judged as being academically inadequate and assigned to special category, low academic, or vocational-track curricula. As these students fall behind their age group, they become stigmatized as slow learners and socially isolated in schools. Teachers tend to have low expectations of achievement for delayed students. Together, these situations increase failure rates and the chances that the affected students will become dropouts.

Even for students of color who remain in school and attend racially mixed schools, the likelihood of the greater number of them receiving educational equality is dubious. The academic achievement levels of all students of color, except some Asian Americans, is significantly lower than the national averages. These differences exist on all measures for every age group at all levels of schooling, in every region of the country, and at every socioeconomic level (Gougis, 1986). However, reports from the National Assessment of Educational Progress (NAEP), the College Entrance Examination Board, and the National Center for Educational Statistics indicate that the performance of African Americans, Latinos, and Native Americans on standardized tests and academic proficiency measures is improving.

On closer inspection, these improvements are not as positive as we might hope, for several reasons. First, while the overall performance of all groups of color students on standardized tests increased between 1983 and 1993, they remain significantly lower than that of European Americans. A case in point is Scholastic Aptitude Test (SAT) scores, which increased from 893 to 902 during this decade. As Table 9.1 shows, while the SAT scores of students of color also increased, they continue to be lower than those of European Americans and the national average, with the exception of Asian Americans.

The greatest gains occurred among Asian Americans, whose scores increased 21 points on the math and 20 points on the verbal portions of the SAT test. Native Americans also made impressive gains between 1983 and 1993—12 points on the verbal and 22 points on the math scores, as did African Americans (14 verbal and 19 math).

The gaps among ethnic groups on the SAT continue to be significant. Although the combined scores of African Americans increased by 33 points, they continue to be lower than any other group. There was a 35 point gap between them and Puerto Ricans, the group whose performance is closest to theirs, and 209 point differential between African Americans and Asian Americans, who perform the highest on the SAT. The verbal SAT scores of all groups except European and Mexican Americans

Table 9.1 Scholastic Aptitude Test (SAT) Scores by Selected Ethnicity for 1983 and 1993

| Group | Composite Verbal and Math Scores | | |
	1983	1993	Point Difference
African Americans	708	741	+33
American Indians	813	847	+34
Asian Americans	909	950	+41
European Americans	927	948	+9
Mexican Americans	793	802	+9
Puerto Ricans	761	776	+21
All Students	893	902	+9

Source: The Conditions of Education. (1994). Washington, DC: U.S. Department of Education, Office of Educational Research and Improvement.

also increased; however, they remain significantly lower than the math scores. Despite achieving the overall greatest gains between 1983 and 1993, the largest gaps occurred for Asian Americans. There was a difference of 120 points between their verbal (415) and math (535) SAT scores. For African Americans the difference was 35 points; Mexican Americans, 54; Puerto Ricans, 42, and American Indians, 47. These differences compare to a 54-point difference between the verbal and math scores for all students, and a 50 point difference for European Americans (U.S. Department of Education, 1994d).

The National Assessment of Educational Progress (NAEP) presents achievement data for nine-, thirteen-, and seventeen-year-olds on a regular basis in seven skill areas. Known as "Report Cards," reading and mathematics proficiency is assessed every two years, science and writing every four years, and geography, literature, and U.S. history every six years. Achievement profiles are routinely presented by gender and for European, African, and Latino ethnic groups, but not for Native Indian/Alaskans and Asian/Pacific Islanders. The National Center for Education Statistics explains that because American Indians and Alaska Natives comprise only 1 percent of U.S. school enrollments,

> these students and the schools and teachers who serve them are almost never represented in sufficient numbers in national education studies to permit reliable and valid generalizations about their characteristics. Furthermore, because of factors such as tribal and linguistic diversity, geographic dispersion, and preponderance in remote rural areas, most

national studies have found it too costly to add supplemental
samples to address issues of concern to American Indian and
Alaska Native education. (U.S. Department of Education,
1995, p. iii)

In the 1986 assessment of eleventh graders in literature, African Americans and
Latinos scored similarily (267.5 and 264.8), but significantly lower than the national
average (285.0) and European Americans (289.9). The same pattern was evident in
1988 on the geography proficiency tests. Twelfth-grade African Americans who were
tested received an average score of 258.4 compared to 271.8 for Latinos, and 301.1
for European Americans. The 1988 U.S. History report card indicated that the performance of twelfth-grade Latinos (273.9) and African Americans (274.9) was only
slightly higher than eighth-grade European Americans (270.4), and at least 25 points
below their White peers (301.1). African Americans scored (199.5) lower than Latinos
(202.7) in the fourth grade, but slighly higher in the eighth grade (246.0 and 244.3,
respectively). In all three grades tested, the performance of both groups was significantly lower than that of European Americans. On a scoring scale that ranges from 0
to 500, these performance levels mean that students knew a variety of factual information but were unable to understand major concepts, integrate ideas, or engage successfully in complex problem solving or critical thinking (U.S. Department of
Education, 1994d).

These achievement patterns were substantiated further by a study (*American
Memory*, 1987; Heller, 1987) based on a nationwide survey of 7,812 high school juniors
that was funded by the National Endowment for the Humanities and conducted by the
National Assessment of Educational Progress. It found that more than two-thirds of
the students were unable to locate the Civil War within the correct half century or to
identify the Reformation and the Magna Carta. The vast majority also were unfamiliar
with major European-origin authors such as Dante, Chaucer, Dostoevsky, Whitman,
and Hawthorne.

The 1986–88 and 1992 achievement scores in science, math, reading, and writing
are summarized in Table 9.2. They are based on statistics reported by the U.S. Department of Education (1994a, 1994b, 1994d) and the U.S. Bureau of the Census (1994).

Two major trends are evident in these data. First, patterns similar to those established in geography, history, and literature exist in these subjects as well. That is, the
performance of students of color is significantly lower than European Americans.
Second, there is both cautiously good news and disturbingly bad news relative to
improvements in these four areas. Slight improvements are apparent for all groups in
math and science, but the degree varies by age level and ethnic group. There has been
no significant improvement in reading proficiency for any group since 1984. For most
groups it has either stabilized or declined. In writing a similar trend is apparent for
nine- and seventeen-year-olds; however, improvements occurred for thirteen-year-olds
in all three ethnic groups from 1988 to 1992.

Mathematics test scores between 1986 and 1992 showed an increase of 6 points for
nine-year-old African Americans and 7 points for Latinos, compared to an 8-point gain
for European Americans. Gains also occurred for thirteen-year-olds in all three eth-

Table 9.2 Achievement Proficiency by Subject, Age, and Ethnicity, 1986, 1988, and 1992

Subject and Ethnicity	9 Yr. Olds		13 Yr. Olds		17 Yr. Olds	
SCIENCE	1986	1992	1986	1992	1986	1992
Total	224	231	251	258	288	294
European Americans	232	239	259	267	298	304
African Americans	196	200	222	224	253	256
Latinos	199	205	226	238	259	270
MATHEMATICS	1986	1992	1986	1992	1986	1992
Total	222	230	269	273	302	307
European Americans	227	235	274	279	308	312
African Americans	202	208	249	254	249	286
Latinos	205	212	254	259	283	292
READING	1988	1992	1988	1992	1988	1992
Total	212	210	258	260	290	290
European Americans	218	218	261	266	295	297
African Americans	188	184	243	238	274	261
Latinos	194	192	240	239	271	271
WRITING	1988	1992	1988	1992	1988	1992
Total	206	207	264	274	291	287
European Americans	215	217	269	279	296	294
African Americans	173	175	246	258	275	263
Latinos	190	189	250	265	274	274

Source: NAEP 1992 Trends in Academic Progress: Achievement of U. S. Students in Science 1969 to 1992, Mathematics 1973 to 1992, Reading 1971 to 1992, Writing 1984 to 1992. Report No. 23-TROI. (1994). Washington, DC: U.S. Department of Education, Office of Research and Improvement.

nic groups, but at an even lower rate—5, 5, and 3 points, respectively. Improvement in the math proficiency of seventeen-year-olds was slightly better for students of color. African Americans increased by 7 points, Latinos by 9, and European Americans by 4. Students in all groups at all three ages performed better in areas of mathematical knowledge (recalling and recognizing facts) and skills (performing computations and manipulations) than in applications (reasoning and problem solving).

According to the 1988 reports on science achievement, Native Americans/Indians (46.9 percent), African Americans (47.7 percent), and Latinos (37.8 percent) were more highly represented in the lowest quartile, and more underrepresented in the upper quartile (8.3, 10.3, and 6.3 percent, respectively). By comparison, Asian American students (30.3 percent) slightly outnumbered European Americans (29.6 percent) in the upper quartile, as well as in the lower one (22.0 percent for Asians and 19.2 percent for Whites) (*Equity and Excellence*, 1985; U.S. Department of Education, 1989). According to *The 1990 Science Report Card* (U.S. Department of Education, 1992), the proficiency of European and Asian/Pacific Islander Americans is comparable at grades four, eight, and twelve and is the highest of all groups. The relative status of the other three ethnic groups, in descending order, are American Indians, Latinos, and African Americans. This sequence prevailed across the three age-levels tested. For example, twelfth-grade American Indians achieved a score of 286 compared to 273 for Latinos, and 256 for African Americans.

The 1992 science test results indicated that the proficiency of all ethnic groups (for whom data were available) has increased since 1986. However, the gains are small and the patterns across groups remain unchanged. African Americans in all age groups continue to perform lower than all other groups; the range of their gains was only 2 to 4 points across grade levels. The greatest gains occurred for Latinos, especially among thirteen-year-olds (12 points) and seventeen-year-olds (11 points). Thirteen-year-old European Americans also had a slightly greater gain than did the two other age groups. For African Americans, the increase in science achievement was a little better for nine-year-olds. Neither the performance of African American nor Latinos *in any age group* reached the national averages. The differences for African American nine-, thirteen-, and seventeen-year-olds were 31, 34, and 38 points, respectively.

The scores of Latinos were equally as disturbing, but not quite as extreme. Their science scores were 26, 20, and 24 points below the national averages of nine-, thirteen-, and seventeen-year-olds. Furthermore, the performance of none of these ages or ethnic groups, with the exception of seventeen-year-old European Americans, reached a level of proficiency (300 points) that NAEP has declared is necessary for students to be able to analyze and interpret scientific data. Although no data were reported for Asian/Pacific Islanders and American Indians in 1992, it can be assumed that their relative standing remained the same as in 1990. This is a reasonable conclusion, given that the achievement patterns of ethnic groups are long-standing and that the gains made by other groups between 1990 and 1992 were too small to change them.

The reading achievement of nine-year-old African Americans declined by 4 points between 1988 and 1992, compared to a 2-point loss for Latinos, and no changes for European Americans. While some improvement was evident for thirteen-year-old European Americans (+5 points), this was not the case for seventeen-year-olds (-2 points), nor for thirteen (-5 points) or seventeen-year-old African Americans (-7 points). The performance of these two Latino age groups remained virtually the same between 1988 and 1992. An even more problematic fact is that the reading performance of seventeen-year-old African Americans (261 points) was lower than that of thirteen-year-old European Americans (266), and well below the level that NAEP has deemed indicative of the ability to understand relatively complicated information (300 points).

In its 1986 Writing Report Card NAEP explained that writing achievement cor-
relates highly with reading achievement. Better readers also are better writers. In all
grades (four, eight, and twelve), African American, Latinos, and students from disadvantaged urban communities performed at a substantially lower level than did
European Americans, Asian Americans, and advantaged suburban students on all writing skills assessed (informative, persuasive, and imaginative). All students in all ethnic
groups and grade levels were deficient in higher-order thinking skills, as evidenced by
difficulty in performing adequately on analytical and persuasive writing tasks.

Although some improvements at all three grade-levels were evident for each ethnic group in 1988 and again in 1992, the other previously estalished patterns prevailed.
The greatest gains occurred among thirteen-year-olds—by 10 points for European
Americans, 12 for African Americans, and 15 for Latinos. NAEP suggests that
although these changes "were pervasive across several measures of writing achievement;...such a large gain may be considered quite surprising, and the prudent
approach is to wait and see if subsequent assessments through the 1990s confirm this
improvement" (U.S. Department of Education, 1994b, p. 7). Nine-year-old African
and European Americans made minor improvements (2 points) while the scores of
their seventeen-year-old counterparts declined by 2 and 12 points, respectively. The
scores of nine-year-old Latinos declined by 1 point, while those of seventeen-year-olds
remained the same. The writing skills of twelfth-grade Latinos and African Americans
continue to be lower than eighth-grade European Americans. African Americans had
the lowest performance of all groups. As was the case with math, science, and reading, none of the groups reached the level of writing proficiency (a score of 300), which
indicates that they can write effective responses containing supportive details and can
synthesize information from specialized reading materials.

MIXED SIGNALS IN ACHIEVEMENT PATTERNS

The overall academic achievement profiles of students of color send mixed messages.
The fact that NAEP and the National Center for Education Statistics do not track and
report the performance of Asian/Pacific Islanders and Native Indians/Alaskans as routinely and thoroughly as they do for European, African, and Latino Americans leaves
the educational status of these groups virtually unknown and therefore untreatable.

It is encouraging to see that the significant declines that all groups experienced in
the 1984–86 assessment period were counteracted by some recovery during
1988–1992. The fact that students of color in all three age-groups tested made small
but steady gains in science and mathematics achievement is also encouraging. It is
disheartening and troublesome that this pattern is not true for reading and writing.
In general Latinos seem to be making more academic progress than are African
Americans even though their dropout rates are higher. Consequently, the gaps between
their achievement levels and those of European American students are decreasing
somewhat, while those of African Americans remain about the same. Although recent
improvements by students of color on standardized tests show that they are making
some gains on low-level cognitive skills, such as decoding, computation, factual recog-

nition, and recall, they are not developing high-level skills, such as making inferences, critical thinking, analyzing and synthesizing information, logical reasoning, and creative expression.

Another good-news, bad-news dilemma associated with the achievement profiles is that the data are largely not disaggregated. These are composite profiles for large groups and large clusters of skills. As such, they do not identify what aspects of the various subjects and skills were easy or difficult for students taking the tests. Nor do they give any detailed information on how individuals within ethnic groups were distributed across the range of skills included in the various tests. For instance, it is impossible from the scores to discern whether comprehension, vocabulary, making inferences, or some other component skill of reading was most challenging for Mexican Americans, Puerto Ricans, or Cuban Americans. How individuals' membership in ethnic groups is assigned and where they are placed for analysis also may distort some of the achievement patterns. In government documents on educational attainment, data for European and African Americans often are accompanied with notation that these groups "include persons of Hispanic origin." Other times distinctions, such as "White, non-Hispanic" and "Black, non-Hispanic" are made. Yet, the Asian American ethnic group is not separated into such components as Japanese, Chinese, Koreans, or Vietnamese.

The variability of performance patterns across the subscales of standardized tests within ethnic groups is very evident among Asian Americans. Often considered the model minority, they are commonly perceived to be high achievers who perform well in all aspects of schooling and on all measures of achievement. This positive stereotype overlooks the immense national origins diversity of Asian American ethnic groups, the serious language and adjustment problems that recent Southeast Asian refugees and new immigrants encounter, and the special educational needs of individual students.

The bimodal pattern of educational achievement that actually exists among Asian American students dispels this myth of universal high performance. It reveals that they are more likely than other groups to enroll in college preparatory programs, to maintain heavier high school course loads, to take more foreign languages and more high-level mathematics and science, to spend more time on homework, and to have higher educational aspirations. Their math and science proficiency is much greater than their verbal and writing skills, as is apparent in their 1993 SAT scores, where math performance exceeded verbal by 120 points. This spread has not varied by more than 6 points over the last ten years. It contradicts the premise that the achievement of these students is unequivocally exceptional and improving significantly.

Dropout rates, limited English proficiency, discipline problems, and various special education needs are high and growing among some students from Asian ethnic groups, particularly those who have not been in the United States for very long. When entering school, many Vietnamese, Hmong, and Cambodian students are placed in classes below modal grade level (Miller-Lachmann & Taylor, 1995). The social stigma and isolation associated with this placement increase their dropout rates. Even high academic-achieving Asian American students are not necessarily socially and emotionally well-adjusted. They do not feel as positive about their physical features and stature as do their White peers. Many also have psychological problems because of stress associated with pressure for high performance, learning to cope with failure, and ethnic identity conflicts (Gibbs & Nahme-Huang, 1989; Pang, Mizokawa, Morishima, & Olstad, 1985; Yu, Doi, & Chang, 1986). The inflated image of Asian American students' success leads some educators to conclude that these students no longer face serious racial discrimination and do not need to be treated like a minority or marginal group. This may be the reason agencies that compile statistics on educational attainments frequently do not report separate data for them. Osajima (1991, pp. 130–131) cautions that

> beneath the awards and accomplishments lie struggles, conflicts, and uncertainities that manifest racism's hidden and subtle impacts…. The quiet demeanor of Asian students, which has heretofore only garnered praise, may in fact be problematic, for this survival mechanism could also leave them isolated with their doubts about identity and belonging.

How can the mixed results that are apparent in the achievement profiles of students of color be explained? One possible explanation is that teachers and instructional programs are still not acknowledging and responding to these students' unique cultural orientations, values, and learning styles. The failure to do so is negatively affecting their achievement outcomes. As Boateng (1990) explains, the "deculturalization" of students of color in schools interferes with their ability to focus on and master academic tasks.

Achievement patterns may be a direct result of the curriculum differentiations that exist for students of color and for European American students in elementary and secondary schools. These students are not necessarily enrolled in similar kinds of courses; nor are they receiving equal status instruction. It is not surprising, then, that there is so much variance in their academic achievement. Another possibility is that all students are not receiving the best quality education possible. This idea is prompted by the fact that there is more achievement variance among groups within than across proficiency levels. Rarely do any ethnic groups achieve higher-order academic skills in any subjects. Therefore, the achievement differences may be more a matter of degree than quality.

It seems that the pattern of differential educational achievement among ethnic groups is firmly established by grade four and it prevails thereafter. The achievement gaps are greater at this age and for seventeen-year-olds, than for thirteen-year-olds. This pattern may be only a temporary occurrence due to the unusual performance pattern of eighth graders in 1988. For example, in 1992 the difference in the math achievement of African Americans and European American fourth graders was 39 points; eighth graders, 43 points; and eleventh graders, 48 points. The differences for reading in the same year were 34, 28, and 38 points.

Other possible explanations of these variations in achievement may be found in students' attendance patterns and dropout rates. Many of the most problematic students of color may have dropped out of school before age seventeen. This should mean that those left are more like their European counterparts and, therefore, have achievement levels similar to theirs. This possibility may be counteracted by disproportionately low percentages of high school students of color enrolled in academic courses of study. The combination of these possibilities give credence to the contention that the longer African American, Latino, and American Indian youths stay in school, the further they fall behind academically. Ralph, Keller, and Crouse (1994) explained this phenonemon further with the example that even after eight additional years of schooling seventeen-year-olds who are at the 10th percentile in math and the 25th percentile in reading and science at age nine still have not attained achievement scores equal to those of the 95th percentile of their cohort at age nine.

Another explanation is that students of color know much more than standardized achievement test scores indicate. Despite their frequent use, these tests may not be valid measures to use in determining the academic abilities of culturally and ethnically different students. The lack of sensitivity of these techniques, in both their content and administration procedures, to the cultural nuances of students of color may have a negative effect on their total scores. In other words, lack of test-taking skills and other preferred performance styles may mediate against some ethnic groups doing well on the SAT and NAEP tests of academic proficiency. Measures of achievement that are culturally sensitive, employ diverse techniques, and access multidimensional "sites" of performance, such as curriculum content and classroom instructional interactions, may produce very different results.

The unequal curriculum and instruction systems that exist in U.S. schools undoubtedly account for much of the disparaties in achievement among students of color and European Americans. This inequity has been firmly established by research. For example, in its *Mexican-American Education Study*, conducted between 1971 and 1974, the U.S. Civil Rights Commission (1971–1974) attributed quality and equality of educational experiences to the opportunities different students receive to participate in classroom interactions with teachers. It found that Mexican Americans were not receiving as many opportunities as European Americans to participate in classroom interactions, as evidenced by fewer and lower-level questions asked of them, the time allowed to give responses, and the praise and encouragement teachers gave for students' efforts. Gay's (1974) similar findings for African American students' interactions with both African and European American teachers led her to conclude that these teachers act more alike than differently in their classroom treatment of students. All teachers tended to give preferential treatment and more quality opportunities to participate in the substance of instruction to European American students.

Other disparities in curriculum options and instructional interactions available to racially and ethnically different groups have been reported by Goodlad (1984), Oakes (1985), and Persell (1977). They indicate that students of color are disproportionally enrolled in special education programs, vocational courses, and low-track classes and are underrepresented in high-track and college preparatory programs (see chapter 15 for further details). Furthermore, the placement of students of color in vocational courses occurs earlier, and the programs differ substantially in kind and content from those for European Americans. Students of color are assigned to vocational programs that train specifically for low-status occupations (e.g., cosmetology, mill and cabinet shop, building maintenance, television repair, retail sales, clerical jobs). By comparison, European American students enroll more often in vocational courses that offer managerial training, business finance, and general industrial arts skills. To receive their training, youths of color must leave the school campus more often than Whites, thus isolating them from many of the social activities of the school (Oakes, 1985).

The enrollment of students of color in academic programs also is unequally distributed. They are highly underrepresented in college preparatory and in gifted and talented programs. In its 1985 report on the educational status of African Americans, the College Entrance Examination Board found that most African American seniors had taken fewer years of coursework in mathematics, physical sciences, and social studies than had European Americans. Even in subjects in which the years of coursework are similar, the content of the courses differs substantially. Although college-bound African American and Latino seniors are as likely as European Americans to have taken three or more years of mathematics, they are less likely to have taken algebra, geometry, trigonometry, and calculus and more likely to have taken general and business math (U.S. Department of Education, 1994c). In 1992 American Indians, African Americans, and Latinos compiled fewer academic units (16.0, 16.7, and 16.9, respectively) than did European (17.6) and Asian Americans (18.5). The number of vocational course units all students took declined between 1982 and 1992. Yet, the number of vocational course units of African Americans (4.0) and American Indians (4.8) continued to be above the national average (3.8). Those of Latinos equalled it. Furthermore, students in low-income and predominately children-of-color schools have less access to microcomputers, have fewer qualified teachers trained in the use of computers, and tend to use microcomputers more for drill and practice in basic skills than for conceptual knowledge or programming instruction (*Equity and Excellence*, 1985; U.S. Department of Education, 1994d; Winkler, Stravelson, Stasz, Robyn, & Fiebel, 1984).

The system of tracking routinely used to organize students for instruction is probably the most effective means of denying educational equality to students of color. In general, tracking differentiates access to knowledge, content and quality of instruction, expectations of teachers, and classroom climates for learning between upper and lower tracks. The studies of school tracking conducted by Oakes, Goodlad, Rosenbaum, Morgan, and others present convincing and devastating proof of the extent to which this practice perpetuates educational inequities along race, ethnic, and socioeconomic lines. These inequities include emphasizing compliance-type behaviors and attitudes for low-track enrollees, and leadership and intellectual skills for high track students; better teachers, equipment, materials, and more provocative instructional strategies assigned to higher tracks; higher-order intellectual, critical thinking, and problem-solving skills in high-track classes; high expectations of achievement for high-track and low expectations for low-track students; and more time allocated to academic tasks in high tracks, compared to classroom management and discipline issues in low tracks (Goodlad, 1984; Morgan, 1977; Oakes, 1985; Persell, 1977; Rosenbaum, 1976; Verdugo, 1986). These disparities are discussed in greater detail in chapter 4.

Because African Americans, Latinos, and American Indians are over-represented in lower-track curriculum programs, they are consistently and systematically denied equal access to the *substance* of quality education. *In effect, tracking is a process for the legitimation of the social inequalities that exist in the larger society.* It serves the instrumental functions of social selection, creating castes among students and closing off paths for personal advancement for those in the lower levels (Morgan, 1977). Through this practice, students learn to accept the unequal patterns of social and political participation in society and all its institutions as the natural order of things.

The under-enrollment of students of color in high-track and academic programs evident in kindergarten through grade twelve also exists in baccalaureate and graduate college degree programs. In fact, the higher the level of education, the greater is the degree of underrepresentation. Students of color are underrepresented in all fields of college study except the social sciences and education. However, in 1991 there was an increase in the number of African Americans who received bachelor's degrees in business and management, computer and information sciences, natural sciences, engineering, and the health sciences, while the number in the humanities and education declined. Degrees granted to Latinos increased in the same fields with the exception of engineering and business and management. Asian American degrees continue to be clustered heavily in the sciences and technical fields. While the number receiving degrees in education also declined, there were slight increases in the humanities and social sciences (U.S. Department of Education, 1994d).

In the final analysis, it is the kinds of access students of color have to high-status knowledge and the quality of instructional interactions between students and teachers in individual schools and classrooms that define educational quality and indicate who receives educational equality. These processes are what ultimately determine which students are educated for intellectual rigor, personal self-determination, and social empowerment, and which ones are trained for a life of institutional compliance, economic dependence, and the social underclass (*Equality and Excellence*, 1985). The current educational status of students of color in the United States suggests that too many of them are being educated for the underclass.

WHY EDUCATIONAL INEQUALITY EXISTS FOR STUDENTS OF COLOR

Wherever students of color attend school, whether in predominantly minority or racially mixed settings, in urban or suburban environments, in poor or middle-class communities, in the Northern, Eastern, Southern, or Western United States, issues of educational inequality prevail. These issues concern access to excellence and equity of educational opportunities and outcomes, with the focus of access being the substance of the educational process. The pivotal question is how to make the total educational enterprise more responsive to the histories, heritages, life experiences, and cultural conditioning of students of color in all of its policy-making, program-planning, and instructional practices.

The quality of the various resources used in the educational process has a direct effect on the level and quality of student achievement. When different groups of students are exposed to qualitatively different resources, their achievements also differ. In the debate on educational equality, a crucial question is whether the resources used in teaching students of color are comparable to those used with European Americans on measures of accuracy, technical quality, relevance, and appropriateness. These resources include facilities, personnel, financing, instructional materials and programs, and environmental settings.

The relative value of instructional resources cannot be determined independently of environmental context, intended users, and expected outcomes. School resources are preferentially allocated to high-track and academic programs and to middle-class, European American students. Even when students of color receive similar educational resources as Whites, the effects are not identical. Sometimes the same resources that benefit and facilitate European-origin students' development block or retard the educational development of students of color. How is this possible? One way is how school systems and personnel generally perceive and treat these curricular and instructional options that are highly populated by students of color relative to performance expectations and resource allocations. They receive fewer laboratory facilities, fewer out-of-classroom learning experiences, lesser qualified teachers, and less commitment, concern, and effort from teachers.

But not all students of color are enrolled in low-track, nonacademic, and special education programs. Most are enrolled in regular classrooms and programs across a wide spectrum of curriculum options, including general education, academic, and college preparatory courses. If educational resources are allocated by programs and if these programs receive a fair share of them, then how is it possible to claim that students of color are being denied comparable access? Several ways are possible. First, the sameness of educational resources for diverse individuals and groups does not constitute comparability of quality or opportunity. Teachers, materials, and teaching environments that work well for European American students do not necessarily work equally well for children of color. To believe that they do is to assume that African American, Latino, American Indian, Asian American, and European origin students are identical in personal, social, cultural, historical, and family traits.

Second, most graduates of typical teacher education programs know little about the cultural traits, behaviors, values, and attitudes that different children of color bring to the classroom, and how they affect the ways these students act in and react to instructional situations. They do not know how to understand and use the school behaviors of these students, which differ from their normative expectations, as aides to teaching. Therefore, they tend to misinterpret them as deviant and treat them punitively. Because teachers' cultural backgrounds and value orientations are highly compatible with middle-class and European American culture, they can use these cultural connections to facilitate the learning of White students. This is done routinely and without conscious or deliberate intentions. It is their shared cultural orientations that make instruction more relevant and personally meaningful. The absence of these for students of color places them at a learning disadvantage.

Third, like teacher education, most curriculum designs and instructional materials are Eurocentric. As such, they reflect the middle-class experiences, perspectives, and value priorities in which the macroculture of the United States is grounded. These educational initiatives are likely to be more relevant to life experiences, aspirations, and frames of reference of European Americans than to those of students of color who are not part of the mainstream culture. Thus, when attempting to learn academic tasks, European American students may not have the additional burden of working across irrelevant instructional materials and methods. More of their efforts and energies can be directed toward mastering the substance of teaching. Students of color are often placed in double academic jeopardy. They must divide their energies and efforts between coping with curriculum materials and instructional methods that are not culturally relevant to their learning styles or reflective of their life experiences and mastering the academic knowledge and tasks being taught. Because this division of efforts dissipates their concentration on learning tasks, they do not receive educational opportunities to learn the substances of teaching that are comparable to those of European Americans.

Fourth, the school environments in which students live and learn are not comparable for racially majority and minority students. When students and teachers arrive at school they do not leave their cultural backgrounds at home. This is not a problem for most European Americans, since school culture and rules of behavior are reflections and extensions of their home cultures. A high degree of cultural congruency exists between middle-class European American culture and school culture. These students do not experience much social-code incompatibility or need for cultural style shifting to adjust to the behavioral rules and expectations of schools. The converse is true for students of color. Many of the social codes for succeeding in school are unfamiliar to them, or are diametrically opposed to the codes they have learned in their home cultures. When learning situations do not reflect the cultures of the students, gaps exist "between the contexts of learning and the contexts of performing" (John-Steiner & Leacock, 1979, p. 87). These gaps are greatest for students from ethnic cultures and communities that are not part of the mainstream culture and can mediate against effective teaching and learning. Therefore, the causes of many of the disparities that are apparent in the educational attainment of different ethnic groups are situated in cultural, procedural, and contextual incompatibilities.

Most educators do not think to teach students skills for how to survive and succeed in school—for example, how to study across ethnic learning styles, how to adjust talking styles to accommodate school expectations, how to interact appropriately with school administrators and classroom teachers, and how to identify and adjust to the procedural rules for functioning in different instructional classrooms. Instead, educators tend to operate on the assumption that school codes of behavior are universal and commonly understood and are acquired from simply living in the broader culture that surrounds schools. What most of them forget is that many students of color live only marginally in mainstream culture. Furthermore, their parents may not be able to pass on to them a legacy of how to "do" schooling successfully because they did not experience it themselves.

The effect of these differences in socialization among European, African, Latino, Native, and Asian Americans in how to survive in school is another example of the differential use of personal energies and efforts. Students have to learn how to survive in school while simultaneously learning what is taught. If they fail to master the social codes, they may never get a chance to try the academic tasks. As Holliday (1985) suggests, mastery of the social protocols and managerial procedures of schooling is frequently a prerequisite to receiving opportunities to participate in substantive instructional interactions and for academic learning to occur.

The school failure of students of color because of their inability to master social codes of behavior is much more frequent than for European Americans. So is their in-class success measured more often by social skill mastery (such as compliance to institutional expectations and having pleasant or accommodating personality traits) than by academic performance. Teachers tend to give more credit to "being nice, cooperative, and not trouble-makers," "feeling sorry for students," and "work being neat, if not of very high substantive quality" in the assessment of students' of color performance. In comparison, the performance of European American students is assessed more on academic criteria ("he studies hard," "she is a good thinker," "they are very attentive in class," "she asks provocative questions," "his writing is clear and cogent"). Inequalities exist in these assessment habits because the success or failure of students of color is a matter of social competence, while that of European Americans depends on academic competence. Thus, as some students are acquiring skills for institutional adaptation, being followers, and minimizing their options and opportunities beyond school, others are being groomed to maximize their long-term options and to be thinkers, leaders, and continuous intellectual learners (Holliday, 1985; Oakes, 1985).

Closely related to the issue of comparable quality resources is the role of teacher attitudes, expectations, and competencies in perpetuating educational inequality for students of color. The essence of this issue is, How can teachers who have grown up in ethnically isolated communities and in a racist society teach students whom they do not know, may not value, and may even fear? This question is crucial in equations of educational equality, especially when most teachers are racially White, culturally Eurocentric, middle class, female, and whose professional preparation is grounded almost exclusively in Eurocentric cultural orientations. Therefore, they enter the profession assuming that all students can be taught as if they were European Americans. Teachers of color who receive the same kind of professional socialization frequently begin their careers with the same kind of expectations, attitudes, and values.

Most teachers know little about different ethnic groups' life-styles or learning habits and preferences. Many are insecure and uncertain about working with African American, Latino, Asian, and American Indian students and have low expectations of achievement for them. Too many teachers still believe that students of color are either culturally deprived and should be remediated by using middle-class Whites as the appropriate norm, or do not have the aspirations or capacities to learn as well as European Americans. Some Asian groups, such as Japanese, Chinese, and Koreans, are exempted from these negative expectations, but they are treated as unfairly by teachers' unrealistic high academic expectations. They are expected to be stellar performers in every dimension of learning and schooling. Research shows that "Teachers form expectations about children based directly upon race and social class . . . pupil test scores, appearance, language style, speed of task performance, and behavior characteristics which are themselves culturally defined. Moreover, teacher expectations are more influenced by *negative* information about pupil characteristics than positive data" (Persell, 1977, p. 112). Teachers transmit these attitudes and expectations in what they say and do in the classroom. Students respond to these expectations in ways that become self-fulfilling prophecies. Many children of color come to believe that they are destined to fail, and they act accordingly. Most European American students internalize the high expectations teachers have of them, accordingly believe they are destined to succeed, and they do.

Educators tend to discriminate their school behaviors according to their performance expectations of different students. For example, teachers who do not have high academic expectations for students of color ask them low-level memory, recall, and convergent questions, do not praise or encourage them as often as European Americans, use lower standards for judging the quality of their work, and do not call on them as frequently. Guidance counselors who do not believe students of color can master high-level math and science skills do not schedule them into these classes. School teachers and administrators who expect greater discipline problems from students of color tend to treat their rule infractions with harsher punishment. In general, low expectations of educators cause them to feed African Americans, Latinos, American Indians, and some Southeast Asians (notably Vietnamese and Cambodians) academic pabulum. They then wonder why these students do not do well on standardized measures of school achievement.

Special-purpose instruction for students of color tends to be remediation; for European Americans, it tends to be enrichment. For example, Asians and Latinos are enrolled in bilingual education or English as a second language, while European American students take "foreign languages." Disproportionately large numbers of African and Native Americans (especially males) receive Chapter 1 and learning disability services, while enrollments in gifted and talented programs favor European Americans and, in some instances, Japanese, Korean, and Chinese Americans. Students of color for whom educators have low expectations are suspected of dishonesty and cheating when they defy these expectations by performing well. When they actualize these expectations, their teachers make comments such as "What else can you expect?" Presumed high-achieving European American students who do not live up to expectations are described as underachievers, and low-performing students who exceed expectations are called overachievers. These attitudes cause wide disparities in how educators interact with European Americans and students of color in the day-to-day operations of schools and thereby perpetuate educational inequalities.

The educational inequities in school resources, teacher attitudes, and classroom interactions are reinforced further by culturally biased tests and procedures used to diagnose students' needs and to evaluate their performance. Whether standardized achievement measures, minimum-competency tests, teacher-made tests, classroom observations, criterion-referenced tests, or even portfolios, most assessment approaches currently used discriminate against students of color in content, standardization norms, and administration procedures. For students with limited English proficiency, having to take performance tests in English automatically puts them at a major disadvantage. A similar disadvantage accrues to students whose cultural orientations are directed more toward using oral techniques to demonstrate their skills when they have to show mastery in school almost exclusively in written formats. The time and skills required to formulate responses and translate them back and forth between two or more linguistic and cultural performance systems may interfere with demonstrating content mastery. Consequently, for these students their test scores may be more an indication of their language and cultural code shifting abilities than of their content knowledge. By their nature, tests contribute to the social stratification of students. Because they are designed and used to discriminate differences among and to rank students according to competence, even the most content bias-free tests—especially norm-referenced ones—are tools for sorting students into unequal categories (Grant & Sleeter, 1985; Morgan, 1977; Persell, 1977).

Schools prize verbal learning and written demonstrations of achievement. These styles of demonstrating achievement are consistent with mainstream American and European origin students' cultures, but they are contrary to the performance styles of many groups of color. For African Americans, whose cultural socialization emphasizes aural, verbal, and participatory learning, and for American Indians who are accustomed to imitative learning in their home cultures, it is difficult to transform what they know from one performance style to another (Shade, 1989). When they have to demonstrate their achievement on written tests, the format may be more of a problem for them than are the content and substance of the learning tasks. While they are struggling to translate their knowledge and skill mastery into an unfamiliar expressive style, European American students are busy demonstrating their knowledge of the content. These differences in performance starting points mean that most students of color are at a disadvantage from the beginning of formal schooling. Not understanding the problems they are having with performance formats and styles, teachers conclude that their failure is due totally to their inability to master the instructional content. The effects of these misdiagnoses and misevaluations become cumulatively greater for students of color as they advance in school. Until they receive starting points comparable to those of European Americans in terms of alternative diagnostic and performance criteria, and until the assessment techniques and tools are more compatible with their cultural and learning styles, inequities in educational opportunities will continue to exist for African, Latino, Native, and Asian American students.

A similar argument holds for the content and substance of student evaluations. All achievement tests are designed to determine what students know. Presumably they reflect what is taught in schools. This is a reasonable expectation, and there would be no issue of ethnic inequality if schools taught equally relevant curricula equally well to all students. But they do not. Although progress has been made in the last three decades to make school curricula more inclusive of ethnic and cultural diversity, most of the knowledge taught, and consequently the achievement tests, continue to be Eurocentric. Even skill mastery is transmitted through Eurocentric contexts. For instance, achievement tests may embed skills in scenarios about situations that are not relevant to the cultural backgrounds and life experiences of students of color. These students then have to decipher the contexts in order to extrapolate the skill content. One example is asking immigrant students from the Caribbean who have never experienced snow to engage in problem solving from a composition on the challenges and dilemmas of a blizzard. They may know the skill, but unfamiliarity with the contextual scenario (problems associated with snow) interferes with their effectively demonstrating their ability to do problem solving. Most European Americans students do not have these kinds of "contextual interference" problems. Both the context and the performance format are familiar to them because they are extracted from cultural orientations they share. If they know the skill, they therefore are advantaged in demonstrating their mastery.

This is not to say that students of color should not take achievement tests, that their school performance should not be evaluated, or that high levels of achievement should not be expected of them. Rather, it is to suggest that to avoid perpetuating educational inequality through assessment procedures, these students should not always be expected to demonstrate mastery in culturally incompatible styles and formats. A wide variety of measures should be used so that no single one that is highly advantageous to one ethnic group over another is used consistently. Both the content and process of curriculum, teaching, and testing should be revised to incorporate more fully the cultural contributions, experiences, orientations, and styles of the full range of ethnic groups in the United States.

ACHIEVING EDUCATIONAL EQUALITY

The College Entrance Examination Board (*Equity and Excellence*, 1985, p. 4) concluded its report with the observation that "excellence for Black students will not become a reality until they receive enriched curricular opportunities in elementary and secondary schools, sufficient financial assistance to pursue higher education opportunities, and instruction from well-qualified teachers." John-Steiner and Leacock (1979, pp. 87–88) believe that "when the background of the teacher differs greatly from that of the children she works with, a setting results which is alien and tension-producing for the teacher or the student or both."

To these observations can be added the fact that unfriendly, tension-filled, and culturally incompatible classroom climates—what is frequently referred to as the absence of "safe, supportive, and caring learning communities" (McCaleb, 1994)—substantially reduce the potential for educational equality for students who live and function in them. This is too often the fate of students of color in U.S. schools. Casso (1979, p. 121) argues that "it is the educational system which needs to be changed and restructured rather than the Mexican-American child...lest it keep compounding the crime of attempting to remold every brown child into a cog for the white middle class machine." Fantini (1979) proposes that efforts to bring about equality focus on providing equal access to quality education. Gay (1994) suggests that the existence of equal access to educational opportunities is contingent on *comparability in culturally relevant learning experiences for ethnically diverse students, instead of treating them identically.* It is impossible to provide this comparability without using pedagogical plurality that is centered in cultural diversity.

The achievement of these proposals requires (1) institutional reforms aimed at creating school structures, content, and processes that respond positively to human and cultural diversity; (2) developing a policy of quality that views diverse learners as significant educational consumers with some fundamental rights; and (3) creating an ethic of educational equality and excellence grounded in cultural pluralism. Miller-Lachmann and Taylor (1995, p. 97) lend additional support to these ideas with the explanation that

> while increased funding will help in meeting [the needs of
> diverse students], it is not the only, or even necessarily the
> most important, factor. Greater diversity within schools and
> within classes, increased awareness of and sensitivity to each
> child's cultural heritage, a more inclusive curriculum, school
> staffs that more closely reflect the backgrounds of the stu-
> dents, and a more open, accessible, and democratic leader-
> ship structure contribute as well to the educational success of
> children of color.

Implicit in these suggestions and the issues of inequality discussed earlier in this chapter is that educational equality cannot be achieved without massive schoolwide reform. The reform efforts should begin with a redefinition of educational equality for students of color as access to *a variety of instructional processes that are informed by and responsive to their cultural orientations and learning styles.* In operational terms, this means affirming that problems in learning are located not so much in the inabilities of students as in culturally unequal, insensitive, and hegemonic practices used in the schools they attend. It also means refocusing schools toward being more responsive to human variability, spending less time manipulating students of color to make them comply to institutional structures, and implementing programs and processes that empower students through access to high-quality, high status, and high power knowledge and experiences (Fantini, 1979, p. 147). This will be a significant departure from most current notions of equality as access to uniform school resources for diverse students.

Such conceptions of educational equality require reform in teacher preparation, curriculum design, classroom instruction, grouping of students for instruction, school climates, and how students' needs are diagnosed and their achievement assessed. All of these issues cannot be discussed in great detail here. Because of the crucial role teachers play in determining the quality of learning opportunities students receive in classrooms, more attention is given to their professional preparation.

All forms of tracking should be eliminated entirely. Even under the best of circumstances, tracking denies equal educational opportunities to students of color and also to others who populate the lower levels. It closes rather than opens pathways to social and academic advancement, and it commits some students early to a permanent educational and social underclass. Tracking should be replaced with flexible and frequently changed cooperative and heterogeneous groupings of students for specific instructional tasks or skill development purposes. For example, students grouped together to learn geographical directions should remain together only until that skill is mastered. Then other kinds of arrangements should be constructed to deal with new learning skills, tasks, and experiences.

Norm-referenced standardized tests for evaluating student achievement should be used infrequently, cautiously, and only in conjunction with other performance measures. More emphasis should be placed on evaluating students against their own records, with *range of improvement between different points of reference being the focus of attention*, as opposed to performance at isolated points in time. This requires that schools and classrooms use multiple techniques and procedures, including academic, social, psychological and emotional measures, as well as verbal, visual, observational, participatory, and kinetic means, to assess students' school performance.

These approaches should always serve diagnostic and developmental functions and be culturally responsive. That is, they should be used to determine how and why students are proceeding with specific learning tasks, and the formats they take should reflect the cultural orientations and nuances of the students being assessed. They should be administered frequently, and instructional programming should be changed according to the results obtained. Thus, students of color should be put on self-referenced and self-paced programs to complete their schooling. Narrative reports, developmental profiles, student-teacher-parent conferences, and anecdotal records should replace or complement letter and symbol grades for reporting student progress.

School curricula, too, must be reformed if equal educational opportunities are to be assured for students of color. However, emphases of the various commission studies and proposals for school reform released in the 1980s and 1990s that emphasize greater curriculum quantity as the measure of educational quality is not the answer. More of the same irrelevant school subjects will not improve the quality of schooling and the educational attainment for any students of color. Instead, they increase the likelihood of ever-greater school failure. If Latinos, Native Americans, and African Americans are already failing science, simply taking more of it without multiculturalizing any of its content or techniques means that these students will have even greater opportunities to fail. If low-track students are already taking substantially different kinds of mathematics courses than high-track students, then the gap in the substantive content they are learning widens as the high-track students take even more advanced courses, and the low-track students take even more remedial math courses.

What schools consider to be essential knowledge and skills for all students to learn and how these skills are understood and taught—that is, the canons of U.S. education—need to be revised to incorporate cultural pluralism. These revisions should reflect the comprehensive demographic, social, cultural, and linguistic realities of U.S. society and the world, not just the technological, economic, and political sides of life. This means, first, that school curricula should demonstrate and emulate the interdisciplinary nature of human life, knowledge, values, skills, and experiences. Second, they should teach and model the interdependence of the world—a world in which Whites are a small numerical minority, and one in which the control of natural resources, social aspirations, and power negotiations is gradually shifting from Western to non-Western, non-White nations. Third, a concerted effort should be made to achieve a greater balance between technological developments and humanistic concerns, where skills in ethics, morality, and aesthetics are as important as cognition. These kind of curricular reform emphases increase the possibility that the experiences, cultures, and contributions of groups of color in the United States will be included across the various subject matter content areas; that students of color will identify with and relate better to the substance of school curricula; that they will have a greater sense of ownership in the schooling enterprise; and that more African Americans, Asians Americans, Latinos, and American Indians will have opportunities comparable to those of European American students to establish personally enabling connections with schools and thereby improve their overall academic achievement.

Because teachers play such a central role in the kinds of educational opportunities students of color receive in classrooms, their reeducation and training are fundamental to providing educational equality. This training should have four primary emphases. The first is *self-knowledge.* Teachers, counselors, and administrators need to become conscious of their own cultural values and beliefs, how these affect their attitudes and expectations toward different ethnic groups, and how these are habitually exhibited in their school behaviors. They also need to understand the effects of these on students, relative to their self-concepts, academic abilities, educational opportunities, and achievement outcomes.

Spindler and Spindler (1993) offer a model for how teacher self- knowledge can be facilitated. Called "cultural therapy," it is "a process of bringing one's own culture, in its manifold forms—assumptions, goals, values, beliefs, and communicative modes—to a level of awareness that permits one to perceive it as a potential bias in social interaction and in the acquisition or transmission of skills and knowledge" (p. 28). It has elements of self-reflection, self-monitoring, and self-transcendence. This cultural consciousness is imperative "so that potential conflicts, misunderstandings, and blind spots in the perception and interpretation of behavior can be anticipated" (p. 28), and unequal power relationships in school and the larger society that are instigated by cultural preferences or dominance can be explicated. For teachers, cultural therapy can be the first step in changing insensitive biased behaviors, attitudes, and assumptions that are detrimental to students whose cultural backgrounds are different from their own. It helps them to identify, understand, and analyze reasons they may find the values and behaviors of culturally different students—especially those of color—objectionable, shocking, and irritating (Spindler & Spindler, 1993). The ultimate goal of cultural therapy is to empower teachers, not indict them. It is based on the idea that social reform begins with the individual.

Merely telling teachers about how their cultural assumptions can lead to low expectations and negative consequences for students of color receiving educational equality will not suffice. Nor will reading the impressive body of research that documents these effects. These approaches seem too much like personal indictments and tend to cause individuals to become defensive and alienated. Teachers need to be *shown* how they behave toward culturally diverse students in their classrooms. This can be done by projecting mirror images of or replaying their classroom behaviors back to them, training teachers how to be participant observers of their own classroom dynamics, and how to use different techniques systematically to analyze their instructional behaviors. Inexpensive technology, such as camcorders, makes it possible to do this with ease and expediency. Audio- and videotapes of teaching behaviors are invaluable for showing teachers what they actually do in classrooms. They are much better than outside observers, because recorders and cameras do not interpret or misrepresent what actually occurs. Training in ethnographic techniques, interactional analysis, questioning strategies, frame analysis, self-reflection, feedback mechanisms, and participatory action research can help teachers to look systematically at these recorded behaviors and to monitor their change efforts.

In addition to learning how to culturally decode their attitudes and behaviors from an insider's viewpoint, teachers need to learn how to analyze them from the perspectives of "others," especially those of their students of color. These skills are not acquired automatically; they must be deliberately taught. Without training, most educators cannot see the cultural biases and prejudices of their routine school behaviors. Suggestions to the effect that they are not treating students of color and European Americans equally tend to be associated with deliberate and blatant acts of discrimination. Teachers do not understand how thoroughly and subtly cultural nuances permeate all of their behavior and can generate negative effects in instructional actions toward students who do not share their cultural frames of reference.

These cultural influences need to be counteracted by developing skills in critical consciousness and culturally appropriate pedagogy for use with diverse students. Several contributing authors (Lamawaima, Lee and Defoe, Garcia, and Foster) to the *Handbook of Research on Multicultural Education* (Banks & Banks, 1995) explain what this means specifically for Native, African, and Mexican Americans. Their descriptions, along with those offered by Ladson-Billings (1994) and Hollins, King, and Hayman (1994), include teaching about the cultural heritages and contributions of ethnic groups of concern; social and interpersonal relationships between students and teachers that convey a sense of personal kindredness, interdependence, connectedness, and caring; using cultural frames of reference to make the content of teaching personally meaningful to students; concern for the affective and moral as well as cognitive development of students; and cultivating social and cultural consciousness, solidarity, and responsibility. Thus, culturally appropriate or responsive pedagogy "empowers students intellectually, socially, emotionally, and politically by using cultural referents to impart knowledge, skills, and attitudes" (Ladson-Billings 1992, p. 382).

A second emphasis in teacher reeducation for educational equality is understanding the differences in cultural values and behavioral codes between themselves as middle-class European Americans and students of color, and how instructional processes can be restructured to better accommodate them. Teachers cannot begin to treat African, Latino, Indian, Asian, and European American students equitably until they accept that they all have comparable human worth and that differences do not automatically mean inferiorities. This acceptance begins with acquiring knowledge about ethnic groups' cultural backgrounds, life experiences, and interactional styles to replace racial myths and stereotypes. Once teachers understand the structures and motivations behind these cultural behaviors, they can begin to design more culturally compatible instructional options and thereby improve the quality of the learning experiences for students of color. This is the logic behind Pai's (1990) and Gay's (1994) contentions that knowledge of cultural diversity is an essential foundation for equality and excellence in both the processes and outcomes of education. These ideas are further endorsed and elaborated by the research reported in *Readings in Equal Education: Qualitative Investigations into Schools and Schoolings* (Foster, 1991). The findings consistently indicate that "cultural connectedness" in the educational process improves the academic achievement of students of color.

The third focus of teacher reeducation should be the development of technical instructional skills that are more appropriate for use with students of color. The point of departure for this training should be understanding the specific traits of different teaching styles and ethnic learning styles. This knowledge should be combined with learning how to diversify teaching strategies culturally; to create more supportive environments for learning and demonstrating achievement; to reduce stress, tension, and conflict in ethnically pluralistic classrooms; to select materials that have high-quality interest appeal for different ethnic groups; and to develop and use learning activities that are meaningful, involving, enabling, and empowering for students of color. In other words, teachers need to learn how to ethnically integrate their structural arrangements for teaching, to culturally diversify their instructional and assessment strategies, to multiculturalize the substance of learning, and to democratize the environments constructed for learning. These general skills can be operationalized by helping teachers learn how to use specific instructional skills with students of color, such as questioning, feedback and reinforcement, cooperative learning, inductive teaching, social context learning, and auditory and visual learning.

The approaches used in teacher training to develop these skills should be four-dimensional, including *diagnosis, development and implementation, analytical debriefing and reflection*, and *refinement*, with teachers-in-training actively involved in each aspect. The training process should begin with a careful assessment of the value of and problems associated with using various instructional strategies with students of color. Examples of actual teaching behaviors should be used for this purpose. The training should then proceed to having teachers develop alternative curriculum designs and instructional strategies that incorporate cultural diversity and try them out in real or simulated teaching situations and under careful supervision. After these development efforts have been piloted or field-tested, they should be examined thoroughly through the filters of some *established* cultural diversity design and implementation criteria in order to determine their strengths and weaknesses. Central to this analysis should be discerning features of the new teaching strategies that facilitate or continue to inhibit the improvement of educational opportunities and achievement for students of color. Finally, the insights gained from these experiences and analyses should be used to further refine the multicultural curriculum designs and instructional strategies.

A fourth emphasis in the retraining of teachers, counselors, and school administrators for educational equality is public relations skill development. Major reform is needed in how educators are prepared to communicate and interact with parents of color and to mobilize their community resources to help in the educational process. Currently, there is a strong tendency for educators to blame the school failure of students on the lack of involvement of their parents in school affairs. This buck-passing is counter productive to improving the education of students. It is a form of blaming and indicting the victims and of educators abdicating their own responsibility for teaching youths of color.

Certainly, parents of color should be more actively involved in their children's education, but it is understandable why they are reluctant or unable to do so. The schools that are failing their children are the same ones that failed many of them when they were students and that still treat them in paternalistic ways. Educators usually approach parents about their children only when the children get into trouble with the school system. This punitive, adversarial posture is not conducive to cooperation among educators and parents of color. Furthermore, teachers and administrators do not fully understand or appreciate the fact that many parents do not have the time, the personal resources, or the technical skills to assist in the education of their children in ways they typically expect. How can parents effectively supervise their children's homework or come to the schools on demand when they are unfamiliar with the latest pedagogical strategies used in schools and when they are working at hourly wage or low-salaried jobs that do not permit them to take time off without significant cost? How can a non- or limited English-speaking Hmong mother or father even understand the children's language arts assignments, least of all supervise and help them complete it? Teacher education programs should help educators understand these real-life social and cultural factors, how they affect how parents react to invitations and challenges to being educational partners, and to work toward developing novel strategies to overcome these obstacles.

This retraining process should begin with the inclusion of culturally appropriate public relations skill development for use with different ethnic communities. It should be a part of all levels of professional preparation, undergraduate and graduate, preservice and in-service. It should start with acquiring an accurate knowledge base about the cultural dynamics of different ethnic communities, who the power brokers are in these communities, and how interactions and relationships are negotiated. It should also include specific strategies and skills about how to establish credibility and trust with different ethnic communities and parents. Specifically, these might include such skills as identifying and accessing the informal community networks of influence; understanding different ethnic groups' interactional protocols and decorums; establishing consultancy relations with parents and community organizations; establishing equal-status relationships with parents of color and other community members; being cultural brokers or mediators across the cultural systems of homes and schools; diffusing the threat and intimidation often associated with schools for parents of color; and translating educational jargon into language styles that are meaningful for parents from different ethnic, social, and linguistic backgrounds.

Instead of always expecting parent-school interactions to take place in schools (which often are alien and hostile territories for parents and students of color), educators need to locate their efforts to increase parental involvement more within ethnic communities, or at least in neutral territories. The places and times of school-parent interactions, discussions, conferences, and consultations are important symbolic statements about the sincerity of schools' commitments to involving parents as fully enfranchised, equal-status partners in the education of their children. Parents having always to go to the school at educators' convenience conveys an implicit message of super-subordination, with the educators in the position of power and privilege. This kind of relationship does not facilitate parental involvement in *significant* school affairs; nor does it serve well the advancement of educational equality for students of color.

All of these are elements of *cultural diplomacy* that classroom teachers, guidance counselors, and school administrators need to master in order to develop more constructive and cooperative relations with parents and communities of color. They, like the components of cultural therapy, literacy in ethnic and cultural diversity, and culturally appropriate pedagogy, are fundamental to improving the quality of educational opportunities and outcomes for students of color.

CONCLUSION

Educational attainment among most students of color continues to be disturbingly low, even after more than four decades of deliberate legal reforms and funding policies designed to improve it. Some improvements are apparent; but, across the entire spectrum of measures used to assess school achievement these changes are not significant enough to alter the overall patterns. Consistently across time, place, and as indicators of achievement, African Americans have the lowest academic proficiency levels of all ethnic groups, followed in sequence by Latinos and Native Americans. These trends are unequivocal in the math, science, reading, writing, history, geography, and literature report cards issued at two-, four-, and six-year intervals by the National Assessment of Educational Progress (NAEP). The fact that their school attendance and graduation rates are surpassed only by European and Asian Americans (while those of Latinos and American Indians are lower) makes this even more troubling. If staying in school has positive consequences for mediating educational, social, and economic disadvantaged conditions, as theory claims, then as graduation rates increase and dropout rates decline African Americans should be expected to perform academically much better than they are.

The failure of most students of color to achieve significant educational improvements from year to year gives credence to the position taken by Miller-Lachmann and Taylor (1995) that while funds and laws are necessary variables in providing educational equality, they are not sufficient. Something significantly different from what has been tried in the past must be done to provide education equality for students of color. A crucial focus of future reform efforts should be improving the *quality* of the instructional interactions that occur between students of color and teachers in the classroom. Culturally responsive pedagogy and multicultural education offer ideologies and strategies that can facilitate these changes.

Many researchers and scholars agree that the quality of student-teacher interactions in instructional situations is the ultimate test of educational equality. They add that how these are structured and negotiated are determined by cultural attitudes, values, and assumptions. When the cultures of students and teachers are not synchronized, someone loses out. Invariably, it is the students and the effectiveness of their learning, especially if they are members of racially visible groups, such as African, Indian, Latino, and Asian Americans. The lack of teachers' understanding and acceptance of their cultural styles and their inability or unwillingness to use them as instructional tools mean that these students do not have comparable access to high-quality instructional opportunities and interactions as their European American counterparts. It is not surprising, then, that disparities in instructional access produce disparities in achievement outcomes.

These situations will be reversed only when educators accept the fact that culture is a crucial, if not the ultimate, mediating factor in academic achievement. Given that students of color represent culturally pluralistic backgrounds, the only way to assure that they will have maximum opportunities to learn to the best of their abilities is to ensure that the delivery of all of their educational services—whether curriculum, instruction, materials, assessment, counseling, or leadership—are culturally embedded. In other words, *culturally responsive strategies* must be used to educate children of color. As John Goodlad suggests, the central problem of both educational equality and excellence for today and tomorrow is "no longer access to school. It is access to knowledge for all" (Goodlad, 1984, p. 140). This access is not maximally possible for students of color unless their cultural orientations are used as filters for teaching and learning. Therefore, school reform toward improving educational equality for students of color must be centered in the systematic implementation of multicultural education.

Questions and Activities

1. How do popular conceptions of educational equality differ from the view of this concept presented by Gay, the author of this chapter? What unfortunate assumptions, according to Gay, underlie these popular notions of educational equality?

2. In what ways did the educational status of students of color improve between the 1980s and the early 1990s? Why did the educational status of students of color improve during this period?

3. In what ways did the educational status of students of color decline during the 1980s? What are some reasons for this decline?

4. How does the reference to Asian Americans as the model minority oversimplify their educational status? Give specific examples from this chapter to support your response.

5. How do school and curriculum practices such as tracking, vocational courses, and special education classes deny students of color equal educational opportunities?

6. The author argues that students of color are often placed in double jeopardy in school, in part because of differences between their cultures and the culture of the school. Explain what the author means by this concept. How can teachers help reduce the problems students of color experience in the schools?

7. How does testing, according to the author, promote educational inequality for poor students and for students of color? How can assessment programs be changed so they will contribute to educational equality for all students?

8. According to the author, how can curriculum reforms related to ethnic diversity contribute to educational equality?

9. Gay contends that educational equality for students of color cannot be achieved short of "massive schoolwide reform." What factors in the school environment and in teacher education does she think require reform? What specific recommendations does she make for attaining these reforms?

10. Explain why Gay believes that multicultural education has the potential for improving educational equality for students of color.

11. Construct a descriptive profile of the concept of educational equality as developed by the author of this chapter.

12. Observe for several days in a school that has a large percentage of students of color. Look for evidence of the existence of the inequities discussed in this chapter. In what ways do your observations substantiate the conclusions by Gay about the problems that students of color experience in schools? What programs and efforts are being implemented in the school you observed to improve the educational status of students of color, and to what extent are they effective?

References

American Memory: A Report on the Humanities in the Nation's Public Schools. (1987). Washington, DC: National Endowment for the Humanities.

Astin, A. A. (1985). *Achieving Educational Excellence: A Critical Assessment of Priorities and Practices in Higher Education.* San Francisco: Jossey-Bass.

Banks, J. A. and Banks, C. A. M. (Eds.). (1995). *Handbook of Research on Multicultural Education.* New York: Macmillan.

Boateng, F. (1990). Combatting Deculturalization of the African-American Child in the Public School System: A Multicultural Approach. In K. Lomotey (Ed.). *Going to School: The African American Experience* (pp. 73–84). Albany, NY: SUNY Press.

Casso, H. J. (1979). Educating the Linguistically and Culturally Different. In D. A. Wilkerson (Ed.). *Educating All of Our Children: An Imperative for Democracy* (pp. 84–102). Westport, CT: Mediax.

Celis, W. III. (1993, December 14). Study Finds Rising Concentration of Black and Hispanic Students. *New York Times,* A1.

Education That Works: An Action Plan for the Education of Minorities. (1990). Cambridge: Massachusetts Institute of Technology, Quality Education for Minorities Project.

Equality and Excellence: The Educational Status of Black Americans. (1985). New York: College Entrance Examination Board.

Fantini, M. D. (1979). From School System to Educational System: Policy Considerations. In D. A. Wilkerson (Ed.). *Educating All of Our Children: An Imperative for Democracy* (pp. 134–153). Westport, CT: Mediax.

Foster, M. (Ed.). (1991). *Readings on Equal Education: Qualitative Investigations into Schools and Schooling.* Vol. 11. New York: AMS Press.

Gay, G. (1974, January). *Differential Dyadic Interactions of Black and White Teachers with Black and White Pupils in Recently Desegregated Social Studies Classrooms: A Function of Teacher and Pupil Ethnicity.* Washington, DC: Office of Education, National Institute of Education.

Gay, G. (1994). *At the Essence of Learning: Multicultural Education.* West Lafayette, IN: Kappa Delta Pi.

Gibbs, J. T. and Nahme-Huang, L. (Eds.). (1989). *Children of Color: Psychological Interventions with Minority Youth.* San Francisco: Jossey-Bass.

Goodlad, J. I. (1984). *A Place Called School: Prospects for the Future.* New York: McGraw-Hill.

Gougis, R. A. (1986). The Effects of Prejudice and Stress on the Academic Performance of Black Americans. In U. Neisser (Ed.). *The Achievement of Minority Children: New Perspectives* (pp. 145–158). Hillsdale, NJ: Lawrence Erlbaum.

Grant, C. A. and Sleeter, C. E. (1985). Equality, Equity, and Excellence: A Critique. In P. G. Altbach, G. P. Kelly, and L. Weis (Eds.). *Excellence in Education: Perspectives on Policy and Practice* (pp. 139–159). Buffalo, NY: Prometheus Books.

Grant, C. A. and Sleeter, C. E. (1986). *After the School Bell Rings.* Philadelphia: Falmer Press.

Heller, S. (1987, September 16). 17-Year-Olds Get 'Failing Marks' in Their Knowledge of Great Works of Literature and Historical Events. *Chronicle of Higher Education, 34*(3), A35, A38.

Holliday, B. G. (1985). Towards a Model of Teacher-Child Transactional Processes Affecting Black Children's Academic Achievement. In M. B. Spencer, G. K. Brookins, and W. R. Allen (Eds). *Beginnings: The Social and Affective Development of Black Children* (pp. 117–130). Hillsdale, NJ: Lawrence Erlbaum.

Hollins, E. R., King, J. E., and Hayman, W. C. (Eds.). (1994). *Teaching Diverse Populations: Formulating a Knowledge Base.* Albany, NY: SUNY Press.

John-Steiner, V. P. and Leacock, E. (1979). Transforming the Structure of Failure. In D. A. Wilkerson (Ed.). *Educating All of Our Children: An Imperative for Democracy* (pp. 79–91). Westport, CT: Mediax.

Kominski, R. and Adams, A. (1994). *Education Attainment of the U.S. March 1993 and 1992.* Washington, DC: U.S. Bureau of the Census, Current Population Reports, P 20–476, U.S. Government Printing Office.

Ladson-Billings, G. (1992). Liberatory Consequences of Literacy: A Case of Culturally Relevant Instruction for African American Students. *The Journal of Negro Education, 61*(3), 378–391.

Ladson-Billings, G. (1994). *The Dreamkeepers: Successful Teachers of African-American Children.* San Francisco: Jossey-Bass.

McCaleb, S. P. (1994). *Building Communities of Learning: A Collaboration among Teachers, Students, Families, and Community.* New York: St. Martin's Press.

Miller-Lachmann, L. and Taylor, L. S. (1995). *Schools for All: Educating Children in a Diverse Society.* New York: Delmar Publishers.

Morgan, E. P. (1977). *Inequality in Classroom Learning: Schooling and Democratic Citizenship.* New York: Praeger.

Nielsen, F. (1986). Hispanics in High School and Beyond. In M. A. Olivas (Ed.). *Latino College Students* (pp. 71–103). New York: Teachers College Press.

Nieto, S. (1995). A History of the Education of Puerto Rican Students in U.S. Mainland Schools: "Losers," "Outsiders," or "Leaders"? In J. A. Banks and C. A. M. Banks (Eds.). *Handbook of Research on Multicultural Education* (pp. 388–411). New York: Macmillan.

Oakes, J. (1985). *Keeping Track: How Schools Structure Inequality.* New Haven, CT: Yale University Press.

Olivas, M. A. (1986). Research on Latino College Students: A Theoretical Framework and Inquiry. In M. A. Olivas (Ed.). *Latino College Students* (pp. 1–25). New York: Teachers College Press.

Orum, L. S. (1986, August). *The Education of Hispanics: Status and Implications.* Washington, DC: National Council of La Raza. ERIC Document, ED 274753.

Osajima, K. (1991). Breaking the Silence: Race and the Educational Experiences of Asian-American College Students. In M. Foster (Ed.). *Readings on Equal Education: Qualitative Investigations into Schools and Schooling* Vol. 11 (pp. 115–134). New York: AMS Press.

Pai, Y. (1990). *Cultural Foundations of Education.* New York: Merrill.

Pang, V. O., Mizokawa, D. T., Morishima, J. K., and Olstad, R. G. (1985, March). Self-Concept of Japanese American Children. *Journal of Cross-Cultural Psychology, 16*, 99–108.

Persell, C. H. (1977). *Education and Inequality: A Theoretical and Empirical Synthesis.* New York: Free Press.

Ralph, J., Keller, D., and Crouse, J. (1994). How Effective Are American Schools? *Phi Delta Kappan, 76*(2), 144–150.

Rosenbaum, J. E. (1976). *Making Equality: The Hidden Curriculum in High School Tracking.* New York: John Wiley & Sons.

Santiago, I. S. (1986). The Education of Hispanics in the United States: Inadequacies of the Melting Pot Theory. In D. Rothermund and J. Simon (Eds.). *Education and the Integration of Ethnic Minorities* (pp. 151–185). New York: St. Martin's Press.

Shade, B. J. R. (Ed.). (1989). *Culture, Style, and the Educative Process.* Springfield, IL: Charles C Thomas.

Spindler, G. and Spindler, L. (1993). The Processes of Culture and Person: Cultural Therapy and Culturally Diverse Schools. In P. Phelan and A. L. Davidson (Eds.). *Renegotiating Cultural Diversity in American Schools* (pp. 27–51). New York: Teachers College Press.

Teachers' Views on Equity and Excellence. (1983). Washington, DC: National Education Association.

USA Today. (1986, May 13). 1.

U.S. Bureau of the Census. (1993). *The 1990 Census of Population, Social and Economic Characteristics, United States, 1990.* CP-2-1. Washington, DC: U.S. Government Printing Office.

U.S. Bureau of the Census. (1994). *Statistical Abstract of the United States.* Washington, DC: U.S. Government Printing Office.

U.S. Civil Rights Commission. (1971–1974). *Mexican-American Educational Study, Reports I–VI.* Washington DC: Government Printing Office.

U.S. Department of Education. (1989). *Digest of Statistics.* Washington, DC: U.S. Government Printing Office.

U.S. Department of Education. (1990). *The Condition of Education,* Vol. 1, *Elementary and Secondary Education.* Washington, DC: U.S. Government Printing Office.

U.S. Department of Education. (1991). *Characteristics of the 100 Largest Public Elementary and Secondary School Districts in the United States: 1988–1989.* Washington, DC: U.S. Government Printing Office.

U.S. Department of Education. (1992, March). *The 1990 Science Report: NAEP's Assessment of Fourth, Eighth, and Twelfth Graders.* Washington, DC: U.S. Government Printing Office.

U.S. Department of Education. (1993, May). *America's Teachers: Profile of a Profession.* NCES 93-025. Washington, DC: U.S. Government Printing Office.

U.S. Department of Education. (1994a). *Digest of Education Statistics.* Washington, DC: U.S. Government Printing Office.

U.S. Department of Education. (1994b). *NAEP 1992 Trends in Academic Progress.* Washington, DC: U.S. Government Printing Office.

U.S. Department of Education. (1994c). *Progress of Education in the United States of America 1990 through 1994.* Washington, DC: U.S. Government Printing Office.

U.S. Department of Education. (1994d). *Condition of Education, Elementary and Secondary Education.* Washington, DC: U.S. Government Printing Office.

U.S. Department of Education. (1995). *Characteristics of American Indian and Alaska Native Education.* Washington, DC: U.S. Government Printing Office.

Verdugo, R. R. (1986). Educational Stratification and Hispanics. In M. A. Olivas (Ed.). *Latino College Students* (pp. 325–347). New York: Teachers College Press.

Winkler, J. D., Stravelson, R. J., Stasz, C., Robyn, A., and Fiebel, W. (1984). *How Effective Teachers Use Microcomputers in Instruction.* Santa Monica, CA: Rand Corporation.

Yu, E. S. H., Doi, M., and Chang, C. (1986, November). *Asian American Education in Illinois: A Review of the Data.* Springfield: Illinois State Board of Education.

Chapter 10

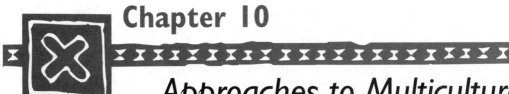

Approaches to Multicultural Curriculum Reform

James A. Banks

THE MAINSTREAM-CENTRIC CURRICULUM

The United States is made up of many different racial, ethnic, religious, and cultural groups. In many school curricula, textbooks, and other teaching materials, most of these groups are given scant attention. Rather, most curricula, textbooks, and teaching materials focus on White Anglo-Saxon Protestants. This dominant cultural group in U.S. society is often called mainstream Americans. A curriculum that focuses on the experiences of mainstream Americans and largely ignores the experiences, cultures, and histories of other ethnic, racial, cultural, and religious groups has negative consequences for both mainstream American students and students of color. A mainstream-centric curriculum is one major way in which racism and ethnocentrism are reinforced and perpetuated in the schools and also in society at large.

A mainstream-centric curriculum has negative consequences for mainstream students because it reinforces their false sense of superiority, gives them a misleading conception of their relationship with other racial and ethnic groups, and denies them the opportunity to benefit from the knowledge, perspectives, and frames of reference that can be gained from studying and experiencing other cultures and groups. A mainstream-centric curriculum also denies mainstream American students the opportunity to view their culture from the perspectives of other cultures and groups. When people view their culture from the point of view of another culture, they are able to understand their own culture more fully, to see how it is unique and distinct from other cultures, and to understand better how it relates to and interacts with other cultures.

A mainstream-centric curriculum negatively influences students of color, such as African Americans, Hispanics, and Asian Americans. It marginalizes their experiences and cultures and does not reflect their dreams, hopes, and perspectives. Students learn best and are more highly motivated when the school curriculum reflects their cultures, experiences, and perspectives. Many students of color are alienated in the school in part because they experience cultural conflict and discontinuities that result from the cultural differences between their school and community. The school can help students of color mediate between their home and school cultures by implementing a curriculum that reflects the culture of their ethnic groups and communities. The school can and should make effective use of the community cultures of students of color when teaching them such subjects as writing, language arts, science, and mathematics (Grant & Gomez, 1996).

In the mainstream-centric approach, events, themes, concepts, and issues are viewed primarily from the perspective of middle-class Anglo-Americans and Europeans. Events and cultural developments such as the European explorations in the Americas and the development of American music are viewed from Anglo and European perspectives and are evaluated using mainstream-centric criteria and points of view.

When the European explorations of the Americas are viewed from a Eurocentric perspective, the Americas are perceived as having been "discovered" by the European explorers such as Columbus and Cortes (Loewen, 1995). The view that native peoples in the Americas were discovered by the Europeans subtly suggests that Indian cultures did not exist until they were "discovered" by the Europeans and that the lands occupied by the American Indians were rightfully owned by the Europeans after they settled on and claimed them. The Anglocentric view, below, of the settlement of Fort Townsend in the state of Washington appears on a marker in a federal park on the site where a U.S. Army post once stood. With the choice of words such as *settlers* (instead of *invaders), restive,* and *rebelled,* the author justifies the taking of the Indian's lands and depicts their resistance as unreasonable.

Fort Townsend

A U.S. Army Post was Established on this Site in 1856.
In mid-nineteenth century the growth of Port Townsend
caused the Indians to become restive. Settlers started a home
guard, campaigned wherever called, and defeated the Indians
in the Battle of Seattle. Indians rebelled as the government
began enforcing the Indian Treaty of 1854, by which the
Indians had ceded most of their territory. Port Townsend, a
prosperous port of entry on Puget Sound, then asked protection of the U.S. army.

When the formation and nature of U.S. cultural developments, such as music and dance, are viewed from mainstream-centric perspectives, these art forms become important and significant only when they are recognized or legitimized by mainstream critics and artists. The music of African American musicians such as Chuck Berry and Little Richard was not viewed as significant by the mainstream society until White singers such as the Beatles and Rod Stewart publicly acknowledged the significant ways their own music had been deeply influenced by these African American musicians. It often takes White artists to legitimize ethnic cultural forms and innovations created by Asian Americans, African Americans, Hispanics, and Native Americans.

EFFORTS TO ESTABLISH A MULTICULTURAL CURRICULUM

Since the civil rights movement of the 1960s, educators have been trying, in various ways, to better integrate the school curriculum with ethnic content and to move away from a mainstream-centric and Eurocentric curriculum (Banks, 1995). These have proven to be difficult goals for schools to attain for many complex reasons. The strong assimilationist ideology embraced by most U.S. educators is one major reason (Banks, 1994). The assimilationist ideology makes it difficult for educators to think differently about how U.S. society and culture developed and to acquire a commitment to make the curriculum multicultural. Individuals who have a strong assimilationist ideology believe that most important events and developments in U.S. society are related to the nation's British heritage and that the contributions of other ethnic and cultural groups are not very significant by comparison. When educators acquire a multicultural ideology and conception of U.S. culture, they are then able to view the experiences and contributions of a wide range of cultural, ethnic, and religious groups as significant to the development of the United States.

Ideological resistance is a major factor that has slowed and is still slowing the development of a multicultural curriculum, but other factors have also affected its growth and development. Political resistance to a multicultural curriculum is closely related to ideological resistance. Many people who resist a multicultural curriculum believe that knowledge is power and that a multicultural perspective on U.S. society challenges the existing power structure. They believe that the dominant mainstream-centric curriculum supports, reinforces, and justifies the existing social, economic, and political structure. Multicultural perspectives and points of view, in the opinion of many observers, legitimize and promote social change and social reconstruction.

In recent years a heated debate has occurred about the extent to which the curriculum should be Western and European-centric and to which it should reflect the cultural, ethnic, and racial diversity in the United States. At least three major positions in this debate can be identified. The Western traditionalists argue that the West, as defined and conceptualized in the past, should be the focus in school and college curricula because of the major influence of Western civilization and culture in the United States and throughout the world (Ravitch, 1990; Schlesinger, 1991). Afrocentric scholars contend that the contributions of Africa and of African peoples should receive major emphasis in the curriculum (Asante, 1991; Asante & Ravitch, 1991). The multiculturalists argue that although the West should receive a major emphasis in the curriculum, the West should be reconceptualized so that it reflects the contributions that people of color have made to the West (Zinn & Kirschner, 1995). In addition to teaching about Western ideals, the gap between the ideals of the West and its realities of racism, sexism, and discrimination should be taught (Parekh, 1986). Multiculturalists also believe that in addition to learning about the West, students should study other world cultures, such as those in Africa, Asia, the Middle East, and America, as they were before the Europeans arrived.

Other factors that have slowed the institutionalization of a multicultural curriculum include the low level of knowledge about ethnic cultures that most educators have and the heavy reliance on textbooks for teaching. Teachers must have an in-depth knowledge about ethnic cultures and experiences to integrate ethnic content, experiences, and points of view into the curriculum. Many teachers tell their students that Columbus discovered America and that America is a "new world" because they know little about the diverse Native American cultures that existed in the Americas more than 40,000 years before the Europeans began to settle in the Americas in significant numbers in the sixteenth century.

Many studies have revealed that the textbook is still the main source for teaching, especially in such subjects as the social studies, reading, and language arts (Goodlad, 1984; Social Science Education Consortium, 1982). Some significant changes have been made in textbooks since the civil rights movement of the 1960s. More ethnic groups and women appear in textbooks today than in those of yesteryear (Garcia, 1993). However, the content about ethnic groups in textbooks is usually presented from mainstream perspectives, contains information and heroes that are selected using mainstream criteria, and rarely incorporates information about ethnic groups throughout the text in a consistent and totally integrated way (Sleeter & Grant, 1991). Information about ethnic groups is usually discussed in special units, topics, and parts of the text. Because most teachers rely heavily on the textbook for teaching, they approach the teaching of ethnic content in a fragmented fashion.

LEVELS OF INTEGRATION OF MULTICULTURAL CONTENT

The Contributions Approach

Four approaches to the integration of ethnic and multicultural content into the curriculum that have evolved since the 1960s can be identified (see Figure 10.1). The *contributions approach* to integration (level 1) is one of the most frequently used and is often used extensively during the first phase of an ethnic revival movement. It is also frequently used when a school or district first attempts to integrate ethnic and multicultural content into the mainstream curriculum.

The contributions approach is characterized by the insertion of ethnic heroes/heroines and discrete cultural artifacts into the curriculum, selected using criteria similar to those used to select mainstream heroes/heroines and cultural artifacts. Thus, individuals such as Crispus Attucks, Benjamin Bannaker, Sacajawea, Booker T. Washington, and Cesar Chavez are added to the curriculum. They are discussed when mainstream American heroes/heroines such as Patrick Henry, George Washington, Thomas Jefferson, Betsey Ross, and Eleanor Roosevelt are studied in the core curriculum. Discrete cultural elements such as the foods, dances, music, and artifacts of ethnic groups are studied, but little attention is given to their meanings and importance within ethnic communities.

An important characteristic of the contributions approach is that the mainstream curriculum remains unchanged in its basic structure, goals, and salient characteristics. Prerequisites for the implementation of this approach are minimal. They include basic knowledge about U.S. society and knowledge about ethnic heroes/heroines and their roles and contributions to U.S. society and culture.

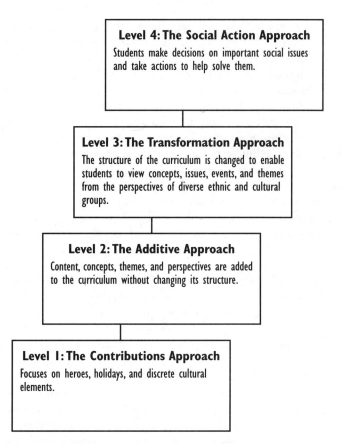

Figure 10.1 Levels of Integration of Multicultural Content

Individuals who challenged the dominant society's ideologies, values, and conceptions and advocated radical social, political, and economic reform are seldom included in the contributions approach. Thus, Booker T. Washington is more likely to be chosen for study than is W. E. B. Du Bois, and Sacajawea is likely to be chosen than is Geronimo. The criteria used to select ethnic heroes/heroines for study and to judge them for success are derived from the mainstream society and not from the ethnic community. Consequently, use of the contributions approach usually results in the study of ethnic heroes/heroines who represent only one important perspective within ethnic communities. The more radical and less conformist individuals who are heroes/heroines only to the ethnic community tend to be ignored in textbooks, teaching materials, and activities used in the contributions approach.

The heroes/heroines and holidays approach is a variant of the contributions approach. In this approach, ethnic content is limited primarily to special days, weeks, and months related to ethnic events and celebrations. Cinco de Mayo, Martin Luther King Jr.'s Birthday, and African American History Week are examples of ethnic days and weeks celebrated in the schools. During these celebrations, teachers involve students in lessons, experiences, and pageants related to the ethnic group being commemorated. When this approach is used, the class studies little or nothing about the ethnic group before or after the special event or occasion.

The contributions approach (level 1 in Figure 10.1) provides teachers with a way to integrate ethnic content into the curriculum quickly, thus giving some recognition to ethnic contributions to U.S. society and culture. Many teachers who are committed to integrating their curricula with ethnic content have little knowledge about ethnic groups and curriculum revision. Consequently, they use the contributions approach when teaching about ethnic groups. These teachers should be encouraged, supported, and given the opportunity to acquire the knowledge and skills needed to reform their curricula by using one of the more effective approaches described later in this chapter.

There are often strong political demands from ethnic communities for the school to put their heroes/heroines, contributions, and cultures into the school curriculum. These political forces may take the form of demands for heroes and contributions because mainstream heroes, such as Washington, Jefferson, and Lincoln, are highly visible in the school curriculum. Ethnic communities of color want to see their own heroes/heroines and contributions alongside those of the mainstream society. Such contributions may help give them a sense of structural inclusion, validation, and equity. Curriculum inclusion also facilitates the quests of marginalized ethnic and cultural groups for a sense of empowerment and efficacy. The school should help ethnic-group students acquire a sense of empowerment and efficacy. These factors are positively correlated with academic achievement (Coleman, Campbell, Hobson, McPartland, Mood, Weinfeld, & York, 1966).

The contributions approach is also the easiest approach for teachers to use to integrate the curriculum with ethnic content. However, this approach has several serious limitations. When the integration of the curriculum is accomplished primarily through the infusion of ethnic heroes/heroines and contributions, students do not attain a global view of the role of ethnic and cultural groups in U.S. society. Rather, they see ethnic issues and events primarily as an addition to the curriculum and consequently as an appendage to the main story of the development of the nation and to the core curriculum in the language arts, the social studies, the arts, and other subject areas.

Teaching ethnic issues with the use of heroes/heroines and contributions also tends to gloss over important concepts and issues related to the victimization and oppression of ethnic groups and their struggles against racism and for power. Issues such as racism, poverty, and oppression tend to be avoided in the contributions approach to curriculum integration. The focus tends to be on success and the validation of the Horatio Alger myth that all Americans who are willing to work hard can go from rags to riches and "pull themselves up by their bootstraps."

The success stories of ethnic heroes such as Booker T. Washington, George Washington Carver, and Jackie Robinson are usually told with a focus on their success, with little attention to racism and other barriers they encountered and how they succeeded despite the hurdles they faced. Little attention is also devoted to the process by which they become heroes/heroines. Students should learn about the process by which people become heroes/heroines as well as about their status and role as heroes/heroines. Only when students learn the process by which individuals become heroes/heroines will they understand fully how individuals, particularly individuals of color, achieve and maintain hero/heroine status and what the process of becoming a hero/heroine means for their own lives.

The contributions approach often results in the trivialization of ethnic cultures, the study of their strange and exotic characteristics, and the reinforcement of stereotypes and misconceptions. When the focus is on the contributions and unique aspects of ethnic cultures, students are not helped to view them as complete and dynamic wholes. The contributions approach also tends to focus on the life-styles of ethnic groups rather than on the institutional structures, such as racism and discrimination, that strongly affect their life chances and keep them powerless and marginalized.

The contributions approach to content integration may provide students with a memorable one-time experience with an ethnic hero/heroine, but it often fails to help them understand the role and influence of the hero/heroine in the total context of U.S. history and society. When ethnic heroes/heroines are studied separate and apart from the social and political context in which they lived and worked, students attain only a partial understanding of their roles and significance in society. When Martin Luther King, Jr., or Rosa Parks are studied outside the social and political context of institutionalized racism in the U.S. South in the 1940s and 1950s, and without attention to the more subtle forms of institutionalized racism in the North during this period, their full significance as social reformers and activists is neither revealed nor understood by students.

The Additive Approach

Another important approach to the integration of ethnic content to the curriculum is the addition of content, concepts, themes, and perspectives to the curriculum without changing its basic structure, purposes, and characteristics. The *additive approach* (level 2 in Figure 10.1) is often accomplished by the addition of a book, a unit, or a course to the curriculum without changing it substantially. Examples of this approach include adding a book such as *The Color Purple* to a unit on the twentieth century in an English class, the use of the film *Miss Jane Pittman* during a unit on the 1960s, and the addition of a unit on the internment of the Japanese Americans during a study of World War II in a class on U.S. history.

The additive approach allows the teacher to put ethnic content into the curriculum without restructuring it, a process that would take substantial time, effort, training, and rethinking of the curriculum and its purposes, nature, and goals. The additive approach can be the first phase in a transformative curriculum reform effort designed to restructure the total curriculum and to integrate it with ethnic content, perspectives, and frames of reference.

However, this approach shares several disadvantages with the contributions approach. Its most important shortcoming is that it usually results in the viewing of ethnic content from the perspectives of mainstream historians, writers, artists, and scientists because it does not involve a restructuring of the curriculum. The events, concepts, issues, and problems selected for study are selected using mainstream-centric and Eurocentric criteria and perspectives. When teaching a unit such as The Westward Movement in a fifth-grade U.S. history class, the teacher may integrate the unit by adding content about the Oglala Sioux Indians. However, the unit remains mainstream-centric and focused because of its perspective and point of view. A unit called The Westward Movement is mainstream and Eurocentric because it focuses on the movement of European Americans from the Eastern to the Western part of the United States. The Oglala Sioux were already in the West and consequently were not moving westward. The unit might be called *The Invasion from the East*, from the point of view of the Oglala Sioux. Black Elk, an Oglala Sioux holy man, lamented the conquering of his people, which culminated in their defeat at Wounded Knee Creek on December 29, 1890. Approximately 200 Sioux men, women, and children were killed by U.S. troops. Black Elk said, "The [Sioux] nation's hoop is broken and scattered. There is no center any longer, and the sacred tree is dead" (Neihardt, 1972, p. 230).

Black Elk did not consider his homeland "the West," but rather the center of the world. He viewed the cardinal directions metaphysically. The Great Spirit sent him the cup of living water and the sacred bow from the West. The daybreak star and the sacred pipe originated from the East. The Sioux nation's sacred hoop and the tree that was to bloom came from the South (*Black Elk's Prayer*, 1964). When teaching about the movement of the Europeans across North America, teachers should help students understand that different cultural, racial, and ethnic groups often have varying and conflicting conceptions and points of view about the same historical events, concepts, issues, and developments. The victors and the vanquished, especially, often have conflicting conceptions of the same historical event. However, it is usually the point of view of the victors that becomes institutionalized within the schools and the mainstream society. This happens because history and textbooks are usually written by people who won the wars and gained control of the society, and not by the losers—the victimized and the powerless. The perspectives of both groups are needed to help us fully understand our history, culture, and society.

The people who are conquered and the people who conquered them have histories and cultures that are intricately interwoven and interconnected. They have to learn each others' histories and cultures to understand their own fully. White Americans cannot fully understand their own history in the Western United States and in America without understanding the history of the American Indians and the ways their histories and the histories of the Indians are interconnected. James Baldwin (1985) insightfully pointed out that when White Americans distort African American history, they do not learn the truth about their own history because the history of Blacks and Whites in the United States is tightly bound together. This is also true for African American history and Indian history. The history of African Americans and Indians in the United States is closely interconnected, as Katz (1986) documents in his book *Black Indians: A Hidden Heritage*. The additive approach fails to help students view society from diverse cultural and ethnic perspectives and to understand the ways that the histories and cultures of the nation's diverse ethnic, racial, cultural, and religious groups are interconnected.

Content, materials, and issues that are added to a curriculum as appendages instead of being integral parts of a unit of instruction can become problematic. Problems might result when a book such as *The Color Purple* or a film like *Miss Jane Pittman* is added to a unit when the students lack the concepts, content background, and emotional maturity to deal with the issues and problems in this material. The effective use of such emotion-laden and complex materials usually requires that the teacher help students acquire, in a sequential and developmental fashion, the content background and attitudinal maturity to deal with them effectively. The use of both of these materials in different classes and schools has resulted in major problems for the teachers using them. A community controversy arose in each case. The problems developed because the material was used with students who had neither the content background nor the attitudinal sophistication to respond to them appropriately. Adding ethnic content to the curriculum in a sporadic and segmented way can result in pedagogical problems, trouble for the teacher, student confusion, and community controversy.

The Transformation Approach

The *transformation approach* differs fundamentally from the contributions and additive approaches. In these two approaches, ethnic content is added to the mainstream core curriculum without changing its basic assumptions, nature, and structure. The fundamental goals, structure, and perspectives of the curriculum are changed in the transformation approach.

The transformation approach (level 3 in Figure 10.1), however, changes the basic assumptions of the curriculum and enables students to view concepts, issues, themes, and problems from several ethnic perspectives and points of view. The mainstream-centric perspective is one of only several perspectives from which issues, problems, concepts, and issues are viewed. It is neither possible nor desirable to view every issue, concept, event, or problem from the point of view of every U.S. ethnic group. Rather, the goal should be to enable students to view concepts and issues from more than one perspective and from the point of view of the cultural, ethnic, and racial groups that were the most active participants in, or were most cogently influenced by, the event, issue, or concept being studied.

The key curriculum issues involved in multicultural curriculum reform is not the addition of a long list of ethnic groups, heroes, and contributions, but the infusion of various perspectives, frames of references, and content from various groups that will extend students' understandings of the nature, development, and complexity of U.S. society. When students are studying the revolution in the British colonies, the perspectives of the Anglo revolutionaries, the Anglo loyalists, African Americans, Indians, and the British are essential for them to attain a thorough understanding of this significant event in U.S. history (see Figure 10.2). Students must study the various and sometimes divergent meanings of the revolution to these diverse groups to understand it fully (Gay & Banks, 1975).

In the language arts, when students are studying the nature of U.S. English and proper language use, they should be helped to understand the rich linguistic and language diversity in the United States and the ways that a wide range of regional, cultural, and ethnic groups have influenced the development of U.S. English. Students should also examine how normative language use varies within the social context, the region, and the situation. The use of Black English is appropriate in some social and cultural contexts and inappropriate in others. This is also true of standard U.S.

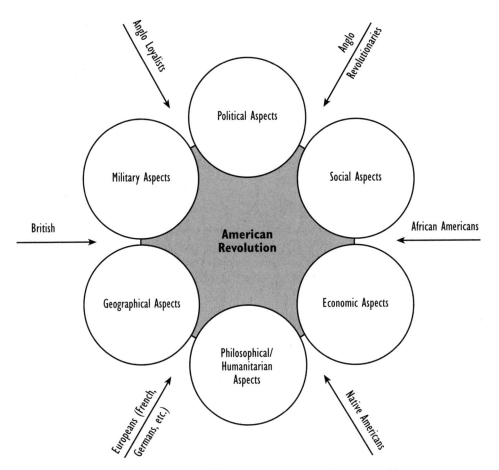

Figure 10.2 A Multicultural Interdisciplinary Model for Teaching the American Revolution

Source: Reprinted with permission from Geneva Gay and James A. Banks, "Teaching the American Revolution: A Multiethnic Approach," *Social Education*, 7 (November–December 1975): 462.

English. The United States is rich in languages and dialects. The nation has more than twenty million Hispanic citizens; Spanish is the first language for most of them. Most of the nation's approximately thirty million African Americans speak both standard English as well as some form of Black English or Ebonics (Baugh, 1983). The rich language diversity in the United States includes more than twenty-five European languages; Asian, African, and Middle-Eastern languages; and American Indian languages. Since the 1970s, languages from Indochina, spoken by groups such as the Hmong, Vietnamese, Laotians, and the Cambodians, have further enriched language diversity in the United States.

When subjects such as music, dance, and literature are studied, the teacher should acquaint students with the ways these art forms among U.S. ethnic groups have greatly influenced and enriched the nation's artistic and literary traditions. The ways that African American musicians such as Bessie Smith, W. C. Handy, and Leontyne Price have influenced the nature and development of U.S. music should be examined when the development of U.S. music is studied. African Americans and Puerto Ricans have significantly influenced the development of American dance. Writers of color, such as Langston Hughes, Toni Morrison, N. Scott Momaday, Carlos Bulosan, Maxine Hong Kingston, Rudolfo A. Anaya, and Piri Thomas, have not only significantly influenced the development of American literature, but have also provided unique and revealing perspectives on U.S. society and culture (Gillan & Gillan, 1994; Harris, 1992; Rico & Mano, 1995).

When studying U.S. history, language, music, arts, science, and mathematics, the emphasis should not be on the ways that various ethnic and cultural groups have contributed to mainstream U.S. society and culture. *The emphasis, rather should be on how the common U.S. culture and society emerged from a complex synthesis and interaction of the diverse cultural elements that originated within the various cultural, racial, ethnic, and religious groups that make up U.S. society.* I call this process multiple acculturation, and I argue that even though Anglo-Saxon Protestants are the dominant group in the United States—culturally, politically, and economically—it is misleading and inaccurate to describe U.S. culture and society as an Anglo-Saxon Protestant culture (Banks, 1994). Other U.S. ethnic and cultural groups have deeply influenced, shaped, and participated in the development and formation of U.S. society and culture. African Americans, for example, profoundly influenced the development of the U.S. Southern culture, even though they had very little political and economic power (Abbott, 1986). One irony of conquest is that those who are conquered often deeply influence the cultures of the conquerors.

A multiple acculturation conception of U.S. society and culture leads to a perspective that views ethnic events, literature, music, and art as integral parts of the common, shared U.S. culture. Anglo-Saxon Protestant culture is viewed as only a part of this larger cultural whole. Thus, to teach American literature without including significant writers of color, such as those named above, gives a partial and incomplete view of U.S. literature, culture, and society.

The Social Action Approach

The *social action approach* (level 4 in Figure 10.1) includes all the elements of the transformation approach but adds components that require students to make decisions and take actions related to the concept, issue, or problem studied in the unit. Major goals of instruction in this approach are to educate students for social criticism and social change and to teach them decision-making skills. To empower students and help them acquire political efficacy, the school must help them become reflective social critics and skilled participants in social change. The traditional goal of schooling has been to socialize students so they would accept unquestioningly the existing ideologies, institutions, and practices within society and the nation-state (Newmann, 1968).

Political education in the United States has traditionally fostered political passivity rather than political action. A major goal of the social action approach is to help students acquire the knowledge, values, and skills they need to participate in social change so that victimized and excluded ethnic and racial groups can become full participants in U.S. society and so the nation will move closer to attaining its democratic ideals. To participate effectively in democratic social change, students must be taught social criticism and must be helped to understand the inconsistency between our ideals and social realities, the work that must be done to close this gap, and how students can, as individuals and groups, influence the social and political systems in U.S. society. In this approach, teachers are agents of social change who promote democratic values and the empowerment of students. Teaching units organized using the social action approach have the components described below.

1. *A decision problem or question.* An example of a question is: What actions should we take to reduce prejudice and discrimination in our school?

2. *An inquiry that provides data related to the decision problem.* The inquiry might consist of these kinds of questions:

   a. What is prejudice?

   b. What is discrimination?

   c. What causes prejudice?

   d. What causes people to discriminate?

   e. What are examples of prejudice and discrimination in our nation, community, and school?

   f. How do prejudice and discrimination affect the groups below? How does each group view prejudice? Discrimination? To what extent is each group a victim or a perpetuator of prejudice and discrimination?

   g. How has each group dealt with prejudice and discrimination? (Groups: White mainstream Americans, African Americans, Asian Americans, Hispanic Americans, Native Americans.)

The inquiry into the nature of prejudice and discrimination would be interdisciplinary and would include readings and data sources in the various social sciences, biography, fiction, poetry, and drama. Scientific and statistical data would be used when students investigated how discrimination affects the income, occupations, frequency of diseases, and health care within these various groups.

3. *Value inquiry and moral analysis.* Students are given opportunities to examine, clarify, and reflect on their values, attitudes, beliefs, and feelings related to racial prejudice and discrimination. The teacher can provide the students with case studies from various sources, such as newspapers and magazines. The case studies can be used to involve the students in discussions and role-playing situations that enable them to express and to examine their attitudes, beliefs, and feelings about prejudice and discrimination.

Poetry, biography, and powerful fiction are excellent sources for case studies that can be used for both discussion and role playing. Countee Cullen's powerful poem "Incident" describes the painful memories of a child who was called "nigger" on a trip to Baltimore. Langston Hughes's poem "I, Too" poignantly tells how the "darker brother" is sent into the kitchen when company comes. The teacher and the students can describe verbally or write about incidents related to prejudice and discrimination they have observed or in which they have participated. The following case, based on a real-life situation, was written by the author for use with his students. After reading the case, the students discuss the questions at the end of it.

Trying to Buy a Home in Lakewood Island

About a year ago, Joan and Henry Green, a young African American couple, moved from the West Coast to a large city in the Midwest. They moved because Henry finished his Ph.D. in chemistry and took a job at a big university in Midwestern City. Since they have been in Midwestern City, the Greens have rented an apartment in the central area of the city. However, they have decided that they want to buy a house. Their apartment has become too small for the many books and other things they have accumulated during the year. In addition to wanting more space, they also want a house so that they can receive breaks on their income tax, which they do not receive living in an apartment. The Greens also think that a house will be a good financial investment.

The Greens have decided to move into a suburban community. They want a new house and most of the houses within the city limits are rather old. They also feel that they can obtain a larger house for their money in the suburbs than in the city. They have looked at several suburban communities and decided that they like Lakewood Island better than any of the others. Lakewood Island is an all-White community, which is comprised primarily of lower-middle-class and middle-class residents. There are a few wealthy families in Lakewood Island, but they are exceptions rather than the rule.

Joan and Henry Green have become frustrated because of the problems they have experienced trying to buy a home in Lakewood Island. Before they go out to look at a house, they carefully study the newspaper ads. When they arrived at the first house in which they were interested, the owner told them that his house had just been sold. A week later they decided to work with a realtor. When they tried to close the deal on the next house they wanted, the realtor told them that the owner had raised the price $10,000 because he had the house appraised since he put it on the market and had discovered that his selling price was much too low. When the Greens tried to buy a third house in Lakewood Island, the owner told them that he had decided not to sell because he had not received the job in another city that he was almost sure he would receive when he had put his house up for sale. He explained that the realtor had not removed the ad about his house from the newspaper even though he had told him that he had decided not to sell a week earlier. The realtor the owner had been working with had left the real estate company a few days ago. Henry is bitter and feels that he and his wife are victims of racism and discrimination. Joan believes that Henry is paranoid and that they have been the victims of a series of events that could have happened to anyone, regardless of their race.

(Reprinted with permission from James A. Banks, *Teaching Strategies for Ethnic Studies*, 6th ed. Boston: Allyn and Bacon, 1997, pp. 234, 236)

Questions: What should the Greens do? Why?

4. *Decision making and social action* (synthesis of knowledge and values). Students acquire knowledge about their decision problem from the activities in 2, above. This interdisciplinary knowledge provides them with the information they need to make reflective decisions about prejudice and discrimination in their communities and schools. The activities in 3 enable them to identify, clarify, and analyze their values, feelings, and beliefs about prejudice and discrimination: The decision-making process enables the students to synthesize their knowledge and values to determine what actions, if any, they should take to reduce prejudice and discrimination in their schools. They can develop a chart in which they list possible actions to take and their possible consequences. They can then decide on a course of action to take and implement it.

Mixing and Blending Approaches

The four approaches for the integration of multicultural content into the curriculum (see Table 10.1) are often mixed and blended in actual teaching situations. One approach, such as the contributions approach, can be used as a vehicle to move to other, more intellectually challenging approaches, such as the transformation and social action approaches. It is unrealistic to expect a teacher to move directly from a highly mainstream-centric curriculum to one that focuses on decision making and social action. Rather, the move from the first to higher levels of multicultural content integration is likely to be gradual and cumulative.

A teacher who has a mainstream-centric curriculum might use the school's Martin Luther King Jr.'s birthday celebration as an opportunity to integrate the curriculum with ethnic content about King, as well as to think seriously about how content about African Americans and other ethnic groups can be integrated into the curriculum in an ongoing fashion. The teacher could explore with the students these kinds of questions during the celebration:

1. What were the conditions of other ethnic groups during the time that King was a civil rights leader?
2. How did other ethnic groups participate in and respond to the civil rights movement?
3. How did these groups respond to Martin Luther King, Jr.?
4. What can we do today to improve the civil rights of groups of color?
5. What can we do to develop more positive racial and ethnic attitudes?

The students will be unable to answer all the questions they have raised about ethnic groups during the celebration of Martin Luther King, Jr.'s birthday. Rather, the questions will enable the students to integrate content about ethnic groups throughout the year as they study such topics as the family, the school, the neighborhood, and the city. As the students study these topics, they can use the questions they have formulated to investigate ethnic families, the ethnic groups in their school and in schools in other parts of the city, ethnic neighborhoods, and various ethnic institutions in the city such as churches, temples, synagogues, schools, restaurants, and community centers. As a culminating activity for the year, the teacher can take the students on a tour of an ethnic community in the city. However, such a tour should be both preceded and followed by activities that enable the students to develop perceptive and compassionate lenses for seeing ethnic and cultural differences and for responding to them with sensitivity. A field trip to an ethnic community or neighborhood might reinforce stereotypes and misconceptions if students lack the knowledge and insights needed to view ethnic cultures in an understanding and caring way. Theory and research indicate that contact with an ethnic group does not necessarily lead to more positive racial and ethnic attitudes (Allport, 1979; Schofield, 1995). Rather, the conditions under which the contact occurs and the quality of the interaction in the contact situation are the important variables.

GUIDELINES FOR TEACHING MULTICULTURAL CONTENT

The following fourteen guidelines are designed to help you better integrate content about ethnic groups into the school curriculum and to teach effectively in multicultural environments.

1. You, the teacher, are an extremely important variable in the teaching of ethnic content. If you have the necessary knowledge, attitudes, and skills, when you encounter racist content in materials or observe racism in the statements and behavior of students you can use these situations to teach important lessons about the experiences of ethnic groups in the United States. An informative source on racism is Paul Kivel, *Uprooting Racism: How White People Can Work for Racial Justice* (Philadelphia, PA: New Society Publishers, 1995). Another helpful source on this topic is chapter 11 in this book.

Table 10.1 Approaches for the Integration of Multicultural Content

Approach	Description	Examples	Strengths	Problems
Contributions	Heroes, cultural components, holidays, and other discrete elements related to ethnic groups are added to the curriculum on special days, occasions, and celebrations.	Famous Mexican Americans are studied only during the week of Cinco de Mayo (May 5). African Americans are studied during African American History Month in February but rarely during the rest of the year. Ethnic foods are studied in the first grade with little attention devoted to the cultures in which the foods are embedded.	Provides a quick and relatively easy way to put ethnic content into the curriculum. Gives ethnic heroes visibility in the curriculum alongside mainstream heroes. Is a popular approach among teachers and educators.	Results in a superficial understanding of ethnic cultures. Focuses on the life-styles and artifacts of ethnic groups and reinforces stereotypes and misconceptions. Mainstream criteria are used to select heroes and cultural elements for inclusion in the curriculum.
Additive	This approach consists of the addition of content, concepts, themes, and perspectives to the curriculum without changing its structure.	Adding the book *The Color Purple* to a literature unit without reconceptualizing the unit or giving the students the background knowledge to understand the book. Adding a unit on the Japanese American internment to a U.S. history course without treating the Japanese in any other unit. Leaving the core curriculum intact but adding an ethnic studies course, as an elective, that focuses on a specific ethnic group.	Makes it possible to add ethnic content to the curriculum without changing its structure, which requires substantial curriculum changes and staff development. Can be implemented within the existing curriculum structure.	Reinforces the idea that ethnic history and culture are not integral parts of U.S. mainstream culture. Students view ethnic groups from Anglocentric and Eurocentric perspectives. Fails to help students understand how the dominant culture and ethnic cultures are interconnected and interrelated.
Transformation	The basic goals, structure, and nature of the curriculum are changed to enable students to	A unit on the American Revolution describes the meaning of the revolution to Anglo revolutionaries,	Enables students to understand the complex ways in which diverse racial and cultural groups	The implementation of this approach requires substantial curriculum revision, in-service training,

Table 10.1 Continued

Approach	Description	Examples	Strengths	Problems
	view concepts, events, issues, problems, and themes from the perspectives of diverse cultural, ethnic, and racial groups.	Anglo loyalists, African Americans, Indians, and the British. A unit on 20th-century U.S. literature includes works by William Faulkner, Joyce Carol Oates, Langston Hughes, N. Scott Momoday, Saul Bellow, Maxine Hong Kingston, Rudolfo A. Anaya, and Piri Thomas.	participated in the formation of U.S. society and culture. Helps reduce racial and ethnic encapsulation. Enables diverse ethnic, racial, and religious groups to see their cultures, ethos, and perspectives in the school curriculum. Gives students a balanced view of the nature and development of U.S. culture and society. Helps to empower victimized racial, ethnic, and cultural groups.	and the identification and development of materials written from the perspectives of various racial and cultural groups. Staff development for the institutionalization of this approach must be continual and ongoing.
Social Action	In this approach, students identify important social problems and issues, gather pertinent data, clarify their values on the issues, make decisions, and take reflective actions to help resolve the issue or problem.	A class studies prejudice and discrimination in their school and decides to take actions to improve race relations in the school. A class studies the treatment of ethnic groups in a local newspaper and writes a letter to the newspaper publisher suggesting ways that the treatment of ethnic groups in the newspapers should be improved.	Enables students to improve their thinking, value analysis, decision-making, and social-action skills. Enables students to improve their data-gathering skills. Helps students develop a sense of political efficacy. Helps students improve their skills to work in groups.	Requires a considerable amount of curriculum planning and materials identification. May be longer in duration than more traditional teaching units. May focus on problems and issues considered controversial by some members of the school staff and citizens of the community. Students may be able to take few meaningful actions that contribute to the resolution of the social issue or problem.

2. Knowledge about ethnic groups is needed to teach ethnic content effectively. Read at least one major book that surveys the histories and cultures of U.S. ethnic groups. One book that includes historical overviews of U.S. ethnic groups is James A. Banks, *Teaching Strategies for Ethnic Studies*, 6th ed. (Boston: Allyn and Bacon, 1997).

3. Be sensitive to your own racial attitudes, behavior, and the statements you make about ethnic groups in the classroom. A statement such as "Sit like an Indian" stereotypes Native Americans.

4. Make sure that your classroom conveys positive images of various ethnic groups. You can do this by displaying bulletin boards, posters, and calendars that show the racial and ethnic diversity within U.S. society.

5. Be sensitive to the racial and ethnic attitudes of your students and do not accept the belief, which has been refuted by research, that "kids do not see colors." Since the pioneering research by Lasker in 1929, researchers have known that very young children are aware of racial differences and that they tend to accept the evaluations of various racial groups that are normative within the wider society (Banks, 1995). Do not try to ignore the racial and ethnic differences that you see; try to respond to these differences positively and sensitively. Chapter 11 of this book provides thoughtful guidelines for avoiding the "colorblind" phenomenon.

6. Be judicious in your choice and use of teaching materials. Some materials contain both subtle and blatant stereotypes of ethnic groups. Point out to the students when an ethnic group is stereotyped, omitted from, or described in materials from Anglocentric and Eurocentric points of view. A useful guide for teachers of young children is Louise Derman-Sparks and the A. B. C. Task Force, Anti-Bias Curriculum, *Tools for Empowering Young Children* (Washington, DC: National Association for the Education of Young Children). Also see "Ten Quick Ways to Analyze Children's Books for Sexism and Racism," reprinted in James A. Banks, *An Introduction to Multicultural Education* (Boston: Allyn and Bacon, 1994).

7. Use trade books, films, videotapes, and recordings to supplement the textbook treatment of ethnic groups and to present the perspectives of ethnic groups to your students. Many of these sources contain rich and powerful images of the experience of being a person of color in the United States. A large collection of books and videotapes are annotated in James A. Banks, *Teaching Strategies for Ethnic Studies*, 6th ed. (Boston: Allyn and Bacon, 1997).

8. Get in touch with your own cultural and ethnic heritage. Sharing your ethnic and cultural story with your students will create a climate for sharing in the classroom, will help motivate students to dig into their ethnic and cultural roots, and will result in powerful learning for your students.

9. Be sensitive to the possible controversial nature of some ethnic studies materials. If you are clear about the teaching objectives you have in mind,

you can often use a less controversial book or reading to attain the same objectives. *The Color Purple* by Alice Walker (1982), for example, is a controversial book. A teacher, however, who wants her students to gain insights about African Americans in the South can use *Roll of Thunder, Hear My Cry* by Mildred D. Taylor (1976) instead of *The Color Purple*.

10. Be sensitive to the developmental levels of your students when you select concepts, content, and activities related to ethnic groups. Concepts and learning activities for students in kindergarten and the primary grades should be specific and concrete. Students in these grades should study such concepts as *similarities, differences, prejudice,* and *discrimination* rather than higher-level concepts such as racism and oppression. Fiction and biographies are excellent vehicles for introducing these concepts to students in kindergarten and the primary grades. As students progress through the grades, they can be introduced to more complex concepts, examples, and activities.

If you teach in a racially or ethnically integrated classroom or school you should keep the following guidelines in mind.

11. View your students of color as winners. Many students of color have high academic and career goals. They need teachers who believe they can be successful and are willing to help them succeed. Both research and theory indicate that students are more likely to achieve highly when their teachers have high academic expectations for them.

12. Keep in mind that most parents of color are very interested in education and want their children to be successful academically even though the parents may be alienated from the school (Clark, 1983). Do not equate education with schooling. Many parents who want their children to succeed have mixed feelings about the schools. Try to gain the support of these parents and make them partners in the education of their children.

13. Use cooperative learning techniques and group work to promote racial and ethnic integration in the school and classroom. Research indicates that when learning groups are racially integrated, students develop more friends from other racial groups, and race relations in the school improve. A helpful guide is Elizabeth G. Cohen's *Designing Groupwork: Strategies for the Heterogeneous Classroom*, 2nd ed. (New York: Teachers College Press, 1994).

14. Make sure that school plays, pageants, cheerleading squads, school publications, and other formal and informal groups are racially integrated. Also make sure that various ethnic and racial groups have equal status in school performances and presentations. In a multiracial school, if all of the leading roles in a school play are filled by White characters, an important message is sent to students and parents of color whether such a message was intended or not.

SUMMARY

This chapter describes the nature of the mainstream-centric curriculum and the negative consequences it has for both mainstream students and students of color. This curriculum reinforces the false sense of superiority of mainstream students and fails to reflect, validate, and celebrate the cultures of students of color. Many factors have slowed the institutionalization of a multicultural curriculum in the schools, including ideological resistance, lack of teacher knowledge of ethnic groups, and the heavy reliance of teachers on textbooks.

Four approaches to the integration of ethnic content into the curriculum are identified in this chapter. In the *contributions approach*, heroes, cultural components, holidays, and other discrete elements related to ethnic groups are added to the curriculum without changing its structure. The *additive approach* consists of the addition of content, concepts, themes, and perspectives to the curriculum, with its structure remaining unchanged. In the *transformation approach*, the structure, goals, and nature of the curriculum are changed to enable students to view concepts, issues, and problems from diverse ethnic perspectives. The *social action approach* includes all elements of the transformation approach, as well as elements that enable students to identify important social issues, gather data related to them, clarify their values, make reflective decisions, and take actions to implement their decisions. This approach seeks to make students social critics and reflective agents of change. The final part of this chapter presents guidelines to help you teach ethnic content and to function more effectively in multiethnic classrooms and schools.

Questions and Activities

1. What is a mainstream-centric curriculum? What are its major assumptions and goals?

2. Examine several textbooks and find examples of the mainstream-centric approach. Share these examples with colleagues in your class or workshop.

3. How does a mainstream-centric curriculum influence mainstream students and students of color?

4. According to Banks, what factors have slowed the development of a multicultural curriculum in the schools? What is the best way to overcome these factors?

5. What are the major characteristics of the following approaches to curriculum reform: the contributions approach; the additive approach; the transformation approach; the social action approach?

6. Why do you think the contributions approach to curriculum reform is so popular and widespread within schools, especially in the primary and elementary grades?

7. In what fundamental way do the transformation and social action approaches differ from the other two approaches identified above?

8. What are the problems and promises of each of the four approaches?

9. What does the author mean by "multiple acculturation"? Do you think this concept is valid? Why or why not?

10. What problems might a teacher encounter when trying to implement the transformation and social action approaches? How might these problems be overcome?

11. Assume that you are teaching a social studies lesson about the westward movement in U.S. history and a student makes a racist, stereotypic, or misleading statement about Native Americans, such as, "The Indians were hostile to the White settlers." How would you handle this situation? Give reasons to explain why you would handle it in a particular way.

12. Develop a teaching plan in which you illustrate how you would teach a unit incorporating elements of the transformation and social action approaches to curriculum reform.

References

Abbott, D. (Ed.). (1986). *Mississippi Writers: Reflections on Childhood and Youth, II: Nonfiction*. Jackson: University Press of Mississippi.

Allport, G. W. (1979). *The Nature of Prejudice* (25th anniversary ed.). Reading, MA: Addison-Wesley.

Asante, M. K. (1991). The Afrocentric Idea in Education. *Journal of Negro Education, 60*(2), 170–180.

Asante, M. K. and Ravitch, D. (1991, Spring). Multiculturalism: An Exchange. *The American Scholar, 60*(2), 267–276.

Baldwin, J. (1985). *The Price of the Ticket: Collected Nonfiction 1948–1985*. New York: St. Martin's Press.

Banks, J. A. (1994). *Multiethnic Education: Theory and Practice* (3rd ed.). Boston: Allyn and Bacon.

Banks, J. A. (1995). Multicultural Education: Its Effects on Students' Racial and Gender Role Attitudes. In J. A. Banks and C. A. M. Banks (Eds.). *Handbook of Research on Multicultural Education* (pp. 617–627). New York: Macmillan.

Banks, J. A. (1997). *Teaching Strategies for Ethnic Studies* (6th ed.). Boston: Allyn and Bacon.

Baugh, J. (1983). *Black Street Speech: Its History, Structure, and Survival*. Austin: The University of Texas Press.

Black Elk's Prayer from a Mountaintop in the Black Hills, 1931. (1964). In J. D. Forbes (Ed.). *The Indian in America's Past* (p. 69). Englewood Cliffs, NJ: Prentice-Hall.

Clark, R. M. (1983). *Family Life and School Achievement: Why Poor Black Children Succeed or Fail*. Chicago: University of Chicago Press.

Coleman, J. S., Campbell, E. Q., Hobson, C. J., McPartland, J., Mood, A. M., Weinfeld, F. D., and York, R. L. (1966). *Equality of Educational Opportunity*. Washington, DC: U.S. Government Printing Office.

Garcia, J. (1993). The Changing Image of Ethnic Groups in Textbooks. *Phi Delta Kappan, 75*(1), 29–35.

Gay, G. and Banks, J. A. (1975, November–December). Teaching the American Revolution: A Multiethnic Approach. *Social Education, 39*, 461–465.

Gillan, M. M. and Gillan, J. (Eds.). (1994). *An Anthology of Contemporary Multicultural Poetry*. New York: Penguin.

Goodlad, J. I. (1984). *A Place Called School*. New York: McGraw-Hill.

Grant, C. A. and Gomez, M. L. (Eds.). (1996). *Making Schooling Multicultural: Campus and Classroom*. Englewood Cliffs, NJ: Merrill.

Harris, V. J. (Ed.). (1992). *Teaching Multicultural Literature in Grades K–8*. Norwood, MA: Christopher-Gordon Publishers, Inc.

Katz, W. L. (1986). *Black Indians: A Hidden Heritage*. New York: Atheneum.

Lasker, B. (1929). *Race Attitudes in Children*. New York: Henry Holt.

Loewen, J. W. (1995). *Lies My Teacher Taught Me: Everything Your American History Textbook Got Wrong*. New York: The New Press.

Neihardt, J. G. (1972). *Black Elk Speaks*. New York: Pocket Books.

Newmann, F. N. (1968). Discussion: Political Socialization in the Schools. *Harvard Educational Review, 38*, 536–545.

Parekh, B. (1986). The Concept of Multicultural Education. In S. Modgil, G. K. Verma, K. Mailick, and C. Modgil (Eds.). *Multicultural Education: The Interminable Debate* (pp. 19–31). London: Falmer Press.

Ravitch, D. (1990, Spring). Diversity and Democracy: Multicultural Education in America. *American Educator, 16–48*.

Rico, B. R. and Mano, S. (Eds.). (1995). *American Mosaic: Multicultural Readings in Context* (2nd ed.). Boston: Houghton Mifflin.

Schlesinger, A. M. Jr. (1991). *The Disuniting of America: Reflections on a Multicultural Society*. Knoxville, TN: Whittle Direct Books.

Schofield, J. W. (1995). Improving Intergroup Relations among Students. In J. A. Banks and C. A. M. Banks (Eds.). *Handbook of Research on Multicultural Education* (pp. 635–646). New York: Macmillan.

Sleeter, C. E. and Grant, C. A. (1991). Race, Class, Gender, and Disability in Current Textbooks. In M. W. Apple and L. K. Christian-Smith (Eds.). *The Politics of the Textbook* (pp. 78–110). New York: Routledge.

Social Science Education Consortium. (1982).*The Current State of Social Studies: A Report of Project SPAN*. Boulder, CO: Author.

Taylor, M. (1976). *Roll of Thunder, Hear My Cry*. New York: Dial.

Walker, A. (1982). *The Color Purple*. New York: Harcourt Brace.

Zinn, H. and Kirschner, G. (1995). *A People's History of the United States: The Wall Charts*. New York: The New Press.

Chapter 11

Causes and Consequences of the Colorblind Perspective

Janet Ward Schofield

INTRODUCTION

Although the motivational and cognitive approaches to understanding intergroup attitudes and behavior as exemplified by Gaertner and Dovidio (1986), Hamilton and Trolier (1986), I. Katz, Wackenhut, and Hass (1986), Linville, Salovey, and Fischer (1986), McConahay (1986), and Miller and Brewer (1986) come out of rather different research traditions and focus on somewhat different issues, they share an important but often unemphasized assumption—that the context in which intergroup attitudes develop and in which they are expressed in behavior has a very real influence on such attitudes and behavior. For example, Gaertner and Dovidio (1977), who clearly emphasize motivational factors, have demonstrated that many liberal Whites discriminate mainly in situations in which their negative response can be justified with a non-race-related rationale. Similarly, McConahay's (1986) finding that less old-fashioned racism is expressed in the presence of a Black than of a White experimenter suggests the power of contextual factors, as does his general point that old-fashioned racism is apparently on the wane because in many milieus it is no longer socially acceptable.

The research on which this paper is based was funded by the author's contract with the National Institute of Education (Contract 400-76-0011). Other expenses relating to the chapter's preparation were covered by the Learning Research and Development Center, which is partly funded by NIE. However, all opinions expressed herein are solely those of the author and no endorsement of the ideas by NIE is implied or intended.
Source: Reprinted with permission from J. F. Dovidio & S. L. Gaertner (Eds.) (1986). *Prejudice, Discrimination, and Racism.* New York: Academic Press, pp. 231–253. Copyright © 1986 by Academic Press, Inc.

Cognitive theories about intergroup relations also take account of contextual factors. For example, Hamilton (1979), and Hamilton and Trolier (1986), describe the way in which distinctiveness, which is to some extent a function of context, influences individual's conceptions about the extent to which two factors, such as minority group status and the propensity for aggressive behavior, are perceived as correlated. An even more clear-cut demonstration of the effect of context on cognitive processes occurs in research on the solo effect, which shows how perceptions of an individual are influenced by the mere fact that that person is the only member of a particular social category, such as women or Blacks, in a given situation (Taylor & Fiske, 1978).

Although both the motivational and cognitive approaches to intergroup relations touch on the importance of the social context, neither of them typically systematically explores this issue in nonlaboratory contexts. The purpose of this chapter is to utilize an in-depth study of intergroup relations in a desegregated school to discuss the ways in which context can and does influence the course of intergroup relations. Previous work stemming from the cognitive and motivational perspectives has tended to confine itself to assessing the impact of experimentally manipulated context effects on various aspects of intergroup attitudes and behavior. This chapter takes a radically different approach. It examines the development of one specific aspect of context in an ongoing social situation, a desegregated school, and analyzes both its functions in that situation and its consequences. The aspect of context examined is the existence of a belief system which Rist (1974) has characterized as the colorblind perspective. The basis for the analysis presented is a four-year ethnographic study of peer relations in a desegregated school. Before proceeding to this analysis, I both discuss the main components of the colorblind perspective and describe the study on which the analysis is based.

Rist (1974) defines *the colorblind perspective* as a point of view which sees racial and ethnic group membership as irrelevant to the ways individuals are treated. Taking cognizance of such group membership in decision making is perceived as illegitimate and likely to either lead to discrimination against the minority group or reverse discrimination in its favor. Neither of these is viewed as desirable. From this perspective, school desegregation is an effort to provide all children, regardless of their background, with equal educational opportunities in order to assure that they have a fair chance to compete with others as they make their way in American society. Thus, school desegregation is a mechanism for class assimilation because it functions to facilitate social mobility on the part of Blacks who are to be treated exactly like their White peers.

The class assimilation view of school desegregation is very much in tune with a widely held American democratic philosophy: people are to be judged as individuals and not as members of ethnic or racial groups; they should be rewarded on the basis of their behavior rather than of social category membership; and the American economic and social system should be open to all those willing to work hard and strive for advancement. As Rist points out, however, this view does not grant any positive status to lower-class values or modes of behavior. Regardless of whether these values and behaviors reflect pathological reactions to a deprived childhood or creative adaptations to a lower-class environment, they are seen as a problem, standing in the way of the child's success at school and in the larger society (see Jones, 1986).

I would argue that two basic factors make study of the implications of the colorblind perspective worthwhile. First, there is evidence that this perspective is widespread in American schools, either as part of official policy or as an informal but nonetheless powerful social norm (Sagar & Schofield, 1984). It is also frequently espoused as a goal to be sought for in many other realms such as employment practices, judicial proceedings, and the like. Second, although in many ways the colorblind perspective is appealing because it is consistent with a long-standing American emphasis on the importance of the individual, it easily leads to a misrepresentation of reality in ways which allow and sometimes even encourage discrimination against minority group members, as later parts of this chapter demonstrate.

THE RESEARCH SITE: WEXLER MIDDLE SCHOOL

In choosing a site for the research, I adopted a strategy that Cook and Campbell (1976) have called generalizing to target instances. The aim was not to study what happens in a typical desegregated school, if such an entity can even be said to exist. Rather, it was to explore peer relations under conditions that theory suggests should be relatively conducive to positive relations between Blacks and Whites.

Over forty years ago in his classic book, *The Nature of Prejudice*, Allport (1954) proposed that intergroup contact may reinforce previously held stereotypes and increase intergroup hostility unless the contact situation is structured in a way that (1) provides equal status for minority and majority group members, (2) encourages cooperation toward shared, strongly desired goals, and (3) provides institutional support for positive relations. These ideas, as elaborated and refined by more recent theoretical and empirical work (Amir, 1969, 1976; Cook, 1969, 1985; Pettigrew, 1967, 1969), constitute a useful foundation for understanding the likely outcomes of interracial contact. For example, although equal status may be neither an absolutely necessary prerequisite nor a sufficient condition for change, it does appear to be very helpful (Amir, 1969, 1976; Cohen, 1975; Cohen, Lockheed, & Lohman, 1976; Cook, 1978, 1985; Riordan, 1978). In addition, a rapidly growing body of research suggests that cooperation toward mutually desired goals is indeed generally conducive to improved intergroup relations (Aronson, Blaney, Stephan, Sikes, & Snapp, 1978; Ashmore, 1970; Cook, 1978, 1985; Johnson & Johnson, 1982; Johnson, Johnson, & Maruyama, 1984; Johnson, Maruyama, Johnson, Nelson, & Skon, 1981; Sharan, 1980; Sherif, 1979; Slavin, 1980, 1983a, 1983b, 1985; Worchel, 1979).

Wexler Middle School, which serves 1200 children in sixth through eighth grades, was chosen for study because the decisions made in planning for it suggested that it would come reasonably close to meeting the conditions specified by Allport and the more recent theorists who have built on his work. The school's strong efforts to provide a positive environment for interracial education can be illustrated by examination of its staffing policy. The administration, faculty, and staff of the school are biracial, with about 25 percent of the faculty being Black. The top four administrative positions are filled by two Blacks and two Whites, clearly symbolizing the school's commitment to providing equal status for members of both groups.

The extent to which Wexler met the conditions specified by Allport and his intellectual heirs as conducive to the development of improved intergroup relations has been discussed at length elsewhere (Schofield, 1982). Here, I merely report the conclusion drawn in that discussion—that Wexler came considerably closer to these criteria than most desegregated public schools. Yet, it fell seriously short of meeting them completely in a number of ways, many of which were the direct result of societal conditions over which Wexler had little or no control. For example, in spite of Wexler's commitment to a staffing pattern which would provide equal formal status for Blacks and Whites, the proportion of Black teachers on its staff was considerably lower than the proportion of Black students in the school because the school system did not want to put too high a proportion of its Black teachers in one school. In sum, Wexler made stronger than usual efforts to foster positive relations between Blacks and Whites, but fell markedly short of being a theoretically ideal milieu for the accomplishment of this goal.

Wexler is located in a large industrial northeastern city. Just over 20 percent of the city's population is Black. The school was constructed to serve as a model of high quality integrated education. When it first opened its doors, its student body was almost precisely 50 percent Black and 50 percent White, mirroring closely the proportion of Black and White students in the school system of which Wexler was a part. A large majority of Wexler's White students came from middle- or upper-middle-class homes. Although some of the Black children were middle class, the majority came from either poor or working-class families.

DATA GATHERING

The analysis that follows is based on an intensive four-year study of peer relations at Wexler. The basic data-gathering strategy was *intensive* and *extensive* observation in Wexler's classrooms, hallways, playgrounds, and cafeteria. Observers used the full field-note method for recording the events they witnessed (Olson, 1976). A large number of events were observed because they were representative of the events that filled most of the school day at Wexler. However, an important subgroup of events was over-sampled in relation to their frequency of occurrence because of their direct relevance to the study's focus. This strategy, which Glaser and Strauss (1967) call theoretical sampling, led to oversampling certain activities, such as affective education classes, designed to help students get to know each other, and meetings of Wexler's interracial student advisory group set up to handle the special problems students may face in a desegregated school. Over the course of the study, more than 500 hours were devoted to observation of students and staff at Wexler.

A wide variety of other data-gathering techniques ranging from sociometric questionnaires to experimental work was also used (Sagar & Schofield, 1980; Schofield, 1979; Schofield & Francis, 1982; Schofield & Sagar, 1977; Schofield & Whitley, 1983; Whitley & Schofield, 1984). Interviews were employed extensively. For example, randomly selected panels of students participated in open-ended interviews twice a year. Teachers and administrators were also interviewed repeatedly. In addition, graffiti in the bathrooms and on the school walls were routinely recorded, school bulletins were collected, and careful note was taken of such things as wall decorations and public address system announcements.

Space does not allow full discussion of the many varied techniques which were employed in collecting and analyzing the data on which this chapter is based. However, two general principles which guided the research must be mentioned. First, both data-gathering and analysis were as rigorous and systematic as possible. For example, sampling techniques were employed where appropriate; trained coders, who were unaware of the race and sex of particular respondents, coded the open-ended interviews using reliable systems developed for this research; field notes were carefully indexed so that all notes relevant to a given topic could be examined, et cetera. Second, because it is often impossible to achieve extremely high levels of precision and control in field research, strong efforts were made to triangulate the data (Webb, Campbell, Schwartz, & Sechrest, 1966). Great care was taken to gather many different types of information bearing on the same issue, to minimize the potential problems with each data source, and to be sensitive in analyzing and interpreting the data to biases which could not be completely eliminated. The basic approach used in the analysis of the qualitative data is outlined in works such as Becker and Greer (1960), Bogdan and Taylor (1975), Campbell (1975), and Glaser and Strauss (1967). Fuller details on data-gathering and analysis are presented elsewhere, as is information on the strategies used to minimize observer reactivity and bias (Schofield, 1982; Schofield & Sagar, 1979).

THE COLORBLIND PERSPECTIVE AND ITS COROLLARIES

Wexler's faculty clearly tended to subscribe to the colorblind view of interracial schooling. Interviews with both Black and White teachers suggested that the majority of both groups tended to see Wexler as an institution which could help impart middle-class values and modes of behavior to lower-class students so that they could break out of the cycle of poverty and become middle-class persons themselves. Even though the bulk of these lower-class students were Black, race was seen as quite incidental to the class assimilation process.

A Black administrator, with perhaps more candor than many similarly oriented White administrators and teachers, made her class assimilation goals explicit and, at the same time, made it clear just which students needed to be so assimilated:

> I really don't address myself to group differences when I am dealing with youngsters. . . . I try to treat youngsters, I don't care who they are, as youngsters and not as Black, White, green or yellow. . . . Many of the Black youngsters who have difficulty are the ones who . . . have come from communities where they had to put up certain defenses and these defenses are the antithesis of the normal situation . . . like they find in school. It is therefore [difficult] getting them to become aware that they have to follow these rules because [they] are here . . . not over there in their community. . . . I think that many of the youngsters [from the] larger commu-

> nity have a more normal set of values that people generally
> want to see, and therefore do not have [as] much difficulty in
> coping with their school situation. . . . [The Black children]
> do have difficulty in adjusting because they are just not used
> to it. Until we can adjustively counsel them into the right
> types of behavior . . . I think we're going to continue to have
> these types of problems.

The only thing atypical in the preceding remarks is the frank acknowledgment that the children perceived as lacking the "normal set of values that people generally want to see" are indeed "our Black youngsters." More usually, this was implicit in remarks emphasizing the negative effects of growing up in a poor family or a low-income neighborhood.

As a reaction to the invidious distinctions which have traditionally been made in the United States on the basis of race, the colorblind perspective is understandable and, from a social policy standpoint, it seems laudable. However, this orientation was accompanied at Wexler by a number of other logically related beliefs, which taken together with it had some important though largely unrecognized negative consequences. These beliefs and their basis in the ongoing social reality at Wexler are discussed individually. Then the consequences of such a belief system are discussed in some detail.

Race as an Invisible Characteristic

It is not a very great leap from the colorblind perspective, which says that race is a social category of no relevance to one's behavior and decisions, to a belief that individuals should not or perhaps even do not *notice* each other's racial group membership. At Wexler, acknowledging that one was aware of another's race was viewed by many as a possible sign of prejudice, as illustrated by the following excerpt from project field notes:

> When I was arranging the student interviews, I men-
> tioned to Mr. Little [White] that I thought there was only
> one White girl in one of his classes. I asked if I was right
> about this and he said, "Well, just a minute. Let me check."
> After looking through the class roster in his roll book he
> said, "You know, you're right. I never noticed that. . . . I
> guess that's a good thing."

Our data suggest that teachers not only denied that they noticed children's race when the researchers were present, but also did so among themselves. For example, when one White teacher was complying with our request to mark down the race of his students on a class roster to enable the research team to learn students' names more quickly, he remarked, "Did you ever notice those teachers who say, 'I never notice what they are?'"

Although there was less unanimity on the issue of whether students noticed the race of others than of whether teachers did, a substantial proportion of Wexler's faculty asserted that the students rarely noticed race. This point of view is exemplified by the following excerpt from an interview with a Black science teacher:

> Ms. MONROE: You know, I hear the things the students usually fight about. As I said before, it's stupid things like someone taking a pencil. It's not because [the other person] is Black or White. . . . At this age level . . . I don't think it's Black or White.
>
> INTERVIEWER: There's something I'm wondering about. It is hard to believe, given the way our society is, that you can just bring kids together and they won't be very much aware—
>
> Ms. MONROE: They just go about their daily things and don't . . . I don't think they think about it really. . . . I see them interacting with one another on an adult basis. . . . They are not really aware of color . . . or race or whatever.
>
> INTERVIEWER: You really don't see that as a factor . . . in their relationships?
>
> Ms. MONROE: No.

Although the faculty at Wexler saw themselves and to a lesser extent their students as oblivious to the race of others, there are a wide variety of data suggesting that this view was not accurate. Most removed from the specific situation at Wexler but nonetheless pertinent is a substantial body of data from research on stereotyping and person perception. This work suggests that individuals tend to utilize preexisting categories in perceiving and responding to others (Taylor, 1981). More specifically, there is research suggesting that individuals spontaneously utilize the physical appearance of others as a basis for categorizing them by race. Further, this categorization has an impact on how individuals are perceived and on how others respond to them (Duncan, 1976; I. Katz, Wackenhut, & Hass, 1986; P. Katz, 1976; Malpass & Kravitz, 1969; Sagar & Schofield, 1980; Taylor, Fiske, Etcoff, & Ruderman, 1978). The teachers and students at Wexler were to some extent self-selected members of an interracial institution and thus might conceivably be less prone to utilize race as a category for processing information about others than the college student populations utilized in most of the studies on person perception. However, given the importance of race as a social category in many aspects of life in the U.S., it seems highly unlikely that the prevailing tendency at Wexler was for individuals not even to notice each other's race.

Interviews with students made it clear that many of them were very conscious of their race or of the race of other students, which is hardly surprising given the fact that interracial schooling was a new and somewhat threatening experience for many of them. The following excerpt from an interview in which the interviewer had not herself previously mentioned race suggests just how salient racial categories were to the children.

> INTERVIEWER: Can you tell me who some of your friends are?
>
> BEVERLY (BLACK): Well, Stacey and Lydia and Amy, even though she's White.

Similarly, students' awareness of racial group membership is illustrated by an excerpt from field notes taken in a seventh-grade class which had a higher-than-average proportion of Black students in it because the teachers had decided to put many of the lower-achieving children in a class by themselves.

> Howard, a White male, leaned over to me *(a White female observer)* and said, "You know, it just wasn't fair the way they set up this class. There are sixteen Black kids and only nine White kids. I can't learn in here." I said, "Why is that?" Howard replied "They copy and they pick on you. It just isn't fair."

Race as a Taboo Topic

Before proceeding to discuss why the view that they and their students tended not even to notice race gained considerable popularity among Wexler's teachers in spite of everyday indications that this was often not the case, I would like to discuss two other phenomena closely related to the development of the colorblind perspective. The first of these was the development of a norm strong enough to be labeled a virtual taboo against the utilization of the words *white* and *black* in a context in which they referred to racial group membership. Thus, for example, in almost 200 hours of observations in classrooms, hallways, teachers meetings, et cetera during Wexler's first year, fewer than 25 direct references to race were made by school staff or students (Schofield, 1982). Any use of the words *black* and *white* in a context in which they referred to an individual or group was classified as a reference to race, as were racial epithets, and words and phrases used almost exclusively within one group to express solidarity (e.g., "Hey, Brother") or the like.

The extremely infrequent reference to race was all the more surprising when one considers that our observations included a wide variety of formal and informal situations, ranging from workshops funded by the Emergency School Assistance Act, federal legislation which provides funds to desegregating schools to help them handle special problems that may arise as a result of desegregation, to informal student interactions on the playgrounds and in the hallways.

Students' awareness of the taboo is shown clearly in the following field notes, which recount a conversation with a White social worker whose work at Wexler on the extracurricular program was funded by a local foundation concerned with race relations. Perhaps not surprisingly under these circumstances, she showed much less reluctance than most staff to deal in a straightforward manner with the issue of race.

> Ms. Fowler said that a short while ago she had heard from Martin *(Black)* that another child had done something wrong. The offense was serious enough so that she wanted to track down this individual. She asked Martin to describe the child who had committed the offense. Martin said, "He has black hair and he's fairly tall." He didn't give the race of the other person even though he went on to give a fairly complete description otherwise. Finally, Ms. Fowler asked,

> "Is he Black or White?" Martin replied, "Is it all right for me
> to say?" Ms. Fowler said that it was all right. . . . Martin then
> said, "Well, the boy was White."

Students were well aware that making references to race displeased many of their teachers and might also offend peers.

> INTERVIEWER: You know the other day I was walking around the school and heard a sixth grade student describing a student from the seventh grade to a teacher who needed to find this student in order to return something she had lost. The sixth grader said the seventh grader was tall and thin. She described what the girl had been wearing and said her hair was dark, but she didn't say whether the girl was Black or White. . . . Why do you think she didn't mention that?
>
> SYLVIA (BLACK): The teacher might have got mad if she said whether she was White or Black.
>
> INTERVIEWER: Do some teachers get mad about things like that?
>
> SYLVIA: Some do . . . they holler. . . .
>
> INTERVIEWER: Now when you talk to kids who are Black, do you ever mention that someone is White or Black?
>
> SYLVIA: No.
>
> INTERVIEWER: What about when you're talking with kids who are White?
>
> SYLVIA: Nope.
>
> INTERVIEWER: You never mention race? Why not?
>
> SYLVIA: They might think I'm prejudiced.

Social Life as a Web of Purely Interpersonal Relations

Consistent with the view that race is not, or at least should not be, a salient aspect of other individuals and with the practice of not speaking about race was a tendency to conceptualize social life as a web of interpersonal rather than intergroup relations and to assume that interpersonal relations are not much influenced by group membership. As one teacher put it,

> Peer group identity here in middle school . . . has nothing to do with race. There's a strong tendency to group that exists independent of . . . racial boundaries. . . . We started in September with these students letting them know we weren't going to fool around with that. . . . You're a student and we don't care what color you are.

This tendency to minimize the potential importance of intergroup processes was illustrated clearly during an in-service training session, the stated purpose of which was to help teachers deal effectively with the racially heterogeneous student body. The facilitator, a White clinical psychologist employed by a local foundation, started the session off by making some general statements about the importance of understanding cultural differences between students. Although the facilitator kept trying to nudge and finally to push the group to discussing ways in which the biracial nature of the student body influenced peer relations, appropriate curricular materials, and the like, the group ended up discussing issues such as the problems caused by individual children who acted out aggressively in the classroom, the difficulty that overweight children have in gaining peer acceptance, and the fact that handicapped children were sometimes taunted by their classmates.

Contrasting sharply with the teachers' tendency to insist that they and their students reacted to each other exclusively as individuals and to de-emphasize the importance of intergroup as opposed to interpersonal processes was the students' willingness to discuss with interviewers the importance race played in Wexler's social life.

> INTERVIEWER: I have noticed . . . that [in the cafeteria] very often White kids sit with White kids and Black kids sit with Black kids. Why do you think that is?
>
> MARY (WHITE): Cause the White kids have White friends and the Black kids have Black friends. . . . I don't think integration is working. . . . Blacks still associate with Blacks and Whites still associate with Whites. . . .
>
> INTERVIEWER: Can you think of any White kids that have quite a few Black friends or of any Black kids who have quite a few White friends?
>
> MARY: Not really.

The tendency for students to group themselves by race in a variety of settings was very marked. For example, on a fairly typical day at the end of the school's second year of operation 119 White and 90 Black students attended the seventh-grade lunch period. Of these over 200 children, only 6 sat next to someone of the other race (Schofield & Sagar, 1977).

Of course, it is possible that it was not race itself which was a factor in producing such interaction patterns, but something correlated with race such as socioeconomic status, academic achievement, or the opportunity for previous contact with each other. Such factors did appear to reinforce the tendency to prefer intragroup interactions, and were often cited by teachers as the actual cause of the visually apparent tendency of students to cluster with those of their own race. Yet, the results of an experiment conducted at Wexler demonstrate that race itself was a real factor in peer relations. In this study, eighty male sixth graders were presented with carefully drawn pictures of a number of ambiguously aggressive types of peer interactions which were quite common at Wexler, such as poking another student with a pencil. For each type of interaction, some students were shown pictures in which both students were Black, others saw pictures in which both students were White, and still others saw mixed race dyads with the Black student shown as either the initiator of the behavior or as the student to whom it was directed. The results suggested that the race of the person initiating the behavior influenced how mean and threatening it was interpreted as being (Sagar & Schofield, 1980) (see Table 11.1). Such a finding is, of course, inconsistent with the notion that students take no notice of others' race. It is also incompatible with the idea that intergroup processes have no influence on students' reactions to their peers because the data suggest that the perception of an individual's behavior is influenced by the group membership of the person performing it.

Table 11.1 Mean Ratings of Both White and Black Actors' Ambiguously Aggressive Behaviors by White and Black Subjects

Subject Group	Actor Race	Rating Scale: Mean/Threatening
White	White	8.28
	Black	8.99
Black	White	7.38
	Black	8.40

Note. Means are based on sums of paired 7-point scales indicating how well the given adjective described the behaviors, from 1 (not at all) to 7 (exactly). N = 40 in each group. Each subject rated two White and two Black actors (e.g., the perpetrator of the ambiguously aggressive act) and two White and Black targets. The 4 x 4 nature of the Latin square required treating the race permutations as four levels of a single factor. Significant F values on this factor provided justification for testing actor race, target race, and interaction effects with simple contrasts, using the error variance estimate generated by the ANOVA. The significant main effect of race permutations on the summed mean/threatening scales, $F(3,192) = 3.02$, $p < .05$, was found to reflect, as predicted, tendency for subjects to rate the behaviors by Black actors more mean/threatening than identical behaviors by White actors, $t(144) = 2.90$, $p < .01$. Means are not broken down by target race because no statistically significant main effects or interactions were found for this variable.

Source: From Sagar, H. A., and Schofield, J. W. (1980). Racial and Behavioral Cues in Black and White Children's Perceptions of Ambiguously Aggressive Acts. *Journal of Personality and Social Psychology, 39*(4), 590–598. Copyright 1980 by the American Psychological Association. Adapted with permission.

THE FUNCTIONS AND CONSEQUENCES OF THE COLORBLIND PERSPECTIVE AND ITS COROLLARIES

Regardless of the fact that the colorblind perspective and its corollaries were not completely accurate views of the social processes occurring at Wexler, they appeared to influence the development of the social fabric at Wexler in ways which had a number of important consequences, some positive and some negative. The following discussion of the functions of this set of beliefs suggests why the colorblind perspective was attractive to teachers and how it affected both the education and social experiences of Wexler's students.

Reducing the Potential for Overt Conflict

One concern that typifies many desegregated schools, and which is often especially salient in newly desegregated situations, is a desire to avoid dissension and conflict which are or could appear to be race related (Sagar & Schofield, 1984). The adopting of colorblind policies is often seen as useful in achieving this goal because if such policies are implemented fully they can help protect the institution and those in positions of responsibility in it from charges of discrimination. This is not to say that such policies lead to equal outcomes for members of all groups. Indeed, when there are initial group differences on criteria relevant to success in a given institution, such policies are likely to lead to differential outcomes, a situation that some would characterize as institutional racism (Jones, 1972, 1986). However, as noted earlier, the colorblind perspective is consistent with notions of fairness which have long held sway in the U.S. and thus can be relatively easily defended. Policies which give obvious preference to either minority or majority group members are much more likely to spark controversy and conflict.

An example from Wexler illustrates the way in which the operation of the colorblind perspective helps to minimize overt conflict in situations where the outcomes for Blacks and Whites as a whole are extremely different. The suspension rate for Black students at Wexler was roughly four times that for White students. The strong correlation between race and socioeconomic background at Wexler made it predictable that the Black students' behavior would be less consistent than that of White students with the basically middle-class norms prevailing in the school. However, the colorblind perspective appeared instrumental in helping to keep Wexler's discipline policies from becoming a major focus of contention. To my knowledge, the disparity in suspension rates was never treated as a serious issue which needed attention. When researchers asked faculty and administrators about it, some, perhaps not altogether candidly, denied having noticed it. Others argued that it was not a problem in the sense that individual students were generally treated fairly. In fact, teachers often emphasized strongly the effort they made to treat discipline problems with White and Black students in exactly the same way.

On the relatively rare occasions in which charges of discrimination were raised by students unhappy with the way a teacher had dealt with them, teachers tended to discount the complaints by reiterating their commitment to the colorblind perspective.

> Ms. WILSON (WHITE): I try not to let myself listen to it (the charge of discrimination). Maybe once in a while I ask myself "Well, why would he make that statement?" But I know in my mind that I do not discriminate on the basis of race. . . . And I will not have someone create an issue like that when I know I have done my best not to create it.

Only an occasional teacher, more often than not Black, suggested that the colorblind perspective actually worked to help create the disparity, an issue which is addressed in a later part of this chapter. Be this as it may, the colorblind perspective clearly fostered an atmosphere which minimized the chances that the disparity itself was likely to become the focus of overt discontent or constructive action.

Minimizing of Discomfort or Embarrassment

Many of the faculty and students at Wexler had little prior experience in desegregated schools. Also, most of them lived in neighborhoods which were either heavily White or heavily Black. Thus, for many, there was an initial sense of awkwardness and anxiety, like the intergroup anxiety Stephan and Stephan (1985) discuss. Under such circumstances, avoiding mention of race and contending that it rarely influenced relations between individuals seemed to minimize the potential for awkward or embarrassing social situations. This is related to the aforementioned conflict-avoidance function of these beliefs but can be distinguished conceptually because feelings of awkwardness and embarrassment can but do not always lead to conflict. In fact, these beliefs and norms seemed to help to maintain the veneer of politeness which Clement, Eisenhart, and Harding (1979) have argued is part of the etiquette of race relations in some desegregated situations.

One way to illustrate the ways in which the colorblind perspective and the associated beliefs and norms helped to smooth social relations between Blacks and Whites is to compare the situation at Wexler to another sort of interaction which is often rather strained, at least initially, i.e., interaction between individuals who are visibly handicapped and those who are not. In a fascinating analysis of this latter situation, Davis (1961) argues that the emotion aroused in the nonhandicapped person by the sight of a handicapped one creates tension and an uncertainty about what is appropriate behavior that interferes with normal interaction patterns. There is a tendency for the handicap to become the focus of attention and to foster ambiguity about appropriate behavior. Davis argues that the initial reaction to this situation is often a fictional denial of the handicap and of its potential effect on the relationship—that is, a tendency to pretend to ignore the existence of the handicap, which at least temporarily relieves the interactants of the necessity of dealing with its implications. Analogously, one can think of the racial group membership of individuals in a biracial interaction, be they Black or White, as a sort of visually apparent handicap. Like a handicap, one's group membership may well provoke an affective response in others which predisposes them to avoidance or at least raises questions about appropriate behavior. Of course, just as some individuals will feel more awkward than others when interacting with a handicapped person, so some individuals will more likely be more affected by interacting with someone of the other race. However, to the extent that either is a potential threat to a smooth, relaxed, and pleasant interaction, one way of handling that threat is to pretend one is unaware of the attribute which creates it.

Although Davis argues that initial interactions between the handicapped and others are characterized by a fictional denial of the handicap, he also suggests that with time this fiction is discarded because based on an obvious falsehood, it is inherently unstable and in the long run dysfunctional. Similarly, I would argue that although this colorblind perspective and the accompanying taboo may have made the initial adjustment to Wexler easier, in the long run they tended to inhibit the development of positive relations between Black and White students. These students were vividly aware of differences and tensions between them which were related to their group membership. Yet such issues could not be dealt with in a straightforward manner in the colorblind climate. Thus, anger sometimes festered and stereotypes built when fuller discussion of the situation might have made it easier for individuals to see each other's perspectives. This is not to suggest that schools have the responsibility to function as giant T-groups or as therapeutic institutions. Rather, it is to say that the refusal of many of Wexler's faculty to recognize the fundamental role that race played in peer relationships meant that they played a less constructive role than they might have in guiding students through a new and sometimes threatening experience.

Increasing Teachers' Freedom of Action

The colorblind perspective and its corollaries undoubtedly gained some of their appeal because they tended to simplify life for Wexler's staff and to increase their freedom of action. An example can illustrate both points. After being asked by one of the research team about the outcome of a closely contested student council election, a White teacher disclosed that she had purposely miscounted votes so that a "responsible child" (a White boy) was declared the winner rather than the "unstable child" (a Black girl) who had actually received a few more votes. The teacher seemed ambivalent about and somewhat embarrassed by her action, but the focus of her concern was her subversion of the democratic process. She reported that she had looked at the two children as individuals and decided that one was a more desirable student council representative than the other. As far as I could tell from an extended discussion with her, she did not consciously consider the race of the students involved. Further, she did not appear to consider the fact that her action had changed the racial composition of the student council.

The failure to consider such issues clearly simplified the decision-making process because there was one less item, and an affect-laden one at that, to be factored into it. Related to this, such a colorblind approach increased teachers' freedom of action because actions which appeared acceptable if one were to think about them in a colorblind way often appeared much less acceptable from a perspective which is not colorblind. Indeed, the colorblind perspective and its corollaries fostered an environment which two related lines of work would suggest is conducive to discriminatory behavior, at least on the part of certain types of individuals. First, work by Snyder, Kleck, Strenta, and Mentzer (1979) demonstrates that people are more likely to act in accordance with feelings they prefer not to reveal when they can appear to be acting on some other basis than when no other obvious explanation for their behavior is available. Specifically, they found that individuals avoided the physically handicapped when such avoidance could easily be attributed to preference for a certain kind of movie. However, when the situation did not provide this sort of rationale for avoidance behavior, the tendency to avoid handicapped others disappeared. Thus, by analogy, one might expect that an environment which minimizes the importance of race and even forbids overt consideration or discussion of the topic would free individuals whose basic tendency is to discriminate (a normatively unacceptable orientation at Wexler) to do so. The vast majority of Wexler's faculty espoused basically equalitarian racial attitudes and would quite rightly be insulted by the idea that they would intentionally discriminate against their Black students. Yet, the work of Gaertner and Dovidio (1981; 1986) demonstrates that one need not be an old-fashioned racist to discriminate against Blacks when the conditions are conducive to it.

Specifically, Gaertner and Dovidio argue that a great many liberal Whites these days are highly motivated to maintain an image of themselves as egalitarian individuals who neither discriminate against others on the basis of race nor are prejudiced. However, the desire to maintain such an image is coupled with some negative affect and with certain beliefs which predispose them to react negatively to Blacks. This predisposition is expressed primarily in circumstances in which it does not threaten an egalitarian self-concept. One important relevant circumstance is the availability of non-race-related rationales for the behavior in question (Gaertner & Dovidio, 1986). It is precisely this aspect of the situation which is influenced by the colorblind perspective and its corollaries. To the extent they help to remove awareness of race from conscious consideration, they make other explanations for one's behavior relatively more salient. Thus, they free the aversive racist to act in a discriminatory fashion. Further, to the extent the taboo at Wexler inhibited individuals from challenging others' behaviors as racist in outcome or intent, it removed a potential barrier to racist behavior because it minimized the probability that such behavior would pose a threat to a liberal self-concept.

Ignoring the Reality of Subjective Culture

Although the colorblind perspective and its corollaries served some useful purposes such as minimizing social awkwardness in certain situations, they also had several unrecognized negative effects, as indicated. One important consequence of this mind set was a predisposition to ignore or deny the possibility of cultural differences between White and Black children which influenced the way they functioned in school. For example, the differential suspension rate for Black and White children may have stemmed partially from differences between the White and Black students in what Triandis, Vassiliou, Vassiliou, Tanaka, and Shanmugam (1972) would call their subjective culture. Specifically, data from the Sagar and Schofield (1980) experiment described earlier suggested that Black boys saw certain types of ambiguously aggressive acts as less mean and threatening and more playful and friendly than their White peers. These behaviors were ones which sometimes began conflicts between students which resulted in suspensions. Awareness of the differential meaning of such behaviors to White and Black students might at least have suggested ways of trying to reduce the disproportionate suspension of Black students. Other research suggests that Black-White differences in subjective culture are not limited to this one area (Jones, 1986). Kochman (1981) has argued convincingly that Black and White students utilize widely differing styles in classroom discussion and that misunderstanding of the cultural context from which students come can lead peers and teachers to misinterpret involvement for belligerence. Heath's (1982) research suggests that the type of questions which teachers typically pose in elementary school classrooms are quite similar to those asked in White middle-class homes but differ substantially from those typically addressed to young children in poor Black homes. Thus, there is reason to think that in assuming a completely colorblind perspective teachers may rule out awareness of information which would be useful in deciding how best to structure materials for their students as well as in interpreting many aspects of their behavior.

Failing to Respond to and Capitalize on Diversity

There were numerous less subtle ways in which the colorblind perspective and the accompanying de-emphasis on the biracial nature of the school worked to the disadvantage of Wexler's students, and more often to the disadvantage of Black than of White ones. One of the more obvious of these concerned the extent to which efforts were made to provide instructional materials which were likely to reflect the interests and life experiences of Wexler's Black students. Wexler operated as part of a school system which made some effort to utilize multicultural texts. In addition, a number of teachers, a disproportionate number of whom were Black, took special care to relate class work to the concerns and interests of Black students by assigning class projects like essays on the TV movie *Roots*. Yet, the prevailing tendency was to abjure responsibility for making sure instructional materials reflected the biracial nature of the student body. Interviews with teachers suggested that many saw no reason to try to locate or develop instructional materials which reflected Black Americans' participation in our society. For example, one math teacher who used a book in which all individuals in the illustrations were White contended that "math was math" and that an interview question about the utilization of biracial or multicultural materials was irrelevant to his subject matter. Similar claims were made by other teachers, including some who taught topics like reading, language arts, and social studies.

The colorblind perspective and its corollaries not only made it more likely that individual faculty members would ignore the challenge of presenting students with materials which related in motivating ways to their own experience, but actually led to a constriction of the education provided to students. For example, in a lesson on the social organization of ancient Rome, one social studies teacher discussed the various classes in Roman society, including the nobles and plebeians at length but avoided all reference to slaves. Another teacher included George Washington Carver on a list of great Americans from which students could pick individuals to learn about but specifically decided not to mention he was Black for fear of raising racial issues. In the best of all worlds, there would be no need to make such mention, because children would have no preconceptions that famous people are generally White. However, in a school where one White child was surprised to learn from a member of our research team that Martin Luther King was Black, not White, it would seem reasonable to argue that highlighting the accomplishments of Black Americans and making sure that students do not assume famous figures are White is a reasonable practice. Such constriction based on a desire to avoid racial problems is not unique at Wexler. For example, Scherer and Slawski (1979) report that a desegregated high school they studied eliminated the lunch hour and study halls to minimize the sort of loosely supervised contact between students which seemed to be likely to lead to conflict. However, the nature of the constriction at Wexler was influenced by the colorblind perspective and its corollaries. At Wexler, the tendency was to ignore or avoid certain topics. Such a tendency, while undeniably a low-risk one, failed to take advantage of the diversity of experiences and perspectives of its students as a resource for the educational process.

CONCLUSIONS

Since Supreme Court Justice Harlan first spoke of a colorblind society as a goal to be striven for, such a perspective has often been held up as a needed antidote to the virulent racism in our society which traditionally consigned certain individuals to subordinate positions on the basis of their color and their color alone. However, this chapter takes the position that the colorblind perspective is not without some subtle dangers. It may ease initial tensions and minimize the frequency of overt conflict. Nonetheless, it can also foster phenomena like the taboo against ever mentioning race or connected issues and the refusal to recognize and deal with the existence of intergroup tensions. Thus, it fosters an environment in which aversive racists, who are basically well-intentioned, are prone to act in a discriminatory manner. Further, it makes it unlikely that the opportunities inherent in a pluralistic institution will be fully realized and that the challenges facing such an institution will be dealt with effectively.

Acknowledgments

The author wishes to express her deep appreciation to the students and staff of Wexler School.

Questions and Activities

1. According to the author, how does the social context influence the expression of racism and discrimination?

2. What is the *colorblind perspective?* Give some examples of it. On what major beliefs and assumptions is it based?

3. In what ways does the colorblind perspective contribute to racial discrimination and institutionalized racism in schools? Give specific examples.

4. How does the colorblind perspective often lead to what the author calls a "misrepresentation of reality"? Which realities are often misrepresented by the colorblind perspective?

5. Why did the teachers at Wexler deny that they were aware of the race of their students? What were some of the consequences of their denial? How was their denial inconsistent with many realities related to race in the school?

6. What did the interviews with the students at Wexler reveal about their conceptions of race? How did their conceptions of race differ from those of the teachers? Why?

7. Why do teachers often embrace the colorblind perspective? According to the author, what are its benefits and costs?

8. How does the colorblind perspective make it easier for liberal White teachers to discriminate? Give specific examples from this chapter and from your own observations and experiences in schools and in other settings and contexts.

9. How does the colorblind perspective negatively affect the development of a multicultural curriculum? What are the most promising ways to counteract the colorblind perspective? Give specific examples.

References

Allport, G. W. (1954). *The Nature of Prejudice.* Cambridge, MA: Addison-Wesley.

Amir, Y. (1969). Contact Hypothesis in Ethnic Relations. *Psychological Bulletin, 71*(5), 319–342.

Amir, Y. (1976). The Role of Intergroup Contact in Change of Prejudice and Ethnic Relations. In P. A. Katz (Ed.). *Towards the Elimination of Racism* (pp. 245–308). New York: Pergamon.

Aronson, E., Blaney, N., Stephan, C., Sikes, J., and Snapp, M. (1978). *The Jigsaw Classroom.* Beverly Hills, CA: Sage Publications.

Ashmore, R. (1970). Solving the Problem of Prejudice. In B. E. Collins (Ed.). *Social Psychology* (pp. 246–296). Reading, MA: Addison-Wesley.

Becker, H. S. and Greer, B. (1960). Participant Observations: Analysis of Qualitative Data. In R. N. Adams and J. J. Preiss (Eds.). *Human Organization Research* (pp. 267–289). Homewood, IL: The Dorsey Press.

Bogdan, R. C. and Taylor, S. J. (1975). *Introduction to Qualitative Research Methods: A Phenomenological Approach to the Social Sciences.* New York: Wiley.

Campbell, D. T. (1975). Degrees of Freedom and the Case Study. *Comparative Political Studies, 8*(2), 178–193.

Clement, D. C., Eisenhart, M., and Harding, J. R. (1979). The Veneer of Harmony: Social-Race Relations in a Southern Desegregated School. In R. C. Rist (Ed.). *Desegregated Schools* (pp. 15–62). New York: Academic Press.

Cohen, E., Lockheed, M., and Lohman, M. (1976). The Center for Interracial Cooperation: A Field Experiment. *Sociology of Education, 49*, 47–58.

Cohen, E. G. (1975). The Effects of Desegregation on Race Relation. *Law and Contemporary Problems, 39*(2), 271–299.

Cook, S. W. (1969). Motives in the Conceptual Analysis of Attitude-Related Behavior. In W. J. Arnold and D. Levine (Eds.). *Nebraska Symposium on Motivation,* Vol. 17 (pp. 179–235). Lincoln: University of Nebraska Press.

Cook, S. W. (1978). Interpersonal and Attitudinal Outcomes in Cooperating Interracial Groups. *Journal of Research and Development in Education, 12*(1), 97–113.

Cook, S. W. (1985). Experimenting on Social Issues: The Case of School Desegregation. *American Psychologist, 40*, 452–460.

Cook, T. and Campbell, D. (1976). The Design and Conduct of Quasi-Experiments and True Experiments in Field Settings. In M. Dunnette (Ed.). *Handbook of Organizational Psychology* (pp. 223–281). Chicago: Rand McNally.

Davis, F. (1961). Deviance Disavowal: The Management of Strained Interaction by the Visibly Handicapped. In H. S. Becker (Ed.). *The Other Side: Perspectives on Deviance* (pp. 119–137). New York: The Free Press.

Duncan, B. L. (1976). Differential Racial Perception and Attribution of Intergroup Violence. *Journal of Personality and Social Psychology, 35*, 590–598.

Gaertner, S. L. and Dovidio, J. F. (1977). The Subtlety of White Racism, Arousal and Helping Behavior. *Journal of Personality and Social Psychology, 34*, 691–707.

Gaertner, S. L. and Dovidio, J. F. (1981). Racism among the Well-Intentioned. In E. Clausen and J. Bermingham (Eds.). *Pluralism, Racism, and Public Policy: The Search for Equality* (pp. 208–222). Boston: G. K. Hall.

Gaertner, S. L. and Dovidio, J. F. (1986). The Aversive Form of Racism. In J. F. Dovidio and S. L. Gaertner (Eds.). *Prejudice, Discrimination, and Racism* (pp. 61–89). Orlando, FL: Academic Press.

Glaser, B. G. and Strauss, A. L. (1967). *The Discovery of Grounded Theory: Strategies for Qualitative Research.* Chicago: Aldine.

Hamilton, D. L. (1979). A Cognitive-Attributional Analysis of Stereotyping. In L. Berkowitz (Ed.). *Advances in Experimental Social Psychology, 12*, pp. 53–84. New York: Academic Press.

Hamilton, D. L. and Trolier, T. K. (1986). Stereotypes and Sterotyping: An Overview of the Cognitive Approach. In J. F. Dovidio and S. L. Gaertner (Eds.). *Prejudice, Discrimination, and Racism* (pp. 127–163). Orlando, FL: Academic Press.

Heath, S. B. (1982). Questioning at Home and at School: A Comparative Study. In G. Spindler (Ed.). *Doing the Ethnography of Schooling: Educational Anthropology in Action* (pp. 102–131). New York: Holt, Rinehart and Winston.

Johnson, D. W. and Johnson, R. T. (1982). The Study of Cooperative, Competitive, and Individualistic Situations: State of the Area and Two Recent Contributions. *Contemporary Education: A Journal of Reviews, 1*(1), 7–13.

Johnson, D. W., Johnson, R. T., and Maruyama, G. (1984). Goal Interdependence and Interpersonal Attraction in Heterogeneous Classrooms: A Meta-Analysis. In N. Miller and M. B. Brewer (Eds.). *Groups in Contact: The Psychology of Desegregation* (pp. 187–212). Orlando, FL: Academic Press.

Johnson, D. W., Maruyama, G., Johnson, R. T., Nelson, D., and Skon, L., (1981). Effects of Cooperative, Competitive, and Individualistic Goal Structures on Achievement: A Meta-Analysis. *Psychological Bulletin, 89*, 47–62.

Jones, J. M. (1972). *Prejudice and Racism.* Reading, MA: Addison-Wesley.

Jones, J. M. (1986). Racism: A Cultural Analysis of the Problem. In J. F. Dovidio and S. L. Gaertner (Eds.). *Prejudice, Discrimination, and Racism* (pp. 279–313). Orlando, FL: Academic Press.

Katz, I., Wackenhut, J., and Hass, R. G. (1986). Racial Ambivalence, Value Duality, and Behavior. In J. F. Dovidio and S. L. Gaertner (Eds.). *Prejudice, Discrimination, and Racism* (pp. 35–59). Orlando, FL: Academic Press.

Katz, P. A. (1976). The Acquisition of Racial Attitudes. In P. Katz (Ed.). *Toward the Elimination of Racism* (pp. 125–156). New York: Pergamon Press.

Kochman, T. (1981). *Black and White Styles of Conflict.* Chicago: University of Chicago Press.

Linville, P. W., Salovey, P., and Fischer, G. W. (1986). Stereotyping and Perceived Distributions of Social Characteristics: An Application to Ingroup-Outgroup Perception. In J. F. Dovidio and S. L. Gaertner (Eds.). *Prejudice, Discrimination, and Racism* (pp. 165–207). Orlando, FL: Academic Press.

Malpass, R. S. and Kravitz, J. (1969). Recognition for Faces of Own and Other Races. *Journal of Personality and Social Psychology, 13*, 330–334.

McConahay, J. B. (1986). Modern Racism, Ambivalence, and the Modern Racism Scale. In J. F. Dovidio and S. L. Gaertner (Eds.). *Prejudice, Discrimination, and Racism* (pp. 91–125). Orlando, FL: Academic Press.

Miller, N. and Brewer, M. B. (1986). Categorization Effects on Ingroup and Outgroup Perception. In J. F. Dovidio and S. L. Gaertner (Eds.). *Prejudice, Discrimination, and Racism* (pp. 209–229). Orlando, FL: Academic Press.

Olson, S. (1976). *Ideas and Data: Process and Practice of Social Research.* Homewood, IL: The Dorsey Press.

Pettigrew, T. (1967). Social Evaluation Theory: Convergences and Applications. In D. Levine (Ed.). *Nebraska Symposium on Motivation*, Vol. 5 (pp. 241–315). Lincoln: University of Nebraska Press.

Pettigrew, T. (1969). Racially Separate or Together. *Journal of Social Issues, 25*(1), 43–69.

Riordan, C. (1978). Equal-Status Interracial Contact: A Review and Revision of the Concept. *International Journal of Intercultural Relations, 2*(2), 161–185.

Rist, R. C. (1974). Race, Policy and Schooling. *Society, 12*(1), 59–63.

Sagar, H. A. and Schofield, J. W. (1980). Racial and Behavioral Cues in Black and White Children's Perceptions of Ambiguously Aggressive Acts. *Journal of Personality and Social Psychology, 39*(4), 590–598.

Sagar, H. A. and Schofield, J. W. (1984). Integrating the Desegregated School: Problems and Possibilities. In M. Maehr and D. Bartz (Eds.). *Advances in Motivation and Achievement: A Research Annual.* Greenwich, CT: JAI Press.

Scherer, J. and Slawski, E. J. (1979). Color, Class, and Social Control in an Urban Desegregated School. In R. C. Rist (Ed.). *Desegregated Schools* (pp. 117–153). New York: Academic Press.

Schofield, J. W. (1979). The Impact of Positively Structured Contact on Intergroup Behavior: Does It Last under Adverse Conditions? *Social Psychology Quarterly, 42*(3), 280–284.

Schofield, J. W. (1982). *Black and White in School: Trust, Tension or Tolerance?* New York: Praeger.

Schofield, J. W. and Francis, W. D. (1982). An Observational Study of Peer Interaction in Racially-Mixed "Accelerated" Classrooms. *The Journal of Educational Psychology, 74*(5), 722–732.

Schofield, J. W. and Sagar, H. A. (1977). Peer Interaction Patterns in an Integrated Middle School. *Sociometry. 40*(2), 130–138.

Schofield, J. W. and Sagar, H. A. (1979). The Social Context of Learning in an Interracial School. In R. Rist (Ed.). *Inside Desegregated Schools: Appraisals of an American Experiment* (pp. 155–199). San Francisco: Academic Press.

Schofield, J. W. and Whitley, B. E. (1983). Peer Nomination Versus Rating Scale Measurement of Children's Peer Preferences. *Social Psychology Quarterly, 46*(3), 242–251.

Sharan, S. (1980). Cooperative Learning in Teams: Recent Methods and Effects on Achievement, Attitudes and Ethnic Relations. *Review of Educational Research, 50*(2), 241–272.

Sherif, M. (1979). Superordinate Goals in the Reduction of Intergroup Conflict: An Experimental Evaluation. In W. G. Austin and S. Worchel (Eds.). *The Social Psychology of Intergroup Relations* (pp. 257–261). Monterey, CA: Brooks/Cole Publishing Company.

Slavin, R. E. (1980). Cooperative Learning. *Review of Educational Research, 50*(2), 315–342.

Slavin, R. E. (1983a). *Cooperative Learning.* New York: Longman.

Slavin, R. E. (1983b). When Does Cooperative Learning Increase Student Achievement? *Psychological Bulletin, 94*, 429–445.

Slavin, R. E. (1985). Cooperative Learning: Applying Contact Theory in Desegregated Schools. *Journal of Social Issues, 41*(3), 45–62.

Snyder, M. L., Kleck, R. E., Strenta, A., and Mentzer, S. J. (1979). Avoidance of the Handicapped: An Attributional Ambiguity Analysis. *Journal of Personality and Social Psychology, 12*, 2297–2306.

Stephan, W. G. and Stephan, C. W. (1985). Intergroup Anxiety. *Journal of Social Issues, 41*(3), 157–175.

Taylor, S., Fiske, S., Etcoff, N., and Ruderman, A. (1978). Categorical and Contextual Basis of Person Memory and Stereotyping. *Journal of Personality and Social Psychology, 36*(7), 778–793.

Taylor, S. E. (1981). A Categorical Approach to Stereotyping. In D. Hamilton (Ed.). *Cognitive Processes in Stereotyping and Intergroup Behavior* (pp. 83–114). Hillsdale, NJ: Erlbaum.

Taylor, S. E. and Fiske, S. T. (1978). Salience, Attention and Attribution: Top of the Head Phenomena. In L. Berkowitz (Ed.). *Advances in Experimental Social Psychology*, Vol. 11 (pp. 249–288). New York: Academic Press.

Triandis, H. C., Vassiliou, V., Vassiliou, G., Tanaka, Y., and Shanmugam, A. (Eds.). (1972). *The Analysis of Subjective Culture.* New York: Wiley.

Webb, E. J., Campbell, D. T., Schwartz, R. D., and Sechrest, L. (1966). *Unobtrusive Measures: Nonreactive Research in the Social Sciences.* Chicago: Rand McNally.

Whitley, B. E. and Schofield, J. W. (1984). Peer Preference in Desegregated Classrooms: A Round Robin Analysis. *Journal of Personality and Social Psychology, 46*(4), 799–810.

Worchel, S. (1979). Cooperation and the Reduction of Intergroup Conflict: Some Determining Factors. In W. G. Austin and S. Worchel (Eds.). *The Social Psychology of Intergroup Relations* (pp. 262–273). Monterey, CA: Brooks/Cole Publishing Company.

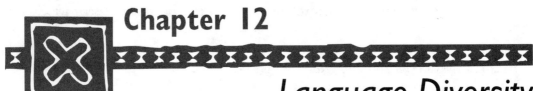

Chapter 12

Language Diversity and Education

Carlos J. Ovando

Language is a shared and sharing part of culture that cares little about formal classifications and much about vitality and connection, for culture itself perishes in purity or isolation.

Carlos Fuentes (1988, p. 27)

Language diversity has a strong influence on the content and process of schooling practices for both language minority and majority students in the United States. Language, as a system of communication linking sound, written or visual symbols, and meaning, is an indispensable bridge for sharing knowledge, skills, values, and attitudes within and across cultures. It has tremendous power as the paramount instrument of cognitive development, and it can open or close the door to academic achievement. How, then, is the educational inequality often experienced by language minority students related to the degree of their ability to understand, speak, read and write standard English?

To present an overview of how language diversity is related to educational outcomes, this chapter is organized in three sections. In the first section we consider what language is and how children and adults acquire their first and second languages. In the second section we survey varieties of nonstandard English as well as non-English-language diversity in the United States. In the third section we address classroom adaptations to meet the needs of language minority students.

THE SOCIOCULTURAL NATURE OF LANGUAGE AND LANGUAGE ACQUISITION

Language is a powerful and transformative part of culture. As with culture, language is learned, it is shared, and it evolves and changes over time. It is much more than a set of words and grammar rules. It is a forceful instrument for giving individuals, groups, institutions, and cultures their identity. Through language we communicate our values, attitudes, skills, and aspirations as bearers of culture and as makers of future culture.

Language can be analyzed from many different points of view. For instance, at the physical level, it is a system of sounds and movements made by the human body and decoded by the listener's auditory system. From the cognitive point of view, it is a tool for the expression of thought. From the anthropological point of view, it is an intricate and pervasive component of culture. From the semiotic point of view, language can also be studied as a system of signs and symbols that have socially determined meanings (Shaumyan, 1987).

From the pedagogical point of view, what has an individual learned when he or she is said to have gained communicative competence in a particular language? To begin with, there are the more familiar components of language that have to be developed:

1. Phonetics and phonology—the sound system
2. Morphology—the way in which units of meaning are formed into words
3. Syntax—the grammar of sentence formation
4. Lexicon—the vocabulary

Beyond these components, however, are other culture-related domains to be mastered for communicative competence. These domains illustrate the subtleties and sociocultural aspects of the process of learning a language.

1. Discourse. How the language is organized in speech and writing beyond the sentence level; for example, how paragraphs or conversations are structured.

2. Appropriateness. The way language use is adjusted according to the social situation; for example, "Hit the lights, will ya?" versus "Would you mind turning the lights off, please?"

3. Paralinguistics. Distance between speakers, intonation, volume and pitch of speech, gestures, facial expressions and other body language.

4. Pragmatics. The interaction of discourse, appropriateness, and paralinguistics; for example, pragmatics involve implicit and explicit cultural norms for when it is and is not appropriate to talk, how speech is paced, the correct way to listen, when to be direct and when to be indirect, how to take turns in conversation, and how to adapt language according to roles, social status, attitudes, settings, and topics.

5. Cognitive-academic language proficiency (Cummins, 1979, 1981, 1991). Mastery of the language skills needed to learn and develop abstract concepts in such areas as mathematics, science, and social studies (Ovando & Collier, 1985).

Even such a cursory listing of these language components and domains clearly suggests that language acquisition is a complicated, subtle, culture-specific, and life-long process. Educators thus need to realize that the difference between English and

Spanish, for example, or even between standard English and Black English, is much more than a difference in phonology, morphology, syntax, and lexicon. It has often been said that learning basic communication in one's first language is a simple process—child's play, so to speak. However, when examined carefully, even one's full development of the first language—including literacy skills and knowledge about the structure and function of the language—is a complex process in which it takes years to reach communicative competence. Knowing this, teachers are more likely to develop respect for and sensitivity to students who arrive in the classroom speaking anything other than standard English. For non-English speakers in particular, teachers should be realistic as to the years of language development needed for speakers to move from basic communication in English to full communicative competence.

Languages grow and develop as tools of communication within a given environment. In this sense, there is no such thing as "right" or "wrong" language, only language that is appropriate or inappropriate in a given context. Languages and language varieties develop and thrive because they meet the needs of communities. If a given community of speakers finds it necessary to maintain a language because it satisfies spiritual, social, intellectual, technical, scientific, economic, or political needs, then the chances that a particular linguistic community will survive are greatly enhanced. Thus, for example, Yupik (an Eskimo Aleut language) is alive in Akiachak, Alaska, despite the powerful influence of English, because it fulfills the people's need for continuity with their heritage. Within the domain of English itself, the United States teems with a variety of linguistic microcultures representing a diversity of experiences—American Indian varieties of English, Creoles, Black English, and a broad array of regional accents, vocabularies, and styles.

Because through multicultural education we seek to promote equity and excellence across such variables as race, ethnicity, nationality, gender, social class, regional groups, religion, exceptionality, literacy background, age, and language background, it is vital for educators to understand the function language can play in either helping or inhibiting the educational fulfillment of individuals. As Hymes (1981) states:

> The law of the land demands that equal educational
> opportunity not be denied because of language.
> "Language" has been understood most readily in terms of
> "languages," such as Spanish, and structurally definable
> varieties of a language, such as Black English Vernacular.
> If one defines "language," as I do, in terms of ways of
> speaking, as involving both structure and ways of using
> structure, there are even deeper implications, implications
> not yet legally explored. One's language affects one's
> chances in life, not only through accent, but also through
> action. Access to opportunities in the form of access to
> schools, jobs, positions, memberships, clubs, and homes,
> may depend on ways of using language that one has no
> chance to master, or chooses not to master. (pp. vii–viii)

Within and outside the school setting, it becomes important to consider how persons come to acquire and value the particular types of first and second languages they prefer to use in formal and informal situations. Therefore, we now turn to research on first and second language acquisition and its application in classrooms. We focus here on the process by which non-English speakers acquire English language skills.

First and Second Language Acquisition

For the past thirty years, linguists and cognitive psychologists have made considerable progress in understanding first and second language acquisition. It would be impossible to provide here a complete overview of this complex field of study. (See Masahiko & Ovando, 1995, for a more extensive examination of this field.) Therefore, we focus our discussion more on aspects of language acquisition that relate closely to the effective education of language minority students.

The research indicates that language learning is a developmental process that goes through predictable stages. We acquire our first language as children, in the context of natural, interesting, and meaningful interactions within the social and physical environment. In such an environment, the child is exposed day after day to peer and adult language models in a context that gives meaning to language. Because of this strongly contextualized environment, speakers tend to learn communication shortcuts such as incomplete responses and many nonverbal cues.

Although it is now referred to more commonly as social or playground language, Cummins initially refers to this type of language as basic interpersonal communicative skills (BICS). Doing research with English language learners in Canada, Cummins suggested that an average non-English-speaking student could learn to communicate at this level in English after about two years of instruction in an acquisition-rich environment similar to that of a child learning a first language (Cummins, 1981). This ability to get along in the world conversationally enables English language learners to make everyday conversational contact with their English-speaking peers. Such contact, in turn, provides a pivotal function in the acculturation of such students, especially to the school culture. In addition, such face-to-face communication serves as an initial platform for building a self-concept in social relationships. In other words, the acquisition of such social language serves a powerful and important sociolinguistic function in the lives of persons learning their second languages.

However, even though a student of limited English proficiency may seem to be making rapid progress in the acquisition of English, such control of social language does not necessarily equip the student for the curriculum's more cognitively demanding tasks. Cognitive tasks require a second developmental level beyond conversational language that consists of the language used in school and many facets of adult life. Here, the context is less clear. Instead, communication depends on a speaker's (or writer's) ability to manipulate the vocabulary and syntax and discourse style with precision (Ovando, 1983). Cummins has referred to this type of language competence as cognitive academic language proficiency (CALP). Again, research by Cummins indicates that, as measured by standardized tests, children with little or no prior schooling experience attain native-like cognitive-academic language proficiency in English in about five to seven years (Cummins, 1981). For the past ten years, Cummins's research reported in 1981 has been replicated and expanded in a series of studies by Collier and Thomas (see Collier, 1995, for a synthesis of their work.) Affirming Cummins's earlier research, they conclude (cited in Collier, 1995):

> In our studies we have found that in U.S. schools where all instruction is given through the second language (English), non-native speakers of English with no schooling in their first language take 7–10 years or more to reach age and grade-level norms of their native English-speaking peers. Immigrant students who have had 2–3 years of first language in their home country before they come to the U.S. take at least 5–7 years to reach typical native-speaker performance. (p. 8)

Just because a child speaks little or no English does not mean that he or she comes to school as a blank tablet. Such children come to school with a wealth of home experiences and of skills and competence in their home language. All of this provides a basis for future learning. Again, Cummins (1981) concludes that prior acquired knowledge and skills in the home language transfer to the new language. This is known as the common underlying proficiency (CUP). Thus, for example, a Filipino student who already knows in Tagalog how to manipulate the language involved in the solution of word problems will be able to transfer those skills into the second language as she acquires new mathematical vocabulary in English. In other words, knowledge acquired through the student's first language is not only useful but also crucial in the continuous cognitive development of the student in the second language (Ramirez, 1991). In fact, ample research evidence suggests that cognitive and academic development in the first language can have a very positive effect on second-language schooling. (See Collier, 1995, for a synthesis of the research on the role of the first language on second-language schooling.) Of importance to language minority educators is Cummins's (1981) conclusion on the instructional use of both the home language (L1) and English (L2):

> The results of research on bilingual programs show that minority children's L1 can be promoted in school at no cost to the development of proficiency in the majority language: . . .
>
> The data clearly show that well-implemented bilingual programs have had remarkable success in developing English academic skills and have proved superior to ESL-only programs in situations where direct comparisons have been carried out. (p. 28)

Tracking and expanding on the work of Cummins, Collier (1995) reports:

> In our examination of large datasets across many different research sites, we have found that the most significant student background variable is the amount of formal schooling students have received in their first language. Across all

program treatments, we have found that non-native speakers being schooled in second language for part or all of the school day typically do reasonably well in the early years of schooling (kindergarten through second or third grade). But from fourth grade on through middle school and high school, when the academic and cognitive demands of the curriculum increase rapidly with each succeeding year, students with little or no academic and cognitive development in their first language do less and less well as they move into the upper grades. . . .

What about students schooled bilingually in the U.S.? It still takes a long time to demonstrate academic proficiency in second language comparable to a native speaker. But the difference in student performance in a bilingual program, in contrast to an all-English program, is that students typically score at or above grade level in their first language in all subjects areas, while they are building academic development of second language. When students are tested in their second language, they typically reach and surpass native speakers' performance across all subject areas after 4–7 years in a quality bilingual program. Because they have not fallen behind in cognitive and academic growth during the 4–7 years that it takes to build academic proficiency in second language, bilingually schooled students typically sustain this level of academic achievement and outperform monolingually schooled students in the upper grades. (p. 9)

Thus, native language support in a quality bilingual program can provide academic development through comprehensible instruction. This development can then be applied to their academic and language growth in English.

LANGUAGE VARIETY IN THE UNITED STATES

As a language laboratory, the United States is truly remarkable. Of the scores of American Indian languages existing prior to European contact, about 175 Native American languages have survived the overwhelming assimilative powers of the English language in the United States and about 35 such languages in Canada (Krauss, 1995). Languages other than English used by colonizers of North America—such as Spanish and French—continue not only to survive but also to serve as lively communicative and cultural instruments in various regions of the country. The successive waves of immigrants to the United States have also made the nation linguistically rich. Today the nation's language assets range from such languages as Navajo—still spoken in the same communities in which it was spoken hundreds of years ago—to Hmong, spoken by recent refugees from the highlands of Laos, Thailand, and Cambodia.

In addition to the varied mix of languages, language contact in the United States has produced many indigenous language varieties known as pidgin, creole, and dialect. Pidgin is a type of language that evolves through contact between groups speaking different languages. It mixes components of the contact languages and has its own grammar system. Creole is the adoption of a pidgin as the accepted language of a community. As Anttila puts it, "this happened often on the plantations of the New World, where slaves from different language backgrounds were forced to use a pidgin among themselves, and between themselves and the masters. After escape, freedom, or revolution the pidgin was all they had, and it had to become the first language of the community" (Anttila, 1972, p. 176). Three examples of creole varieties in the United States are (1) Gullah, a creole of English and West African origin which is spoken on the Sea Islands, from the Carolinas to northern Florida; (2) Louisiana French Creole, which coexists with two local varieties of French and another local variety of English; and (3) Hawaiian Creole, which has been influenced by Hawaiian, Japanese, Chinese, Portuguese, English, and Ilocano. Complementing the rich indigenous creole traditions of the United States is Black English, spoken by a large segment of the African American population. To understand better these indigenous language varieties, we look more closely at the nature of Gullah, Louisiana French Creole, Hawaiian Creole, and Black English.

Gullah

Gullah is geographically associated with African Americans who initially settled in South Carolina in the 1700s. Nichols has estimated that in the early 1980s there were about 300,000 African Americans who spoke Gullah in an area including South Carolina, Georgia, and parts of lower North Carolina and Northern Florida (Nichols, 1981). Ties between Gullah and its West African language ancestors include similar vowel sounds and some vocabulary items, such as *goober* for "peanut," *cooter* for "turtle," and *buckra* for "White man" (Nichols, 1981, p. 75). Structurally, Gullah also differs from standard English. For example, instead of using he and she, the neuter pronoun *ee* is used for both male and female. *Fuh* is used to indicate an infinitive clause, as in "I came *fuh* get my coat." Progressive action can be indicated by *duh* plus the verb: "Greg *duh* hide" instead of "Greg is hiding" (Nichols, 1981, pp. 73–75).

Most members of the Gullah-speaking community are not strictly creole speakers. What is found instead are individuals "who show greater or lesser use of creole features along a continuum of language use ranging from creole to a dialect of English" (Nichols, 1981, p. 73). Not surprisingly, there is a strong association of Gullah use with age and amount of formal schooling. For example, the very old and the very young tend to use Gullah more extensively. School-age children tend to switch back and forth between Gullah—referred to as "country talk"—and the prestige variety of standard English, especially for the benefit of teachers, who usually do not understand Gullah.

Gullah has been analyzed extensively by linguists, and much is known about its phonology, grammar, vocabulary, and sociolinguistic usage. Gullah has also been popularized through literature such as the stories of Ambrose González (Nichols, 1981) and the novels and Gullah sketches of Pulitzer Prize winner Julia Peterkin (Nichols, 1981). Yet the children who speak Gullah have been stigmatized in the schools, and there has not been a vigorous effort to incorporate their language into the curriculum to create bridges to standard English. Although some teachers are addressing literacy development for such children through such means as the language-experience approach, by and large such creole-speaking children may not be receiving equal educational opportunities in classrooms in which standard English is the accepted medium of instruction.

Louisiana French Creole

Like Gullah, Louisiana French Creole reflects a linguistic structure that sets it apart from English. Louisiana Creole speakers may have difficulty understanding English, and vice versa. Louisiana French Creole, a contemporary of Gullah, seems to have evolved via West African slaves who were introduced by French colonists to Southern Louisiana and needed a common language to communicate with each other. Louisiana French Creole has structural similarities with English-related creoles such as Gullah. For example, the pronoun li is used for both he and she. Also, like Gullah, no verb "to be" is used in equative clauses. However, unlike Gullah, most of the Louisiana French Creole vocabulary is derived from French rather than from English, with some use of African vocabulary items (Nichols, 1981).

Although Acadian and standard French are officially affirmed in the school curriculum in Louisiana, Louisiana French Creole traditionally has not had the same status. Like Gullah-speaking children, children who speak Louisiana French Creole therefore run the risk of not receiving equal educational opportunities. Furthermore, they and their parents may interpret the neglect of their primary language as a devaluation of their sociolinguistic background in the eyes of school personnel and society at large.

Hawaiian Creole

Hawaiian Creole is a relative newcomer into the family of indigenous creoles in U.S. society. Its use dates back to the late nineteenth century. Unlike Louisiana French Creole, there is considerably more careful scholarly documentation about its origin, structure, and function (Nichols, 1981). Hawaiian Creole evolved as a pidgin during the late nineteenth century, when plantations were developed and the Hawaiian Islands came under the influence of English speakers from the United States mainland. Similar to Gullah, Hawaiian Creole is English-related, and its lexicon is predominantly English, with the aforementioned influence from Hawaiian, Japanese, Chinese, Portuguese, and Ilocano. This rich linguistic mixture in the Hawaiian Islands has led language scholars to view Hawaiian English "in terms of three coexistent systems—a pidgin, Creole, and dialect of English—none of which occurs in unadulterated forms but only in combinations of different proportions" (Nichols, 1981, p. 48). Whether Hawaiian English is a dialect of English or a creole language is a complex issue. Somewhat like Gullah, its degree of similarity to English ranges on a continuum depending on the community and the context. For example, linguists note a highly decreolized language variety in the more urbanized population centers like Oahu and more creolized traditional patterns in the more remote islands of Kauai and Hawaii (Nichols, 1981).

In any event, Hawaiian Creole is a lively language that plays a key role in the lives of many Hawaiian children both socially and academically. As with Gullah and Louisiana French Creole, Hawaiian Creole, or Pidgin English, as it is known by island residents, is a highly stigmatized language variety that until the 1970s had been singled out by educational policy makers as a cause of the many academic problems experienced by Hawaiian students. According to Nichols, the policy was to decreolize the students' language. Because such a posture toward Hawaiian Creole did not produce the desired result of eliminating it from the lives of students, education policies since then have tended toward acceptance of the language in the lives of the students. However, there has remained a sense that it is a "deficient language" and thus in need of correction (Nichols, 1981, p. 86). The attempt in Hawaii to eradicate Hawaiian Creole confirms once more that when something as important as a language is threatened, its users tend to protect and defend it. This is what happened in the islands, where Hawaiian Creole speakers began to view their use of creole as an important symbol of solidarity in their community.

Black English

Black English, although a dialect of English rather than a creole language, shows parallels in historical development with creole languages. Black English reflects influence from British and American English as well as English-based pidgin from sixteenth-century West Africa. In situations involving language contact, one has to understand the nature of social relationships both within and outside the involved communities. The inhumanity of master-slave relationships were certainly not conducive to an egalitarian communicative process. But it is in this type of socially strained context that Black English and White English coexisted and influenced each other. From the late 1700s until the early 1900s, approximately 90 percent of the African American population in the United States lived in the Southern states (Whatley, 1981). With such a high concentration of speakers, Black English was able to mature into a highly sophisticated and rule-governed "subsystem within the larger grammar of English" (Whately, 1981, p. 64).

Unlike Gullah, Louisiana French Creole, and Hawaiian Creole, Black English spread throughout the United States. In the twentieth century, many African Americans began to migrate to the large urban centers of the North. Through this two-way connection between Black communities in the rural South and the industrial North, Black English continued to evolve. As Whatley observes, "Funerals, homecoming celebrations at churches, and family reunions took northerners 'down home' at least annually" (Whatley, 1981, p. 94). Strong regional and familial ties between the rural South and the industrial North generated much cross-fertilization of old and new communication patterns.

On the other hand, de facto segregation in the large urban centers of the North tended to insulate African American and White communities from each other. That meant that, given the social distance created between the speakers of Black English and White English, both languages had minimal influence on one another. Thus, Black English tended to continue developing its own set of structures, functional patterns, and styles.

Despite the presence of Black English throughout the United States, many Americans have a highly distorted perception of the nature of Black English. As Whatley points out, much of what the nation has come to understand as Black English has come about through Hollywood and the electronic media, with all of its distortions and stereotypic tendencies. Thus, the world of entertainment has given us a highly stylized version of Black speech—jiving, copping, playing the dozens, boasting, preaching, and fussing, for example. However, the impression that television, radio, theater, and musicals have given U.S. audiences regarding Black communities is just the tip of the linguistic iceberg. As Whatley indicates, there are many aspects of Black English other than those portrayed in the media (Whatley, 1981).

As with any type of language use, there is great speech variation among speakers of Black English. Also, speech behavior is highly contextualized. That is, individuals tend to assess the communicative situation and respond accordingly. Most speakers of English use a variety of styles of language in their daily lives, these variations being determined by degrees of formality and social status. Within the African American experience, praising, fussing, teasing, lying, preaching, jiving, boasting, or joking are carefully determined by the age, gender, and status of speakers. For example, the eldest members of the African American community tend to have greater latitude and prestige in language use, and children are the lowest-ranking members of the speech community (Whatley, 1981). This, of course, does not mean that African American children are not allowed to interact with adults in creative and expressive ways. What it does mean, however, is that there is a certain speech protocol that is sensitive to such variables as age, social status, gender, and formal and informal settings.

Because of African Americans' historical status as an oppressed minority, Whites have tended to perceive Black English as "a mass of random errors committed by Blacks trying to speak English" (Labov, Cohen, Robins & Lewis, 1968, p. 366). However, the language varieties used by African Americans are valid linguistic systems. They have an internal linguistic infrastructure and a set of grammar rules just as any other language does. For example, the use of the verb "to be" follows different rules in Black English than in standard English. Speakers of standard English tend to contract forms of the verb "to be," as in the sentence, "She's tall" instead of "She is tall." Black English deletes "is" entirely so that the sentence becomes "She tall." Black English also has a use for "be" that standard English does not. The sentences "He always be walkin' on a desert on TV" and "He jus' be walkin' dere sometime" use what linguists call the "invariant be." This use of the verb refers to action that takes place habitually over a period of time, and for this there is no exact standard English equivalent (Whatley, 1981).

Multiple negation is perhaps one of the most stigmatized aspects of Black English when speakers enter the formal school system. Yet there is no logical basis for such stigmatization. Acceptance or nonacceptance of the double negative as a socially correct form is essentially a historical accident. According to language scholars, multiple negation was an integral part of the English language up to the time of Shakespeare. Also, it is useful to know that although Latin is credited for having influenced the single negation in English, other Romance languages such as Spanish, French, and Italian use the double negative as part of their respective standard speech patterns (Whatley, 1981).

A fair curricular process is one that builds on the sociocultural and linguistic backgrounds the students bring with them. Yet use of Black English has had many negative consequences for Black students. Many African American youth have not prospered in U.S. schools, and in the process of searching for reasons for this, some educators have singled out their Black English communication patterns as an important part of the cause for their academic failure. In the past, a common perception among educators, although not necessarily articulated, has been that speakers of Black English are language deficient. Use of Black English, from this point of view, is seen as being detrimental to the student's cognitive development. However, thinking skills can be demonstrated in any language; they are not the exclusive domain of standard English. Consider as an example the following conversation between two young speakers of Black English:

A: Do you know 'bout factors and all that stuff?

B: Yeah, I know all that.

A: Well, how come you only made a 50 on that test?

B: That test was tough—she ain't no good teacher anyway.

A: But you have been in the other math class, the one dat ain't done factors like we have.

B: Yeah, but I can do spelling—and you can't.

(Whatley, 1981, p.99)

Whatley (1981) interprets the above playful interaction as follows:

> It is clear in this boasting episode that child A had collected highly specific information to support his boast, and he set child B up to a challenge by a seemingly innocent question. The strategies and information to support these were planned in advance. Child A wins this sequence, because child B must shift topic and begin another boast. (p. 30)

From the above boasting episode, it is apparent that although the children are not using standard English, they are certainly not language deficient. If anything, the pair reflect a high level of creativity and spontaneity with language behavior, which is highly desirable for cognitive development. The children's language is different from standard English, but the language they use is not deficient. Their linguistic behavior and vocabulary inventory serve their communication needs extremely well.

Gullah, Louisiana French Creole, Hawaiian Creole, and Black English have much in common. They are rule-governed and they are legitimate linguistic expressions, just as standard English is. They are a link to our past, and they have a birthright to exist and to be accepted. Yet they are not given much recognition in the larger society. Rather, they are viewed by many people as aberrant and inferior language varieties. Consequently, a great unfounded fear exists on the part of educators that affirmation of such languages will perpetuate school failure in the lives of such students. Because teaching practices are not always linguistically enlightened, language can become a main source of inequality surrounding the lives of students who come to school marked with a stigmatized speech variety.

Cognitive psychologists, on the other hand, tell us that we build our cognitive repertoire on prior knowledge, experiences, attitudes, and skills (Wertsch, 1985). It is a layering process. Educators, therefore, dare not destroy what was there before. The goal should be to build on and add to what is already present in the lives of students. Creative bridges using the early socialization patterns of the home language and culture can be useful in motivating students to learn. This, of course, means that such students will come to see their teachers as professionals who understand the value of their nonstandard languages. Such teachers, while respecting the structure and function of the home language, will help to build another layer of linguistic skill that will enable these students to negotiate the prestige variety of English in the larger society and thus to have more options in their lives. Now that we have surveyed a few nonstandard language varieties found in the United States, we can complete our portrait of language variety by looking at the backgrounds of students from non-English-speaking communities.

The Demographics of Students from Non-English-Language Backgrounds

As a result of shifting demographics, the United States is currently experiencing an increasing representation of English language learners in its schools. Since the passage of the 1968 Title VII Bilingual Education Act and the landmark U.S. Supreme Court Decision *Lau* v. *Nichols* (Waugh & Koon, 1974), which provided a legal basis for equitable treatment of non-English-speaking-background students in U.S. schools, educational policy for non-English-language communities has put linguistic minorities in the national spotlight. Non-English-background students in U.S. schools come from an astounding variety of backgrounds. For example, many foreign-born children come to U.S. schools speaking only the language of their home country. Their families may be voluntary immigrants or involuntarily uprooted refugees, such as the Hmong. They may reside in the United States legally or as undocumented immigrants. There are also U.S.-born language minority students for whom the United States is their home country. This group includes speakers of American Indian languages. It also includes groups who have maintained over generations the use of colonial and early immigration languages such as Spanish, French, German and Swedish. And today it includes the offspring and subsequent generations of immigrants of virtually every nationality. Upon entering school, all of these students may fall anywhere on a broad continuum of language status. The child may be entirely monolingual in the non-English language; he or she may be bilingual in the home language and English; or the child may be dominant in English, with only a few fragmentary skills in the ancestral language.

The diversity of languages in the United States is truly amazing. For example, in remote Anchorage, Alaska, students speaking more than 100 different languages, from virtually every region of the world, have been identified in the local school district's bilingual education program. As of 1992, the Los Angeles School District, whose identified language minority students spoke at least 80 different languages, offered bilingual instruction in Spanish, Cantonese, Vietnamese, Korean, Filipino, and Armenian. With its large language minority population, California has become the Ellis Island of the 1990s. By the year 2000, the state is projected to have a minority population between 40 and 50 percent (Cortés, 1986). If these figures are examined in relation to school-age populations, it is projected that in the year 2000, 52 percent of students in California will be ethnic minorities (Cortés, 1986).

Other data show that during the ten years between 1980 and 1990, U.S. society became increasingly multiracial, multicultural, and multilingual. The demographic trend shows that in these ten years the total population of the United States grew by 9.8 percent. However, groups in which most language minority students are found were growing at a much faster rate. The American Indian population (including Eskimo and Aleut) grew by 37.9 percent, Asian and Pacific Islanders by 107.8 percent, Hispanic Americans by 53 percent, and "Others" by 45.1 percent (NABE, n.d., p. 1). Increased immigration from both Latin America and Asia as well as high fertility rates within these populations are some of the major factors contributing to this demographic shift.

The upswing in immigration has resulted in large numbers of school entrants whose first language is not English (Masahiko & Ovando, 1995). Summarizing the most recent census data concerning demographic changes from 1980 to 1990, the *New York Times* of April 28, 1993 (Barringer, 1993), reports that the number of U.S. residents for whom English is a foreign/second language increased nearly 40 percent to 32 million. In 1992 the U.S. Department of Education (1992) estimated that in 1990–1991 approximately 2.3 million children lived in language-minority households, made substantial use of minority languages, and were of limited proficiency in English. According to the Stanford Working Group (1993), the number of such children is much greater, perhaps as many as 3.3 million children between the ages of five and seventeen. Language-minority children are now the fastest-growing group in schools in the United States (McKeon, 1992). Among language-minority groups, Spanish-speaking households are the fastest-growing sector and are expected to become this country's largest minority in the not-so-distant future.

While these figures are useful in giving at least an imperfect glimpse at the approximate number of children from language minority homes, they do not begin to scratch the surface when it comes to figuring out who is eligible for bilingual services and how long they are to be served. Thus, as Ulibarri (1986) suggests,

> Differences in estimates of the limited-English-proficient population derive from efforts to count the number of children according to different definitions and interpretations of eligibility for services. At issue are the criteria for determining which language minority children are in need of

English and native language related services. Thus, the problem is not simply one of differences in number of eligible
children, but one in which the actual definition of who is eligible also varies. (p. 57)

Although there is great variation depending on the student's background and
schooling opportunities, a disproportionate number of English language learners do
not achieve well academically. In fact, they are all too often overrepresented at the bottom of the test score ladder. Despite the research-based knowledge we have gained
over the past thirty years about how individuals learn their first and second languages
and about how acculturative and assimilative forces work with immigrants and indigenous groups, there is still a wide gap between theory and practice. Consider, for example, the strong resistance that bilingual instruction has received in educational circles
despite the evidence indicating that English language learners who develop a strong
sociocultural, linguistic, and cognitive base in their primary language tend to transfer
those attitudes and skills to the other language and culture. Moreover, the chronically
poor track record schools have had in educating American Indians, for example, suggests that the schooling of most language minorities has generally been surrounded
by a great deal of political and ideological controversy at the expense of sustained and
well-founded curricular development.

ADDRESSING LANGUAGE NEEDS IN THE MULTICULTURAL CLASSROOM

The basis for the debate surrounding the schooling of language minority students has
to do essentially with the kind of citizens we want and need in our society. Should the
school curriculum affirm cultural and linguistic pluralism through an additive process?
Or should the schools pursue an ideologically conservative agenda of assimilating
language minorities into mainstream U.S. society by subtracting their ancestral cultures and languages?

These questions raise some pointed and difficult issues regarding the nature and
extent of cultural and linguistic pluralism in U.S. society. However, rather than thinking in either/or terms of pluralism or assimilation, perhaps it would be useful to view
U.S. society as a dynamic and complex cultural and linguistic organism—one that is
constantly undergoing evolution and change according to the nature of circumstances.
With this framework, we can envision a constructive pluralism in which cultural and
linguistic maintenance, diversification, and assimilation are taking place simultaneously
under varying circumstances. Within such an environment of constructive pluralism, it
cannot be acceptable to blame the student's genetic, environmental, cultural, or linguistic background for lack of academic success in the English-dominated classroom.
Programs and practices can be implemented to redress some of the past inequities
experienced by all language minority students—both English-background students
who come to our schools speaking stigmatized nonstandard versions of English as
well as students whose primary language is not English. Given the political climate of
the late 1990s, implementation of such programs, however, can resemble paddling a

canoe against a powerful and recurring tide with strong, cold winds buffeting it from the sides. Not to do so, on the other hand, suggests abdicating responsibility for the basic tenets of sound multicultural education.

A good place to start in designing quality programs for language minority students is by examining effective teaching and learning classroom climates for students in general, taking into account the important school reform movements currently evolving. Summarizing and endorsing the case for constructivist classrooms in the educational reform efforts of the 1990s, Fosnot (1993) states that

> constructivism is not a theory about teaching. It's a theory about knowledge and learning. Drawing on a synthesis of current work in cognitive psychology, philosophy, and anthropology, the theory defines knowledge as temporary, developmental, socially and culturally mediated, and thus, non-objective. Learning from this perspective is understood as a self-regulated process of resolving inner cognitive conflicts that often become apparent through concrete experience, collaborative discourse, and reflection. (p. vii)

Fosnot, in Brooks and Brooks (1993), identifies five key principles of such constructive pedagogy: (1) posing problems of emerging relevance to learners; (2) structuring learning around "big ideas" or primary concepts; (3) seeking and valuing students' points of view; (4) adapting curriculum to address students' suppositions; and (5) assessing student learning in the context of teaching (Fosnot, in Brooks & Brooks, 1993, pp. vii–viii).

These principles provide an important reminder of certain basic pedagogical practices that may have validity for all students, regardless of language background, and such practices should not be overlooked when trying to create a "special" program for language-minority students. Nevertheless, a variety of language issues in classroom instruction are unique to addressing the needs of language-minority students.

One unique issue regarding the education of speakers of nonstandard English varieties, such as Black English, Appalachian English, or Hawaiian Creole, is whether their language varieties should be used formally in the classroom. Also, should students be trained to be bidialectical, that is, to be able to switch from their home variety of English to standard English according to the situation? Some educators interpret bidialectalism as a waste of educational effort, suggesting that students need to discard their home language and replace it with standard English, preferably by the time they leave kindergarten. And yet most linguists keep reminding us that suppressing such dialects is confusing and detrimental to the academic and social well-being of students. As proven by the repeated attempts to eradicate nonstandard English varieties for the past fifty years in the schools, such efforts have not been positively correlated with the achievement gains of language-minority students (Ovando & Collier, 1985). The use of nonstandard English itself cannot be singled out as the cause for school failure. As Torrey puts it, "teachers should not judge children's language abilities by their schoolyard grammar" (Torrey, 1983, p. 627). Instead, among the sources of poor academic performance are the school's reaction and approach to nonstandard English. A more positive pedagogical position, states Torrey (1983), is one that affirms the importance of home dialect and its appropriate use within the community in which it is spoken while at the same time students are taught the standard variety. Affirming home language means that students may produce utterances in the classroom in native dialect without being told that they are wrong or that what they say is vulgar or bad. Instead, the teacher analyzes with the students the differences between their dialect and the standard variety: grammatical patterns, pronunciation, vocabulary items, varying social contexts, and so on. (p. 627)

Of course, the challenge for English-language learners is not that they speak a stigmatized variety of English, but rather that their first language is one other than English. A variety of important instructional approaches have been developed to meet the unique needs of these students. Such curricular approaches support the idea that creating bridges between the world of the language-minority student and that of the school will produce positive cognitive, linguistic, and cultural outcomes. For example, in 1980, the California Office of Bilingual Education launched the Case Studies Project, based on leading theories of cognitive development, second-language acquisition, and cross-cultural communication. An integrated curriculum incorporating home language instruction, communication-based sheltered English, and mainstream English has produced excellent results in reading, language arts, and mathematics for language-minority students. Five principles serve as the pedagogical platform for the Case Studies Project:

1. Language development in the home language as well as in English has positive effects on academic achievement.

2. Language proficiency includes proficiency in academic tasks as well as in basic conversation.

3. A LEP student should be able to perform a certain type of academic task in his or her home language before being expected to perform the task in English.

4. Acquisition of English language skills must be provided in contexts in which the student understands what is being said.

5. The social status implicitly ascribed to students and their languages affects student performance. Therefore, majority and minority students should be in classes together in which cooperative learning strategies are used. English speakers should be provided with opportunities to learn the minority languages, and teachers and administrators should model using the minority languages for some noninstructional as well as instructional purposes. (Crawford, 1987)

A two-way bilingual program is one specifically designed to give both languages equal status. In such a program, the English-speaking children learn the minority language at the same time that the language-minority students are learning English.

Collier (1995) found the following five elements to be important for effective two-way bilingual instruction. It is interesting and important to note the important role of sociocultural issues and community involvement among these elements for a successful bilingual program.

> (1) integrated schooling, with English speakers and language minority students learning academically through each others' languages; (2) perceptions among staff, students, and parents that it is a "gifted and talented" program, leading to high expectations for student performance; (3) equal status of the two languages achieved, to a large extent, creating self-confidence among language minority students; (4) healthy parent involvement among both language minority and language majority parents, for closer home-school cooperation; and (5) continuous support for staff development, emphasizing whole language approaches, natural language acquisition through all content areas, cooperative learning, interactive and discovery learning, and cognitive complexity for all proficiency levels. (Collier, 1995, pp. 15–16)

Bilingual programs by definition include an English as a second language (ESL) component, since one of the main goals is to develop the language minority student's proficiency in English. However, many communities do not or are unable to provide bilingual instruction for all language minority students. This occurs for a mixture of reasons involving such factors as politics, the availability of bilingual teachers, and demographics. In such situations, English-language learners are provided with ESL instruction alone, without any significant instruction in their home language. Among the skills important to the ESL teacher are 1) a sound knowledge of theory and methods of language acquisition; 2) an understanding of the relationship between culture and language, identity and adjustment to the new school environment; and 3) the ability to design instruction in such a way to help students become as proficient as possible in content areas such as math, science and social studies at the same time that they are learning English.

Regarding the knowledge of language acquisition, the ESL teacher strives to enable the English-language learner to develop phonology, morphology, syntax, and vocabulary primarily through real communicative activities rather than through such approaches as lecture and drills (Heath, 1986). Crawford (1987) describes such language-rich instruction as follows:

> (a) Content is based on the students' communicative needs; (b) instruction makes extensive use of contextual clues; (c) the teacher uses only English, but modifies speech to students' level and confirms student comprehension; (d) students are permitted to respond in their native language when necessary; (e) the focus is on language function or content, rather than grammatical form; (f) grammatical accuracy is

> promoted, not by correcting errors overtly, but by providing
> more comprehensible instruction; and (g) students are
> encouraged to respond spontaneously and creatively. (p. 43)

With respect to cultural knowledge, effective ESL teachers do not necessarily need to speak the first languages of their students, but they do need to have as broad an understanding as possible of the history, folklore, traditions, values, attitudes and current sociocultural situation of the cultural groups with which they work. This knowledge helps the teacher to understand better the behavior of ESL students as they adjust to life in the United States, and, equally important, it shows the students and their parents that the teacher values the family's cultural background and recognizes that students do not come to him or her as blank tablets but rather as unique individuals with a rich background.

Looking now at the third broad area of expertise for the ESL teacher, we consider the role of the ESL teacher in enabling English-language learners to develop cognitive-academic language proficiency. Two such curricular and instructional approaches are communication-based sheltered English classes and the Cognitive Academic Language Learning Approach (CALLA). Sheltered English is an immersion type of methodology which "shelters" English language learners from "input beyond their comprehension, first in subjects that are less language-intensive, such as mathematics, and later in those that more so, such as social studies" (Crawford, 1987, p. 177). In sheltered English classes, teachers, who may be familiar with the students' first languages and cultures, adjust subject matter content and methodology for students who represent a variety of linguistic backgrounds and who are at about the same level of competence in the target language (Richard-Amato, 1988). As reflected in the Case Studies design, sheltered English classes require that

> teachers change their speech register by slowing down; limiting their vocabulary and sentence length; repeating,
> emphasizing, and explaining key concepts, and using examples, props, visual clues, and body language to convey and
> reinforce meaning carried by the language of instruction.
> (cited in Crawford, 1989, p. 132)

Like sheltered English, CALLA is a content-based ESL instructional model originally developed by Chamot and O'Malley (1986) in response to the lack of academic success of English-language learners. The model supports the notion that by adding academic content to the ESL curriculum and following a specific set of instructional strategies, English-language learners can be prepared for grade-level content classrooms (Chamot & O'Malley, 1994). Buttressed by cognitive theory, research, and ongoing classroom use, CALLA is aimed at English-language learners who are at the advanced beginning and intermediate levels of English-language proficiency. As developed by Chamot and O'Malley (1994), CALLA is compatible with such instructional approaches as language across the curriculum, language experience, whole language, process writing, cooperative learning, and cognitive instruction.

Reflecting the bilingual and ESL principles discussed throughout this section, the California Commission on Teacher Credentialing (1993) has adopted a new design for the preparation of teachers who serve English-language learners. The new design includes two credential variations—a Cross-Cultural, Language and Academic Development (CLAD) emphasis for nonbilingual contexts, and the Bilingual Cross-Cultural, Language and Academic Development (BCLAD) emphasis for bilingual contexts. The CLAD/BCLAD credentials include the following six domains of knowledge and skills in which teachers must show competence: 1) language structure and first- and second-language development; 2) methodology of bilingual, English-language development and content instruction; 3) culture and cultural diversity; 4) methodology for primary language instruction; 5) the culture of emphasis; and 6) the language of emphasis. (The culture and language of emphasis refer to the particular group with whom the teacher is preparing to work, such as Vietnamese, Korean, or Chinese.)

Whether we are talking about speakers of nonstandard varieties of English or non-English speakers, and whether we are talking about bilingual programs, ESL programs, or mainstream classrooms, two common threads run through this entire section on how to address language needs in the multicultural classroom. First, the language the child brings to the classroom must be respected and used as a valuable cognitive tool and as a bridge for development of the language skills that will enable him or her to succeed academically. Second, all language-minority students need rich opportunities to develop the complex language skills they will use in literacy-related school activities and throughout their lives as lifelong learners and thinking, active citizens. In other words, it is insufficient for students to be able to converse with their peers only on the playground or in the halls, or to be able to recite a few rules about standard English. They need to be able to use the context-reduced language associated with extracting meaning from the printed word, for synthesizing and evaluating materials, and for writing. The importance of the development of such high-level skills is illustrated in Collier's research on non-English-speaking students who entered school in the United States at seventh grade and who were not provided with native-language content instruction. Even though they may have had a solid academic background in their home language, in the U.S. school system they tended to fall behind in standardized test norms, except in mathematics, by the time they reached the eleventh grade. Collier (1987) points out that

> as they master enough BICS and develop a wide enough
> range of vocabulary in English to move into deeper develop-
> ment of CALP in second language, they have in the mean-
> time lost 2–3 years of CALP development at their age-grade
> level. This puts them significantly behind in mastery of the
> complex material required for high school students. (p. 12)

The Sociolinguistic Context of Classroom Language Development

An important principle to keep in mind when working with all language minority students—either English or non-English-speaking—is that their cognitive development must be launched from within a given sociolinguistic context. There are no such things as exportable models that work everywhere without adaptation. As Heath (1986) points out, language arts curricula are based on an assumption of a path of language development that is the same for all children, regardless of ethnic origin. Yet the research that establishes such lines of development is predominantly based on middle-class English-speaking families. Only in recent years have ethnographers working in language-minority communities begun to identify culturally different patterns of language socialization experienced by children. One implication of this variation in language development is that the academic success of language-minority students may hinge to some degree on how these children are able to manipulate language in a variety of contexts and for different purposes, rather than on the specific language they use.

In describing the nature of language earlier in this chapter, we listed the culturally influenced domains of language beyond phonology, morphology, syntax and vocabulary—such things as body language, degrees of formality, organizational styles, styles of speech, and appropriate speaking and listening etiquette. Related to these domains is Heath's research on genres. Regarding the specific linguistic elements that are essential for academic success in school regardless of language background, Heath (1986) has summarized the research on genre, which she defines as the

> kind of organizing unit into which smaller units of language, such as conversations, sentences, lists, or directives may fit. Each cultural group has fundamental genres that occur in recurrent situations; and each genre is so patterned as a whole that listeners can anticipate by the prosody or opening formulae what is coming—a joke, a story, or a recounting of shared experiences. Moreover, each sociocultural group recognizes and uses only a few of the total range of genres that humans are capable of producing. (pp. 168–170)

Heath (1986) then argues that in order for students to function well in formal U.S. school settings, they must be able to use a variety of genres typical to U.S. pedagogy, such as label quests, meaning quests, recounts, accounts, event casts, and stories. Label quests are activities in which adults ask children to say their name or to identify an item—"What's that?" or "What kind of _____ is that?" Meaning quests are activities in which an unstated or partly stated meaning is inferred from an oral or written language source. For example, a teacher might ask, "What did the author mean when she wrote, 'Andy kicked the book out of his way'?" In recounts, the child retells an experience that is already known to the teller and the listener. The speaker may be prompted with guiding questions by the adult. Accounts are activities in which the child provides new information to the listener. Accounts are often judged by their logical sequence and their truthfulness. Such accounts are the predecessors of research and creative writing assignments in the upper grades. Event casts are running narratives of events occurring or about to occur. For example, making a gelatin dessert may be accompanied by the mother's sequenced narrative (Heath, 1986).

Heath (1986) indicates that such genres exist in mainstream U.S. school-based activities in a predictable and consistent manner, but that genres may or may not all be consistently present in the same way in the language-minority child's home context.

Heath suggests that it is the school's responsibility to help students acquire these genres by working closely with the ethnolinguistic community. In doing so, teachers can broaden cross-culturally the base of linguistic experiences to maximize their students' opportunities for acquiring such genres. Language-minority students should have access first to these genres in their dominant language. Also, parents who have a limited grasp of English should be encouraged to use their primary language rather than English with their children. Given their limited command of the English language, they will not be able to use English across the variety of suggested genres and thus will limit the quality and range of linguistic interaction with their children. Instead, such parents ideally should concentrate on engaging their children in conversations in their home language that are interesting and also representative of the variety of genres—written and oral—that schools require. Heath suggests that teachers in a creative partnership with ethnolinguistic communities should make a sustained and creative effort to expose students to these school-valued genres, at the same time capitalizing on community genres available.

As noted earlier, there is no single model for addressing the cognitive, linguistic, and cultural needs of all language-minority students. But the principles and designs, and their practical implications discussed here can help educators who are genuinely interested in putting into practice in their classrooms what we have learned over the past thirty years or so about how children acquire their first and second languages, about how they develop cognitively in their primary and secondary languages, and about how they adjust socioculturally to the dominant culture.

Language diversity, as a powerful and ubiquitous ingredient of the U.S. multicultural mosaic, enriches the lives of those who use such languages. It also enriches the lives of monolingual English speakers as they live, study, and work with people of non-English-language background. As educators we have much power to assure that the valuable and varied sociolinguistic experiences of language minorities do not continue to be translated into negative cognitive, cultural, and linguistic outcomes. As suggested in this chapter, we now have some of the conceptual, programmatic, and curricular tools with which to begin the job.

SUMMARY

Throughout this chapter I have stressed the power that language issues have to affect schooling outcomes for language-minority students. In the first section I discussed how language is interwoven with cultural styles and values. As such, language comprises more than grammar rules, vocabulary, and a sound system. To have communicative competence in a language requires not only these things but also many others, such as the appropriate facial and body gestures, the use of varying levels of formality in the appropriate contexts, correct styles of conversation, and the ability to express abstract concepts.

By studying how children learn language, psycholinguists and cognitive psychologists have determined that language learning is a developmental process that goes through predictable stages. Researchers such as Cummins and Collier and Thomas have identified two levels of language proficiency that are particularly important when designing educational programs for language minority students: social language skills, which take approximately two years to develop, and cognitive academic language proficiency, which may take five to seven years or longer to acquire. Equally important is the common underlying proficiency (CUP) proposed by Cummins, the notion that skills learned in the first language will transfer to the second language. This concept is one of the major underpinnings for the value of bilingual instruction.

In the second section of the chapter I surveyed the extensive nature of language variety in the United States. An examination of nonstandard English and Creole languages emphasizes that language changes fulfill sociohistorical needs. Likewise, the language varieties resulting from these changes have their own grammatical and phonological rules and appropriate cultural styles and they are valid means of expression rather than "deficient" language systems. This section also documented that the number of students from non-English-speaking backgrounds continues to increase in the United States, and these students are present in significant numbers throughout the country.

In the final section of the chapter, I described some principles for the instruction of language minority students. In the case of nonstandard English speakers, the home language cannot be blamed for school failure. On the contrary, one cause for language-related school failure is the educator's negating approach toward the home language. Through an additive process, the value of the home language can be affirmed while models are also provided for use of the standard language in appropriate contexts.

For students who come from non-English-speaking backgrounds, an active, hands-on teaching style rather than a lecture style is needed, with frequent checking for understanding. Concepts, knowledge base, and thinking skills ideally should be developed in the home language through bilingual instruction, which, of course, includes an ESL component. Regarding ESL instruction, social communicative skills—which may be acquired fairly rapidly—are not sufficient for academic success. Schools must continue to provide support for language-minority students to achieve cognitive-academic language proficiency in English.

Finally, there is a need for the continued development and maintenance of social and cultural bridges between the language-minority student's home life and school life. An awareness of how language is used in the home community will enable educators to be sensitive to school genres that are different. Efforts to equalize the social and linguistic status of majority and minority students within the school setting will also produce positive results for all students in the classroom and, ultimately, in society.

Questions and Activities

1. What are some of the major characteristics of a language? What role does language play in the maintenance of a culture?

2. How can teachers draw on the home experiences of non-English speakers and speakers of nonstandard varieties of English to help these students develop competence in standard English?

3. What are some common misconceptions about Black English and how can they be overcome? How can a knowledge of the nature of Black English be helpful to teachers of African American students?

4. What special problems do language-minority students experience in schools? What programs and practices can schools implement to help these students experience educational success?

5. Prepare a debate on the pros and cons of bilingual education.

6. Interview officials in a nearby school district to get a profile of local language diversity. Find out how many different languages are spoken by the students in the district and what programs are being implemented to address the needs of these students.

7. Identity some principles for working effectively with language-minority students. What support and training might teachers need to implement these principles in the classroom? Interview an ESL teacher, a bilingual teacher, or a teacher who has many nonstandard English speakers in his or her classroom. Discuss what concepts, principles, and methods this teacher uses for students' language and academic development.

References

Anttila, R. (1972). *An Introduction to Historical and Comparative Linguistics.* New York: Macmillan.

Barringer, F. (1993, April 28). Immigration in 80's Made English a Foreign Language for Millions. *New York Times*, A1, A10.

Brooks, J. G. and Brooks, M. G. (Eds.). (1993) *In Search of Understanding: The Case for Constructivist Classrooms.* Alexandria, VA: ASCD.

California Commission on Teacher Credentialing. (1993, May 19). *CLAD/BCLAD: California's New Design for the Preparation and Credentialing of Teachers of Limited-English-Proficient Students.* Sacramento: Author.

Chamot, A. U. and O'Malley, J. M. (1986). *A Cognitive Academic Language Learning Approach: An ESL Content-Based Curriculum.* Washington, DC: National Clearinghouse for Bilingual Education.

Chamot, A. U. and O'Malley, J. M. (1994). *The CALLA Handbook: Implementing the Cognitive Academic Language Learning Approach.* Reading, MA: Addison-Wesley.

Collier, V. P. (1987, April 23). Age and Rate of Acquisition of Cognitive-Academic Second Language Proficiency. Paper presented at the American Educational Research Association Meeting.

Collier, V. P. (1995). Second Language Acquisition for School: Academic, Cognitive, Sociocultural and Linguistic Processes. Paper presented at the Georgetown University Round Table (GURT).

Cortés, C. E. (1986). The Education of Language Minority Students: A Contextual Interaction Model. In California State Department of Education. *Beyond Language: Social and Cultural Factors in Schooling Language Minority Students.* Los Angeles: Evaluation, Dissemination, and Assessment Center, California State University.

Crawford, J. (1987, April 1). Bilingual Education: Language, Learning, and Politics. *Education Week: A Special Report*, 43.

Cummins, J. (1979). Cognitive/Academic Language Proficiency, Linguistic Interdependence, the Optimal Age Question, and Some Other Matters. *Working Papers on Bilingualism, 9,* 1–43.

Cummins, J. (1981). The Role of Primary Language Development in Promoting Educational Success for Language Minority Students. In California State Department of Education. *Schooling and Language Minority Students: A Theoretical Framework.* Los Angeles: National Evaluation, Dissemination, and Assessment Center, California State University.

Cummins, J. (1991). Interdependence of First- and Second-Language Proficiency in Bilingual Children. In E. Bialystok (Ed.). *Language Processing in Bilingual Children* (pp. 70–89). Cambridge: Cambridge University Press.

Fosnot, C. T. (1993). Preface. In J. G. Brooks and M. G. Brooks (Eds.). *In Search of Understanding: The Case for Constructivist Classrooms.* Alexandria, VA: ASCD.

Fuentes, C. (1988). *Myself with Others: Selected Essays.* New York: Farrar, Straus & Giroux.

Heath, S. B. (1986). Sociocultural Contexts of Language Development. In California State Department of Education. *Beyond Language: Social & Cultural Factors in Schooling Language Minority Students.* Los Angeles: National Evaluation, Dissemination, and Assessment Center, California State University.

Hymes, D. H. (1981). Foreword. In C. A. Ferguson and S. B. Heath (Eds.). *Language in the USA.* Cambridge: Cambridge University Press.

Krauss, M. (1995, February 3). Keynote Address: *Endangered Languages: Current Issues and Future Prospects.* Dartmouth College, Hanover, NH.

Labov, W., Cohen, P., Robins, C., and Lewis, J. (1968). *A Study of the Non-Standard English of Negro and Puerto Rican Speakers in New York City, Report. on Cooperative Research Project 3288.* New York: Columbia University.

Masahiko, M. and Ovando, C. J. (1995). Language Issues in Multicultural Contexts. In J. A. Banks and C. A. M. Banks (Eds.). *Handbook of Research on Multicultural Education* (pp. 427–444). New York: Macmillan.

McKeon, D. (1992). Introduction. In *TESOL Resource Packet* (p. i). Alexandria, VA: TESOL.

National Association for Bilingual Education. (n.d.). *Fact Sheet Need for Additional Funding for the Federal Bilingual Education Act.* Washington, DC: Author.

Nichols, P. (1981). Creoles of the USA. In C. A. Ferguson and S. B. Heath (Eds.). *Language in the USA.* Cambridge: Cambridge University Press.

Ovando, C. J. (1983, April). Bilingual/Bicultural Education: Its Legacy and Its Future. *Phi Delta Kappan, 64*(8), 566.

Ovando, C. J. and Collier, V. P. (1985). *Bilingual and ESL Classrooms: Teaching in Multicultural Contexts.* New York: McGraw-Hill.

Ramírez, D. (1991, March 15). Study Finds Native Language Instruction Is a Plus. *NABE News, 14*(5), 1.

Richard-Amato, P. A. (1988). *Making It Happen: Interaction in the Second Language Classroom.* New York: Longman.

Shaumyan, S. (1987). *A Semiotic Theory of Language.* Bloomington: Indiana University Press.

Torrey, J. W. (1983, Winter). Black Children's Knowledge of Standard English. *American Educational Research Journal, 20*(4), 627.

Ulibarri, D. M. (1986). Issues in Estimates of the Number of Limited English Proficient Students. In *A Report of the Compendium of Papers on the Topic of Bilingual Education of the Committee on Education and Labor House of Representatives, 99th Congress, 2D Session*. Washington, DC: U.S. Government Printing Office.

U.S. Department of Education. (1992). *The Condition of Bilingual Education: A Report to the Congress and the President*. Washington, DC: U.S. Government Printing Office.

Waugh, D. and Koon, B. (1974). *Breakthrough for Bilingual Education*. Washington, DC: U.S. Commission on Civil Rights.

Wertsch, J. V. (1985). *Vygotsky and the Social Formation of Mind*. Cambridge: Harvard University Press.

Whatley, W. (1981). Language among Black Americans. In C. A. Ferguson and S. B. Heath (Eds.). *Language in the USA*. Cambridge: Cambridge University Press.

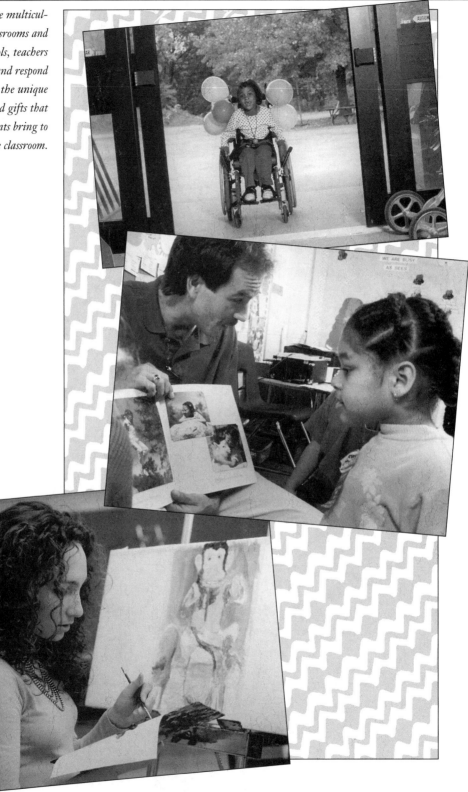

In effective multicultural classrooms and schools, teachers recognize and respond effectively to the unique talents and gifts that such students bring to the classroom.

Exceptionality

Expanded rights for students with disabilities was one major consequence of the civil rights movement of the 1960s and 1970s. The Supreme Court's Brown decision, issued in 1954, established the principle that to segregate students solely because of their race is inherently unequal and unconstitutional. This decision, as well as other legal and social reforms of the 1960s, encouraged advocates for the rights of students with disabilities to push for expanded rights for them. If it were unconstitutional to segregate students because of their race, it was reasoned, segregating students because they were disabled could also be challenged.

The advocates for the rights of students with disabilities experienced a major victory in 1975 when Congress enacted Public Law 94-142, The Education for All Handicapped Children Act. This act was unprecedented and revolutionary in its implications. It requires free public education for all children with disabilities, nondiscriminatory evaluation, and an individualized education program (IEP) for each student with a disability. The act also stipulates that each student with a disability should be educated in the least restricted environment. This last requirement has been one of the most controversial provisions of Public Law 94-142. Most students who are classified as disabled—about 90 percent—are mildly disabled. Consequently, most students with disabilities—about two-thirds—spend at least part of the school day in regular classrooms. Students with disabilities who are taught in the regular classroom are mainstreamed; this process is called mainstreaming.

Exceptionality intersects with factors such as gender and race or ethnicity in interesting and complex ways. Males and students of color are more frequently classified as special education students than are females and White mainstream students. Nearly twice as many males as females are classified as special education students. Consequently, males of color are the most likely group to be classified as mentally retarded or learning disabled. The higher proportion of males and students of color in special education programs is related to the fact that mental retardation is a socially constructed category (see chapter 1).

Disabled as well as gifted students are considered exceptional. Exceptional students are those who have learning or behavioral characteristics that differ substantially from most other students and that require special attention in instruction. Concern for U.S. students who are gifted and talented increased after the Soviet Union successfully launched Sputnik in 1957. A Gifted and Talented Children's Education Act was passed by Congress in 1978. However, the nation's concern for the gifted is ambivalent and controversial. In 1982, special funding for gifted education was consolidated with twenty-nine other educational programs. The controversy over gifted education stems in part from the belief by many people that it is elitist. Others argue that gifted education is a way for powerful mainstream parents to acquire a special education for their children in the public schools. The fact that few students of color are classified as gifted is another source of controversy. Despite the controversies that surround programs for gifted and talented youths, schools need to find creative and democratic ways to satisfy the needs of these students.

The chapters in this part describe the major issues, challenges, and promises involved in creating equal educational opportunities for students who are exceptional—those with mental retardation as well as those who are intellectually gifted and talented.

Chapter 13

Educational Equality for Students with Disabilities

William L. Heward and Rodney A. Cavanaugh

Children differ from one another. Place yourself as a casual observer in any classroom in any school and you will immediately notice differences in children's height, weight, style of dress, hair and skin color, and other physical characteristics. Look a bit closer and you will see some obvious differences in children's language and their interpersonal and scholastic attributes. Look closer still and you will begin to recognize how individual children respond differently to the content of academic and social curricula and to the pedagogy of the classroom.

Children also differ from one another in ways that are usually not apparent to a casual observer. Differences in the educational opportunities children receive and the benefits they derive from their time in school are two examples. The educational implications of gender, race, social class, religion, ethnicity, and language diversity not only influence how children may respond to curriculum and instruction but also affect the structure and design of educational systems in general.

While gender, social class, race, ethnicity, and language differences increasingly characterize U.S. classrooms and influence equitable access to the benefits of educational programs, every classroom can also be characterized by students' *skill diversity*. Some children learn quickly and easily apply what they learn to new situations. Other children must be given repeated practice to master a simple task and then may have difficulty successfully completing the same task the next day. Some children are popular and have many friends. Others are ostracized because they have not learned how to be friendly. Some children can run fast, while others cannot run at all.

The skill differences among most children are relatively small, allowing most children to benefit from the general education program offered by their schools. When the physical, social, and academic skills of children differ to such an extent that typical school curricula or teaching methods are neither appropriate nor effective, however, equitable access to and benefits from educational programs are at stake.

Since 1975, federal legislation has mandated educational equality for learners with disabilities through individualized programs of special education. Like the rest of the chapters in your text, this chapter is not about surface or educationally irrelevant differences among individual children. Nor does it propose that teachers are casual observers. Teachers must have the knowledge and skills to recognize and to be appropriately responsive to the diversity their students represent. This chapter extends the concept of diversity to include children with disabilities and to lay the foundation for teachers to examine educational equity for learners with diverse skills.

In this chapter we briefly outline the history of exclusion and educational inequality experienced by many students with disabilities in the nation's schools. We also examine the progress made during the past two decades, paying particular attention to the Individuals with Disabilities Education Act (IDEA), federal legislation that requires that all children, regardless of the type or severity of their disabilities, be provided with appropriate educational programs. We look at the key features of this landmark law, the outcomes of its implementation, and the major barriers that still stand in the way of true educational equity for students with disabilities. But first, let us take a closer look at the concept of disability and examine when skill diversity necessitates special education.

WHO ARE STUDENTS WITH DISABILITIES?

When the term *exceptional* is used to describe students, it includes both children who have difficulty learning and children whose performance is advanced. The performance of children who are exceptional differs from the norm (either above or below) to such an extent that individualized programs of special education are necessary to meet their diverse needs. *Exceptional* is an inclusive term that describes not only students with severe disabilities but also students who are gifted and talented. This chapter focuses on children with disabilities—those for whom learning is a significant challenge.

The term *disability* refers to the loss or reduced function of a certain body part or organ; impairment is often used synonymously with disability. A child with a disability cannot perform certain tasks (e.g., walking, speaking, seeing) in the same way in which most nondisabled children do. A disability does not constitute a handicap, however, unless the disability leads to educational, personal, social, vocational, or other challenges for the individual. For example, a child with one arm who can function in and out of school without special support or accommodations is not considered handicapped. Similarly, a child, who may not read as fluently as his or her classmates, but whose progress in his or her grade-level curriculum is commensurate with his or her peers, is not handicapped.

Handicap refers to the challenges a person with a disability experiences when interacting with the environment. Some disabilities pose a handicap in some environments but not in others. The child with only one arm may be handicapped when playing with nondisabled classmates on the playground, but having the use of only one arm might not pose a handicap in the classroom. Unlike the term *exceptional*, the term *handicapped* does not include students who are gifted and talented.

Children not currently identified as handicapped, but who are considered to have a higher-than-normal chance of developing a handicap, are referred to as *at risk*. This term is used with infants and preschoolers who, because of difficulties experienced at birth or conditions in the home environment, may be expected to have developmental problems as they grow older. Some educators also use the term to refer to students who are having learning problems in the regular classroom and are therefore "at risk" of being identified as handicapped and in need of special education services. Physicians also use the terms *at risk* or *high risk* to identify pregnancies in which there is a higher-than-usual probability of the baby's being born with a physical or developmental disability.

When a physical, behavioral, or cognitive disability adversely affects the learning and development of a student, it is considered an educational handicap. Students with disabilities are entitled to special education and related services because their physical or behavioral attributes conform to one or more of the following categories of disability:

- Mental retardation or developmental disabilities (Beirne-Smith, Patton, & Ittenbach, 1994)

- Learning disabilities (Mercer, 1992)

- Behavior disorders or emotional disturbance (Kauffman, 1993)

- Communication (speech and language) disorders (Shames, Wiig, & Secord, 1994)

- Hearing impairments (Paul & Quigley, 1994)

- Visual impairments (Barraga & Erin, 1992)

- Physical and other health impairments (Bigge, 1991)

- Severe and multiple disabilities (Meyer, Peck, & Brown, 1991; Snell, 1993)

- Autism (Matson, 1994)

- Traumatic brain injury (Gerring & Carney, 1992)

It is beyond the purpose and scope of this chapter to describe the defining characteristics and educational implications of each type of exceptionality. Interested readers should refer to the sources identified in the References to obtain information about each area.

Regardless of the terms used to refer to students who exhibit diversity in academic, vocational, and social skills, it is incorrect to believe that there are two kinds of students—those who are exceptional and those who are typical. All children differ from one another to some extent. Exceptional students are those whose skill diversity is significant enough to require a specially designed program of instruction in order to achieve educational equality.

Students who are exceptional are more like other students than they are different from them. All students are alike in that all students can benefit from an appropriate education, an education that empowers students to do things they were previously unable to do and to do them with greater independence and enjoyment.

Disability as a Social Construct

The proposition that some (perhaps all) disabilities are social constructs merits attention in any discussion of educational equity for exceptional children (Coleman, 1966; Danforth, 1995; Sleeter, 1986). The issue is perhaps particularly relevant to a text about multicultural education (Huebner, 1994).

The establishment of membership criteria in any group is, by definition, socially constructed because the criteria have been created by human beings (Banks & Banks, 1993). How educational communities respond to the cultural- , ethnic- , gender- , and class-specific attributes children bring to the classroom is more important than how they perceive the establishment of membership criteria for a particular group. Education's response to the diversity children represent will influence their achievement as well as the professional and societal judgments about that achievement.

Children who are poor or whose ethnicity is not White European American are generally underrepresented in programs for children who are gifted and talented and overrepresented in programs for children who experience learning difficulties (Correa & Heward, 1996). There is evidence that some children's so-called disabilities are primarily the result of culture, class, or gender influences that are at odds with the culture, class, or gender that has established a given category of disability and the assessment procedures used to make those determinations (Grossman, 1995). As we discuss later in this chapter, a significant focus of special education litigation and legislation has dealt directly with these inequities.

Deconstructing the traditional sociopolitical view of exceptionality, changing social group membership, or passing legislation will not, however, eliminate the real challenges students with disabilities experience in acquiring fundamental academic, self-help, personal-social, and vocational skills. While the criteria for determining the presence or absence of a disability may be hypothetical social constructions, the handicaps created by educational disabilities are not (Fuchs & Fuchs, 1995a).

Our discussion of students with disabilities and of the role special education plays in addressing their needs assumes that a child's physical, behavioral, or cognitive skill diversity is influenced by, but also transcends, other variables such as ethnicity and social class. We also assume that the educational challenges students with disabilities experience represent real and significant barriers to their ability to experience independence and personal satisfaction across a wide range of life experiences and circumstances. Many factors will contribute to educational equality for children with disabilities. Among the most important of these factors is carefully planned and systematically delivered instruction with meaningful and future-oriented curricula.

Classification of Exceptional Students

The classification of students according to the various categories of exceptionality is done largely under the presumption that students in each category share certain physical, behavioral, and learning characteristics that hold important implications for planning and delivering educational services. It is a mistake, however, to believe that once a child has been identified as belonging to a certain disability category, his or her educational needs and the manner in which those needs should be met have also been identified.

The classification and labeling of exceptional students have been widely debated for many years. Some educators believe that a workable system of classification is necessary to obtain the special educational services and programs that are prerequisite to educational equality for exceptional students. Others argue that the classification and labeling of exceptional students serve only to exclude them from the mainstream of educational opportunities. The classification of exceptional students is a complex issue affected not only by educational considerations, but by social, political, and emotional concerns as well. Research conducted to assess the effects of labeling has been of little help, with most of the studies contributing inconclusive and contradictory evidence (MacMillan, 1988). Here is a summary of the most common arguments given for and against the labeling of students who are exceptional (Heward, 1996).

Possible Advantages of Labeling

- Categories can relate diagnosis to specific treatment.
- Labeling helps professionals communicate with one another and to classify and assess research findings.
- Funding of special education programs is often based on specific categories of exceptionality.
- Labels allow special-interest groups to promote specific programs and to spur legislative action.
- Labeling helps make the special needs of exceptional children more visible to the public.

Possible Disadvantages of Labeling

- Labels usually focus on negative aspects of the child, causing other people to think about the child only in terms of inadequacies or defects. Labels tend to identify what the child cannot do rather than what the child can or might be able to learn to do.
- Labels may cause other people to react to and hold low expectations of a child based on the label, resulting in a self-fulfilling prophecy.
- Labels that describe a child's performance deficit often mistakenly acquire the role of explanatory constructs (e.g., "Sherry acts that way because she is emotionally disturbed.").
- Labels suggest that learning problems are primarily the result of something wrong within the child, thereby reducing the systematic examination of and accountability for instructional variables as the cause of performance diversity. This is an especially damaging outcome when the label provides educators with a built-in excuse for ineffective instruction (e.g., "Jalen hasn't learned to read because he's _____.")
- A label may contribute to a child to development of a poor self-concept.

- Labels may lead peers to reject or ridicule the labeled child.
- Labels have a certain permanence about them. Once labeled as retarded or learning disabled, a child has difficulty ever achieving the status of being just like the other kids.
- Labels often provide a basis for keeping students out of the regular classroom.
- The classification of exceptional children requires the expenditure of much professional and student time that could be better spent in planning, delivering, and receiving instruction.

There are many reasons both for and against the classification and labeling of students who are exceptional. At one level, classification can be seen as a way to organize the funding and administration of special education programs in the schools. In fact, the federal government and most states and school districts allocate money and resources according to the number of students in each category of exceptionality. To receive an individualized program of educational services to meet his or her needs, a student must first be identified as having a disability and then, with few exceptions, be further classified into one of the categories, such as for learning disabilities or visual impairment. So, in practice, being labeled as belonging to a given disability category, and therefore being exposed to all of the potential disadvantages that label carries with it, is prerequisite to receiving the special education services necessary to achieve educational equality. Many educators are aware of this problem and argue that the classification and labeling of exceptional students by category of condition actually interfere with the kind of assessment and instruction most needed by the student. Stainback and Stainback (1984), for example, contend that

> these categories often do not reflect the specific educational needs and interests of students in relation to such services. For example, some students categorized as visually handicapped may not need large print books, while others who are not labeled visually impaired and thus are ineligible for large print books could benefit from their use. Similarly, not all students labeled behaviorally disordered may need self-control training, while some students not so labeled may need self-control training as a part of their educational experience. Such categories . . . actually interfere with providing some students with the services they require to progress toward their individual educational goals. Eligibility for educational and related services should be based on the abilities, interests, and needs of each student as they relate to instructional options and services, rather than on the student's inclusion in a categorical group. (p. 105)

The benefits and detriments of labeling children with disabilities may be summed up with two contrasting outcomes. Classification generally has a positive impact for groups of exceptional children because of funding structures for special education services and because of facilitated organizational and advocacy efforts by educators, parents, and persons with disabilities. On the other hand, classification may have a negative impact on individual children because of the connotation labels carry and the limited value for guiding instructional practice and policy. A major challenge facing education today lies in determining how to meet the individual needs of exceptional students without subjecting them to the negative outcomes that labeling fosters.

Regardless of what labels may or may not do for children with disabilities, labels don't teach. Becker, Engelmann, and Thomas's (1971) advice is still pertinent today: "For the most part the labels are not important. They rarely tell the teacher who can be taught in what way. One could put five or six labels on the same child and still not know what to teach him or how" (pp. 435–436).

How Many Exceptional Students Are There?

It is impossible to know for certain how many students with disabilities there are in U.S. schools. Six reasons for this uncertainty are:

1. State and local school systems use different criteria for identifying exceptional students.

2. The identification of students with disabilities is not completely systematic because of the less-than-exact nature of screening and assessment procedures.

3. The significant role played by subjective judgment in interpreting the results of referral and assessment data makes identification inconsistent from case to case.

4. The number of students with disabilities identified by a given school is affected by the school's relative success in providing instructional support to the regular classroom teacher so that a student who is at-risk does not become a student with a disability.

5. The relative ability of a school system to provide special education services for every student identified as having a disability (a requirement of federal legislation) may affect how diligently the school system works to identify students with exceptional needs.

6. A student might be identified as disabled at one time and as not disabled (or included in another disability category) at another time (e.g., Halgren & Clarizio, 1993; Wolman, Thurlow, & Bruininks, 1989).

In spite of the difficulty these and other factors pose in determining the actual number of students with disabilities, data are available showing how many students with disabilities receive special education services in the United States. Each year, the U.S. Department of Education, Office of Special Education and Rehabilitation Services (OSERS), submits a report to Congress on the education of children with disabilities. The most recent information available is for the 1992–1993 school year (U.S. Department of Education, 1994).

Consider these eight statements about students with disabilities and the extent to which they receive special education in the United States:

- More than 5.1 million children with disabilities, or 7.4 percent of the resident population from birth to age twenty-one, received special education services during the 1992–1993 school year.

- The number of children and youth who receive special education has increased every year since a national count was begun in 1976, with an overall increase of 39 percent since 1976–1977. New early intervention programs have been major contributors to the increases since 1986. During 1992–1993, 459,728 preschoolers (4 percent of the population age three to five) and 143,392 infants and toddlers (1.2 percent of all children from birth through age two) were among those receiving special education.

- Children with disabilities in special education represent approximately 8 percent of the entire school-age population.

- The number of children who receive special education increases from age three through age nine. The number served decreases gradually with each successive age year after age nine until age seventeen. After age seventeen, the number of students receiving special education decreases sharply.

- Nearly 94 percent of all school-age children receiving special education are reported under four disability categories: learning disabilities (52.4 percent), speech and language impairment (22.2 percent), mental retardation (10.9 percent), and emotional disturbance (8.3 percent).

- The percentage of school-age students receiving special education under the learning disabilities category has grown dramatically (from 23.8 percent to 52.4 percent), while the percentage of students with mental retardation has decreased (from 24.9 percent to 10.9 percent) since the federal government began collecting and reporting child count data in 1976–1977.

- About twice as many males as females receive special education.

- The vast majority—approximately 90 percent—of school-age children receiving special education have "mild disabilities."

HISTORY OF EDUCATIONAL EQUALITY FOR STUDENTS WITH DISABILITIES

If a society can be judged by the way it treats people who are different, our educational system would not be judged very favorably. Students who are different, whether because of race, culture, language, gender, or exceptionality, have often been denied equal access to educational opportunities. For many years, educational opportunity of any kind did not exist for many students with disabilities. Students with severe disabilities were completely excluded from public schools. Before 1970, many states had laws permitting local school districts to deny access to children whose physical or intellectual disability caused them, in the opinion of school officials, to be unable to benefit from instruction.

Most students with disabilities were enrolled in school, but perhaps half of the nation's children with disabilities were denied an appropriate education through what H. R. Turnbull (1993) calls "functional exclusion." The students were allowed to come to school but were not participating in an educational program designed to meet their special needs. Students with mild learning and behavior problems remained in the regular classroom but were given no special help. If they failed to make satisfactory progress in the curriculum, they were called "slow learners"; if they acted-out in class, they were called "disciplinary problems" and were suspended from school.

For students who did receive a program of differentiated curriculum or instruction, special education usually meant a separate education in segregated classrooms and special schools isolated from the mainstream of education. These children were labeled *mentally retarded, crippled,* or *emotionally disturbed.* Special education often meant a classroom specially reserved for students who could not measure up in the regular classroom. The following passage exemplified what was too often a common occurrence:

> I accepted my first teaching position in a special education class in a basement room next door to the furnace. Of the fifteen "educable mentally retarded" children assigned to work with me, most were simply nonreaders from poor families. One child had been banished to my room because she posed a behavior problem to her fourth-grade teacher. My class and I were assigned a recess spot on the opposite side of the play yard, far away from the "normal" children. I was the only teacher who did not have a lunch break. I was required to eat with my "retarded" children while the other teachers were permitted to leave their students. (Aiello, 1976, p. 14)

As society's concepts of equality, freedom, and justice have expanded, education's response to students with disabilities has changed slowly but considerably over the past several decades. Educational opportunity has gradually shifted from a pattern of exclusion and isolation to one of integration and participation. But change has not come easily, nor has it occurred by chance. Judiciary and legislative authority has been necessary to begin to correct educational inequities for children with disabilities.

Today's efforts to ensure educational equality for students with disabilities can be viewed as an outgrowth of the civil rights movement. All of the issues and events that helped shape society's attitudes during the 1950s and 1960s affected the development of special education for exceptional students, particularly the 1954 landmark case of *Brown* v. *Board of Education of Topeka* (1954). This case challenged the practice, common in 1954, of segregating schools according to the race of the children. The U.S. Supreme Court ruled that education must be available to all children on equal terms, and that it is unconstitutional to operate segregated schools under the premise that they are separate but equal.

The *Brown* decision initiated a period of intense questioning by parents of children with disabilities who wondered why the same principles of equal access to education did not also apply to their children. Numerous cases challenging the exclusion and isolation of children with disabilities by the schools were brought to court by parents and advocacy groups. At issue in these cases were numerous questions, including (1) the fairness of intelligence testing and the legitimacy of placing children in special education classes solely on the basis of those tests, (2) intelligence testing and other assessment instruments that were not administered in a child's native language or were otherwise culturally biased, and (3) arguments by schools that they could not afford to educate exceptional students. One of the most influential court cases in the development of educational equality for exceptional students was the 1972 *Pennsylvania Association for Retarded Children v. Commonwealth of Pennsylvania* (1972). The association (PARC) brought the class-action suit to challenge a state law that enabled public schools to deny education to children they considered "unable to profit from public school attendance."

The attorneys and parents who represented PARC argued that it was neither rational nor necessary to assume that the children were uneducable. Because the state could neither prove that the children were uneducable nor demonstrate a rational basis for excluding them from public school programs, the court decided that the children were entitled to a free public education. Other court cases followed with similar rulings—children with disabilities, like all other people in the United States, are entitled to the same rights and protection under the law as guaranteed in the Fourteenth Amendment, which declares that people may not be deprived of their equality or liberty on the basis of any classification such as race, nationality, or religion.

The phrase *"progressive integration"* (Reynolds, 1989) has been used to describe the history of special education and the gradual but unrelenting progress of ensuring equal educational opportunity for all children. Of the many court cases involving education for children with disabilities, no case resulted in sweeping educational reform. With each instance of litigation, however, the assembly of what was to become the Individuals with Disabilities Education Act (IDEA) became more complete. Together, all of these developments contributed to the passage of a federal law concerning educational equality for students with disabilities.

THE INDIVIDUALS WITH DISABILITIES EDUCATION ACT: A LEGISLATIVE MANDATE FOR EDUCATIONAL EQUALITY FOR STUDENTS WITH DISABILITIES

Public Law 94-142 (1975), originally titled the Education for All Handicapped Children Act, but since amended as the Individuals with Disabilities Education Act (IDEA), was reluctantly signed by President Gerald Ford, who expressed concern that the federal government was promising more than it could deliver. This legislation represented the culmination of the efforts of a great many parents, educators, and legislators to bring together under one comprehensive law the requirements and safeguards deemed necessary if students with disabilities were to experience educational equality.

Many parents and educators expected PL 94-142 to improve educational opportunities for students with disabilities (Turnbull, 1993). These predictions proved accurate, as IDEA is a landmark piece of legislation that changed the face of education in this country. This law has affected every school in the country and has changed the roles of regular and special educators, school administrators, parents, and many others who are involved in the educational process.

As it does with other comprehensive federal laws, Congress periodically reauthorizes and amends PL 94-142. Since its passage, the law has been amended three times. In 1982, the administration attempted to revise some of the rules and regulations governing the law's implementation. Had these changes been successful, the law would have been weakened in several respects. Advocacy groups composed of parents and professionals rallied to voice their opposition to these proposed changes. As a result, in 1983, when the law was amended for the first time (PL 98-199), Congress reaffirmed all of the major provisions of the law and included language that would expand research and services aimed at easing the transition from school to work for high school students. This initial amendment also provided for increases in funding for a number of programs.

Three years later, Congress passed the Education Amendments of 1986. This legislation was aimed at expanding special educational services to three- to five-year-old children. These amendments required school districts to provide full educational services to this population of young children by the beginning of the 1990-1991 school year. In addition, financial incentives were established to encourage schools to initiate programs for children from birth through age two.

In 1990, Congress changed the law's title to the Individuals with Disabilities Education Act (IDEA). This law (PL 101-476) retained all of the basic provisions of PL 94-142. It also made several important additions, including "autism" and "traumatic brain injury," to the categories of exceptionality covered by the original legislation, and specific requirements for helping secondary students make the transition from school to adult life.

There have also been numerous legal challenges to the IDEA. These challenges have focused primarily on what constitutes a free, appropriate education in the least restrictive environment. In spite of these challenges, the basic rules it originally outlined still govern the education of students with disabilities.

Major Components of the Individuals with Disabilities Education Act (IDEA)

The IDEA mandates that all children with disabilities between the ages of three and twenty-one, regardless of the type or severity of their disability, shall receive a free, appropriate public education. This education must be provided at public expense—that is, without cost to the child's parents. The IDEA is directed primarily at the states, which are responsible for providing education to their citizens. Each state education agency must comply with the law by locating and identifying all children with disabilities. The majority of the many rules and regulations defining how the IDEA operates are related to six major principles that have remained unchanged since 1975 (Strickland, & Turnbull, 1993; Turnbull, 1993).

Zero Reject

Schools are prohibited from excluding any child solely because the child has a disability. This fundamental requirement of the law is based on the proposition that all children with disabilities can learn and benefit from an appropriate education, and that schools, therefore, do not have the right to deny any child access to equal educational opportunity.

The principle of zero reject means more than schools not denying children educational opportunities. When designing educational programs for children with disabilities, the intent of the term *equality* is not limited to equal access alone. The definition is broader in that children with disabilities are also entitled to different types of services because their disabilities justify special educational approaches (Turnbull, 1993).

Nondiscriminatory Evaluation

The IDEA requires that students with disabilities be evaluated fairly. Assessment must be nondiscriminatory. This requirement of IDEA is particularly important because of the disproportionate number of children from non-White and non-English-speaking cultural groups who were identified as having disabilities, often solely on the basis of a score from standardized intelligence tests. Both of the intelligence tests that have been used most often in the identification of students with learning problems had been developed based on the performance of White, middle-class children. Because of their Anglocentric nature, the tests are often considered to be unfairly biased against children from diverse cultural groups who have had less of an opportunity to learn the knowledge sampled by the test items (Mercer, 1973). The IDEA states clearly that the results of one test cannot be used as the sole criterion for placement into a special education program. Ortiz and Garcia (1988) have developed a prereferral process for preventing inappropriate placements of culturally diverse students in special education.

In addition to nondiscriminatory assessment, testing must be multifactored to include as many tests and observational techniques as necessary to fairly and appropriately identify an individual child's strengths and weaknesses.

A child who has been referred for a multifactored assessment for a learning disability, for example, must be evaluated by several individuals across several different social and academic areas. The school psychologist may administer several different tests in order to obtain reliable data about the child's ability and achievement levels. The school counselor may observe the child in various academic settings as well as nonacademic settings such as the playground and lunchroom. Observational data from the child's teachers and samples of the child's work should be compiled. A speech and language therapist, occupational therapist, rehabilitation counselor, or social worker may also be included in the assessment process. Finally, parental input and the child's own perceptions of his or her needs should be obtained and documented. The result of these efforts should be an accurate picture of the child's current levels of performance, with clear indications as to what type of educational program will be most appropriate.

Individualized Education Program

Perhaps the most significant aspect of the IDEA is the requirement that an *individualized education program (IEP)* be developed and implemented for each child with a disability. The law is very specific in identifying the kind of information an IEP must include and who is to be involved in its development. Each IEP must be created by a child-study team consisting of (at least) the child's teacher(s), a representative of the local school district, the child's parents or guardians, and, whenever appropriate, the child. For suggestions on how students with disabilities can participate in the IEP process, see Peters (1990) and Van Reusen and Bos (1990, 1994).

Many child-study teams include professionals from various disciplines such as school psychology, physical therapy, and medicine. Special education experts believe that an interdisciplinary team whose members represent varied training, experience, and points of view is best able to determine the special educational and related services that many students with disabilities need (Thomas, Correa, & Morsink, 1995).

The particular formats of IEPs vary from school district to school district, but all must include the following content:

1. A statement of the child's present level of educational performance.

2. A statement of the annual goals to be achieved by the end of the school year in each area requiring specially designed instruction.

3. Short-term objectives stated in measurable, intermediate steps between the present level of performance and the annual goals.

4. The specific educational and related services (e.g., transportation, physical therapy) needed by the child, including the physical education program and any special instructional media and materials that are needed.

5. The date by which those services will begin and the anticipated length of time the services will be provided.

6. A description of the extent to which the child will participate in the regular education program of the school.

7. A statement of the needed transition services (e.g., community-based work experience) for students, beginning no later than age sixteen and annually thereafter (when determined appropriate for the individual, beginning at age fourteen or younger), including, when appropriate, a statement of the interagency responsible or linkages (or both) before the student leaves the school setting.

8. Objective criteria, procedures, and schedules for determining, at least annually, whether the short-term objectives are being achieved.

9. A justification for the type of educational placement being recommended for the child.

10. A list of the individuals responsible for implementing the IEP.

Although the IEP is a written document signed by both school personnel and the child's parents, it is not a legally binding contract. That is, parents cannot take their child's teachers or the school to court if all goals and objectives stated in the IEP are not met. However, schools should be able to document that the services described in the IEP have been provided in a systematic effort to meet those goals. IEPs must be reviewed by the child-study team at least annually.

The IEP is the foundation of the special education and related services a child with a disability receives. Special education is, by definition, an individualized approach to teaching children whose skill diversity prohibits them from acquiring academic, social and vocational competencies as other students typically do. A carefully and collaboratively prepared IEP specifies the skills the child needs to learn in relation to his or her present levels of performance, the procedures that will be used to occasion that learning, and the means of determining the extent to which learning has taken place (Bierly, 1978; Strickland & Turnbull, 1993). Too often there is a discrepancy between what is written on the IEP and the instructional programs students actually receive (Algozzine, 1993; Nevin, McCann, & Semmel, 1983; Smith, 1990). It is important to remember that the IEP itself does not teach. If the IEP is to benefit a child, its objectives must be systematically taught and routinely and directly evaluated.

Least Restrictive Environment

As described earlier, the 1972 PARC class-action case was settled by a ruling that it was neither rational nor necessary to exclude or segregate students from regular education programs solely because of a disability. The IDEA made this finding of the PARC case the law by mandating that students with disabilities must be educated in the *least restrictive environment (LRE)*. Specifically, the law states that

> to the maximum extent appropriate, children with disabilities, including children in public or private institutions or other care facilities, [be] educated with children who are not disabled, and that special classes, separate schooling, or other removal of children with disabilities from the regular educational environment [occur] only when the nature or severity of the disability is such that education in regular classes with the use of supplementary aids and services cannot be achieved satisfactorily. (Public Law 94-192, Section 612 (5) B)

The LRE requirement has been one of the most controversial and least understood aspects of the IDEA. During the first few years after its passage, some professionals and parents erroneously interpreted the law to mean that all children with disabilities, regardless of type or severity of their disabilities, had to be placed in regular classrooms. Instead, the LRE principle requires that each child with a disability be educated in a setting that most closely resembles a regular class placement and in which his or her individual educational needs can be met. Although some people argue that any decision to place a child with a disability in a special class or school is inappropriate, most educators and parents realize that a regular classroom placement can be overly restrictive if the child's academic and social needs are not met. Two students who have the same disability should not necessarily be placed in the same setting. LRE is a relative concept; the least restrictive environment for one student with a disability would not necessarily be appropriate for another.

A number of factors should be considered when determining the restrictiveness of a particular educational environment. These factors include the extent to which the child has opportunities to acquire new skills, the availability of the regular education teacher to all students, and the opportunity a child with a disability has to establish relationships with other students (Heron & Skinner, 1981).

To provide an appropriate LRE for each child with a disability, most schools must offer a continuum of services made up of a range of placement and instructional options. Figure 13.1 shows a continuum of placement options as it is most often depicted. The regular classroom is at the bottom of the pyramid and is widest to show that the greatest number of exceptional students should be placed there. Moving up from the bottom of the pyramid, each successive placement option represents an environment in which increasingly more restrictive, specialized, and intensive instructional and related services can be offered. The more severe a child's disability, the greater the need for specialized services. As we have noted, however, the majority of students who receive special education services experience mild disabilities; hence, the pyramid grows smaller at the top to show that more restrictive settings are required for fewer students.

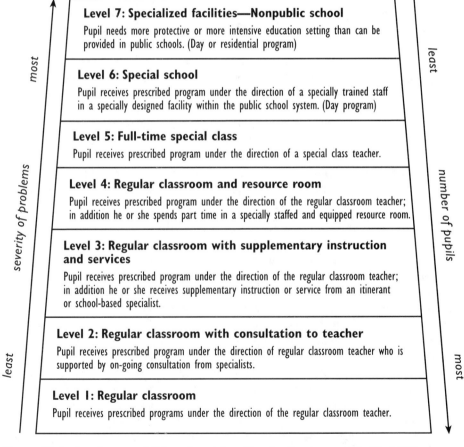

Figure 13.1 Continuum of Educational Services for Students with Disabilities

Source: From Montgomery County Public Schools, Rockville, MD. Reprinted by permission.

The continuum-of-services concept is meant to be flexible. That is, decisions regarding the placement of students with disabilities should not be considered permanent, but should be reviewed periodically. A student may be moved to a more restrictive setting for a limited time, but when certain performance objectives have been met, the student should be returned to the more integrated setting as soon as possible.

Although the continuum-of-services model represents well-established practice in special education, it is not without controversy. A number of specific criticisms have been leveled at this tradition of providing services to exceptional students (e.g., Taylor, 1988). Some have argued that the continuum overly legitimizes the use of restrictive placements, implies that integration of persons with disabilities can take place only in least-restrictive settings, and may infringe on the rights of people with disabilities to participate in their communities. In addition, the model suggests that

> people move through the continuum in a developmental, step-wise fashion, ignoring transitional states between steps. Perhaps the feature of the continuum that is least useful is its preoccupation with the physical setting in which education takes place, rather than with the quality of services provided. As special education continues to improve the effectiveness of its instructional methods, the most restrictive options of the continuum will rarely be considered as proper placements. . . . In this writer's view, we are prepared now to lop off the top two levels of the continuum; . . . it is now well demonstrated that we can deliver special education and related services within general school buildings and at a continuum level no higher than the special class. Thus, we can foresee the undoing or demise of special schools (day and residential) as delivery mechanisms for special education—at least in the United States. (Reynolds, 1989, pp. 7–11)

Maynard Reynolds, who was among the first to propose the continuum of services concept, believes it is time to make some changes in the model—specifically, to do away with the two most restrictive placements.

Not all special educators would agree with Reynolds. As we see throughout this text, the relative value of providing services to students with disabilities outside of the regular classroom, and especially in separate classrooms and schools, is a hotly contested issue in special education (Fuchs & Fuchs, 1994, 1995b; Kauffman & Hallahan, 1995; O'Neil, 1995; Shanker, 1995; Taylor, 1995).

Note that in the first three placement options, students with disabilities spend the entire school day in regular classes with their nondisabled peers. In fact, two-thirds of all students with disabilities receive at least part of their education in regular classrooms with their nondisabled peers (see Figure 13.2). Many of these students, however, spend a portion of each school day in a resource room (level 4 in Figure 13.1), where they receive individualized instruction from a specially trained teacher. Approximately one of every four students with disabilities is educated in a separate classroom in a regular public school. Special schools provide the education for about one in twenty children with disabilities, usually students with the most severe disabilities.

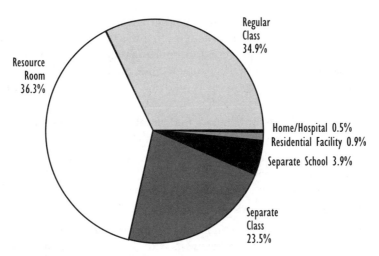

Figure 13.2 Percentage of All Students with Disabilities Ages Six through Twenty-One Served in Six Educational Placements

Notes: Separate school includes both public and private separate school facilities. Residential facility includes both public and private residential facilities.

Source: From *Sixteenth Annual Report to Congress on the Implementation of the Individuals with Disabilities Education Act*, p. 12, 1994, U.S. Department of Education.

Neither the IDEA nor the regulations that accompany it specify exactly how a school district is to determine LRE. After reviewing the rulings on litigation in four LRE suits that have reached the U.S. Courts of Appeals, Yell (1995) concluded that the courts have held that IDEA does not require the placement of students with disabilities in the regular classroom, but fully supports the continuum of services.

Lane's (1992) study of LRE litigation suggests that the courts have viewed the general education classroom as the appropriate placement for some students but not necessarily for all. The courts have resolved issues of LRE in some cases by weighing the benefits of including a child with a disability in a general education classroom against the degree to which that setting can provide an appropriate education.

Due Process Safeguards

The IDEA acknowledges that students with disabilities are people with important legal rights. The law makes it clear that school districts do not have absolute authority over exceptional students. Schools may not make decisions about the educational programs of children with disabilities in a unilateral or arbitrary manner. Due process is a legal concept that is implemented through a series of procedural steps designed to assure fairness of treatment among school systems, parents, and students. Specific due process safeguards have been incorporated into the IDEA because of past educational abuses of children with disabilities (Meyen, 1978). In the past, special education placements were often permanent, void of periodic reviews, and made solely on the basis of teacher recommendations. Further, students with severe and profound disabilities were automatically excluded from public school programs and placed in residential programs where the quality of instructional programs often was very poor. The fact that children from minority cultural groups were disproportionately placed into special education programs was another factor in mandating the due process procedures.

Key elements of due process as it relates to special education are the parents' right to

- Be notified in writing before the school takes any action that may alter the child's program (testing, reevaluation, change in placement)
- Give or withhold permission to have their child tested for eligibility for special education services, reevaluated, or placed in a different classroom or program
- See all school records about their child
- Have a hearing before an impartial party (not an employee of the school district) to resolve disagreements with the school system
- Receive a written decision following any hearing
- Appeal the results of a due process hearing to the state department of education (school districts may also appeal)

Ann and Rud Turnbull (1990), who are special educators and parents of a young man with disabilities, describe due process as the legal technique that seeks to achieve fair treatment, accountability, and a new and more equal "balance of power" between professionals, who have traditionally wielded power, and families, who have felt they could not affect their children's education.

Parent Participation

The IDEA recognizes the benefits of active parent participation. Parents not only have a right to be involved in their child's education, but parents also can help professionals select appropriate instructional goals and can provide information that will help teachers be more effective in working with their children. As noted, parents are to take an active role as full members of the child-study team that develops the IEP for their child. Of course, parents cannot be forced to do so and may waive their right to participate. In addition to involving parents in IEP development, the IDEA requires each state to include parents of students who are exceptional on their special education advisory panel that is responsible for helping the state education agency develop its overall plan and policies for meeting the needs of students with disabilities.

Section 504 of the Rehabilitation Act of 1973

Another important law that extends civil rights to people with disabilities is Section 504 of the Rehabilitation Act of 1973. This regulation states, in part, that "no otherwise qualified handicapped individual shall, solely by reason of his handicap, be excluded from the participation in, be denied the benefits of, or be subjected to discrimination in any program or activity receiving federal financial assistance." This law, worded almost identically to the Civil Rights Act of 1964 (which prohibited discrimination based on race, color, or national origin), promises to expand opportunities to children and adults with disabilities in education, employment, and various other settings. It calls for provision of "auxiliary aides for students with impaired sensory, manual, or speaking skills"—for example, readers for blind students, interpreters for deaf students, and people to assist physically disabled students in moving from place to place. This requirement does not mean that schools, colleges, and employers must have *all* such aids available at *all* times; it simply demands that no person with disabilities may be excluded from a program because of the lack of an appropriate aid.

Architectural accessibility for students, teachers, and other people with physical and sensory impairments is an important feature of Section 504; however, the law does not call for a completely barrier-free environment. Emphasis is on accessibility to programs, not on physical modification of all existing structures. If a chemistry class is required for a premedical program of study, for example, a college might make this program accessible to a student with physical disabilities by reassigning the class to an accessible location or by providing assistance to the student in traveling to an otherwise inaccessible location. All sections of all courses need not be made accessible, but a college should not segregate students with disabilities by assigning them all to a particular section, regardless of disability. Like the IDEA, Section 504 calls for nondiscriminatory placement in the "most integrated setting appropriate" and has served as the basis for many court cases over alleged discrimination against individuals with disabilities, particularly in their right to employment.

Americans with Disabilities Act

The Americans with Disabilities Act (PL 101-336) was signed into law on July 26, 1990. Patterned after Section 504 of the Rehabilitation Act of 1973, the Americans with Disabilities Act (ADA) extends civil rights protection to persons with disabilities in private sector employment, all public services, and in public accommodations, transportation, and telecommunications. A person with a disability is defined in the ADA as a person (1) with a mental or physical impairment that substantially limits that person in a major life activity (e.g., walking, talking, working, self-care); (2) with a record of such an impairment (such as a person who no longer has heart disease but is discriminated against because of that history); or (3) who is regarded as having such an impairment (a person with significant facial disfiguration due to a burn who is not limited in any major life activity but is discriminated against). The major provisions of the ADA are as follows:

- Employers with fifteen or more employees may not refuse to hire or promote a person because of a disability if that person is qualified to perform the job. Also, the employer must make reasonable accommodations that will allow a person with a disability to perform essential functions of the job. Such modifications in job requirements or situation must be made if they will not impose undue hardship on the employer.

- All new vehicles purchased by public transit authorities must be accessible to people with disabilities. All rail stations must be made accessible, and at least one car per train in existing rail systems must be made accessible.

- It is illegal for public accommodations to exclude or refuse persons with disabilities. Public accommodations are the everyday businesses and services such as hotels, restaurants, grocery stores, parks, and so on. All new buildings must be made accessible, and existing facilities must remove barriers if the removal can be accomplished without much difficulty or expense.

- Companies offering telephone service to the general public must offer relay services to individuals who use telecommunications devices for the deaf (such as TDDs) twenty-four hours a day, seven days a week.

EDUCATIONAL EQUALITY FOR STUDENTS WITH DISABILITIES: SOME PROGRESS AND REMAINING CHALLENGES

What effect has the IDEA had? The most obvious effect is that many more students with disabilities are receiving special education and related services than before the law's passage. But this is what the law requires and is only one aspect of its impact. Educational equality for students with disabilities is also evidenced in the ways that today's schools function as complex human services agencies. Since the passage of the IDEA, there has been a dramatic increase in the number of both special education teachers and support staff. Providing the related services necessary to meet the diverse needs of students with disabilities requires that the number of nonclassroom professionals be nearly equal to that of special education teachers. School psychologists, social workers, speech and language therapists, occupational therapists, physical therapists, audiologists, recreational therapists, adaptive physical educators, vocational specialists, and mental health professionals all lend support and expertise to the education of learners with special needs.

Perhaps the law has had its most dramatic effect on students with severe disabilities, many of whom had been completely denied the opportunity to benefit from an appropriate education. No longer can schools exclude students with disabilities on the premise that they are ineducable. Indeed, the IDEA states clearly that all students can benefit from an appropriate education, and that the local school has the responsibility to make the modifications in curriculum content and teaching method dictated by the unique needs of each student. In essence, the law requires schools to adapt themselves to the needs of students rather than allowing schools to deny educational equality to students who do not fit the school.

Most people would agree that the IDEA has contributed positively to the education of students with disabilities, but significant barriers remain to full educational equality for exceptional students in the United States. We briefly examine five of these issues. If a truly appropriate educational opportunity is to be a reality for students with disabilities, U.S. schools must work hard to (1) encourage cooperation and collaboration between special and regular educators, (2) move beyond simple compliance with the law to effective instruction, (3) provide more and better early intervention programs for young children with disabilities, (4) increase the success of young adults with disabilities as they make the transition from school to community, and (5) ensure relevant, individualized education to students with disabilities from culturally and linguistically diverse backgrounds.

Regular and Special Education Partnerships

The Individuals with Disabilities Education Act has had a tremendous impact on education. The law requires that all students with disabilities be provided an appropriate education in the least restrictive environment. As noted, most children with disabilities spend at least part of each school day in regular classrooms and increasingly inclusive educational options for students with disabilities are expanding.

Traditionally, regular and special education have been viewed as separate disciplines, each serving different student populations. With the passage of the IDEA, general and special education teachers are becoming partners in meeting the needs of all learners. The concept of "your kids" and "my kids" is gradually being replaced by "our kids."

Some people argue that special and regular education should merge their respective talents and methods to create an approach more efficient than the dual system commonly practiced. Creating a general education system that services the needs of all students by combining the most effective practices of regular and special education was originally referred to as the "regular education initiative" (Reynolds, Wang, & Walberg, 1987; Stainback & Stainback, 1987; Wang & Walberg, 1988). Others argue that such a merger would not be in the best interests of exceptional students until teacher training and professional practice improve and child-centered curricula become more common (Kauffman, Gerber, & Semmel, 1988; Lieberman, 1985; Mesinger, 1985).

Mainstreaming has traditionally been thought of as the process of integrating students with disabilities into regular schools and classes. Today, the term *inclusive education* is changing not only the language of special education reform, but its intent as well. Inclusive education can be successful only with full cooperation and collaboration among those responsible for the educational programs of students with disabilities (Giangreco, Cloninger, Dennis, & Edelman, 1994; Putnam, 1993; Stainback & Stainback, 1992). The IDEA does not specifically mention mainstreaming or inclusion, but it does require that educational services be provided in the least restrictive environment and that cooperation between regular and special education facilitates those placements.

The effects of the IDEA on regular education are neither entirely clear nor without controversy. This dissonance is further complicated by the tone and content of many discussions about how special education can or should reform while ensuring that the best interests of students with disabilities are appropriately served (Fuchs & Fuchs, 1994, 1995a, 1995b; Taylor, 1995). What is clear, however, is that the entire educational community has the responsibility to do the best job it can in meeting the needs of children with diverse skills. In the final analysis, issues of labeling, classification, placement, and teaching assignments are secondary to the quality of instruction that takes place in the classroom (Keogh, 1990; Lovitt, 1996).

Effective Instruction

Educational equality for students with disabilities is required by the IDEA. The letter of the law can be met by following the mandates for multifactored evaluations, IEPs, due process, and placements in the least restrictive environment. None of these mandated processes, however, teach. Educational equality can be achieved only through effective instruction.

In practice, the spirit of the law sets the stage for educational equality. The procedures and results of multifactored assessments must be scrutinized. Members of the child-study teams must ask, "Do these results provide the means of making placement decisions that will truly benefit the child?" The spirit of the law requires that IEPs be more than correctly completed forms that get filed away and never consulted. The IEP must be a collective effort by teachers, parents, administrators, and other professionals that guides the education of children with disabilities. The spirit of the law requires that due process safeguards be more than a formality. They must protect the wishes of parents and the needs of children throughout the process of securing special education services.

Equally important is the law's intent concerning least restrictive environments. Children's academic and social needs must both be addressed through opportunities to interact with nondisabled students to the greatest extent possible and to interact with meaningful curricula and instruction that is purposeful and powerful.

Teachers, of course, are ultimately responsible for providing effective instruction to exceptional students. With this responsibility comes several obligations. With the support of the school administration, teachers must (1) use direct assessment and observation of students' performance as a means of designing instruction and evaluating its effectiveness (Bushell & Baer, 1994; McLoughlin & Lewis, 1994); (2) use empirically validated methods of instruction (Gardner et al., 1994; Lovitt, 1995); (3) teach so that newly learned skills are useful outside of the classroom (Horner, Dunlap, & Koegel, 1988); (4) change an instructional program when it does not promote achievement and success (Howell, Fox, & Morehead, 1993); (5) consult with their regular education colleagues and their student's parents (Heron & Harris, 1993); (6) be an advocate for the needs of exceptional learners in the school as a whole; and (7) command a professional knowledge base that can generate multiple solutions to the diverse needs of their learners (Lovitt, 1995, 1996).

> Teachers must demand effectiveness from their instructional approaches. For many years conventional wisdom has fostered the belief that it takes unending patience to teach children with disabilities. I believe this view is a disservice to students with special needs and to the educators—both special and general education teachers—whose job it is to teach them. Teachers should not wait patiently for exceptional students to learn, attributing lack of progress to some inherent attribute or faulty process within the child, such as mental retardation, learning disability, ADD, or emotional disturbance. Instead, the teacher should use direct and frequent

> measures of the student's performance as the primary guide
> for modifying the instructional program in order to improve
> it effectiveness. This, I believe, is the real work of the educa-
> tor. (Heward, 1996, p. 2)

Although the IDEA does not state that the job of a teacher is to change behavior, that is what a teacher does. When a teacher helps children who previously could not add, spell, compose, tie their shoes, apply for a job, or make a friend, and they learn to do so, behavior has been changed. Effective instruction does not change children's behavior by chance. Effective instruction is deliberate in its intent. Chance has no place in assuring children's equal opportunity to lead productive, independent, and satisfying lives.

Early Intervention

The years from birth to school age are very important to a child's learning and development. The typical child enters school with a large repertoire of intellectual, language, social, and physical skills on which to build. Unfortunately, for many children with disabilities, the preschool years represent a long period of missed opportunities. Without systematic instruction, most young children with disabilities do not acquire many of the basic skills their nondisabled peers seemingly learn without effort. Parents concerned about their child's inability to reach important developmental milestones have often been told by professionals, "Don't worry. He'll probably grow out of it before too long." Many children with disabilities, as a result, fall further and further behind their nondisabled peers, and minor delays in development often become major delays by the time the child reaches school age.

Two decades ago, there were virtually no early intervention programs for children with disabilities from birth to school age; today, early childhood special education is the fastest-growing area in the field of education. As with special education of school-age exceptional students, federal legislation has played a major role in the development of early intervention programs. By passing Public Law 99-457, the Education of the Handicapped Act Amendments of 1986, Congress reaffirmed the basic principles of the original PL 94-142 and added two major sections concerning early intervention services.

Only about 70 percent of the preschoolers aged three to five with disabilities were being served under the incentive provisions of the IDEA (which did not require states to provide a free, public education to children with disabilities under the age of six years). PL 99-457 requires each state to show evidence of serving all three- to five-year-old children with disabilities in order to receive any preschool funds.

The second major change brought about by PL 99-457 is that incentive grants are available to states for developing systems of early identification and intervention for infants and toddlers with disabilities from birth to age two. The services must be planned by a multidisciplinary team that includes the child's parents and must be implemented according to an individualized family services plan that is similar in concept to the IEP for school-aged students with disabilities.

Nearly every special educator today now realizes the critical importance of early intervention for both children who are at risk and who have disabilities, and most also agree that the earlier intervention is begun, the better. Fortunately, many educators are working to develop the programs and services so desperately needed by the increasing numbers of babies and preschoolers, especially as a result of prenatal exposure to drugs and alcohol (Carta, 1996; Howard & Williams, & McLaughlin, 1994). These programs are necessary to give these children a fighting chance to experience educational equality when they enter school.

Transition from School to Adult Life

If the degree of educational equality afforded to students who are exceptional is to be judged, as we think it should, by the extent to which students with disabilities can function independently in everyday environments, then we still have a long way to go. Follow-up studies of young adults who have graduated or left public school secondary special education programs have produced disquieting results. Only about 60 percent find work, and much of the work is part time and at or below minimum wage (Edgar, 1985). The probability of a person with moderate or severe disabilities finding real work in the community is much lower. One study of 117 young adults with moderate, severe, or profound mental retardation found an unemployment rate of 78.6 percent (Wehman, Kregel, & Seyfarth, 1985). Of the 25 who had jobs, only 14 were in the community; 11 were working in sheltered workshops. Only 8 of those working earned more than $100 per month.

Employment problems are not the only difficulties faced by adults with disabilities. In a statewide follow-up study of graduates of secondary special education programs in Iowa, Sitlington, Frank, and Carson (1993) found only 5.8 percent of 737 students with learning disabilities, 5 of 142 students with mental retardation (3.5 percent), and just 1 of 59 students with behavior disorders could be judged as having made a "successful adult adjustment" (p. 230) one year after they had completed high school. A national survey found that 56 percent of Americans with disabilities indicated that their disabilities prevented them from doing many everyday activities taken for granted by nondisabled people, such as getting around the community, attending cultural or sporting events, and socializing with friends outside their homes (U.S. Department of Education, 1986, p. xiv).

Education cannot be held responsible for all of the difficulties faced by adults with disabilities, but the results of these and other studies make it evident that many young people leave public school special education programs without the skills necessary to function in the community. Many educators today see the development of special-education programs that will effectively prepare exceptional students for adjustment and successful integration in the adult community as the ultimate measure of educational equality for students with disabilities.

Special Education in a Diverse Society

Both special and general educators face major challenges in providing relevant, individualized education to students with disabilities from culturally diverse backgrounds (Baca & Cervantes, 1989; Correa & Heward, 1996). Many students with disabilities experience discrimination or experience inadequate educational programs because their racial, ethnic, social class, or gender is different from the majority. Students from culturally and linguistically diverse backgrounds are often under- or overrepresented in educational programs for exceptional children (Correa, Blanes-Reyes, & Rapport, 1995). For example:

- Asian Pacific students are generally underrepresented in disability categories and overrepresented in gifted and talented programs.

- African American students still tend to be overrepresented in classrooms for students with mild mental retardation.

- Latinos are overrepresented in programs for students with learning disabilities and speech language impairments (Finn, 1982; Harry, 1992a, as cited in Artiles & Trent, 1994).

- Native Americans are in classes for students with learning disabilities in disproportionately high numbers, whereas their representation in classes for students who are gifted is consistently low (Chinn & Hughes, 1987).

- Ethnically diverse students constitute about 27 percent of the general school population but only about 18 percent of all students who are identified as gifted and talented (Chinn & McCormick, 1986).

- Approximately one-half million migrant students live in the United States, but only 10.7 percent of them with mild disabilities appear to be identified (Smith & Luckasson, 1995).

- Twenty-six percent of African American and 18 percent of Hispanic children are labeled mentally retarded, while only 11 percent of White children have this label (U.S. Department of Education, 1990).

While a student's ethnicity or language should never be the basis for inclusion in or exclusion from special education programs, increased numbers of students from culturally and linguistically diverse backgrounds will require that educators attend to several important issues.

First, the adequacy of assessment and placement procedures must be assured. Multifactored assessments must be conducted in ways that will be appropriately sensitive to the students' culture and language to ensure that a special education placement is a function of the student's documented needs rather than biased referral and assessment practices.

Second, providing appropriate support services that are responsive to the cultural and linguistic needs of the student may enhance the child's educational program. For example, bilingual aides, inservice training for teachers, and multicultural education for peers may be necessary to ensure that the child's education is meaningful and maximally beneficial.

Third, teachers and other school staff may need to learn about the values and standards of behavior present in the child's home. Since most teachers are White (Ladson-Billings, 1994), learning not only to understand but also to respect and appreciate the child's culture as it is reflected in his or her home will be important to understanding the child's behavior in the classroom and in communicating with parents.

Good intentions or token attempts at cultural sensitivity, of course, will do little in the way of providing an appropriate individualized educational program for students with disabilities from culturally diverse backgrounds. The instructional materials educators use and the methods they employ while teaching must be responsive to the differing cultural background of their students.

Does this mean that a teacher with students from four different cultural backgrounds needs four different methods of teaching? The answer is both "no" and "yes." For the first answer, it is our view that systematic instruction benefits children from all cultural backgrounds. When students with disabilities must also adjust to a new or different culture or language, it is especially important for the teacher to plan individualized activities, convey expectations clearly, observe and record behavior precisely, and give the child specific, immediate feedback during instruction. When coupled with a respectful attitude, these procedures will increase the motivation and achievement of most students.

Good teachers must also be responsive to changes (or lack of change) in individual students' performance. So it can also be argued that the effective teacher needs as many different ways of teaching as there are students in the classroom. Cultural diversity just adds another dimension to the many individual characteristics students present each day. While the basic methods of systematic instruction apply to all learners, teachers who will be most effective in helping children with disabilities from culturally diverse backgrounds achieve will be those who are sensitive to and respectful of their students' heritage and values.

As with all children with disabilities, the teacher of culturally diverse students must be flexible in teaching style, establish a positive climate for learning, and use a variety of approaches to meet individual student needs. Through careful assessment and observation of behavior, and the use of appropriate materials and community resources, the teacher can do a great deal to help culturally and linguistically diverse children with disabilities and their families experience success in school.

SUMMARY

The task of providing educational equality for students with markedly diverse skills is enormous. By embracing the challenge, U.S. schools have made a promise to exceptional students, to their parents, and to society. Progress has been made, but, as we have seen, significant challenges must still be overcome if the promise is to be kept. The views of our society are changing and continue to be changed by people who believe that our past practice of excluding people with disabilities was primitive and unfair. As an institution, education reflects the attitudes of society.

There is, however, still much room for change. The 24th Annual Gallup/Phi Delta Kappa Poll of the Public's Attitudes Toward the Public Schools (Elam, Lowell, & Gallup, 1992) contained two questions about placement alternatives for students with disabilities. One question asked whether students with mental handicaps should be in the same classrooms as other (nondisabled) students or in their own classrooms. The second question asked whether students with physical handicaps should be in the same classrooms as other (nondisabled) students or in their own classrooms. Sixty-seven percent of the respondents from the national total believed that children with mental handicaps should be in special classes, while 22 percent of the respondents believed that students with mental handicaps should be in the same classrooms as other students.

The national results reflected opposite opinions for students with physical handicaps. Sixty-five percent of the respondents said these students should be in the same classrooms as their nondisabled peers, and 27 percent believed that they should be in separate classrooms. The public's view that some groups of exceptional learners are better suited for equal educational opportunity than are others is cause for concern. The author's narrative summary of the results, however, is alarming. The authors state, "The public is of two minds on this question, but the majority took the 'commonsense' view that physically handicapped children can be successfully integrated with nonhandicapped peers, whereas mentally handicapped children cannot" (Elam et al., 1992, p. 50).

"Common sense" ought to dictate that all children are entitled to educational equality; but the history of exclusion and inequality for students with disabilities tells us that no such sense of equity, common or otherwise, has driven educational policy. The "common sense" assertion that children with mental handicaps cannot be successfully integrated with nonhandicapped peers not only ignores years of collaborative and documented progress by educators, family members, and students with disabilities, but it also legitimizes separateness as the only realistic choice for some students with disabilities. In the absence of alternatives from which professionals, parents, and students can choose, equity is impossible.

Uninformed common sense and popular consensus have no place in decisions that will have life-long implications for children and their families. Decisions about educational placement and program options must reflect the best interests of individual children and must be solidly anchored in objective data, not opinion. While much progress has been made in achieving educational equality for students with disabilities, much work remains to be done.

Providing educational equality for students with disabilities does not mean either ignoring a child's disability or pretending that it does not exist. Children with disabilities do have differences from children who do not have disabilities. But, as we state at the beginning of this chapter, students who are exceptional are more like than unlike other students. Every exceptional student must be treated first as an individual, not as a member of a labeled group or category.

There is a limit to how much educational equality can be legislated, for in many cases it is possible to meet the letter of the law but not necessarily the spirit of the law. Treating every student with a disability as a student first and as an individual with a disability second may be the most important factor in providing true educational equality. This approach does not diminish the student's exceptionality, but instead it might give us a more objective and positive perspective that allows us to see a disability as a set of special needs. Viewing exceptional students as individuals with special needs tells us a great deal about how to help them achieve the educational equality they deserve.

Questions and Activities

1. Why are both children who are learning disabled and those who are gifted considered exceptional?

2. In what ways are exceptional students similar to and different from other students?

3. Name ten categories of disability. Identify community and school resources from which teachers can receive help when working with students who are exceptional.

4. What are the advantages and disadvantages of labeling and classifying students with disabilities? Be sure to consider the views of educators, parents, and students.

5. Interview a local special education school administrator to determine (a) how many students in the district receive special education services; (b) how many of these students are bilingual, males, females, or are students of color; (c) how many students are in each of the ten categories of disability; (d) how many special education students are mainstreamed, the portion of the school day in which they are mainstreamed, and the classes in which mainstreamed students participate.

6. How did the civil rights movement influence the movement for educational equality for students with disabilities?

7. What is an IEP and how can it benefit students with disabling conditions? Visit a special education classroom and ask to review some of the student IEPs. Talk with the special education teacher about how an IEP may influence regular classroom teachers when students are mainstreamed.

8. Are all students with disabling conditions mainstreamed? Why or why not? How does the concept of least restrictive environment (LRE) influence alternative placements for students with disabling conditions?

9. How does your state support special programs and services for students who are gifted? Are state funds provided for gifted education?

10. In your view, which of the challenges facing the education of exceptional students is the most critical? What suggestions would you make for meeting that challenge?

References

Aiello, B. (1976, April 25). Up from the Basement: A Teacher's Story. *New York Times*, 14.

Algozzine, B. (1993). Splitting Hairs and Loose Ends: Answering Special Education's Wake-Up Call. *Journal of Special Education, 26*, 462–468.

Artiles, A. J. and Trent, S. C. (1994). Overrepresentation of Minority Students in Special Education: A Continuing Debate. *The Journal of Special Education, 27*, 410–437.

Baca, L. M. and Cervantes, H. T. (1989). *The Bilingual Special Education Interface* (2nd ed.). Columbus, OH: Merrill.

Banks, J. A. and Banks, C. A. M. (Eds.). (1993). *Multicultural Education: Issues and Perspectives* (2nd ed.). Boston: Allyn and Bacon.

Barraga, N. C. and Erin, J. N. (1992). *Visual Handicaps and Learning* (3rd ed.). Austin, TX: Pro-Ed.

Becker, W. C., Engelmann, S., and Thomas, D. R. (1971). *Teaching: A Course in Applied Psychology.* Chicago: Science Research Associates.

Beirne-Smith, M., Patton, J. R., and Ittenbach, R. (1994). *Mental Retardation* (4th ed.). New York: Macmillan.

Bierly, K. (1978, September). Public Law 94-142: Answers to the Questions You're Asking. *Instructor, 87,* 63–67.

Bigge, J. L. (1991). *Teaching Individuals with Physical and Multiple Disabilities* (3rd ed.). Columbus, OH: Merrill.

Brown v. *Board of Education of Topeka.* (1954). 347 U.S. 483.

Bushell, D. Jr. and Baer, D. M. (1994). Measurably Superior Instruction Means Close, Continual Contact with the Relevant Outcome Data. Revolutionary! In R. Gardner III, D. M. Sainato, J. O. Cooper, T. E. Heron, W. L. Heward, J. Eshleman, and T. A. Grossi (Eds.). *Behavior Analysis in Education: Focus on Measurably Superior Instruction* (pp. 3–10). Pacific Grove, CA: Brooks/Cole.

Carta, J. J. (1996). Perspectives on Educating Young Children Prenatally Exposed to Illegal Drugs. In W. L. Heward, *Exceptional Children: An Introduction to Special Education* (5th ed.). Englewood Cliffs, NJ: Prentice-Hall/Merrill.

Chinn, P. C. and Hughes, S. (1987). Representation of Minority Students in Special Education Classes. *Remedial and Special Education, 8,* 41–46.

Chinn, P. C. and McCormick, L. (1986). Cultural Diversity and Exceptionality. In N. G. Haring & L. McCormick (Eds.). *Exceptional Children and Youth* (4th ed.) (pp. 95–117). Columbus, OH: Merrill.

Coleman, J. S. (1966). *Equality of Educational Opportunity.* Washington, DC: U.S. Government Printing Office.

Correa, V. I., Blanes-Reyes, M., and Rapport, M. J. (1995). Minority Issues. In H. R. Turnbull and A. P. Turnbull. (Eds.). *A Compendium Report to Congress.* Lawrence, KS: Beach Center.

Correa, V. I. and Heward, W. L. (1996). Special Education in a Culturally and Linguistically Diverse Society. In W. L. Heward, *Exceptional Children: An Introduction to Special Education.* Englewood Cliffs, NJ: Prentice-Hall/Merrill.

Danforth, S. (1995). Toward a Critical Theory Approach to Lives Considered Emotionally Disturbed. *Behavioral Disorders, 20*(2), 136–143.

Edgar, E. (1985). How Do Special Education Students Fare after They Leave School? A Response to Hasazi, Gordon, and Roe. *Exceptional Children, 51,* 470–473.

Elam, S. M., Lowell, C. R., and Gallup, A. M. (1992). The 24th Annual Gallup/Phi Delta Kappa Poll of the Public's Attitudes toward the Public Schools. *Phi Delta Kappan, 74*(1), 41–53.

Fuchs, D. and Fuchs, L. S. (1994). Inclusive Schools Movement and the Radicalization of Special Education Reform. *Exceptional Children, 60,* 294–309.

Fuchs, D. and Fuchs, L. S. (1995a). What's "Special" about Special Education? *Phi Delta Kappan, 76*(7), 531–540.

Fuchs, D. and Fuchs, L. S. (1995b). Sometimes Separate Is Better. *Educational Leadership, 52*(4), 22–25.

Gardner, R. III, Sainato, D. M., Cooper, J. O., Heron, T. E., Heward, W. L., Eshleman, J., and Grossi, T. A. (Eds.). (1994). *Behavior Analysis in Education: Focus on Measurably Superior Instruction.* Monterey, CA: Brooks/Cole.

Gerring, J. P. and Carney, J. M. (1992). *Head Trauma: Strategies for Educational Reintegration.* San Diego, CA: Singular.

Giangreco, M. F., Cloninger, C., Dennis, R., and Edelman, S. (1994). Problem-Solving Methods to Facilitate Inclusive Education. In J. S. Thousand, R. A. Villa, and A. I. Nevin (Eds.). *Creativity and Collaborative Learning* (pp. 322–346). Baltimore: Paul H. Brookes.

Grossman, H. (1995). *Special Education in a Diverse Society.* Boston: Allyn and Bacon.

Halgren, D. W., and Clarizio, H. F. (1993). Categorical and Programming Changes in Special Education Services. *Exceptional Children, 59,* 547–555.

Heron, T. E. and Harris, K. C. (1993). *The Educational Consultant: Helping Professionals, Parents, and Mainstreamed Students* (3rd ed.). Austin, TX: PRO-ED.

Heron, T. E. and Skinner, M. E. (1981). Criteria for Defining the Regular Classroom as the Least Restrictive Environment for LD Students. *Learning Disability Quarterly, 4,* 115–121.

Heward, W. L. (1996). *Exceptional Children: An Introduction to Special Education* (5th ed.). Englewood Cliffs, NJ: Prentice-Hall/Merrill.

Horner, R. H., Dunlap, G., and Koegel, R. L. (1988). *Generalization and Maintenance: Life-Style Changes in Applied Settings.* Baltimore: Paul H. Brookes.

Howard, V. F., Williams, B. F., and McLaughlin, T. F. (1994). Children Prenatally Exposed to Alcohol and Cocaine: Behavioral Solutions. In R. Gardner III, D. M. Sainato, J. O. Cooper, T. E. Heron, W. L. Heward, J. Eshleman, & T. A. Grossi (Eds.). *Behavior Analysis in Education: Focus on Measurably Superior Instruction* (pp. 131–146). Pacific Grove, CA: Brooks/Cole.

Howell, K. W., Fox, S. L., and Morehead, M. K. (1993). *Curriculuum-Based Education.* Pacific Grove, CA: Brooks/Cole.

Huebner, T. A. (1994). Understanding Multiculturalism. *Journal of Teacher Education, 45*(5), 375–377.

Kauffman, J. M. (1993). *Characteristics of Emotional and Behavioral Disorders of Children and Youth* (5th ed.). New York: Macmillan.

Kauffman, J. M., Gerber, M. M., and Semmel, M. I.. (1988). Arguable Assumptions Underlying the Regular Education Initiative. *Journal of Learning Disabilities, 21,* 6–11.

Kauffman, J. M. and Hallahan, D. K. (1995). *The Illusion of Full Inclusion: A Comprehensive Critique of a Current Special Education Bandwagon.* Austin, TX: PRO-ED.

Keogh, B. K. (1990). Narrowing the Gap between Policy and Practice. *Exceptional Children, 57,* 186–190.

Ladson-Billings, G. (1994). What We Can Learn from Multicultural Education Research. *Educational Leadership, 51,* 22–27.

Lane, J. (1992). The Use of the Least Restrictive Environment Principle in Placement Decisions Affecting School-Age Students with Disabilities. *University of Detroit Mercy Law Review, 69,* 291–322.

Lieberman, L. (1985). Special Education and Regular Education: A Merger Made in Heaven. *Exceptional Children, 51,* 513–516.

Lovitt, T. C. (1995). *Tactics for Teaching* (2nd ed.). Englewood Cliffs, NJ: Prentice-Hall.

Lovitt, T. C. (1996). What Special Educators Need to Know. In W. L. Heward, *Exceptional Children: An Introduction to Special Education* (5th ed.). Englewood Cliffs, NJ: Prentice-Hall/Merrill.

MacMillan, D. L. (1988). New EMRs: Chapter One. In G. A. Robinson (Ed.). *Best Practices in Mental Disabilities* (p. 24). Des Moines: Iowa State Department of Public Instruction. (ERIC Document Reproduction Services No. ED304 828)

Matson, J. L. (Ed.). (1994). *Autism in Children and Adults: Etiology, Assessment, and Intervention.* Pacific Grove, CA: Brooks/Cole.

McLoughlin, J. A. and Lewis, R. B. (1994). *Assessing Special Students* (4th ed.). New York: Macmillan.

Mercer, C. D. (1992). *Students with Learning Disabilities* (4th ed.). New York: Macmillan.

Mercer, J. R. (1973). *Labeling the Mentally Retarded.* Berkeley: University of California Press.

Mesinger, J. F. (1985). Commentary on a Rationale for the Merger of Special and Regular Education or, Is It Time for the Lamb to Lie Down with the Lion? *Exceptional Children, 51,* 510–512.

Meyen, E. L. (Ed.). (1978). *Exceptional Children and Youth: An Introduction.* Denver: Love.

Meyer, L., Peck, C., and Brown, L. (Eds.) (1991). *Critical Issues in the Lives of People with Severe Disabilities.* Baltimore: Paul H. Brookes.

Nevin, A., McCann, S., and Semmel, M. I. (1983). An Empirical Analysis of the Regular Classroom Teacher's Role in Implementing IEP's. *Teacher Education and Special Education, 6,* 235–246.

O'Neil, J. (1995). Can Inclusion Work? A Conversation with Jim Kauffman and Mara Sapon-Sevin. *Educational Leadership, 52*(4), 7–11.

Ortiz, A. A. & Garcia, S. (1988). A Prereferral Process for Preventing Inappropriate Referrals of Hispanic Students to Special Education. In A. Ortiz and B. A. Ramirez (Eds.). *Schools and the Culturally Diverse Exceptional Student: Promising Practices and Future Directions* (pp. 6–18). Reston, VA: Council for Exceptional Children.

Paul, P. V. and Quigley, S. P. (1994). *Language and Deafness* (2nd ed.). San Diego, CA: Singular Publishing Group.

Pennsylvania Association for Retarded Children v. *Commonwealth of Pennsylvania.* (1972). 343 F., Supp. 279.

Peters, M. T. (1990, Summer). Someone's Missing: The Student as an Overlooked Participant in the IEP Process. *Preventing School Failure, 34,* 32–36.

Public Law 94–192: The Education of All Handicapped Children Act. (1975). Section 612(5)B.

Putnam, J. W. (1993). *Cooperative Learning and Strategies for Inclusion: Celebrating Diversity in the Classroom.* Baltimore: Paul H. Brookes.

Reynolds, M. C. (1989). An Historical Perspective: The Delivery of Special Education to Mildly Disabled and At-Risk Students. *Remedial and Special Education, 10,* 6–11.

Reynolds, M. C., Wang, M. C., and Walberg, H. J. (1987). The Necessary Restructuring of Special and Regular Education. *Exceptional Children, 53,* 391–398.

Shames, G. H., Wiig, E. H., and Secord, W. A. (1994). *Human Communication Disorders* (4th ed.). New York: Macmillan.

Shanker, A. (1995). Full Inclusion Is Neither Free nor Appropriate. *Educational Leadership, 52*(4), 18–21.

Sitlington, P. L., Frank, A. R., and Carson, R. (1993). Adult Adjustment among High School Graduates with Mild Disabilities. *Exceptional Children, 59*, 221–233.

Sleeter, C. E. (1986). Learning Disabilities: The Social Construction of a Special Education Category. *Exceptional Children, 53*(1), 46–54.

Smith, D. D. and Luckasson, R. (1995). *Introduction to Special Education: Teaching in an Age of Challenge* (2nd ed.). Boston: Allyn and Bacon.

Smith, S. W. (1990). Individualized Education Programs (IEP's) in Special Education—from Intent to Acquiescence. *Exceptional Children, 57*, 6–14.

Snell, M. E. (Ed.). (1993). *Instruction of Students with Severe Disabilities* (4th ed.). New York: Macmillan.

Stainback, S. and Stainback, W. (1987). Integration versus Cooperation: A Commentary on Educating Children with Learning Problems: A Shared Responsibility. *Exceptional Children, 54*, 66–68.

Stainback, S. and Stainback, W. (1992). *Curriculum Considerations in Inclusive Classrooms: Facilitating Learning for All Students.* Baltimore: Paul H. Brookes.

Stainback, W. and Stainback, S. (1984, October). A Rationale for the Merger of Special and Regular Education. *Exceptional Children, 51*, 102–111.

Strickland, B. B. and Turnbull, A. P. (1993). *Developing and Implementing Individualized Education Programs* (3rd ed.). New York: Macmillan.

Taylor, S. J. (1988). Caught in the Continuum: A Critical Analysis of the Principle of Least Restrictive Environment. *The Journal of the Association for Persons with Severe Handicaps, 13*, 41–53.

Taylor, S. J. (1995). On Rhetoric: A Response to Fuchs and Fuchs. *Exceptional Children, 61*, 301–302.

Thomas, C. C., Correa, V. I., and Morsink, C. V. (1995). *Interactive Teaming: Consultation and Collaboration in Special Programs.* Englewood Cliffs, NJ: Prentice-Hall/Merrill.

Turnbull, A. P. and Turnbull, H. R. (1990). *Families, Professionals, and Exceptionality: A Special Partnership* (2nd ed.). New York: Macmillan.

Turnbull, H. R. III. (1993). *Free Appropriate Public Education: The Law and Children with Disabilities* (4th ed.). Denver: Love.

U.S. Department of Education. (1986). *Eighth Annual Report to Congress on the Implementation of the Education of All Handicapped Children Act.* Washington, DC: U.S. Government Printing Office.

U.S. Department of Education. (1990). *Twelfth Annual Report to Congress on the Implementation of the Education of All Handicapped Children Act.* Washington, DC: U.S. Government Printing Office.

U.S. Department of Education. (1994). *Sixteenth Annual Report to Congress on the Implementation of the Individuals with Disabilities Education Act.* Washington, DC: U.S. Government Printing Office.

Van Reusen, A. K. and Bos, C. S. (1990). IPLAN: Helping Students Communicate in Planning Conferences. *Teaching Exceptional Children, 22*(4), 30-32.

Van Reusen, A. K. and Bos, C. (1994). Facilitating Student Participation in Individualized Education Programs through Motivation Strategy Instruction. *Exceptional Children, 60*, 466–475.

Wang, M. C. and Walberg, H. J. (1988). Four Fallacies of Segregationism. *Exceptional Children, 55*, 497–502.

Wehman, P., Kregel, J., and Seyfarth, J. (1985). Employment Outlook for Young Adults with Mental Retardation. *Rehabilitation Counseling Bulletin, 5*, 343–354.

Wolman, C., Thurlow, M. L., and Bruininks, R. H. (1989). Stability of Categorical Designation for Special Education Students: A Longitudinal Study. *The Journal of Special Education, 23*, 213–222.

Yell, M. L. (1995). Least Restrictive Environment, Inclusion, and Students with Disabilities: A Legal Analysis. *Journal of Special Education, 28*, 389–404.

Chapter 14

School Inclusion and Multicultural Issues in Special Education

Luanna H. Meyer, Beth Harry, and Mara Sapon-Shevin

Public Law 94-142 (now the Individuals with Disabilities Act, or IDEA) was passed by Congress in 1975 to prevent discrimination and the exclusion of children with disabilities from the public school system. Previously, children with disabilities could be refused entry to school or, if they were allowed to attend, they were virtually ignored as no accommodations were made to the general education curriculum that would enable them to succeed in school and graduate to meaningful adult roles. IDEA now requires that all children be provided with a free and appropriate education. In addition, various due process protections are included in the law to ensure that school districts must attend to the diverse needs of students who had not previously fit within an age-graded curriculum. Thus, special education can be viewed as a systemic response to extend equal educational opportunities to all children, with no exceptions. This is the generous and idealistic interpretation of special education.

Richardson (1994) describes another view of the development of special education. She discusses three worlds: the common, the delinquent, and the special. The introduction of compulsory education linked the three worlds, as students who were previously either voluntarily absent or systematically excluded began to come to school. The experiences of the state of California—a leader in the early special education movement—illustrate the relationship well.

In 1947, a "separation of races" clause that had existed unchallenged since 1883 was under attack as justification for segregating Mexican Americans in school. The

Preparation of this chapter was supported in part by Cooperative Agreement No. H086A2003, the Consortium for Collaborative Research on Social Relationships, awarded to Syracuse University (Luanna Meyer, Principal Investigator) from the U.S. Department of Education. However, the opinions expressed herein are not necessarily those of the Department of Education, and no official endorsement should be inferred.

court ruled that because they did not represent one of the "great races of man," Mexican Americans could not be segregated. Richardson (1994) presents evidence that this judicial decision was the impetus for the establishment in California of special education classes for students who were then formally labeled educably mentally retarded, or EMR. Further, as both the overall school-age population and school attendance continued to increase, there occurred a dramatic increase in the use of long-term suspensions for reasons such as low motivation, poor adjustment, and other forms of withdrawal (Divergent Youth, 1963; Richardson, 1994). The original function of special education as a program focused on intellectual disabilities was expanded to include new behavioral categories. Writes Richardson (1994), "In a culmination of hearings and investigations into youth divergence, the special education provision for educationally handicapped minors was formally enacted in 1963" (p. 713).

From this second perspective, special education emerged not primarily as a strategy to meet individual needs but, instead, to provide a mechanism for sending some children to school elsewhere, apart from their nondisabled peers. Dunn (1968) argued this point in his influential article, "Special Education for the Mildly Retarded: Is Much of It Justifiable?" He noted that segregated programs for students with mental retardation grew at the same time that the *Brown* v. *Board of Education* decision was otherwise challenging racial segregation during the 1950s and 1960s. Further, he highlighted the disproportionate overrepresentation of children of color in segregated special education classes and presented evidence that children in the segregated programs did less well academically than similar children who had remained in general education with no special education services. Special education was being used, Dunn (1968) charged, as a strategy for continued racial segregation. It was a scathing critique and widely discussed for many years.

Yet, states Richardson, special education "occupies the high ground of many contemporary educational debates" located at "the forefront of pedagogical innovation and judicial reform" (Richardson, 1994, p. 713). Special education rose to the challenge of developing diverse instructional strategies that resulted in significant educational attainment even in children once labeled "uneducable" (Horner, Meyer, & Fredericks, 1986). This occurred at a time when general education continued, for the most part, to maintain the myth of homogeneity. Within the broader educational community, movements that acknowledge diversity are seen as recent and even controversial, such as multicultural education and instructional innovations based on theories of multiple intelligences and diverse learning styles (Banks & Banks, 1995).

Which interpretation is correct? Is special education the villian—or the savior? Is it leading the way for a general education system that is finally ready to accept diversity and teach children as they are—not as we want them to be? The overall theme of this chapter is that both interpretations ring true. We believe that it is critical to acknowledge that the major motivation for systemic support of special education may have been the exclusion of children who were seen as different and who challenged the system. Unless we recognize this possibility, we cannot fully appreciate how difficult and important it will be to accomplish their re-entry. Special educators who accepted the challenge to educate children excluded from general education have generated principles, perspectives, and instructional strategies of value. Special education was allowed to exist and even thrive for many of the wrong reasons, but the strategies that emerged must be incorporated into the general education system in order to educate, enrich, and nurture the educational and socioemotional development of all children. This is the basic premise of the movement for quality inclusive schooling.

We begin this chapter with a brief overview of the overrepresentation issue and the linkages between cultural inclusion and quality inclusive schooling for various marginalized populations of students. We then discuss the role of the family and home-school involvement in inclusive schools and end this section with recommendations for ideal parental participation. Next, we describe what quality inclusive schooling looks like and discuss the process of building school communities and changing teacher education accordingly. Finally, we challenge the reader to consider the consequences of continued fragmentation and splintering of structures and resources in U.S. education. We call for a better balance between the responsibility to meet individual as well as interpersonal needs to produce not only an educated but also a socially responsible citizenry.

THE OVERREPRESENTATION OF CHILDREN OF COLOR

Concern over the disproportionate representation of children of color in special education continues to be an issue (Artiles & Trent, 1994; Dunn, 1968). In California's early special education programs, many more African American and Hispanic students were diagnosed as "Educably Mentally Retarded" (EMR) than would have been expected based on their representation in the general population (Finn, 1982; Kirp, 1973; Mercer, 1973; Walker, 1987). Mercer's (1973) research offered a major and seminal critique of the concept of educable mental retardation. She suggested that the diagnosis was accurate only for Anglo children who displayed learning difficulties both at home and at school. In contrast, the majority of African American and Hispanic children who were labeled "retarded" by their school system during the school day showed no impairment in adaptive behavior in their home, neighborhood, and community. The phrase "six-hour retarded child" was used tongue-in-cheek throughout ensuing discussions of this discrepancy to note the irony of being labeled retarded by teachers while doing just fine outside of school.

Mercer (1973) argued that both the school structure itself and the nature of cognitive measures (such as IQ) used to identify mental retardation were culturally biased in favor of Anglo children and against children of color. The majority of the children of color who had the label "EMR" were not retarded at all—they were simply mislabeled by discriminatory assessment practices and measures. Mercer (1979) developed and validated the *System of Multicultural Assessment (SOMPA)*, which became a model for culture-free cognitive assessment. Her pioneering work was also instrumental in the design of certain procedural safeguards incorporated into IDEA, with key provisions requiring nondiscriminatory assessment and the use of both intellectual and adaptive behavior evaluations to establish eligiblity for special education services.

What happened next was a shift in the pattern of diagnosis. The population of children with the label "educable mental retardation" declined dramatically during the 1970s and 1980s, and, in parallel, the population of children receiving services as learning disabled or educationally handicapped increased just as dramatically. Smith (1983) noted that African Americans continued to be overrepresented in EMR classes, and that where there were decreases, children of color were increasingly placed in LD classrooms. By the 1990s, overrepresentation of children of color that had occurred in EMR classes now was present in the learning disability (LD) label (Argulewicz, 1983; MacMillan, Jones, & Meyers, 1976; Tucker, 1980).

Disproportionate representation also occurred in other categories. Meier, Stewart, and England (1989) reported the results of a large-scale study conducted in nearly 200 school districts that examined the effects of socioeconomic status and race on educational opportunities. They found widespread evidence of what they referred to as "second-generation discrimination," including various sorting practices resulting in overrepresentation of African American students in special education classrooms. African American students were also disproportionately punished or suspended through disciplinary sanctions. In contrast, "a white student was 3.2 times more likely to be assigned to a gifted class than is a black student" (Meier et al., 1989, p. 5).

Gottlieb, Alter, Gottlieb, and Wishner (1994) reported data from several large-scale studies showing that children attending special education classes in urban districts between 1984 and 1993 were overwhelmingly poor. Most were labeled "learning disabled," and of these, 19 percent were foreign born and an additional 44 percent were from homes where English was not the primary language spoken by caregivers. Gottlieb and his colleagues also demonstrated that only a small percentage of LD students (15 percent) in a 1992 sample actually fit the clinical definition for this disability; instead, most were poor children with low achievement and low scores on cognitive measures (Gottlieb et al., 1994, p. 458). What is happening, according to these authors, is that special education is being asked to accept "regular education *fallout*" (original emphasis), adding: "The current state of urban education, so woefully underfunded relative to its needs, provides students little access to intensive resources outside of special education" (Gottlieb et al., 1994, p. 459).

THE INFLUENCE OF PARENT PARTICIPATION

Parental involvement in education is not unique to special education. However, there are two reasons parental involvement is even more crucial for children with disabilities than for other children. First, students with disabilities are more vulnerable as their performance and behavior may be misinterpreted through the use of inappropriate and incorrect assessments. Students with cognitive and language impairments may not be able to report negligent or abusive practices to their parents. Parental input is therefore essential to ensure professional understanding of the student as well as to protect the student. Second, the historical fact that students with significant disabilities were traditionally excluded altogether from schools has necessitated greater specification of student rights and, consequently, parental rights to ensure adequate provision of educational services to which the child is entitled.

For children of color, parental involvement becomes even more critical within the context of their overrepresentation in special education services. Parental involvement can function as a protection against the misinterpretion of cultural behavioral differences by White professionals. Yet, by all reports in the literature and in the common parlance of school personnel, low-income and minority parents are the very parents who are described as being the least participatory (Harry, 1992).

In this section, we analyze the way parental participation plays out for these families in special education. Understanding why these parents are apparently disempowered in the special education system may help us develop alternative strategies enabling families to advocate effectively for their children's needs.

The Structure of Parent Participation in Special Education

Policy makers, practitioners, researchers, and theorists in special education envisaged a parent-professional interaction that would function as an equitable "partnership" (Turnbull & Turnbull, 1990). IDEA specifies due process requirements for this partnership that must be observed in the referral, evaluation, placement, and instruction of a student with a disability:

- At the point that a child is referred to special education, parental permission must be received for an evaluation.

- If the evaluation recommends special education placement, parental permission must be received for such placement, but if the parent disagrees with the evaluation he or she is entitled to seek an independent evaluation that must be paid for by the district if the results do not concur.

- Once the child is placed in a special education program, an individualized program is developed and parents must be invited annually to help develop and approve this plan.

- Each student must receive a full reevaluation every three years, and parents must be notified of this, although their permission for the reevaluation is not required.

Ideally, this legal mandate would result in meaningful parent participation. The language of the law, however, does not require the ideal. Rather, it reflects a legal discourse that focuses on objectively verifiable acts between parents and professionals, such as the receipt by parents of "notification" of certain intentions and the receipt by school systems of "informed consent" from the parents. These very formalistic notions of legal accountability differ considerably from the interaction syles familiar to most families. The process becomes even less helpful for families as school districts have institutionalized legalistic procedures to meet the parent participation requirements of the law; this process is discussed next.

The Influence of the Legal Framework on Parental Participation

The most important feature of parent-professional communication, as currently practiced, is written documentation. This includes informing parents of their legal rights, gaining parental consent, and gaining evidence of waivers of rights, such as the right to receive notice of a meeting within the time specified by the state regulations. The paperwork involved is time-consuming for teachers and overwhelming, even confusing or alienating, for many parents (Correa, 1987; Figler, 1981; Harry, 1992; Harry, Allen, & McLaughlin, 1995).

In most school systems, sharing these written records at the required annual review conference has become the centerpiece of communication with parents. The purposes of the conference are to review the student's performance and to develop a new Individualized Educational Program (IEP) for the coming academic period. However, the IEP is almost always prespecified by professionals and presented to the parents for their consent and signature. Exemplary conferences include reports from all professionals who provide services to the child, including the special education teacher and related services personnel. However, in practice, parents are seldom provided an opportunity to speak with the entire team. Most important, there is no explicit expectation of the parental role at these conference. Research (Evans, Salisbury, Palombaro, & Goldberg, 1994) on parent conferences shows that it is very common for professionals to hold low expectations of parent involvement at these meetings, and, indeed, observations of meetings show that parents are not generally expected to participate in any active way. Rather, the agenda is usually structured in such a way as to relegate the parent to the position of recipient of professional opinions and signatory to their recommendations.

In a three-year study of the participation of African American parents of preschoolers (Harry et al., 1995), one mother summarized the process in these words: "They lay it out [the IEP]. If you have a question, you can ask them. Then you sign it." This view of the process has been corroborated by several studies (Bennett, 1988; Harry, 1992; Mehan, Hartwick, & Meihls, 1986).

The Influence of the Medical Framework on Parental Participation

The medical model continues to dominate special education. Within this model, disabilities are seen as phenomena that reside within individuals, and can, therefore, be identified, assessed, and treated by experts using objective measures and methods. Professionals continue to promulgate this medical model even for categories as ambiguous as Attention Deficit Hyperactivity Disorder (ADHD), where there will be virtually no organic signs to identify the disability, along with considerable evidence that boys, and particularly certain ethnic groups of boys (e.g., African American boys), are greatly overrepresented (Gottlieb & Alter, 1995).

The scientific belief in objectivity is central to this process. Professionals are trained to value only information that has the appearance of objectivity and to use language that reflects this value. The resulting form of discourse is, therefore, what Hall (1977) has referred to as "low context," a form of communication that excludes information that may be construed as ambiguous or imprecise. Parental participation is very difficult to achieve within this mode, and the ideal of a "partnership" is almost impossible, since the input of professionals is considered essential while that of parents is seen as subjective by nature and thus lacking credibility (for detailed analyses of the implicit imbalance of power in this relationships, see Gliedman & Roth, 1980, and Mehan, Hartwick, & Meihls, 1986).

The irony of this preference for scientific knowledge is that only a small percentage of disabilities can be delineated by the methods of science and revealed through physical or organic evidence such as sensory impairments, motor damage, or genetic disorders mapped organically. The vast majority of children receiving special education services have so-called handicapping conditions that defy biological evidence—their existence relies completely on clinical judgment and reflects the values of the society. In their model program serving Latino language minority children, Ruiz, Rueda, Figueroa, and Boothroyd (in press) note that teachers with a great deal of special education training tended to use a medical model deficit-based approach to describe children with learning disabilities. As they became more versed in instructional strategies reflecting holistic and constructivist principles of teaching and learning, they shifted their perspective to viewing the children's learning problems as within-school and not within-child (Poplin, 1988). As Mercer (1973) had reported years earlier, for the majority of children in special education, disability exists only in the eyes of the school—not within any biological process or deficit in the child. The "cultural discontinuity" noted by Grant and Secada (1990) between students of color and general education teachers who are predominately White increases the potential for cultural misunderstandings to turn into false labels and removal from the classroom to segregated programs.

Cultural Discontinuity in Parent Participation

The special education structure of written communication and formal face-to-face conferences assigns a passive respondent role to parents unless they possess the professional language and monocultural, legalistic skills integral to the process. The distinct middle-class quality of these events is a source of discomfort for many low-income and working-class parents. Add to this the likelihood that virtually the entire educational team facing the family will be themselves White and middle class, while most parents of children with disabilities are neither White nor middle class. Neither within nor outside these two sets of events is there any avenue for the voice of parents who do not use the language of this system.

The present situation may satisfy the requirements of the law but in reality serves to disenfranchise rather than empower parents who do not have the cultural capital to negotiate the system. Indeed, even White, middle-class parents find this challenge difficult. For example, in her well-known guide for parents, Coyne Cutler (1993), herself a parent, exhorts parents to develop various skills to advocate for their children in the following ways: making effective telephone calls and writing formal letters to school principals and school district administrators, reviewing school records, and keeping records. The productive assertiveness and productive confrontation framework in which these activities are suggested illustrate how difficult such advocacy would be for a parent whom professionals perceive as being of low social status and less educated and whose literacy skills or experience with U.S. schools and bureaucracies are not adequate to these tasks.

Research on the participation of minority families commonly points to logistical concerns such as transportation and child-care needs. But these instrumental barriers may be easily surmountable and relatively insignificant in comparison to the numerous barriers related to the structure and process of the special education system itself. Bennett (1988), for example, used ethnographic data with Caribbean Hispanic families to illustrate how school personnel determined what could be discussed at the IEP conference, and, in so doing, effectively excluded a parent's concern with classroom climate as a factor in her child's education. Studies by Harry (1992) and Harry et al. (1995) of the perspectives of Puerto Rican and African American families offer a vivid picture of parents gradually withdrawing from interaction with professionals because of the alienating influence of two factors: (a) the legal and medical frameworks outlined above and (b) their incompatibility with the more personal and less technological cultural frameworks from which parents came. Similarly, Figler (1981) showed the alienating influences of written communication and misunderstanding among Puerto Rican parents. All of these studies also identified a pattern of deferential parental behavior that masked their real reactions to the process.

Another aspect of the medical model that creates confusion for many minority and low-income parents is the disability classification system. While middle-class parents have fought to gain recognition of mild disability categories such as learning disabilities and attention deficit disorder (and even gifted learning disabilities), low-income parents maintain a broader perspective. They accept a wider variation in ability and development as part of the spectrum of human variation and do not necessarily think of most variations as disabilities (Mercer, 1973). Mild mental retardation, for example, has been described by low-income Puerto Rican and African American parents as too severe a term for students who can read and write and may live relatively independent lives (Harry, 1992; Harry et al., 1995; Smith-Lewis, 1993). The Puerto Rican parents in Harry's study also rejected the notion of learning disabilities, attributing their children's difficulties to second-language acquisition or to family characteristics.

One final, overarching aspect of the effects of existing practice on minority parents is that the field of education has traditionally cast certain minority groups in a deficit role. This is notably the case for African Americans and Native Americans. The parent education movement throughout the twentieth century has increasingly represented middle-class beliefs and values about appropriate child-rearing techniques. For example, ideals such as democratic yet structured parent-child interactions or the promotion of personal individuality and the value of competition for even young children have become entrenched as correct beliefs. Many minority and low-income families differ from these practices. An African American family may continue to adhere to traditional parent-child interactional styles (Delpit, 1988), and a Native American tribe's tradition of a relatively unrestrictive mode of child rearing is often interpreted as negligence by mainstream professionals (Cunningham, Cunningham, & O'Connell, 1986; Medicine, 1981).

Further, middle-class assumptions about family structures have been based on a vision of the nuclear family upheld as the ideal to which other types of family arrangements are (unfavorably) compared. Such cultural discontinuities lead to the belief that families who do not adhere to mainstream patterns and traditions need training to inculcate the appropriate behaviors and patterns of child-rearing. The deficit view continues to be another souce of alienation for minority families. Not only are they seen as falling short of meaningful participation in the parental involvement models central to the special education system, they also are viewed as failing in their own primary child-rearing responsibilities (Ball & Harry, 1993).

Toward the Ideal in Parent Participation

There are several sources of difficulty in the parent-school relationship that intersects with the special education system. Harry (1992) presents considerable evidence that the legalistic and formalistic nature of the mandates designed to promote parent involvement in special education are actually culturally biased—favoring Anglo and middle-class parents. Effective practices that would ensure representation of family members of color will require strategies that begin with trust between parents and professionals. Such strategies are not likely to be illustrated solely through the more narrow framing of participation required by law such as attendance and signatures at certain meetings arranged by professionals. They are far more likely to be evidenced by ongoing communication between teachers and family members.

If that is true, another issue that must be addressed is the cultural discontinuity between the teacher—most often White and middle class as well as English-speaking—and the family—increasingly ethnically diverse and speaking a primary language other than English. Harry (1992) and Harry et al. (in press) have reported strategies that professionals can and do use even where such cultural discontinuities exist in order to nevertheless carry out exemplary parent-teacher conferences. Successful conferences seemed to be the result of sensitive responding of individual professionals or teams to the concerns expressed by parents during those meetings. Of course, truly exemplary conferences must be based on a systemic structure that incorporates parental participation, rather than relying on the good will and personality characteristics of individual professionals and the initiative of parents (Correa, 1987; Goldstein & Turnbull, 1982; Malmberg, 1984; Thompson, 1982). However, we still need a great deal of information about what such conference communication strategies might be. It is possible that they can be described and taught to teachers and teacher trainees as part of their teacher education programs (Harry & Kalyanpur, 1994).

Yet, in many instances, the gap between professional and parent may be insurmountable. Linguistic differences, particularly in urban and rural school districts enrolling large new immigrant populations, are unlikely to be satisfactorily addressed by sensitive communication strategies where the language of the home is not spoken by any professional in school—at least for several years. Harry (1992) described how one school district increased the participation of a group of Puerto Rican parents by hiring a family liaison whose primary job was to personalize and clarify the entire special education process for parents. Such efforts must be accompanied by effective professional development in effective communication and understanding of multicultural issues related to families and cultural perspectives on disabilities (Harry, 1992; Marion, 1979).

Evans, Okifuji, and Thomas (1995) describe the role of school partners. School partners were paraprofessional staff hired by their school district to serve as mediators and go-betweens, to advocate for both parents and teachers, and to interpret each group's needs. These school partners worked at primary-grade levels. Evidence of their effectiveness was sufficient to ensure continued staffing throughout the early phases of budget reductions (Evans et al., 1995). Such positions are now being eliminated as part of cost cutting. Paraprofessional personnel are staffed in special education programs, but little has been published regarding their role in inclusive programs.

QUALITY INCLUSIVE SCHOOLING: BUILDING SCHOOL COMMUNITIES

Recognizing that students are diverse in many ways and that diversity should be celebrated rather than denied has implications for how school programs are organized and services delivered. We are committeed to the creation and support of school communities that are inclusive. Inclusive schools are purposely heterogeneous and attempt to meet individual educational needs within a shared, common social context, without the requirement or expectation that a child must go elsewhere for services (Meyer, 1994a; Roach, 1994). The movement for quality inclusive schooling began with a focus on enabling students with disabilities to attend their neighborhood schools and classrooms, instead of segregated, handicapped-only schools and programs (Giangreco & Putnam, 1991; Will, 1986). However, the inclusive schooling movement is now centered within the broader agenda of de-tracking and merging previously fragmented and categorical services for children (Cohen, 1994; Roach, 1994; Sapon-Shevin, 1994, 1994/1995). From this perspective, inclusion entails a system that responds sensitively and appropriately to racial, ethnic, religious, and all student differences within a cohesive school community (Ayres, 1993).

Ramsey's (1987) eight goals for teaching from a multicultural perspective represent the kinds of interpersonal and intrapersonal attitudes and behaviors also regarded as critical to quality inclusive schooling. These goals include teaching children to appreciate and value the contributions of others, to see themselves as members of a larger society, to respect different perspectives, and to accept responsibility for their social environment and society (Ramsey, 1987). Teaching children to be knowledgeable about differences, supportive of others, and active in changing structures that are oppressive to various groups can begin within inclusive classrooms. We now have a rich data base demonstrating the benefits to the individual children (all children, not only those with disabilities), professional school personnel, and the community as a function of the development of quality inclusive schooling and meaningful social interactions between children with and without disabilities (Meyer, 1994a). We have documentation of effective strategies to meet the educational needs of even students with the most significant disabilities enrolled in quality inclusive programs with their nondisabled peers (Giangreco & Putnam, 1991; York & Vandercook, 1990).

The integration of support services within general education reflects best practices in special education. It also represents a commitment to addressing all of a child's needs without pullout or removal from that child's peer group and community and makes those services available to support other, nonlabeled children as well. Finally, a classroom that openly and directly addresses the interests, needs, and possibilities of all its members provides children with the best, direct experience of democratic structures that empower and support all learners.

A major implication of this philosophy is that special services to children be delivered within the general education context. For example, Shakira may need speech therapy, but rather than being sent elsewhere to receive that help (to a speech therapist down the hall for a fifteen-minute lesson), the speech therapist plans with the general education classroom teacher how to meet Shakira's speech needs within the regular classroom. The speech therapist may come in and work with Shakira and a small group of other children—who can also be positive speech models for her—or she may coach the teacher on how to work with Shakira during her usual reading group activities. But Shakira, as an African American student, may have other educational needs as well. The speech therapist must be sensitive to issues of Shakira's dialect of English as she plans what speech patterns do and do not require remediation. Shakira must be viewed as a person with multiple identities, and these identities must be dealt with in an integrated fashion within the classroom.

Inclusive Schools: The School as Community

What does it mean to be a community? A community is a group of people who are joined for a common purpose, with the contribution of each member valued and respected. Within a given school community, teaching, extra-curricular activities, and the curriculum itself must be organized to support positive social interactions and the valuing of differences. The Child Development Project (CDP) model described by Solomon, Schaps, Watson, and Battistich (1992) is unique in that its primary goal is not the improvement of academic skills, but the creation of school communities to promote interpersonal responsibility and foster growth and development in the areas of social and moral development. Within that context, extensive academic growth occurs, but the organizing variable is caring. Write Solomon et al. (1992):

> The goal of the CDP school-wide program is to create an ethos in which care and trust are emphasized above restrictions and threats, and where each person is asked to try to live up to the ideals of kindness, fairness, and responsibility. Rather than telling students what the rules are, and what happens to them if they break them, we try to involve students in deciding what kind of school they all want, and in working to make it that kind of school. This implies a certain degree of trust in the goodwill of students, and in their capacity to support one another and to be able to see the benefits of working and learning in a caring environment. (p. 51)

Inclusion advocates are keenly aware that the culture of the school must be one that supports diversity, mutual regard, and caring as well as the need to adapt instruction in ways that do not stigmatize or separate students. For a community to be fully functional, it must provide each of the following: (a) the safety to show oneself as an individual; (b) opportunities to know others beyond a superficial level; and (c) structures that promote positive interaction and interdependence.

The Safety to Show Oneself as an Individual

In order for individuals to contribute to a community and derive full benefits from membership in that community, they must feel safe to reveal themselves fully, free of the threat of humiliation or reproach. Teachers and administrators create that kind of safety by supporting risk-taking, providing positive feedback, and eliminating or minimizing negative competition and failure. All individuals are multifaceted. Banks (see chapter 1) emphasizes that all individuals bring with them to any interaction a racial identity, an ethnic background, their gender, their age, their religion, their social class, as well as other group identities. Mee Wong is a ten-year-old girl. She is also Korean, lives in the city, has two working-class parents, and is a practicing Buddhist. Having a learning disability may be part of her identity, but it does not define who she is. All of her characteristics help define who she is and must be respected in the classroom. Having a learning disability should not preclude her from being fully accepted in the general education classroom any more than being Buddhist should exclude her from her peer group and neighborhood.

Grant and Sleeter in chapter 3 explain that race, social class, and gender are used to construct major groups of people in society. Because all students are members of all three status groups, each of these groups and the interactions among these groups affect students' perceptions and actions. When issues of disability are added to these categories, the number of interactions and spheres of influence increases exponentially. Adapting a Christmas craft activity for Joshua, who has cerebral palsy and uses a communication board, may not be an appropriate or adequate response to his individual identity when we know that Joshua is Jewish and does not celebrate Christmas. If we define Joshua according to only one dimension of his identity, we cannot meet his needs and treat him with respect. Shamika is African American, lives with her mother, and has difficulties reading. When she is given reading books at her level, we should be thoughtful about not limiting the reading materials to books that portray only European American, two-parent families. We should create classroom environments in which children are comfortable revealing all aspects of their backgrounds and experiences that matter to them. Classrooms must support the diversity of students by responding to each of their identities, and not stereotyping students according to unidimensional and narrow notions of who they are.

Opportunities to Know One Another

Within a classroom community, students must have opportunities to learn about their classmates in ways that honor the full range of experiences and differences that each child brings to the classroom. Children differ in terms of age, size, ethnic and racial background, skills and abilities, religion, and family structure. A teacher cannot mandate instant trust and connection, but he or she can structure situations and interaction opportunities that allow students to learn about one another. Students must be provided with occasions to talk about their family situations, cultural experiences and values, religion, leisure-time activities, and other aspects of their personal lives. Educational theorists emphasize how critical social context is for virtually all learning and the value of a child's experience for the mastery of everything new (Tharp & Gallimore, 1989; Vygotsky, 1978). Putting those theories into action will require that we reference children's personal and social lives throughout their academic lives.

Sapon-Shevin (1992) has detailed the ways in which teachers can structure their classrooms so that students learn about racial, cultural, family, gender, religious, and skill differences as part of the curriculum. This information need not be limited to learning facts about other groups, but can be extended so that students are actively working to understand and combat prejudices and stereotypes they encounter in school and society. Louise Derman-Sparks's (1989) *Anti-Bias Curriculum* provides numerous examples of how even very young children can be empowered to challenge injustices and inequities in society.

Structures That Promote Helping and Positive Interaction

Inclusive classroom communities must provide multiple occasions for students to work with one another and provide positive peer support. Inflexible hierarchies of skill or status in which certain children are consistently the givers and others the receivers must be transformed into more reciprocal peer relationships in which all students have the opportunity to teach, help, and support their classmates (Meyer, 1991). Peer tutoring opportunities and models such as reciprocal teaching both within the classroom and across classroom settings, shared projects, and a general classroom atmosphere that encourages and supports positive student interactions are necessary to enhance the classroom community. Rules that discourage student interaction (such as strict teacher control over talking, seating patterns, and movements within the classroom) must be modified so that students can look to one another for support.

Villa and Thousand (1992) have detailed many ways in which students can be involved in helping and teaching one another in classroom settings. Students can function as part of teaching teams that allow any student to receive intensive instructional support within the classroom. Same-age and cross-age partner learning systems can also be established within a single classroom, or across classrooms or the entire school. A wide variety of cooperative learning strategies also enable students to learn how to support one another while they learn, rather than teaching them to learn in competition with one another (Putnam, 1993; Sapon-Shevin, Ayres, & Duncan, 1994). The benefits to students receiving instruction from peers include academic gains, opportunities to develop friendships that can emerge from working together over time, the development of personal social skills in the context of structured peer interactions, and heightened self-esteem. Furthermore, the child being tutored is not the only one to benefit: the child who is the tutor also benefits as a result of the opportunity to practice leadership skills, to improve communication skills, and to develop higher level metacognitive thinking and problem-solving skills.

INCLUSIVE CLASSROOMS, INCLUSIVE PEDAGOGY

To speak of a classroom as inclusive requires not only that a full range of students are represented and respected within the classroom context, but also that the teaching strategies employed are responsive to and inclusive of those differences. Narrow, inflexible teaching practices that assume that all student learn best in the same way and

bring the same expriences, background, learning style, and interests to the task are neither inclusive nor sensitive to student needs. Inclusive pedagogy can be described in
terms of both the content of what is taught and the process.

Inclusive Curricula

Banks, in chapter 10, discusses the ways in which the "mainstream-centric curriculum"
can be modified to incorporate multiple perspectives, and he describes four levels of
integration of multicultural content (see chapter 10 for a more extensive discussion of
these levels). Issues of ability-disability can be incorporated into the practices of teaching and learning at each of these four levels:

- At the level of Contributions, focusing on heroes, holidays, and discrete
  cultural elements, this approach has been reflected in having the class read
  a book about Helen Keller and teaching a unit on blindness. Students may
  come to appreciate that persons who are blind can make important contributions, but they are not being challenged to question the more fundamental notions of segregation and exclusion of *most* people who are blind
  who are not seen as making exemplary contributions.

- At the Additive level, "content, concepts, themes, and perspectives are
  added to the curriculum without changing its structure" (Banks, 1993,
  p. 199). A special education parallel to this approach is to mainstream students with special education needs while leaving the curriculum of the
  classroom intact. Special activities may be implemented for the students
  with disabilities, but these activities are not integrated into the main life
  and curriculum of the classroom. Operationally, an island in the mainstream is the result, consisting of a special education student or small
  group working with a special educator on a separate activity while classmates are engaged in the larger group activity. Early exemplars of integration differed from today's inclusive efforts in their fundamental practices
  of creating small tutorials within the general education classroom rather
  than modifying ongoing instructional activities to enable the student with
  disabilities to participate fully.

- In the Transformational approach, "the structure of the curriculum is
  changed to enable students to view concepts, issues, events, and themes
  from the perspectives of diverse ethnic and cultural groups" (Banks, 1993,
  p. 199). This approach from an inclusive perspective involves not only
  having students with special needs become part of the classroom, but also
  rethinking and reinventing the curriculum so that it is inclusive and multilevel. All students—across a diverse range of abilities and needs—would be
  engaged in educational experiences appropriate to their level but as part of
  a common topic, focus, and lesson (Putnam, 1993).

- The Social Action approach "includes all the elements of the transformation approach but adds components that require students to make decisions and take actions related to the concept, issue, or problem studied in

the unit" (Banks, 1993, p. 205). This would require both reshaping and reinventing the nature of general education classrooms and making them multilevel and inclusive as well as thinking about how schools and teaching can be part of a broader social goal of changing arbitrary and limiting notions of ability, expectations, and the need for segregation. This level has implications for school-based decisions about outcomes evaluation, diplomas, testing of students, and curriculum design, as exemplified by the National Council of the Teachers of Mathematics (1993) standards that reconceptualize broader outcomes such as critical thinking and problem solving. These goals relate meaningfully to the use of mathematics in life and can be readily adapted to represent the wide range of mathematics skill levels of students found in any given classroom. Thus, students with and without disabilities might be working on their problem-solving skills in mathematics, but each student would have an individually appropriate learner objective and the instructional unit would be adapted accordingly. Again, one model for accomplishing this in inclusive classrooms has been cooperative learning (Putnam, 1993; Sapon-Shevin, Ayres, & Duncan, 1994). There may be many others, and the challenges of the coming years will be to consider major changes in how curriculum is designed and implemented to better meet the diverse needs of students.

Inclusive Pedagogy

Inclusive pedagogy can be described as a set of teaching practices and structures that acknowledge student differences and are responsive to that diversity. Banks's (1993) transformation and social action levels represent inclusive pedagogy. Cooperative learning and other strategies to support multilevel instruction are examples of pedagogy that can be structured inclusively. In cooperative learning structures, students work together to achieve common goals. Social skills (listening, compromising, asking questions, encouraging) are taught both formally and informally, and the task is structured so that students must work together in order to achieve a successful product. A cooperatively structured math lesson, for example, may involve students generating and then solving their own multistep math problems. A student with a disability who cannot write could contribute to the task as the checker for the group, doing the problem on a calculator and confirming the group's answer. Tasks can be structured so that students generate problems related to their own lives and experiences. Because students are working together, student differences can contribute to successful task completion, rather than being viewed as obstacles to some standard curriculum.

Multilevel instruction involves structuring lessons so that different modalities, different content areas, and different levels of performance can be accommodated within current educational practices (Putnam, 1993). For example, a thematic unit on families could involve math activities (graphing family demographics), language (writing biographies of family members, taking oral histories), and exploring music and arts activities related to different cultures. All students could be involved in reading, writing, and math activities appropriate to their levels and interests, so that even a student with the most profound disabilities could be meeting his or her educational objective in such a unit.

For example, a student with multiple disabilities might be working on operating a switch to activate a computer, small appliances, or a tape recorder. Depending on the student's communication goals, two needs could be met within the context of this hypothetical family unit. First, the student could be telling a biography of a family member by listing some descriptive facts about a brother or sister—this might be part of a communication goal for that student involving describing important personal characteristics and using an augmentative communication system to write this list. Second, the student could be working on operating a switch to activate a tape recording of that list read out by a classmate, so that when it is that student's turn to read the biography to the class, the student must operate the switch to start the recording and then again to stop it at the end. There are numerous examples of successfully including students with special needs through adaptations to good instruction and educational best practices for all students (Meyer, Williams, Harootunian, & Steinberg, 1995; Salisbury, Palombaro, & Hollowood, 1993; Sapon-Shevin, Ayres, & Duncan, 1994; Scruggs & Mastropieri, 1994).

INCLUSIVE SOCIAL SUPPORTS WITHIN THE SCHOOL COMMUNITY

Ideally, the inclusive nature of the classroom community is paralleled by an inclusive school community that encourages and supports the full participation of all parents and staff members. In many schools, decision making is noncollaborative and top-down, placing the majority of participants in the role of receiving information and responding to policy decisions that have already been made. Alternative decision-making models are needed that involve participants from the beginning, before policy is made. Models of Task Force planning and team decision making within special education must be expanded in scope to encompass broader issues of an inclusive school system.

For example, the group process described in Schnorr, Ford, Davern, Park-Lee, and Meyer (1989) for curricular planning by parents and teachers on behalf of students with significant disabilities has been revised to incorporate systems-change planning by school districts implementing their first inclusive programs (Black, Meyer, & Giugno, 1993). The Task Force approach begins by selecting or recruiting participating members who represent the relevant constituents of an educational change, such as district administrators, building principal, both general and special education teachers, and one or more parents. Depending on the focus, other members might also be involved. For example, therapists (occupational, physical, and speech) should participate in planning to involve students with multiple and communication disabilities. Similarly, school psychologists and mental health professionals should participate in models to include students with emotional and behavioral needs in general education environments.

In addition to collaboration by professionals and adults in school planning, a number of models involve peers and students in the process. Pugach and Johnson

(1990) describe a model for peer collaboration through which teachers work together to clarify problems, generate possible interventions, and then evaluate outcomes. They report that although the model was originally designed for the specific purpose of addressing the needs of individual students who were not having successful school experiences, teachers and principals found the process to be effective for addressing an array of needs regarding curricular issues, schoolwide management issues, coordinated scheduling of specialist time, and the use of resources (Pugach & Johnson, 1990).

Other such collaborative teamwork models are described by Vandercook and York (1990), Thousand and Villa (1990), and Meyer and Henry (1993). Meyer and Henry (1993) emphasize that students' perceptions of the schooling experience can be so powerful that educators must become more interested in and sensitive to those perceptions. Rather than assuming that students benefit from school efforts at inclusion and support structures, processes such as student interviews and student focus group discussions can provide the school team with information on whether such innovations are working as planned from the students' perspectives (Henry, 1994). Students do not always perceive school practices as fair (Brantlinger, 1991; Evans, et al., 1994; Henry, 1994).

Supports for students can also be de-professionalized to good advantage. Student support groups that meet on a regular basis to discuss school and personal concerns and to problem solve have been very successful in promoting positive social interaction and caring among students. In Johnson City, New York, children have been taught to engage in a model called Collaborative Problem Solving (Salisbury & Palombaro, 1991; Salisbury, Palombaro, & Evans, 1993). The students respond to the dilemmas posed by the inclusion of students with severe disabilities in their classrooms and are able to generate solutions that will allow these classmates to be full participants in the life of the classroom. If the students notice, for example, that a child with a physical disability is not able to fully participate in playground activities, the students might generate ideas for alternatives, evaluate whether the ideas are feasible, try out the most promising solution, and then evaluate their success as a group. Even very young children are able to do this and often generate more creative ideas than the adults (Salisbury & Palombaro, 1991).

Along similar lines, Villa and Thousand (1992) reported the results of supporting students as peer advocates: "Peer support, in its various forms, can quickly become the norm within a school. Recently, in a school where peer support systems have been functioning for two years, over 25 percent of the junior high school body volunteered to be buddies for a new seventh grader whose primary school experiences had been in segregated special education classes" (p. 134).

It is important, of course, that these peer support structures are reciprocal. Students with disabilities must be given opportunities to teach, help, and assist other students as well as being recipients of such help and support. If we do not attend to the reciprocity of peer tutoring and peer buddy systems, our peer support structures may be little more than training students to become little special educators for their peers who have disabilities. Hierarchical role relationships may have unintended negative consequences in the long run in addition to the short-term positive outcomes of helping that we see. In a longitudinal follow-up of a large sample of nondisabled teenagers ages sixteen to eighteen who had been Special Friends to students with severe disabilities years earlier in elementary school, there were a number of negative memories associated with having been asked to perform caregiver and teacher-type roles in those interactions (Kishi & Meyer, 1994).

INCLUSIVE TEACHER EDUCATION

Prior to the concept of quality inclusive schooling, the delivery of special education services occurred in separate schools, classrooms, and/or resource rooms. In contrast, quality inclusive schooling entails the delivery of special education services and supports to children in the general education classroom. In principle, including students with disabilities as full participants in their schools and communities should signify an acceptance of individual differences that would generalize to enhancing the capacity of the school and its professional staff to accommodate a wide range of learning styles and needs. In practice, models of quality inclusive schools include access to special education services and supports for all students who might benefit—regardless of whether a child has a label or has been through the diagnostic process.

A major argument advanced in support of quality inclusive schooling is capacity building: schools and teachers within those schools would be committed to and capable of delivering effective instruction to all children, not only to those judged to be typical or tracked according to various criteria (Gartner & Lipsky, 1987; Meyer, 1994b; Roach, 1994; Sapon-Shevin, 1994). But who will staff those schools and classrooms? What are the implications of staffing inclusive schools with professionals who were themselves trained in programs tracked for either special or general education? We believe that just as cultural diversity demands preparation in multicultural education for all teachers, individual learning differences (including disabilities) demands the preparation of a new generation of teachers with a repertoire of values and strategies that match the demands of inclusive classrooms.

Today's teachers are not confident of their abilities to manage and accommodate the diverse range of student characteristics in their classrooms. Gottlieb et al. (1994) reported that 63 percent of the teachers who referred children out of the classroom to special education said they did not know what resources would enable them to teach those children within their classrooms. Only 16 percent believed they could be trained with the skills to enable them to teach children whom they had referred. Only 10 percent of the referring general education teachers could even describe a curricular adaptation they might make to accommodate the child. It is no wonder, then, that Gottlieb and his colleagues conclude that without "massive staff development efforts," the mainstreaming movement was unlikely to improve children's academic status (Gottlieb et al., 1994, p. 462). Similarly, in their 1994 study in New York City—again showing disproportionate referrals to special education for students whose needs were not much different from others—referring classroom teachers had made only one attempt to address the learner's needs prior to seeking placement elsewhere. That one attempt did not involve making curricular adaptations, modifying instruction, or even seeking additional professional technical assistance from within their school or district: What they did was call home and ask the parent to fix the problem. Given stressed economic circumstances and both cultural and language differences from that of the school professional staff, it is difficult to envision what parents would be expected to do to address academic learning and behavioral difficulties their children were experiencing in school.

The National Association of State Boards of Education (1992) recognized the implications of inclusion on teacher preparation programs and called for the development of new directions in teacher education consistent with the merger of special and general education in the classroom. Historically, many preservice teacher education programs have included dual certification options in both general and special education, but a truly merged program incorporating multicultural education as well as both special and general education training remains a rarity (National Association of State Boards of Education, 1994). We have described the components of the program initiated at the undergraduate level at Syracuse University in 1990; this continues to be the only provisional certification training program available to teacher education majors in elementary and special education (Meyer, Mager, Yarger-Kane, & Hext-Contreras, 1995). It is our belief that teachers entering the teaching profession must begin with this expanded commitment and increased capacity to serve all students, rather than seeing themselves as serving only one type of child. Our first graduates finished the program in 1994, but our feedback from them as well as various other constituent groups is promising with regard to whether the approach is preparing teachers for diversity and for the changes in our school population (Meyer et al., 1995).

DIVERSITY AND CARING COMMUNITIES: OUTCOMES FOR THE SOCIAL GOOD

We believe that the existence and perpetuation of pull-out solutions to student differences inevitably generates (and reflects) some perhaps unintended but very real side effects:

1. As long as the belief persists that general education classrooms are homogeneous, the cycle of referral for differences will continue and will, ultimately, exceed the resources of marginalized systems.

Our current dual system of general and special education encourages the school to conceptualize homogeneous typical groupings as the only functional structures for teaching and learning. Systems that allow and even encourage narrowing of commitment and capacity to serve diverse needs; that expect children to fit curriculum rather than adapting schooling to meet children's needs; and that institutionalize the identification of difference through segregation and tracking will increasingly reduce tolerance for differences and restrict the range of those who are viewed as being typical and who are seen as belonging. This is particularly dysfunctional at a time in U.S. history when new immigrant groups, increased poverty, and proportionately greater numbers of culturally and linguistically diverse students and families are a fact of life. The inevitable result will be an increasing cycle of referrals that will ultimately exceed the resources of the various special systems that are both marginalized and devalued by the mainstream society.

2. In the long run, efforts to reduce class size and restrict general education enrollment to smaller groups of students ready to learn will fail. Instead, as children leave the mainstream, resources will follow, and the cycle will repeat.

Gottlieb et al. (1994) note that the current system of special education reduces any need for the general education system to develop meaningful instructional and student support programs and services for children in the general education classroom. Teachers seemed to believe that the only mechanism available to them to reduce class size and the instructional challenges confronting them in the short run was to fully access referrals to special education—which, in large urban areas, continued to mean placement in a separate educational environment. But as children do leave the general education enrollment, resources must be provided to them at their new destination—and those resources must come from somewhere. Increasingly, resources have declined in general education as our many entitlement programs have increased. While the relationship may not be a simple one, we believe that declining resources will be spread ever more thinly—and ultimately, those resources will come from the same budget and class size will increase once again. A major argument advanced by proponents of quality inclusive schooling is that our educational system cannot afford separate and fragmented systems. Children with disabilities must return to general education classroom and attend school with their peers. But the resources supporting those children must return as well—and those resources must be restructured and capacities enhanced to better serve all children, those with and without disabilities.

3. When children with and without disabilities grow up in isolation from one another, they sacrifice much. Children will "Do as I do, and not as I say," and if we model segregation and rejection from a social system as central to our democratic institution as the public schools, we will have a great deal to answer for when those exclusionary models play out in the domains of daily living.

When children with disabilities are segregated from their nondisabled peers, they lose social context as a major teaching and learning environment. They become increasingly dependent on teacher-directed, highly structured learning and on adults in particular as the source of all new knowledge and support. On the other hand, they give up peer groups and participation in their neighborhood and community. Increasingly, as natural supports are prevented and thwarted from developing, persons with disabilities become more and more dependent on costly professional and paid services to fill the void.

Almost fifty years ago, Adorno, Frenkel-Brunswik, Levinson, and Sanford (1950) advanced their theory that one's attitudes toward persons who are viewed as different was part of a consistent pattern that affected all aspects of the individual's behavior and beliefs. Their studies of racial prejudice and political conservatism were premised on the theory that cultural acceptance would be associated with democratic principles, and that the promotion of cultural acceptance would thus have broad benefits for the social good. The movement for multiculturalism in education makes a similar point while acknowledging the futility of ignoring a pluralism that now dominates the population of U.S.

school children. Learning to accept individual differences and to celebrate diversity as an enriching experience are broad principles consistent with democratic values and the creation of caring schools that support children's growth and development.

In addition to multicultural education, various other general education reform movements emphasize the need for caring school communities. Berman (1990) builds a case for such school communities if we are to address the basic societal needs of our democracy for the "nurturing in young people of a sense of social responsibility and social efficacy" (p. 1); he notes with irony that "We teach reading, writing, and math by doing them, but we teach democracy by lecture" (p. 2). In her writings, Noddings (1992) has long emphasized that the creation of educational environments that support learning involves the creation of caring communities, where teachers supplement the emphasis on academic excellence with relational ethics and moral education. She emphasizes that teachers must model caring throughout their teaching and interactions with students, a concern that can be traced to John Dewey's writings.

Wells and Crain (1994) note that a thirty-year research literature on school desegregation has most often focused on the immediate effects of racial integration on individual students—their achievement, their self-esteem, and their intergroup relations. They argue that another perspective focused on life chances of African American students requires a long-term outlook. According to a sociological perspective referred to as *perpetuation theory*, "the goal of desegregation is also to break the cycle of segregation and increase access to high status institutions and the powerful social networks within them" (p. 531). What is the purpose of our educational system and public education in the United States? Is it exclusively intended to meet the needs of each individual child? We think not. At least in part, our educational system was conceptualized as a pathway to a democratic community and the betterment of all its citizenry. Our challenge is, of course, to examine the rhetoric and practices within education with the goal of reaching a better balance between meeting unique needs and building community.

Questions and Activities

1. Why, according to the authors, are students of color and low-income students overrepresented in special education classes and programs?

2. Why is it especially important for parents of color and low-income parents to be involved in special education programs for their children? What are some effective ways in which these parents can become involved in special education programs?

3. Why do parents, especially low-income parents and parents of color, often find it difficult to participate meaningfully in special education programs even though laws exist to ensure their participation?

4. In what ways do the research and assessment work by Jane R. Mercer reveal that special education is a social construction? Give specific examples from this chapter to support your response.

5. According to the authors, what are some of the major characteristics of qualitative *inclusive* schools? On what major assumptions and beliefs are they based?

How do inclusive schools exemplify and foster the idea of "the school as a community" described by the authors?

6. What do the authors mean by "inclusive pedagogy"? Give specific examples of this concept.

7. The authors believe that special education students should be educated in the same schools and classrooms as general education students. What problems and opportunities does this notion pose for classroom teachers? What guidelines, tips, and insights do the authors provide that may help teachers deal with the challenges and problems posed by the inclusive approach to schooling?

References

Adorno, T. W., Frenkel-Brunswik, E., Levinson, D. J., and Sanford, R. N. (1950). *The Authoritarian Personality*, Vols. 1 & 2. New York: John Wiley & Sons.

Argulewicz, E. N. (1983). Effects of Ethnic Membership, Socioeconomic Status, and Home Language on LD, EMR, and EH Placements. *Learning Disabilities Quarterly, 6*, 195–200.

Artiles, A. J. and Trent, S. C. (1994). Overrepresentation of Minority Students in Special Education: A Continuing Debate. *The Journal of Special Education, 27*, 410–437.

Ayres, B. J. (1993). *Equity, Excellence, and Diversity in the "Regular" Classroom.* Unpublished doctoral dissertation, Syracuse University, Syracuse, NY.

Ball, E. W. and Harry, B. (1993). Multicultural Education and Special Education: Parallels, Divergencies, and Intersections. *Educational Forum, 57*, 430–437.

Banks, J. A. (1993). Approaches to Multicultural Curriculum Reform. In J. A. Banks and C. A. McGee Banks (Eds.). *Multicultural Education: Issues and Perspectives*, (2nd ed.) (pp. 195–214). Boston: Allyn & Bacon.

Banks, J. A. and Banks, C. A. M. (Eds.). (1995). *Handbook of Research on Multicultural Education.* New York: Macmillan.

Bennett, A. T. (1988). Gateways to Powerlessness: Incorporating Hispanic Deaf Children and Families into Formal Schooling. *Disability, Handicap and Society, 3*(2), 119–151.

Berman, S. (1990). The Real Ropes Course: The Development of Social Consciousness. *ESR Journal: Educating for Social Responsibility, 1*, 1–18.

Black, J., Meyer, L. H., and Giugno, M. (1993). *A Task Force Model for Statewide Systems Change.* Syracuse: New York Partnership for Statewide Systems Change.

Brantlinger, E. (1991). Social Class Distinctions in Adolescents: Reports of Problems and Punishment in School. *Behavioral Disorders, 17*, 36–46.

Cohen, F. (1994, December/1995, January). Prom Pictures: A Principal Looks at Detracking. *Educational Leadership, 52*(4), 85–86.

Correa, V. I. (1987). Involving Culturally Diverse Families in the Educational Process. In S. H. Fradd and M. J. Weismantel (Eds.). *Meeting the Needs of Culturally and Linguistically Different Students: A Handbook for Educators* (pp. 130–144). Boston: College Hill.

Coyne Cutler, B. (1993). *You, Your Child, and "Special" Education: A Guide to Making the System Work.* Baltimore: Paul H. Brookes.

Cunningham, K., Cunningham, K., and O'Connell, J. C. (1986). Impact of Differing Cultural Perceptions on Special Education Service Delivery. *Rural Special Education Quarterly, 8*(1), 2–8.

Delpit, L. D. (1988). The Silenced Dialogue: Power and Pedagogy in Educating Other People's Children. *Harvard Educational Review, 3,* 280–298.

Derman-Sparks, L. and the ABC Task Force. (1989). *Anti-Bias Curriculum: Tools for Empowering Young Children.* Washington, DC: National Association for the Education of Young Children.

Divergent Youth. (1963). (Report of the Senate Fact Finding Committee on Education: Subcommittee on Special Education). Washington, DC: U. S. Government Printing Office.

Dunn, L. (1968). Special Education for the Mildly Retarded: Is Much of It Justifiable? *Exceptional Children, 35,* 5–22.

Evans, I. M., Okifuji, A., and Thomas, A. D. (1995). Home-School Partnerships: Involving Families in the Educational Process. In I. M. Evans, T. Cicchelli, M. Cohen, and N. P. Shapiro (Eds.). *Staying in School: Partnerships for Educational Change* (pp. 23–40). Baltimore: Paul H. Brookes.

Evans, I. M., Salisbury, C., Palombaro, M., and Goldberg, J. S. (1994). Children's Perception of Fairness in Classroom and Interpersonal Situations Involving Peers with Disabilities. *Journal of the Association for Persons with Severe Handicaps, 19,* 326–332.

Figler, C. S. (1981, February). *Puerto Rican Families with and without Handicapped Children.* Paper presented at the Council for Exceptional Children Conference on the Exceptional Bilingual Child, New Orleans. (ERIC Document Reproductgion Service No. ED 204 876.)

Finn, J. D. (1982). Patterns in Special Education Placement as Revealed by the OCR Surveys. In K. A. Heller, W. H. Holtzman, and S. Mesrick (Eds.). *Placing Children in Special Education: A Strategy for Equity* (pp. 322–381). Washington, DC: National Academy Press.

Gartner, A. and Lipsky, D. K. (1987). Beyond Special Education: Toward a Quality System for All Students. *Harvard Educational Review, 57,* 367–395.

Giangreco, M. and Putnam, J. (1991). Supporting the Education of Students with Severe Disabilities in Regular Education Environments. In L. H. Meyer, C. A. Peck, and L. Brown (Eds.). *Critical Issues in the Lives of People with Severe Disabilities* (pp. 245–270). Baltimore: Paul H. Brookes.

Gliedman, J. and Roth, W. (1980). *The Unexpected Minority: Handicapped Children in America.* New York: Harcourt Brace Jovanovich.

Goldstein, S. and Turnbull, A. P. (1982). The Use of Two Strategies to Increase Parent Participation in IEP Conferences. *Exceptional Children, 48,* 360–361.

Gottlieb, J. and Alter, M. (1995). *Overrepresentation of Children of Color Referred to Special Education.* New York: New York University Department of Teaching and Learning.

Gottlieb, J., Alter, M., Gottlieb, B. W., and Wishner, J. (1994). Special Education in Urban America: It's Not Justifiable for Many. *Journal of Special Education, 27,* 453–465.

Grant, C. A. and Secada, W. G. (1990). Preparing Teachers for Diversity. In W. R. Houston (Ed.). *Handbook of Research on Teacher Education* (pp. 403–422). New York: Macmillan.

Hall, E. T. (1977). *Beyond Culture.* New York: Anchor.

Harry, B. (1992). *Cultural Diversity, Families, and the Special Education System: Communication for Empowerment.* New York: Teachers College Press.

Harry, B., Allen, N., and McLaughlin, M. (1995). Communication vs. Compliance: African American Parents' Involvement in Special Education. *Exceptional Children, 61,* 364–377.

Harry, B., Grenot-Scheyer, M., Smith-Lewis, M., Park, H. S., Xin, F., and Schwartz, I. (In press). Developing Culturally Inclusive Services for Individuals with Severe Disabilities. *Journal of the Association for Persons with Severe Handicaps.*

Harry, B. and Kalyanpur, M. (1994). The Cultural Underpinnings of Special Education: Implications for Professional Interactions with Culturally Diverse Families. *Disability, Handicap, and Society, 9*(2), 145–166.

Henry, L. A. (1994). *At-Risk: Students' Perceptions of the Middle Level Schooling Experience.* Unpublished doctoral dissertation, Syracuse University, Syracuse, NY.

Horner, R. H., Meyer, L. H., and Fredericks, H. D. B. (Eds.). (1986). *Education of Learners with Severe Handicaps: Exemplary Service Strategies.* Baltimore: Paul H. Brookes.

Kirp, D. (1973). Schools as Sorters: The Constitutional and Policy Implications of Student Classification. *University of Pennsylvania Law Review, 121,* 705–797.

Kishi, G. S. and Meyer, L. H. (1994). What Children Report and Remember: A Six-Year Follow-Up of the Effects of Social Contact between Children with and without Severe Disabilities. *Journal of the Association for Persons with Severe Handicaps, 19,* 277–289.

MacMillan, D. L., Jones, R. L., and Meyers, C. E. (1976). Mainstreaming the Mildly Retarded: Some Questions, Cautions, and Guidelines. *Mental Retardation, 14,* 3–10.

Malmberg, P. A. (1984). *Development of Field Tested Special Education Placement Committee Parent Education Materials.* Unpublished doctoral dissertation, Virginia Polytechnic Institute and State University, Blacksburg.

Marion, R. (1979). Minority Parent Involvement in the IEP Process: A Systemtic Model Approach. *Focus on Exceptional Children, 10*(8), 1–16.

Medicine, B. (1981). American Indian Family: Cultural Change and Adaptive Strategies. *Journal of Ethnic Studies, 8*(4), 13–23.

Mehan, H., Hartwick, A., and Meihls, J. L. (1986). *Handicapping the Handicapped: Decision-Making in Students' Educational Careers.* Stanford, CA: Stanford University Press.

Meier, K. J., Stewart, J., and England, R. E. (1989). *Race, Class, and Education: The Politics of Second-Generation Discrimination.* Madison: The University of Wisconsin Press.

Mercer, J. R. (1973). *Labeling the Mentally Retarded: Clinical and Social System Perspectives on Mental Retardation.* Berkeley: University of California Press.

Mercer, J. R. (1979). *System of Multicultural Pluralistic Assessment: Technical Manual.* Cleveland: The Psychological Corporation.

Meyer, L. H. (1991). Advocacy, Research, and Typical Practices: A Call for the Reduction of Discrepancies between What Is and What Ought to Be, and How to Get There. In L. H. Meyer, C. A. Peck, and L. Brown (Eds.). *Critical Issues in the Lives of People with Severe Disabilities* (pp. 629–649). Baltimore: Paul H. Brookes.

Meyer, L. H. (1994a). Editor's Introduction: Understanding the Impact of Inclusion. Special Issue of *Journal of the Association for Persons with Severe Handicaps, 19,* 251–252.

Meyer, L. H. (1994b, October). Quality Inclusive Schooling: How to Know It When You See It. *TASH Newsletter, 21*(10), 18–22.

Meyer, L. H. and Henry, L. A. (1993). Cooperative Classroom Management: Student Needs and Fairness in the Regular Classroom. In J. W. Putnam (Ed.). *Cooperative Learning and Strategies for Inclusion* (pp. 93–121). Baltimore: Paul H. Brookes.

Meyer, L. H., Mager, G. M., Yarger-Kane, G., and Hext-Contreras, G. (1995). *Inclusive Teacher Education for Inclusive Schooling.* Paper submitted for publication consideration.

Meyer, L. H., Williams, D. R., Harootunian, B., and Steinberg, A. (1995). An Inclusion Model to Reduce At-Risk Status among Middle School Students: The Syracuse Experience. In I. M. Evans, T. Chicchelli, M. Cohen, and N. P. Shapiro (Eds.). *Staying in School: Partnerships for Educational Change* (pp. 83–110). Baltimore: Paul H. Brookes.

National Association of State Boards of Education (1992). *Winners All: A Call for Inclusive Schools.* Alexandria, VA: Author.

National Association of State Boards of Education. (1994). *Winning Ways.* Alexandria, VA: Author.

National Council of Teachers of Mathematics. (1993). *Curriculum and Evaluation Standards for School Mathematics.* Reston, VA: Author.

Noddings, N. (1992). *The Challenge to Care in Schools: An Alternative Approach to Education.* New York: Teachers College Press.

Poplin, M. S. (1988). Holistic/Constructivist Principles of the Teaching/Learning Process: Implications for the Field of Learning Disabilities. *Journal of Learning Disabilities, 21,* 401–416.

Pugach, M. C. and Johnson, L. J. (1990). Meeting Diverse Needs through Professional Peer Collaboration. In W. Stainback and S. Stainback (Eds.). *Support Networks for Inclusive Schooling: Interdependent Integrated Education.* Baltimore: Paul H. Brookes.

Putnam, J. W. (Ed.). (1993). *Cooperative Learning and Strategies for Inclusion: Celebrating Diversity in the Classroom.* Baltimore: Paul H. Brookes.

Ramsey, P. G. (1987). *Teaching and Learning in a Diverse World: Multicultural Education for Young Children.* New York: Teachers College Press.

Richardson, J. G. (1994). Common, Delinquent, and Special: On the Formalization of Common Schooling in the American States. *American Educational Research Journal, 31,* 695–723.

Roach, V. (1994, November). The Superintendent's Role in Creating Inclusive Schools. *The School Administrator, 52*(4), 64–70.

Ruiz, N. T., Rueda, R., Figueroa, R. A., and Boothroyd, M. (In press). Shifting Paradigms of Bilingual Special Education Teachers: Complex Responses to Education Reform. *Journal of Learning Disabilities.*

Salisbury, C. L. and Palombaro, M. (1991, November). Fostering Inclusion through Collaborative Problem Solving: The Johnson City Experience. Paper presented at the Annual Conference of the Association for Persons with Severe Handicaps, Washington, DC.

Salisbury, C. L., Palombaro, M. M., and Evans, I. M. (1993). *Collaborative Problem Solving: Instructor's Manual.* Binghamton: State University of New York at Binghamton.

Salisbury, C. L., Palombaro, M. M., and Hollowood, T. M. (1993). On the Nature and Change of an Inclusive Elementary School. *Journal of the Association for Persons with Severe Handicaps, 18,* 75–84.

Sapon-Shevin, M. (1992). Celebrating Diversity, Creating Community: Curriculum That Honors and Builds on Differences. In S. Stainback and W. Stainback (Eds.). *Curriculum Considerations in Inclusive Classrooms: Facilitating Learning for All Students* (pp. 19–36). Baltimore: Paul H. Brookes.

Sapon-Shevin, M. (1994). *Playing Favorites: Gifted Education and the Disruption of Community.* Albany: State University of New York Press.

Sapon-Shevin, M. (1994, December/1995, January). Why Gifted Students Belong in Inclusive Schools. *Educational Leadership, 52*(4), 64–70.

Sapon-Shevin, M., Ayres, B., and Duncan, J. (1994). Cooperative Learning and Inclusion. In J. Thousand, R. Villa, and A. Nevin (Eds.). *Creativity and Collaborative Learning: A Practical Guide to Empowering Students and Teachers* (pp. 45–58). Baltimore: Paul H. Brookes.

Schnorr, R., Ford, A., Davern, L., Park-Lee, S., and Meyer, L. H. (1989). *The Syracuse Curriculum Revision Manual: A Group Process for Developing a Community-Referenced Curriculum Guide.* Baltimore: Paul H. Brookes.

Scruggs, T. E. and Mastropieri, M. A. (1994). Successful Mainstreaming in Elementary Science Classes: A Qualitative Study of Three Reputational Cases. *American Educational Research Journal, 31,* 785–811.

Smith, G. R. (1983). Desegregation and Assignment of Children to Classes for the Mildly Retarded and Learning Disabled. *Integrated Education, 21,* 208–211.

Smith-Lewis, M. (1993). [What Is Mental Retardation? Perceptions from the African American Community.] Unpublished raw data.

Solomon, D., Schaps, E., Watson, M., and Battistich, V. (1992). Creating Caring School and Classroom Communities for All Students. In R. A. Villa, J. S. Thousand, W. Stainback, and S. Stainback (Eds.). *Restructuring for Caring and Effective Education: An Administrative Guide for Creating Heterogeneous Schools* (pp. 41–60). Baltimore: Paul H. Brookes.

Tharp, R. G. and Gallimore, R. (1989). *Rousing Minds to Life: Teaching, Learning, and Schooling in Social Context.* Cambridge: Cambridge University Press.

Thompson, T. M. (1982). An Investigation and Comparison of Public School Personnel's Perception and Interpretation of P.L. 94–142. *Dissertation Abstracts Interantional, 43,* 2840A.

Thousand, J. S. and Villa, R. A. (1990). Sharing Expertise and Responsibilities through Teaching Teams. In W. Stainback and S. Stainback (Eds.). *Support Networks for Inclusive Schooling: Interdependent Integrated Education* (pp. 151–166). Baltimore: Paul H. Brookes.

Tucker, J. A. (1980). Ethnic Proportions in Classes for the Learning Disabled: Issues in Nonbiased Assessment. *Journal of Special Education, 14,* 93–105.

Turnbull, A. P. and Turnbull, H. R. (1990). *Families, Professionals, and Exceptionality* (2nd ed.). Columbus, OH: Merrill.

Vandercook, T. and York, J. (1990). A Team Approach to Program Development and Support. In W. Stainback and S. Stainback (Eds.). *Support Networks for Inclusive Schooling: Interdependent Integrated Education* (pp. 105–128). Baltimore: Paul H. Brookes.

Villa, R. A. and Thousand, J. S. (1992). Student Collaboration: An Essential for Curriculum Delivery in the 21st Century. In S. Stainback and W. Stainback (Eds.). *Curriculum Considerations in Inclusive Classrooms: Facilitating Learning for All Students* (pp. 117–142). Baltimore: Paul H. Brookes.

Vygotsky, L. S. (1978). *Mind in Society: The Development of Higher Psychological Processes.* M. Cole, V. John-Steiner, S. Scribner, and E. Souberman, Eds. & Trans. Cambridge: Harvard University Press.

Walker, L. J. (1987). Procedural Rights in the Wrong System: Special Education Is Not Enough. In A. Gartner and T. Joe (Eds.). *Images of the Disabled, Disabling Images* (pp. 95–115). New York: Praeger.

Wells, A. S. and Crain, R. L. (1994). Perpetuation Theory and the Long-Term Effects of School Desegregation. *Review of Educational Research, 64,* 531–555.

Will, M. (1986). Educating Children with Learning Problems: A Shared Responsibility. *Exceptional Children, 52,* 411–415.

York, J. and Vandercook, T. (1990). Strategies for Achieving an Integrated Education for Middle School Students with Severe Disabilities. *Remedial and Special Education, 11*(5), 6–15.

Chapter 15

Teaching Gifted Students in a Multicultural Society

Rena F. Subotnik

Children with breathtaking problem-solving acuity can be found in every neighborhood, school, and community. This chapter discusses how these exceptional individuals function within schools and deal with societal expectations regarding their success. It also discusses why some gifted children may not achieve to their full potential. Issues involving the identification and nurturing of gifted students from diverse racial, cultural, and ethnic groups are also discussed.

WHAT ARE THE PURPOSES OF GIFTED EDUCATION?

Schooling that focuses on the development of talent should help gifted children interact successfully with the mainstream culture and should nurture abilities that may be valued by themselves or their communities (Maker & Schiever, 1989). Although every child with exceptional gifts deserves consideration for special talent development programming, barriers to fulfilling this societal obligation include misguided identification processes, inappropriate curriculum, and inadequate counseling. These obstacles can be reduced by using the scholarship generated in the multicultural and gifted education literature, renewed community support, and the advocacy of informed educators.

A common misconception is that gifted students do not require special attention to be successful in school. Because they tend to learn more quickly and comprehensively, they need educational modifications presented at an appropriate speed and level of comprehension. Far too frequently, gifted students spend hours in school covering material they already know and answering simplistic questions about complex issues. Gifted students who complete assignments ahead of classmates may be sent to the library for unsupervised reading or research, allocated more seat work, or asked to help fellow students. Although these options are not intrinsically problematic and in some cases are effective, gifted students deserve to have at least some portion of both the school curriculum and the teacher's attention focused on their educational needs. Gifted students who are in a minority in terms of ability, SES, race, ethnicity, or language have special needs for teacher support and recognition.

THE GIFTED EDUCATION MOVEMENT: A BRIEF HISTORY

Until the 1920s, most people in the United States did not enroll in high school, and certainly not in college. Secondary and postsecondary education was therefore geared to the academically able, most often from among the White privileged classes. On the elementary school level, exceptional youngsters were double-promoted (i.e., skipped a grade). In the early 1920s, Lewis Terman developed a test designed to measure intelligence based on the work of French psychologist Alfred Binet; he named it the Stanford-Binet Intelligence Test. To validate his hypothesis that a high IQ would predict adult genius, he established a longitudinal study of nine- to eleven-year-olds who scored in the 99th percentile and above on the Stanford-Binet (IQ 140+) (Terman & Oden, 1925). Followed up in adulthood, these high IQ individuals proved in fact to be exceptionally productive compared to individuals of the same fairly high social and economic background. Most became prominent academics, writers, lawyers, and business executives.

If Terman (Terman & Oden, 1925) could be considered the "father" of the movement in the United States to recognize and serve high-I.Q.-type gifted children, the "mother" would be Leta Hollingworth (Silverman, 1995). Much of Hollingworth's efforts were channeled into creating educational environments that were designed to meet the educational and psychological needs of these learners (Hollingworth, 1927). Based on the powerful influence of Terman's and Hollingworth's work on the psychological and education communities, several experimental programs, including the Hunter College Elementary School and the Speyer School in New York City, were developed using the Stanford-Binet to identify gifted children.

By 1947, Terman and his colleagues realized that IQ was not a sufficient predictor of exceptional achievement (Subotnik, Kassan, Summers, & Wasser, 1993; Terman & Oden, 1947). None of his study subjects had achieved true eminence; many could even be classified as adult underachievers. Clearly, other variables were important to the fulfillment of great potential.

Psychologists J. P. Guilford (1967) and E. P. Torrance (1965) pursued investigations into the measurement of creativity, with the goal of persuading the scholarly community that IQ and creativity were not directly related. They argued that if high IQ was viewed as the sole predictor of adult creativity, many gifted individuals would be overlooked in the admission to special programs designed for talent development.

In the 1970s, the impact of the civil rights movement and the advent of special-education legislation led theorists and researchers in the field to focus on discovering and nurturing gifted children who had been underserved because of poverty, racism, sexism, or disabilities. The commitment to identifying and supporting gifted students outside the mainstream, middle-class, White culture was generally absent until that time. However, it is important to note that scholars of color have written about exceptional individuals within their race. W. E. B. Du Bois (1903), for example, termed the Black intelligensia the "Talented Tenth."

In 1992 Commissioner Sidney Marland entered into the public record the definition of giftedness proposed by the United States Office of Education (USOE) for use by state and local agencies in developing policies for serving gifted children:

> Children capable of high performance include those with demonstrated achievement and/or potential ability in any of the following areas, singly or in combination:

1. general, intellectual ability
2. specific academic aptitude
3. creative or productive thinking
4. leadership ability
5. visual and performing arts
6. psychomotor ability. (pp. 10–11)

As a result of the continued struggle to recognize the special needs of gifted students, particularly those from groups underrepresented in special programs, a follow up to the Marland Report was commissioned in the 1990s. This document, entitled *National Excellence: A Case for Developing America's Talent* (Ross, 1993), featured the following declaration: "Outstanding talents are present in children and youth from all cultural groups across all economic strata, and in all areas of human endeavor" (p. 26). This key statement was derived from both the recognition that participants of special programs for the gifted remained disproportionately White and middle class, and from the emerging conceptions of giftedness developed in the last two decades.

CURRENT CONCEPTIONS OF GIFTEDNESS

Scholars and educators have proposed a variety of theoretical frameworks that seek to expand the conception of giftedness beyond the notion of high IQ. Definitions by Renzulli (1978), Sternberg (1986), and Gardner (1993) are the most widely discussed in the field; they are briefly described in the following paragraphs.

Based on a biographical review of eminent creators, Renzulli (1978) claimed that earlier notions of giftedness ignored the important role of motivation, drive, and persistence in the manifestation of talent. IQ had served a purpose, according to Renzulli, in drawing attention to "school-house" giftedness but could not explain the derivation of seminal ideas and beautiful creations. Further, he argued that creativity and persistence were more important than very high IQ. He feared that exceptionally able children were being excluded from special services because programs focused exclusively on school-house giftedness rather than on the development of talent that is most valuable to our society.

Finally, Renzulli proposed that we reframe our thinking about gifted individuals and focus on gifted behaviors that can be enhanced by opportunities in schools. Given appropriately stimulating environments, students who apply above-average ability, creativity, and motivation (the three rings) to carry out creative tasks are exhibiting gifted behaviors. These students should then be provided with the educational resources to carry out those tasks (Renzulli, 1977). Renzulli and his colleagues designed a wide array of tools to assist in the development of identification schemes and curriculum development built on the principles of the three-ring definition.

Sternberg's (1986) triarchic theory of intellectual giftedness also includes three components. The first subtheory addresses gifted individuals' executive skills in planning, learning, and carrying out given tasks. The second subtheory speaks to gifted individuals' insight into novel ideas and situations. The third subtheory incorporates contextual and practical decision-making skills, such as knowing when it is better to pursue or drop a project, to widen or narrow one's focus, or think reflectively rather than quickly.

Sternberg (1986) believes that the three components of intelligence described in the triarchic theory can be taught. Gifted individuals, according to the theory, know how to capitalize on their strengths and use their executive skills, creativity, and practical intelligence to the solution of real life problems. Gardner (1983, 1993) has proposed a theory of multiple intelligences that acknowledges a variety of human capacities and propensities. Each intelligence uses the manipulation of symbol systems to solve problems or create ideas or products. The seven intelligences in Gardner's framework are the linguistic, logical mathematical, spatial, musical, bodily kinesthetic, interpersonal, and intrapersonal. The least familiar concept in multiple intelligence theory is intrapersonal intelligence, which Gardner defines as the capacity to develop accurate insights about one's own thinking, feeling, and behaving.

According to Gardner, the intelligences are raw biological potentials that need to be identified and nurtured so that people can maximize their intellectual abilities to meet vocational and avocational goals. Two principles are key to the application of the Multiple Intelligence theory approach. One is the recognition that intelligences are manifested and valued differentially in different cultures and community settings (Baldwin, 1994). The second important point is that the best way to identify children's intelligences is to provide naturalistic scenarios for exploring each domain. Children's propensities can then be noted and developed (Gardner, 1993).

The instruments needed to carry out an identification program based on Sternberg's or Gardner's theories are not yet widely available. However, their ideas are circulating in the education community and serving as stimuli to renew discussion of such important questions as "What is giftedness?" and "How is it manifested?"

IDENTIFICATION OF GIFTED STUDENTS

There are no federally mandated definitions of giftedness. The identification of students for special programming is therefore tied to local definitions adopted by the school, school district, or state. Most U.S. school systems focus on serving gifted children who, because of their exceptional intellectual, creative, or academic abilities, need modification of the regular curriculum. Recognition is also given to giftedness in leadership and in visual and performing arts, although much less frequently. This policy is based on the belief that assessment of talent in leadership and in the visual and performing arts is too subjective, whereas standardized tests are available for use in the identification of intellectual, academic, and creative aptitude. In addition, the arts and leadership studies are not considered central to the mission and responsibility of schools. However, methods such as portfolios and auditions commonly used in the arts and leadership studies could open new ways to identify gifted students.

Incorporating these and other such methods into identifying gifted students would bring the field closer to the paradigm proposed by Howard Gardner (1993). Nevertheless, standardized test scores remain pervasive among the requirements for placement in gifted programs. In addition, the more removed a gifted child is from middle- to upper-middle-class mainstream culture the less likely it is for the student to be identified and served by the educational system (Colangelo, 1985; Oden, Kelly, Ma, & Weikart, 1992).

Why do standardized tests weigh so heavily in the labeling process? Some psychometricians believe that of all the ways we have to predict success in school or college, carefully designed tests are the most valid. Indeed, a very high score on such an instrument should be noted. Conversely, however, low scores do not necessarily reflect a person's lack of potential or ability. In fact, critics such as Helms (1992) point out that tests of general intelligence may be viewed as instruments that merely assess a White style of thinking. Clearly, other data need to be collected to make fair and accurate judgments about talent and educational needs.

For financial and political reasons, school districts set aside a limited number of seats in programs no matter now many students need special services. Test scores are used to cull potential candidates down to a manageable size because they are perceived by the public as being more objective than teacher recommendation or grade point averages. If indeed our goal is to assist in the development of children's full potential, educators should try to serve all children who would benefit from admission to a special program or set of services (Barkan & Bernal, 1991; Callahan & McIntyre, 1994; Kerr, Colangelo, Maxey, & Christensen, 1992).

A multicultural perspective can provide a more intellectually legitimate identification scheme by highlighting those abilities and skills that are universally valued and indicating how those abilities are manifested in various cultures and communities (Baldwin, 1991; Frasier, 1991a; Kirschenbaum, 1988; Tonemah, 1991, 1992). According to Frasier and her colleagues (1991a, 1991b; Frasier, Garcia, & Passow, 1995; Frasier & Passow, 1994), a clear statement of the characteristics and behaviors associated with giftedness might include intense motivation, extraordinary quantitative or communication skills, superior memory capacity, exceptional problem-solving abilities, and high-level creativity. These characteristics may be expressed differently based on the form of analogical reasoning and symbol systems held valuable by the subculture (Oden, Kelly, Ma, & Weikart, 1992).

In response to the array of literature on alternative forms of assessment, Frasier and Passow (1994) contend that formulating special constructs, watering down criteria, or seeking different areas of talent are not the way to increase the representation of African American, Latino, and American Indian children in gifted programs. They argue that we must attend to how cultural differences and environmental contexts affect performance on the measures that are used.

More equitable and accurate identification can be made by focusing on outstanding performance in one or two domains rather than across many (Gardner, 1993; House & Lapan, 1994; Kay & Subotnik, 1994; Miserandino, Subotnik, & Ou, 1995; Roedell, Jackson, & Robinson, 1980). Emphasis on the latter may mask outstanding abilities in one talent area at the expense of high levels of competence in many. Some of the data sources that may go into labeling a child as gifted are described below. Each has advantages and disadvantages.

Achievement Tests

Each year, most public school students take a battery of tests used to compare their academic standing with those of students in the same grade throughout the country. Results of these tests can pinpoint students who are significantly above the national norm. Raw scores are translated into percentiles or stanines, and children who score above a predetermined cutoff, such as the 91th percentile or the 9th stanine, may become candidates for further assessment.

One drawback inherent in the use of achievement tests for the identification of gifted students is the ceiling effect. If tests are not challenging enough, too many scores get bunched at the very top percentiles. The use of off-level tests, those appropriate for students at higher grade levels, provide teachers and admissions committees with clearer insights into students' maximum capabilities. Another drawback is the excessive dependence on reading ability for success on even the mathematics portion of the test. The scores of children who have learning disabilities or are LEP (limited English proficient) may not reflect their true aptitude for mathematics or the aural comprehension of language (Barkan & Bernal, 1991). Finally, lack of exposure and practice in test-taking skills may depress the achievement test scores of children whose schools do not provide such training (Ford, 1994b).

Individual Intelligence Tests

Individually administered IQ tests remain the most widely used instruments for admission to gifted programs. Test items draw on students' problem-solving skills, such as reproducing block patterns. They also draw on educational and cultural experiences, such as vocabulary, memory for facts, and basic arithmetic. Individual IQ tests are expensive to administer and tend to underestimate the intellectual potential of children who are economically disadvantaged or LEP. Test bias can also occur because of poor tester-testee rapport and variability in exposure to vocabulary and experiences appearing on the test.

Most scholars today recommend more dynamic forms of assessment (Borland & Wright, 1994; Ford & Harris, 1994; Frasier, 1991b; Helms, 1992). Dynamic assessment involves exposing children to a new task and demonstrating problem-solving methods for them and then noting how well children can apply the demonstrated skill or concept to a similar challenge (Feuerstein, 1973).

Behavior Checklists

Useful information can be collected about specific students from teachers, parents, peers, and the student. These instruments are not effective, however, unless they clearly delineate the behaviors and characteristics that define the gifts and talents being sought.

Teachers

Teachers' reliability as identifiers of gifted students is influenced by their understanding of the school district's definition of giftedness. Without a set of descriptions of desired student characteristics, teachers tend to nominate academically able students who are obedient, attractive, bright, and socially adept, while missing students who are shy, bored, less popular, and of a lower socioeconomic level (Gallagher & Gallagher, 1994). Furthermore, teachers are too often focused on children's deficits to notice their strengths, particularly with African American, Latino, and American Indian students (Banks, 1995; Callahan & McIntyre, 1994; House & Lapan, 1994). If the identifying characteristics are made explicit and teachers are culturally and racially sensitive and informed, teachers are a valuable source of referrals (Borland & Wright, 1994; Gear, 1976).

Parents

Depending on their cultural background, parents may over- or underrate their children's abilities (Callahan & McIntyre, 1994; Davis & Rimm, 1985; Ford, 1994b; Scott, Perou, Urbano, Hogan, & Gold, 1992). However, a well-designed behavior checklist filled out by parents can provide invaluable assistance to teachers and administrators by describing children's interests and accomplishments outside school (Borland & Wright, 1994; Ford, 1993a, 1994b; Frasier, 1991b).

Peers

An excellent source of candidates for possible special programming is peers. School districts, such as the Seattle Public Schools, have devised instruments that ask for the names of schoolmates who best fit one or more of the following categories: (1) learns quickly and easily, (2) has creative ideas, (3) is concerned with fairness, and (4) tells the wildest stories (see Renzulli, Reis, & Smith, 1981). Obviously, these data are valid only if students have spent a period of time together in school. If school assignments change from year to year, it may be necessary to delay peer nomination procedures until new students are at least fairly well integrated into the school population.

Self

Some students, because of their reticent personality, lack of social skills, interests that take place outside both the school and home, or cultural disinclination to draw attention to themselves (Callahan & McIntyre, 1994; Frasier, 1991a; Kitano, 1991), will not be noticed by parents, peers, or teachers. Self-nomination provides such individuals with the opportunity to describe their activities to specialists who can use the information for possible placement in a gifted program.

The information derived directly from children may be especially enlightening in terms of identifying those gifted African American children whose academic effort is not commensurate with their ability, despite an achievement orientation (Ford, 1993b).

Work Samples

Direct examples of creative work that go beyond academic expectations are sometimes used for placement into special programs (Tonemah, 1991, 1992). These products are direct reflections of youngsters' creative ability and motivation and in this way have more content validity than do tests purported to *measure* potential to be creatively productive. This work can take the form of science projects, art work, dance or music performances, games, or essays. These portfolios can be used even with preschool-age children and can include both teacher- and student-selected materials (Coleman, 1994; Wright & Borland, 1993). To reduce bias in judgments of submitted products, it is important to use more than one rater.

In conclusion, a responsible and effective identification procedure uses as much information as possible to help raters make decisions about serving students. Furthermore, opportunities for placement in programs should be continuous and ongoing from kindergarten through grade twelve (Ford & Harris, 1994). Too often, placement decisions are made based on available space rather than educational need. Generally it is better to err in the direction of inappropriately admitting a student into a program than to leave out a student on the basis of a single test score cutoff.

ADDRESSING GIFTED STUDENTS' INTELLECTUAL CHARACTERISTICS IN SCHOOL SETTINGS

Gifted children and adults from all socioeconomic and ethnic backgrounds exhibit some or all of the following intellectual characteristics: accelerated pace of learning due to superior memory; quantitative skills; communication skills; capacity for seeing relationships and patterns; and intense motivation (Frasier & Passow, 1994). Each individual has a unique profile of strengths drawn from this list. The characteristics become most visible when applied to a specific area, such as mathematics, music, creative writing, or chess.

Accelerated Pace of Learning

The primary characteristic of giftedness noticed by classroom teachers and parents is the speed with which these children learn. Students who learn mathematical concepts, vocabulary, and reading skills after minimal exposure are using their extraordinary ability to memorize, strategize, and concentrate. If a class dwells on a simple concept for too long, the gifted child may become bored and disruptive. It is not uncommon, however, for a stellar mathematics student to be a competent but uncreative writer. In fact, some gifted students have serious academic problems that require special planning and may be due to learning disabilities. Teachers who work with intellectually and academically gifted students learn to compact portions of the curriculum according to the profile of strengths presented by the students.

Capacity for Seeing Relationships and Patterns

Teachers have the opportunity to draw their students' attention to concepts and patterns that are central to one or more academic disciplines (e.g., power, beauty, change) so that students can make generalizations, solve complex problems, and devise creative insights. In addition, students who are skilled at seeing relationships and patterns can be taught two or more concepts at once, increasing the complexity of the lesson as well as saving time for enrichment. In beginning foreign language instruction, for example, both gender notations and tense can be taught together instead of separately (VanTassel-Baska, 1994).

Gifted specialists encourage students to view themselves as producers rather than as mere consumers of knowledge (Passow, 1985). The producer sees relationships where they did not exist before and translates those insights into products that give pleasure, satisfy a need, or generate new ideas. Creative children want to try different ways to solve problems (e.g., a new way to learn the multiplication tables, take attendance, sell cereal, breed fruit flies, end racism). Although we may admire our most creative students, their nontraditional approach to classroom life can sometimes be troublesome, particularly in a large heterogeneous class.

Class assignments can be designed to promote the notion of student-as-producer by requiring the inclusion of some original dimension to every major assignment. For example, a research report should not simply describe the history of the scholarship on the topic but should also incorporate the student's reactions to the literature described. Science reports could not only delineate the procedures of the experiment, but also encompass a section on follow-up questions or alternative hypotheses.

Intense Motivation

Gifted students tend to be extremely curious about many topics and concepts to which they are exposed, such as music composition, historical examples of racism, computer programming, or product invention. Once a child becomes captivated by a project, it may be difficult to tear him or her away to do anything else, even to eat or sleep. Such a child may become disgruntled when an interesting point in class is passed over by classmates who are satisfied with a superficial explanation. Scheduling, when possible, should include blocks of time in the class or resource room for students to pursue in-depth discussion or projects.

AFFECTIVE CHARACTERISTICS

Many gifted children have an extraordinary ability to read people and situations. They may not know how to handle what they see or hear, nor will they necessarily use the ability for the benefit of other people. Some of the ways gifted children manifest this sensitivity include high expectations for themselves and others, low tolerance for lags between intellectual and physical development, and concern with inconsistencies between ideal and real behavior. Problematic behavior derived from these attending characteristics (not requiring outside therapy or medication) are best handled in individual or small-group counseling sessions with other gifted students led by counselors familiar with the constellation of problems found most typically among gifted students from varied backgrounds.

High Expectations of Self and Others

At the elementary school level, many gifted children learn relatively effortlessly, and if not adequately challenged will lower their personal standards and submit hastily conceived work (Ford, 1992; Matthew, Golin, Moore, & Baker, 1992). Others may refuse to participate in cooperative groups with classmates who are satisfied to achieve competence and not mastery of a particular task or assignment. In the course of private conversation gifted students may tell you that they find it exhausting to work on behalf of the other group members to achieve personal standards.

High expectations can be placed on others in the social realm as well. Gifted students tend to be extraordinarily concerned with issues of fairness and are devastated when friends fail to live up to the principles of behavior they hold up for themselves in relationships. Furthermore, African American, Latino, and American Indian children may encounter teacher expectations that far underestimate their capabilities (Banks, 1995), causing painful confusion. Peer counseling groups and other support systems must be in place that prevent inaccurate and harmful teacher perceptions from being internalized (Ford, 1994a, 1994b; Kitano, 1995; Noble, Subotnik, & Arnold, in press).

Impatience with Lags in Physical Development

Many gifted children try to engage in activities and solve problems normally associated with older children. Primary-age gifted children are particularly prone to frustration when they can visualize problem solutions but do not have the agility or vocabulary to carry them out. For example, a first grader may want to explore the properties of a paper geodesic dome model but may not be able to manage the necessary cutting. The same holds true for the youngster who dreams up elaborate stories for a book but does not yet have the motor coordination to write. A friend from a sixth-grade classroom, the teacher, or teacher assistant can lend a literal helpful hand by doing the necessary cutting or writing.

Gifted adolescents may be extremely interested and well read in topics such as death but do not have the emotional maturity to achieve more than an intellectual understanding of the topic. Discussing their thoughts with uninterested age mates or with adults uncomfortable with the paradox of intellectual precocity and emotional immaturity can be problematic. Peer groups organized by school counselors or educators that can bring together gifted students for sessions around these topics can be very effective in reducing students' sense of isolation.

Noticing Inconsistencies between Ideal and Real Behavior

Gifted children can also be victims of a phenomenon called existential depression, or carrying the burden of the world on their shoulders (Webb, Meckstroth, & Tolan, 1986). Becoming aware of hypocrisies such as racism found in everyday life can leave such a child numb or cynical. Frank discussions with compassionate teachers and counselors are essential to supporting the self-concept of sensitive adolescents, particularly those who have been the direct recipients of the debilitating effects of racism. Activism and idealism modeled by a parent, teacher, or friend can help channel these concerns constructively.

SUGGESTIONS FOR CURRICULAR AND INSTRUCTIONAL MODIFICATIONS

Identification processes must be justified by providing high-quality services designed to foster the intellectual, academic, and creative strengths of participating students and *retaining* students in those programs (Ford, 1994b). The regular curriculum was designed to be a basic foundation for all students. Differentiating the regular curriculum for use with gifted students requires a combination of acceleration, enrichment, and the use of interdisciplinary themes; the proportions should be determined by the individual student's academic and talent profiles and interests (Van Tassel-Baska, 1994).

Acceleration

Although the term *acceleration* is often associated with grade skipping, it can also be used to mean moving more rapidly through the year's required curriculum to create more time for higher-level enrichment activities. The teacher must first assess the skill and knowledge levels of the students, allowing those who have already mastered the initial topics to begin at a more advanced stage. Continuous monitoring for mastery is, of course, necessary. Some subjects, like mathematics, foreign language, grammar, and reading skills are more conducive to this kind of acceleration because of their sequential nature (Van Tassel-Baska, 1994).

Many school subjects are taught as a series of incremental steps toward the acquisition of a higher goal. Acceleration works best when that goal is presented in the beginning as the object of the upcoming series of lessons, much like pieces of a jigsaw puzzle fit together to create a picture. If the real goal is understanding the picture, and the pieces are simply building blocks to reaching the goal, then the student and teacher can work together to determine the minimum amount of pieces the student needs to see the picture.

Another method of acceleration is to reduce the number of practice exercises a student must successfully complete to demonstrate mastery. If, after instruction, a child can do the last ten problems in the unit, he or she should not have to do the first forty.

Gifted children from underrepresented groups have a special need for appropriately paced curriculum, as underachievement has been shown to be the result of insufficient challenge and a paucity of exercise in academic discipline and study skills (Frasier & Passow, 1994; Miserandino et al., 1995; Oden et al., 1992). Academic talent, therefore, needs to be recognized and served as early as possible (Borland & Wright, 1994; Ford, 1992; Matthew et al., 1992).

Enrichment

Enrichment should be an essential component of schooling for all students. Since children can best demonstrate their talents in a highly stimulating environment, an enriched curriculum not only provides exciting academic experiences, but also creates additional opportunities for identification of gifted students (Frasier & Passow, 1994).

Curriculum can be enriched for students from all backgrounds in a number of ways. One important way is to introduce content that extends the regular curriculum through multicultural education (Ford, 1994b). Two examples include (1) the study of biographies of female and culturally diverse scientists, mathematicians, or writers whose work contributed to the skills and knowledge learned in the science, mathematics, and language arts curriculum; (2) the collection of stories from various ethnic community newspapers covering a topic under examination in social studies. Enrichment topics and ideas are usually generated from the available expertise of teachers, community or parent mentors, or the students themselves.

Developing new skills traditionally not taught in the regular curriculum is another enrichment technique. Advanced research topics such as survey development, interviewing, finding primary resources, organizing case studies, and elementary statistics can be introduced to young students for use in establishing their "careers" as producers of knowledge. According to Renzulli (1977), students who respond to enriched curriculum by proposing independent or small-group projects are exhibiting gifted behaviors.

Barkan and Bernal (1991) question why all bright U.S. school children are not trained to be bilingual. Schools in Europe, Canada, and Latin America expect graduates to be competent in more than one language. If bilingualism were viewed as a positive and valued outcome of schooling, the stigma placed on Limited English Proficient (LEP) students in the United States could be transformed into an advantage, especially if exposure to dual language use began in the primary years.

Providing enrichment to gifted students in the regular classroom requires that the teacher answer three questions:

1. What topics from the regular curriculum are most conducive to extension and enrichment?

2. How much time for enrichment can be derived from acceleration or compacting of the regular curriculum?

3. What are the talents, interests, and availability of the students, staff members, parents, and community members who might be involved in independent projects that are outgrowths of the enrichment experience?

Contracts for time to work on independent projects can be negotiated with clearly established time limitations and criteria for evaluation. The expected outcome of enrichment is for students to synthesize their newly gained knowledge and skills into the design and completion of an individual or small-group investigation to be evaluated by experts within the school and the community (Renzulli, 1977).

Interdisciplinary Themes and Concepts

Teachers rarely use interdisciplinary frameworks in planning curricula for the gifted. This is unfortunate because the technique capitalizes on the gifted child's ability to see relationships and make generalizations. The real world, of course, is not divided up into academic subject areas. When we develop an impression of an event, place, or person, we do not think in terms of subtraction, verbs, spelling, or data-retrieval charts. Instead, we find ourselves intrigued because that object, person, or event is, among other things, *beautiful, revolutionary, adaptive,* or *powerful.* Teachers can take advantage of students' ability to organize their thinking around major concepts by pointing them out when they appear in the regular curriculum. For example, the concept of power can be explored in the social studies through the balance of power in the U.S. system of government, in science by the generation of electricity, in language arts by persuasive language, in art by political cartoons or posters, and in mathematics by symbol systems (e.g., powers of 10) that allow us to describe elegantly enormously large or small numbers.

ADMINISTRATIVE OPTIONS

Once identified, gifted students can be served by the schools in a variety of ways, depending on local policy. The options differ by the degree to which gifted students are segregated from their regular classroom peers. Ironically, while advocates for gifted education struggle to create and maintain options for gifted children to work with ability peers, the education establishment is pursuing the placement of all children in the regular classroom. Placement decisions, however, are best made on an individual child's needs rather than on politics or philosophy. Some gifted children can thrive in the regular classroom with a teacher who is prepared and able to differentiate the curriculum where necessary and where there are one or more gifted classmates for shared group work and discussion. Other gifted children require too many academic adjustments and experience too much social isolation to warrant placing them in a regular classroom.

Specialized Schools

Some states such as North Carolina have established residential schools for extremely talented students from all over the state. Metropolitan areas with large school-age populations have also created schools for highly intellectually or artistically gifted children. Because even students within these special schools have varied profiles of talent and academic strengths, regular (and even remedial) to very advanced classes must be offered in nearly all academic subjects. Special resource teachers make arrangements for individual students to work in their areas of strength with community, corporate, or university mentors. A drawback to this arrangement, however, is that some students suffer from lowered academic self-concepts within classes that are composed entirely of academically talented peers (Marsh, Chessor, Craven, & Roche, 1995). Comparisons to their peers can lead to underachievement and related negative outcomes.

Special Groupings within Schools

When there are enough identified gifted students on a grade level to form a class, they may be grouped together for most of their school subjects: science, mathematics, language arts, foreign language, and social studies. Music, art, industrial arts, and physical education may be shared with other students in the building. Separate classes within a school can either be a boon to the school or a divisive force. Gifted classes with appropriately trained teachers, students identified in a nonarbitrary manner—with continuous opportunities for the admission of new members—may set a dynamic tone throughout the school. When the program is weak, however, staff and students outside the program may see the special class as an excuse for placating powerful parents or politicians.

Pull-Out Programs

The pull-out model is the most common administrative option for gifted children (Cox, Daniel, & Boston, 1985). A trained specialist meets with small groups of identified students for from one to five hours per week to focus on the unique interests and talents of the individual students rather than on the required curriculum. Students generally learn research and intellectual skills needed to conduct small-group and individual investigations and to make contact with adults in the community who can serve as mentors. Gifted students remain in contact with their age peers for most of their time in school.

Many regular classroom teachers resent the disruptions caused by children leaving the classroom to attend sessions with specialists. Other problems that stem from the pull-out arrangement include doubling up of homework from both special and regular classes and the difficulty of maintaining continuity in the special program when there are week-long breaks between sessions.

The special school, special class, and pull-out options allow gifted children to be inoculated against school and peer culture that subverts studiousness and the pursuit of academic excellence. In the case of females and ethnic and cultural groups underrepresented in science, homogeneous grouping has encouraged enrollment in advanced coursework (Casserly, 1980; Miserandino et al., 1995; Smith, LeRose, & Clasen, 1991) and realistic preparation for the competition encountered in postsecondary institutions (Seymour & Hewitt, 1994).

Conversely, segregated programs tend to reduce academic self-concept among participants when they compare themselves to equally talented peers (Marsh, Chessor, Craven, & Roche, 1995). Such comparisons can be devastating, particularly in adolescence.

Regular Classroom with Consulting Teacher

Many school districts and counties hire a gifted specialist to serve the entire system. The specialist arranges in-service courses, organizes curriculum-writing teams, and visits with individual teachers who seek advice. If the person provides quality service, regular classroom teachers can derive help and ideas for meeting the needs of gifted children within their classroom. The strength of this arrangement lies in the social integration of gifted students into the mainstream school culture. The drawbacks include the additional strain on teachers to specialize their curriculum and instructional strategies and the academic isolation of gifted students. Without modification, gifted students are often left to fend for themselves (Archambault, Westberg, Brown, Hallmark, Emmons, & Zhang, 1993).

INFLUENCES ON THE FULFILLMENT OF TALENT POTENTIAL

Being identified as gifted and placed in a program are no guarantees that a student will fulfill his or her potential. In addition to the role of task commitment and motivation addressed by Renzulli, other factors can negatively influence the productivity of a gifted child, including lack of support from parents, teachers, peers, one's subculture, or counselors.

Parents

Parents with high ambitions for their gifted child will ensure that the child receives the highest-quality education possible. However, most parents prefer to have a bright but not gifted child with good social skills. The special child's needs can be intrusive on family life in many ways: reduction of attention to nongifted siblings, parental intimidation by their child's superior intellect, and fear that the gifted child will reject family culture to some degree if not altogether (Baldwin, 1987; Colangelo, 1985; Davis, 1977), particularly if their child will be a minority, ethnically or socioeconomically, in a program (Callahan & McIntyre, 1994; Ford, 1994b; Kitano, 1991).

Successful programs must include an effective parent participation component (Ford, 1994b; Kerr et al., 1992; Maker & Schiever, 1989). Parents, particularly those distrustful of schools as an institution or concerned about removing their child from familiar contexts, need to be included in the discussion of program goals and must be convinced of the importance of their emotional support to their child's continuing participation in the gifted program (Oden et al., 1992; Scott et al., 1992).

It is also essential to avoid making assumptions about parental values based on socioeconomic status, race, or ethnicity. Variability is great among members of ethnic groups based on language, socioeconomic status, country of origin, generations in the United States, and the degree to which one subscribes to mainstream values (Kitano, 1991). Factors that are of major importance to the nurturing of giftedness by parents include expectations for achievement, language modeling, academic guidance, and intellectuality of the home (Frasier, 1991a; VanTassel-Baska, 1989). These characteristics are not exclusive to any one cultural, racial, or ethnic group.

Teachers

Teachers can help a gifted child by providing a source of support in schools that insufficiently recognize intellectual or academic achievement. Teachers can excite and stimulate children by modeling intellectual curiosity and can help students feel comfortable with their intellectual strengths. Teachers can actively recruit children who may be reluctant to be labeled as gifted due to concerns about standing out from peers or community members (Kitano, 1991). Teachers can seek out high-achieving role models from the African American, Latino, and American Indian communities to serve as guides and mentors in the classroom (Ford, 1994b; Maker & Schiever, 1989). On the secondary and middle school levels, teachers must ensure that challenging courses are available so that students in rural or inner-city schools can enroll in gatekeeper courses to the college-bound tracks like algebra and calculus (Miserandino et al., 1995; Oakes, 1990; Oden et al., 1992; Seymour & Hewitt, 1994). Study groups in advanced courses have been shown to be effective in raising achievement, particularly with gifted African American students (Olszenski-Kubilius, Grant, & Seibert, 1994; Treisman, 1992).

Peer Group Membership

When children believe they must choose between a drive for excellence and a desire for friendship, they experience tremendous stress (Ford, 1992; Griffin, 1992; Kerr, 1994). Arguments for the segregation of gifted students into homogeneous groups is particularly salient in systems where the school culture is not supportive of academic brilliance (Gallagher, 1986; Krueger, 1978). Homogeneous grouping into special schools, classes, or pull-out programs is especially effective for African American, Latino, and American Indian children if a critical mass of gifted ethnic peers are also participating. The stress of being a minority within a gifted program can to some degree be as stressful as being isolated intellectually in an age peer group (Cooley, Cornell, & Lee, 1991; Ford & Harris, 1994; Maker & Schiever, 1989).

Subculture

To succeed both in school and at home, language minority students are challenged with becoming bilingual-bicultural and learning how to "play the game" in the mainstream culture (Baldwin, 1991; Barkan & Bernal, 1991; Clark, 1991; Ford, 1994b; Fordham & Ogbu, 1986; Kitano, 1991; Ogbu, 1995). This means, for example, that a Mexican American youngster brought up speaking Spanish must also learn to operate comfortably in English and, most important, to know when each language is most appropriately used. Inability to function as a so-called border crosser (Giroux & McLaren, 1994) can impinge on successful competition for jobs, scholarships, and university entrance. Conversely, masterful border crossing can lead to brilliant new insights derived from perspectives not shared by mainstream classmates.

Feuerstein (1973), a pioneering Israeli psychologist, explained the inordinate numbers of intelligent non-European Israelis being labeled as retarded because of their lack of familiarity with Western-oriented academic tasks. Gifted children baffled by an unfamiliar school system need to be shown how it functions; they need, for example, test-taking skills (Ford, 1994b; Oden et al., 1992; Olszenski-Kubilius, Grant, & Seibert, 1994). Teachers and school counselors can provide invaluable assistance by sensitively helping students know when to call on their cultural and ethnic ways of speaking, thinking, playing, and learning, and when to call on their proficiency with mainstream forms of expression and problem solving.

Counseling Needs

Gifted African American, Latino, and American Indian children are subject to several psychological stresses that are unique from those of their White peers. Methods for addressing and even alleviating these stresses have been derived from research with high-achieving African American, Latino, and American Indian adults (Banks & Banks, 1995; Griffin, 1992; Kerr, 1994; Kitano, 1995; Ponterotto, Casas, Suzuki, & Alexander, 1995) and can serve to enhance the methodology of all counselors.

Gifted children may not allow themselves the possibility of occasional failure and mistakes (Griffin, 1992; Kitano, 1995), particularly when they are a minority in an educational situation like a gifted program (Ford & Harris, 1994). They need assistance in learning to anticipate and resist internalizing limiting messages of inferiority (Ford, 1993a; Kitano, 1995; Noble, Subotnik, & Arnold, in press). Examples of resilience in the face of adversity can then be highlighted and encouraged (Ford, 1994a: Noble et al., in press; Wang & Gordon, 1994). Most important, with proper guidance, gifted African American, Latino, and American Indian children can transform adversity into creative productivity by learning that adversity is the emotional source of much of humanity's greatest ideas and inventions (Ochse, 1990; Simonton, 1994).

CONCLUSION

Great thinkers derive their ideas from nontraditional viewpoints. The greatest gift we can give to children is exposure to the multiple perspectives derived from the myriad cultures and ethnicities that make up the U.S. population. The greatest gift we can give ourselves as educators is to reformulate our traditional views of identifying and serving gifted children so that we can prevent the tragedy of lost talent that persists to this day.

Questions and Activities

1. What were some of the social and political factors that led to the development of gifted education in the United States?

2. What sources of data are used to identify gifted students? Identify some of the problems associated with each source.

3. Form a group with several of your classmates. Research and report on ways students gifted in various areas such as language arts, mathematics, and science can be served in the regular classroom.

4. What are the characteristics associated with gifted children, regardless of their ethnicity or socioeconomic status? How might these characteristics be expressed in different cultural or economic milieus?

5. What resources and training will you need to teach gifted students?

6. Write a brief paper on how the concept of ability grouping is applied to teaching gifted students in regular classrooms, pull-out programs, specialized classes, and specialized schools. What are some benefits and disadvantages of each setting?

7. Using a lesson that you would normally teach, give examples of how the concepts of acceleration and enrichment can be applied in your classroom. What benchmarks would you use to determine when acceleration was appropriate? How would you identify the students who would participate in enrichment activities? Give examples of acceleration and enrichment activities that can be used with the lesson.

8. Educators have a special responsibility to identify and provide services to gifted students who are bilingual, culturally and ethnically diverse, and from low-income homes. Research the policies of your local gifted programs to see whether there exists a commitment to identifying and serving gifted children from diverse racial, ethnic, and cultural groups.

References

Archambault, F. X., Westberg, K. L., Brown, S. W., Hallmark, B. W., Emmons, C. L., and Zhang, W. (1993). *Regular Classroom Practices with Gifted Students: Results of a National Survey of Classroom Teachers*. Research Monograph 93102. Storrs, CT: National Research Center on Gifted and Talented.

Baldwin, A. Y. (1987). Undiscovered Diamonds: The Minority Gifted Child. *Journal for the Education of the Gifted, 10*(4), 271–285.

Baldwin, A. Y. (1991). Ethnic and Cultural Issues. In N. Colangelo and G. A. Davis (Eds.). *Handbook of Gifted Education* (pp. 416–427). Boston: Allyn and Bacon.

Baldwin, A. Y. (1994). The Seven Plus Story: Developing Hidden Talent among Students in Socioeconomically Disadvantaged Environments. *Gifted Child Quarterly, 38*(2), 80–84.

Banks, J. A. (1995). Multicultural Education: Historical Development, Dimensions, and Practice. In J. A. Banks and C. A. M. Banks (Eds.). *Handbook of Research on Multicultural Education* (pp. 3–24). New York: Macmillan.

Banks, J. A. and Banks, C. A. M. (Eds.). (1995). *Handbook of Research on Multicultural Education.* New York: Macmillan.

Barkan, J. H. and Bernal, E. M. (1991). Gifted Education for Bilingual and LEP Students. *Gifted Child Quarterly, 35*(3), 144–147.

Borland, J. H. and Wright, L. (1994). Identifying Young, Potentially Gifted, Economically Disadvantaged Students. *Gifted Child Quarterly, 38*(4), 164–171.

Callahan, C. M. and McIntyre, J. A. (1994). *Identifying Outstanding Talent in American Indian and Alaska Native Students.* PIP 94-1219. Washington, DC: U.S. Government Printing Office.

Casserly, P. L. (1980). Factors Affecting Female Participants in Advanced Placement Programs in Mathematics, Chemistry, and Physics. In L. H. Fox, L. Brody, and D. Tobin (Eds.). *Women and the Mathematical Mystique* (pp. 138–163). Baltimore: The Johns Hopkins University Press.

Clark, M. L. (1991). Social Identity, Peer Relations, and Academic Competence of African American Adolescents. *Education and Urban Society, 24*(1), 41–52.

Colangelo, N. (1985). Counseling Needs of Culturally Diverse Gifted Students. *Roeper Review, 8,* 33–35.

Coleman, L. J. (1994). Portfolio Assessment: A Key to Identifying Hidden Talents and Empowering Teachers of Young Children. *Gifted Child Quarterly, 38*(2), 65–69.

Cooley, M. R., Cornell, D. G., and Lee, C. (1991). Peer Acceptance and Self Concept of Black Students in a Summer Gifted Program. *Journal for the Education of the Gifted, 14*(2), 166–177.

Cox, J., Daniel, N., and Boston, B. (1985). *Educating Able Learners: Programs and Promising Practices.* Austin: University of Texas Press.

Davis, G. (1977). Bitters in the Brew of Success. *Black Enterprise, 8,* 31–35.

Davis, G. A. and Rimm, S. B. (1985). *Education of the Gifted and Talented.* Englewood Cliffs, NJ.: Prentice-Hall.

Du Bois, W. E. B. (1903). The Talented Tenth. In *The Negro Problem: A Series of Articles by Representative Negroes of Today.* New York: James Pratt.

Feuerstein, R. (1973). *Instrumental Enrichment.* Baltimore: University Park Press.

Ford, D. Y. (1992). Determinants of Underachievement as Perceived by Gifted, Above Average, and Average Black Students. *Roeper Review, 14*(3), 130–136.

Ford, D. Y. (1993a). An Investigation of the Paradox of Underachievement among Gifted Black Students. *Roeper Review, 6*(2), 78–84.

Ford, D. Y. (1993b). Support for the Achievement Ideology and Determinants of Achievement as Perceived by Gifted, Above Average, and Average Black Students. *Journal for the Education of the Gifted, 16*(3), 280–298.

Ford, D. Y. (1994a). Nurturing Resilience in Gifted Black Youth. *Roeper Review, 17*(2), 80–85.

Ford, D. Y. (1994b). *The Recruitment and Retention of African American Students in Gifted Education Programs: Implications and Recommendations.* Research Monograph No. 9406. Storrs, CT: National Research Center for the Gifted and Talented.

Ford, D. Y., and Harris III, J. (1994). Reform and Gifted Black Students: Promising Practices in Kentucky. *Journal for the Education of the Gifted, 17*(3), 216–240.

Fordham, S. and Ogbu, J. (1986). Black Students' School Success: Coping with the Burden of 'Acting White.' *The Urban Review, 18*(3), 176–203.

Frasier, M. M. (1991a). Response to Kitano: The Sharing of Giftedness between Culturally Diverse and Non-Diverse Gifted Students. *Journal for the Education of the Gifted, 15*(1), 20–30.

Frasier, M. M. (1991b). Disadvantaged and Culturally Diverse Gifted Students. *Journal for the Education of the Gifted, 14*(3), 234–245.

Frasier, M. M., Garcia, J. H., and Passow, A. H. (1995). *A Review of Assessment Issues in Gifted Education and Their Implications for Identifying Gifted Minority Students.* Research Monograph 95204. Storrs, CT: National Research Center on the Gifted and Talented.

Frasier, M. M. and Passow, A. H. (1994). *Toward a New Paradigm for Identifying Talent Potential.* Research Monograph 94112. Storrs, CT: National Research Center on the Gifted and Talented.

Gallagher, J. J. (1986). The Conservation of Intellectual Resources. In A. J. Cropley, K. K. Urban, H. Wagner, and W. Wieczerkowski (Eds.). *Giftedness: A Continuing Worldwide Challenge* (pp. 21–30). New York: Trillium Press.

Gallagher, J. J. and Gallagher, S. A. (1994). *Teaching the Gifted Child* (4th ed.). Boston: Allyn and Bacon.

Gardner, H. (1983). *Frames of Mind.* New York: Basic Books.

Gardner, H. (1993). *Multiple Intelligences: The Theory into Practice.* New York: Basic Books.

Gear, G. H. (1976). Accuracy of Teacher Judgment in Identifying Intellectually Gifted Children: A Review of the Literature. *Gifted Child Quarterly, 20,* 278–289.

Giroux, H. A. and McLaren, P. (1994). *Between Borders: Pedagogy and the Politics of Cultural Studies.* New York: Routledge.

Griffin, J. B. (1992). Catching the Dream for Gifted Children of Color. *Gifted Child Quarterly, 36*(3), 126–130.

Guilford, J. P. (1967). *The Nature of Human Intelligence.* New York: McGraw-Hill.

Helms, J. E. (1992). Why Is There No Study of Cultural Equivalence in Standardized Cognitive Ability Testing? *American Psychologist, 47,* 1083–1101.

Hollingworth, L. (1927). *Gifted Children: Their Nature and Nurture.* New York: Macmillan.

House, E. R. and Lapan, S. (1994). Evaluation of Programs for Disadvantaged Gifted Students. *Journal for the Education of the Gifted, 17*(4), 441–466.

Kay, S. I. and Subotnik, R. F. (1994). Talent beyond Words: Unveiling Spatial, Expressive, Kinesthetic and Musical Talent in Young Children. *Gifted Child Quarterly, 38*(2), 70–74.

Kerr, B. A. (1994). *Smart Girls Two: A New Psychology of Girls, Women, and Giftedness.* Dayton: Ohio Psychology Press.

Kerr, B. A., Colangelo, N., Maxey, J., and Christensen, P. (1992). Characteristics of Academically Talented Minority Students. *Journal of Counseling and Development, 70*(5), 606–670.

Kirschenbaum, R. J. (1988). Methods for Identifying the Gifted and Talented American Indian Student. *Journal for the Education of the Gifted, 11*(3), 53–63.

Kitano, M. K. (1991). A Multicultural Educational Perspective on Serving the Culturally Diverse Gifted. *Journal for the Education of the Gifted, 15*(1), 4–19.

Kitano, M. K. (1995). Lessons from Gifted Women of Color. *Journal of Secondary Gifted Education, 6*(2), 176–187.

Krueger, M. L. (Ed.). (1978). *On Being Gifted.* New York: Walker.

Maker, C. J. and Schiever, S. W. (1989). *Cultural Issues in Gifted Education: Defensible Programs for Cultural and Ethnic Minorities.* Austin, TX: Pro-Ed.

Marland, S. P., Jr. (1972). *Education of the Gifted and Talented,* Vol. 1: Report to the Congress of the United States by the United States Commissioner of Education. Washington, DC: U.S. Government Printing Office.

Marsh, H. W., Chessor, D., Craven, R., and Roche, L. (1995). The Effects of Gifted and Talented Programs on Academic Self-Concept: The Big Fish Strikes Again. *American Educational Research Journal, 32*(2), 285–319.

Matthew, J. L., Golin, K. G., Moore, M. W., and Baker, C. (1992). Use of SOMPA in the Identification of Gifted African American Children. *Journal for the Education of the Gifted, 15*(4), 344–356.

Miserandino, A., Subotnik, R. F., and Ou, K. (1995). Identifying and Nurturing Mathematical Talent in Urban School Settings. *Journal of Secondary Gifted Education, 6*(4), 245–257.

Noble, K. D., Subotnik, R. F., and Arnold, K. D. (in press). A New Model for Adult Female Talent Development. In K. D. Arnold, K. D. Noble, and R. F. Subotnik (Eds.). *Remarkable Women: Perspectives on Female Talent Development.* Cresskill, NJ: Hampton Press.

Oakes, J. (1990). *Multiplying Inequalities: The Effects of Race, Social Class, and Tracking on Opportunities to Learn Mathematics and Science.* Santa Monica, CA: Rand.

Ochse, R. (1990). *Before the Gates of Excellence: Determinants of Creative Genius.* New York: Cambridge University Press.

Oden, S., Kelly, M. A., Ma, Z., and Weikart, D. P. (1992). *Challenging the Potential: Programs for Talented Disadvantaged Youth.* Ypsilanti, MI: High Scope.

Ogbu, J. (1995). Understanding Cultural Diversity and Learning. In J. A. Banks and C. A. M. Banks (Eds.). *Handbook of Research in Multicultural Education* (pp. 582–593). New York: Macmillan.

Olszenski-Kubilius, P., Grant, B., and Seibert, C. (1994). Social Support System and the Disadvantaged Gifted: A Framework for Development Programs and Services. *Roeper Review 17*(1) 20–25.

Passow, A. H. (1985). Intellectual Development of the Gifted. In F. R. Link (Ed.). *Essays on the Intellect* (pp. 23–43). Alexandria, VA: ASCD.

Ponterotto, J. G., Casas, J. M., Suzuki, L. A., and Alexander, C. M. (Eds.). (1995). *Handbook of Multicultural Counseling.* Thousand Oaks, CA: Sage.

Renzulli, J. (1977). *Enrichment Triad Model.* Mansfield Center, CT: Creative Learning Press.

Renzulli, J. (1978). What Makes Giftedness: Reexamining a Definition. *Phi Delta Kappan, 58,* 180–184.

Renzulli, J., Reis, S. M., and Smith, L. H. (1981). *The Revolving Door Identification Model.* Mansfield Center, CT: Creative Learning Press.

Roedell, W. C., Jackson, N. E., and Robinson, H. B. (1980). *Gifted Young Children.* New York: Teachers College Press.

Ross, P. O. (1993). *National Excellence: A Case for Developing America's Talent.* PIP 93-1201. Washington, DC: Office of Educational Research and Improvement.

Scott, M. S., Perou, R., Urbano, R., Hogan A., and Gold, S. (1992). The Identification of Giftedness: A Comparison of White, Hispanic, and Black Families. *Gifted Child Quarterly, 36*(3), 131–139.

Seymour, E., and Hewitt, N. M. (1994). *Talking about Leaving: Factors Contributing to High Attrition Rates among Science, Mathematics, and Engineering Undergraduate Majors.* Boulder: University of Colorado Bureau of Sociological Research.

Silverman, L. K. (1995). Why Are There So Few Eminent Women? *Roeper Review, 18*(1), 5–13.

Simonton, D. K. (1994). *Greatness: Who Makes History and Why?* New York: Guilford.

Smith, J., LeRose, B., and Clasen, R. E. (1991). Underrepresentation of Minority Students in Gifted Programs: Yes It Matters. *Gifted Child Quarterly, 35*(2), 81–83.

Sternberg, R. J. (1986). A Triarchic Theory of Intellectual Giftedness. In R. J. Sternberg and J. E. Davidson (Eds.). *Conceptions of Giftedness* (pp. 223–243). New York: Cambridge University Press.

Subotnik, R. F., Kassan, L., Summers, E., and Wasser, A. (1993). *Genius Revisited: High IQ Children Grown Up.* Norwood, NJ: Ablex.

Terman, L. M. and Oden, M. (1925). *Genetic Studies of Genius: Mental and Physical Traits of a Thousand Gifted Children.* Stanford, CA: Stanford University Press.

Terman, L. M. and Oden, M. (1947). *Genetic Studies of Genius: The Gifted Child Grows Up.* Stanford, CA: Stanford University Press.

Tonemah, S. A. (1991). Philosophical Perspectives of Gifted and Talented American Indian Education. *Journal of American Indian Education, 31*(1), 3–9.

Tonemah, S. A. (1992). American Indian Students and Alaska Native Students. In P. Cahape and C. B. Howley (Eds.). *Indian Nations At Risk: Listening to the People* (pp. 81–85). Charleston, WV: ERIC Clearinghouse on Rural Education and Small Schools.

Torrance, E. P. (1965). *Rewarding Creative Behavior: Experiments in Classroom Creativity.* Englewood Cliffs, NJ.: Prentice-Hall.

Treisman, U. (1992). Studying Students Studying Calculus: A Look at the Lives of Minority Mathematics Students in College. *The College Mathematics Journal, 23*(5), 362–372.

VanTassel-Baska, J. (1989). The Role of Family in the Success of Disadvantaged Gifted Learners. In J. VanTassel-Baska and P. Olszenski-Kubilius (Eds.). *Patterns of Influence on Gifted Learners: The Home, the Self, the School* (pp. 60–80). New York: Teachers College Press.

VanTassel-Baska, J. (1994). *Comprehensive Curriculum for Gifted Learners* (2nd ed.). Boston: Allyn and Bacon.

Wang, M. C. and Gordon, E. W. (Eds.). (1994). *Educational Resilience in Inner-City America: Challenges and Prospects.* Hillsdale, NJ: Lawrence Erlbaum.

Webb, J. T., Meckstroth, E. A., and Tolan, S. S. (1986). *Guiding the Gifted Child* (2nd ed.). Columbus: Ohio Psychology Publishers.

Wright, L. and Borland, J. H. (1993). Using Early Childhood Developmental Portfolios in the Identification and Education of Young, Economically Disadvantaged, Potentially Gifted Students. *Roeper Review, 15*(4), 205–210.

Students from diverse racial, ethnic, and social-class groups experience academic and social success in the effectively reformed multicultural school.

School Reform

Reforming schools so that all students have an equal opportunity to succeed requires a new vision of education and social actors who are willing to advocate for and participate in change. The two chapters in Part Six discuss effective ways to conceptualize and implement school reform within a multicultural framework. In chapter 16, Sonia Nieto presents and analyzes five conditions that will promote student achievement within a multicultural perspective. According to Nieto, school should (1) be antiracist and antibiased; (2) reflect an understanding and acceptance of all students as having talents and strengths that can enhance their education; (3) be considered within the parameters of critical pedagogy; (4) involve those people most intimately connected with teaching and learning; and (5) be based on high expectations and rigorous standards for all learners.

Cherry A. McGee Banks, in chapter 17, discusses ways to involve parents in schools. She argues that parent involvement is an important factor in school reform and student achievement and that parents can be a cogent force in school reform. Parents, perhaps more than any other group, can mobilize the community to support school reform. Parents have first-hand knowledge about the school's effectiveness and can be vocal advocates for change. As consumers of educational services, parents can raise questions that are difficult for professional educators and administrators to raise, such as: "What is the proportion of males in special education classes?" and "What is the ethnic breakdown of students enrolled in higher-level math and science classes?"

Banks argues that parents are more willing to work for school reform when they are involved in schools. They are more likely to become involved in schools when parent involvement opportunities reflect their varied interests, skills, and motivations. Banks suggests ways to expand traditional ideas about parent involvement and to increase the number and kinds of parents involved in schools.

Chapter 16

School Reform and Student Achievement: A Multicultural Perspective

Sonia Nieto

Student learning is the primary purpose of schooling. As such it is necessary to look at school reform in light of whether, to what extent, and how students learn. Without this kind of inquiry, educational reform becomes an empty exercise in bureaucratic shuffling or external imposition of city, state, and federal policies that have little to do with the actual learning, or lack of learning, that goes on in classrooms.

Many school reform policies, especially as espoused in the past decade, have unfortunately more often than not been characterized by punishing those schools, teachers, districts, and ultimately students who have not measured up to predetermined norms of success. Longer school days and years, more high-stakes testing (that is, tests used as the sole or primary criterion for such crucial decisions as placement in ability groups and college admission), and less attention to pedagogy and curriculum have been the result.

This chapter begins with the assumption that student learning can be positively influenced by changes in school policies and practices that are part of systemic school reform measures. Nevertheless, there is no simple cause-effect relationship between school reform and learning. Given the social nature of schooling, it is difficult to ascribe a fixed causal relationship between student learning and schooling. Many complex forces influence student learning, including personal, psychological, social, cultural, community, and institutional factors (Erickson, 1993). That is, we cannot simply say that eliminating tracking will help all students succeed, or that native language instruction is the one element that will help all language minority students learn. Neither can we state that making pedagogy more culturally relevant is always the answer. These changes may in fact substantially improve educational outcomes for many more students than are now achieving academic success. However, taken in isolation, these changes fail to reflect the complex nature of student learning.

A comprehensive view of student learning that takes into account the many internal and external influences on achievement may help explain why some students succeed academically while others do not. For example, in one study of dropouts, it was found that 68 percent of the Puerto Rican students who had never been in bilingual programs dropped out of school, while only 39 percent of those who had been in bilingual classrooms for at least part of their school experience dropped out (Frau-Ramos & Nieto, 1993). The difference in dropout rates was dramatic, but a 39 percent dropout rate is still unacceptably high; it suggests that other issues were at work, including students' perceptions of fitting in, teachers' limited awareness of their students' backgrounds, and other school policies that led some students to feel like outsiders (Frau-Ramos & Nieto, 1993). In this case, bilingual education was important in mediating the school retention of some students, but it was not sufficient to help all students succeed academically.

Culturally responsive education, an approach based on using students' cultures as an important source of their education, can go a long way in improving the education of students whose cultures and backgrounds have been maligned, denied, or omitted in school curricula (Au & Kawakami, 1994; Ladson-Billings, 1994a, 1994b; Delpit, 1995). This approach offers crucial insights for understanding the lack of achievement of students from culturally subordinated groups. Nevertheless, by itself culturally responsive pedagogy cannot guarantee that all students will learn. For example, it is important to remember that there are cases in which culturally marginalized students have been successfully educated *in spite* of what might be considered culturally incompatible settings. Catholic schools, for example, might seem at first glance to be culturally inappropriate for some children because bilingual programs are seldom offered, classes are usually overcrowded, and formal environments stress individual excellence rather than cooperation. These kinds of policies may be considered culturally inappropriate for Latino and African American students, yet many students from culturally dominated backgrounds who attend Catholic schools have been academically successful (Bryk, Lee, & Holland, 1993; Hill, Foster, & Gendler, 1990).

It is therefore necessary to look beyond only cultural responsiveness to help explain student academic success. Because of generally restricted resources, Catholic schools tend to offer *all* students a less differentiated curriculum, less tracking, and more academic classes, in addition to having clear, uncomplicated missions and strong social contracts (Bryk, Lee, & Holland, 1993). Thus, what at first glance appears to be incongruous in terms of cultural compatibility is explained as a result of school structures that imply similarly high expectations for all students. These examples help explain the complex relationship of academic success to a multiplicity of conditions, and they indicate that there is no one simple solution to academic failure.

In this chapter, I explore the meaning of school reform with a multicultural perspective and consider implications for student learning. I begin by defining school reform with a multicultural perspective, including how policies and practices are viewed within this perspective. I then describe a set of five interrelated conditions for successful school reform within a multicultural perspective. It is arbitrary to consider these conditions as separate issues because they are intimately interconnected. With this in mind and for the purpose of expediency, however, I explain the five conditions separately, with implications for increasing student achievement.

SCHOOL REFORM WITH A MULTICULTURAL PERSPECTIVE

Multicultural education is often assumed to be little more than isolated lessons in sensitivity training or prejudice reduction, or separate units about cultural artifacts or ethnic holidays. Sometimes, it is used to mean education geared for inner-city schools or, more specifically, for African American students. If conceptualized in this way, multicultural education will have little influence on total school reform.

When conceptualized as broad-based school reform, multicultural education can have a major influence on how and to what extent students learn. When it focuses on factors that can contribute to student underachievement, multicultural education allows educators to explore alternatives to systemic problems that lead to academic failure for many students and it fosters the design and implementation of productive learning environments, diverse instructional strategies, and a deeper awareness of how cultural and language differences can influence learning.

School reform with a multicultural perspective thus needs to begin with an understanding of multicultural education within a *sociopolitical context* (Nieto, 1996). A sociopolitical context underscores that education is part and parcel of larger societal and political forces, such as inequality based on stratification due to race, social class, gender, and other differences. Given this perspective, educational decisions concerning such policies as tracking, testing, language use, curriculum, and pedagogical approaches all must be understood as influenced by broader social policies. As we are reminded by Paulo Freire (1985), every educational decision, whether made at the classroom, city, state, or national level, is imbedded within a particular ideological framework. Such decisions can be as simple as to whether a classroom should be arranged in rows with all students facing the teacher, or with tables of groups of students to encourage cooperative work, or in a variety of ways depending on the task at hand. Alternatively, these decisions can be as far-reaching as eliminating tracking within an entire system, or teaching language minority students by using their native language and English, or by using English only. Imbedded within each educational decision are assumptions about the nature of learning, about what students are capable of achieving, about whose language is valued, and about who should be at the center of the educational process. Thus, even seemingly innocent decisions carry an enormous amount of ideological and philosophical baggage, which is in turn communicated to students either directly or indirectly.

As I state more extensively elsewhere, I define multicultural education within a sociopolitical context as (Nieto, 1996)

> a process of comprehensive school reform and basic education for all students. It challenges and rejects racism and other forms of discrimination in schools and society and accepts and affirms the pluralism (ethnic, racial, linguistic, religious, economic, and gender, among others) that students, their communities, and teachers represent. Multicultural education permeates the curriculum and instructional strategies used in schools, as well as the interac-

> tions among teachers, students, and parents, and the very
> way that schools conceptualize the nature of teaching and
> learning. Because it uses critical pedagogy as its underlying
> philosophy and focuses on knowledge, reflection, and action
> (praxis) as the basis for social change, multicultural education
> promotes the democratic principles of social justice. (p. 307)

This definition of multicultural education assumes a comprehensive school reform effort rather than superficial additions to the curriculum or one-shot treatments with a focus on diversity, such as workshops for teachers or assembly programs for students. As such, it is used as the lens through which to view the conditions for systemic school reform that can help improve the learning of all students.

CONDITIONS FOR SYSTEMIC SCHOOL REFORM WITH A MULTICULTURAL PERSPECTIVE

Education reform cannot be envisioned without taking into account both micro- and macrolevel issues that may affect student learning. Microlevel issues include the cultures, languages, and experiences of students and their families and how these are taken into account in determining school policies and practices (Cummins, 1989; Hollins, King, & Hayman, 1994; Ladson-Billings, 1994a). Macrolevel issues include the racial stratification that helps maintain inequality, and the resources and access to learning that are provided or denied by schools (Ascher & Burnett, 1993; Kozol, 1991; Weinberg, 1990). In addition, how students and their families view their status in schools and society must be considered. Ogbu (1994), for instance, has argued that school performance gaps persist because the forces of racial stratification and the unequal treatment of dominated groups, as well as the responses of dominated groups to these experiences, also continue.

Conditions such as inequitable school financing (Darling-Hammond, 1995; Kozol, 1991), unrepresentative school governance (Meier & Stewart, 1991), and large class size (Glass, 1982) may play a powerful role in promoting student underachievement. For example, Ascher and Burnett (1993) found that disparities among rich and poor states, and among rich and poor districts in the same state, actually grew in the 1980s. Yet reform strategies such as longer school days, more rigorous graduation standards, and increased standardized testing often do not take such issues into account. Equalizing just two conditions of schooling—funding and class size—would probably result in an immediate and dramatic improvement in the learning of students who have not received the benefits of these two conditions (Glass, 1982; Kozol, 1991).

School reform strategies that do not acknowledge such macrolevel disparities are sometimes little more than wish lists because they assume that all schools begin with a level playing field. The conditions described below, while acknowledging these disparities, nevertheless provide hope for school systems where such changes as equitable funding or small class size may not happen in the near future. Rather than wait for these changes to happen, schools themselves can begin to improve the conditions for successful student learning. Five conditions needed to improve student achievement are described below. These conditions, along with changes in funding and resource allocation, would help create schools where all students have a better chance to learn.

School Reform Should Be Antiracist and Antibiased

An antiracist and antibias perspective is at the core of multicultural education (Banks & Banks, 1995). This is crucial because too often it is believed that multicultural education automatically takes care of racism; but this is far from the reality (Weinberg, 1990). In fact, multicultural education without an explicit antiracist focus may perpetuate the worst kinds of stereotypes if it focuses on only superficial aspects of culture and the addition of ethnic tidbits (see chapter 10). In contrast, being antiracist means paying attention to all areas in which some students may be favored over others, including the curriculum, choice of materials, sorting policies (Oakes, 1990), and teachers' interactions and relationships with students and their communities (Cummins, 1989). Educators committed to multicultural education with an antiracist perspective need to closely examine both school policies and the attitudes and behaviors of its staff to determine how these might be complicitous in causing academic failure. The kind of expectations that are held for students (Nieto, 1994b), whether native language use is permitted or punished (Cummins, 1989), how sorting takes place (Oakes & Guiton, 1995; Spring, 1989), and how classroom organization, pedagogy, and curriculum might influence student learning (Haberman, 1991; Lee, Bryk, & Smith, 1993) each need to be considered.

To become antiracist, schools need to examine as well how the curriculum may perpetuate negative, distorted, or incomplete images of some groups while exalting others as the makers of all history. Unfortunately, many textbooks and children's books are still replete with racist and sexist images and with demeaning portrayals of people from low-income communities. Although the situation is improving, there are still too many examples of negative portrayals (García, 1993; Harris, 1992; Loewen, 1995; Sleeter & Grant, 1991). Furthermore, most of the women and men presented as heroes or heroines in the standard curriculum are in the mainstream or are considered safe even though they may be from nondominant cultures.

Others who have fought for social justice are ignored, omitted, or made safe by downplaying their contributions. For example, a now-classic article by Kozol (1975) graphically documents how schools bleed the life and soul out of even the most impassioned and courageous heroes, such as Helen Keller and Martin Luther King, Jr., in the process making them boring and less-than-believable caricatures. A more recent article by Kohl (1993) demonstrates how Rosa Parks, the mother of the civil rights movement, has been made palatable to the mainstream by portraying her not as a staunch civil rights crusader who consciously battled racist segregation, but rather as a tired woman who simply did not want to give up her seat on the bus (Kohl, 1993). Taking another example, few children learn about the slave revolt led by Nat Turner (Aptheker, 1943/1987), although most learn that "Abraham Lincoln freed the slaves." These are examples of at best distorted, and at worst racist, representations.

Through this kind of curriculum, students from dominant groups learn that they are the norm, and consequently they often assume that anyone different from them is culturally or intellectually disadvantaged. On the other hand, students from subordinated cultures often internalize the messages that their cultures, families, languages, and experiences have low status, and they may consequently learn to feel inferior (Cummins, 1989; Darder, 1991). All students suffer as a result, but the learning of students from dominated groups is the most negatively affected.

The issue of institutional power is also at play here. Discussions of racism tend to focus on individual biases and negative perceptions of some people toward members of other groups. This perception conveniently skirts the issue of how institutions themselves, which are much more powerful than individuals, develop harmful policies and practices that victimize American Indians, African Americans, Latinos, poor European Americans, females, and others from powerless groups (Winant, 1994). The major difference between *individual racism* and *institutional racism* is the wielding of power because it is primarily through the power of the people who control institutions such as schools that oppressive policies and practices are reinforced and legitimated (Tatum, 1992; Weinberg, 1990). That is, when racism is understood as a systemic problem, not just as an individual dislike for a particular group of people, we can better understand its negative and destructive effects.

I do not wish to minimize the powerful effect of individual prejudice and discrimination, which can be personally very painful, nor to suggest that individual discrimination occurs only in one direction, for example, from Whites to African Americans. No group monopolizes prejudice and discrimination; they occur in all directions, and even within groups. But interethnic hostility, personal prejudices, and individual biases, while certainly hurtful, do not have the long-range and life-limiting effects of *institutional* racism and bias (King, 1991). Testing practices, for example, may be institutionally discriminatory because they label students from culturally and socially dominated groups as inferior as a result of their performance on these tests (Mercer, 1989). Rather than critically examining the tests themselves, the underlying purpose of such tests, or their damaging effects, the students themselves are often blamed (Medina & Neill, 1990).

An antiracist perspective is also apparent in schools when students are permitted, and even encouraged, to speak about their experiences with racism and other biases. Many White teachers feel great discomfort when racism is discussed in the classroom for several reasons: their lack of experience in confronting such a potentially explosive issue, the conspiracy of silence about racism (as if not speaking about it will make it disappear), the guilt they may feel being a member of the group that has benefited from racism, and the generally accepted assumption that we live in a colorblind society (see chapter 11), or a combination of these reasons (Fine, 1991; Sleeter, 1992; Tatum, 1992). Yet when students are given time and support for expressing their views, the result can be powerful because their experiences are legitimated and used in the service of their learning.

Donaldson (1994) describes how urban high school students used the racism they and their peers experienced in school as the content of a peer education assembly program. The result was a powerful and critical examination of the impact that race can have on their education. A similar result was documented by Zanger (1993), when she brought together a group of high-achieving Latino and Latina Boston high school students to talk about their experiences with discrimination. In the subsequent dialogue, students discussed such meaningful issues as their feelings of exclusion and subordination and their cultural invisibility in the school. They also proposed specific solutions that have profound implications for school policies and practices, including the kinds of program options that schools offer for learning English. In the words of one young woman (cited in Zanger, 1993),

> I think we should try to learn English, but not lose our
> Spanish. They want us to learn English and lose our cultural
> backgrounds. And I think there's a way they can work up on
> our *already* [existing] culture. And build it to be strong and
> better than what they are and we are. Two things combined
> can be very good. I mean we take the Spanish culture and a
> little bit of the English culture, we can be great students, we
> can be great people, we can be great leaders of this country.
> (p. 175; emphasis added)

Another example comes from an extensive study that took place over a one-year period in which numerous students, staff, and parents in California schools were consulted and interviewed (Poplin & Weeres, 1992). The researchers found that, in spite of the fact that racism is rarely discussed in their classes, most students described racist incidents in school and could easily relate them to racism in the larger society. In addition, and probably not coincidentally, most young people expressed an intense interest in knowing about one another's cultures and backgrounds, but they learned very little about these in school. In a similar vein, a qualitative research study by Kiang and Kaplan (1994) explored the views of Vietnamese students on their exclusion in discussions about racial conflict after a violent clash between African American and White students. Not only did the students feel left out of these important discussions, but more important, they also felt that their involvement might help improve the race relations and the quality of life in the school.

In my own research on the views of academically successful students concerning their schooling, racism and other examples of discrimination on the part of fellow students and teachers were mentioned (Nieto, 1994a). Manuel, a Cape Verdean student who moved to the United States at age eleven, described how it felt to be the butt of jokes from his peers: "When American students see you, it's kinda hard [to] get along with them when you have a different culture, a different way of dressing and stuff like that. So kids really look at you and laugh, you know, at the beginning" (p. 414). Avi, a Jewish American young man, discussed a number of incidents of anti-Semitism, including one in which a student walked by him and whispered, "Are you ready for the Second Holocaust?" Other students talked about discrimination on the part of teachers. Marisol, a Puerto Rican student, and Vinh, who was Vietnamese, specifically mentioned language discrimination as a major problem. In Marisol's case, it happened when a teacher did not allow her to use Spanish in the classroom. For Vinh, it concerned teachers' attitudes about his language. He explained: "Some teachers don't understand about the language. So sometimes, my language, they say it sounds funny" (p. 414).

As these examples make clear, an antiracist perspective in schools is essential if all students are to be given equitable environments for learning. An antiracist perspective is an important lens through which to analyze a school's policies and practices, including the curriculum, pedagogy, testing and tracking, discipline, faculty hiring, student retention, and attitudes about and interactions with parents.

School Reform Should Reflect an Understanding and Acceptance of All Students as Having Talents and Strengths That Can Enhance Their Education

It has been amply documented that many educators believe that students from culturally subordinated groups have few experiential or cultural strengths that can benefit their education (Ginsburg, 1986; Haberman, 1991; Ryan, 1972). Such students, generally low-income children of all groups and children of color specifically, are considered to be "walking sets of deficiencies" (Nieto, 1994b). They may be considered "culturally deprived," a patronizing term popularized in the 1960s to shift the blame for student failure from schools and society to students and their families (Reissman, 1962). Students may be labeled *culturally deprived* because they speak a language other than English as their native language, have just one parent, live in poverty, or simply because of their race or ethnicity.

Rather than begin with this kind of deficit view, it makes more sense to begin with a more positive and, in the end, more realistic view of students and their families. School reform measures based on the assumption that children of all families bring cultural and community strengths to their education would go a long way in providing more powerful learning environments for a greater number of youngsters. Luis Moll's (1992) research on incorporating "funds of knowledge" into the curriculum, that is, using the experiences and skills of all families to encourage student learning, is a more hopeful and productive way of approaching families than is the viewpoint that they have only deficits that must be repaired.

Beginning with the premise that students and their families have important talents that can help their children achieve has important implications for school policies and practices. This premise implies that teachers need to learn culturally responsive ways of teaching all of their students (Darder, 1991; Hollins, King, & Hayman, 1994; Ladson-Billings, 1994a). Instead of placing the blame solely on students, teachers need to consider how their students best learn, how their cultural backgrounds may influence learning, and how teachers' own pedagogical practices need to change as a result.

Teachers also need to consider how the language spoken by students may influence their academic achievement. For instance, it is common practice in schools to try to convince parents whose native language is other than English that they should speak only English with their children. This recommendation makes little sense for at least three reasons. First, these parents often speak little English themselves, and their children are thus provided with less than adequate models of English. Second, this practice often results in cutting off, rather than stimulating, communication between parents and children (Campos & Keatinge, 1988; Cummins, 1981). Third, if young people are encouraged to learn English at the expense of their native language, rather than in conjunction with it, they may lose important connections that help maintain close and loving relations with family members (Rodríguez, 1983).

In this regard, a nationwide survey of more than 1,000 families for whom English was a second language found evidence of serious disruptions of family relations when young children learned English in school and lost their native language (NABE No-Cost Study on Families, 1991). Thus, a more reasonable recommendation, and one that would honor the contributions parents can make to their children's education, is to encourage rather than discourage them to speak their native language with their children, to speak it often, and to use it consistently. In schools, this means that students would not be punished for speaking their native languages; rather, they would be encouraged to do so, and to do so for learning. A rich communicative legacy, both in school and at home, would be the result (Cummins, 1981; McLaughlin, 1992).

Another example of failing to use student and community strengths can be found in the curriculum. Young children are frequently presented with images of community helpers who may be unrelated to their daily lives. A perspective that affirms the talents and experiences of students and their families would expand the people and roles included in the curriculum. Not only would children study those community helpers traditionally included, such as police officers, mail carriers, and teachers, but they might also learn about their local merchants, community social service activists, and street vendors. These people are also community helpers, although they have not generally been sanctioned as such by the official curriculum.

A further consideration concerning the talents and strengths of students and their families is what Cummins (1994) has called the "relations of power" in schools. In proposing a shift from "coercive" to "collaborative" relations of power, Cummins argues that traditional teacher-centered transmission models can limit the potential for learning, especially among students from dominated communities whose cultures and languages are devalued by the dominant canon. For instance, the previously cited in-depth study of schools by Poplin and Weeres (1992) found that students frequently reported being bored and seeing little relevance in the school curriculum to their lives and futures. Furthermore, the researchers concluded that as the curriculum, texts, and assignments became more standardized, students became even more disengaged in their learning (Poplin & Weeres, 1992). That is, the more school experiences were unrelated to their own community experiences, the less relevant schooling became for students. Their findings suggest that using students and their families as collaborators in developing the curriculum would help promote student learning. By encouraging collaborative relations of power, schools can begin to recognize other sources of legitimate knowledge that have been overlooked, and this practice can in turn positively affect the degree to which students learn.

School Reform Should Be Considered within the Parameters of Critical Pedagogy

The connection between critical pedagogy and a multicultural perspective has recently been explored, and it is a promising avenue for expanding and informing both of these philosophical frameworks (Nieto, 1996; Shor, 1992; Sleeter & McLaren, 1995). According to Banks (1997), the main goal of a multicultural curriculum is to help students develop decision-making and social-action skills. When students learn to view situations and events from a variety of viewpoints, critical thinking, reflection, and action are promoted. Critical pedagogy is an approach through which students and teachers are encouraged to view what they learn in a critical light, in the words of Paulo Freire (1970), by learning to read both "the word and the world." According to Freire, the opposite of a critical or empowering approach is "banking education," where students learn to regurgitate and passively accept the knowledge they are given. A critical education, on the other hand, expects students to seek their own answers, to be curious, and to question.

Most students do not usually have access to a wide range of viewpoints, but this is essential if they are to develop the important critical judgment and decision-making skills they will need to become productive members of a democratic society. Because a critical perspective values diverse viewpoints and encourages critical thinking, reflection, and action, students are empowered as learners because they are expected to become problem-solvers. Furthermore, critical pedagogy is based on using students' present reality as a foundation for their further learning, rather than on doing away with or belittling what they know and who they are. Critical pedagogy thus acknowledges cultural and linguistic diversity instead of suppressing it.

Shor's (1992) analysis concerning critical pedagogy is instructive. He begins with the assumption that no curriculum can be truly neutral. Therefore, it is the responsibility of schools to present students with the broad range of information they will need to learn to read and write *critically* and in the service of social change. He writes: "Knowledge is the power to know, to understand, but not necessarily the power to do or to change. . . . Literacy and awareness by themselves do not change oppressive conditions in school and society. Knowledge is power only for those who can use it to change their condition" (p. 6).

Given this perspective, it is clear that critical pedagogy is not simply the transfer of knowledge from teacher to students, even though it may be important knowledge that has heretofore not been made available to them. A critical perspective does not simply operate on the principle of substituting one truth for another; instead, students are expected to reflect on multiple and contradictory perspectives to understand reality more fully (Giroux, 1983; Shor, 1992). For instance, learning about the internment of Japanese citizens and residents in the United States during World War II is not in itself critical pedagogy; it only becomes so when students analyze different viewpoints and use them to understand the inconsistencies they uncover (Daniels, 1971). They can then begin to understand the role played by racist hysteria, economic exploitation, and propaganda as catalysts for the internment, and they can judge this action vis à vis the stated ideals of our nation.

Without a critical perspective, reality is often presented to students as if it were static, finished, and flat; underlying conflicts, problems, and inherent contradictions are omitted. Textbooks in all subject areas generally exclude information about unpopular perspectives, or the perspectives of disempowered groups in society (Sleeter & Grant, 1991). Few of the books to which students have access present the viewpoints of people who have built our country, from enslaved Africans to immigrant labor to other working-class people, even though they have been the backbone of society (Apple & Christian-Smith, 1991; Zinn, 1995). Likewise, the immigrant experience, shared by many groups in the United States, is generally treated, if at all, as a romantic and successful odyssey instead of as a more complicated process that has been also a wrenching experience of loss. In addition, the European immigrant experience is generally presented as the sole model for all other immigrants, although the historical context, the racial hostility, and the economic structures awaiting more recent immigrants are very different and more complicated than was true for the vast majority of Europeans who arrived during the late nineteenth and early twentieth centuries (Carnoy, 1994).

Using critical pedagogy as a basis for school reform renders very different policies for schools than do traditional models of school reform. Even more important than just increasing curricular options, critical pedagogy helps to expand teachers' and schools' perspectives about what their students know and what their intellectual capabilities might be. When a critical perspective is used, students can be helped to become agents of their own learning and can use what they learn in productive and critical ways. The knowledge they learn can be used to explore the reasons for certain conditions in their lives and to design strategies for changing them.

A number of eloquent accounts of critical pedagogy in classrooms are compelling examples of the positive and empowering influence that teachers' guidance can have on student learning. For instance, Mercado (1993), working collaboratively with a middle-school teacher and her students, designed a project in which the young people became researchers about conditions in their Bronx neighborhood. Students learned a variety of sophisticated academic skills at the same time that they learned to think more deeply about the reasons for situations such as drug abuse, homelessness, teenage pregnancy, and intergenerational conflicts. In many cases, students used their research skills in social action projects to improve their community.

Sylvester (1994), a teacher in an urban Philadelphia school, described how he put critical pedagogy into practice with his mostly Latino and African American third-grade students. Conceptualizing education as a means to change social structures rather than merely replicate them, he created an economy that he and his students named "Sweet Cakes Town." This classroom-based system provided students with real-life situations in which they focused on issues such as unemployment, homelessness, injustice, cooperation, and entrepreneurship in the service of the community. For instance, Sylvester recounts what happened after one particular reading by his students:

> After we read a biography of Cesar Chavez, student workers created their own union, which they named JBS Local 207 (standing for John Barnes School, room 207). It took a while for them to coordinate collective action. At first when I lowered their wages, one of them said, "I'm on strike," to which I replied, "OK, who wants her job?" At this point, many of the students raised their hands, and the striker backed down. Trying to make this as realistic as possible, I lowered their wages again and again. Eventually they realized that their individual good was dependent on each other, and except for two die-hard scabs, the workers waged a strike. The union leaders and I reached a bargain over lunch, and later the bargain was ratified by the rank and file. (p. 316)

Of the many lessons Sylvester learned from this project were that students need opportunities to imagine themselves in new roles, that teachers need to provide students, particularly African American and Latino students, with positive images that challenge academic success as "acting White" (Fordham & Ogbu, 1986), and that the curriculum should present reality to students as something to be questioned and analyzed.

In another example, Peterson (1991) wrote about how he uses critical pedagogy with his elementary school students to teach literacy, debunk myths, and provide a rich environment for learning. He describes, for instance, how class meetings become "problem-posing" exercises (Freire, 1970) as students list the concerns or problems they want to discuss and then decide which one to tackle on a particular day. He describes the five-step plan they use by listing a series of questions they need to answer:

1. What is the problem?
2. Are you sure about it?
3. What can we do about it?
4. Try it.
5. How did it work? (p. 166)

Peterson (1991) does not propose this process as a panacea. Instead, he states, "While many of the problems poor and minority children and communities face cannot be easily or immediately 'solved,' a 'problem-posing' pedagogy can encourage a questioning of why things are the way they are and the identification of actions, no matter how small, to begin to address them" (p. 166).

Other accounts of critical pedagogy in action, all written by classroom teachers, are contained in a recent publication by Rethinking Schools (Bigelow et al., 1994). In these powerful accounts, which discuss specific curricular and pedagogical innovations, critical pedagogy is the force behind student learning.

The People Most Intimately Connected with Teaching and Learning (Teachers, Parents, and Students Themselves) Need to Be Meaningfully Involved in School Reform

Research on involvement by parents, students, and teachers in decisions affecting education have consistently indicated that such involvement can dramatically improve student learning (Abi-Nader, 1993; Fine, 1991; Henderson & Berla, 1995; Soo Hoo, 1993). Yet the people who are closest to learners are often excluded from discussions and policy implications and from the implementation of school reform measures. Schools usually are not organized to encourage the involvement of these groups, but instead take their cue from school boards and state and national guidelines.

Cummins (1989) reviewed programs that included student empowerment as a goal and concluded that students who are encouraged to develop a positive cultural identity through interactions with their teachers experience a sense of control over their own lives and develop the confidence and motivation to succeed academically. In the case of teachers, Lee, Bryk, and Smith (1993) reported that teachers who have more control over classroom conditions consider themselves more efficacious. An analysis of a number of programs by Fruchter, Galletta, and White (1993) stressing effective parent involvement found that all the programs reviewed shared the following components: a commitment to involve low-income parents, family empowerment as a major goal, and a stated desire to reduce the gap between home and school cultures by designing programs that respond to and build on the values, structures, languages, and cultures of students' homes.

School reform measures that stress the meaningful involvement of students, teachers, and parents would probably look quite different from traditional approaches. They would begin with the assumption that these groups have important and insightful perspectives about student learning. Thus, rather than thinking of ways to bypass their ideas, school reformers would actively seek their involvement in developing, for instance, disciplinary policies, curriculum development, and decisions concerning tracking and the use of tests.

Including teachers in meaningful ways can be a powerful way to reflect the realities of the classroom in school-based reform (Throne, 1994). Likewise, allowing time in the curriculum, for example, for students to engage in critical discussions about how the language of some communities is devalued would no doubt help to affirm the legitimacy of the discourse of all students. At the same time, these kinds of discussions would also acknowledge the need to learn and become comfortable with the discourse of the larger society (Delpit, 1992). In addition, involving parents in curriculum development would enrich the curriculum in general, affirm what families have to offer, and help students overcome their embarrassment about their cultures, languages, and values, an all-too-common attitude for students from culturally subordinated groups (Delgado-Gaitán, 1993).

School Reform Needs to Be Based on High Expectations and Rigorous Standards for All Learners

Many students cope on a daily basis with complex and difficult problems, including poverty, violence, racism, abuse, families in distress, and lack of health care and proper housing (Kozol, 1991; Nieto, 1994b). In addition to such situations, many students come to school with conditions that some teachers and schools consider to place them at risk for learning, including speaking a language other than English or simply belonging to a nondominant racial or ethnic group. Unfortunately, these conditions are sometimes used as a rationalization for low expectations of what students are capable of learning. Just the opposite should be the case. That is, schools in our society have been expected to provide an equal and equitable education for all students, not just for those who have no problems in their lives or who fit the image of successful students due to race, class, or language ability. Unfortunately, the promise of an equal education for all has not been realized, as is evident from a number of critiques of the myth of our schools as "the great equalizer" (Bowles & Gintis, 1976; Katz, 1975; Spring, 1989). Nevertheless, the ideal of equitable educational opportunity is worth defending and vigorously putting into practice.

It is undeniably true that many students come to our schools with incredibly difficult problems, and the school itself cannot be expected to solve them. Neither can we dismiss the heroic efforts of many teachers and schools who, with limited financial and other material resources, teach students who live in dire circumstances under what can best be described as challenging conditions. Nevertheless, the difficult conditions in which some students live need not be viewed as insurmountable barriers to their academic achievement. It is too often the case that society's low expectations of students, based on these situations, often pose even greater barriers. For example, if students do not speak English, an assumption is often made that they cannot learn (Flores, Cousin, & Díaz, 1991); or if they do not have consistent experiences with or access to libraries, museums, or other cultural institutions that are considered essential for preparing students for schools, the assumption that they are not even ready to learn may be made (Haberman, 1991).

If we are serious about giving all students more options in life, particularly students from communities denied the necessary resources with which to access these options, then we need to begin with the assumption that these students are academically capable, both individually and as a group. Too many students have been dismissed because they were not born with the material resources or family conditions considered important for learning. The attitude that students who do not arrive at school with such benefits are therefore incapable of learning is further promoted by claims of race-based genetic inferiority (Herrnstein & Murray, 1994), a renewed trend reminiscent of previous arguments that made similar claims (Jensen, 1969).

The numerous examples of dramatic success in the face of adversity are powerful reminders that great potential exists in all students. Consider, for example, the case of Garfield High School. Here, the mostly Mexican American students taught by Jaime Escalante, the protagonist of the popular film *Stand and Deliver,* were tremendously successful in learning advanced mathematics. In fact, when they took the Advanced Placement (AP) calculus test, they did so well that the test makers assumed they had cheated. As a result, they had to take it a second time, and this time their performance was even better.

The success of the Algebra Project in Cambridge, Massachusetts (Moses, Kamii, Swap, & Howard, 1989), is another example. In this project, young people who had previously been denied access to algebra because they were thought to be incapable of benefiting from it became high achievers in math. When they went on to high school, fully 39 percent of the first graduating class of the project were placed in honors geometry or honors algebra classes; incredibly, none of the graduates was placed in a lower-level math course. The success of the project was explained by the authors: "Teachers and parents in the Open Program came to believe that ability grouping in mathematics seriously impaired the capacity of middle school students of color and females to learn as well as they might" (p. 45).

In a study about Central Park East Elementary School in East Harlem, New York, a school with a student body made up overwhelmingly of Latino and African American students, Meier (1993, 1995) provides another example of academic success among youngsters who might not have been thought capable of succeeding. The school, which accepts students from the neighborhood and not from elite or favored groups, has documented astonishing success: an in-depth study of the first seven graduating classes of the school revealed that 90 percent earned high school diplomas, and two-thirds went on to college, nearly double the rate for the city as a whole.

Conditions in students' lives that might be considered barriers to learning, such as speaking a language other than English or being a member of a culturally dominated group, are not necessarily problems or roadblocks, although they have generally been defined as such by the general population. These conditions may in fact enrich the lives of students, but they are often perceived as handicaps to learning by an assimilationist society that encourages cultural and linguistic homogeneity. Numerous success stories of students who speak other languages or use their cultural values and traditions as strengths rather than deficits have been reported in the educational research literature (Díaz Soto, 1993; Hakuta, 1990; Nieto, 1996; Willig & Ramírez, 1993). This leads us to the inevitable conclusion that before fixing what may be considered problems that impede student learning, schools and society need to change their own perceptions of these conditions and view them as potential benefits.

CONCLUSION

There is no simple formula for increasing student learning. A step-by-step blueprint for school reform is both unrealistic and inappropriate because each school differs from all others in its basic structure, goals, and human dimensions. In addition, inequitable conditions such as school funding and the distribution of resources for learning are major factors that help explain academic failure or success (Darling-Hammond, 1995). However, certain conditions can dramatically improve the learning of many students who are currently marginalized from the center of learning because of school policies and practices based on deficit models. If we begin with the assumptions that students cannot achieve at high levels, that their backgrounds are riddled with deficiencies, and that multicultural education is a frill that cannot help them to learn, we will end up with school reform strategies that have little hope for success.

In this chapter, I have presented and analyzed five conditions to promote student achievement within a multicultural perspective.

1. School reform should be antiracist and antibiased.
2. School reform should reflect an understanding and acceptance of all students as having talents and strengths that can enhance their education.
3. School reform should be considered within the parameters of critical pedagogy.
4. The people most intimately connected with teaching and learning (teachers, parents, and students themselves) need to be meaningfully involved in school reform.
5. School reform needs to be based on high expectations and rigorous standards for all learners.

Thus, I began this chapter with assumptions based on student, family, and teacher strengths, and on the possibility that a comprehensive and critical approach to multicultural education can provide an important framework for rethinking school reform. Given these assumptions, we have a much more promising scenario for effective learning and for the possibility that schools can become places of hope and affirmation for students of all backgrounds and situations.

Questions and Activities

1. What does the author mean by "culturally responsive education"? Why does she think it is important? According to the author, is culturally responsive education sufficient to guarantee academic success for students of color and low-income students? Why or why not?

2. What does the author mean when she states that multicultural education takes place within a sociopolitical context? What social, political, and economic factors must be considered when multicultural education is being implemented? How can a consideration of sociopolitical factors help multicultural school reform to be more effective?

3. What five conditions does the author believe are needed to improve students' academic achievement? How are these factors interrelated?

4. How does the author distinguish *individual* and *institutional racism?* Why does she think this distinction is important? Give examples of each type of racism from your personal experiences and observations.

5. What, according to the author, is an antiracist perspective? Why does she believe that an antiracist perspective is essential for the implementation of multicultural education? Give specific examples of antiracist teaching and educational practices.

6. The author briefly describes Luis Moll's concept of incorporating community knowledge into the curriculum. How does this concept help teachers to implement "culturally sensitive" teaching?

7. What is critical pedagogy? How, according to the author, can it be used to enrich and strengthen multicultural education?

8. According to the author, what positive contributions can parents and students make to creating an effective multicultural school? Give specific examples in your response.

References

Abi-Nader, J. (1993). Meeting the Needs of Multicultural Classrooms: Family Values and the Motivation of Minority Students. In M. J. O'Hair and S. Odell (Eds.). *Diversity and Teaching: Teacher Education Yearbook I* (pp. 212–236). Forth Worth: Harcourt Brace Jovanovich.

Apple, M. W. and Christian-Smith, L. K. (Eds.). (1991). *The Politics of the Textbook.* New York: Routledge and Chapman Hall.

Aptheker, H. (1943/1987). *American Negro Slave Revolts.* New York: International Publishers.

Ascher, C. and Burnett, G. (1993). *Current Trends and Issues in Urban Education.* New York: ERIC Clearinghouse on Urban Education, Teachers College, Columbia University.

Au, K. A. and Kawakami, A. J. (1994). Cultural Congruence in Instruction. In E. R. Hollins, J. E. King, and W. C. Hayman (Eds.). *Teaching Diverse Populations: Formulating a Knowledge Base* (pp. 5–24). New York: State University of New York Press.

Banks, J. A. (1997). *Teaching Strategies for Ethnic Studies* (6th ed.). Boston: Allyn and Bacon.

Banks, J. A. and Banks, C. A. M. (Eds.). (1995). *Handbook of Research on Multicultural Education.* New York: Macmillan.

Bigelow, B., Christensen, L., Karp, S., Miner, B., and Peterson, B. (Eds.). (1994). *Rethinking Our Classrooms: Teaching for Equity and Justice.* Milwaukee: Rethinking Schools.

Bowles, S. and Gintis, H. (1976). *Schooling in Capitalist America: Educational Reform and the Contradictions of Economic Life.* New York: Basic Books.

Bryk, A. S., Lee, V. E., and Holland, P. B. (1993). *Catholic Schools and the Common Good.* Cambridge: Harvard Educational Review Press.

Campos, S. J. and Keatinge, H. R. (1988). The Carpinteria Language Minority Student Experience: From Theory, to Practice, to Success. In T. Skutnabb-Kangas and J. Cummins (Eds.). *Minority Education: From Shame to Struggle* (pp. 299–307). Clevedon, England: Multilingual Matters.

Carnoy, M. (1994). *Faded Dreams: The Politics and Economics of Race in America.* New York: Cambridge University Press.

Cummins, J. (1981). The Role of Primary Language Development in Promoting Educational Success for Language Minority Students. In Office of Bilingual Bicultural Education, *Schooling and Language Minority Students: A Theoretical Framework* (pp. 28–41). Sacramento: Evaluation, Dissemination, and Assessment Center, California State University.

Cummins, J. (1989). *Empowering Minority Students.* Sacramento: California Association for Bilingual Education.

Cummins, J. (1994). From Coercive to Collaborative Relations of Power in the Teaching of Literacy. In B. M. Ferdman, R.-M. Weber, and A. G. Ramírez (Eds.). *Literacy across Languages and Cultures* (pp. 295–331). Albany: State University of New York Press.

Daniels, R. (1971). *Concentration Camps, U.S.A.: Japanese Americans and World War II.* New York: Holt.

Darder, A. (1991). *Culture and Power in the Classroom: A Critical Foundation for Bicultural Education.* New York: Bergin & Garvey.

Darling-Hammond, L. (1995). Inequality and Access to Knowledge. In J. A. Banks and C. A. M. Banks (Eds.). *Handbook of Research on Multicultural Education* (pp. 465–483). New York: Macmillan.

Delgado-Gaitán, C. (1993). Research and Policy in Reconceptualizing Family-School Relationships. In P. Phelan and A. L. Davidson (Eds.). *Renegotiating Cultural Diversity in American Schools* (pp. 139–158). New York: Teachers College Press.

Delpit, L. (1992). The Politics of Teaching Literate Discourse. *Theory into Practice, 31,* 285–295.

Delpit, L. (1995). *Other People's Children: Cultural Conflict in the Classroom.* New York: The New Press.

Díaz Soto, L. (1993). Native Language for School Success. *Bilingual Research Journal, 17*(1 & 2), 83–97.

Donaldson, K. (1994). Through Students' Eyes. *Multicultural Education, 2*(2), 26–28.

Erickson, F. (1993). Transformation and School Success: The Politics and Culture of Educational Achievement. In E. Jacob and C. Jordan (Eds.). *Minority Education: Anthropological Perspectives* (pp. 27–51). Norwood, NJ: Ablex Publishing Corporation.

Fine, M. (1991). *Framing Dropouts: Notes on the Politics of an Urban Public High School.* Albany: State University of New York Press.

Flores, B., Cousin, P. T., and Díaz, E. (1991). Transforming Deficit Myths about Learning, Language, and Culture. *Language Arts, 68*(5), 369–379.

Fordham, S. and Ogbu, J. U. (1986). Black Students' School Success: Coping with the 'Burden of Acting White.' *Urban Review, 18*(3), 176–206.

Frau-Ramos, M. and Nieto, S. (1993). "I Was an Outsider": An Exploratory Study of Dropping Out among Puerto Rican Youths in Holyoke, Massachusetts. In R. Rivera and S. Nieto (Eds.). *The Education of Latino Students in Massachusetts: Issues, Research, and Policy Implications* (pp. 147–169). Boston: Gastón Institute.

Freire, P. (1970). *Pedagogy of the Oppressed.* New York: Seabury Press.

Freire, P. (1985). *The Politics of Education: Culture, Power, and Liberation.* South Hadley, MA: Bergin & Garvey.

Fruchter, N., Galletta, A., and White, J. L. (1993). New Directions in Parent Involvement. *Equity and Choice, 9*(3), 33–43.

García, J. (1993). The Changing Image of Ethnic Groups in Textbooks. *Phi Delta Kappan, 75*(1), 29–35.

Ginsburg, H. (1986). The Myth of the Deprived Child: New Thoughts on Poor Children. In U. Neisser (Ed.). *The School Achievement of Minority Children: New Perspectives* (pp. 169–189). Hillsdale, NJ: Lawrence Erlbaum.

Giroux, H. A. (1983). *Theory and Resistance in Education: A Pedagogy for the Opposition.* South Hadley, MA: Bergin & Garvey.

Glass, G. V. (1982). *School Class Size: Research and Policy.* Beverly Hills, CA: Sage Publications.

Haberman, M. (1991). The Pedagogy of Poverty versus Good Teaching. *Phi Delta Kappan, 73*, 290–294.

Hakuta, K. (1990). *Bilingualism and Bilingual Education: A Research Perspective*, No. 1. Washington, DC: National Clearinghouse for Bilingual Education.

Harris, V. J. (Ed.). (1992). *Teaching Multicultural Literature in Grades K–8.* Norwood, MA: Christopher-Gordon Publishers.

Henderson, A. T. and Berla, N. (1995). *A New Generation of Evidence: The Family Is Crucial to Student Achievement.* Washington, DC: Center for Law and Education.

Herrnstein, R. J. and Murray, C. (1994). *The Bell Curve: Intelligence and Class Structure in American Life.* New York: The Free Press.

Hill, P. T., Foster, G. E., and Gendler, T. (1990). *High Schools with Character.* Santa Monica, CA: Rand Corporation.

Hollins, E. R., King, J. E., and Hayman, W. C. (Eds.). (1994). *Teaching Diverse Populations: Formulating a Knowledge Base.* Albany: State University of New York Press.

Jensen, A. R. (1969). How Much Can We Boost I.Q. and Scholastic Achievement? *Harvard Educational Review, 39*, 1–123.

Katz, M. B. (1975). *Class, Bureaucracy, and the Schools: The Illusion of Educational Change in America.* New York: Praeger.

Kiang, P. N. and Kaplan, J. (1994). Where Do We Stand? Views of Racial Conflict by Vietnamese American High-School Students in a Black-and-White Context. *The Urban Review, 26*(2), 95–119.

King, J. E. (1991). Dysconscious Racism: Ideology, Identity, and the Miseducation of Teachers. *Journal of Negro Education, 60*(2), 133–146.

Kohl, H. (1993). The Myth of "Rosa Parks the Tired." *Multicultural Education, 1*(2), 6–10.

Kozol, J. (1975, December). Great Men and Women (Tailored for School Use). *Learning Magazine,* 16–20.

Kozol, J. (1991). *Savage Inequalities: Children in America's Schools.* New York: Crown.

Ladson-Billings, G. (1994a). *The Dreamkeepers: Successful Teachers of African American Children.* San Francisco: Jossey-Bass Publishers.

Ladson-Billings, G. (1994b). Who Will Teach Our Children? Preparing Teachers to Successfully Teach African American Students. In E. R. Hollins, J. E. King, and W. C. Hayman (Eds.). *Teaching Diverse Populations: Formulating a Knowledge Base* (pp. 129–142). Albany: State University of New York Press.

Lee, V. E., Bryk, A. A., and Smith, J. B. (1993). The Organization of Effective Secondary Schools. In L. Darling-Hammond (Ed.). *Review of Research in Education,* Vol. 19 (pp. 171–267). Washington, DC: American Educational Research Association.

Loewen, J. W. (1995): *Lies My Teacher Taught Me: Everything Your American History Textbook Got Wrong.* New York: The Free Press.

McLaughlin, B. (1992). *Myths and Misconceptions about Second Language Learning: What Every Teacher Needs to Unlearn.* Santa Cruz, CA: National Center for Research on Cultural Diversity and Second Language Learning.

Medina, N. and Neill, D. M. (1990). *Fallout from the Testing Explosion,* (3rd ed.). Cambridge: FairTest.

Meier, D. (1993). Transforming Schools into Powerful Communities. In R. Takanishi (Ed.). *Adolescence in the 1990s: Risk and Opportunity* (pp. 199–202). New York: Teachers College Press.

Meier, D. (1995). *The Power of Their Ideas: Lessons for America from a Small School in Harlem.* Boston: Beacon Press.

Meier, K. J. and Stewart, J., Jr. (1991). *The Politics of Hispanic Education: Un Paso Pa'lante y Dos Pa'tras.* New York: State University of New York Press.

Mercado, C. I. (1993). Caring as Empowerment: School Collaboration and Community Agency. *Urban Review, 25*(1), 79–104.

Mercer, J. (1989). Alternative Paradigms for Assessment in a Pluralistic Society. In J. A. Banks and C. A. M. Banks (Eds.). *Multicultural Education: Issues and Perspectives.* (pp. 289–304). Boston: Allyn and Bacon.

Moll, L. (1992). Bilingual Classroom Studies and Community Analysis: Some Recent Trends. *Educational Researcher, 21*(2), 20–24.

Moses, R. P., Kamii, M., Swap, S. M., and Howard, J. (1989). The Algebra Project: Organizing in the Spirit of Ella. *Harvard Educational Review, 59*(4), 24–47.

NABE No-Cost Study on Families. (1991). *NABE News, 14*(4), 7, 23.

Nieto, S. (1994a). Lessons from Students on Creating a Chance to Dream. *Harvard Educational Review, 64*(4), 392–426.

Nieto, S. (1994b). What Are Our Children Capable of Knowing? *The Educational Forum, 58*(4), 434–440.

Nieto, S. (1996). *Affirming Diversity: The Sociopolitical Context of Multicultural Education* (2nd ed.). White Plains, NY: Longman.

Oakes, J. (1990). Opportunities, Achievement, and Choice: Women and Minority Students in Science and Mathematics. In C. B. Cazden (Ed.). *Review of Research in Education*, Vol. 16, (pp. 153–222). Washington, DC: American Educational Research Association.

Oakes, J. and Guiton, G. (1995). Matchmaking: The Dynamics of High School Tracking Decisions. *American Educational Research Journal, 32*(1), pp. 3–33.

Ogbu, J. U. (1994). Racial Stratification and Education in the United States: Why Inequality Persists. *Teachers College Record, 96*(2), 264–298.

Peterson, R. E. (1991). Teaching How to Read the World and Change It: Critical Pedagogy in the Intermediate Grades. In C. E. Walsh (Ed.). *Literacy as Praxis: Culture, Language, and Pedagogy* (pp. 156–182). Norwood, NJ: Ablex.

Poplin, M. and Weeres, J. (1992). *Voices from the Inside: A Report on Schooling from Inside the Classroom.* Claremont, CA: Claremont Graduate School, Institute for Education in Transformation.

Reissman, F. (1962). *The Culturally Deprived Child.* New York: Harper & Row.

Rodríguez, R. (1983). *Hunger of Memory: The Education of Richard Rodríguez.* Boston: David R. Godine.

Ryan, W. (1972). *Blaming the Victim.* New York: Vintage Books.

Schofield, J. W. (1986). Causes and Consequences of the Colorblind Perspective. In J. F. Dovidio and S. L. Gaertner (Eds.). *Prejudice, Discrimination and Racism* (pp. 231–253). New York: Academic Press.

Shor, I. (1992). *Empowering Education: Critical Teaching for Social Change.* Chicago: University of Chicago Press.

Sleeter, C. E. (1992). *Keepers of the American Dream: A Study of Staff Development and Multicultural Education.* London: Falmer Press.

Sleeter, C. E. and Grant, C. A. (1991). Race, Class, Gender and Disability in Current Textbooks. In M. W. Apple and L. K. Christian-Smith (Eds). *The Politics of the Textbook* (pp. 78–110). New York: Routledge & Chapman Hall.

Sleeter, C. E. and McLaren, P. L. (1995). *Multicultural Education, Critical Pedagogy, and the Politics of Difference.* New York: State University of New York Press.

Soo Hoo, S. (1993). Students as Partners in Research and Restructuring Schools. *The Educational Forum, 57*(4), 386–393.

Spring, J. (1989). *The Sorting Machine Revisited: National Educational Policy since 1945.* White Plains, NY: Longman.

Sylvester, P. S. (1994). Elementary School Curricula and Urban Transformation. *Harvard Educational Review, 64*(3), 309–331.

Tatum, B. D. (1992). Talking about Race, Learning about Racism: The Application of Racial Identity Development Theory in the Classroom. *Harvard Educational Review, 62*, 1–24.

Throne, J. (1994). Living with the Pendulum: The Complex World of Teaching. *Harvard Educational Review, 64*(2), 195–208.

Weinberg, M. (1990). *Racism in the United States: A Comprehensive Classified Bibliography.* Westport, CT: Greenwood Press.

Willig, A. C. and Ramírez, J. D. (1993). The Evaluation of Bilingual Education. In M. B. Arias and U. Casanova (Eds.). *Bilingual Education: Politics, Practice, Research* (pp. 65–87). Chicago: University of Chicago Press.

Winant, H. (1994). *Racial Conditions: Politics, Theory, Comparisons.* Minneapolis: University of Minnesota Press.

Zanger, V. V. (1993). Academic Costs of Social Marginalization: An Analysis of Latino Students' Perceptions at a Boston High School. In R. Rivera and S. Nieto (Eds.). *The Education of Latino Students in Massachusetts: Issues, Research and Policy Implications* (pp. 167–187). Boston: Gastón Institute.

Zinn, H. (1995). *A People's History of the United States.* (rev. ed.). New York: Harper & Row.

Chapter 17

Parents and Teachers: Partners in School Reform

Cherry A. McGee Banks

Parent-community involvement is a dynamic process that can encourage, support, and provide opportunities for parents and educators to cooperate in the education of students. An important goal of parent-community involvement is to improve student learning. In a comprehensive review of research on parent involvement, Anne Henderson (1987) found that there is compelling evidence that parent involvement improves student achievement. Effective parent involvement can also improve student attendance and social behavior.

To be effective, parent involvement must be conceptualized broadly. It must provide opportunities for parents to be involved in different settings and at different levels of the educational process (Mannan & Blackwell, 1992). Some parents may want to focus their energies on working with their own children at home. Other parents may want to work on committees that make decisions affecting students throughout the school district.

Parent-community involvement is also an important component of school reform (Mannan & Blackwell, 1992). Many tasks involved in restructuring schools, such as setting goals and allocating resources, are best achieved through a collaborative problem-solving structure that includes parents, community members, and educators.

Parents and community groups help form what John Goodlad (1984) calls "the necessary coalition of contributing groups" (p. 293). Educational reform needs the support, influence, and activism of parents and community groups. Schools are highly dependent on and vulnerable to citizens who can support or impede change. Parents and community leaders can validate the need for educational reform and can provide an appropriate forum for exploring the importance of education. They can also extend the discussion on school improvement issues beyond formal educational networks and help generate interest in educational reform in the community at large. Parents and community leaders can help provide the rationale, motivation, and social action necessary for educational reform.

WHY IS PARENT-COMMUNITY INVOLVEMENT IMPORTANT?

Parent involvement is important because it acknowledges the importance of parents in the lives of their children, recognizes the diversity of values and perspectives within the school community, provides a vehicle for building a collaborative problem-solving structure, and increases the opportunity for all students to learn in schools.

Parents are often children's first and most important teachers. Students come to school with knowledge, values, and beliefs they have learned from their parents and communities. Parents directly or indirectly help shape their children's value system, orientation toward learning, and view of the world in which they live. Parents can help teachers extend their knowledge and understanding of their students. Through that knowledge and understanding, teachers can improve their teaching effectiveness.

Most parents want their children to succeed in school. Schools can capitalize on the high value most parents put on education by working to create a school environment that reflects an understanding of the students' home and community (Diaz, Moll & Mehan, 1986; Hidalgo, Bright, Sau-Fong, Swap, and Epstein, 1995). When schools conflict with their students' home and community, they can alienate students from their families and communities and cause stress and confusion. For example, many African American (Delpit, 1988) and White working-class parents use direct language when they interact with their children. A working-class parent who wants her child to share a cookie may say, "Joyce, give Barbara half of your cookie." Teachers, however, frequently use indirect language when they issue directives. A teacher who wants Joyce to share her cookie may say, "Joyce, wouldn't you like to share your cookie with Barbara?" The teacher's veiled command may suggest to Joyce that she has a choice when in fact she does not.

To create a harmonious environment between the school, home, and community, teachers need to understand their students' community and home life. Teachers need to be knowledgeable about parents' educational expectations for their children, languages spoken at home, family and community values and norms, as well as how children are taught in their homes and communities. Parents also need information about the school. Parents need to know what the school expects their children to learn, how they will be taught, and the required books and materials their children will use in school. Most important, parents need to know how teachers will assess their children and how they can support their children's achievement.

Students, parents, and teachers all benefit from parent involvement in schools (Comer & Haynes, 1991). When parents become involved, students perform better in school (Clark, 1983). Parental involvement can enable and support students' educational success by providing opportunities for parents to model school-related values and behaviors, can reinforce behaviors that are important for school success, and can provide direct instruction to their children (Hoover-Dempsey & Sandler, 1995). Parental involvement increases the number of people who are supporting the child's learning. Such involvement can also increase the amount of time the child is involved in learning activities. Parent involvement allows parents and teachers to reinforce skills and provide an environment that has consistent learning expectations and standards.

Parents also become more knowledgeable about their child's school, its policies, and the school staff when they are involved in schools. Perhaps most important, parent involvement provides an opportunity for parents and children to spend time together. During that time, parents can communicate a high value for education, the importance of effort in achievement, and high positive regard for their children.

Teachers and principals who know parents treat them with greater respect and show more positive attitudes toward their children (Clark, 1983). Teachers generally see involved parents as concerned individuals who are willing to work with them. They often believe that parents who are not involved in school do not value education.

Parent involvement helps both parents and teachers become more aware of their need to support student learning. Student improvements that result from parents and teachers working together can increase teachers' sense of professionalism and each parents' sense of parenting skills. A cooperative relationship between teachers and parents increases the good will of parents and promotes positive community relations.

Historical Overview

While parent involvement in education is not new, its importance and purpose have varied at different times in American history. In the early part of the nation's history, families were often solely responsible for educating children. Children learned values and skills by working with their families in their communities.

When formal systems of education were established, parents continued to influence their children's education. During the Colonial period, schools were viewed as an extension of the home. Parental and community values and expectations were reinforced in the school. Teachers generally came from the community and often knew their students' parents personally and shared their values.

At the beginning of the twentieth century, when large numbers of immigrants came to the United States, schools were used to compensate for the perceived failures of parents and communities. Schools became a major vehicle to assimilate immigrant children into U.S. society (Banks, 1997). In general, parents were not welcomed in schools. Students were taught that their parents' ways of speaking, behaving, and thinking were inferior to what they were taught in school. In his 1932 study of the sociology of teaching, Waller (1965) concluded that parents and teachers lived in a state of mutual distrust and even hostility.

As society changed, education became more removed from the direct influence of parents. Responsibility for transmitting knowledge from generation to generation was transferred from the home and community to the school. Education was seen as a job for trained professionals. Schools were autonomous institutions staffed by people who were often strangers in their students' home communities. Teachers did not necessarily live in their students' neighborhood, know the students' parents, or share their values.

Over time, schools were given more and more duties that traditionally had been the responsibility of the home and community. For example, parental responsibility for sex education was delegated partly to the schools (Coleman, 1987). Schools operated under the assumption of *in loco parentis*, and educators were often asked to assume the role of both teacher and substitute parent.

In a pluralist society, what the school teaches as well as who and how the school teaches can create tensions between parents and schools. Issues ranging from what the school teaches about the role of women in our society to mainstreaming students with disabilities point to the need for educators, parents, and communities to work together. Today, more and more parents, educators, and community leaders are calling for parent involvement in schools. Parents and educators are concerned about parent involvement, and a majority of both groups feel that it is important and necessary (Williams, 1984). However, parents and educators are frequently unsure about what forms this involvement should take. Often the views of parents and teachers conflict about meaningful ways to involve parents in the educational process (Lightfoot, 1978).

Parent and Community Diversity

Student diversity mirrors parent and community diversity. Just as teachers are expected to work with students from both genders and from different ethnic groups and social classes, parent involvement challenges teachers to work with a diverse group of parents. Some parents with whom teachers work are from different racial and ethnic groups. Others are single parents, parents with special needs, low-income parents, parents with disabilities, or parents who do not speak English. Some parents are members of several of these groups.

Diversity in parent and community groups can be a tremendous asset to the school. However, it can also be a source of potential conflicts and frustrations. Some parents are particularly difficult to involve in their children's education. They resist becoming involved for several reasons (Harry, 1992). In a national survey parents indicated that a lack of time was the number one reason they were not involved in their children's schools (Clark, 1995). The pressures to earn a living and take care of a home and children can put a great deal of stress on parents. At the end of the day, some parents just want to rest. Other parents do not believe they have the necessary educational background to be involved in their children's education. They feel intimidated by educators and believe that education should be left to the schools. Others feel alienated from the school because of negative experiences they have had there or because they believe the school does not support their values (Berger, 1987; Clark, 1995; Rasinski, 1990). In addition, some parents are products of the "me" generation. These parents are primarily concerned with narcissistic endeavors. They are involved in self-development and career-advancement activities. They have limited time available for school involvement because it is not a priority in their lives (Coleman, 1987).

The increase in the number of grandparents who are providing primary care to their grandchildren is another example of parent diversity. Approximately 3.2 million children under the age of eighteen live with their grandparents (U.S. Bureau of the Census, 1989). Twelve percent of African American, 5.8 percent of Latino, and 3.6 percent of White children live with grandparents (U.S. Bureau of the Census, 1989).

Three groups of parents who tend not to be included in school involvement activities are described below. These include parents with special needs, single-parent families, and low-income families. These groups were selected to illustrate particular problem areas for parent involvement. The specific groups of parents discussed should not be interpreted as an indication that only parents from these groups are difficult to involve in schools or that all parents from these groups are difficult to involve in schools. Parents from all groups share many of the concerns discussed here, and there are examples of parents from each group discussed who are actively involved in schools.

Parents with Special Needs

Families with special needs include a wide range of parents. They are found in all ethnic, racial, and income groups. Chronically unemployed parents, parents with long-term illness in the family, abusive parents, and parents with substance-abuse problems are examples of parents with special needs. Although parents with special needs have serious problems that cannot be addressed by the school, teachers should not ignore the importance of establishing a relationship with them. Knowing the difficulties students are coping with at home can help teachers create environments that are supportive during the time students are in school (Swadener & Niles, 1991). Schools can help compensate for the difficult circumstances students experience at home. For some students, the school is the only place during the day where they are nurtured.

Abusive parents require special attention from the school. Most schools have developed policies on how to treat suspected cases of child neglect or abuse. The policies should be written and available to all school personnel. It is generally helpful for one person to be in charge of receiving reports and other information. All states require schools to report suspected cases of child abuse.

Working with special-needs families requires district or building support to develop a list of community outreach agencies for referral. Although some special-needs parents may resist the school's help, they need to know that their problems can negatively affect their children's success in school. Working with these parents can show students who are in difficult home environments that they are not alone. Most parents want to feel that they are valued and adequate human beings and that they can help their children succeed. They are willing to be involved in school, but they do not want to be embarrassed (Berger, 1987). Some parents with special needs will be able to be actively involved in schools, but many will be unable to become involved on a regular basis.

An important goal for working with parents with special needs is to keep lines of communication open. Try to get to know the parents. Do not accept a stereotypical view of them without ever talking to them. Encourage parents to be involved whenever and however they feel they are able to participate. Be prepared to recommend appropriate community agencies to the family. Try to develop a clear understanding of your student's home environment so that you can provide appropriate intervention at school.

Members of the community who are involved in school may be willing to serve as intermediaries between the school and uninvolved parents. In an ethnography of an inner-city neighborhood, Shariff (1988) found that adults shared goods and services and helped each other in an effort to help children in other families. Educators can build on the sense of extended family that may exist in some neighborhoods to form community support groups for students whose parents cannot be involved in school. However, regardless of the circumstances students confront at home, teachers have a responsibility to help them perform at their highest level at school.

Single-Parent Families

One of the most significant social changes in the United States in the last thirty years is the increase in the percentage of children living with one parent. In 1970, 13 percent of children under age eighteen lived with one parent. By 1993, 30 percent of children under eighteen lived with one parent (U.S. Bureau of the Census, 1994b). This increase was particularly significant in the African American community. The number of African American children under eighteen living with one parent increased from 36 percent in 1970 to 52 percent in 1980, to 63 percent in 1993 (U.S. Bureau of the Census, 1994b). There was also an increase in the number of White children under eighteen living with one parent between 1970 and 1980. In 1970, 10 percent of White children under eighteen lived with one parent compared to 17 percent in 1980. However, by 1993, 25 percent of White children under eighteen lived with one parent (U.S. Bureau of the Census, 1994b).

Most children who live with one parent are from divorced homes or are the children of unwed parents. In 1991, 49.87 percent of all marriages in the United States ended in divorce (U.S. Bureau of the Census, 1993). Teenage wives had a divorce rate almost twice as high as that of wives ages thirty-five to thirty-nine (U.S. Bureau of the Census, 1989). The number of premaritally conceived births and births to unmarried women has continued to increase. In 1990, 12.8 percent of the children born in the United States were born to teenage mothers and 26.6 percent of children born in the United States were born to unmarried women (U.S. Bureau of the Census, 1993).

Single-parent families share many of the hopes, joys, and concerns about their children's education that are found in two-parent families. However, because they have a lower rate of attendance at school functions, they are frequently viewed as not supporting their children's education. When teachers respond sensitively to the needs and limitations of single parents, they can be enthusiastic partners with teachers. Four suggestions for working with single parents are listed below. Many of these suggestions apply to other groups of parents as well.

1. Provide flexible times for conferences, such as early mornings, evenings, and weekends.
2. Provide baby-sitting service for activities at the school.
3. Work out procedures for acknowledging and communicating with noncustodial parents. For instance, under what circumstances are noncustodial parents informed about their children's grades, school behavior, or attendance? Problems can occur when information is inappropriately given to or withheld from a noncustodial parent.
4. Use the parents' correct surname. Students will sometimes have different names from their parents.

Low-Income Families

A family of four, in 1993, with total money income less than $14,763.00 was considered below the poverty level (U.S. Bureau of the Census, 1994a). The poverty level is an official governmental estimate of the income necessary to purchase a minimally acceptable standard of living. In 1990, the Census Bureau noted that the number of people in the United States living below the poverty level was rising. The poverty rate in the United States was 12.8 percent in 1989, 13.5 percent in 1990, and 15.1 percent in 1993 (DeParle, 1991; U.S. Bureau of the Census, 1994a). The percentage of people living in poverty in 1990 was higher than at any time during the 1970s (DeParle, 1991). In addition, there were 2.7 million more people in the United States living in poverty in 1991 than in 1990 (U.S. Bureau of the Census, 1994b).

The median family income of African Americans was $21,548.00 in 1991 compared to $23,895.00 for Hispanics and $37,783.00 for White families (U.S. Bureau of the Census, 1994b). Although the increase in the poverty rate of African Americans was below that of Whites and Hispanics, in 1993 more Blacks lived in poverty than either Whites or Hispanics. The poverty rate for African Americans in 1993 was 33.1 percent compared to 12.2 percent for Whites and 30.6 percent for Hispanics (U.S. Bureau of the Census, 1994a).

The poverty rate for children is also rising. In 1993, the poverty rate for children under age eighteen rose to 22.7 percent compared to 17.9 percent in 1980 and 14.9 percent in 1970 (U.S. Bureau of the Census, 1993). The number of children living in poverty is related to the number of female-headed households. In 1993, the poverty rate for married couples with children under eighteen was 9.0 percent compared to 46 percent for single mothers (U.S. Bureau of the Census, 1994a).

Almost 77 percent of homeless families were headed by a single parent in 1988 (U.S. Bureau of the Census, 1989). That parent was usually a female who has two or three children. A 1988 study conducted by the U.S. Conference of Mayors found that 25 percent of the homeless were children (Wright, 1990). These children were members of homeless families, runaways, or children rejected by their parents. Runaways and children who were rejected by their parents accounted for 10 percent of the homeless population in such cities as Denver, Los Angeles, New Orleans, and San Francisco (Wright, 1990). In 1988, the Department of Education estimated that there were 220,000 homeless school-age children in the United States (Wright, 1990). Of those children, more than 65,000 do not attend school regularly (Wright, 1990).

Low-income parents are generally strong supporters of education. They see education as a means to a better life for their children. However, they are often limited in their ability to buy materials and make financial commitments that can enable them to participate in activities such as field trips or extracurricular programs. Many of the suggestions listed for single-parent families also apply to low-income families. Schools can provide workbooks and other study materials for use at home as well as transportation for school activities and conferences. This will increase the ability of low-income families to become more involved in their children's education. The school can also support low-income families by establishing community service programs. For example, students can help clean up neighborhoods and distribute information on available social services. The schools can provide desk space for voter registration and other services.

Perhaps the most important way for schools to work with low-income parents is to recognize that low-income parents can contribute a great deal to their children's education. While those contributions may not be in the form of traditional parent involvement, they can be very beneficial to teachers and students. The values and attitudes parents communicate to their children and their strong desire for their children to have a better chance in life than they had are important forms of support for the school.

TEACHER CONCERNS WITH PARENT-COMMUNITY INVOLVEMENT

Many teachers are ambivalent about parent and community involvement in education. Even though teachers often say they want to involve parents, many are suspicious of parents and are uncertain of what parents expect from them. Some teachers wonder if parents will do more harm than good. They think parents may disrupt their routine, may not have the necessary skills to work with students, may be inconvenient to have in the classroom, and may show interest only in helping their own child, not the total class. Even teachers who think they would like to involve parents are not sure they have the time or the skill and knowledge to involve parents. Many teachers believe that they already have too much to do and that working with parents would make their overburdened jobs impossible.

Many of these concerns result from a limited view of the possibilities for parent involvement. Frequently when parents and teachers think of parent involvement, they think it means doing something for the school, generally at the school, or having the school teach parents how to become better parents. In today's society, a traditional view of parent involvement inhibits rather than encourages parents and teachers to work together. Traditional ideas about parent involvement have a built-in gender and social class bias and are a barrier to most males and low-income parents.

When parent involvement is viewed as a means of getting support for the school, parents are encouraged to bake cookies, raise money, or work at the school as unpaid classroom, playground, library, or office helpers. This form of parent involvement is generally directed to mothers who do not work outside the home. However, the number of mothers available for this form of involvement is decreasing. In 1992, 31.4 percent of the mothers of kindergarten children were employed full-time outside the home (U.S. Bureau of the Census, 1994b).

When parent involvement is viewed as a means to help deficient parents, the school provides parents with information on how to become better parents (Linn, 1990). This view of parent involvement is often directed toward minority and low-income parents (Jennings, 1990). This approach often makes parents feel they are the cause of their children's failure in school. Teachers are presented as more skilled in parenting than parents. Parents and teachers may even become rivals for the child's affection (Lightfoot, 1978).

Cultural perspectives play an important role in the traditional approach to parent involvement. Bullivant (1993) points out the importance of understanding a social group's cultural program. To be effective, parent and community involvement strategies should reflect what Bullivant calls the core of the social group's cultural program. He states that the core consists of the knowledge and conceptions embodied in the group's behaviors and artifacts and the values subscribed to by the group.

The parent-as-helper idea is geared toward parents who have the skills, time, and resources to become school helpers. Not all parents want to or feel they can or should do things for the school. Whether parents are willing to come to school is largely dependent on the parents' attitude toward school. This attitude results in part from their own school experiences.

Involvement efforts based on "the parent in need of parenting skills" assumes that there is one appropriate way to parent and that parents want to learn it. Both "the parent as helper" and "the parent in need of parenting skills" are conceptualizations derived from questionable assumptions about the character of contemporary parents and reflect a limited cultural perspective.

STEPS TO INCREASE PARENT-COMMUNITY INVOLVEMENT

Teachers are a key ingredient in parent-community involvement. They play multiple roles, including facilitator, communicator, and resource developer. Their success in implementing an effective parent-community involvement program relates to their skill in communicating and working with parents and community groups. Teacher attitude is also very important. Parents are supportive of the teachers they believe like their children and want their children to succeed. Teachers who have a negative attitude toward students will likely have a similar attitude toward the students' parents. Teachers tend to relate to their students as representatives of their parents' perceived status in society. Teachers use such characteristics as class, race, gender, and ethnicity to determine students' prescribed social category (Lightfoot, 1978).

Below are five steps you can take to increase parent-community involvement in your classroom. These steps involve establishing two-way communication, enlisting support from staff and students, soliciting support from the community, developing resource materials for home use, and broadening the activities included in parent involvement.

Establish Two-Way Communication between the School and Home

Establishing two-way communication between the school and home is an important step in involving parents. Most parents are willing to become involved in their children's education if you let them know what you are trying to accomplish and how parents can help. Teachers should be prepared to engage in outreach to parents and not to wait for them to become involved. Actively solicit information from parents on their thoughts about classroom goals and activities. When you talk with parents and community members, be an active listener. Listen for their feelings as well as for specific information. Listed below are seven ways you can establish and maintain two-way communication with parents and community members.

1. If possible, have an open-door policy in your classroom. Let parents know they are welcome. When parents visit, make sure they have something to do.

2. Send written information home about school assignments and goals so that parents are aware of what is going on in the classroom. Encourage parents to send notes to you if they have questions or concerns.

3. Talk to parents by phone. Let parents know when they can reach you by phone. Also, call parents periodically and let them know when things are going well. Have something specific to talk about. Leave some time for the parent to ask questions or make comments.

4. Report problems to parents, such as failing grades, before it is too late for them to take remedial action. Let parents know what improvements you expect from their children and how they can help.

5. Get to know your students' community. Take time to shop in their neighborhoods. Visit community centers and attend religious services. Let parents know when you will be in the community and that you are available to talk to them in their home or at some other location.

6. If you teach in an elementary school, try to have at least two in-person conferences a year with parents. When possible, include the student in the conference. Let the parent know in specific terms how the student is doing in class. Find out how parents feel about their children's level of achievement, and let them know what you think about the students' achievement level. Give parents some suggestions on what their student can do to improve and how they can help.

7. Solicit information from parents on their views on education. Identify their educational goals for their children, ways they would like to support their children's education, and their concerns about the school. There are a number of ways to get information from parents, including sending a questionnaire home and asking parents to complete it and return it to you, conducting a telephone survey, and asking your students to interview their parents.

Enlist the Support of Other Staff Members and Students

Teachers have some flexibility in their classrooms, but they are not able to determine some of the factors that influence their ability to have a strong parent involvement program. For instance, the type and amount of supplies available for student use can determine whether a teacher can send home paper, pencils, and other materials for parents to use with their children. If teachers are allowed to modify their schedules, they can find free time to telephone parents, write notes, and hold morning or evening conferences with parents. The school climate also influences parent involvement. However, school climate is not determined by one individual; it is influenced by students, teachers, the principal, and the school secretary. Teachers need support from staff, students, the principal, and district-level staff to enhance their parent involvement activities.

Your students can help solicit support for parent and community involvement from staff and other students. Take your class on a tour of the school. Ask the class to think about how their parents would feel if they came to the school. Discuss these two questions: Is there a place for visitors to sit? Are there signs asking visitors to go directly to the office? Ask your students to list things they could do to make the school a friendlier place for parents.

Invite your building principal to come to your classroom and discuss the list with your students. Divide the class into small groups and have them discuss how they would like their parents involved in their education. Ask them to talk to their parents and get their views. Have each group write a report on how parents can be involved in their children's education. Each group could make presentations to students in the other classrooms in the building on how they would like to increase parent involvement in their school.

If funds or other support is needed from the district office for your parent involvement activities, have the students draw up a petition and solicit signatures from teachers, students, and parents. When all of the signatures are gathered, they can be delivered to an appropriate district administrator.

Building principals and district administrators can give you the support you need to:

1. Help create and maintain a climate for positive parent-community involvement. This can include supporting flexible hours for teachers who need to be out of the classroom to develop materials or to work with parents. Teachers can be given time out of the classroom without negatively affecting students. Time can be gleaned from the secondary teacher's schedule by combining homerooms one day a week, by team-teaching a class, or by combining different sections of a class for activities such as chapter tests. At the elementary school level, team teaching, released time during periods when students are normally out of the classroom for specialized subjects such as music and art, or having the principal substitute in the classroom are ways to provide flexible hours for teachers.

2. Set up a parent room. The parent room could be used for a number of functions, including serving as a community drop-in center where parents could meet other parents for a cup of coffee, or as a place for parents to work on school activities without infringing on the teachers' lounge. It could also be used as a waiting room for parents who need to see a student or a member of the school staff.

3. Host parent nights during which parents can learn more about the school, the curriculum, and the staff.

4. Send a personal note to students and to their parents when a student makes the honor roll or does something noteworthy.

5. Develop and distribute a handbook that contains student names and phone numbers, PTA or other parent group contact names, and staff names and phone numbers.

6. Ask the school secretary to make sure visitors are welcomed when they come to the school and are given directions as needed.

7. Encourage students to greet visitors and help them find their way around the building.

Enlist Support from the Community

To enlist support from the community, you need to know something about it. The following are some questions you should be able to answer.

1. Are there any drama, musical, dance, or art groups in the community?
2. Is there a senior-citizen group, a public library, or a cooperative extension service in the community?
3. Are employment services such as the state employment security department available in the community?
4. Are civil rights organizations such as the Urban League, Anti-Defamation League, or NAACP active in the community?
5. What is the procedure for referring people to the Salvation Army, Goodwill Industries, or the State Department of Public Assistance for emergency assistance for housing, food, and clothing?
6. Does the community have a mental-health center, family counseling center, or crisis clinic?
7. Are programs and activities for youth such as Boys and Girls Clubs, Campfire, Boy Scouts, Girl Scouts, YMCA, and the YWCA available for your students?

As you learn about the community, you can begin developing a list of community resources and contacts that can provide support to families, work for your students, and provide locations for students to perform community service projects. Collecting information about your students' community and developing community contacts should be viewed as a long-term project. You can collect information as your schedule permits and organize it in a notebook. This process can be shortened if several teachers work together. Each teacher could concentrate on a different part of the community and share information and contacts.

Community groups can provide support in several ways. They can develop big sister and big brother programs for students, provide quiet places for students to study after school and on weekends, donate educational supplies, help raise funds for field trips, set up mentor programs, and tutor students.

Community groups can also provide opportunities for students to participate in community-based learning programs. Community-based learning programs provide an opportunity for students to move beyond the textbook and experience real life (McClure, Cook, & Thompson, 1977). They give students an opportunity to see how knowledge is integrated when it is applied to the real world. It puts them in touch with a variety of people and lets them see how people cope with their environment.

Community-based learning also enhances career development. It can help students learn about themselves, gain confidence, and better understand their strengths and weaknesses. Students can learn to plan, make decisions, negotiate, and evaluate their plans. Here are some examples of community work (McClure, Cook, & Thompson, 1977). Students can:

- Paint an apartment for an ill neighbor
- Clean alleys and backyards for the elderly
- Write letters for people who are ill

- Read to people who are unable to read
- Prepare an empty lot as a play area for young children
- Plant a vegetable garden for the needy
- Collect and recycle newspapers

Develop Learning Resources for Parents to Use at Home

Many of the learning materials teachers use with students at school can be used by parents at home to help students improve their skills. The materials should be in a format suitable for students to take home and should provide clear directions for at-home completion. Parents could let the teacher know how they liked the material by writing a note, giving their child a verbal message for the teacher, or by calling the school. Clark (1987) has written a series of math home-involvement activities for kindergarten through eighth grade. The activities are included in a booklet and are designed to help students increase their math skills. Parents are able to use the creative activities to reinforce the skills their children learn at school. These kinds of materials are convenient for both parents and teachers to use.

It is important for teachers to have resources available for parents to use. This lets parents know that they can help increase their children's learning and that you want their help. Simply telling parents they should work with their children is not sufficient. Parents generally need specific suggestions. Once parents get an idea of what you want them to do, some will develop their own materials. Other parents will be able to purchase materials. You can suggest specific books, games, and other materials for parents to purchase and where these learning materials are available.

Some parents will not have the financial resources, time, or educational background to develop or purchase learning materials. With your principal's help or help from community groups, you can set up a learning center for parents. The learning center could contain paper, pencils, books, games, a portable typewriter, a portable computer, and other appropriate resources. The learning center could also have audiocassettes on such topics as instructional techniques, classroom rules, educational goals for the year, and oral readings from books. Parents and students could check materials out of the learning center for use at home.

Broaden the Conception of Parent and Community Involvement

Many barriers to parent-community involvement can be eliminated by broadly conceptualizing parent-community involvement. Parents can play many roles, depending on their interests, skills, and resources. It is important to have a variety of roles for parents so that more parents will have an opportunity to be involved. It is also important to make sure that some roles can be performed at home as well as at school. Below are five ways parents and community members can be involved in schools. Some of the roles can be implemented by the classroom teacher. Others need support and resources from building principals or central office administrators.

Parents Working with Their Own Children

Working with their own children is one of the most important roles parents can play in the educational process. Parents can help their children develop a positive self-concept and a positive attitude toward school as well as a better understanding of how their effort affects achievement. Most parents want their children to do well in school and are willing to do whatever they can to help them succeed. Teachers can increase the support they receive from their students' homes by giving parents a better understanding of what is going on in the classroom, by letting parents know what is expected in the classroom, and by suggesting ways they can support their child's learning.

You can work with parents to support the educational process in these three ways:

1. Involve parents in monitoring homework by asking them to sign homework papers.

2. Ask parents to sign a certificate congratulating students for good attendance.

3. Give students extra points if their parents do things such as sign their report card, attend conferences, or read to them.

Some parents want a more active partnership with the school. These parents want to help teach their children. Below are three ways you can help parents work with their children to increase their learning.

1. Encourage parents to share hobbies and games, discuss news and television programs, and talk about school problems and events with their children.

2. Send information home on the importance of reading to children and include a reading list. A one-page sheet could be sent home stating, "One of the best ways to help children become better readers is to read them. Reading aloud is most helpful when you discuss the stories, learn to identify letters and words, and talk about the meaning of the words. Encourage leisure reading. Reading achievement is related to the amount of reading kids do. It increases vocabulary and reading fluency." Then list several books available from the school library for students to check out and take home.

3. You can supply parents with materials they can use to work with their children on skill development. Students can help make math games, crossword puzzles, and other materials that parents can use with them at home.

Professional Support Person for Instruction

Many parent and community members have skills that can be shared with the school. They are willing to work with students as well as teachers. These people are often ignored in parent and community involvement programs. A parent or community member who is a college professor could be asked to talk to teachers about a topic that interests them or to participate in an in-service workshop. A bilingual parent or community member could be asked to help tutor foreign language students or to share books or magazines written in their language with the class. Parents who enjoy reading or art could be asked to help staff a humanities enrichment course before or after school or to recommend materials for the course. Parents and community members who perform these kinds of duties could also serve as role models for your students and would demonstrate the importance of education in the community.

Review the list below and think of how you could involve parents and community members in your classroom. Parents and community members can:

- Serve as instructional assistants
- Correct papers at home or at school
- Use carpentry skills to build things for the school
- Tutor during school hours or after school
- Develop or identify student materials or community resources
- Share their expertise with students or staff
- Expand enrichment programs offered before, after, or during school, such as Great Books and art appreciation
- Sew costumes for school plays
- Type and edit a newsletter

General Volunteers

Some parents are willing to volunteer their time but they do not want to do a job that requires specific skills. When thinking of activities for general volunteers, be sure to include activities that can be performed at the school as well as activities that can be performed at home. Some possible activities include:

- Working on the playground as a support person
- Working in the classroom as a support person
- Working at home preparing cutouts and other materials that will be used in class
- Telephoning other parents to schedule conferences

Decision Makers

Some parents are interested in participating in decision making in the school. They want to help set school policy, select curriculum materials, review budgets, or interview perspective staff members. Roles for these parents and community members include school board member, committee member, and site council member. Serving on a site council is an excellent way for parents to participate in decision making. Site councils are designed to increase parent involvement in schools, empower classroom teachers, and allow the people who implement educational decisions to make them.

The Comer (1988) model is an effective way to involve parents, classroom teachers, and other educators in decision making. Comer believes schools can be more effective when they are restructured in ways that encourage and support cooperation among parents and educators. Comer did much of his pioneering work on parent involvement and restructuring schools in Prince Georges County, Maryland. There he implemented two committees—the School Planning and Management Team (SPMT) and the Student Staff Services Team (SSST).

The SPMT included the school principal, classroom teachers, parents, and support staff. Consensus was used to reach decisions. The committee also had a no-fault policy, which encouraged parents not to blame the school and educators not to blame parents. The SPMT provided a structure for parents and educators to create a common vision for their school, reduce fragmentation, and develop activities, curriculum, and in-service programs. It also developed a comprehensive school plan, designed a schoolwide calendar of events, and monitored and evaluated student progress. The SPMT met at least once a month. Subcommittees of the SPMT met more frequently.

The second committee that Comer implemented was the Student Staff Services team (SSST). The SSST was composed of the school principal, guidance counselor, classroom teachers, and support staff, including psychologists, health aides, and other appropriate personnel. Teachers and parents were encouraged to join this group if they had concerns they believed should be addressed. The SSST brought school personnel together to discuss individual student concerns. The SST brought coherence and order to the services that students receive.

SUMMARY

Parent and community involvement is a dynamic process that encourages, supports, and provides opportunities for teachers, parents, and community members to work together to improve student learning. Parent and community involvement is also an important component of school reform and multicultural education. Parents and community groups help provide the rationale, motivation, and social action necessary for educational reform.

Everyone can benefit from parent-community involvement. Students tend to perform better in schools and have more people supporting their learning. Parents know more about what is going on at school, have more opportunities to communicate with their children's teacher, and are able to help their children increase their learning. Teachers gain a partner in education. Teachers learn more about their students through their parent and community contacts and are able to use that information to help increase their students' performance.

Even though research has consistently demonstrated that students have an advantage in school when their parents support and encourage educational activities, not all parents know how they can support their child's education or feel they have the time, energy, or other resources to be involved in schools. Some parents have a particularly difficult time supporting their children's education. Three such groups are parents who have low incomes, single parents, and parents with special needs. Parents from these groups are often dismissed as unsupportive of education. However, most of them want their children to do well in school and are willing to work with the school when the school reaches out to them and responds to their needs.

To establish an effective parent-community involvement program you should establish two-way communication with parents and community groups, enlist support from the community, and have resources available for parents to use in working with their children. Expanding how parent-community involvement is conceptualized can increase the number of parents and community members able to participate. Parents can play many roles. Ways to involve parents and community members include parents working with their own children, parents and community members sharing their professional skills with the school, parents and community groups volunteering in the school, and parents and community members working with educators to make decisions about school.

Questions and Activities

1. Compare the role of parents in schools during the Colonial period to that of students today. Identify and discuss changes that have occurred and changes you would like to see occur in parent involvement.

2. Consider this statement: Regardless of the circumstances students experience at home, teachers have a responsibility to help them perform at their highest level at school. Do you agree? Why or why not?

3. Interview a parent of a bilingual, ethnic minority, religious minority, or low-income student to learn more about the parent's views on schools and the educational goals for his or her children. This information cannot be generalized to all members of these groups, but it can be an important departure point for learning more about diverse groups within our society.

4. Consider this statement: All parents want their children to succeed in school. Do you agree with the statement? Why or why not?

5. Interview a classroom teacher and an administrator to determine his or her perceptions of parent-community involvement.

6. Write a brief paper on your personal views of the benefits and drawbacks of parent-community involvement.

7. Form a group with two other members of your class or workshop. One person in the group will be a teacher, the other a parent, and the third an observer. The teacher and the parent will role-play a teacher-parent conference. After role-playing the conference, discuss how it felt to be a parent and a teacher. What can be done to make the parent and teacher feel more comfortable? Was the information shared at the conference helpful? The observer can share his or her view of the parent and teacher interaction.

References

Banks, J. A. (1997). *Teaching Strategies for Ethnic Studies* (6th ed.). Boston: Allyn and Bacon.

Berger, E. H. (1987). *Parents as Partners in Education: The School and Home Working Together* (2nd ed.). Columbus, OH: Merrill.

Bullivant, B. M. (1993). Culture: Its Nature and Meaning for Educators. In J. A. Banks and C. A. M. Banks, *Multicultural Education: Issues and Perspectives* (2nd ed.) (pp. 29–47). Boston: Allyn and Bacon.

Clark, C. S. (1995). Parents and Schools. *CQ-Researcher, 5*(3). 51–69.

Clark, R. M. (1987). *Home Involvement Activities*. Boston: Houghton Mifflin.

Clark, R. M. (1983). *Family Life and School Achievement: Why Poor Black Children Succeed or Fail*. Chicago: University of Chicago Press.

Coleman, J. S. (1987). Families and Schools. *Educational Researcher, 16*(6), 32–38.

Comer, J. (1988). Educating Poor Minority Children. *Scientific American, 259*, 42–48.

Comer, J. P. and Haynes, N. M. (1991). Parent Involvement in Schools: An Ecological Approach. *The Elementary School Journal, 91*(3), 271–277.

Delpit, L. D. (1988). The Silenced Dialogue: Power and Pedagogy in Educating Other People's Children. *Harvard Educational Review, 58*(3), 280–298.

DeParle, J. (1991, September 27). Poverty Rate Rose Sharply Last Year as Incomes Slipped. *New York Times*, 1, 11.

Diaz, S., Moll, L. C., and Mehan, H. (1986). Sociocultural Resources in Instruction: A Context Specific Approach. In *Beyond Language: Social & Cultural Factors in Schooling Language Minority Students* (pp. 187–230). Los Angeles: California State University.

Goodlad, J. I. (1984). *A Place Called School: Prospects for the Future*. New York: McGraw-Hill.

Harry, B. (1992). Restructuring the Participation of African-American Parents in Special Education. *Exceptional Children, 59*(2), 123–131.

Henderson, A. (1987). *The Evidence Continues to Grow: Parent Involvement Improves Student Achievement*. Columbia, MD: National Committee for Citizens in Education.

Hidalgo, N. M., Bright, J. A., Sau-Fong, S., Swap, S. M., and Epstein, J. L. (1995). Research on Families, Schools, and Communities: A Multicultural Perspective. In J. A. Banks and C. A. M. Banks (Eds.). *Handbook of Research on Multicultural Education* (pp. 498–524). New York: Macmillan.

Hoover-Dempsey, K. and Sandler, H. M. (1995). Parental Involvement in Children's Education: Why Does It Make a Difference? *Teachers College Record, 97*(2), 310–331.

Linn, E. (1990). Parent Involvement Programs: A Review of Selected Models. *Equity Coalition, 1*(2), 10–15.

Jennings, L. (1990, August 1). Parents as Partners. *Education Week*, 23, 35.

Lightfoot, S. L. (1978). *Worlds Apart: Relationships between Families and Schools*. New York: Basic Books.

Mannan, G. and Blackwell, J. (1992). Parent Involvement: Barriers and Opportunities. *The Urban Review, 24*(1), 219–226.

McClure, L., Cook, S. C., and Thompson, V. (1977). *Experience-Based Learning: How to Make the Community Your Classroom*. Portland, OR: Northwest Regional Educational Laboratory.

Rasinski, T. (1990). Reading and the Impowerment of Parents. *The Reading Teacher, 42*, 226–231.

Shariff, J. W. (1988). Free Enterprise and the Ghetto Family. In J. S. Wurzel (Ed.). *Toward Multiculturalism: A Reader in Multicultural Education*. Yarmouth, ME: Intercultural Press.

Swadener, B. B. and Niles, K. (1991). Children and Families "At Promise": Making Home-School-Community Connections. *Democracy and Education*, 13–18.

U.S. Bureau of the Census. (1989). *Statistical Abstract of the United States, 1989* (109th ed.). Washington, DC: U.S. Government Printing Office.

U.S. Bureau of the Census. (1993). *Statistical Abstract of the United States* (113th ed.). Washington, DC: U.S. Government Printing Office.

U.S. Bureau of the Census. (1994a). *Current Population Reports. Special Studies*, Series P-23, No. 188. Washington, DC: U.S. Government Printing Office.

U.S. Bureau of the Census. (1994b). *Statistical Abstract of the United States* (114th ed.). Washington, DC: U.S. Government Printing Office.

Waller, W. (1965). *The Sociology of Teaching*. New York: Wiley.

Williams, D. L. Jr. (1984, May). Highlights from a Survey of Parents and Educators Regarding Parent Involvement in Education. Paper presented at the Seventh National Symposium on Building Family Strengths, Lincoln, NE.

Wright, J. W. (1990). *The Universal Almanac, 1991*. New York: Andrews and McMeel.

Appendix

Multicultural Resources

Issues and Concepts

Baker, G. C. (1994). *Planning and Organizing for Multicultural Instruction* (2nd ed.). Menlo Park, CA: Addison-Wesley.

Banks, J. A. (1994). *An Introduction to Multicultural Education*. Boston: Allyn and Bacon.

Banks, J. A. (1994). *Multiethnic Education: Theory and Practice* (3rd ed.). Boston: Allyn and Bacon.

Banks, J. A. (Ed.). (1996). *Multicultural Education, Transformative Knowledge, and Action: Historical and Contemporary Perspectives*. New York: Teachers College Press.

Banks, J. A. & Banks, C. A. M. (Eds.). (1995). *Handbook of Research on Multicultural Education*. New York: Macmillan.

Cyrus, V. (Ed.). (1993). *Experiencing Race, Class, and Gender in the United States*. Mountain View, CA: Mayfield Publishing Company.

Garcia, E. (1994). *Understanding and Meeting the Challenge of Student Cultural Diversity*. Boston: Houghton Mifflin.

Gay, G. (1994). *At the Essence of Learning: Multicultural Education*. West Lafayette, IN: Kappa Delta Pi.

Gollnick, D. M. & Chinn, P. C. (1990). *Multicultural Education in a Pluralistic Society* (4th ed.). New York: Merrill.

Grant, C. A. & Gomez, M. L. (Eds.). (1996). *Making Schooling Multicultural: Campus and Classroom*. New York: Merrill.

King, E. W., Chipman, M., & Cruz-Janzen, M. (1994). *Educating Young Children in a Diverse Society*. Boston: Allyn and Bacon.

McCarthy, C. & Crichlow, W. (Eds.). (1993). *Race Identity and Representation in Education*. New York: Routledge.

Nieto, S. (1996). *Affirming Diversity: The Sociopolitical Context of Multicultural Education* (2nd ed.). White Plains, NY: Longman.

Ponterotto, J. G., Casas, J. M., Suzuki, L. A., & Alexander, C. M. (Eds.). (1995). *Handbook of Multicultural Counseling*. Thousand Oaks, CA: Sage Publications.

Secada, W. G., Fennema, E., & Adajian, L. B. (Eds.). (1995). *New Directions for Equity in Mathematics Education*. New York: Cambridge University Press.

Sleeter, C. E. & McLaren, P. L. (Eds.). (1995). *Multicultural Education, Critical Pedagogy, and the Politics of Difference*. Albany: State University of New York Press.

Social Class

Anderson, E. (1990). *Street Wise: Race, Class, and Change in an Urban Community*. Chicago: The University of Chicago Press.

Carnoy, M. (1994). *Faded Dreams: The Politics and Economics of Race in America*. New York: Cambridge University Press.

Cose, E. (1993). *The Rage of a Privileged Class*. New York: HarperCollins.

Davis, P. (1995). *If You Came This Way: A Journey through the Lives of the Underclass*. New York: John Wiley & Sons.

Eron, L. D., Gentry, J. H., & Schlegel, P. (Eds.). (1994). *Reason to Hope: A Psychosocial Perspective on Violence and Youth*. Washington, DC: American Psychological Association.

Gans, H. (1995). *The War against the Poor: The Underclass and Antipoverty Policy*. New York: Basic Books.

Jencks, C. & Peterson, P. E. (Eds.). (1991). *The Urban Underclass*. Washington, DC: The Brookings Institution.

Jones, J. (1992). *The Dispossessed: Amercia's Underclass from the Civil War to the Present*. New York: Basic Books.

Kotlowitz, A. (1991). *There Are No Children Here: The Story of Two Boys Growing Up in the Other America*. New York: Doubleday.

Kozol, J. (1991). *Savage Inequalities: Children in America's Schools*. New York: Crown Publishers.

Landry, B. (1987). *The New Black Middle Class*. Berkeley: University of California Press.

Orfield, G. & Ashkinaze, C. (1991). *The Closing Door: Conservative Policy and Black Opportunity*. Chicago: The University of Chicago Press.

Schorr, L. G. with Schorr, D. (1988). *Within Our Reach: Breaking the Cycle of Poverty*. New York: Doubleday.

Religion

Collie, W. E. & Smith, L. H. (Eds.). (1981, January). Teaching about Religion in the Schools: The Continuing Challenge. *Social Education, 45*, 15–34.

Crim, K., Bullard, R., & Shinn, L. D. (Eds.). (1981). *The Perennial Dictionary of World Religions*. San Francisco: HarperSan Francisco.

Elaide, M. (Ed.). (1993). *The Encyclopedia of Religion* (6 vols.). New York: Macmillan.

Engel, D. E. (Ed.). (1974). *Religion in Public Education*. New York: Paulist Press.

Herberg, W. (1960). *Protestant-Catholic-Jew: An Essay in American Religious Sociology*. New York: Anchor Press.

Lincoln, C. E. & Mamiya, L. H. (1990). *The Black Church in the African American Experience*. Durham, NC: Duke University Press.

Melton, J. G. (Ed.). (1991). *The Encyclopedia of American Religions*. Tarrytown, NY: Triumph Books.

Smart, N. (1991). *The Religious Experience* (4th ed.). New York: Macmillan.

Smart, N. & Hecht, R. D. (Eds.). (1990). *Sacred Texts of the World: A Universal Anthology*. New York: Crossroad Publishing Co.

Smith, H. (1994). *The Illustrated World's Religions: A Guide to Our Wisdom Traditions*. San Fransico: HarperSan Francisco.

Smith, J. Z. & Green, W. S. (Eds.). (1995). *The Harper/Collins Dictionary of Religion*. San Francisco: HarperSan Francisco.

Turpin, J. (1990). *Women in Church History: 20 Stories for 20 Centuries*. Cincinnati: St. Anthony Mesenger Press.

Gender

AAUW Report. (1992). *How Schools Shortchange Girls: A Study of Major Findings on Girls and Education*. Washington, DC: AAUW Educational Foundation.

Alarcon, N., Castro, R., Perez, E., Pesquera, B., Riddell, A. S., & Zavella, P. (Eds.). (1993). *Chicana Critical Issues*. Berkeley, CA: Third Woman Press.

Allen, P. G. (1992). *The Sacred Hoop: Recovering the Feminine in American Indian Traditions*. Boston: Beacon Press.

Amott, T. L. & Matthaei, J. A. (1991). *Race, Gender and Work: A Multicultural Economic History of Women in the United States*. Boston: South End Press.

Andersen, M. L. & Collins, P. H. (Eds.). (1995). *Race, Class, and Gender: An Anthology* (2nd ed.). Belmont, CA: Wadsworth Publishing Company.

Anzaldua, G. (1989). *Borderlands/La Frontera*. San Francisco: Spinsters/Aunt Lute Book Company.

Anzaldua, G. (Ed.). (1990). *Making Face, Making Soul: Haciendo Caras, Creative and Critical Perspectives by Women of Color*. San Francisco: Aunt Lute Foundation Books.

Asian Women United of California. (1989). *Making Waves: An Anthology of Writings by and about Asian American Women*. Boston: Beacon Press.

Belenky, M. F., Clinchy, B. M., Goldberg, N. R., & Tarrule, F. M. (1986). *Women's Ways of Knowing: The Development of Self, Voice, and Mind*. New York: Basic Books.

Bell, R. P., Parker, B. J., & Guy-Sheftall, B. (1979). *Sturdy Black Bridges: Visions of Black Women in Literature*. New York: Avon Books.

Benedek, E. (1995). *Beyond the Four Corners of the World: Navajo Woman's Journey*. New York: Knopf.

Bly, R. (1990). *Iron John: A Book about Men*. Reading, MA: Addison-Wesley.

Boyd, H. & Allen, R. L. (Eds.). (1995). *Brotherman: The Odyssey of Black Men in America—An Anthology*. New York: Ballantine Books.

Butler, J. E. & Walter, J. C. (Eds.). (1991). *Transforming the Curriculum: Ethnic Studies and Women's Studies*. Albany: State University of New York Press.

Castillo-Speed, L. (Ed.). (1995). *Latina: Women's Voices from the Borderlands*. New York: Touchstone/Simon & Schuster.

Collins, P. H. (1990). *Black Feminist Thought: Knowledge, Consciousness, and the Politics of Empowerment*. New York: Routledge.

Crawford, V. L., Rouse, J. A., & Woods, B. (Eds.). (1993). *Women in the Civil Rights Movement: Trailblazers and Torchbearers, 1941–1965*. Bloomington: Indiana University Press.

DuBois, E. C. & Ruiz, V. L. (1994). *Unequal Sisters: A Multicultural Reader in U.S. Women's History* (2nd ed.). New York: Routledge.

Frankenberg, R. (1993). *White Women, Race Matters: The Social Construction of Whiteness*. Minneapolis: University of Minnesota Press.

Franklin, C. W. (1984). *The Changing Definition of Masculinity*. New York: Plenum Press.

Gilligan, C. (1982). *In a Different Voice: Psychological Theory and Women's Development*. Cambridge: Harvard University Press.

Guy-Sheftall, B. (Ed.). (1995). *Words of Fire: An Anthology of African-American Feminist Thought*. New York: The New Press.

Hine, D. C., King, W., & Reed, L. (Eds.). (1995). *"We Specialize in the Wholly Impossible": A Reader in Black Women's History*. Brooklyn, NY: Carlson Publishing.

Jones, J. (1985). *Labor of Love, Labor of Sorrow, Black Women, Work and the Family from Slavery to the Present*. New York: Vintage Books.

Katz, J. (Ed.). (1995). *Messengers of the Wind: Native American Women Tell Their Life Stories*. New York: Ballantine Books.

Maher, F. A. & Tetreault, M. K. (1994). *The Feminist Classroom*. New York: Basic Books.

Mankiller, W. & Wallis, M. (1993). *Mankiller: A Chief and Her People*. New York: St. Martin's Press.

Morrison, T. (Ed.). (1992). *Race-ing, Justice, and En-gendering Power: Essays on Anita Hill, Clarence Thomas, and the Construction of Social Reality*. New York: Pantheon.

Sadker, M. & Sadker, D. (1994). *Failing at Fairness: How Amercia's Schools Cheat Girls*. New York: Scribner's.

Stone, L. (Ed.) (1994). *The Education Feminism Reader*. New York: Routledge.

Tsuchida, N. (Ed.). (1982). *Asian and Pacific American Experiences: Women's Perspectives*. Minneapolis: University of Minnesota Press.

Yung, J. (1986). *Chinese Women of America: A Pictorial History*. Seattle: University of Washington Press.

Ethnicity and Language

Aponte, J. F., Rivers, R. Y., & Wohl, J. (Eds.). (1995). *Psychological Interventions and Cultural Diversity*. Boston: Allyn and Bacon.

Au, K. H. (1993). *Literacy Instruction in Multicultural Settings*. New York: Harcourt Brace.

Banks, J. A. (1997). *Teaching Strategies for Ethnic Studies* (6th ed.). Boston: Allyn and Bacon.

Banks, J. A. & Banks, C. A. M. (Eds.). (1995). *Handbook of Research on Multicultural Education*. New York: Macmillan.

Bialystok, E. & Hakuta, K. (1994). *In Other Words: The Science and Psychology of Second-Language Acquisition*. New York: Basic Books.

Crawford, J. (1992). *Hold Your Tongue: Bilingualism and the Politics of "English Only."* Reading, MA: Addison-Wesley.

Cross, W. E., Jr. (1991). *Shades of Black: Diversity in African-American Identity*. Philadelphia: Temple University Press.

Dana, R. H. (1993). *Multicultural Assessment Perspectives for Professional Psychology.* Boston: Allyn and Bacon.

Delpit, L. (1995). *Other People's Children: Cultural Conflict in the Classroom.* New York: The New Press.

Hale, J. E. (1994). *Unbank the Fire: Visions for the Education of African American Children.* Baltimore: The Johns Hopkins University Press.

Heath, S. B. (1983). *Ways with Words: Language, Life, and Work in Communities and Classrooms.* New York: Cambridge University Press.

Hill, H. & Jones, J. E., Jr. (Eds.). (1993). *Race in America: The Struggle for Equality.* Madison: The University of Wisconsin Press.

Hollins, E. R., King, J. E., & Hayman, W. C. (Eds.). (1994). *Teaching Diverse Populations: Formulating a Knowledge Base.* Albany: State University of New York Press.

hooks, b. (1995). *Killing Rage Ending Racism.* New York: Henry Holt.

Igoa, C. (1995). *The Inner World of the Immigrant Child.* New York: St. Martin's Press.

Jacob, E. & Jordan, C. (Eds.). (1993). *Minority Education: Anthropological Perspectives.* Norwood, NJ: Ablex Publishing Corporation.

Ladson-Billings, G. (1994). *The Dreamkeepers: Successful Teachers of African American Children.* San Francisco: Jossey-Bass.

Lomotey, K. (Ed.). (1990). *Going to School: The African-American Experience.* Albany: State University of New York Press.

Minami, M. & Kennedy, B. P. (Eds.). (1991). *Language Issues in Literacy and Bilingual/Multicultural Education* (Reprint Series No. 22). Cambridge: Harvard Educational Review.

Philips, S. U. (1993). *The Invisible Culture: Communication in Classroom and Community on the Warm Springs Indian Reservation.* Prospect Heights, IL: Waveland Press, Inc.

Schuja, M. W. (Ed.). (1994). *Too Much Schooling, Too Little Education: A Paradox of Black Life in White Schools.* Trenton, NJ: Africa World Press.

Wang, M. C. & Gordon, E. W. (Eds.). (1994). *Educational Resilience in Inner-City America: Challenges and Prospects.* Hillsdale, NJ: Lawrence Erlbaum.

Williams, P. J. (1995). *The Rooster's Egg: On the Persistence of Prejudice.* Cambridge: Harvard University Press.

Exceptionality

Baca, L. M. & Almanza, E. (1991). *Language Minority Students with Disabilities.* Reston, VA: Council for Exceptional Children.

Baum, S. M., Owens, S. V., & Dixon, J. (1991). *To Be Gifted and Learning Disabled: From Definitions to Practical Intervention Strategies.* Storrs, CT: Creative Learning Press.

Bireley, M. (1995). *Crossover Children: A Sourcebook for Helping Children Who Are Gifted and Learning Disabled* (2nd ed.). Reston, VA: Council for Exceptional Children.

Carrasquillo, A. L. & Rodriguez, V. (1995). *Language Minority Students in the Mainstream Classroom.* Bristol, PA: Taylor & Francis.

Colangelo, N. & Davis, G. D. (1991). *Handbook of Gifted Education.* Boston: Allyn and Bacon.

Cumins, J. (1984). *Bilingualism and Special Education: Issues in Assessment and Pedagogy.* Bristol, PA: Taylor & Francis.

Gallagher, J. J. (1994). *Teaching the Gifted Child* (4th ed.). Boston: Allyn and Bacon.

George, D. (1995). *Gifted Education: Identification and Provision.* Bristol, PA: Taylor & Francis.

Golomb, C. (Ed.). (1995). *The Development of Artistically Gifted Children: Selected Case Studies.* Hillsdale, NJ: Lawrence Erlbaum.

Goodlad, J. I. & Lovitt, T. C. (Eds.). (1993). *Integrating General and Special Education.* New York: Macmillan.

Grossman, H. (1994). *Special Education in a Diverse Society.* Boston: Allyn and Bacon.

Heward, W. L. (1996). *Exceptional Children: An Introduction to Special Education* (5th ed.). Columbus, OH: Merrill.

Mercer, J. R. (1973). *Labeling the Mentally Retarded.* Berkeley: University of California Press.

Potts, P., Armstrong, F., & Masterton, M. (Eds.). (1994). *Equality and Diversity in Education: Learning, Teaching, and Managing in Schools.* New York: Routledge.

Putnam, J. W. (Ed.). (1993). *Cooperative Learning and Strategies for Inclusion: Celebrating Diversity in the Classroom.* Baltimore: Brookes Publishing Company.

Sapon-Shevin, M. (1994). *Playing Favorites: Gifted Education and the Disruption of Community.* Albany: State University of New York Press.

Thornton, C. A. & Bley, N. S. (Eds.). (1994). *Windows of Opportunity: Mathemtics for Students with Special Needs.* Reston, VA: National Council of Teachers of Mathematics.

Toward a Common Agenda: Linking Gifted Education and School Reform. Reston, VA: Council for Exceptional Children.

Williams, P. (Ed.). (1984). *Special Education in Minority Communities.* Bristol, PA: Taylor & Francis.

School Reform

Apple, M. W. & Christian-Smith, L. K. (Eds.). (1991). *The Politics of the Textbook.* New York: Routledge.

Comer, J. P. (1980). *School Power: Implications of an Intervention Project.* New York: The Free Press.

Freedman, S. G. (1990). *Small Victories: The Real World of a Teacher, Her Students and Their High School.* New York: Harper and Row.

Gardner, H. (1983). *Frames of Mind: The Theory of Multiple Intelligences.* New York: Basic Books.

Hidalgo, N. M. , Bright, J. A., Sau-Fong, S., Swap, S. M., & Epstein, J. L. (1995). Research on Families, Schools, and Communities: A Multicultural Perspective. In J. A. Banks & C. A. M. Banks (Eds.). *Handbook of Research on Multicultural Education* (pp. 498–524). New York: Macmillan.

Johnson, S. M. (1990). *Teachers at Work: Achieving Success in Our Schools.* New York: Basic Books.

Kennedy, M. M. (Ed.). (1991). *Teaching Academic Subjects to Diverse Learners.* New York: Teachers College Press.

Levine, D. U. & Lezotte, L. W. (1995). Effective Schools Research. In J. A. Banks & C. A. M. Banks (Eds.). *Handbook of Research on Multicultural Education* (pp. 525–547). New York: Macmillan.

Meier, D. (1995). *The Power of Their Ideas: Lessons for America from a Small School in Harlem.* Boston: Beacon Press.

Miller, L. S. (1995). *An American Imperative: Accelerating Minority Educational Advancement.* New York: Yale University Press.

Perkins, D. (1995). *Outsmarting IQ: The Emerging Science of Learnable Intelligence.* New York: The Free Press.

Presseisen, B. Z. (1985). *Unlearned Lessons: Current and Past Reforms for School Improvement.* Philadelphia: The Falmer Press.

Rethinking Our Classrooms: Teaching for Equity and Justice. (1994). Milwaukee: Rethinking Schools.

Sleeter, C. E. (1992). *Keepers of the Dream: A Study of Staff Development and Multicultural Education.* Washington, DC: The Falmer Press.

Walsh, C. E. (1991). *Pedagogy and the Struggle for Voice: Issues of Language, Power, and Schooling for Puerto Ricans.* New York: Bergin & Garvey.

Weis, L., Farrar, E., & Petrie, H. G. (1989). *Dropouts from School: Issues, Dilemmas, and Solutions.* Albany: State University of New York Press.

Weis, L. & Fine, M. (Eds.). (1993). *Beyond Silenced Voices: Class, Race, and Gender in United States Schools.* Albany: State University of New York Press.

Glossary

African Americans United States residents and citizens who have an African biological and cultural heritage and identity. This term is used synonymously and interchangeably with *Black* and *Black American*. These terms are used to describe both a racial and a cultural group. There were about 30 million African Americans in the United States in 1990. The number of African Americans increased by 13 percent between 1980 and 1990 to about 12 percent of the U.S. population. They are the nation's largest ethnic group of color.

Afrocentric curriculum A curriculum approach in which concepts, issues, problems, and phenomena are viewed from the perspectives of Africans and African Americans. It is based on the assumption that students learn best when they view situations and events from their own cultural perspectives. (*References:* Molefi Kete Asante, "The Afrocentric Idea in Education," *The Journal of Negro Education*, Vol. 60, No. 2 (Spring 1991): 170–180; Molefi Kete Asante, *The Afrocentric Idea*. Philadelphia: Temple University Press, 1987.)

American Indian See *Native American*.

Anglo-Americans Americans whose biological and cultural heritage originated in England, or Americans with other biological and cultural heritages who have assimilated into the dominant or mainstream culture in the United States. This term is often used to describe the mainstream United States culture or to describe most White Americans.

Antiracist education A term used frequently in the United Kingdom and Canada to describe a process used by teachers and other educators to eliminate institutionalized racism from the schools and society and to help individuals to develop nonracist attitudes. When antiracist educational reform is implemented, curriculum materials, grouping practices, hiring policies, teacher atitudes and expectations, and school policy and practices are examined and steps are taken to eliminate racism from these school variables. A related educational reform movement in the United States that focuses more on individuals than on institutions is known as *prejudice reduction*.

Asian Americans Americans who have a biological and cultural heritage that originated on the continent of Asia. The largest groups of Asian Americans in the United States in 1990 were Chinese, Filipinos, Japanese, Asian Indians, Koreans, and Vietnamese. Other groups include Laotians, Thai, Cambodians, Pakistanis, and Indonesians. Asians are the fastest-growing ethnic group in the United States. They increased 99 percent between 1980 and 1990. There were about 7 million Asian Americans in the United States in 1990.

Cultural assimilation Takes place when one ethnic or cultural group acquires the behavior, values, perspectives, ethos, and characteristics of another ethnic group and sheds its own cultural characteristics.

Culture The ideations, symbols, behaviors, values, and beliefs that are shared by a human group. Culture can also be defined as a group's program for survival and adaptation to its environment. Pluralistic nation-states such as the United States, Canada, and Australia are made up of an overarching culture, called a macroculture, that all individuals and groups within the nation share. These nation-states also have many smaller cultures, called microcultures, that differ in many ways from the macroculture or that contain cultural components manifested differently than in the macroculture. (See chapters 1 and 2 for further discussions of *culture*.)

Disability The physical or mental characteristics of an individual that prevent or limit him or her from performing specific tasks.

Discrimination The differential treatment of individuals or groups based on categories such as race, ethnicity, gender, sexual orientation, social class, or exceptionality.

Ethnic group A microcultural group or collectivity that shares a common history and culture, common values, behaviors, and other characteristics that cause members of the group to have a shared identity. A sense of peoplehood is one of the most important characteristics of an ethnic group. An ethnic group also shares economic and political interests. Cultural characteristics, rather than biological traits, are the essential attributes of an ethnic group. An ethnic group is not the same as a racial group. Some ethnic groups, such as Puerto Ricans in the United States, are made up of individuals who belong to several different racial groups. White Anglo-Saxon Protestants, Italian Americans, and Irish Americans are examples of ethnic groups. Individual members of an ethnic group vary considerably in the extent to which they identify with the group. Some individuals have a very strong identity with their particular ethnic group, whereas other members of the group have a very weak identification with it.

Ethnic minority group An ethnic group with several distinguishing characteristics. An ethnic minority group has distinguishing cultural characteristics, racial characteristics, or both, which enable members of other groups to identify its members easily. Some ethnic minority groups, such as Jewish Americans, have unique cultural characteristics. African Americans have unique cultural and physical characteristics. The unique attributes of ethnic minority groups make them convenient targets of racism and discrimination. Ethnic minority groups are usually a numerical minority within their societies. However, the Blacks in South Africa, who are a numerical majority in their nation-state, are often considered a sociological minority group by social scientists because they have little political and economic power.

Ethnic studies The scientific and humanistic analysis of behavior influenced by variables related to ethnicity and ethnic-group membership. This term is often used to refer to special school, university, and college courses and programs that focus on specific racial and ethnic groups. However, any aspects of a course or program that includes a study of variables related to ethnicity can accurately be referred to as ethnic studies. In other words, ethnic studies can be integrated within the boundaries of mainstream courses and curricula.

Eurocentric curriculum A curriculum in which concepts, events, and situations are viewed primarily from the perspectives of European nations and cultures and in which Western civilization is emphasized. This approach is based on the assumption that Europeans have made the most important contributions to the development of the United States and the world. Curriculum theorists who endorse this approach are referred to as *Eurocentrists* or *Western traditionalists*.

European Americans See *Anglo-Americans*.

Exceptional Used to describe students who have learning or behavioral characteristics that differ substantially from most other students and that require special attention in instruction. Students who are intellectually gifted or talented as well as those who have disabilities are considered exceptional.

Gender Consists of behaviors that result from the social, cultural, and psychological factors associated with masculinity and femininity within a society. Appropriate male and female roles result from the socialization of the individual within a group.

Gender identity An individual's view of the gender to which he or she belongs and his or her shared sense of group attachment with other males or females.

Global education Concerned with issues and problems related to the survival of human beings in a world community. International studies is a part of global education, but the focus of global education is the interdependence of human beings and their common fate, regardless of the national boundaries within which they live. Many teachers confuse global education and international studies with ethnic studies, which deal with ethnic groups within a national boundary, such as the United States.

Handicapism The unequal treatment of people who are disabled and related atitudes and beliefs that reinforce and justify discrimination against people with disabilities. The term *handicapped* is considered negative by some people. They prefer the term *disabled*. *People with disabilities* is considered a more sensitive phrase than *disabled people* because the word *people* is used first and given emphasis.

Hispanic Americans Americans who share a culture, heritage, and language that originated in Spain. The word *Latinos* is sometimes used to refer to Hispanic Americans in certain regions of the nation. Most Hispanics in the United States speak Spanish and are mestizos. A mestizo is a person of mixed biological heritage. Most Hispanics in the United States have an Indian as well as a Spanish heritage. Many of them also have an African biological and cultural heritage. The largest groups of Hispanics in the United States are Mexican Americans (Chicanos), Puerto Ricans, and Cubans. In 1990, there were more than 22 million documented Hispanics in the United States, which was about 9 percent of the U.S. population. In 1990, Mexicans made up 61 percent of Hispanics in the United States; Puerto Ricans, 12 percent; Cubans, 5 percent; and Central and South Americans, 12 percent. Persons who identified themselves only as Hispanics made up 8 percent. Hispanics are one of the nation's fastest-growing ethnic groups of color. They increased 49 percent between 1980 and 1990, from 14.6 to 22.4 million. The nation's non-Hispanic population increased almost 7 percent during this period. It is misleading to view Hispanics as one ethnic group. Some Hispanics believe that the word *Hispanics* can help to unify the various Latino groups and thus increase their political power. The primary identity of most Hispanics in the United States, however, is with their particular group, such as Mexican American, Puerto Rican, or Cuban.

Mainstream American A United States citizen who shares most of the characteristics of the dominant ethnic and cultural group in the nation. Such an individual is usually White Anglo-Saxon Protestant and belongs to the middle class or a higher social-class status.

Mainstream-centric curriculum A curriculum that presents events, concepts, issues, and problems primarily or exclusively from the points of view and perspectives of the mainstream society and the dominant ethnic and cultural group in the United States, White Anglo-Saxon Protestants. The mainstream-centric curriculum is also usually presented from the perspectives of Anglo males.

Mainstreaming The process that involves placing students with disabilities into the regular classroom for instruction. They might be integrated into the regular classroom for part or all of the school day. This practice was initiated in response to Public Law 94-142 (passed by Congress in 1975), which requires that students with disabilities be educated in the least restricted environment.

Multicultural education A reform movement designed to change the total educational environment so that students from diverse racial and ethnic groups, both gender groups, exceptional students, and students from each social-class group will experience equal educational opportunities in schools, colleges, and universities. A major assumption of multicultural education is that some students, because of their particular racial, ethnic, gender, and cultural characteristics, have a better chance to succeed in educational institutions as they are currently structured than do students who belong to other groups or who have different cultural and gender characteristics.

Multiculturalism A philosophical position and movement that assumes that the gender, ethnic, racial, and cultural diversity of a pluralistic society should be reflected in all of the institutionalized structures of educational institutions, including the staff, the norms and values, the curriculum, and the student body.

Multiethnic education A reform movement designed to change the total educational environment so that students from diverse racial and ethnic groups will experience equal educational opportunities. Multiethnic education is an important component of multicultural education.

Native American United States citizens who trace their biological and cultural heritage to the original inhabitants in the land that now makes up the United States. *Native American* is used synonymously with *American Indian*. There were about 2 million Native Americans in the United States in 1990. Only four tribes, the Cherokee, Navajo, Chippewa, and Sioux, had more than 100,000 persons in 1990. Most tribes had a population of less than 10,000. The two largest tribes were the Cherokee (308,000) and the Navajo (219,000).

People of color Groups in the United States and other nations who have experienced discrimination historically because of their unique biological characteristics that enabled potential discriminators to identify them easily. African Americans, Asian Americans, and Hispanics in the United States are among the groups referred to as people of color. Most members of these groups still experience forms of discrimination today.

Positionality An idea that emerged out of feminist scholarship stating that variables such as an individual's gender, class, and race are markers of her or his relational position within a social and economic context and influence the knowledge that she or he produces. Consequently, valid knowledge requires an acknowledgment of the knower's position within a specific context. (See chapter 7 in this book.)

Prejudice A set of rigid and unfavorable attitudes toward a particular individual or group that is formed without consideration of facts. Prejudice is a set of attitudes that often leads to discrimination, the differential treatment of particular individuals and groups.

Race Refers to the attempt by physical anthropologists to divide human groups according to their physical traits and characteristics. This has proven to be very difficult because human groups in modern societies are highly mixed physically. Consequently, different and often conflicting race typologies exist.

Racism A belief that human groups can be validly grouped according to their biological traits and that these identifiable groups inherit certain mental, personality, and cultural characteristics that determine their behavior. Racism, however, is not merely a set of beliefs but is practiced when a group has the power to enforce laws, institutions, and norms, based on its beliefs, that oppress and dehumanize another group.

Religion A set of beliefs and values, especially about explanations that concern the cause and nature of the universe, to which an individual or group has a strong loyalty and attachment. A *religion* usually has a moral code, rituals, and institutions that reinforce and propagate its beliefs.

Sex The biological factors that distinguish males and females, such as chromosomal, hormonal, anatomical, and physiological characteristics.

Sexism Social, political, and economic structures that advantage one sex group over the other. Stereotypes and misconceptions about the biological characteristics of each sex group reinforce and support sex discrimination. In most societies, women have been the major victims of sexism. However, males are also victimized by sexist beliefs and practices.

Social class A collectivity of people who have a similar socioeconomic status based on such criteria as income, occupation, education, values, behaviors, and life chances. *Lower class, working class, middle class,* and *upper class* are common designations of social class in the United States.

Contributors

Cherry A. McGee Banks is associate professor of education at the University of Washington, Bothell. Her current research interest focuses on race and gender in educational leadership. She has contributed to such journals as the *Phi Delta Kappan, Social Studies and the Young Learner, Educational Policy, Theory Into Practice*, and *Social Education*. Professor Banks is associate editor of the *Handbook of Research on Multicultural Education*, contributing author of *Education in the 80s: Multiethnic Education*, and co-author of *March Toward Freedom: A History of Black Americans*. She serves on several national committees and boards including the American Bar Association's Special Committee on Youth Education for Citizenship and the Board of Examiners for the National Council for the Accreditation of Teacher Education. Professor Banks serves on the editorial boards of *The Social Studies* and *Educational Foundations*.

James A. Banks is professor and director of the Center for Multicultural Education at the University of Washington, Seattle. He has written or edited fifteen books in multicultural education and in social studies education. His books include *Teaching Strategies for Ethnic Studies; Multiethnic Education: Theory and Practice; Teaching Strategies for the Social Studies;* and *An Introduction to Multicultural Education*. He is the editor of the *Handbook of Research on Multicultural Education*.

Professor Banks has received fellowships from the National Academy of Education, the Kellogg Foundation, and the Rockefeller Foundation. In 1986, he was named a Distinguished Scholar/

Researcher on Minority Education by the American Educational Research Association (AERA). In 1994, he received the AERA Research Review Award. A past president of the National Council for the Social Studies, he received an honorary Doctorate of Humane Letters (L.H.D.) from the Bank Street College of Education in 1993. In 1996, he became President-elect of AERA and President in 1977.

Johnnella E. Butler is professor of American ethnic studies and adjunct professor of English and Women Studies at the University of Washington, Seattle. She was formerly on the faculty of Smith College, where she served as chairperson of the Afro-American Studies Department. Professor Butler is a specialist in African American literature and American ethnic literature and criticism and is particularly interested in the relationship between ethnic studies and women's studies. The author of *Black Studies: Pedagogy and Revolution: A Study of the Teaching of Afro-American Literature in the Liberal Arts Curriculum*, she has contributed to several books, including *Women's Place in the Academy: Transforming the Liberal Arts Curriculum; Gendered Subjects;* and *Toward a Balanced Curriculum*. She is co-editor with John C. Walter of *Transforming the Curriculum: Ethnic Studies and Women's Studies*. Professor Butler is a member of the executive board of the American Studies Association, 1995–1998.

Rodney A. Cavanaugh is assistant professor of special education at the State University of New York at Plattsburgh. A former teacher of students with learning and behavior disorders in Michigan and

Ohio, he currently teaches graduate and undergraduate courses in special education and supervises preservice teaching practica. He is vice-president of the New York State Council for Exceptional Children Division of Mental Retardation/Developmental Disabilities. His current research interests and publications involve effective teaching strategies for learners with disabilities and action research in teacher education. Professor Canavaugh was named the 1995 New York State Professor of the Year by the Carnegie Foundation for the Advancement of Teaching.

Frederick Erickson is the Judy and Howard Berkowitz Professor of Education in the Graduate School of Education at the University of Pennsylvania, where he teaches the anthropology of education and directs the Cantor Center for Research on Diversity in Education and the Center for Urban Ethnography. He convenes the annual Ethnography in Education Forum. His publications include *The Counselor as Gatekeeper: Social Interaction in Interviews; Sights and Sounds of Life in Schools;* a chapter in the *Handbook of Research on Teaching* (3rd edition); and articles on ethnicity and on ethnographic description in *Sociolinguistics: An International Handbook of the Science of Language and Society.* He is a past president of the Council on Anthropology and Education of the American Anthropological Association. He received the Council's George and Louise Spindler Award for outstanding scholarly contributions to educational anthropology in 1991. He is a past editor of the *Anthropology and Education Quarterly.*

Geneva Gay is professor of education and associate of the Center for Multicultural Education at the University of Washington, Seattle. She received the 1990 Distinguished Scholar Award, presented by the Committee on the Role and Status of Minorities in Educational Research and Development of the American Educational Research Association, and the 1994 Multicultural Educator Award, presented by the National Association of Multicultural Education. She is known nationally and internationally for her scholarship on multicultural education, particularly as it relates to curriculum design, classroom instruction, staff development, and the culture and learning of students of color. Her writings include more than ninety-five articles and book chapters, the co-editorship of *Expressively Black: The Cultural Basis of Ethnic Identity,* and author of *At the Essence of Learning: Multicultural Education.*

Carl A. Grant is a Hoefs-Bascom professor at the University of Wisconsin–Madison. He has written or edited seventeen books in multicultural teacher education. These books include *Making Schooling Multicultural: Campus and Classroom* (with Mary L. Gomez), 1995; *Educating for Diversity,* 1995; *Making Choices for Multicultural Education* (with Christine E. Sleeter), 1994; *Research and Multicultural Education,* 1993; and *After the School Bell Rings* (with Christine E. Sleeter), 1986. Professor Grant has written more than 100 articles and book chapters. His writings and programs that he directed have received awards. He is a former teacher and administrator. He was a Fulbright Scholar in England and was chosen by the Association of Teacher Education as a leader in teacher education. In 1993, he became the president of the National Association for Multicultural Education (NAME).

Beth Harry entered the field of special education as a parent of a child with cerebral palsy. She is associate professor of special education at the University of Miami, Florida, and her particular interests are in families and cultural issues. Her research and teaching focus on the impact of culture and social status on the needs and perspectives of families of children with disabilities, and on professionals' interactions with such families. She uses ethnographic research methods to investigate these issues, with particular regard to African American and Hispanic parents. She is the author of *Cultural Diversity, Families and the Special Education System,* a study of Puerto Rican parents' perspectives, and of several articles published in leading educational journals.

William L. Heward is professor of special education at the Ohio State University, where he coordinates the doctoral program in applied behavior analysis. In 1985 he received OSU's highest honor for teaching excellence, the Alumni Association's Distinguished Teaching Award. He has had several opportunities to teach abroad, most recently in 1993, when he served as a Visiting Professor at Keio University in Tokyo, Japan. Professor Heward's current research interests focus on "low tech" methods teachers can use to increase the frequency with which each student actively responds and participates during large group instruction. His books include *Exceptional Children: An Introduction to Special Education,* 5th edition, and the forthcoming *A Dozen Teaching Mistakes and What To Do Instead.*

Lynette Long is a psychologist in private practice in Bethesda, Maryland. A former high school teacher and university professor, she has contributed articles to numerous journals and has written and co-authored six books, including *Unparented: American Teens on Their Own; The Handbook for Latchkey Children and Their Parents;* and *Questioning: Skills for Helping Processes.* Dr. Long has done research and training in several areas, including human relations, sex equity, and latchkey children.

Luanna H. Meyer is professor of education and coordinator of the Inclusive Elementary and Special Education Program at Syracuse University. She also directs the Consortium for Collaborative Research on the Social Relationships of Children and Youth and the New York Partnership for Statewide Systems Change. She is a Fellow of the American Association on Mental Retardation, has been an executive board member of AAMR and TASH, and is internationally known for her work in special education and the inclusion of students with significant disabilities into their schools and communities. She has published more than 100 books, book chapters, and journal articles, and she edits a new book series entitled *Children, Youth, and Change: Sociocultural Perspectives.*

Sonia Nieto is professor of education in the cultural diversity and curriculum reform program at the University of Massachusetts, Amherst. Her professional interests focus on multicultural and bilingual education and on the social and cultural context of education. She is co-editor of *The Education of Latino Students in Massachusetts: Issues, Research, and Policy Implications* (with R. Rivera, 1993) and author of *Affirming Diversity: The Sociopolitical Context of Multicultural Education* (2nd ed., 1996). She has published many book chapters as well as articles in such journals as the *Harvard Educational Review, Educational Forum,* and *Multicultural Education.* Professor Nieto has served on many local, regional, and national boards that focus on educational equity and social justice, and she has received numerous awards for her community service.

Carlos J. Ovando is professor of education at Indiana University, Bloomington. He has taught at Oregon State University, University of Alaska, Anchorage, and University of Southern California. Professor Ovando specializes in bilingual and multicultural education and has contributed to numerous publications in these fields. He has served as guest editor of two special issues of the *Educational Research Quarterly* and contributed to the *Handbook of Research on Multicultural Education, Peabody Journal of Education, Bilingual Research Journal, Phi Delta Kappan, Educational Leadership, Kappa Delta Pi Record,* and the *Harvard Educational Review.* He is the co-author of *Bilingual and ESL Classrooms.* Professor Ovando has presented papers in Canada, Egypt, England, Guam, Mexico, Nicaragua, the Netherlands, and the Philippines.

Caroline Hodges Persell is professor of sociology at New York University. She is president of the Eastern Sociological Society and has received grants from the National Science Foundation, the Danforth Foundation, the Fund for the Improvement of Post-Secondary Education, and the U.S. Office of Education. She has received a Faculty Development Award from the National Science Foundation, the Hans O. Mauksch Award for Contributions to Undergraduate Sociology from the American Sociological Association, and the first Annual Women Educators' Research Award, and she was named the first Robin M. Williams, Jr., Distinguished Lecturer by the Eastern Sociological Society. Her books include *Understanding Society: An Introduction to Sociology; Preparing for Power: America's Elite Boarding Schools* (with Peter W. Cookson, Jr.); and *Education and Inequality.*

David Sadker is a professor at the American University in Washington, DC. His research and writing document sex bias from the classroom to the boardroom. His work has been reported in hundreds of newspapers and magazines, including *USA Today, Business Week, The Washington Post, The London Times, The New York Times, Time,* and *Newsweek.* Professor Sadker received the American Educational Research Association's award for the best review of research published in the United States in 1991, its professional service award in 1995, and The Eleanor Roosevelt award from the American Association of University Women in 1995. David Sadker's most recent book, *Failing at Fairness: How Our Schools Cheat Girls* (1995), was published by Touchstone Press.

Myra Sadker was a professor of education at The American University in Washington, DC, and director of the Master of Arts in Teaching program. She also served as dean of the School of Education and director of the Teacher Preparation Progams. Professor Sadker, who was a language arts teacher, contributed to numerous journals and books and offered workshops on sex equity in more than forty states. She and Professor David Saker co-authored a number of books, including *Sex Equity Handbook for Schools* and *Failing at Fairness: How Our Schools Cheat Girls.*

Janet Ward Schofield is professor of psychology and a senior scientist in the Learning Research and Development Center at the University of Pittsburgh. She has also served as a faculty member at Spelman College. She received her Ph.D. from Harvard University in 1972. Professor Schofield is a social psychologist whose major interest for more than twenty years has been social processes in desegregated schools. She has published more than two dozen papers in this area as well as two books. One of these, *Black and White in School:*

Trust, Tension or Tolerance? was awarded the Society for the Psychological Study of Social Issues' Gordon Allport Intergroup Relations Prize. She is a contributing author of the *Handbook of Research on Multicultural Education.* Professor Schofield's work in her other major area of interest, the impact of computer technology on classroom processes, has resulted in numerous publications, including the book, *Computers and Classroom Culture.*

Mara Sapon-Shevin is professor of education in the Teaching and Leadership Division of the School of Education at Syracuse University. She teaches in the university's Inclusive Elementary and Special Education Teacher Education Program, which prepares teachers for inclusive, heterogeneous classrooms. She is active in working with schools to promote the full inclusion of all students and the creation of cooperative school communities. She is co-president of the International Association for the Study of Cooperation in Education and gives workshops on cooperative learning and cooperative games for the classrooms. The author of many articles and book chapters on cooperative learning, full inclusion, diversity education, and the politics of gifted education, she is the author of *Playing Favorites: Gifted Education and the Disruption of Community.*

Christine E. Sleeter is a professor and planning faculty member at California State University, Monterey Bay. Previously she was a professor of teacher education at the University of Wisconsin–Parkside. She was a recent recipient of the National Association for Multicultural Education Research Award and also of the AERA Committee on the Role and Status of Minorities in Education Distinguished Scholar Award. She has published numerous books and articles in multicultural education. Her most recent books include *Keepers of the American Dream; Developing Multicultural Teacher Education Curricula* (with Joseph Larkin); and *Multicultural Education, Critical Pedagogy and the Politics of Difference* (with Peter McLaren).

Rena F. Subotnik, specialist in gifted education at Hunter College and research/curriculum consultant to the Hunter College Campus Schools, has been awarded research and training grants with the National Science Foundation, the Javits Grant Program of the U.S. Department of Education, and the Spencer Foundation. She was the winner of the 1990 Early Scholar Award of the National Association for Gifted Children and currently serves on the editorial boards of the *American Educational Research Journal, Journal for Secondary Gifted Education,* and the *Roeper Review.* Dr. Subotnik is first author of *Genius Revisited: High IQ Children Grown Up* (Ablex, 1993), co-editor of *Beyond Terman: Contemporary Longitudinal Studies of Giftedness and Talent* (Ablex, 1994), and the forthcoming *Remarkable Women: Perspectives on Female Talent Development* (Hampton Press).

Mary Kay Thompson Tetreault is vice president for Academic Affairs at California State University, Fullerton, where she previously held the position of dean of the School of Human Development and Community Service. She also worked as a professor of secondary education, a department chair and an assistant dean at Lewis and Clark College, and taught social studies in high schools near Boston and Chicago. Tetreault received her B.A. in history from Benedictine College, a Master of Arts in Teaching from the University of Chicago, and her doctorate in Social Education and Women's Studies from Boston University. Mary Kay Tetreault is the author (with Frances Maher) of *The Feminist Classroom,* published in 1994 by Basic Books. She also edited *Women in America: Half of History,* a collection of primary source materials for secondary school students.

James K. Uphoff is professor and chair of teacher education at Wright State University, Dayton, OH. He has been an educator for more than thirty-six years, serves as the editor for the ASCD Religion and Public Education Network, is a Malone Faculty Fellow in Arab-Islamic Studies, was co-founder of the Public Education Religion Studies Center at WSU, and has been honored by his university for both his scholarship and service. He is also the author of several books on early childhood education, including School Readiness and Transition Programs: Real Facts from Real Schools, 1995. He has also been a local school board member since 1989.

Index